W9-BFX-028

Laos .

Joe Cummings

dradav@aol.com

DISTRIBUTED BY
ASIA BOOKS

Laos

3rd edition

Published by
Lonely Planet Publications
Head Office: PO Box 617, Hawthorn, Vic 3122, Australia
Branches: 150 Linden Street, Oakland, CA 94607, USA
    10a Spring Place, London NW5 3BH, UK
    71 bis rue du Cardinal Lemoine, 75005 Paris, France

Printed by
SNP Printing Pte Ltd, Singapore

Photographs by

Jerry Alexander	Joe Cummings
Bethune Carmichael	Bernard Napthine
Frank Carter	Carly Hammond
Juliet Coombe (La Belle Aurore)	

Front cover: Wat Mai Suwannaphumaham, Luang Prabang (Jerry Alexander)

First Published
January 1994

This Edition
October 1998

National Library of Australia Cataloguing in Publication Data

Cumming, Joe.
  Laos.

  3rd ed.
  Includes index.
  ISBN 0 86442 617 8.

  1. Laos - Guidebooks. I. Title.

915.940442

Joe Cummings

Joe Cummings became involved in South-East Asian studies while a political science student at Guilford College, a Quaker school in North Carolina, and then later as a Peace Corps volunteer in Thailand. Since then he has worked as a translator/interpreter of Thai in San Francisco, finished a master's degree in Thai language and Asian art history at the University of California, has been an East-West Center scholar in Hawaii, taught English at a Malaysian university, served as a Lao bilingual studies consultant in Oakland, and led one of the first American group tours to visit Laos after the 1975 Revolution.

Fluent in Thai and Lao, Joe is the author of Lonely Planet's *Thailand* guidebook (winner of the 1995 Lowell Thomas Best Guidebook award) and the *Thai* and *Lao* phrasebooks, along with the Lonely Planet travel atlases for these two countries. He is also author and photographic contributor to Asia Books' *Laos* pictorial guide and author of the upcoming *Royal Cities of Laos*, published by Teak House. He also writes for *Asian Wall Street Journal*, *Geographical*, *The Nation*, *Outside*, *South China Morning Post*, *World & I* and others.

From Joe

Special thanks to Sousath Phetrasy (who enlightened me on many aspects of Xieng Khuang Province – and tried but failed to convince me on others!), Vixian Viengkeo (for help in Attapeu), Oliver Bandmann (who generously provided the Vang Vieng Caves map and other information), Yoi Soumpholphakdy, Somphone & Mayulee, tireless archaeologist Thongsa Sayavongkhamdy, Patrizia Zolese (who along with Berenice Bellina and Jean-Pierre Message of the Lao Archaeological Project kindly provided information on the UNESCO project in Champasak), Michael Hodgson and Hu Li Cheng (whose Raintrees bookshops continue to capture a sizable chunk of my income every time I visit Laos), *bon vivant* Santi Inthavong, the inspirational Christopher Kremmer, Lynne Cummings (whose proofreading and fact-checking made this a better book), fun travel companions Jerry and Loma Alexander, stylish René Sepul and Cici Olssen, fearless fact-checkers Steven Martin, Frank Carter and Tara Sauvage, l'Ecole Française d'Extrême-Orient, Teak House, and all the Lonely Planet readers who took the time to write with comments and suggestions.

From the Publisher

This third edition of *Laos* was edited in Lonely Planet's Melbourne gulag by Richard Plunkett with help from Martin Hughes, while Anne Mulvaney and Greg Alford handled the proofing. Quentin Frayne did the Language chapter, while Ratry Chanty typeset the Lao script. The mapping and design was handled by Tim Fitzgerald, while David Kemp designed the cover. Jenny Bowman contributed illustrations, while librarian Leonie Mugavin sourced some of the illustration material. Adam McCrow, Katrina Browning and Chris Love checked the book in the final production stages. Thanks to Kristin Odijk and Sue Galley for their help and ideas.

Warning & Request

Things change – prices go up, schedules change, good places go bad and bad places go bankrupt – nothing stays the same. So, if you find things better or worse, recently opened or long since closed, please tell us and help make the next edition even more accurate and useful. We value all the feedback we receive from travellers. Julie Young coordinates a small team which reads and acknowledges every letter, postcard and email, and ensures every morsel finds its way to the appropriate authors, editors and publishers.

Everyone who writes to us will find their name in the next edition of the appropriate guide and will receive a free subscription to our quarterly newsletter, *Planet Talk*. The very best contributions will be rewarded with a free Lonely Planet guide.

Excerpts from your correspondence may appear in new editions of this guide; in our newsletter, *Planet Talk*; or in updates on our Web site or email newsletter – so please let us know if you don't want your letter published or your name acknowledged.

Thanks

Many thanks to the following travellers who took the time and trouble to write to us about their experiences in Laos:

Vic Adams, Karen Agate-Hilton, Phannara Aing, Simon Aliwell, Christian Alpers, E Amon, Paulina Axelson, Rupert Baker, Joan Becich, Linda Bennett, Bruno Bernardin, Jan Beukema, Paul Bodler, David Boyall, Josianne Braver, Saskia Brinks, Melissa Brown, Michael Bussman, Andy Carvin, Nicolas Chagnon, Toby Charnaud, Dudu Cohen, Barbie Cole, Cameron Cooper, Pam Cunneyworth, Sophie Davies, Dennis Dearth, Marco Del Corona, Vreni & Peter Demuth, Esther de Vries, Patrick D'Haese, Beingeie Didier, G Diers, Jean-Benoit Dunckel, Paul Durham, Steve Epstein, Derek Evans & Ingrid Evans-Schloss.

Brian Farrelly, Norbert Fesser, Hanne Finholt, James Fink, Simon Finnigan, Rune Fisker, Cuthbert Fitzclune, Jack Fowlie, Martin Fritze, Dave Fuller, Linda Gault, Michelle Gelsimino, Don Geramom, Lorne Goldman, Elizabeth Gowans, David Gowlett, Moses Graubard, Martine & Bruno Grosjean, David Grossman, Michael Grossmann, Nigel Hall, Jan Hamilton, B Hammersley, Helle Hansen, Richard Harnetty, S Harpfer, Diane Harthing, John Haseman, Jim & Annie Hershberg, TE Hesse, Chris Hilburn, David Hogarth, Chris Holland, Ken Howard, John & Alison Howie, MJ & HG Humphreys, Ian Hunt, Denise Hutton, Michael Johansson & I Judd.

Jeff Kaye, Margo Kerkvliet, Kathy & Warren Kreuger, Mike Krosin, David Kulka, Linc Kyhn, Mr Lane, Karol Lapsley, Hannah Lawrence, Marc Lemieux, Keith Liker, Ron Lish, Christine Lutz, Martin Lykke, Richard Mabbitt, Paula MacNamara, Mark Mason, Hajime Matsuzaki, C McFarlane, Heather Merriam, Dan Michaelis, Andrew Ming, Carlos Mock, Kai Monkkonen, Ana Moore, Dave Mountain, Taka Muraoka, Dean Myerson, Baan Nantaporn, Sandra & Andy Neeve, Annette Nielsen, Susan Oakden & Ross Orton.

Luca Paietta, Gloria & Jim Patterson, Piergiorgio Pescali, Claes Petersen, Duncan Priestley, I Rafael, Sean Ramsay, Eduard Reitsema, J Ribbans, Mark Robinson, Sherry Ronick & Grade 3, Ron Rook, Kellt Row, HH Saffery, MD Santoni, Ralf Schramm, Caitriona Shanahan, Michael Shinners, Tina & Kevin Shirley, Paul Sidwell, David Smith, Gerard Snowball, Teresa Sobieszczyk, Burt Sutherland, Dan Tamir, Jan-Pieter Tanis, Mike Taylor, Monica Thom, Lisette Thresh, Melita Tickner & Jim Turner.

Derek Uram, Pascal Vanhove, Jan van Jeew, Eva van Marcke, Johnny Valentine, Harold van Voornveld, Sandra Velthuis, Frans Verbruggen, Willy Verspay, NH & Rene Voyer, Lee Walker, Russell & Barbara Wiemers, Don Williams, I Wilson, Stephen Yates, Alexander Zumdieck & Suzanne Zyla.

Contents

Map Legend

BOUNDARIES

—··—··—··—··—	International Boundary
—·—·—·—·—·—	Provincial Boundary
— — — — —	Disputed Boundary

ROUTES

═══A25═══	Freeway, with Route Number
═══════	Major Road
───────	Minor Road
─ ─ ─ ─ ─	Minor Road - Unsealed
───────	City Road
───────	City Street
───────	City Lane
├──┼──●──┼──┤	Train Route, with Station
╫─╫─╫─╫─╫─╫─╫	Cable Car or Chair Lift
─ ─ ─ ─ ─	Ferry Route
─ ─ ─ ─ ─	Walking Track
· · · · · · ·	Walking Tour

AREA FEATURES

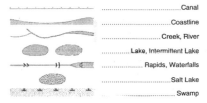

	Building
	Cemetery
	Desert
	Market
	Park, Gardens
	Pedestrian Mall
	Reef
	Urban Area

HYDROGRAPHIC FEATURES

	Canal
	Coastline
	Creek, River
	Lake, Intermittent Lake
	Rapids, Waterfalls
	Salt Lake
	Swamp

SYMBOLS

◉	CAPITAL	National Capital	✈	Airport	←	One Way Street	
◎	CAPITAL	Provincial Capital	✝	Airfield	)(	Pass	
●	CITY	City		Ancient or City Wall	ⓟ	Petrol Station	
●	Town	Town	∴	Archaeological Site	★	Police Station	
●	Village	Village	ⓢ	Bank	✉	Post Office	
			🏛	Cathedral, Church	❖	Shopping Centre	
■		Place to Stay	⌒	Cave	◎	Spring	
▲		Camping Ground		Cliff or Escarpment	🏛	Stately Home	
⌂		Hut or Chalet	◑	Embassy	⅄	Stupa	
			✛	Hospital	⊞	Swimming Pool	
▼		Place to Eat	※	Lookout	☎	Telephone	
🍺		Pub or Bar	☾	Mosque	■	Temple or Wat	
			▲	Mountain or Hill	▣	Tomb	
			⚱	Monument	❶	Tourist Information	
			🏛	Museum	◒	Transport	
			⚓	Nature Reserve	🐘	Zoo	

Note: not all symbols displayed above appear in this book

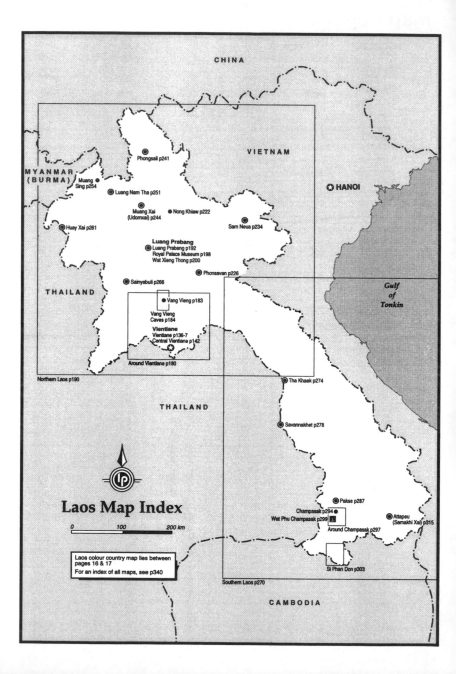

CHINA

VIETNAM

MYANMAR
(BURMA)

● Phongsali p241

Muang ●
Sing p254

◉ Luang Nam Tha p251

✪ HANOI

◉ Muang Xai
(Udomxai) p244

● Nong Khiaw p222

● Huay Xai p261

◉ Sam Neua p234

Luang Prabang
◉ Luang Prabang p192
Royal Palace Museum p198
Wat Xieng Thong p200

◉ Phonsavan p226

THAILAND

◉ Sainyabuli p266

*Gulf
of
Tonkin*

● Vang Vieng p183

Vang Vieng
Caves p184

Vientiane
Vientiane p136-7
Central Vientiane p142

✪

Around Vientiane p180

Northern Laos p190

◉ Tha Khaek p274

THAILAND

◉ Savannakhet p278

Laos Map Index

0   100   200 km

Laos colour country map lies between
pages 16 & 17
For an index of all maps, see p340

◉ Pakse p287

Champasak p294 ●
Wat Phu Champasak p299

◉ Attapeu
(Samakhi Xai) p315

Around Champasak p297

Si Phan Don p303

Southern Laos p270

CAMBODIA

Introduction

Known in antiquity as Lan Xang (Million Elephants), and by Indochina War-era journalists as the Land of a Million Irrelevants, this sparsely populated country is finally enjoying peace after nearly 300 years of war with Annam, Burma, China, Siam, France and the USA.

Traditionally the least developed and most enigmatic of the three former French Indochina states, Laos has emerged as the frontrunner in economic and political reform. Free markets and private foreign investment have been the norm since 1989, yet most development moves at a snail's pace. While Thailand speeds headlong into the 21st century, Cambodia suffers from deep internal divisions and Vietnam rapidly industrialises in order to provide work for its teeming population, Laos seems content to remain an Asian backwater while slowly developing one of the most stable, low-profile economic and political systems in the region.

After nearly 20 years of virtual isolation, landlocked Laos has in the 1990s become more open towards the outside world, though the numbers of foreign visitors are kept down by tangles of red tape and a general lack of infrastructure. More a blessing than a curse, the overall lack of foreign influence offers travellers an unparalleled glimpse of old South-East Asia. From the fertile lowlands of the Mekong valley to the rugged Annamite highlands, travellers who have made it to

Laos – even if only for a few days in transit to or from Vietnam – are almost unanimous in their admiration of the country. Many visitors have found Laos to be a highlight of their South-East Asian journeys.

Facts about Laos

HISTORY
Summary

For centuries Laos was used as a pawn in a strategic game between neighbouring states and, later, world powers. Despite this, and perhaps due to the Lao's devout Buddhism and tolerance, nationalist aspirations were slow to develop and the shaping of Laos as a modern nation state can only be traced back to 1945.

WWII, and Japan's temporary occupation of French Indochina, kick-started Laos' drive for independence, which was gained from France in 1949. Laos then became a microcosm for the global struggle between left and right-wing ideologies with the US and Vietnam funding and supporting opposing sides in the contest for Laos' allegiance.

Following the end of the Vietnam War in 1975, the Pathet Lao revolutionary movement set up the Lao People's Democratic Republic (LPDR) and remains the authority in Laos today.

Prehistory

The Mekong River valley and Khorat Plateau areas which today encompass significant parts of Laos, Cambodia and Thailand were inhabited as far back as 10,000 years ago. Virtually all of the ethnic groups in these areas, both indigenous and immigrant, belong to the Austro-Thai ethnolinguistic family. Historically in Laos, these are mostly subgroups identified with the Thai-Kadai and Miao-Yao (Hmong-Mien) language families.

The Thai-Kadai is the most significant ethno-linguistic group in all of South-East Asia, with 72 million speakers extending from the Brahmaputra River in India's Assam state to the Gulf of Tonkin and China's Hainan island. To the north, there are Thai-Kadai speakers well into the Chinese provinces of Yunnan and Guangxi, and to the south they extend as far as the northern Malaysian state of Kedah. In Thailand and Laos they are the majority populations, and in China, Vietnam and Myanmar (Burma) they are the largest minorities. The major Thai-Kadai groups are the Ahom (Assam), the Siamese (Thailand), the Black Thai or Thai Dam (Laos and Thailand), the Thai Yai or Shan (Myanmar and Thailand), the Thai Neua (Laos, Thailand and China), the Thai Lü (Laos, Thailand and China) and the Yuan (Laos and Thailand). All of these groups belong to the Thai half of Thai-Kadai; the Kadai groups are relatively small (numbering less than a million) and include such comparatively obscure languages in southern China as Kelao, Lati, Laha, Laqua and Li.

When tracing the origins of the current inhabitants of Laos, we must consider the fact that their predecessors belonged to a vast, nonunified zone of Austro-Thai influence that involved periodic migrations along several different geographic lines.

Austro-Thai Migration

A linguistic map of southern China, northwestern India and South-East Asia clearly shows that the preferred zones of occupation by the Austro-Thai – collectively called 'Tai' by many scholars – have been river valleys, from the Red River (Hong River) in southern China and Vietnam to the Brahmaputra River in Assam. At one time, the main access points into what is now Thailand and Laos were the Yuan Jiang and other river areas in Yunnan and Guangxi and the Chao Phraya River in Thailand. These are areas where the populations remain quite concentrated today. Areas in mainland South-East Asia lying between these points were intermediate migrational zones and have always been far less populated.

The Mekong River valley between Thailand and Laos was one such intermediate zone, as were river valleys along the Nam Ou, Nam Seuang and other rivers in modern Laos (Myanmar's Shan States also fall into this category). As far as historians have been able to piece together from the scant linguistic and anthropological evidence, significant numbers of Austro-Thai peoples in southern China or north Vietnam began migrating southward and westward in small groups as early as the 8th century AD, but most certainly by the 10th century. These groups established local polities along traditional Tai lines according to *meuang* (roughly principality or district) under the hereditary rule of chieftains or sovereigns called *jao meuang*.

Each meuang was based in a river valley or section of a valley. Some meuang were loosely collected under one jao meuang or an alliance of several. One of the largest collections of meuang (though not necessarily united) is thought to have emanated from southern China's Guangxi Province and/or Vietnam's Dien Bien Phu area, a theory favoured by pronunciation patterns today found along the Guangxi-Vietnam-Laos-Thailand-Myanmar axis.

In the mid-13th century, the rise to power of the Mongols under Kublai Khan in China caused a more dramatic south-westward migration of Austro-Thai peoples. Wherever the Tai met indigenous populations of Tibeto-Burmans and Mon-Khmers in the move south (into what is now Myanmar, Thailand, Laos and Cambodia), they were somehow able to displace, assimilate or co-opt them without force. This seems to puzzle many historians, but the most simple explanation is probably that there were already Tai peoples in the area. This supposition finds considerable support in current research on the development of Austro-Thai language and culture.

In Lao legend, the mythic figure Khun Borom (Bulom) cut open a gourd somewhere in the vicinity of Dien Bien Phu (north-western Vietnam) and out came seven sons who spread the Austro-Thai family from east to west. Although previous theory had placed the original centre of Austro-Thai culture in south-western China or even Indonesia, recent evidence suggests the possibility they may originally have emanated from the Dongson/Tonkin culture

in northern Vietnam – a theory perhaps confirmed in the Khun Bulom myth. Among tribal Thais, Dien Bien Phu is known as Muang Theng.

Southern Laos, on the other hand, was an early centre of the Mon-Khmer Funan Kingdom (1st to 6th centuries) and the Chenla Kingdom (6th to 8th centuries), both of which extended from Champasak into north-western Cambodia. Farther north two Mon kingdoms called Sri Gotapura (centred at present-day Tha Khaek) and Muang Sawa (at Luang Prabang) flourished from the 8th to the 12th century. These kingdoms were superseded by the Angkor Empire and later by Lao and Siamese principalities.

Lan Na Thai & Lan Xang

Until the 13th century, there were several small, independent Tai and Mon meuang in what is today northern Thailand and Laos. In the mid-13th century, a Tai rebellion against the Khmers resulted in the consolidation of a number of meuang to create the famous Sukhothai Kingdom in northern Thailand. Sukhothai's King Ram Khamhaeng supported Chao Mengrai of Chiang Mai and Chao Khun Ngam Muang of Phayao (Chiang Mai and Phayao were both meuang in northern Thailand) in the formation of Lan Na Thai (Million Thai Rice Fields), sometimes written simply as Lanna. Lanna extended across north-central Thailand to include the meuang of Sawa (Luang Prabang) and Wieng Chan (Vientiane).

Debate about whether Lanna was essentially Lao or Thai – or whether such a distinction even existed at the time – has become a hot topic in Laos today. There is evidence that both 'Lao' and 'Thai' were terms used by the people of this kingdom to describe themselves; nationalistic citizens of Thailand and Laos today make it a point to emphasise one over the other when writing and rewriting the history of the era.

In the 14th century, as Lanna declined under pressure from the kingdom of Ayuthaya in central Siam, a Lao warlord named Chao Fa Ngum (also spelt Fa Ngoum) took Wieng Chan with the support

Historical Summary

1353	Fa Ngum declares himself King of the Lao Kingdom, Lan Xang.
1421	Death of Fa Ngum's son and successor, Samsenthai. Lan Xang lapses into warring factions for next century.
1520	King Phothisarat comes to throne and moves capital to Vientiane.
1637	King Suliyna Vongsa takes the throne and rules for 57 years, a period regarded as Laos' 'golden age'.
1694	Death of King Suliyna Vongsa and the break-up of Lan Xang begins.
1885	Following centuries of successive invasions by neighbouring powers the former Lan Xang is by now broken up into a series of states under Siamese control.
1893-1907	Siamese-French treaties lead to the French taking control of all territory east of the Mekong River.
1896-97	Laos' current boundaries take shape through joint commissions with China, Britain and Siam.
1941	WWII; the Japanese occupy Laos.
1945	King Sisavang Vong is forced by the Japanese to declare independence. French paratroopers land in Laos and once again declare it to be a French protectorate.
1945-49	Resistance to French rule widens; Laos grows increasingly unstable.
1949 ·	Laos is recognised as an 'independent associate state' of France.
1950	Communist-inspired Pathet Lao (PL) resistance government formed with Vietnamese support.
1953	Franco-Laotian Treaty grants full sovereignty to Laos.
1957	Formation of first coalition government, the Government of National Union.
1958	Government falls and comes under control of the right-wing, US-backed Committee for the Defence of National Interests (CDNI).
1960	Rightists win national elections rigged by Central Intelligence Agency (CIA). Attempted coup forces resignation of government.
1961	US President John F Kennedy announces that he will intervene to stop perceived Communist takeover of Laos.
1962	Geneva Convention on Laos concludes with agreement to provide for independent, neutral Laos. Vietnamese army remains in Laos defying convention. Second Government of National Union formed.
1964	Series of coups and counter-coups result in the polarisation of the PL on one side and the neutralist and right-wing forces on the other. US bombing of Communist targets in Laos begins.
1964-73	Indochina War intensifies; US bombing of eastern Laos.
1973	Negotiations lead to ceasefire. Provisional Government of National Union (PGNU) formed.
1975	Intimidation leads to rightist leaders and government members fleeing Laos and the PGNU is dismantled. Lao People's Revolutionary Party (LPRP) is declared to be the ruling party of the newly christened Lao People's Democratic Republic (LPDR), with Kaysone Phomvihane as leader.
1975-77	LPRP embarks on a policy of 'accelerated socialism' and curtails the practice of Buddhism. Huge exodus of Lao citizens begins.
1987-88	Three month border war between Laos and Thailand.
1997	Laos becomes full member of the Association of South-East Asian Nations (ASEAN).

of 10,000 Khmer troops. As a child Fa
Ngum had been expelled from Muang Sawa
along with his father, Chao Phi Fa, because
the latter had seduced one of his father's (Fa
Ngum's grandfather's) wives. The pair took
refuge at the Angkor court of Jayavarman
Paramesvara, where Fa Ngum eventually
married the Khmer king's daughter, Nang
Kaew Kaeng Nya. With a declining Khmer
Empire behind him, Chao Fa Ngum took
Wieng Chan, the Phuan kingdom of Xieng
Khuang, the Khorat Plateau (in north-
eastern Thailand) and finally Muang Sawa.
His own father having died during the con-
quest of Sawa, Fa Ngum vanquished his
grandfather in 1353 and declared himself
king of these territories, which he named
Lan Xang Hom Khao (Million Elephants &
White Parasol).

Geographically, Lan Xang was one of the
largest kingdoms in mainland South-East
Asia, although then, as Laos is now, it was
sparsely populated. Although Lan Xang is
considered by many present-day Lao to
have been the first truly Lao nation, it was
clearly created as a Khmer client state. Surviving inscriptions from the era most
frequently refer to inhabitants of the state as
'Thai', further fuelling the debate as to
when the distinction between 'Thai' and
'Lao' began.

Fa Ngum made Theravada Buddhism the
state religion and accepted the Pha Bang, a
gold Buddha image said to have been cast
in Sri Lanka, from the Khmers. The Pha
Bang became a talismanic symbol for the
sovereignty of the Lao kingdom of Lan
Xang and has remained so in Laos today.
The image was kept in Muang Sawa, which
is how the city's name later changed to
Luang Phabang (Great Pha Bang), more
commonly spelt 'Luang Prabang' following
standard Thai pronunciation.

Within 20 years of its founding, Lan
Xang had expanded eastward to Champa
and along the Annamite mountains in
Vietnam. Fa Ngum became known as 'the
Conqueror' because of his constant preoccupation with warfare. Unable to tolerate
his ruthlessness any longer, Fa Ngum's

Lan Xang Monarchs
During the first two centuries of Lan Xang
history the royal seat was in Luang
Prabang, after which it was moved to
Vientiane (during the reign of King Sai
Setthathirat).

Fa Ngum	1353-73
Samsenthai	1373-1416
Lan Kham Deng	1416-27
Phommathat	1428-29
Mun Sai	1430
Fa Khai	1430-33
Kong Kham	1433-34
Yukhon	1434-35
Kham Keut	1435-38
Sao Tiakaphat	1438-79
Theng Kham	1479-86
Lasenthai	1486-96
Som Phu	1496-1501
Wisunalat	1501-20
Phothisarat	1520-48
Sai Setthathirat	1548-71
Sensulinthara	1571-75
Maha Upahat	1575-80
Sensulinthara	1580-81
Nakhon Noi	1582-83
interregnum	*1583-91*
Nokeo Kumman	1591-96
Thammikarat	1596-1622
Upanyuvarat	1622-23
Phothisarat	1623-27
Mon Keo	1627
Upanyuvarat	-*
Ton Kham	-*
Visai	-*
Sulinya Vongsa	1637-94

* The dates of these reigns are not known
exactly.

ministers finally drove him into exile – to
the current Thai province of Nan – in 1373.
He died in Nan five years later.

Fa Ngum's eldest son, Oun Heuan, succeeded him and took the title of Phaya
Samsenthai (the Lord of 300,000 Thai;

derived from a census of adult males living in Lan Xang in 1376). After marrying Thai princesses from Chiang Mai and Ayuthaya, Samsenthai reorganised and consolidated the royal administration of Lan Xang along Siamese lines, building many *wat* (temples) and schools. He developed the economy and during his 43-year reign Lan Xang became an important trade centre. After his death in 1421 at the age of 60, Lan Xang lapsed into warring factions for another century.

Twelve rulers succeeded one another during this period, none ruling more than 20 years, most lasting only a year or two. Seven of these monarchs were installed by Samsenthai's ambitious daughter Nang Kaew Phimpha, who then took the throne herself to become Lan Xang's only female ruler. Deposed by her own ministers after a few months, she was tied to a stone and 'abandoned to the crows and vultures' according to Lao archives.

In 1520 King Phothisarat came to the throne and moved the capital to Wieng Chan to avoid Burmese aggression from the west. In 1545, he subdued the kingdom of Lanna and gained the throne of that kingdom for his son, Setthathirat. When Setthathirat inherited the kingship of Lan Xang three years later, he brought with him the Pha Kaew or so-called Emerald Buddha from Lanna (the Lanna equivalent to Lan Xang's Pha Bang). He had Wat Pha Kaew built in Wieng Chan to house the Pha Kaew (the image was later taken back by the Thais) and also ordered the construction of That Luang, the country's largest Buddhist stupa.

Although Lan Xang was a large and powerful kingdom, its rulers were never able to fully subjugate the highland tribes of mountain Laos. States in north-eastern Laos, such as Xieng Khuang and Sam Neua, remained independent of Lan Xang rule and subject to Chinese or Annamese influence. In 1571, King Setthathirat disappeared somewhere in the mountains on the way back from a military expedition into Cambodia, and it is thought that his troops may have met with rebellious highlanders on an excursion into southern Laos.

Leaderless, Lan Xang declined rapidly over the next 60 years, dissolving into warring factions and subject to intermittent Burmese domination. Finally, in 1637 King Sulinya Vongsa ascended the throne following a dynastic war. He ruled for 57 years, the longest reign of any Lao king, and was able to further expand Lan Xang's frontiers. These years are regarded as Laos' 'golden age' – a historic pinnacle in terms of territory and power.

Fragmentation & War with Siam

When King Sulinya Vongsa died without an heir in 1694, there was a three-way struggle for the throne that led to the break-up of Lan Xang. By the early 18th century, Sulinya's nephew, under the stewardship of Annam (Vietnam), had taken control of the middle Mekong River valley around Wieng Chan. A second, independent kingdom emerged in Luang Prabang under Sulinya's grandsons. A prince in the lower Mekong River area established a third kingdom, Champasak, under Siamese influence.

Between 1763 and 1769 Burmese armies overran northern Laos and annexed the kingdom of Luang Prabang, while the Siamese took Champasak in 1778.

By the end of the 18th century, the Siamese had expanded their influence to include the kingdom of Wieng Chan and were exacting tribute from Luang Prabang. Chao Anou, a Lao prince educated in Bangkok, was installed as the vassal king of Wieng Chan by the Siamese court. Anou restored the capital, encouraged a renaissance of Lao fine arts and literature, and improved relations with Luang Prabang. At the same time, however, Wieng Chan was further pressured by the Vietnamese into paying tribute to the Annamite Empire of Emperor Gia Long. Unable or unwilling to serve two masters, Chao Anou rebelled against Siam in the 1820s, an unsuccessful challenge that resulted in the virtual razing of the Wieng Chan capital and the resettlement of many of its residents to Siam.

Eventually the same fate overtook Luang Prabang and Champasak. By the late 19th century, almost the entire region between the Mekong and the Annamite Chain had been defeated and depopulated.

By the late 19th century Wieng Chan, Luang Prabang and Champasak had become Siamese satellite states. In 1885, after successive invasions by the Annamese and the Chinese Haw (actually a loose affiliation of looting mercenaries of various ethnicities, including Yunnanese, Black Thai, and French army deserters), the neutral states of Xieng Khuang and Hua Phan also agreed to Siamese protection, a service the Siamese were glad to provide since they desired these states as buffers against the expanding influence of the French in Vietnam.

French Rule

In the late 19th century, the French were busy making inroads towards the establishment of French Indochina. After creating French protectorates in Tonkin and Annam, France established a consulate at Luang Prabang (with Siamese permission) and was soon able to convince that state to ask for protectorate status as well. In current Lao history, Luang Prabang monarch Oun Kham is painted as a villain for having agreed to French protectorship, but the bare truth is that his only feasible choice at the time was between French or Siamese rule; some historians claim there would be no Laos today had the territory been carved up by the Chinese and Vietnamese.

Through a succession of Siamese-French treaties between 1893 and 1907, the Siamese eventually relinquished control of all the territory east of the Mekong River, keeping everything to the west for themselves. The French united all of the remaining Lao principalities as one colonial territory according to the western custom of territorial boundaries – before French rule none of the Lao kingdoms had ever been surveyed or mapped. Like the British, they assumed they had little to fear from uniting separate entities that had never been able to integrate

successfully. The nation's present boundaries took shape in 1896-97 through joint commissions with China, Britain (for the Lao-Burmese border) and Siam. In retrospect France's disregard for differences between the cultures west and east of the Annamite Chain – the historic dividing line between the Indianised and Sinicised cultures of South-East Asia – was a major blunder, for almost as soon as the French left the country was at war.

It was the French who gave the country its modern name, Laos, an apparent misapprehension of *le Laos* for *les Laos*, the plural of Lao, in reference to the several Lao kingdoms that existed side by side (in the Lao language, the country and people are both simply 'Lao').

Laos was never very important to France except as a buffer state between British-influenced Thailand (and British-occupied Burma) and the more economically important Annam and Tonkin. An 1866 French survey concluded that the Mekong was useless for commercial navigation, that no precious metals were readily available and that the country was too mountainous for large-scale plantations.

Nevertheless the French installed *corvée*, a system of draft labour in which every Lao male was forced to contribute 10 days of manual labour per year to the colonial government. In spite of producing tin, rubber and coffee, Laos never accounted for more than just 1% of French Indochina's exports (opium was by far the most lucrative) and by 1940 only 600 French citizens lived in Laos.

Throughout the Francophone world Laos was known as the land of the lotus-eaters, and resident *fonctionnaires* (civil servants) were regarded as among the most dissolute in the French Empire for their adoption of native mores. But the presence of the French undermined the traditional flexibility of Lao interstate relations and severed the most populous part of the Champasak Kingdom by conceding Isaan (north-eastern Thailand, predominantly Lao in population) to Siam. Hence the French involvement in

Laos, however benign it may have initially appeared (there was never any French military action against the Lao people until 1946), resulted in a weakening of Lao states that probably could not have been achieved even by warfare.

The French also stifled the indigenous modernisation of Laos by imposing a Vietnamese-staffed civil service (just as the British did in Burma with an Indian-staffed civil service). Even the current Lao government labours under the legacy of the French and Vietnamese administrative styles.

WWII & Independence

In 1941, the Japanese occupied French Indochina with the support of the Vichy regime. The Lao mounted very little resistance against the occupation but were able to gain more local autonomy than they enjoyed under the French.

Towards the end of the war, the Japanese forced the French-installed King Sisavang Vong to declare independence in spite of his loyalty to France. The prime minister and viceroy, Prince Phetsarat, didn't trust the King and formed a resistance movement called Lao Issara (Free Lao) to ensure that the country remained free of French colonial rule once the Japanese left.

When French paratroopers arrived in Vientiane and Luang Prabang in 1945, they had King Sisavang Vong relieve Prince Phetsarat of his official positions and once again declared Laos to be a French protectorate. Phetsarat and the Lao Issara formed the Committee of the People and in October 1945 drew up a new constitution proclaiming Laos independent of French rule. When the King refused to recognise the new document, he was deposed by the National Assembly.

Eventually Sisavang Vong came around to the Lao Issara view of things and was reinstated as king in April 1946 (the first time any Lao monarch actually ruled all of Laos). Two days after his coronation, French and Lao guerrillas who called themselves the 'Free French' took Vientiane and smashed Lao Issara forces (as well as resistance

forces sent to Laos from Vietnam by Ho Chi Minh). Phetsarat and many of the Lao Issara fled to Thailand, where they set up a government-in-exile with Phetsarat acting as regent. This brutal suppression of the Lao Issara sent many recruits in Ho Chi Minh's direction.

By late 1946, the French were willing to concede autonomy to Laos and invited the Lao Issara to enter into formal negotiations. But the Lao Issara split into three factions in response to the offer. One faction, under Phetsarat, refused to negotiate with the French, insisting on immediate independence according to Lao Issara terms only. The second was headed by Phetsarat's half-brother, Prince Souvanna Phouma, who wanted to negotiate with the French in forming an independent Laos. The third faction was led by another half-brother, Prince Souphanouvong, who wanted to work out a deal with the Viet Minh under Ho Chi Minh.

The French proceeded without the co-operation of the Lao Issara and in 1949 held

King Sisavang Vong was reluctant to declare independence from the French in 1945, but changed his mind after being briefly deposed.

BERNARD NAPTHINE

CARLY HAMMOND

BERNARD NAPTHINE

Young Laos
Top: A pause in the rice paddies of southern Laos' Si Phan Don riverine archipelago.
Left: Hill tribe Laotians such as this girl form a significant proportion of the population.
Right: With shaved head and saffron robes, serving as a monk is an important traditional
rite of passage for Lao males.

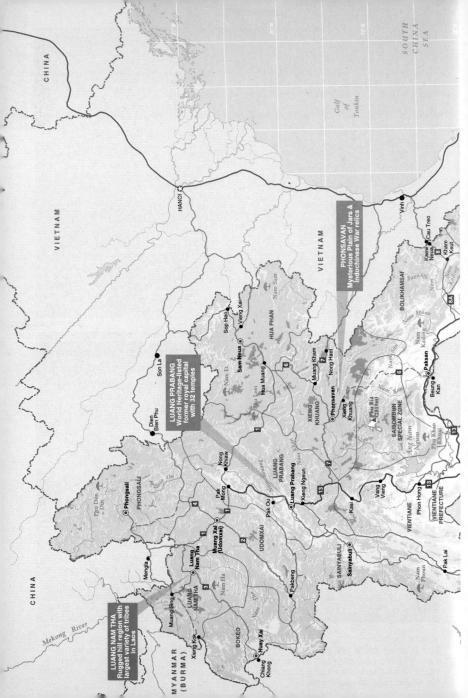

CHINA

SOUTH
CHINA
SEA

VIETNAM

Gulf of
Tonkin

HANOI

Vinh

PHONSAVAN
Mysterious Plain of Jars &
Indochinese War relics

Kaew
Neua
Cau Treo

Kham
Kout

BOLIKHAMSAI

Son La

Dien
Bien Phu

Sop Hao

Vieng Xai

HUA PHAN

Sam Neua

Nam Et

Hua Muang

6

Muang Kham
7
Nong Haet

Paksan

Beung
Kan

8A

LUANG PRABANG
World Heritage-listed
former royal capital
with 32 temples

1

XIENG
KHUANG

Phonsavan
Xieng
Khuang

Phu Bia
(2817m)

SAISOMBUN
SPECIAL ZONE

Phu Khao
Khuai

13

Phongsali

PHONGSALI

Phu Den
Din

Nong
Khiaw

LUANG
PRABANG

Luang Prabang

Xieng Ngeun

13

Kasi

Vang
Vieng

Phon Hong

VIENTIANE

(VIENTIANE
PREFECTURE)

13

Pak
Mong

4

Pak Ou

7

Mengla

Muang Xai
(Udomxai)

1

UDOMXAI

2

CHINA

Luang
Nam Tha

Nam Ha

Pakbeng

SAINYABULI

Sainyabuli

Pak Lai

LUANG NAM THA
Rugged hill region with
largest variety of tribes
in Laos

Muang
Sing

LUANG
NAM THA

3

Nam Tha

BOKEO

Xieng Kok

Huay Xai

Chiang
Khong

MYANMAR
(BURMA)

Mekong River

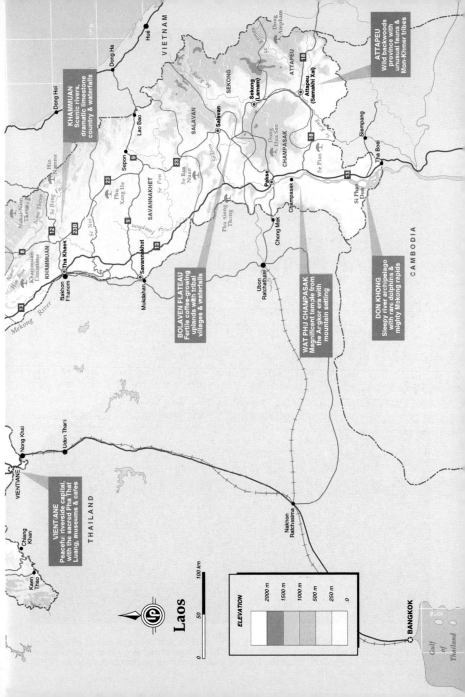

Laos

ELEVATION

2000 m
1500 m
1000 m
500 m
250 m
0

0   50   100 km

VIENTIANE
Peaceful, riverside capital, with the sacred Pha That Luang, museums & gates

KHAMMUAN
Scenic rivers, dramatic limestone country & waterfalls

ATTAPEU
Wild backwoods province with unusual fauna & Mon-Khmer tribes

BOLAVEN PLATEAU
Fertile coffee-growing uplands with tribal villages & waterfalls

WAT PHU CHAMPASAK
Magnificent temple from the Angkor era with mountain setting

DON KHONG
Sleepy river archipelago with rare dolphins & mighty Mekong rapids

VIETNAM

THAILAND

CAMBODIA

Gulf of Thailand

KHAMMUAN

SAVANNAKHET

SALAVAN

SEKONG

CHAMPASAK

ATTAPEU

Hué
Dong Ha
Dong Hoi
Lao Bao
Sepon
Salavan
Sekong (Lamam)
Attapeu (Samakhi Xai)
Siempang
Tha Boei
Pakse
Champasak
Chong Mek
Ubon Ratchathani
Nakhon Ratchasima
BANGKOK
Mukdahan
Savannakhet
Nakhon Phanom
Tha Khaek
VIENTIANE
Nong Khai
Udon Thani
Chiang Khan
Kaen Thao

Mekong River

Se Bang Fai
Se Noi
Se Bang Hieng
Se Pon
Se Don
Se Ban Nuan
Se Kong
Se Pian
Se Kaman

Si Phan Don

Nam Theun
Nam Ngum
Nam Hin Bun
Nam Kading

Khammuan Limestone
Nakai–Nam Theun

Phu Xang He
Phu Sieng Thong
Phu Xiang Thong

Dong Hua Sao
Dong Phu Vieng
Dong Ampham

12
13
23
23B
9
18

17°N
101°E

Elderly woman in Luang Prabang wearing an interesting and colourful mix of Hmong and western garb. The ethnic groups which inhabit Laos' highlands have resisted assimilation into mainstream Lao society for centuries, and maintained their animist faiths and traditional crafts and agricultural practices.

a French-Lao convention in which Laos was recognised as an 'independent associate state' that remained part of the French Union. The treaty gave Laos the right to become an independent member of the United Nations and for the first time Laos was recognised by the world as a separate nation. The Lao Issara dissolved, but Phetsarat remained in Thailand for most of the rest of his life.

Four years later, France granted full sovereignty to Laos via the Franco-Laotian Treaty of October 1953. By this time, the French were heavily preoccupied with the Viet Minh offensives in Vietnam and were looking to reduce their colonial burden in an attempt to preserve what little remained of the French Empire.

Rise of the Pathet Lao

Prior to the late 1940s and early 1950s, the only Lao association with the Communist liberation movement had been through the membership of Prince Souphanouvong and Viet Minh organiser Kaysone Phomvihane in Ho Chi Minh's Indochinese Communist Party (ICP). In 1948, Prince Souphanouvong went to Hanoi to gain support from the Viet Minh for a Lao Communist movement. At about the same time, Kaysone Phomvihane (who later became Secretary-General of the Lao People's Revolutionary Party and Prime Minister of the LPDR) was making headway among tribal minorities in the mountain districts of eastern Laos on behalf of the ICP.

In 1950, the Viet Minh-supported Free Lao Front (FLF, Neo Lao Issara, often incorrectly translated as Lao Freedom Front) and the Lao Resistance Government under Prince Souphanouvong were founded in eastern Laos to fight the French.

The next 25 years which ended in the Lao Communist takeover in 1975 encompassed a somewhat bewildering succession of political changes – just keeping track of all the name changes requires an almost prodigious memory. First, the ICP reconstituted itself as the Vietnamese Workers Party in 1951, with plans to organise separate covert parties in Laos (the Lao People's Party) and Cambodia

Kaysone Phomvihane led the life of a guerilla for 30-odd years, enduring the huge American military assault before seizing power in 1975.

(the Cambodian People's Party) as well. The first use of the term Pathet Lao (Land of the Lao) came in an international communiqué released by the Free Lao Front in 1954 and referred specifically to the tactical forces of the FLF (and later the Patriotic Lao Front). In 1965, the name was changed to the Lao People's Liberation Army (LPLA) but, for the international media, the term Pathet Lao (PL) became generally applied to the Vietnamese-supported liberation movement in Laos.

In 1953-54, the kingdom of Laos was governed by a constitutional monarchy along European lines. A French-educated elite ran the government, while the Lao resistance in the countryside increased, especially following the defeat of the French by Viet Minh troops at Dien Bien Phu in 1954. The US government, anxious to counter the Viet Minh influence in South-East Asia, began pouring aid into Laos to ensure loyalty to the 'democratic cause'. During this same period,

Viet Minh and PL troops claimed the north-eastern Lao provinces of Hua Phan and Phongsali following the Geneva Conference of 1954, which sanctioned the takeover 'pending political settlement'.

In 1955, a clandestine Communist party was officially formed in Sam Neua (Hua Phan Province) under the name Lao People's Party (LPP), consisting of 25 former ICP members. In reality, this group had existed since 1951 when the ICP split into three groups representing Vietnam, Laos and Cambodia. The LPP set up a national front in early 1956 called the Lao Patriotic Front (LPF, known in Lao as Neo Lao Hak Sat or NLHS – which ought really to be translated as Patriotic Lao Front). The LPP, like its counterpart in Cambodia, was a member of the Indochinese United Front, which was led by the Vietnamese Workers Party. In reality, all of these groups were either fronts for, or tactical extensions of, the latter organisation.

Coalition & Dissolution

In 1957, the participants at the Geneva Conference had finally reached a settlement. The LPF and the Royal Lao Government agreed to a coalition government (under the RLG's Prince Souvanna Phouma) known as the Government of National Union. Two LPF ministers and their deputies were admitted at the national level.

According to the Geneva agreement, the 1500 PL troops in the north-east were supposed to be absorbed into the Royal Lao Army, but disagreements over rank precluded a successful merger. When a 1958 National Assembly election in the two north-eastern provinces demonstrated unexpected LPF support among the general populace (13 out of 21 seats), there was a right-wing reaction that led to the arrest of LPF ministers and deputies, and the re-entrenchment of PL troops in the countryside. This government action was undoubtedly fuelled by the US government's withdrawal of all aid to Laos (which by this point made up the bulk of the Lao national budget) following the electoral results.

The fall of the Government of National Union left the Vientiane government under the dominance of the Committee for the Defence of National Interests (CDNI), which was made up of extreme right-wing military officers and French-educated elites. The CDNI had powerful US backing. Phoui Sananikone was installed as prime minister and Prince Souvanna Phouma was made the Lao ambassador to France. But within a year of their arrest, Prince Souphanouvong and his LPF colleagues had escaped and were again leading the resistance in the countryside.

When a 1959 UN investigation declared that the PL were not using regular North Vietnamese troops, the Vientiane government was strongly advised to adopt a more neutral policy towards the LPF.

However the PL was definitely receiving North Vietnamese support in the form of resident political and military advisors during this period. The North Vietnamese, in fact, virtually took control of the sparsely populated eastern Laos to use as a supply route (the 'Ho Chi Minh Trail') to the Viet Cong in South Vietnam. In the north and north-east, the North Vietnamese assisted the PL in gaining control over the tribal mountain dwellers.

Once again, to counter the North Vietnamese presence, the USA began pouring aid into Laos – this time mostly for direct military use. In the summer of 1959 fighting broke out between the Pathet Lao (and their North Vietnamese military advisors) and the royal government at the strategic Plain of Jars. Shortly thereafter, the US dispatched Special Forces teams to train government troops in Laos, and in March 1960 the CIA's infamous Air America took delivery of four helicopters in Laos.

Coup & Counter-Coup

In August 1960, a neutralist military faction led by Kong Le seized Vientiane in a coup d'état and recalled Prince Souvanna Phouma from France to serve as prime minister. Rightist General Phoumi Novasan (cousin to Thailand's Marshal Sarit) at first agreed to support the new government and to allow LPF participation, but in a few months changed his mind and withdrew with his troops to southern Laos. Supplied with US guns and ammunitions, in December he launched an attack on Vientiane and wrested control from the neutralists in a CIA-rigged election. Kong Le and his troops retreated to Xieng Khuang, where they joined forces with the PL and North Vietnamese. The USSR supplied this new coalition with armaments and by 1961 they held virtually all of northern and eastern Laos.

A superpower confrontation threatened to erupt when US president John F Kennedy, in his first enunciation of the famous 'domino theory', announced that he would intervene with US troops to prevent what was perceived as a Communist takeover of Laos. A 14-nation conference convened in Geneva in May 1961 to try and halt the crisis. Both sides held their ground, awaiting the outcome of the conference. In July 1962, after long internal and international negotiations, a set of agreements were signed which provided for an independent, neutral Laos. The observance of these agreements was to be monitored by the International Commission for Supervision & Control (ICSC).

A second Government of National Union was formed the following month, a coalition of Prince Boun Oum (representing the rightist military), Prince Souphanouvong (for the PL) and Prince Souvanna Phouma (for the neutralist military). The US, meanwhile, complied with the Geneva agreement by pulling out all 666 of its military advisors and support staff. Seven thousand North Vietnamese ground troops, on the other hand, remained in Laos, completely ignoring Geneva and the ICSC.

The second attempt at a coalition government didn't last long. Minor skirmishes occurred between PL and neutralist troops over the administration of the north-east. The PL seriously upset the tripartite balance of power with an unprovoked attack against Kong Le's neutralist headquarters in Xieng Khuang, thus forcing Kong Le into an alliance with the rightists to avoid defeat.

In 1964, there was a rapid series of coups and counter-coups that resulted in the final alignment of the PL on the one side and the neutralist and right-wing factions on the other. From this point on, the PL leadership refused to participate in any offers of coalition or national elections, quite justifiably believing that they would never be given a voice in governing the country as long as either of the other two factions were in power. Instead they continued to look towards the north Vietnamese, eventually allowing as many as seven North Vietnamese Army (NVA) divisions into north-eastern Laos in direct contravention of the Geneva accords.

War of Resistance

From 1964 to 1973, the war in Indochina heated up. US air bases were established in Thailand, and US bombers were soon crisscrossing eastern and north-eastern Laos on their way to and from bombing missions in North Vietnam and along the Ho Chi Minh trail. Secret saturation bombing of PL and NVA strongholds was carried out, but the PL simply moved their headquarters into caves near Sam Neua. Even without specific targets, B-52 captains would empty their bomb bays over civilian centres in eastern Laos when returning from Vietnamese air strikes so that their orders to release all bombs would be fulfilled. The USA, in fact, dropped more bombs on Laos than they did worldwide during WWII; Laos has earned the distinction of being the most heavily bombed nation, on a per capita basis, in the history of warfare.

As guerrilla resistance in South Vietnam increased, the US military leadership feared that bombing Laos wasn't enough, so they began forming a special CIA-trained army in the country to counter the growing influence of the Pathet Lao. This army of 10,000 was largely made up of Hmong tribesmen under the direct command of the Royal Lao Army (RLA) General Vang Pao, himself a Hmong. These troops were a division of the RLA that was trained for mountain warfare and were not, as has been claimed, mercenaries in the true sense of the term. Like the South Vietnamese, however, they were US-trained (in

The Secret War & Its Legacy

From 1964 to 1973 Laos was a battlefield in a war that most of the western world didn't know about. Basically a continuation of a struggle whose roots extended back centuries, the historic antagonists were the relatively peaceful Indianised cultures west of the Annamite Chain and the more expansionist Sinicised Vietnamese. These enemies were superseded by modern opponents playing native pawns – the Hmong and the Pathet Lao – against one another while committing thousands of their own troops in support.

Both the USA and North Vietnam (along with China) acted in direct contravention of the Geneva Accord of 1962, which recognised the neutrality of Laos and forbade the presence of all foreign military personnel. To evade the Geneva agreement, the USA placed CIA agents in foreign aid posts and temporarily turned air force officers into civilian pilots. The war was so secret that the name of the country was banished from all official communications; participants simply referred to operations in Laos as 'the Other Theater'.

As Christopher Robbins, in his well-researched book *The Ravens* (a code name for US pilots in Laos), has described:

> The pilots in the Other Theater were military men, but flew into battle in civilian clothes: denim cutoffs, T-shirts, cowboy hats and dark glasses ... They fought with obsolete aircraft ... and suffered the highest casualty rate of the Indochina War, as high as 50% ... Each pilot was obliged to carry a small pill of lethal shellfish toxin, especially created by the CIA, which he had sworn to take if he ever fell into the hands of the enemy.

However, US military 'technicians' were in Laos as early as 1959, when they began training the Royal Lao Army (RLA) as well as Hmong hill tribe guerrillas under the charismatic Vang Pao. First used as anti-insurgent armies by the French in Vietnam (a CIA case officer was sent to study French methodology while the French were still embroiled in Indochina), the Hmong became perhaps the most important human component of the US-financed Secret War. The so-called Armée Clandestine grew to 9000 troops by mid-1961 with nine CIA specialists, nine Special Forces officers ('Green Berets') and 99 CIA-trained Thai 'special service' officers in command of a force of Hmong, Lao and Thai footsoldiers. To this day the CIA effort in Laos remains the largest and most expensive paramilitary operation ever conducted by the United States.

Long Tieng (actually Long Chen in Lao), a name which didn't appear on any maps even though with the American-Hmong military presence it became the second-largest city in the country and one of the busiest airports in the world, was the clandestine headquarters for the Other Theatre. Sitting high in the mountains about halfway between Vientiane and the Plain of Jars, Long Tieng was never referred to by its geographic name but by the Air America code name 'Alternate', the Raven nickname 'Shangri-La' or the USAF designation LS ('Lima Site' or Landing Site) 20A.

Other towns and villages around the country with military landing strips were also called 'Lima Sites' and numbered (eg LS 32) and by the early 70s there were over 400 of them. Today Long Tieng is surrounded by the Saisombun Special Zone, a new administrative unit carved out of Luang Prabang and Xieng Khuang provinces by the Lao military due to continuing 'security problems' related to Hmong army remnants in the area who have yet to yield ground to the PL.

Combat planes and bombers used regularly in the Secret War included the Douglas A-1 Skyraider, Vought A-7 Corsair II, Boeing B-52 Stratofortress, McDonnell Douglas F-4 Phantom II and Republic F-105 Thunderchief. The forward air controllers known as the Ravens flew only small, slow prop planes used to fire white phosphorous smoke rockets to mark North Vietnamese Army and Pathet Lao targets for Lao pilots. These included the Cessna O-1 observation aircraft, U-17 (Cessna 185) and longer-range T-28.

The American presence in Royal Lao Goverment-held Laos was so thick when travel writer Paul Theroux passed through while writing *The Great Railway Bazaar* he called Laos 'one of America's expensive practical jokes'.

Of the hundreds of Americans who volunteered to serve in Laos as pilots, intelligence operatives or reconnaissance troops, an estimated 400 died in combat while over 400 others have been classified as 'missing in action' (MIA). The American presence in western Laos, however, paled beside that of the North Vietnamese Army in eastern Laos, a side of the war most western journalists never saw.

On the other side of the battlefield headquartered in the Plain of Jars (Xieng Khuang), Hua Phan and other northern provinces were thousands of Vietnamese-trained Pathet Lao, backed by tens of thousands of North Vietnamese regulars, who didn't bother to disguise themselves as civilians.

The illegal Vietnamese occupation was far greater than the US presence from beginning to end. By 1969 the entire North Vietnamese 316th Division was deployed in Laos, fielding a total of 34,000 combat troops, 18,000 support troops, 13,000 army engineers and 6,000 advisors for the purpose of placing Long Tieng under siege.

Outnumbered and outmanoeuvred, the US-Hmong Thai forces lost Long Tieng and scored few strategic victories during the nine-year Secret War, in spite of the fact that they had superior firepower. They also had the opportunity to ignore virtually all the 'rules of engagement' (aka ROEs, nicknamed 'Romeos') that had to be observed in Vietnam (where they were often cited as an excuse for the US defeat). In Vietnam, for example, the ROEs prohibited bombing within 500m of a temple while in Cambodia there was a 1km limit. In Laos, bombardiers were free to decimate temples, hospitals and any other building that came into their sights.

In support of Vang Pao's army alone, the Ravens and their native cohorts flew 1.5 times the number of air sorties flown in all of Vietnam. Totalling 580,944 sorties by 1973, the secret air force dropped an average of one planeload of bombs every eight minutes, 24 hours a day, for nine years! This cost US taxpayers around US$2 million per day.

After US President Johnson halted all bombing raids on North Vietnam in November 1968, the bombing of Laos increased as more air power became available. An American pilot quoted in *The Ravens* recollects:

> Many times we got so much air we couldn't handle it all. Even before the bombing halt there were times when the weather was so bad over North Vietnam that they would come back (to Laos) in waves. They were damn near out of gas and they wanted to make one pass and get rid of their bombs ... Often you ended up doing saturation bombing in the area you happened to be at the time the first flight got in (to Laos).

In 1970 US President Richard Nixon, on the advice of Henry Kissinger, authorised massive B-52 air strikes in Laos, all of which remained highly classified until years later. Between 1964 and 1969 about 450,000 tonnes of ordnance had been let loose on the country, but afterwards that amount was fielded every year through to the end of 1972. By the war's end the bombing amounted to approximately 1.9 million metric tonnes in all, equalling 10 tonnes per sq km, or over a half-tonne for every man, woman and child living in Laos.

Defoliants and herbicides were also dropped on Laos by the secret air force. During 1965-66, 200,000 gallons of herbicides were deposited along the Ho Chi Minh Trail near Sepon, laying bare all vegetation, poisoning civilian crops and rendering the water system unusable even for irrigation, much less drinking. Dubbed 'Agent Orange' and 'yellow rain' in the modern media, the toxic substance is still responsible for a large number of infirmities suffered by the inhabitants of eastern Laos. The Lao government itself allegedly used Agent Orange captured from the RLG against its own citizens in central Laos for two years following the 1975 PL takeover.

the case of Laos, also Thai-trained) and US-paid. By the end of the 1960s, there were more Thais and Lao Theung than Hmong in the RLA.

In addition, a rotating number of US Air Force pilots, stationed in Long Tieng (the French spelling of Long Chen) and Savannakhet, flew missions in northern and eastern Laos as forward air controllers (FACs), spotting PL and NVA targets for Lao and Thai-piloted tactical bombers.

By 1971 Chinese troops were also engaged in Laos with an air defence force of 6000 to 7000, mostly concentrated along the 'Chinese Road' – actually a complex of roads the Chinese were building in the provinces of Luang Nam Tha, Udomxai and Phongsali. Along with anti-aircraft personnel the Chinese maintained as many as 16,000 Chinese road workers in Laos throughout the war.

Revolution & Reform
In 1973, as the USA began negotiating its way out of Vietnam via the Paris agreements, a ceasefire agreement was reached in Laos. The country was effectively divided into PL and non-PL zones, just as it had been in 1954. Only this time the Communists were in control of 11 out of the 13 provinces instead of two. A Provisional Government of National Union (PGNU) was formed after long negotiations and the two sides began trying to form yet another coalition government. Meanwhile popular support for the PL was growing as the non-PL Vientiane leadership showed signs of corruption and manipulation by the US. The US finally began drawing back from Laos, and the last Air America aeroplane flew across the Mekong River to Thailand in June 1974.

The unexpectedly rapid fall of Saigon and Phnom Penh following US withdrawal in April 1975 led the PL to attack Muang Phu Khun, a strategic RLG and Hmong-defended crossroads between Vientiane and Luang Prabang. It was a crushing defeat for the US-backed forces, and a symbolic final battle in the PL's long struggle.

The LPP applied political pressure to non-PL ministers and generals as well, urging them to resign. Luang Prabang and Vientiane were papered over with threatening posters that left little to the imagination as to what the alternative to resignation might be.

On 4 May 1975, four ministers and seven generals resigned and an exodus of the Lao political and commercial elite across the Mekong into Thailand began. PL forces then seized the southern provincial capitals of Pakse, Champasak and Savannakhet without opposition and on 23 August they took Vientiane in a similar manner.

Lao People's Democratic Republic (LRDP)
Over the following months, the PGNU was quietly dismantled and in December the Lao People's Revolutionary Party (LPRP) was declared the ruling party of the Lao People's Democratic Republic (LPDR). The takeover was bloodless; even the US embassy closed down for only a day.

Kaysone Phomvihane, a protégé of the Vietnamese Communists, served as the Prime Minister of the LPDR until his death in November 1992 at the age of 71. Born Cai Song ('Kaysone' is an approximation of his Vietnamese name in Lao) to a Lao mother and a Vietnamese father in Savannakhet in 1920, Kaysone spent much of his early life in Hanoi, where he studied law. Assisted by the Viet Minh, he helped to organise the Lao Issara resistance movement in the 1940s.

His role in modern Lao politics cannot be overestimated; he was fluent in Lao, Vietnamese, Thai, Shan, French and English, and was considered a highly pragmatic ruler who learned from his mistakes. He was succeeded by former deputy prime minister and defence minister Khamtay Siphandone in the position of prime minister. In 1996 Khamtay was elected president.

Observers of East European politics may notice a close similarity between the 1975 Revolution in Laos and the Communist takeover in Czechoslovakia in 1948. Both involved national fronts, supported by covert Marxist-Leninist parties, which effected semi-legal changes of power through a combination of popular support and armed threats. Furthermore, both countries were in the shadow of intimidating foreign armies stationed at nearby borders, ready to intervene at any moment (the Soviets in the case of Czechoslovakia, the Vietnamese in the case of Laos).

During the first two years of LPRP rule, the harsh political and economic policies caused thousands of refugees to leave the country. The government followed the Vietnamese policy of 'accelerated socialisation' through a rapid reduction of the private sector and a steep increase in agricultural collectivisation.

The practice of the traditional Lao religion, Buddhism, was also severely curtailed (see Religion later in this chapter for more detail).

Military campaigns by the government against its own citizens quickened the exodus of ethnic minorities. Although the war had technically ended in 1975, fighting in the interior continued for another two years, most of it pitting North Vietnamese and PL troops against highlanders in Luang Prabang and Xieng Khuang provinces. The Phu Bia Plateau, a defiant Hmong homeland, was barraged with Soviet artillery, napalm bombs, and chemical weaponry (including trichothecene or 'Yellow Rain'). Many Hmong died (an estimated 10% of all Hmong in the country were killed during the course of the war), while others escaped to Thailand.

Former King Imprisoned After being forced to abdicate the throne despite an earlier proposal by the PL's National Political Consultative Council (headed by 'red' Prince Souphanouvong) endorsing a constitutional monarchy for post-revolution Laos, Savang Vatthana was given a figurehead role in the new government as Supreme Advisor to the President. However in early 1977 anti-Communist rebels briefly seized Muang Nan, 50km south-west of Luang Prabang. When government forces regained

the village, the captured rebels supposedly implicated the former monarchy. Immediately thereafter, the king and his family were banished to a remote area of northern Laos on the Vietnamese border.

Some historical observers today regard the alleged monarchical involvement in the seizure of Muang Nan as disinformation used as an excuse to remove the king from public view.

Although it was announced that the King, Queen, and Crown Prince would be attending a *samana* (re-education camp), they were actually consigned to the cave prisons of Hua Phan, where they perished within four years due to inadequate food rations and the denial of medical treatment. In a 1989 Paris interview, Kaysone Phomvihane replied to a question on the whereabouts of the royal family by saying 'I can tell you now that the King died of natural causes. It happens to all of us'.

The Exodus By mid-1979, this repression had resulted in widespread unrest among the peasants, the traditional power base for Lao communism. As in Vietnam, liberal reforms were undertaken, but in Laos the reforms went further (see Economics and Religion later in this chapter). Unfortunately, the reforms were too little and too late to prevent the further reduction of an already small population. By the end of the 1970s, Lao refugees (including hill tribes) in Thailand constituted 85% of all Indochinese with official refugee status. Unlike the Vietnamese, who had to undertake perilous sea journeys, or the Cambodians, who braved the equally perilous Dang Rek mountains and the 'killing fields' of the Khmer Rouge, Lao refugees had but to cross the Mekong to escape the change of governments.

After 1975 around 300,000 Lao citizens – about 10% of the population – officially resettled abroad. Countless others simply blended into largely Lao-speaking northeastern Thailand. By 1992, approximately 53,000 Lao refugees still resided in six camps in Thailand, and the Thai government set a deadline for all Lao living in

Thailand to return to their homeland or leave for a third country by 1 January 1995. All Lao refugee camps in Thailand are now officially closed, although a few 'holding centres' for hundreds of mostly Hmong refugees in north and north-eastern Thailand remain. These final numbers are undergoing steady repatriation and it is thought the last holding centre will be officially inoperative by the end of 1999.

Laos in the 1980s & 1990s

Samana As many as 40,000 people were sent to re-education camps – known as samana in Lao – and 30,000 imprisoned for 'political crimes' following the 1975 PL takeover (the Union of Lao Organizations in the USA estimate the total number imprisoned at 160,000). One's position in the old regime's hierarchy determined the length of stay; the higher the position, the longer you were subjected to manual labour and daily lectures on the glories of communism.

Since 1989 nearly all camps are reported to have closed and most of the political prisoners – many of whom had been held since 1975 – have been released. At least 30 officials from the former royal government are believed to still be in custody (perhaps double that number have died in camps), and six new prisoners of conscience are known to have received lengthy sentences in Hua Phan camps since 1992.

The influence of the former USSR's glasnost and perestroika policies undoubtedly contributed to further reform in the LPDR during the 1980s in the form of *jintanakan mai* ('new thinking', fancifully translated by some journalists as 'new economic mechanism'). As in other Marxist nations, there has been an ongoing power struggle between the old hardliners and the younger and non-Party leadership, who seek further liberalisation.

In Laos, this is compounded by two conflicting tendencies for policy development. One tendency has been for the Lao leadership to follow the Vietnamese example, the other to implement policies that are developed specifically for the Lao situation.

The second tendency has seemed to gain increasing strength during recent years. But the flourishing of a truly Lao socialism, if such a thing is possible, is still hampered by the direct and unavoidable Vietnamese ideological influence on Lao affairs via high-ranking hardliners in the Lao government who received their military and political training in Hanoi. Younger pragmatists who push for liberalisation always run the risk of being labelled *pátíkạn* (reactionaries).

Relations with Thailand Another very significant influence on modern Laos is its relationship with Thailand. Immediately following the Revolution the Lao government banned practically all things Thai, including Thai university and Buddhist texts – previously central components of educational and religious literature in Laos. Friction grew as Thailand provided resources for huge camps housing thousands of Lao refugees. The conflict culminated in a three-month border war in 1987-88 between the Lao and Thai armies in which over a hundred Lao and Thai soldiers died in combat (the Thai government denies Lao reports that 500 Thai were killed).

The battle seemed to clear the air and the two neighbours have been closer than ever throughout the 1990s; Thai investment is now by far the largest component of the country's foreign portfolio. Some worry that Laos will be overwhelmed by Thai culture and by the Thais' business acumen, and that Laos will eventually become an 'economic province' of Thailand. Others say they would prefer living under Thai economic hegemony to remaining a political vassal of Vietnam.

Preparing for the Future As greater regional economic integration draws Laos into the greater South-East Asian marketplace, the dual influences of Vietnam and Thailand should become more diffuse. Exhibiting their readiness to combine forces with other market economies, government representatives from Laos have been invited to be observers at Association of South-East Asian Nations (ASEAN) meetings since 1992. The country became an ASEAN member in 1997, the eighth full participant in a nine-member organisation that now includes Thailand, Laos, Indonesia, Malaysia, the Philippines, Brunei, Vietnam, Myanmar and Singapore.

As a member of the Mekong River Commission, Laos also signed the 1995 Chiang Rai Accord, an agreement which created joint regulatory roles and mechanisms for settling international disputes with regard to Mekong River use.

Historically, virtually all Lao polities from the early meuang to the LPDR have been dependent on some greater Asian power, whether it be the Siamese, Burmese, Khmer or Vietnamese. Sometimes as many as three of these at one time have exacted tribute, as in the case of 16th century Lan Xang – a vassal of Siam, Myanmar and Vietnam. Add to this the fact that three western powers (France, the USA and the USSR) have contributed greatly to the destabilisation of the Asian balance of power, and the result has been a Laos that has until recently never been able to establish a stable, separate national entity.

When compared with the country's long history of civil and international war, the current state of Lao affairs seems relatively peaceful and stable. Vietnamese and Lao party officials continue to maintain that absolutely no non-Communist Party members will ever be allowed a share in governing any part of Vietnam or Laos. As of 1998 the hardliners still firmly held the upper hand. It remains to be seen whether the Lao will continue to tolerate a Soviet-modelled, one-party system – one of the last to survive the 1989 fall of communism in Russia and Eastern Europe.

GEOGRAPHY

Landlocked Laos shares borders with China, Myanmar, Thailand, Cambodia and Vietnam. It covers 235,000 sq km, an area slightly larger than Great Britain. All of Laos is within the tropics, between latitudes 14°N and 23°N and longitudes 100°E and 108°E. Two main physical features, rivers and mountains, dominate the topography, and their interaction accounts for most of the country's geographic variation. Four biogeographic zones are recognised: the northern Indochina hilly subtropical sector (most of the north); the Annam Trung Son mountain chain (bordering Vietnam from Bulikhamsai Province in the north to Attapeu in the south), the central Indochina tropical lowland plains (along the Mekong River floodplain from Sainyabuli to Champasak) and a small section forming the Indochina transition zone (at the northern tip of Phongsali Province).

Starting 4350km from the sea, 5000m up on the Tibetan Plateau, the Mekong River is known as Lancang Jiang (Turbulent River) in China, Mae Nam Khong (Khong, Mother of Waters) in Thailand, Myanmar and Laos, Tonle Thom (Great Water) in Cambodia and Cuu Long (Nine Dragons) in Vietnam. Half its length runs through China, after which more of the river courses through Laos than through any other South-East Asian country. At its widest, near Si Phan Don, the river can measure 14km across during the rainy season. During the high-water season (July to November) barge trade from China's Yunnan Province brings machinery downriver to Huay Xai and ships timber back up to China. The Mekong's 549km middle reach, what the French colonists called *le bief de Vientiane*, is navigable year-round, from Heuan Hin (north of the Khemmarat Rapids in Savannakhet) to Kok Phong, Luang Prabang, 1074km and 1623km respectively from the sea.

The Mekong Committee (Committee for Coordination of Investigations of the Lower Mekong Basin), set up in 1957 under UN auspices to coordinate development of irrigation, electricity, flood control, fishing and navigation, has recently been revived as the Mekong River Commission. Member states Thailand, Cambodia, Laos and Vietnam have allowed representatives from China and Myanmar to participate in talks since mid-1993.

Mekong River

The 12th longest river in the world – 10th largest in terms of volume – the Mekong is also one of the world's most untamed waterways. Before the completion of the Thai-Lao Friendship Bridge at the end of 1993, not a single span crossed its entire South-East Asian length, and in Laos it is still undammed. Except in Vietnam's Mekong Delta, there are no large cities or industrial zones located anywhere along its banks. Long the main artery of travel within Laos, especially by ferry and speedboat, the Mekong is now increasingly giving way to the all-weather roads that run north and south of Vientiane.

Marco Polo was probably the first European to cross the Mekong, which he accomplished in the 13th century. In the 16th century a group of Portuguese emissaries forded the river at Vientiane, and in the following century the Dutch merchant Geritt van Wuystoff arrived by boat. The Treaty of Bangkok, signed by the French and Siamese on 30 October 1893, officially designated the river as the border between Siam and Indochina.

Now that peace has come to Laos, its hydroelectric and navigation potential will undoubtedly be tapped; a half-dozen hydroelectric facilities and dams are planned, and there is talk of blasting the upper Mekong (north of Luang Prabang) to make it navigable year-round. The river's hydroelectric potential alone is equivalent to the entire petroleum production of Indonesia. Pa Mong, a yet-to-be-built 210m dam planned north of Vientiane, will flood at least 609 sq km and result in the relocation of 43,000 people. Upstream, the Chinese government plans to build over 20 dams along the Mekong and its tributaries over the next 30 years, much to the chagrin of the countries farther down.

Although the six countries each have their own set of priorities, the Chiang Rai Accord signed by the members of the Commission in 1995 now allows them the means to settle disputes, which is an important step in coordinating regional development. Cambodia and Vietnam have the most to lose from exploitation of the Mekong, since they are last in line for its resources. In China, the river's relative remoteness protects it from helter-skelter development. In Thailand a growing environmental movement should temper commercial expansion (though at the same time some Thai companies are looking northward for an escape from conservationist pressures at home). Laos has the most to gain by exploiting the river in ways potentially harmful to the environment, so ultimately it is the key to the river's future.

All the rivers and tributaries west of the Annamite Chain drain into the Mekong. Waterways east of the Annamites (in the provinces of Hua Phan and Xieng Khuang only) flow into the Gulf of Tonkin off the coast of Vietnam.

The Mekong River valley and its fertile floodplains form the country's primary agricultural zones as well, including virtually all of the country's wet-rice lands. The two largest valley sections surround Vientiane and Savannakhet, and these are, as a result, the major population centres. The Mekong and its tributaries are also an important source of fish, a mainstay of the Lao diet.

Major tributaries of the great river include the Nam Ou and the Nam Tha, both of which flow through deep, narrow limestone valleys from the north, and the Nam Ngum, which flows into the Mekong across a broad alluvial plain in Vientiane Province. The latter river is the site of a large hydroelectric plant that is a primary source of power for Vientiane area towns. Electricity generated at the plant is also sold to Thailand and is an important source of revenue for the country. Over 20 other hydroelectric facilities are 'under development' – a term referring to everything from pre-feasibility studies to construction design – for other points along the rivers of Laos.

Mountains and plateaus cover well over 70% of the country. Running about half the length of Laos, parallel to the course of the Mekong River, is the Annamite Chain, a rugged mountain range with peaks averaging 1500 to 2500m in height. Roughly in the centre of the range is the Khammuan Plateau, an area of striking limestone grottoes and gorges. At the southern end of the Annamite Chain stands the 10,000 sq km Bolaven Plateau, an important area for the cultivation of high-yield mountain rice, coffee, tea and other crops that flourish at higher altitudes.

The larger, northern half of Laos is made up almost entirely of broken, steep-sloped mountain ranges. The highest mountains are found in Xieng Khuang Province, where peaks exceeding 2000m are not unusual. Phu Bia, the country's highest peak at 2820m, is found in Xieng Khuang. Just north of Phu Bia stands the country's largest mountain plateau, the Xieng Khuang plateau, which rises 1200m above sea level. The most famous part of the plateau is the Plain of Jars, an area dotted with huge prehistoric stone jars of unknown origin.

CLIMATE
Rainfall
The annual monsoon cycles that affect all of mainland South-East Asia produce a 'dry and wet monsoon climate' with three basic seasons. The south-west monsoon arrives between May and July and lasts into November. Rainfall varies a lot according to latitude and altitude, with the highlands of Vientiane, Bolikhamsai, Khammuan and eastern Champasak provinces getting the most precipitation. The southern peaks of the Annamite Chain receive the heaviest rainfall, over 300cm per year. Luang Prabang, Sainyabuli and Xieng Khuang provinces, for the most part, receive only 100cm to 150cm a year. Vientiane and Savannakhet get about 150 to 200cm, as do Phongsali, Luang Nam Tha and Bokeo.

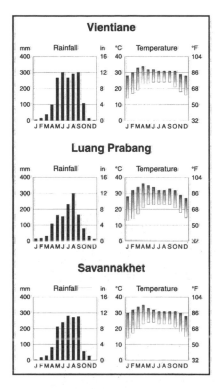

The monsoon is followed by a dry period from November to May, a period that begins with lower relative temperatures (because of the influences of Asia's north-east monsoon, which bypasses Laos but creates cool breezes) through until mid-February. Once the cooling influence of the north-east monsoon has passed, the country experiences much higher relative temperatures from March to May.

Temperatures
As with precipitation, temperatures vary according to altitude. In the humid, low-lying Mekong River valley, as in most parts of Thailand and Myanmar, the highest temperatures occur in March and April (with temperatures approaching 38°C), and the

lowest in December and January (dropping as low as 15°C). In the mountains of Xieng Khuang, however, December to January temperatures can easily drop to 0°C at night; in mountainous provinces of lesser elevation, temperatures may be 5°C to 10°C higher. During most of the rainy season, daytime temperatures average around 29°C in the lowlands and around 25°C in mountain valleys.

ECOLOGY & ENVIRONMENT
The mountains that surround it on every side fortify the land marvellously against the enterprises of foreigners. They render it fertile and abundant in timber for every kind of purpose *and* the Lao have enough left over to provide their neighbours. Whole forests of full grown timber trees grow at the foot of these mountains seeming to have been planted intentionally to serve as a rampart against the great falls of rain which would cause great damage if there were not this natural obstacle.

This prescient observation (and cautionary note) made by Dutch visitor Gerrit van Wuystoff in 1641 holds true for much of Laos today. Although major disruptions were wreaked on the eastern section of the country along the Ho Chi Minh Trail (where herbicides and defoliants – not to mention bombs – were used in abundance during the war), Laos as a whole has one of the most pristine ecologies in mainland South-East Asia. Along with Cambodia, it is also the most understudied country in the region in terms of zoological and botanical research.

Because Laos contains the least exploited, least damaged ecological system in South-East Asia, it's a country of major importance for world wildlife conservation. Many of the plant and animal species found within its borders, though decreasing in numbers, face less risk of extinction than in neighbouring countries mainly due to the comparative lack of population pressure in Laos.

In 1993 the Lao government conferred legal protection upon 17 National Biodiversity Conservation Areas (NBCAs), for a total of 24,600 sq km, or just over 10% of the country's land mass. Most of them are in

southern Laos, which bears a higher percentage of natural forest cover than the north. One of the consulting agencies involved in surveying these areas, the Wildlife Conservation Society, has recommended that an additional 11 sites be added to the list, but so far no further action has been taken.

These NBCA units are not preserves; forests encompassed by this designation, for example, are divided into production forests for timber, protection forests for watershed and conservation forests for pure conservation. The largest of the NBCAs, Nakai-Nam Theun, covers 3710 sq km and is home to the recently discovered *saola* (aka Vu Quang ox, though it bears no relation to an ox) as well as several other species unknown to the scientific world a decade ago.

As in many developing countries, one of the biggest obstacles facing environmental protection is corruption among those in charge of enforcing conservation regulations. Illegal timber felling, poaching and the smuggling of exotic wildlife species would decrease sharply if all officials were held accountable for their civil duties. Lao military personnel themselves are known to use hand grenades and other explosives for catching fish in the nation's lakes and rivers for both recreational and food purposes. Fortunately there is at least some awareness of, and concern for, this type of corruption in Laos. In 1994 the former governor of Attapeu Province was sentenced to 15 years in prison for timber smuggling.

Other threats facing Laos' environment include a widespread lack of awareness of world conservation issues, an absence of legal frameworks, poor definition of authority in conservation areas, lack of communications between national and local governments, and limited funds for conservation purposes.

Most Lao still lead their lives at or just above a subsistence level, consuming comparatively much less of their own natural resources than the people of any 'developed' country. This frugal country ranks 99th in the world with regard to per capita energy consumption by the kilogram-oil-equivalent measure.

Thus the major challenges facing natural Laos today are the internal pressures of economic growth and the external pressures of Laos' more populated and affluent neighbours – particularly China, Vietnam and Thailand – who would like to exploit the country's abundant resources as much as possible.

Over 20 hydroelectric projects, some of which would be contained in the NBCAs, are on the boards for development in the near future. It would be overoptimistic to expect that none of the dams will ever be built, but there is still time for the government to consider cancelling at least some of the projects intended for the more ecologically sensitive areas.

One of the more disturbing aspects of the hydroelectric industry is the way in which companies deliberately apply for concessions in areas zoned for dams, confident in the knowledge that – even if the facility is never constructed – they can usually stall for time long enough to log the valleys intended for inundation. Hence the main profit, whether or not the dams go through, comes from timber. Like solar and wind power, hydropower is a potential source of sustainable and renewable energy when coupled with responsible land/resource planning. The question is, does Laos have the latter?

Tourism, still in its infancy in post-1975 Laos, has thankfully had no major impact on the environment thus far. Until recently the government has wisely avoided giving contracts to companies wishing to develop large-scale resorts. Plans for a huge hotel-casino complex in Champasak Province, financed by a Lao-Thai joint venture and intended for a previously undeveloped area next to the beautiful Khon Phapheng Falls (see Si Phan Don in the Southern Laos chapter for more detail), seems to have been cancelled or at least stalled for the time being. Proponents of the hotel-casino project claimed it would provide job alternatives to local villagers who currently

make their living cutting timber to make charcoal or overfishing the Mekong River to the detriment of the rare Irrawaddy dolphin. Opponents said it would increase overall human activity in the area and lead to environmental degradation. Even the World Bank finally issued a report which concluded the negative ecological consequences of this resort would outweigh any benefits.

Laos has not yet decided to ratify the UN Convention on International Trade in Endangered Species of Wild Flora & Fauna (CITES) although the country does have 'accession' status, meaning it subscribes in principle to the convention but hasn't yet become an official signatory. A traditional trade in rare and endangered species continues unabated, especially in rural areas. While CITES has been somewhat effective in protecting species endangered as a direct result of international trade, the principal cause of species loss worldwide remains habitat destruction.

Doing Your Part

Visitors to Laos can do their bit to conserve the environment in many ways, including: proper disposal of rubbish; avoidance of restaurants which serve threatened or endangered wildlife species; hiking only on established trails; patronising hotels, guesthouses and restaurants which employ 'green' methods of construction and waste disposal as much as possible; and finally by reporting any illegal or unethical environmental practices to international watchdog groups such as the Wildlife Conservation Society (☎ (021) 313133), PO Box 6712, Vientiane, or the International Union for Conservation of Nature & Natural Resources (IUCN, ☎ (021) 216401), 15 Thanon Fa Ngum, Vientiane.

The country's first planned ecological resort, Forespace (☎/fax (021) 217627), PO Box 6679, Vientiane, will design and build a 2km tree-top walkway in the forest canopy of Bokeo Province in north-western Laos. Along with the canopy walkway and tree-top observatories, the blueprint calls for a resources-friendly jungle lodge and herbal sauna. Inspired by similar programmes in South America's Amazonian forests, local hill tribe guides will lead guests on forest walks. A test opening is planned for October 1999.

FLORA & FAUNA
Flora
As in other parts of tropical mainland South-East Asia, with distinctive dry seasons of three months or more, most indigenous vegetation is associated with monsoon forests. Such forests are marked by deciduous tree varieties which shed their leaves during the dry season to conserve water. Rainforests – which are typically evergreen – don't exist in Laos, although non-indigenous rainforest species are commonly seen in the lower Mekong River valley.

Monsoon forests typically exhibit three vegetative layers. Dipterocarps – tall, pale-barked, single-trunked trees that reach as high as 30m – dominate the top canopy of the deciduous monsoon forest, while a middle canopy consists of teak, Asian rosewood and other hardwoods. Underneath are a variety of smaller trees, shrubs, grasses, and – along river habitats – bamboo. In certain plateau areas of the south are dry dipterocarp forests in which the forest canopies are more open, with less of a middle layer and more of a grass-and-bamboo undergrowth layer. Parts of the Annamite Chain are covered by tropical montane evergreen forest, while tropical pine forests can be found on the Nakai Plateau and Sekong area to the south.

According to the IUCN, natural unmanaged vegetation covers 85% of Laos. About half the country (47% to 56% depending on which source you believe) bears natural forest cover. Of these woodlands about half can be classified as primary forest – a very high proportion in this day and age – while another 30% or so represents secondary growth. In South-East Asia, only Cambodia boasts a higher percentage of natural forest cover; worldwide Laos ranks 11th. Although the official export of timber is

tightly controlled, no one really knows how much teak and other hardwoods may be being smuggled out of the country into Vietnam, Thailand, and especially China. During the Indochina War, the Pathet Lao allowed the Chinese to take as much timber as they wanted from the Liberated Zone (11 provinces in all) in return for building roads. Today the Lao army is still taking out huge chunks of forest in Khammuan Province.

Other pressures on the forest cover come from swidden (slash-and-burn) methods of cultivation, in which small plots of forest are cleared, then set afire for nitrogenation of the soil, and farmed intensively for two or three years, after which they are unfarmable. Land processed this way takes eight to 10 years to become fertile again. Environmental researchers are divided among those who believe swidden cultivation is a sustainable agricultural practice that is ultimately less destructive than other forest usages, and those who believe it is not sustainable. Considering the sparse population, swidden cultivation may not be a major threat in Laos – certainly not compared with logging.

In addition to teak and Asian rosewood, the country's flora include a toothsome array of fruit trees (see Food in the Facts for the Visitor chapter), bamboo (more species than any country outside Thailand and China) and an abundance of flowering species such as the orchid. In the high plateaus of the Annamite Chain, extensive grasslands or savanna are common.

Fauna
As in Cambodia, Vietnam, Myanmar and much of Thailand, most of the fauna in Laos belong to the Indochinese zoogeographic realm (as opposed to the Sundaic domain found south of the Isthmus of Kra in southern Thailand or the Paleoarctic to the north in China).

Around 45% of the animal species native to Thailand are shared by Laos, often in greater numbers due to higher forest cover and fewer hunters. Notable **mammals** endemic to Laos include the concolor gibbon, snub-nosed langur, lesser panda, raccoon dog, pygmy slow loris, giant muntjac, Lao marmoset rat and Owston's civet. Other exotic species common to an area that overlaps neighbouring countries in mainland South-East Asia are a number of macaques (such as pig-tailed, stump-tailed, Assamese and rhesus), Phayre's leaf monkey, François' leaf monkey, Douc langur, Malayan and Chinese pangolins, Siamese hare, six species of flying squirrel, 10 species of nonflying squirrel, 10 species of civet, marbled cat, Javan and crab-eating mongoose, spotted linsang, leopard cat, Asian golden cat, bamboo rat, yellow-throated marten, lesser mouse deer, serow (a goat-antelope sometimes called Asian mountain goat), goral (another type of goat-antelope) and 69 species of bats.

According to the latest statistics, around 200 to 500 wild Asiatic elephants roam open-canopy forest areas throughout the country, mainly in Sainyabuli Province west of Vientiane and along the Nakai Plateau in central eastern Laos. In the latter region Vietnamese poachers unfortunately kill the animals for their meat and hides. Around 1100 to 1350 captive or domesticated elephants – used for logging and agriculture can be found scattered around the country, mostly in the provinces of Sainyabuli, Udomxai, Champasak and Attapeu. In total number of work elephants, Laos ranks fourth in Asia after Myanmar, Thailand and India, but in its ratio of elephants to people it ranks first with one elephant per 3920 people; the second closest, Myanmar (which has the largest number of domesticated elephants in the world), has only one per 7130. The Lao PDR government keeps a rare albino (white) elephant in Vientiane as a possible legitimator of its power – just as all Lao kings since Fa Ngum had done. The elephant is rarely seen in public.

More rare are the endangered Asiatic jackal, Asiatic black bear, Malayan sun bear, Malayan tapir, barking deer, sambar (a type of deer), gaur, banteng (both gaur and bantengs are types of wild cattle),

leopard, tiger, clouded leopard and Ir-rawaddy dolphin (see Si Phan Don in the Southern Laos chapter for more detail on these freshwater dolphins).

The most exciting regional zoological discovery of recent years has been the detection of a heretofore-unknown mammal, the spindlehorn (*Pseudoryx nghethingensis*, known as the saola in Vietnam, *nyang* in Laos), a horned animal found in the Anna-mite Chain along the Lao-Vietnamese border. The spindlehorn, which was described in 14th century Chinese journals, was long thought not to exist. The Wildlife Conservation Society has also confirmed another new species of muntjac, plus a rabbit, squirrel, and a warbler. Like the nyang, some of these have also been found in Vietnam, but according to the IUCN 'the prospects for continuing species survival would appear to be better in the Lao PDR than in Vietnam'. A case in point is the recent confirmation in Laos of Vietnam warty pig (*Sus bucclentes*), a species last recorded in Vietnam in 1892 and until recently considered extinct.

A few Javan one-horned and/or Sumatran two-horned rhinos, probably extinct in neighbouring Thailand, are thought to survive in the Bolaven Plateau area of southern Laos. Sightings of kouprey, a wild cattle extinct elsewhere in South-East Asia, have been reported in Attapeu and Champasak provinces as recently as 1993.

Herpetofauna include numerous snake varieties, of which six are venomous: the common cobra, king cobra (hamadryad), banded krait, Malayan viper, green viper and Russell's pit viper. The country's many lizard species include two commonly seen in homes and older buildings, the *túk-kae* (a large gecko) and the *jî-jîan* (smaller house lizards), as well as larger species like the black jungle monitor.

The pristine forests and mountains of Laos harbour a rich selection of resident and migrating **bird** species. Surveys carried out by a British team of ornithologists in 1992-93 recorded 437 species, including eight globally threatened and 21 globally near-threatened species. Notable among these are Siamese fireback, green peafowl, red-collared woodpecker, brown hornbill, tawny fish-owl, Sarus crane, giant ibis and the Asian golden weaver. The urban bird populations are noticeably thin as a result of bird hunting; in downtown Vientiane or Savannakhet it's not uncommon to see someone pointing a long-barrelled musket at upper tree canopies – even on monastery grounds where killing is supposedly not permitted.

Cruelty to Animals

Live frogs in large metal bowls with their legs sewn together (seen at a market in Luang Nam Tha); a live cow tied to the back step of a songthaew (Vang Vieng); a river turtle plucked from the Nam Ou and slung over a fisherman's shoulder by a rope strung through its shell (Nong Khiaw); and live turkeys or chickens carried upside down by their feet (seen all over the country). Would you consider any of the foregoing as 'cruelty to animals'? If so then you're in for a theatre of cruelty in Laos, since – with only the rare slaughterhouse or butcher shop in existence – many rural people deal with all the messy bits involved in transporting and processing animal protein themselves.

Harder to understand, at least for some of us, is the taking of monkeys and other animals from the jungle to be kept as pets – usually tied by a rope or chain to a tree, or confined to cages. Yet this, too, is part of the Lao scene and will probably remain so for some time considering that the average Lao citizen has less than three years of formal education.

Endangered Species

As alluded to above, the distinction between wild animal protein and husbanded animal protein is not yet recognised in Laos, at least not from a moral or ecological perspective. The majority of the population, in fact, derives most of its protein from food culled from nature, not from farms or ranches. How threatening this is to species survival in

Laos is debatable given the nation's extremely sparse population – habitat loss is certainly more of a threat. In the more densely populated areas of the country such as Savannakhet Province, the overfishing of lakes and rivers poses a danger to certain fish species.

The cross-border trade in wildlife is also potentially serious and the largest market at the moment, Vietnam, itself has a very poor record in wildlife management. Much of the poaching that takes place in Laos' NBCAs is in fact carried out by Vietnamese hunters who have crossed into central Laos illegally for the purpose of rounding up such species as pangolins, civets, barking deer, goral and raccoon dogs to sell to their compatriots back home.

Undoubtedly the creature known to be most seriously endangered in Laos at the moment is the Irrawaddy dolphin in the southern Mekong region. At present around a hundred dolphins are thought to survive, but experts say they will all have disappeared within 10 years unless gill-net fishing on the Cambodian side of the border is halted or controlled – not very likely given the current economic and political situation in Cambodia.

The saola and other recently discovered and extremely rare animals in the Nakai Plateau area (see Fauna) are also endangered, but just how much is not known since the population hasn't yet been properly surveyed. Saola horns are a favoured trophy among certain groups on both sides of the Lao-Vietnamese border.

One of the most depressing aspects of discussing animal cruelty or species survival in Laos is knowing that there are no quick fixes available – that, relatively speaking, not much will improve before the country develops a better education system. This will take time, possibly as much as 40 or 50 years if we are to gauge by what has been observed in other nations around the world. Within that time period it is possible that many animal varieties we now know and cherish in Laos will have become extinct.

GOVERNMENT & POLITICS

Since 2 December 1975, the country has been titled the Lao People's Democratic Republic (Sathalanalat Pasathipatai Pasason Lao). Informally, it is acceptable to call the country Laos, or in the Lao language, Páthêt Lao – *páthêt* means land or country, from the Sanskrit *pradesha*. Among English speakers there is a growing tendency to drop the extra 's' added by the French and simply use 'Lao' as the country's shortened unofficial name. Even many western expatriates in the country are now showing a preference for using the name 'Lao'.

Following the 1975 takeover, the former pro-western, monarchical regime was replaced by a government which espoused a Marxist-Leninist political philosophy in alignment with other Communist states, most explicitly the Socialist Republic of Vietnam, the People's Republic of Kampuchea (now the State of Cambodia) and the USSR. The national motto – which appears on all official government stationery – is Peace, Independence, Democracy, Unity & Prosperity (the latter was substituted for 'Socialism' in 1991).

The Party

The central ruling institution in Laos is the Lao People's Revolutionary Party (LPRP), which is modelled on the Vietnamese Communist Party. The LPRP is directed by the Party Congress, which meets every four or five years to elect Party leaders. Other important Party organisations include the nine-member Political Bureau (Politburo), the 49-member Central Committee and the Permanent Secretariat.

The Party ideal is a 'proletarian dictatorship', as proclaimed by the late Secretary General Kaysone Phomvihane in 1977:

To lead the revolution, the working class must act with the help of its general staff, that is to say the political party of the working class, the Marxist-Leninist Party. In our country it is the LPRP which is the sole authentic representative of the interests of the working class, of the working masses of all ethnic groups in the Lao nation.

Despite the claim to proletarianism, membership in the LPRP has consisted mainly of peasant farmers and tribespeople from various ethnic groups, though urban worker membership has increased since the 1975 Revolution. Before the Revolution, Party membership was about 60% Lao Theung (lower mountain dwellers, mostly of proto-Malay or Mon-Khmer descent), 36% Lao Loum (lowland Lao) and 4% Lao Sung (mostly Hmong and Mien hill tribes). Today's percentages are known only by the Party leadership.

The main seat of LPRP power, as in most Communist parties, is the Politburo, which officially makes all policy decisions. In theory, the nine members of the Politburo are selected by the Party Central Committee. In practice, since the Secretary General of the Politburo, the Secretariat and the Central Committee are all the same man, Khamtay Siphandone (who is also the President), virtually all members of these major Party organs are co-opted by this lead position, which has enjoyed the full support of the Vietnamese since the 1940s.

Administration

The LPDR government is structured along Socialist Republic of Vietnam (SRV) lines. The Council of Government, like the SRV's Council of Ministers, consists of twelve ministries (eg the Ministry of Information & Culture). As well as the Council of Government, there is the Office of the Prime Minister, the National Bank, the National Planning Committee and the Nationalities Committee.

The National Assembly (formerly the Supreme People's Assembly) serves as the government's legislative body and is modelled on the SRV's National Assembly and the former USSR's Supreme Soviet. Since the Revolution, total membership in the Assembly has varied and at present totals 99. All but one of the current National Assembly deputies are Communist Party members, and over two-thirds are also members of the Lao Front for National Construction and the Alliance of Lao Patriotic Neutralist Forces

Corruption

The Lao have a saying which they may utter whenever they want to indicate to someone that they're not rich, or that they can't afford a high asking price: 'I'm (one of the) people, not (one of the) government'. In other words *phùu míi sǐi* – 'people with colour' (ie those in uniform) – are generally assumed to have access to wealth denied the average civilian. As in many developing countries, the low salaries paid to government employees understandably motivate some civil servants to seek other sources of income. Some moonlight by working other jobs outside government hours, while others take the easy money offered to them by private interests seeking to navigate the Lao government bureaucracy.

At the everyday level of the common bureaucrat, this takes the form of minor bribes or 'tips' of a few thousand kip here and there, accepted for faster or preferential service, or sometimes simply for doing one's job. At higher levels of government the sums can be vast. Virtually any foreign organisation – governmental or non-governmental, public or private – that wants to do business in Laos participates in the game in one way or another. Bids for government or foreign-aid contracts – especially highway projects, energy programmes and other high-ticket items – face fierce competition in the development world and the deciding factor often comes down to which company pays the best kickback. Unfortunately this sometimes results in substandard project fulfilment since it's not always the best company that gets the contract. Foreign companies and aid organisations also usually have a 'fixer' on staff, a Lao whose job it is to arrange air tickets when the planes are full or to smooth over other inconveniences. Such practices, of course, exacerbate corruption.

Considering that the Lao government is able to collect very little in income taxes from its own citizens, some corruption is understandable as a way to generate income for government works. Most bribes, after all, are a kind of luxury tax on the rich. Through minor corruption, a government uniform provides those who aren't very well educated or very ambitious with an earning potential they couldn't otherwise achieve.

But many Lao privately express the opinion that corruption in Laos is getting a little out of hand. An estimated 40% of all foreign aid goes directly to the government payroll and the more aid and investment funds come into the country, the richer the ministers and their cronies become. Huge chateau-style estates are springing up on the outskirts of Vientiane for high-ranking government officials and their relatives.

Meanwhile the government spends less than 20% of the national budget on social welfare. This mimics exactly the level of government corruption the Pathet Lao (PL) promised to wipe out when they wrested power from the Royal Lao Government in 1975. For those citizens who believed in the socialist ideal of socio-economic equalisation and the redistribution of wealth the increasingly visible signs of corruption are disillusioning.

(a group of military officers aligned with the Lao People's Revolutionary Army). In this the Assembly has become increasingly Party-oriented since the Revolution, when only around two-thirds of the deputies were LPRP members. Assembly deputies are elected by the public; in the last election some 160 candidates competed for the 99 available seats.

The Assembly's main function thus far has been to meet once every year to give approval to the declarations of the prime minister. They also 'elect' both the president and prime minister every five years, though in reality these choices are decided in advance by the 49-member Central Committee of the Party. In spite of the obvious lack of surprise in such an election, the last poll, held in February 1998, took place in total secrecy.

Constitution & Legal Code

For 15 years following the Revolution, the LPDR had no constitution. The first official constitution was drafted in mid-1990 by the Party for the approval of the National Assembly. Interestingly enough, it contains no reference to socialism in the economy but formalises private trade and foreign investment. The constitution also removed the hammer-and-sickle and Communist star from the official national seal to be used on government signs and stationery, replacing it with a likeness of Vientiane's sacred Pha That Luang monument (see the Economy section later in this chapter for more information on the Lao brand of Communism). Red flags bearing the hammer-and-sickle are still raised around the country on National Day (2 December).

The LPDR's first legal code was not enacted until 1988, the same year that Vientiane began searching abroad for foreign

National Symbols

Laos' national seal, often applied to official government publications, features a near-complete circle formed by curving rice stalks which enclose six component symbols of the productive proletarian state: Vientiane's Pha That Luang (which represents religion); a checkerboard of rice fields (agriculture); gear cogs (industry); a dam (energy); a highway (transport); and a grove of trees (forestry). A label in Lao script at the bottom of the seal reads 'Lao People's Democratic Republic'.

The national flag consists of two horizontal bars of red (symbolising courage and heroism), above and below a bar of blue (nationhood) on which is centred a blank white sphere (the light of communism), sometimes also interpreted as a moon. This flag is flown in front of all government offices and by some private citizens on National Day (2 December).

On this holiday the Lao national flag may be joined by a second flag featuring a yellow hammer and sickle centred on a field of red, the international symbol of communism. The latter's display is rather ironic given the fact that the word 'communism' doesn't appear in any government documents, not even the Lao constitution, and considering that the hammer and sickle were wilfully removed from the national seal in the early 90s. Nor are there any public statues of Lenin or Marx anywhere in the country, save for one Lenin bust in Vientiane's Lao Revolutionary Museum.

The late Kaysone Phomvihane, founder of the Lao People's Revolutionary Party, has become the country's foremost national hero. In 1995 the government took delivery of 20 busts of Kaysone from North Korean sculptors who produced similar figures of the late Korean dictator Kim Il Sung. These busts have been placed beneath Lao Buddhist-style pavilions in the centre of newly constructed public memorial squares in every provincial capital as well as in other selected locations around the country.

capital. The new canon set up a court system, prosecutor's office, criminal trial rules and one of Asia's most liberal investment codes. Although the Lao constitution guarantees property rights, the Pathet Lao still holds substantial amounts of private property seized in 1975. Only through direct military connections have many people begun to get their land and houses back.

Lao Front for National Construction

The Lao Front for National Construction (LFNC) was formed in 1979 to take the place of the old Lao Patriotic Front, which had been in existence since 1956 as a political cover for the clandestine Lao People's Party. Its new incarnation was intended to quell unrest among the general population by providing mass participation in a nationalistic effort, much like the Fatherland Front in the SRV. In other words, you don't have to be a Party member to join, as long as you follow Party principles.

The LFNC is comprised of the LPRP, the Federation of Lao Trade Unions, the Federation of Lao Peasants, the Association of Women and other groups originally organised by the Party. The Front is administered by a National Congress (the general membership), a Presidium (headed by President Khamtay Siphandone, elected by the National Assembly), a Secretariat, a Central Committee and local committees at the village, canton, district and provincial levels.

Like the National Assembly, the LFNC has no real power and appears mainly to serve as a rubber stamp apparatus for LPDR policies. There is a potential for pluralism in the Lao government structure, however, which may eventually be realised (assuming eastern European trends are paralleled).

Political Divisions

Laos has been divided up into 16 different *khwāeng* (provinces): Wieng Chan (Vientiane), Sainyabuli, Luang Prabang, Luang Nam Tha, Xieng Khuang, Hua Phan, Phongsali, Bokeo, Udomxai, Bolikhamsai, Khammuan, Savannakhet, Salavan, Sekong, Attapeu and Champasak.

In addition to this, Vientiane (Kamphaeng Nakhon Wieng Chan) is an independent prefecture on an administrative parity with the provinces. The eastern half of Vientiane Province and parts of Xieng Khuang and Bolikhamsai provinces, which have been chronically troubled by armed bandit and/or insurgent attacks, were joined together into the 'Saisombun Special Zone' in 1995 and is administered by the Lao military.

Below the province is the *meúang* (district), which is comprised of two or more *tátséng* (subdistricts or cantons), which are in turn divided into *bâan* (villages).

Ties with Vietnam

The Vietnamese influence on Lao political affairs is still strong, thanks to continuing connections between ageing hardliners educated in Vietnam and their ideological mentors. Several of the high-ranking party members with Vietnamese military and political training – including former presidents Kaysone Phomvihane and Souphanouvong (the 'Red Prince') – died between 1992 and 1995, leading some observers to believe that Vietnamese influence will wane in the future as the hardliners are replaced by younger pragmatists.

The current president, the 71-year-old Khamtay Siphandone, however, was trained in Hanoi and has close links with the Vietnamese military establishment. The prime minister, Choummaly Sayasone, elected in early 1996, formerly served as the country's Defence Minister and is also considered a hardliner who is primarily influenced by Vietnamese political ideology.

Dissent & Insurgency

Unlike in eastern Europe in 1988-90, where popular dissent led to massive political changes, or in China and Myanmar, where widespread dissent has met with harsh suppression, there is currently no significant 'democratic movement' or widespread outspoken discontent in Laos. In part this can be explained by the Lao Buddhist tendency to say *'baw pen nyãng'* ('it doesn't matter') when faced with adversity, and in part because by and large the Lao appear to be satisfied with the post-Revolutionary political system, which has brought them the first extended period of secular peace they've known in three centuries. The threat of being sent to samana certainly silenced most protest during the late 1970s and 1980s.

But probably the most compelling reason dissent is noticeably absent is simply because dissenting Lao have a built-in escape hatch, the Mekong River border with Thailand. Dissenters can vote with their feet, easily crossing the river into north-eastern Thailand, where with little difficulty they blend in with their Lao-speaking Isaan brethren. Ten per cent of the population has left Laos in this fashion since 1975, among them an estimated three-quarters of the country's intelligentsia – perhaps those most inclined to voice political dissatisfaction.

Still, a small insurgent movement – quite possibly several – lurk in the forests and mountains. Some are Hmong warriors who seek to fulfil Vang Pao's dream of creating an independent Hmong district, or who are simply seeking revenge for Pathet Lao defeats or for long stints in re-education camps. Other factions may be armed groups financed by fanatical anti-Communist Thais who had connections with the now-defunct Royal Lao Army, and by US POW/MIA groups hoping to gain information on US airmen lost in Laos during the war. In the early 1990s the US National League of Families, a previously respected POW/MIA advocacy group, were discovered to have diverted US$700,000 to guerrilla training programs, led by a retired American colonel, for Lao and Hmong living in Thailand.

Experts speculate there may be several thousand (estimates vary from a conservative 200 to a ridiculous 10,000) armed insurgents in the hinterland. The Ethnic Liberation Organisation of Laos (ELOL), considered the largest opposition group, is comprised of remnants of a Hmong insurgency called the Chao Fa (Lords of the Sky) who came together in 1975 under Hmong leader Zhong Zhua Her (aka Pa Kao Her). The latter was a senior Hmong resistance

fighter against Pathet Lao and Vietnamese forces in the 1960s and early 1970s. From 1980 until 1984 the Chao Fa received sanctuary, training and weapons from China; after China withdrew support, Zhong Zhua Her reorganised the group in Sainyabuli Province under the name ELOL and reportedly now commands the only outpost in Laos never penetrated by the Communists. As of the mid-1990s the organisation allegedly consisted of 2,000 armed soldiers (plus many more 'trained but unarmed' reserves), but verification of these figures is very difficult to come by.

The second largest insurgency organisation in the country, the Lao National Liberation Front (LNLF), consists of Hmong membership loyal to Vang Pao with a combined force of around 1500 in Xieng Khuang Province. Despite ethnic kinship, the LNLF and ELOL have no alliance and are in fact reported to be hostile towards one another.

A 'Lao United Independence Front' occasionally issues messages to the Thai media proclaiming a 'provisional government' somewhere in Laos, but if this group really exists at all it is probably on Thai soil. Other groups who have issued anti-government decrees include the Free Lao National Liberation Movement, the Free Democratic Lao National Salvation Force and the France-based Movement for Democracy in Laos.

For the most part these rebels – when active at all in Laos – operate sporadically. Nothing exists on the scale of insurgency that goes on, for example, in Cambodia, Myanmar or the Philippines. Meanwhile international support for any such movements steadily wanes as the Pathet Lao government continues to open the country to more political and economic freedoms. For more details on armed rebel activity in Laos, see Dangers & Annoyances in the Facts for the Visitor chapter.

For its part, the Thai government is very sensitive to accusations that Thailand may be harbouring an insurgent movement, however small. In the early 1990s, the US Department of State received complaints from the governments of Thailand and Laos concerning the alleged conduct of US nationals and legal residents who were reportedly involved in efforts to overthrow or otherwise destabilise the Lao government, activities which allegedly took place in Thailand and Laos. That same month, three US citizens and one legal resident were arrested in Thailand for the possession of unauthorised weapons. All four were subsequently deported from Thailand. The Thai government has also issued an outstanding order to place Hmong General Vang Pao – currently residing in the US – under immediate arrest if he comes to Thailand.

ECONOMY
Pre-Revolutionary Economics
Approximately 80% of the Lao population works in agriculture, fishing and forestry; another 10% is employed in the armed forces or in the civil service while an estimated 10% are unemployed. These figures have remained virtually the same both before and after the 1975 Revolution. Laos has been dependent on foreign aid since the 1950s, however, and the amounts and sources of aid have varied greatly over the intervening years.

Between 1968 and 1973, when US aid to the Royal Lao Government (RLG) was at its peak (about US$74.4 million a year), the Lao received as much aid per capita as almost anyone in the world. This aid, of course, was enjoyed by those in the RLG-controlled Vientiane/Luang Prabang/Savannakhet zone and not by those in the Pathet Lao 'liberated zone' (who got US bombs instead). During this period (and back as far as 1964, when the War of Resistance really began), the 11 provinces of the liberated zone existed on a subsistence economy supplemented by commodity assistance from the USSR, China and North Vietnam.

Post-Revolutionary Reforms
After the termination of US aid in 1975, the Vientiane economy collapsed and the new

Lao Economic System
Laos' current economic system can perhaps best be described as a capitalist reality trimmed with socialist ideology. *Jintanakan mai* (new thinking), the Lao version of perestroika, is another term for what the Lao rulership claims is a loyal rendering of Marxism, in which capitalist practices are a way-station on the road to full socialism. When will full socialism be achieved? 'When world conditions are ripe', according to government leaders.

As the Minister for Foreign Affairs told visiting reporters who gathered in Vientiane for the 20th anniversary of the 1975 revolution in December 1995: 'The Lao People's Revolutionary Party is still a party of Marxist-Leninist ideology and the new prosperity being enjoyed by many in the country exists as the product of that ideology, not despite it'.

Observers who would criticise the leadership for what might appear to be hypocrisy should pause to remember that the Lao revolution was more motivated by nationalism than Communist ideology. Because Ho Chi Minh and the North Vietnamese were the only party who would support their struggle, Lao nationalists walked and talked like their ideological masters, but in governing their new state followed a pragmatic path. When collectivisation didn't work, it was quickly abandoned; when the outright suppression of Buddhist monasticism violated the people's mandate, this policy too was relinquished.

One gets the impression that, for all its blunders, the Lao rulers really do have the general population's best interests at heart. Even the restrictive tourism policy – as wrongheaded as it may appear to outsiders – seems an expression of the government's preoccupation with dignity and security over money.

government found itself struggling to manage a virtually bankrupt state. Until 1979, policies of 'accelerated socialisation' (the nationalisation of large private sector businesses and the collectivisation of all agriculture) only made conditions worse. In July 1979, however, the government stopped the creation of new collectives and ordered the consolidation of existing ones, admitting that most Lao peasants were dissatisfied with the system.

Under the new policy, a certain amount of free enterprise was allowed at the village level. For example, families were given permission to cultivate individual rice fields, although major farming activities (clearing fields, planting, weeding and harvesting) were to be done cooperatively. Anyone who is familiar with rice farming in mainland South-East Asia knows that this is exactly how it's done traditionally, even in the more capitalist countries such as Thailand. Rice harvests in Laos are divided into three portions: one for the state, one for the village rice bank, and one for the family (according to a per capita ration system) for sale or consumption.

The LPRP has also made radical changes in monetary policy (allowing a free-floating currency) and commodity pricing (bringing prices closer to free market rates), with the result that by the end of the 1980s the economy appeared to be relatively stable. Both consumer goods and agricultural products are widely available. The exception is in the rural areas of the south, where temporary rice shortages are still common.

In 1987, the government further loosened restrictions on private enterprise. Prior to that year, only about half of the shophouses along Vientiane's main commercial avenue, Thanon Samsenthai, were open. By the end of 1989, at least 75% had opened their doors and today the whole avenue is thriving again. Foreign private investment is now welcome in Laos.

Private land ownership is now legal in Laos. Many farmers and householders (but by no means all) whose family lands had been collectivised since 1975 have been able to reclaim their property. Since 1991 even selected pre-1975 aristocrats – at least those who have the wherewithal to provide 'favours' to the political establishment – have been permitted to reclaim their former villas.

Current Income, Infrastructure & Inflation

But the credit for economic stabilisation can't all be ascribed to the liberalisation of the economy per se. Foreign aid has also greatly increased since 1980, making up as much as 78% of the national budget in certain years. Asian Development Bank (ADB) loans and other kinds of credit have also increased as the country's credit image has improved. UN agencies like UNESCO and the United Nations Development Programme (UNDP) are pouring funds and personnel into Laos as the country again becomes a player in the international development game. Several non-governmental organisations (NGOs) including as Save the Children, Mines Advisory Group and World Concern are also present.

Foreign aid averages over US$150 million per year, around 70% of which comes from multilateral donors such as the ADB, UNDP and UNICEF, 25% from bilateral donors (mainly from Japan, Sweden, Australia, France, Germany, Switzerland and the US) and 5% from NGOs. Russian aid fell by 60% in 1990 and virtually ceased in 1991. The US Congress rescinded a 20 year ban on aid to Laos in 1995. All totalled, foreign aid comprises around 45% of the annual national budget, of which an astounding 40% goes directly to the Lao government payroll.

Yet another reason the economy has developed since 1989 is due to the tolerance of the *talàat mèut* (free, or 'black', market). Markets everywhere in Laos trade freely in untaxed goods from Thailand, China and elsewhere and the changing of international currency (mostly US dollars and Thai baht) is quite open.

A small entrepreneurial class, along with members of the Communist establishment who thrive on bribes and kickbacks, are flourishing in the cities, having attained a privileged economic status reminiscent of the French colonials. Lao and Thai architects are working overtime to design and build huge manors surrounded by gardens and swimming pools for the use of these groups.

On an international scale, however, Laos is still one of the 10 poorest countries in the world, keeping company with such countries as Bhutan, Bangladesh and Rwanda. According to the World Bank definitions, an estimated 46% of Lao citizens fall below the poverty line for Laos.

The annual per capita income in 1998 was US$370 (up from US$135 in 1989), which places Laos ahead of Vietnam and Cambodia (both US$270), but below both China (US$655) and Bhutan (US$420). If income is measured using the 'purchasing power parity' method (which takes into account price differences between countries), the Lao average US$1775 per capita annually, compared to US$8165 in Thailand and US$1430 in Vietnam.

Gross National Product (GNP) growth in 1998 was estimated to be a relatively strong 6.9% per annum (compared with Thailand's -0.4%). Further on the bright side, Laos has one of the lowest foreign debts in Asia, mainly because of heavy international aid. Exports of goods and services grew from 4% of GDP in 1985 to 23% in 1996, followed by an inexplicable decline to single-digit levels in 1997 and 1998 despite the lower price tags (in dollar terms) for export goods.

The economic turmoil that struck the rest of South-East Asia in 1997-98 naturally had an impact on the Lao economy. The Lao national currency (kip) fell into a deflationary tailspin along with the Thai baht and many Thai-financed development projects – such as the Huay Xai-Luang Nam Tha highway – were postponed or even scrapped. To a large extent, however, the Lao economy was cushioned from the full impact of the crash due to the heavy reliance on western aid; the large proportion of the population living at a subsistence level were less affected as well.

Inflation in Laos declined significantly in the early 1990s, from 65% in 1989 to just 6% to 9% between 1992 and 1996. In 1997 and 1998 the real-dollar inflation rate was flat, even deflationary, as the kip continued to decline due to regional pressures on local currencies, especially the Thai baht, and an insatiable demand for dollars. Real-dollar inflation in Vientiane is somewhat higher – perhaps 10% to 12% per annum – due to the heavy influx of foreign aid specialists on expat salaries. It's difficult at this point to assign an accurate inflation rate to the kip itself since the exchange rate was fluctuating wildly through the latter half of 1997 and throughout 1998, but as we went to press the World Bank estimated it had slowed to 6.2%.

Economic Regionalisation

About a third of the population live in the Mekong valley, where trade with Thailand is vital. Another 10% or so live in recently emerging economies in the extreme north (primarily Udomxai, Phongsali and Luang Nam Tha), where trade with China is dominant but where there has been little Lao government control since 1989. A similar situation exists along the Savannakhet-Lao Bao corridor between the Thai and Vietnamese borders, where a three-way trade between Vietnam, Laos and Thailand goes on with little Lao government intervention.

A slim but significant 2% to 3% of all Lao participate in the insulated Luang Prabang economy, where production is growing but self-limited because of the area's isolation from exterior markets. Rising incomes in Luang Prabang are heavily infused with foreign aid money and tourism receipts. Once Route 13 is extended all the way from Luang Prabang to the Chinese border it will become a major trade crossroads (much to the chagrin of those who would like to keep the city quaint and charming).

Between 50% and 60% of the nation's population still live at a subsistence level, largely autonomous from all government involvement, in small villages scattered throughout the country.

Agriculture & Forestry

Only around 7% of the total land area in Laos is considered suitable for agriculture. Cultivation is carried out according to dual patterns, one for the lowlands and one for the highlands.

Lowland agriculture involves permanent farming communities which cultivate irrigated fields; in the highlands, farming communities are to some extent migrational, preferring to use swidden ('slash-and-burn') methods in which forest is cut to the ground and burned in preparation for planting. The Lao government is trying to discourage swidden agriculture among the highland peoples in order to prevent deforestation; current estimates indicate that around a million Lao farmers still practise this form of cultivation.

Important crops in the lowlands include rice, corn, wheat, cotton, tobacco, peanut, soybean, fruits and vegetables. In the mountains, dry rice, tobacco, tea, coffee, maize and opium (by far the country's most lucrative agricultural product) are the major cash crops.

Since about two-thirds of the country is forested, timber and wood products are also important products, comprising up to 25% of Laos' annual exports. Teak is the most important wood for export earnings, followed by secondary forest products like benzoin, a resin which is used to make perfume, and cardamom, a spice.

Minerals

Laos' greatest economic potential lies in its rich mineral resources, which include tin, coal, oil, iron, copper, gold, phosphorite, gypsum, zinc and salt. Many of these are just starting to be exploited. Several international oil companies are currently engaged in petroleum exploration, mostly in southern Laos.

Hydroelectric Power

Laos has 60,400 cubic metres of renewable water resources per capita, more than any other country in Asia (compared with Thailand at 2000 cubic metres, Myanmar 24,000 and Vietnam 5400).

The Nam Ngum dam, 70km north of Vientiane, generates most of the electricity used in the Vientiane valley. In addition, Thailand buys about 850 million kilowatt-hours per year from Laos, via high power lines that stretch across the Mekong to as far away as Udon Thani.

Once the necessary equipment is established along newly paved Route 13, Luang Prabang will join the Vientiane valley power grid. Near Tha Khaek, the Nam Theun-Hin Bun dam project will export all of its 210-megawatt output to power-hungry Thailand by the year 2000, connected to Thailand's main grid via a 95km transmission line to Sakon Nakhon Province. Around 20 other hydropower plants are also in the works. Laos' biggest investment projects are all energy-related: Nam Theun 2 (Thai, French Australian and Lao), Hongsa Lignite (Thai), Nam Ngiep 1 (USA) and Nam Ngum 2 (USA).

Fishing

The rivers in Laos yield a steady supply of fish, an important source of nutrition for the general population. The huge lake (370 sq km) created by the damming of the Nam Ngum is being used for a number of experimental fisheries. If these and other fishery projects are successful, Laos will probably begin exporting freshwater fish to Thailand in the future.

Manufacturing

This sector of the economy is expanding rapidly, with garments and motorcycle assembly capturing the largest segments of the country's export market. Although most of the consumer goods used in the country are imported from Thailand or elsewhere, there are factories in Vientiane which produce soft drinks, beer, cigarettes, bricks and cement. Foreign investment has begun moving from raw materials to joint manufacturing ventures, though Laos doesn't have as large and skilled a labour force as Vietnam, which currently attracts such ventures.

In anticipation of the future, the government has plans to develop Khammuan

Opium & the Golden Triangle

The opium poppy, *Papaver somniferum*, has been cultivated and its resins extracted for use as a narcotic at least since the time of the early Greek Empire. The Chinese were introduced to the drug by Arab traders during the Kublai Khan era (1279-94). It was so highly valued for its medicinal properties that hill tribe minorities in southern China began cultivating the opium poppy in order to raise money to pay taxes to their Han Chinese rulers. Easy to grow, opium became a way for the nomadic hill tribes to raise what cash they needed in transactions (willing and unwilling) with the lowland world. Many of the hill tribes that migrated to Thailand and Laos in the post-WWII era, in order to avoid persecution in Burma and China, took with them their one cash crop, the poppy. The tall flowering plant is well suited to hillside cultivation as it flourishes on steep slopes and in nutrient-poor soils.

The opium trade became especially lucrative in South-East Asia during the 1960s and early 1970s when US armed forces were embroiled in Indochina. Alfred McCoy's *The Politics of Heroin in Southeast Asia* recounts how contact with the GI market not only expanded the immediate Asian market, but provided outlets to world markets. Before this time the source of most of the world's heroin was the Middle East. Soon everyone wanted a piece of the profits and various parties alternately quarrelled over and cooperated in illegal opium commerce. Most notable were the Nationalist Chinese Army refugees living in northern Burma and northern Thailand, and the Burmese anti-government rebels, in particular the Burmese Communist Party, the Shan States Army and the Shan United Army.

The American CIA eventually became involved, using profits from opium and heroin runs aboard US aircraft (the infamous Air America, a CIA front) from Laos to Vietnam and farther afield to finance covert operations throughout Indochina. This led to an increase in the availability of heroin throughout the world, which in turn led to increased production in the remote northern areas of Thailand, Burma and Laos, where there was little government interference. This area came to be known as the 'Golden Triangle' because of fortunes amassed by the 'opium warlords' – mostly Burmese and Chinese military-businessmen who controlled the movement of opium across three international borders.

As more opium was available, more was consumed and the demand increased along with the profits – so the cycle expanded. As a result, opium cultivation became a full-time job for some hill tribe groups within the Golden Triangle. Hill economies were thus destabilised to the point where opium production became a necessary means of survival for thousands of people.

Opium in Laos Opium has been cultivated, processed and used in northern Laos for centuries but the country didn't become a major producer until the passing of the 1971 Anti-Narcotics Law by the Royal Lao Government (at the urging of the US government), a

Province in central Laos – an area rich in mineral and forest resources plus easy access to markets in both Thailand and Vietnam – as an industrial centre.

Tourism

Since the Lao government first began keeping tourism records, the number of annual visitors has increased from 14,400 in 1991 to 403,000 in 1996, the latest year for which statistics are available. Over half (227,600) of the 1996 total comprised visitors from Thailand, many of them on border passes of three days or fewer. Others included 65,500 from Vietnam and 16,700 from China, followed by 11,600 from France, 11,100 from the USA, 6600 from Japan, 6100 from Australia and around move which helped drive regional prices up steeply. This is turn resulted in an increase in criminal activity and in the increased use of heroin among former opium addicts (since heroin could be more easily transported and concealed). Licensed opium dens were permitted until the PL revolution. In 1975 there were over 60 licensed dens in Vientiane, and probably many other unlicensed ones; their current legal status is unclear though opium-smoking dens certainly still exist, even in Vientiane.

Today opium – until 1991 an official export in spite of objections from the USA and neighbouring countries – probably remains the country's biggest export earner. Worldwide the country ranks third in production after Myanmar (Burma) and Afghanistan, with annual crops yielding anywhere from 100 to 200 tonnes of refined opium, surpassing even the figures for colonial Laos under the French. Grown and collected by the Hmong, Akha, Lolo and Mien tribes – experts estimate around 60,000 families in 2200 villages plant poppy – about half the product leaves the country along smuggling routes through Thailand, Cambodia and China, while the other half is consumed in Laos. Some opium is also refined into heroin in clandestine laboratories in the north (and just over the Chinese border in Yunnan), and then smuggled out of the country.

Poppy is cultivated in 10 provinces, particularly throughout the north, although unlike in Myanmar it's not used to finance insurgent armies nor are there opium warlords per se. Instead it's mostly grown in small to medium-size plots, with planting beginning in October and harvesting taking place in January or February. Prices for processed (boiled) opium in Laos fluctuate from US$50 to US$120 per kg depending on the size of the annual harvest. Due to the country's rugged terrain and lack of roads, large-scale poppy cultivation is much tougher to combat here than in Thailand.

In 1987 the Lao and US governments signed an agreement to allow a Lao-American Counter-Narcotics Cooperation programme to be carried out in northern Laos. The UN Drug Control Programme (UNDCP) also operates in the country; four UNDCP workers were killed in an ambush near Phalavek in 1995. The principal thrust of these programmes is to train poppy-growers in crop substitution. Experience with similar projects in Thailand indicates that success only occurs in areas where crop substitution is accompanied by a concentrated effort to indoctrinate the minority ethnic groups into the mainstream lowland culture.

For many ethnicities in Laos, opium plays an important role in traditional medicine. The Lao government doesn't discourage the latter use, instead concentrating on locating and destroying large fields. A recent French study concluded that in villages where opium was produced, only about 11% smoked it regularly and less than five per thousand were addicted to the point where they could no longer work. Among many ethnic groups, raw opium sap, pressed oil and/or poppyseeds also feature significantly in the villagers' daily food intake.

4000 each from the UK and Germany. Other nationalities averaged a thousand visitors or fewer in that year. Also in 1996, 26,200 foreigners (mostly Indians, Sri Lankans, Bangladeshis and Pakistanis) went to Laos seeking visa extensions – most of them for Thailand.

According to the National Tourism Authority of Laos (NTAL), 780,000 visitors are expected to turn up in Laos in 1999 – not an unreasonable expectation given the increases seen between 1991 and 1996. To help meet that expectation the NTAL has mounted a 'Visit Laos 1999' campaign that will involve special exhibits at tourism trade shows around the world as well as a raft of new printed promo materials distributed via embassies and travel agencies.

The total revenue earned from these arrivals in 1996 was estimated to be US$12 million, up from US$2.2 million in 1991. This makes tourism the country's fourth most important source of income, although Laos still lags far behind Thailand.

Foreign Investment in Laos

Laos has one of the most liberal foreign investment codes in the world. Unlike in neighbouring Thailand, where foreign companies are legally limited to a maximum 49% ownership in any enterprise, the Lao government allows 100% foreign ownership in approved projects. Two major conditions apply: investors must operate through a broker to obtain all permits (including business visas) and 100% foreign ownership is limited to 15 years unless an extension is approved.

Working through a broker involves sometimes costly fees (the joke around Vientiane is that most of the country's foreign investment earnings accumulates from brokers' fees) though some investment brokers are better than others. Many foreign investors claim that nothing happens after paying their fees and filing their applications with the appropriate ministries, while other investors have been quite happy with the results.

Standard profit taxes run at 35%, though a lower 20% to 30% rate is available in certain promoted sectors (mostly projects that build infrastructure). Personal income tax is limited to a low 10%. As of the beginning of 1998, the government had granted foreign investment licences totalling US$6.8 billion – over a tenfold increase since 1993. Around three-quarters of this investment was in energy, followed by much smaller investments in tourism, mining, garments/textiles, wood products, import/export and agribusiness.

Investment Profile As of 1996 foreign investment in Laos totalled US$1.3 billion, a figure that outdistanced domestic public investment by a ratio of three to one. Of the 34 countries with companies operating in

Laos, the top five foreign investors by nationality are: Thailand (47%), the USA (27%), Australia (6%), Malaysia (5%) and France (5%).

The top five areas of foreign investment are: transport-communications, industry and handicrafts, electricity, hotels and tourism, and the timber industry.

POPULATION

A 1995 census of Laos taken by the government (with help from the Swedish International Development Agency) recorded a total population of 4.5 million, with an average annual growth rate of 2.4%. Extrapolated to 1998 this means Laos has an estimated current population of 4.7 million. The nation's population density is one of the lowest in Asia, around 20 people per sq km – in other words Laos is roughly the same size as Great Britain with only 8% of Britain's population. By comparison, Vietnam suffers a density of 230 people per sq km, Thailand 120. Roughly 85% of the population lives in rural areas; according to the government's 1995 census, the population of the country's five largest cities and towns are: Vientiane 133,000, Savannakhet 124,000, Pakse 64,000, Luang Prabang 63,000 and Huay Xai 44,000.

Around 10% of the population left the country following the 1975 Communist takeover, over half being lowland Lao and the remainder a mixture of minorities. Of those who emigrated, 66.5% ended up in the USA, 14.5% in France, 8.7% in Canada and 4.9% in Australia. The provinces of Vientiane and Luang Prabang lost the most people, with approximately 25% of the population of Luang Prabang going abroad. The emigration trend has recently reversed itself so that the influx of immigrants – mostly repatriated Lao, but also including Chinese, Vietnamese and other nationalities – now exceeds the number of emigrés.

According to UN statistics, infant mortality in Laos runs at 91 per 1000 live births (about four times higher than in Thailand, thrice as many as in Vietnam). The ratio of

continued on page 50

THE PEOPLES OF LAOS

Laos was once described as 'less a nation state than a conglomeration of tribes and languages ... less a unified society than a multiplicity of feudal societies'. This is still borne out by the country's ethnic mix: Lao traditionally divide themselves into four categories – Lao Loum, Lao Thai, Lao Theung and Lao Sung – roughly classified according to the altitude at which they live.

About half the population are ethnic Lao or Lao Loum. Of the rest, 10% to 20% are tribal Thai, 20% to 30% are Lao Theung (lower mountain-dwellers, mostly of proto-Malay or Mon-Khmer descent) and 10% to 20% are Lao Sung (Hmong or Mien tribes who live higher up). The Lao government has an alternative three-way split, in which the Lao Thai are condensed into the Lao Loum group. Using that system, the percentages are 59.5% Lao Loum, 34% Lao Theung and 9% Lao Sung. This triumvirate is represented on the back of every 1000 kip bill, in national costume, from left to right: Lao Sung, Lao Loum, and Lao Theung.

But which tribes belong to which category? There are officially 68 ethnic groups, classified by many factors – language, history, religion, customs, dress, etc. To divide these groups only by the height they live at (especially since many tribes have been 'invited' down since 1975) is somewhat ludicrous.

Recognising this complexity, ethnographer Laurent Chazee (see Books in the Facts for the Visitor chapter for details) has put forward a scheme of 119 ethnicities divided among Thai-Kadai, Austro-Asiatic (Mon-Khmer), Miao-Yao (Hmong-Mien), Sino-Tibetan and 'Others'. Several in the last category could go in one of the other four.

While the Lao people are a rich mix of various cultural groups, they are still primarily a nation of subsistence farmers using age-old methods, sparsely scattered across Laos' often rugged and forested terrain. The country has one of the lowest population densities in Asia.

BERNARD NAPTHINE

Irrigated rice cultivation is a distinguishing feature of the lowland Lao, or Lao Loum, who inhabit the fertile river plains. Along with the ethnic Lao, they make up about half the Laotian population.

Lao Loum

The Lao Loum (Low Lao) are the ethnic Lao who have traditionally resided in the Mekong River valley or along lower tributaries of the Mekong, and who speak the Lao language. They are an ethnic subgroup of the Austro-Thai peoples who have proliferated throughout South-East Asia, southern China, and the north-eastern Indian subcontinent (see History earlier in this chapter for more detail on Thai migration routes). Under the official government classification they are supposed to be found at elevations between 200m and 400m above sea level.

The Lao Loum culture has traditionally consisted of a sedentary, subsistence lifestyle based on wet-rice cultivation (with *khào nīaw* or glutinous rice the preferred variety). The Lao, like all Austro-Thais, were originally animists (followers of earth spirit cults) who took on Theravada Buddhism as their main religion in the middle of the 1st millennium AD.

The distinction between 'Lao' and 'Thai' is a rather recent historical phenomenon, especially considering that 80% of all ethnic Lao (those speaking a language recognised as 'Lao') living in South-East Asia today reside in north-eastern Thailand. Even Lao living in Laos refer idiomatically to different Lao Loum groups as 'Thai', for example, Thai Luang Phabang (Lao from Luang Prabang), Thai Pakse (from Pakse), Thai Tai (from southern Lao) and Thai Neua (from northern Lao, which is especially confusing since there is also a Thai tribal group known to academics as Thai Neua).

Lao Thai

These are Thai subgroups closely related to the Lao who are more 'tribal' in character; that is, they have resisted absorption into mainstream Lao culture and tend to subdivide themselves according to smaller group distinctions. Like the Lao Loum, they live along river valleys, but the Lao Thai have chosen to reside in upland valleys rather than in the lowlands of the Mekong floodplains.

The Lao Thai cultivate dry or mountain rice as well as wet, or irrigated, rice. Some still practise swidden agriculture. In general, they have maintained animist beliefs and eschewed conversion to Buddhism or Christianity.

The various Lao Thai groups are distinguished from one another by the colour of their clothing or general area of habitation, for example, Black Thai, White Thai, Red Thai, Forest Thai, Northern Thai and so on.

To distinguish between the Siamese Thais and other Austro-Thai ethnic subgroups, a few English-speaking Lao scholars use the spelling 'Tai' to include them all, in spite of the fact that the origins and pronunciation for this word differs not in the slightest from the word 'Thai'. The spelling 'Tai' also poses potential confusion with the Lao-Thai word *tai* or 'south', as in the Lao Tai (or Thai Tai) of southern Laos.

Thai Dam

The predominant Lao Thai tribe is the Thai Dam (Black Thai), who live in the upland valleys of northern and eastern Laos, especially Xieng Khuang and Hua Phan provinces. As their name suggests, black is the preponderant colour of their traditional garb. A fairly large number of Thai Dam, 1950s refugees from North Vietnam's Dien Bien Phu, also live in Vientiane Province.

The Thai Dam have a caste system that divides them into three classes: the *phu tao* (nobility); the *phu noi* (commoners); and the *maw* (priests). Of all the Lao Thai groups, the Thai Dam are considered the most archetypical since their traditions have been so well preserved over the centuries. Among the Lao, they are known for their honesty and industriousness.

Lao Theung

The Lao Theung (Upland Lao) are a loose affiliation of mostly Austro-Asiatic or Mon-Khmer peoples who live on mid-altitude mountain slopes (officially 300m to 900m) in northern and southern Laos. The most numerous group is the Khamu, followed by the Htin, Lamet and smaller numbers of Laven, Katu, Katang, Alak and other Mon-Khmer groups in the south. The Lao Theung are also known by the pejorative term *khàa*, which means slave or servant in the Lao language. This is because they were used as indentured labour by migrating Austro-Thai peoples in earlier centuries and more recently by the Lao monarchy. Today, they still often work as labourers for the Lao Sung.

The Lao Theung have a much lower standard of living than any of the three other groups described here. Most trade between the Lao Theung and other Lao is carried out by barter. Metal tools are not common among the Khamu, Htin and Lamet, who rely mostly on wood, bamboo and stone implements.

Most of the Khamu – of whom there are eight subgroups – originally came from China's Xishuangbanna District (Sipsongpanna in Lao) in Yunnan Province and are now found in all nine northern provinces of Laos. For the most part they are swidden agriculturists who grow mountain rice, coffee, tobacco and cotton. Their villages are established near upland streams; their houses have dirt floors like those of the Hmong, but roofs sport crossed roof-beams similar to the northern Thai *kalae* (locally called *kapkri-aak*). Traditionally they are animists, though many of those living near Lao centres have converted to Theravada Buddhism and a few are Christians.

Many Khamu believe that the human body contains from 30 to 300 spirits; even rice has several different spirits, which are ceremonially bound to the rice during an annual *suu khwān khào* – a special basi ritual for rice.

The Htin (pronounced 'Tin'), numerous in Sainyabuli Province, typically subsist by hunting for wild game, breeding domestic animals and farming small plots of land. Since metal is taboo in their culture, they are particularly skilled at manipulating bamboo to make everything needed around the house; for floor mats and baskets they interweave pared bamboo with a black-coloured grass to create bold geometric patterns. The Htin refer to themselves as 'Phai', and many Lao call them Kha Phai.

The Htin and Khamu languages are closely related, and both groups are thought to have been in Laos long before the arrival of the lowland Lao, tribal Thai or Lao Sung. During the Lao New Year celebrations in Luang Prabang the lowland Lao offer a symbolic tribute to the Khamu as their historical predecessors and as 'guardians of the land'.

Lao Sung

The Lao Sung (High Lao) include those hill tribes who make their residence at altitudes greater than 1000m above sea level. Of all the peoples of Laos, they are the most recent immigrants, having come from Myanmar, Tibet and southern China within the last century.

The largest group are the Hmong, also called Miao or Meo, who probably number around 200,000 in four main subgroups, the White Hmong, Striped Hmong, Red Hmong and Black Hmong (the colours refer to certain clothing details), and are found in the nine provinces of the north plus Bolikhamsai in central Laos.

The agricultural staples of the Hmong are dry rice and corn raised by the slash-and-burn method. They also raise cattle, pigs, water buffalo and chickens. For the most part, theirs is a barter economy in which iron is the medium of exchange. Iron is important for the crafting of machetes for land-clearing and flintlock rifles for hunting. The one Hmong cash crop is opium, which they grow and manufacture more of than any other ethnic group in Laos. The Hmong are most numerous in the provinces of Hua Phan, Xieng Khuang and Luang Prabang, although they can be found over much of northern Laos.

The second-largest group are the Mien (also called Iu Mien, Yao and Man), who number 30,000 to 50,000 and live mainly in Luang Nam Tha, Luang Prabang, Bokeo, Udomxai and Phongsali. The Mien and Hmong have many ethnic and linguistic similarities, but intermarriage is rare. Both groups have a quite sophisticated social structure that extends beyond the village level, and both groups are predominantly animist. The Mien, like the Hmong, are opium poppy cultivators.

The Hmong are considered more aggressive and warlike, however, and as such were perfect for the CIA-trained special Royal

Top: Thai Dam
woman. Many of the
ethnic groups in
Laos have been
given names relating
to their traditional
clothing. The Thai
Dam (Black Thai)
wear clothes which
are predominantly
black. There are also
Black Hmong, as
well as Red, White
and Striped Hmong
sub-groups.

Bottom: Mien
woman. The Mien
are the second
largest Lao Sung or
High Lao ethnic
group after the
Hmong. Like the
Hmong, silver-
smithing and opium
cultivation are
important economic
activities among
these mountain
dwellers.

The Iko (or Akha) hill tribes adorn themselves with colourful and shiny objects. Headgear typically includes metallic decoration, including coins.

ALL PHOTOGRAPHS BY FRANK CARTER

Lao Government forces under General Vang Pao in the 1960s and early 1970s. The resistance groups that still exist are mainly Hmong.

Large numbers of Hmong and Mien left Laos and fled abroad following the 1975 Revolution. It is often claimed that this is because they were 'mercenaries' of the USA (see History earlier in this chapter for more detail). In fact the vast majority of Hmong and Mien who left Laos had no involvement in the war, but they may have expected reprisals because of those who did. Many were also simply following the example of their leader, Vang Pao, who now lives in California. It is estimated that 50,000 Hmong are living in the USA, with another 8000 in other countries. About 2000 Hmong emigrés have returned to Laos since 1991.

Other much smaller Tibeto-Burman hill tribe groups in Laos include the Lisu, Lahu, Lolo, Akha and Phu Noi. Sometimes these are classified as Lao Theung since they live at slightly lower elevations than the Hmong and Mien, but like the Hmong and the Mien they live in the mountains of northern Laos.

Other Asians

As elsewhere in South-East Asia, the Chinese have been migrating to Laos for centuries to work as merchants and traders. Most come direct from Yunnan but more recently many have also been arriving from Vietnam. Estimates of their presence varies from 2% to 5% of the total population. At least half of all permanent Chinese residents in Laos are said to live in Vientiane and Savannakhet. Most businesses in these towns are owned by ethnic Chinese. Thousands of temporary Chinese immigrants from Yunnan also work as skilled labourers in the far north.

Since the Thai-Lao rapprochement of the late 1980s, Thais are coming in ever-increasing numbers. Unlike the Chinese, they only stay for short intervals engaging in business or aid and education projects.

In Vientiane, there is also a small but visible number of northern Indians and Pakistanis who run tailor and fabric shops. Along with Bangladeshis and Burmese, they also seem to make up a good portion of the United Nations teams working in Laos.

In southern Laos, especially in Champasak Province, live small numbers of Cambodians. Most commonly they work as truck drivers and boatmen who are involved in legal and illegal trade between Laos, Cambodia and Thailand. A few Cambodians are stationed in Vientiane as members of regional committees such as the Mekong River Commission.

Vietnamese can be found in substantial numbers in all the provinces bordering Vietnam and in the cities of Vientiane, Savannakhet and Pakse. For the most part Vietnamese residents in Laos work as traders and small businesspeople, though there continues to be a small Vietnamese military presence in Xieng Khuang and Hua Phan provinces. Many of the Vietnamese in urban areas are of ethnic Chinese origin.

continued from page 44
citizens to trained physicians is 4381; by comparison Vietnam has a ratio of 2298 people per doctor, Cambodia 9523.

On the UN Human Development Index – a complex matrix which integrates various statistics concerning income, health, education and living conditions – Laos ranks 133 out of the 173 countries surveyed. Only 20% of the annual national budget goes to the social sector, proportionately far less than most western countries.

Expatriate Community
Most of the expatriate Europeans living in Laos (less than a thousand in all) are temporary contract employees of multilateral and bilateral aid organisations or programmes such as UNESCO, UNDP, FAO, the Lao-Australian Irrigation Project, the Lao-Swedish Forestry Programme and so on. A smaller tally are employed by multinational companies, most numerously those involved in mining, petroleum and hydropower. Virtually all of these groups inhabit huge mansions in eastern Vientiane, just like their compatriots did before 1975. Since the breakup of the USSR the Russian and eastern European presence has shrunk to almost nil. There is also a growing number of foreign non-governmental organisations (NGOs) – around 60 at last count – though their financial presence comprises only about 5% of total foreign aid to Laos.

Very few people of European descent, whether from the west or the east, have been allowed permanent residence in Laos, although quite a few expatriate business-owners have been able to renew temporary residence permits on a yearly basis. About a dozen Europeans – including French and Americans – stayed right through the 1975 Revolution, since small businesses were not nationalised.

EDUCATION
Laos' public school system is organised around five years at the *pathom* (primary) level beginning at age six, followed by three years of *mathayom* (middle) and three

years of *udom* (high) school. In reality less than three years of formal education is the national norm, and most teachers themselves have spent less than five years in school. Seventy percent of all Lao citizens enrol in primary school at some point in their youth, but the dropout rate is 60%. These statistics don't take into account the education provided by the country's Buddhist wats; in rural localities, monastic schooling is the only formal education available, most commonly for boys only.

Private and international schools for the foreign and local elite abound in Vientiane, from a Montessori preschool to the growing Vientiane International School, which takes students through to the age of 14. The country has only two complete universities, Dong Dok University and Phaetsaat University, plus two technical colleges, all four of which are in Vientiane. Together they enrol a very small percentage of the school-age population.

Although the national literacy rate is 84%, if the urban areas (representing only 15% of the population) aren't included, the reading rate drops to around 45%. Age is an important factor in this calculation as well; an estimated 43% of all Lao citizens over age 15 can't read.

ARTS
Architecture
Religious buildings are the cornerstone of traditional Lao architecture (see the special section on Temple Architecture starting on page 203). Colonial architecture in turn-of-the-century urban Laos consisted in the main of thick-walled buildings with shuttered windows and pitched tile roofs in the classic French provincial style. Although many of these structures were torn down or allowed to decay following Lao independence from France, today they are in much demand among foreign and local companies alike.

Shophouses throughout Laos, whether 100 years or 100 days old, share the basic Chinese shophouse design in which the ground floor is reserved for trading purposes while the upper floors contain offices or residences. During most of the post-WWII era, the trend in modern Lao architecture – inspired by the European Bauhaus movement – was towards a boring functionalism in which the average building looked like a giant egg carton turned on its side. The Lao and French aesthetic, once so vibrant, almost disappeared in this characterless style of architecture.

Buildings erected in post-Revolutionary Laos followed the socialist realism school that was enforced in the Soviet Union, Vietnam and China. Straight lines, sharp angles and an almost total lack of ornamentation were the norm for much of the 1970s and early 1980s. Many newer buildings in northern Laos in particular were constructed by Chinese or Vietnamese engineers in this style.

More recently a small trend towards integrating classic Lao architectural motifs with modern functions has taken hold. Prime examples of this movement include Vientiane's National Assembly hall and the new Luang Prabang airport, both of which were designed by Havana and Moscow-trained architect Hongkad Souvannavong. Other design characteristics, such as those represented by the Siam Commercial Bank on Thanon Lan Xang in Vientiane, seek to gracefully reincorporate French colonial features ignored for the last half century.

Sculpture

As in Thailand, Myanmar and Cambodia, the focus of most traditional art in Lao culture has been religious, specifically Buddhist. Unlike the art of these other three countries, Lao art never encompassed a broad range of styles and periods, mainly because Laos has had a much more modest history in terms of power and longevity. Furthermore, since Laos was intermittently dominated by its neighbours, much Lao art was destroyed or carried off by the Chinese, Vietnamese, Siamese or Khmer. Influences from these sponsor states left behind a very strong influence on local sculpture as well. The French, during their colonial stewardship, also carted off much of historical value.

This doesn't mean, however, that what remains isn't worthy of admiration. Though limited in range, Lao art and architecture can be unique and expressive. Most impressive is Lao sculpture of the 16th to 18th centuries, the heyday of the kingdom of Lan Xang. Lao sculptural media usually included bronze, stone or wood and the subject was invariably the Lord Buddha or figures associated with the *jataka* or life stories of the Buddha. Like other Buddhist sculptors, the Lao artisans emphasised the features thought to be peculiar to the historical Buddha, including a beak-like nose, extended earlobes, tightly curled hair and so on.

Two types of standing Buddha images are distinctive to Laos. The first is the 'Calling for Rain' posture, which depicts the Buddha standing with his hands held rigidly at his side, fingers pointing towards the ground. This posture is rarely seen in other South-East Asian Buddhist art traditions. The slightly rounded, 'boneless' look of the image recalls Thailand's Sukhothai style, and the way the lower robe is sculpted over the hips looks vaguely Khmer. But the flat, slab-like earlobes, arched eyebrows and very aquiline nose are uniquely Lao. The bottom of the figure's robe curls upward on both sides in a perfectly symmetrical fashion that is also unique and innovative. The whole image gives the distinct impression of a rocket in flight. Considering that the Lao custom at the end of the dry season is to fire bamboo rockets into the sky in a plea for rain, this may have been the sculptors' desired effect.

The other original Lao image type is the 'Contemplating the Bodhi Tree' Buddha. The Bodhi tree, or 'Tree of Enlightenment', refers to the large banyan tree that the historical Buddha purportedly was sitting beneath when he attained enlightenment in Bodhgaya, India, in the 6th century BC. In this image the Buddha is standing in much the same way as in the 'Calling for Rain' pose except that his hands are crossed at the wrists in front of his body.

The finest examples of Lao sculpture are found in Vientiane's Haw Pha Kaew and

Wat Si Saket, and in Luang Prabang's National Museum.

Although generally uncommon, other styles of sculpture from Siam and Angkor can occasionally be seen in Laos.

Handicrafts

As has been already noted, the Lao are skilful carvers. This applies not only to sim porticoes and gold relief, but to everyday folk art. The most popular carving mediums are wood and bone.

Among the Hmong and Mien hill tribes, silversmithing plays an important role in 'portable wealth' and inheritances. Silversmithing and goldsmithing is a traditional lowland Lao art as well but in recent years these have been in decline.

Mats and baskets woven of various kinds of straw and reed are also common and are becoming a small but important export to Thailand. Among the best baskets and mats are those woven by the Htin.

Paper handcrafted from saa, the bark of a mulberry tree native to northern Laos, has recently become available in Vientiane and Luang Prabang. Saa is a renewable paper resource that needs little processing if compared with wood pulp, and most of the country's supply originates from Luang Prabang Province. Most of the saa harvested in Luang Prabang is transported by river and road to Chiang Mai, Thailand, where saa paper-making is an established cottage industry.

Music & Dance

As in other South-East Asian cultures, music in Laos can be divided into classical and folk traditions. The classical music of Laos is the least interesting, simply because it is so imitative of the classical traditions of Thailand and Cambodia. Lao classical music was originally developed as court music for royal ceremonies and classical dance-drama during the reign of Vientiane's Chao Anou, who had been educated in the Siamese court in Bangkok. The standard ensemble for this genre is called the sep nyai and consists of a set of tuned gongs

called khong wong, a xylophone-like instrument called the ranyat, the khui, or bamboo flute, and the pii, a double-reed wind instrument similar to the oboe – exactly the same instruments as used in the Thai phiphat ensemble.

Nowadays, the only time you'll generally hear this type of music is during the occasional public performance of the Pha Lak Pha Lam, a dance-drama based on the Hindu Ramayana epic. The practice of classical Lao music and drama has been in decline for some time now – 40 years of intermittent war and revolution has simply made this kind of entertainment a low priority among most Lao.

Not so with Lao folk music, which has always stayed close to the people. The principal instrument in the folk genre is the khaen (French spelling: khene), a wind instrument that is devised of a double row of bamboo-like reeds fitted into a hardwood soundbox and made air-tight with beeswax. The rows can be as few as four or as many as eight courses (for a total of 16 pipes), and the instrument can vary in length from around 80cm to 2m in length. Around the turn of the century there were also nine-course khaen but these have all but disappeared. The khaen player blows (as with a harmonica, sound is produced whether the breath is moving in or out of the instrument) into the soundbox while covering or uncovering small holes in the reeds that determine the pitch for each. An adept player can produce a churning, calliope-like music that you can dance to. The most popular folk dance is the lam wong (circle dance) in which couples dance circles around one another until there are three circles in all: a circle danced by the individual, the circle danced by the couple, and one danced by the whole crowd.

The khaen is often accompanied by the saw (sometimes written so), a bowed string instrument. In more elaborate ensembles the khui and khong wong may be added, as well as various hand drums. Khaen music can also incorporate a vocalist. Most Lao pop music is based on vocal khaen music. Melodies are almost always pentatonic, ie they feature five-note scales.

The Lao folk idiom also has its own theatre, based on the *māw lám (mō lám)* tradition. Māw lám is difficult to translate but roughly means something like 'master, or priest, of dance'. Performances always feature a witty, topical combination of talking and singing that ranges across themes as diverse as politics and sex. Very colloquial, even bawdy language is employed; this is one art form that has always bypassed government censors, whether it's the French or the LPRP.

There are four basic types of māw lám. The first, *māw lám lūang* (great māw lám), involves an ensemble of performers in costume, on stage. *Māw lám khuu* (couple māw lám) features a man and woman who engage in flirtation and verbal repartee. *Māw lám chot* (juxtaposed māw lám) has two performers of the same gender who 'duel' by answering questions or finishing an incomplete story issued as a challenge. Finally, *māw lám diaw* (solo māw lám) involves only one performer.

All types of māw lám are most commonly performed at temple fairs and on other festive occasions. You can also commonly hear māw lám khuu and māw lám diaw on radio broadcasts from Laos or from northeastern Thailand.

Literature

Of all classical Lao literature, *Pha Lak Pha Lam*, the Lao version of the Indian epic the *Ramayana*, is the most pervasive and influential in the culture. The Indian source first came to Laos with the Hindu Khmer approximately 900 years ago as stone reliefs which appeared on Wat Phu Champasak and other Angkor-period temples built in what is now central and southern Laos. Oral and written versions may also have been available; eventually, though, the Lao developed their own version of the epic, which differs greatly from the original and from Thailand's *Ramakian*.

Although the main theme remains the same – handsome and virtuous Rama (Pha Lam in Lao) loses his consort Sita (Sii-daa) to evil Ravana, the Lao have embroidered on the *Ramayana* by providing much more biographic detail on the arch-villain Ravana and his evil wife Montho. Rama's brother Laksana (Pha Lak) also has a larger role, as suggested by the inclusion of his name in the Lao epic's title.

Various Thai tribes in Laos have their own renderings of the *Ramayana* story. In the Thai Lü version, for example, Rama is portrayed as an incarnation of Buddha and Ravana is identified with Mara (Buddha's Satan-like tempter in canonical Buddhist mythology).

Also passed on from Indian tradition are the many *jatakas* or life stories (*sáa-tók* in Lao) of the Buddha. Of the 547 jataka tales in the Pali *Tripitaka* (Buddhist canon) – each chronicling a different past life – most appear in Laos almost word-for-word as they were first written down in Sri Lanka. A group of 50 'extra' or apocryphal stories – based on Lao-Thai folk tales of the time – were added by Pali scholars in Luang Prabang 300 to 400 years ago. One of Laos' most popular jatakas is an old Pali original known as the Mahajati or Mahavessandara (Lao: *Mahaa-Vetsanthon*), the story of the Buddha's penultimate life. Interior murals in the sim or ordination chapel of many Lao wats typically depict this jataka and nine others: Temiya, Mahachanaka, Suwannasama, Nemiraja, Mahasotha, Bhuritat, Chantakumara, Nartha and Vithura.

Before the advent of printing, which was introduced by the French, all Lao manuscripts had been inscribed onto palm leaves and other unprocessed natural fibres and, if necessary, then collated into hand-bound volumes.

The reading of palm-leaf manuscripts nowadays is restricted to Buddhist monasteries, where they are considered historical artefacts rather than as a viable way of preserving literature. The use of saa paper (see Handicrafts earlier in this chapter) has been relegated entirely to the tourist market.

SOCIETY & CONDUCT
Traditional Culture

Laos' complex ethnic stratification means that when one speaks of Lao culture, one is truly referring only to the lowland Lao or Lao Loum, who represent only about half the population. Lowland Lao culture predominates in the cities, towns and villages of the Mekong River valley, that is to say in western Laos from Huay Xai to Pakse, but on the official level the customs practised in these areas are in large part taken to be the 'national culture' by the country's rulers.

A hand-painted propaganda billboard standing on a street corner near Wat Si Saket in Vientiane exemplifies this cultural mandate. It depicts a future Vientiane skyline marked by tall, modernistic buildings interspersed with Buddhist wats; in the foreground citizens wearing traditional Lao dress are dancing the lam wong, playing the *khaen*, carrying Buddhist offerings and performing a *basi* ceremony. Hence the true Lao – according to official image propaganda – proudly bear the sartorial and artistic symbols of their culture, practise the majority religion and participate in important ceremonial acts that are deemed 'Lao'.

Dress In many ways the simplified billboard image mentioned above crystallises the perceived traditions of – and expectations for – the Lao people. A good Lao dons some portion of the traditional garb during ceremonies and celebrations – the men only a *phàa biang* or shoulder sash, the women a similar sash, tight-fitting blouse, and *phàa nung* or sarong. In everyday life a man dispenses entirely with the traditional Lao clothing, dressing in the international shirt-and-trousers style, as long as his clothing contributes to a neat and clean appearance, and as long as his hair is neat and short.

Women, on the other hand, are expected to wear the phàa nung on a daily basis except when participating in sports or in a profession which requires a uniform. Other ethnicities living in urban Laos – particularly Chinese and Vietnamese women –

forego the phàa nung as daily wear, but even they must don the Lao sarong when they visit a police or prefecture office; if they don't dress in the prescribed manner they risk having any civic requests denied by Lao bureaucrats – or perhaps won't be served at all.

Cultural Traits To a substantial degree 'Lao-ness' is defined by Buddhism, specifically Theravada Buddhism. More austere and inward-looking than its Mahayana counterpart in northern and eastern Asia, Theravada emphasises the cooling of the human passions and thus strong emotions are a taboo in Lao society (see the special section on Buddhism starting on page 57 for more detail). *Kamma* (karma), more than devotion, prayer or hard work, is believed to determine one's lot in life, hence the Lao tend not to get too worked up over the future. This trait is often perceived by outsiders as a lack of ambition.

The cultural contrast between the Lao and the Vietnamese is an example of how the Annamite Chain separating Laos from Vietnam has also served as a cultural fault line dividing Indic and Sinitic – Theravada and Mahayana – zones of influence. Like their Chinese mentors, the Vietnamese are perceived in Asia as hard workers and aggressive businesspeople. The French coined a saying to highlight the differences among their subjects: 'The Vietnamese plant rice, the Cambodians watch it grow and the Lao listen to it grow.' The Lao have their own proverb that says 'Lao and Viet, like cat and dog'.

Lao commonly express the notion that 'too much work is bad for your brain' and they often say they feel sorry for people who 'think too much'. Education in general isn't highly valued although this attitude is changing quickly with modernisation. Avoiding any undue psychological stress, however, remains a cultural norm. From the typical Lao perspective unless an activity – whether work or play – contains an experiential element of *múan* ('fun'), it will probably lead to stress.

Hence the Lao are quite receptive to outside assistance and foreign investment, since it promotes a certain degree of economic development without demanding a corresponding increase in local productivity. The Lao government wants all the trappings of modern technology – the skyscrapers of the propaganda billboard – without having to give up any of the Lao traditions, among them the múan zeitgeist. The challenge for Laos in the future is to find a balance between cultural preservation and the development of new perceptions and attitudes that will lead the country towards a measure of self-sufficiency.

Etiquette

Visiting Temples The Lao are devout Buddhists; upon visiting Lao Buddhist temples, you owe a measure of respect to the religion and to the people who so graciously allow you to enter their places of worship. Correct behaviour in temples entails several guidelines, the most important of which is to dress neatly and to take your shoes off when you enter religious buildings such as the sim. Shorts or sleeveless shirts are considered improper dress for both men and women; Lao citizens wearing either would be turned away by monastic authorities, but the Lao are often too polite to refuse entry to improperly clad foreigners.

Buddha images are sacred objects, so don't pose in front of them for pictures and definitely do not climb or sit upon them. When sitting in front of a Buddha image, do not point your feet towards the image. The Lao usually employ the 'mermaid pose' when facing an image, which keeps both feet pointed to the rear.

If you want to speak with a monk (the occasional monk can speak English or French), try to keep your head a bit lower than his. If he's sitting, you should sit, too (use the 'mermaid pose' again); if he's standing, you may have to bend down a bit to show proper respect. Women should never touch monks or hand them objects (place an object on a table or other surface in front of a monk instead).

A few of the larger wats in Vientiane charge small entry fees. In other temples, offering a small donation before leaving the compound is appropriate but not mandatory. Usually there are donation boxes near the entry of the sim or next to the central Buddha image at the rear. In rural wats, there may be no donation box available; in these, it's OK to leave money on the floor next to the central image or even by the doorway – no-one is likely to steal it.

Social Gestures Traditionally, the Lao greet each other not with a handshake but with a prayer-like palms-together gesture known as a *nop* or *wài*. If someone nops you, you should nop back (unless it is a child). But nowadays the western-style handshake is just as common and most Lao will offer the same to a foreigner.

The feet are the lowest part of the body (spiritually as well as physically) so don't point your feet at people (you shouldn't even point at objects with your feet). In the same context, the head is regarded as the highest part of the body, so don't touch Lao people on the head either.

When handing things to other people you should use both hands or your right hand only, never the left hand (reserved for toilet ablutions). Books and other written material are given a special status over other secular objects. Hence you shouldn't slide books or documents across a table or counter top, and never place them on the floor – use a chair instead if table space isn't available.

Shoes Shoes are not worn inside people's homes, nor in some guesthouses and shops. If you see a pile of shoes at or near the entrance, you should respect the house custom and remove your shoes before entry. Several Lao have confided in us that they can't believe how oblivious some foreigners appear to be of this simple and obvious custom. For them the wearing of shoes indoors is disgusting and the behaviour of those who ignore the custom is nothing short of boorish.

Visiting Homes The Lao can be very hospitable and although overnight stays in Lao homes are still frowned upon by the government (which requires that any foreigner spending the night be registered with the police), it's not unusual to be invited to a Lao home for a meal or a sociable drink.

Even if your visit is very brief, you will be offered something to eat or drink, probably both – a glass of water, a cup of tea, a piece of fruit, a shot of *lào-láo* (Lao rice liquor), or whatever they have on hand. You are expected to partake of whatever is offered; whether you've already eaten or not, whether you're thirsty or not, to refuse at least a taste is considered quite impolite. In the case of lào-láo, you are expected to drink a full jigger (or the rough equivalent) in one gulp. Subsequent drinks may be refused, but the first cannot. Some hosts will pour a bit of rice liquor onto the floor during such occasions as an offering to the house spirit.

As with temple buildings, you must remove your shoes before entering a Lao home.

Dress & Attitude Shorts – except knee-length walking shorts – sleeveless shirts, tank tops (singlets) and other beach-style attire are not considered appropriate dress in Laos for anything other than sporting events. Such dress is especially counterproductive if worn to government offices (eg when applying for a visa extension). The attitude of 'This is how I dress at home and no-one is going to stop me' gains nothing but disrespect from the Lao.

Sandals or slip-on shoes are OK for almost any but the most formal occasions. Short-sleeved shirts and blouses with capped sleeves likewise are quite acceptable in Laos.

When things go wrong, don't be quick to anger – it won't help matters, since losing one's temper means loss of face for everyone present. Remember that this is Asia, where keeping your cool is the paramount rule. Talking loudly is perceived as rude behaviour by cultured Lao, whatever the situation.

A smile and *sabai-dµi* (the Lao greeting) goes a long way towards calming the initial trepidation that locals may feel upon seeing a foreigner, whether in the city or the countryside.

Upcountry When travelling in minority villages, try to find out what the local customs and taboos are, either by asking someone or by observing local behaviour closely. Here are several other guidelines for minimising the negative impact on the local people.

• Many tribes fear photography, so you should always ask permission – through hand gestures if necessary – before pointing your camera at tribal people and/or their dwellings.
• Show respect for religious symbols and rituals. Avoid touching spirit houses, household altars, village totems (including village gates) and other religious symbols, as this often 'pollutes' them spiritually and may force the villagers to perform purification rituals after you have moved on. Keep your distance from ceremonies being performed unless you're asked to participate.
• Do not enter a village house without the permission or invitation of its inhabitants.
• Practise restraint in giving things to tribespeople or bartering with them. Medicine and medicine are not necessarily appropriate gifts if they result in altering traditional dietary and healing practices. The same goes for clothing. Tribespeople will abandon hand-woven tunics for printed T-shirts if they are given a steady supply. If you want to give something to the people you encounter, the best thing is to make a donation to the village school or some other community fund.

RELIGION
Spirit Cults
In spite of the fact that phĭi worship has been officially banned, it remains the dominant non-Buddhist belief system in the country. Even in Vientiane, Lao citizens openly perform the ceremony called *su khwăn* or *basi (baci* in the common French transliteration) in which the 32 guardian spirits known as *khwăn* are bound to the guest of honour by white strings tied around the

continued on page 64

BUDDHISM

About 60% of the people of Laos are Theravada Buddhists. This proportion is mostly lowland Lao, with a sprinkling of tribal Thais. Buddhism was apparently introduced to Luang Prabang (then Muang Sawa) in the late 13th or early 14th centuries. The first monarch of Lan Xang, King Fa Ngum, was the first to declare Buddhism the state religion, which he did by accepting the Pha Bang Buddha image from his Khmer father-in-law Jayavarman Paramesvara. In 1356 AD, Fa Ngum reportedly built a wat in Muang Sawa to house this famous image.

But Buddhism was fairly slow in spreading throughout Laos, even among the lowland peoples, who were reluctant to accept the faith instead of or even alongside *phīi* (earth spirit) worship.

A bronze casting of Buddha, sitting in the pose in which he reached enlightenment. The image was cast in Laos in the 16th century.

King Setthathirat, who ruled Lan Xang from 1547 to 1571, attempted to make Vientiane a regional Buddhist centre, but it wasn't until the reign of King Sulinya Vongsa in the mid to late 17th century that Buddhism began to be taught in Lao schools. Since the 17th century, Laos has maintained a continuous Theravadin tradition.

Basically, the Theravada school of Buddhism is an earlier and, according to its followers, less corrupted form of Buddhism than the Mahayana schools found in east Asia or in the Himalayan lands. The Theravada (Teaching of the Elders) school is also called the 'Southern' school since it took the southern route from India, its place of origin, through South-East Asia (Myanmar, Thailand, Laos and Cambodia in this case), while the 'Northern' school proceeded north into Nepal, Tibet, China, Korea, Mongolia, Vietnam and Japan. Because the southern school tried to preserve or limit the Buddhist doctrines to only those canons codified in the early Buddhist era, the northern school gave Theravada Buddhism the name Hinayana (Lesser Vehicle). They considered themselves Mahayana (Great Vehicle) because they built upon the earlier teachings, 'expanding' the doctrine so as to respond more to the needs of lay people, or so it is claimed.

Theravada or Hinayana doctrine stresses the three principal aspects of existence: *dukkha* (suffering, unsatisfactoriness, disease), *anicca* (impermanence, transience of all things) and *anatta* (nonsubstantiality or nonessentiality of reality – no permanent 'soul'). Comprehension of anicca reveals that no experience, no state of mind, no physical object lasts. Trying to hold onto experience, states of mind, and objects that are constantly changing creates dukkha. Anatta is the understanding that no part of the changing world can we point to and say 'This is me' or 'This is God' or 'This is the soul'. These concepts, when 'discovered' by Siddhartha Gautama in the 6th century BC, were in direct contrast to the Hindu belief in an eternal, blissful, Self or *Paramatman*, hence Buddhism was originally a 'heresy' against the Brahmanic religion of India.

Gautama, an Indian prince-turned-ascetic, subjected himself to many years of severe austerities to arrive at this vision of the world and was awarded the title of Buddha, 'the Enlightened' or 'the Awakened'. Gautama Buddha spoke of four noble truths which had the power to liberate any human being who could realise them. These four noble truths are:

- The truth of dukkha – 'All forms of existence are subject to dukkha (suffering, unsatisfactoriness, disease, imperfectness)'.
- The truth of the cause of dukkha – 'Dukkha is caused by *tanha* (desire)'.
- The truth of the cessation of dukkha – 'Eliminate the cause of dukkha (ie desire) and dukkha will cease to arise'.
- The truth of the path – 'The eight-fold path is the way to eliminate desire/extinguish dukkha'.

The eight-fold path *(atthangika-magga)* consists of:

* right understanding
* right mindedness (or 'right thought')
* right speech
* right bodily conduct
* right livelihood
* right effort
* right attentiveness
* right concentration.

These eight limbs belong to three different 'pillars' of practice: morality or *sila* (three to five); concentration or *samadhi* (six to eight); and wisdom or *pañña* (one and two).

The path is also called the Middle Way since ideally it avoids both extreme austerity as well as extreme sensuality. Some Buddhists believe the path is to be taken in successive stages, while others say the pillars are interdependent. Another key point is that the word 'right' can also be translated as 'complete' or 'full'.

The ultimate goal of Theravada Buddhism is *nibbana* (Sanskrit: *nirvana)*, which literally means the 'blowing-out' or 'extinction' of all causes of dukkha. Effectively it means an end to all corporeal existence – an end to that which is forever subject to suffering and which is conditioned from moment to moment by *kamma* (action). In reality, most Lao Buddhists aim for rebirth in a 'better' existence rather than the supra-mundane goal of nibbana, which is highly misunderstood by Asians as well as westerners. Many Lao express the feeling that they are somehow unworthy of nibbana. By feeding monks, giving donations to temples and performing regular worship at the local wat they hope to improve their lot, acquiring enough 'merit' (Pali: *punña*; Lao: *bun)* to prevent or at least lessen the number of rebirths.

The making of merit *(hét bun)* is an important social as well as religious activity in Laos. The concept of reincarnation is almost universally accepted by Lao Buddhists, and to some extent even by non-Buddhists, and the Buddhist theory of kamma (Pali) or karma (Sanskrit) is well-expressed in the Lao proverb *'het dji, dâi dji; het sua, dâi sua'* – 'do good and receive good; do evil and receive evil'.

The *Tilatna*, or *Triratna* (Triple Gems), highly respected by Lao Buddhists, include the Buddha, the Dhamma (the teachings) and the Sangha (the Buddhist brotherhood). The Buddha in his sculptural form is found on high shelves or altars in homes and shops as well as in temples, while the Dhamma is chanted morning and evening in every wat. The Sangha is exemplified by the street presence of orange-robed monks, especially in the early morning hours when they perform their alms-rounds.

Lao Buddhism has no particular 'Sabbath' or day of the week when Lao are supposed to make temple visits. Nor is there anything similar to a mass or liturgy over which a priest presides. Instead Lao Buddhists visit the wat whenever they feel like it, most often on *wán pha* (literally 'excellent days') which occur with every full and new moon, ie every 14 days. On such a visit typical activities include the offering of lotus buds, incense and candles at various altars and bone reliquaries around the wat compound, offering food to the temple Sangha (monks, nuns and lay residents – monks always eat first), meditating (individually or in groups), listening to monks chanting *suttas* or Buddhist discourse, and attending a *thêt* or dhamma talk by the abbot or other respected teacher. Visitors may also seek counsel from individual monks or nuns regarding new or ongoing life problems.

Monks & Nuns

Socially, every Lao Buddhist male is expected to become a *khúubạa* (monk) for a short period in his life, optimally between the time he finishes school and starts a career or marries. Men or boys under 20 years of age may enter the Sangha as novices *(samanera* or *naen)* and this is not unusual since a family earns great merit when one of its sons takes robe and bowl. Traditionally the length of time spent in the wat is three months, during the Buddhist lent *(phansãa* or *watsa)* beginning in July, which coincides with the rainy season. However, nowadays men may spend as little as a week or 15 days to accrue merit as monks or novices.

A samanera adheres to 10 precepts or vows, which include the usual prohibitions against stealing, lying, killing, intoxication and

Hundreds of Buddhist monks and nuns take part in the Pha That Luang festival, held each November in Vientiane, receiving alms from the public.

JULIET COOMBE\LA BELLE AURORE

sexual involvement, along with ones forbidding eating after noon; listening to music or dancing; wearing jewellery, garlands or perfume; sleeping on high beds; and accepting money for personal use.

Monks must follow 227 vows or precepts as part of the monastic discipline. All things possessed by a monk must be offered by the lay community. Upon ordination a new monk is typically offered a set of three orange-yellow robes (lower, inner and outer), costing around 16,000 kip for standard grade cloth of cotton or dacron, a bit more for fancier grades. Other possessions he is permitted include a razor, cup, filter (for keeping insects out of drinking water), umbrella and alms bowl. The latter are usually plain black-lacquered steel bowls; monks carry them in shoulder slings to gather their daily food from householders in their monastery precincts.

In monasteries where discipline is lax, monks accumulate a great deal more than the prescribed requisites. Especially in outlying areas of Laos, eg Luang Nam Tha, monastic discipline has declined to the point where monks can be seen drinking liquor at religious festivals in full view of the public.

Many monks are ordained for life. Of these a large percentage become scholars and teachers, while some specialise in healing and/or *sainyasat* (folk magic), although the latter is greatly discouraged by the current ruling party. There is no similar hermetic order for nuns, but women are welcome to reside in temples as *náang síi* (lay nuns), with shaved heads and white robes.

Náang síi only have to follow eight precepts. Because discipline for nuns is much less strenuous than it is for monks, they don't attain quite as high a social status as do monks. However, aside from the fact that they don't perform ceremonies on behalf of other lay persons, they engage in the same basic religious activities (meditation and dhamma study) as monks. The reality is that wats which draw sizeable contingents of eight-precept nuns are highly respected because women don't choose temples for reasons of clerical status − when more than a few reside at one temple it's because the teachings there are considered particularly strong.

Books about Buddhism

If you want to learn more about Theravada Buddhism, recommended titles include:

Buddhist Dictionary by Mahathera Nyanatiloka
Buddhism Explained by Phra Khantipalo
Buddhist Monastic Life by Mohan Wijayaratna
Buddhism in the Modern World edited by Heinrich Dumoulin
Living Dharma: Teachings of Twelve Buddhist Masters edited by Jack Kornfield
Religion and Legitimation of Power in Thailand, Laos, Burma edited by Bardwell L Smith
Theravada Buddhism in Southeast Asia by Robert C Lester
What the Buddha Taught by Walpola Rahula
World Conqueror and World Renouncer by Stanley Tambiah

Post-1975 Buddhism

During the 1964-73 war years, both sides sought to use Buddhism for their own propaganda purposes. In 1968 the Lao Patriotic Front (LPF) included as part of its platform a resolution:

To respect and preserve the Buddhist religion, the purity and freedom of public worship and preaching by monks, to maintain pagodas, to promote unity and mutual assistance between monks and lay followers of different Buddhist sects ...

By the early 1970s, the LPF was winning the propaganda war in the religious sphere, as more and more monks threw their support behind the communist cause.

But major changes were in store for the Sangha following the 1975 takeover. Initially, Buddhism was banned as a primary school subject and people were forbidden to make merit by giving food to monks. Monks were also forced to till the land and raise animals in direct violation of their monastic vows.

Mass dissatisfaction among the faithful prompted the government to rescind their total ban on the feeding of monks in 1976. The giving of rice only was allowed but still the laity was not satisfied, since it was felt that not much merit was to be obtained from the mere offering of rice (which also meant that monks had to continue the cultivation of the soil). By the end of 1976, the government was not only allowing the traditional alms-giving, it was offering a daily ration of rice directly to the Sangha.

In 1992, in what was perhaps its biggest endorsement of Buddhism since the Revolution, the government replaced the hammer-and-sickle emblem which crowned Laos' national seal with a drawing of Pha That Luang, the country's holiest Buddhist symbol.

Today the Department of Religious Affairs (DRA) controls the Sangha and ensures that the teaching of Buddhism is in accordance with Marxist principles. All monks now have to undergo political indoctrination as part of their monastic training. All the canonical and extra-canonical Buddhist texts have been subject to 'editing' by the DRA, who make sure that everything contained therein is congruent with the development of socialism in Laos. Monks are also forbidden to promote phīi worship, which has been officially banned in Laos along with sainyasat (folk magic). The cult of khwǎn (the 32 personal spirits attached to mental/physical functions), however, has not been tampered with.

One of the more major changes in Lao Buddhism was the abolition of the Thammayut sect. Formerly the Sangha in Laos was divided into two sects, the Mahanikai and the Thammayut (as in Thailand). The Thammayut is a minority sect that was begun by Thailand's King Mongkut and patterned after an early Mon form of monastic discipline which the King had practised as a bhikkhu (monk). Although the number of precepts or vows followed is the same for both sects, discipline for Thammayut monks has always been more strictly enforced than that of the Mahanikai sect. Thammayut monks are expected to attain proficiency in meditation as well as Buddhist scholarship or scripture-study; the Mahanikai monks typically 'specialise' in one or the other.

The Pathet Lao objected to the Thammayut sect because it was seen as a tool of the Thai monarchy (and hence US imperialism – even though the Thammayut were in Laos long before the Americans were in Thailand) for infiltrating Lao political culture. The new government not only banned the Thammayut sect but for a few years even banned all Buddhist literature written in the Thai language. This severely curtailed the availability of Buddhist literature in Laos, since Thailand has always been a major source of religious material – as it has for every other kind of written material. The Thammayut ban has also resulted in a much weaker emphasis on meditation *(vipassana)*, considered the spiritual heart of Buddhist practice in most Theravadin countries. Overall monastic discipline has become a great deal more lax as well.

In Laos nowadays there is only one official sect, the 'Lao Sangha' (Song Lao). Former Thammayut monks have either fled to Thailand or renounced their sectarian affiliation. Whether it is due to this exodus or because of the general strictness of policy, the total number of Buddhist monks in Laos declined between 1975 and 1988. Since the economic liberalisation of 1989 – which has made more donor support available to the temples – the number of monks has revived to pre-1975 levels. The ban on Thai Buddhist texts has been rescinded, and nowadays the government even allows Lao monks to study at Mahachulalongkorn Buddhist University at Wat Mahathat in Bangkok.

A multitude of holy Buddha images fill the caves at Pak Ou, on the Mekong about 25km north of Luang Prabang.

BERNARD NAPTHINE

Basi Ceremony

A *māw pháwn* (wish priest) – usually an elder who has spent some time as a monk – presides over the ritual. Those participating in the basi sit on mats around a tiered *phakhuan* (centrepiece), which is decorated with flowers, folded banana leaves and branches with white cotton strings hanging down; pastries, eggs, bananas, liquor and money are placed surrounding the base of the phakhuan as offerings to the spirits in attendance.

After a few words of greeting, the māw pháwn chants in a mixture of Lao and Pali to convey blessings on the honoured guest while all in attendance hold their hands in a prayer-like, palms-together pose. For part of the chanting segment, everyone leans forward to touch the base of the phakhuan; if there are too many participants for everyone to reach the base, it's permissible to touch the elbow of someone who can reach it, thus forming a human chain.

Once the wish priest has finished chanting, each person attending takes two of the white strings from the phakhuan and ties one around each wrist of the honoured guest(s) while whispering a short, well-wishing recitation. When all have performed this action, the guest is left with a stack of strings looped around each wrist and small cups of rice liquor are passed around, sometimes followed by an impromptu *lam wong* (circle dance). For the intended effect, the strings must be kept around the wrists for a minimum of three full days. Some Lao hold that the strings should be allowed to fall off naturally rather than cut off – this can take weeks!

Nowadays, the ceremony appears to have become more of a cheerful formality than a serious ritual, but few Lao would dare to undertake a long journey or initiate an important enterprise without participating.

continued from page 56

wrists. Each of the 32 khwān are thought to be guardians over different organs – mental and physical – in a person's body.

Khwān occasionally wander away from their owner, which isn't thought to be much of a problem except when that person is about to embark on a new project or on a journey away from home, or when they're very ill. Then it's best to perform the basi to ensure that all the khwān are present and attached to the person's body.

Another obvious sign of the popular Lao devotion to phīi can be witnessed in Vientiane at Wat Si Muang. The central image at the temple is not a Buddha figure but the *lák meuang* (city pillar), in which the guardian spirit for the city is believed to reside. Many local residents make daily offerings before the pillar.

Outside the Mekong River valley, the phīi cult is particularly strong among the tribal Thai, especially the Black Thai (Thai Dam), who pay special attention to a class of phīi called *ten*. The ten are earth spirits that preside not only over the plants and soil, but over entire districts as well. The Black Thai also believe in the 32 khwān. Māw, who are specially trained in the propitiation and exorcism of spirits, preside at important Black Thai festivals and ceremonies.

The Khamu tribes have a similar hierarchy of spirits they call *hrooi*. The most important hrooi are those associated with guardianship of house and village. The ceremonies which involve the hrooi have been closed to non-Khamu observers, so very little has been written about them. During the 1960s, some of the Khamu participated in a 'cargo cult' which believed in the millennial arrival of a Messiah figure who would bring them all of the trappings of western civilisation.

JULIET COOMBE/LA BELLE AURORE

JULIET COOMBE/LA BELLE AURORE

JOE CUMMINGS

The national symbol of Laos, Vientiane's Pha That Luang, is the focus of the annual That Luang Festival, which falls in November. The festival, which lasts a week, includes a procession and offerings of floral votives.

BERNARD NAPTHINE

BETHUNE CARMICHAEL

Although the landscape around Vang Vieng is not without rustic charm, most travellers visit for the dramatic karst (limestone) topography and caves. These caverns also captivate the locals: local mythology revolves around them, and are thought to house many spirits.

The Hmong-Mien tribes also practise animism, plus ancestral worship. Some Hmong groups recognise a pre-eminent spirit that presides over all earth spirits; others do not. Some Hmong follow a version of the cargo cult in which they believe Jesus Christ will arrive in a jeep, dressed in combat fatigues. The Akha, Lisu and other Tibeto-Burman groups mix animism and ancestor cults, except for the Lahu, who add a supreme deity called Geusha.

Other Religions

A small number of Lao – mostly those of the remaining French-educated elite – are Christians. Various Christian missionary groups are trying to regain a foothold in Laos. Article 9 of the current Lao constitution, however, reads 'All acts of fomenting division among religions and among the people are prohibited', a clause interpreted to mean that religious proselytising and the distribution of religious materials outside churches, temples or mosques, is illegal. Foreigners caught distributing religious materials may be arrested and held incommunicado or expelled from the country.

Several Christian groups have tried to evade the law by proselytising in Laos under the guise of English-teaching or other aid work. We ran into two French missionaries in Udomxai who were involved in the aid scam, pretending to seek a village that needed humanitarian aid help while actually choosing one based on its remoteness from central authority. This practice has made it somewhat more difficult for legitimate English teachers and small NGOs to obtain the proper permits to enter the country, as anyone from a group whose name isn't already known by the authorities to be legitimate may be suspected of being a Christian front.

A very small number of Muslims live in Vientiane, mostly Arab and Indian merchants whose ancestry dates as far back as the 17th century. Vientiane also harbours a small community of Chams, Cambodian Muslims who fled Pol Pot's Democratic Kampuchea in the 1970s. The latter now have their own mosque in Vientiane. In northern Laos there are also pockets of Muslim Yunnanese, known among the Lao as *jiin háw*.

Facts for the Visitor

PLANNING
When to Go

The best overall time for visiting most of Laos is between November and February – during these months it rains the least and is not too hot. If you plan to focus on the mountainous northern provinces, the hot season (March to May) and early rainy season – say June to July – is not bad either, as temperatures are moderate at higher elevations.

Extensive road travel in remote areas like Attapeu, Phongsali and Sainyabuli may be impossible during the main rainy season, July to October, when roads are often inundated or washed out for weeks, even months at a time. River travel makes a good alternative during these months. If you intend to travel extensively by river November is the best time; flooding has usually subsided yet river levels are still high enough for maximum navigability throughout the country. Between January and June boat services on some rivers – or certain portions of some rivers – may be irregular due to low water levels.

Peak months for tourist arrivals are from December to February and August, although peak season for Laos is a virtual vacuum compared with, say, Chiang Mai in Thailand or Ho Chi Minh City in Vietnam.

Maps

Good maps of Laos are difficult to find. Lonely Planet has a full-colour *Laos* travel atlas. It has 48 pages and includes topographic shading, a 1:1,000,000 scale and the most up-to-date road and place naming scheme for Laos published so far. Travellers might find the travel atlases to the adjacent countries of Vietnam and Thailand handy also.

The National Geographic Service (NGS, Kom Phaen Thii Haeng Saat in Lao, or Service Géographique National in French) has produced a series of adequate maps of Laos and certain provincial capitals. A simple but relatively accurate and up-to-date 1:1,500,000 scale map of the whole country, *Administrative Map of Lao PDR* was last issued by the NGS in 1996 and is available in Vientiane from Raintrees, the State Book Shop, the Lane Xang Hotel and some souvenir shops along Thanon Samsenthai. They can also be purchased direct from the National Geographic Service, which is on a side street to the north of the Patuxai.

The most detailed maps of Laos available – based on Soviet satellite photography from 1981 – were updated for road schemes and place names by the NGS between 1983 and 1986. These topographic maps are labelled in English and French and are often seen on the walls of government offices. The National Geographic Service reprints many of these maps, and will usually sell them to foreigners in spite of the fact that most are marked *En Secret*. When we last visited the office in 1998, however, they required the submission of a letter, on organisation or company letterhead, stating the reason you wanted the maps. This letter then had to be approved by the NGS officials before you could purchase maps. Only a month before that visit we had been able to buy as many maps as we wanted – obviously the policy is changeable.

Occasionally a gift shop in Vientiane will carry a couple of the large NGS 1:5,000,000 scale topographical maps which cover the whole country on one sheet. There is also a set of five topographical maps with a 1:1,000,000 scale, comparable to the Lonely Planet travel atlas in detail though they're about 10 years out of date and each sheet measures 58cm by 75cm! More detailed are the 1986 vintage 1:500,000 scale topographicals, for which there are a total of 11. Only seven of these 11 are available from the NGS, who claim that the missing four are out of print. Other topographical maps in the series decrease in scale to as low as

1:10,000, but anything below the 1:100,000 scale maps (for which it takes 176 to cover the whole country) is overkill unless you plan to drill for oil. Lonely Planet's *Laos* travel atlas or the more general NGS maps are sufficient for most travel purposes.

The National Tourism Authority of Laos (NTAL) now publishes tourist-oriented city maps of Vientiane, Luang Prabang, Tha Khaek, Savannakhet and Pakse. These are reasonably accurate although not much beyond the larger hotels and government offices are marked on them and they are rather out of date. They may be purchased at Raintrees, at the Lane Xang Hotel gift shop and the State Book Shop on Thanon Setthathirat in Vientiane, as well as at the NGS office. For all maps produced in Laos, including the city maps, the lowest prices are available through the NGS. Although this office is supposed to be open Monday to Friday from 8 am to 11.30 am and 2 pm to 4.30 pm, actual opening hours can be erratic.

Map collectors or war historians may find American military maps from 1965 – now rather rare though they may still be available from the Defense Mapping Agency in the US – of some interest. These maps seem fairly accurate for topographic detail but they are woefully out of date with regard to road placement and village names. The same goes for the USA's highly touted Tactical Pilotage Charts, prepared specifically for air travel over Laos and virtually useless for modern ground navigation.

What to Bring

Pack light wash-and-wear, natural-fibre clothes, plus a sweater/pullover and a light jacket for chilly evenings and mornings in the middle of the cool season (December and January) and for the mountainous provinces such as Phongsali and Xieng Khuang any time of year.

Sunglasses are a must for most people and are hard to find in Laos outside Vientiane. Besides filtering sunlight they will protect your eyes from dust when travelling in open vehicles – which means most vehicles in Laos. Bring along a bandanna or scarf for the same situations, to use as a dust screen for nose and mouth. Slip-on shoes or sandals are highly recommended – they are cool to wear and easy to remove before entering a Lao home or temple. A small torch (flashlight) is a good idea, since power blackouts are common. A couple of other handy things are a compass and a fits-all sink plug.

Toothpaste, soap and most other toiletries can be purchased cheaply almost anywhere in Laos. Sunscreen, mosquito repellent, contraceptives and tampons are hard to find, however, so bring enough to last your trip. Tampons, in particular, are almost impossible to find anywhere in Laos. See the Health section later in this chapter for a list of recommended medical items.

SUGGESTED ITINERARIES

A tourist visa allows only 15 days travel in the country, although this term can be extended another 15 days fairly easily. Second extensions can be a little more difficult to obtain; see the Visas section later in this chapter for regulations on visas and extensions. It bears re-emphasising that the sometimes unpredictable nature of travel in Laos – whether by road, river or air – means one can't count on sticking to a set itinerary, no matter how well planned.

If you only have a week to spend in Laos you can easily take in all the major sights in Vientiane and Luang Prabang, provided you fly between these two cities. A popular alternative is to enter the country at Huay Xai in Bokeo Province, opposite Chiang Khong, Thailand, and then to make the river run from Huay Xai to Luang Prabang, continuing south to Vientiane by plane or road. This saves having to backtrack from Luang Prabang to Vientiane.

With a full two weeks you can add side trips north of Vientiane to Vang Vieng and north-east to Xieng Khuang Province. If you want to see a bit of the south, substitute an excursion to the area between Pakse and the Cambodian border, taking in Champasak, Wat Phu and the Si Phan Don area. If Vietnam is next on your schedule, consider entering it by land via Savannakhet and Lao Bao. Yet another alternative is to enter at Huay Xai, continue by road to Luang Nam Tha and Muang Xai, then south by road or river to Luang Prabang and on to Vientiane.

A month's sojourn in Laos – which for tourists will require a visa extension – might begin in the north at Huay Xai and trace a loop through Luang Nam Tha around to Luang Prabang and Xieng Khuang, then on to Vientiane for a break from the rigours of Lao surface travel. From Vientiane (the only place you can extend your visa at this time) you can move down the Mekong valley through the former colonial provincial centres of Tha Khaek, Savannakhet and Salavan before heading east to the remote Sekong and Attapeu provinces. From the latter you could jog back to the Mekong for a laid-back few days in Si Phan Don before exiting the country at Chong Mek, Thailand, near Pakse.

The suggested itineraries above assume you want to see as much of the country as possible within a given interval. A different approach would be to spend more time in a handful of places rather than less time in many. Depending on your inclinations (see the Highlights section following), you might decide to spend a full two weeks or more just exploring the north. If you're into urban culture, a month spent in the towns and cities of the Mekong valley could be very rewarding. Luang Prabang alone is such a pleasant, laid-back city that many people find themselves lingering longer than expected.

HIGHLIGHTS
Although Laos is a relatively small country, time and money constraints will compel most of us to decide – either in advance or as we go along – which parts we're going to see and which parts will have to be left out. Because of the lack of infrastructure it always pays to be under-ambitious with one's travel plans. Don't try to see too much in too little time; you'll have to get used to waiting for buses, boats and planes. In Laos none of these forms of transport keep the back-to-back schedules that are common to

transport in most other parts of Asia. A three hour bus trip can easily turn into a 12 hour one with flat tyres and breakdowns.

Most visitors begin their journey in Vientiane. Depending on how much time you have, you might want to save your capital explorations until after you've seen other parts of the country. That way you'll be sure to have plenty of time upcountry in the 'real' Laos.

Historic Architecture & Museums
The formers royal kingdoms of Vientiane, Luang Prabang, and Champasak offer the most in terms of classic architecture, be it Buddhist temples from the 14th to 19th centuries or French colonial structures from the 19th and 20th centuries. The mysterious Wat Phu Champasak, a Khmer structure in Champasak Province that may once have been the site of human sacrifices, dates back to the Chenla Kingdom (6th to 8th centuries) and the Angkor period (9th to 13th centuries). The enigmatic Plain of Jars near Phonsavan also offers plenty of scope for speculation.

The Lao people are keen to restore older temples, villas and government offices around the country. Colonial architecture is most intact in Luang Prabang, Vientiane, Tha Khaek and Savannakhet. Owing to its rich selection of old temples and French provincial buildings, Luang Prabang was added to UNESCO's World Heritage List in 1995, where it joins such architectural and cultural treasures as the Taj Mahal and Angkor Wat.

Laos isn't a great museum destination yet, but historical museums worth seeing include Vientiane's Haw Pha Kaew and Luang Prabang's Royal Palace.

See the Arts section in the Facts about Laos chapter for more information on art styles and archaeological sites.

Handicrafts
Laos' ethnic diversity means a wide range of handicrafts is available for study or purchase throughout the country. Specialities include silverware, ceramics, woodcarving,

tribal crafts, rattan furniture, textiles and saa paper, nearly all of which can be bought in Vientiane.

North-eastern Laos is famous for Sam Neua-style textiles, which feature rich brocade and dazzling colours. Original silk designs based on these styles are also produced at weaving centres in Vientiane. Simple Lao-style cotton fabrics are abundant in the south near Pakse and Don Khong, while Sekong and Attapeu feature their own styles of weaving unique to the Mon-Khmer tribes in the area.

Hill tribe crafts and jewellery are most abundantly available in Vientiane, though some very interesting work can also be found in Luang Prabang. With some luck, you'll also find good pieces in heavily tribal provinces such as Phongsali, Luang Nam Tha, Hua Phan, Bokeo, Salavan, Sekong and Attapeu. As yet there are few retail outlets in these provinces, so much depends on your initiative in finding village sources on your own.

For information on individual handicrafts, see the Things to Buy section at the end of this chapter.

Culture

Just soaking up the general cultural ambience is one of the highlights of Laos travel, and is an activity which can be enjoyed almost anywhere in the country. You won't see much Lao culture if you spend most of your time sitting around in guesthouses or hanging out in expat restaurants; happily these activities are so far largely restricted to Vientiane and Luang Prabang, so simply escaping these cities will throw you into the real Laos.

For mainstream Lao culture your best venues are towns and villages sited on or near the Mekong River, traditional centres for the lowland Lao. Champasak and Si Phan Don in particular hold fast to older Lao customs. Vientiane and Savannakhet are marching ahead into a transitional mode between the traditional and the modern, though Savannakhet shows far less foreign influence than Vientiane.

Those interested in Hmong-Mien and Thai tribal cultures will want to travel to the far northern provinces of Luang Nam Tha, Bokeo, Udomxai, Phongsali and Hua Phan. The interior of the south – especially Salavan, Sekong and Attapeu provinces – contains lesser-known Mon-Khmer tribes, many of which are also encountered in the highlands of Vietnam.

At least once during your trip, try going to a small town well off the main tourist circuit, staying at a local guesthouse, and eating in Lao rice shops and noodle stands. It's not as easy as going with the crowd but you'll learn a lot about Laos.

Natural Environment

Laos boasts one of the least disturbed ecosystems in Asia due to its overall lack of development and low population density; but, for much the same reason, access to creatures in the wild is limited. With the creation in 1995 of 17 National Biodiversity Conservation Areas (NBCA), the potential for wildlife observation and other eco-tourism pursuits has increased, but so far visitor facilities in these entities have yet to be developed. As with upcountry hill tribe visits, personal initiative is required. Non-government organisations (NGOs) working in Laos, such as the Wildlife Conservation Society, may be able to offer some guidance to those with sincere interests (see the Ecology & Environment section of the Facts about Laos chapter for details). Tour agencies in Vientiane may also be able to help, especially if money's no object. Camping gear is a must, as virtually nothing along these lines is available in Laos.

Probably the two most rewarding areas for wilderness travel are the Nakai-Nam Theun NBCA on the Vietnamese border and the Khammuan Limestone NBCA to the east of Tha Khaek, both in Khammuan Province. The fauna in these areas – from rare birds to wild elephants – is abundant. For flora, parts of Luang Nam Tha and Hua Phan in the north and Attapeu and Champasak in the south offer plenty of primary monsoon forest.

The area around Si Phan Don – a complex of river islands found at the Mekong river's widest point – is of major interest for its riparian habitats and waterfalls. The southernmost reach of Si Phan Don also serves as a fragile home to the rare Irrawaddy dolphin (see the Si Phan Don section of the Southern Laos chapter for details).

TOURIST OFFICES

The National Tourism Authority of Laos (NTAL) was established in Vientiane in the late 1980s as the government-sponsored sole travel agency and tour operator in the country. Following the privatisation of the travel business in the early 1990s, its function as a travel agency has declined substantially although the office can still arrange tours and guides for travel around the country. Private competitors (see the Organised Tours section in the Getting Around chapter) do a better job, however.

The NTAL's senior officials organise endless meetings and seminars to discuss the future of tourism in Laos but in actual fact they wield very little power and as a governing body the office is ineffectual. The NTAL is also supposed to serve as a clearing house on Lao travel information, but they cannot offer much due to a lack of funds and adequately trained personnel. I've noticed a slight increase in the amount of information available at the office over the last few years, but not enough to recommend it as a general information source.

To give an example of NTAL's lack of information and inability to communicate with the provinces, NTAL officials assured me that the Vieng Xai caves in Hua Phan were open to all visitors and that no special permits were necessary for cave entry. Upon arrival in Vieng Xai a few days later the local Vieng Xai officials refused to let me even *look* at the outside of the caves and said a visit would require special permission from Vientiane.

The bottom line is that you're better off going just about anywhere else in Vientiane *but* the NTAL if you're seeking accurate, up-to-date information on travel in Laos.

The NTAL do not supply information by mail and do not maintain any overseas offices. In a few provincial capitals you may find nominal NTAL offices staffed by lone individuals whose major function seems to be extorting money from tour groups visiting the province; the general lack of information at these local offices can be profound. In some remote provinces NTAL officers work in collusion with local authorities to force visitors to hire themselves or their military cronies out as tour guides; although this practice seems to be declining year by year.

Occasionally a local travel agency or guide will try to pass themselves off as NTAL officials or otherwise state that they are 'in charge of tourism' in the province, as has happened repeatedly in Phonsavan in Xieng Khuang Province. Remember that the NTAL has no official regulatory function outside Vientiane (at least not yet) and that you are not required to use any services offered by their representatives, despite any claims to the contrary.

One of NTAL's main functions nowadays seems to be arranging tourist visa extensions. Here again you are not required to visit NTAL for this purpose (although two years ago this wasn't the case). Instead you can now apply directly to the immigration department in Vientiane.

The NTAL head office (☎/fax (021) 212013) is on Thanon Lan Xang opposite the Centre du Langue Française.

VISAS & DOCUMENTS
Passport

Entry into Laos requires a passport valid for at least three months from the time of entry. If you anticipate your passport may expire while you're in Laos, you should obtain a new one before arrival or inquire from your government whether your embassy in Laos (if one exists – see the list of Embassies later in this chapter) can issue a new one.

Visas

Visas for foreigners who want to visit Laos are of the types given below. For all types of visas, the Lao embassy requires that the official one-page visa application form be filled out in triplicate and submitted along with three passport photos and the appropriate fee.

When applying for a visa from outside South-East Asia, you should allow at least two months for the visa process. This is because the embassies must wait for approval from Vientiane before they can issue them. In South-East Asia, the process is much faster – for no apparent reason, since in any case all the embassy has to do is contact Vientiane.

Visa on Arrival Starting on 1 June 1998, the Lao government began issuing 15 day tourist visas on arrival at Wattay international airport in Vientiane and on the Friendship Bridge crossing the Mekong River near Nong Khai, Thailand.

To receive this visa on arrival you must present the following: US$50 cash (travellers cheques and other currencies, including kip, are not accepted); the name of a hotel you will be staying at in Vientiane (pick any one from this guidebook and fill in the blank); and the name of a contact in Vientiane. Most people leave the latter blank unfilled with no problem but if you do know someone in Vientiane, by all means write the name in. For the Wattay airport arrival you're also supposed to possess a valid round-trip air ticket, but so far they haven't checked ours and we haven't heard anyone else say they had their tickets checked either.

It's important to note that you must have US$50 cash in hand when you arrive at Wattay or at the bridge. Moneychangers at either place are unlikely to be able to give you dollars in exchange for Thai baht or any other currency. I've seen several travellers get stuck in airport limbo because they arrived without US dollars to pay for their visa. In such a case the immigration officers may allow you to go into town and try to get dollars from another source. They will, however, keep your passport at the airport in the meantime.

Tourist Visa Until rather recently many Lao embassies and consulates around the world wouldn't issue tourist visas directly but told prospective visitors they had to go through a travel agency authorised to issue such visas. Nowadays most embassies will issue them directly and there's no need to use a travel agency except perhaps for convenience's sake. There is no requirement that you purchase a package tour for Laos in order to obtain a visa, although there is a chance that an unscrupulous travel agency may tell you this is so.

Although in previous years all tourist visas to Laos were limited to 15 days validity (with the possibility of extension inside Laos), as of mid-1998 Lao embassies were authorised to issue 30 day tourist visas. The Lao embassy in Bangkok can usually issue this 30 day visa in 24 hours if you leave your passport overnight. The cost is 750B for the visa plus 300B 'fax fee'. If you only want a 15 day visa, the cost is 250B plus the same fax fee. Some travellers have reported being able to get the shorter visa on the same day of application.

The Lao consulate in Khon Kaen issues 30 day visas for Laos in one to three days for 700B to 1100B, depending on nationality.

In other countries the price of a tourist visa can vary. The going rate in Vietnam and Cambodia as this book went to press was around US$35 for a 30 day visa. In Yangon (Rangoon) the price seemed to vary according to how much the embassy felt like charging that day, usually somewhere between US$38 and US$50.

In Thailand you can easily arrange Lao visas through travel agencies in Bangkok, Chiang Mai, Nong Khai, Chiang Khong, Udon Thani and Ubon Ratchathani. Except in the case of Chiang Khong, costs range from 1500B to 2000B depending on the agency and on the speed of visa delivery. Generally speaking the cheaper services take up to five business days to issue a visa, while the more expensive services usually provide one within 24 hours or less.

In Chiang Khong all agencies charge US$60 or the baht equivalent for a mere

15 day visa. See the Huay Xai section in the Northern Laos chapter for details.

In Vietnam visas are available from agencies in Hanoi and Ho Chi Minh City, at comparable cost. Occasionally one hears of a Vietnamese travel agency which issues a 'cheap' Lao visa for only US$25 or so.

Visit, Non-Immigrant & Business Visas
The visit visa is good for up to 30 days and is the type usually issued to family or friends of foreigners who are working in Laos. Expatriates in Laos must apply on their relative's or friend's behalf from within the country. The application fee for this visa is US$35. It is extendible for a second 30 days. Few people use this type of visa nowadays since tourist visas are so readily obtainable.

A person who has a short-term professional or volunteer assignment in Laos is generally issued a non-immigrant visa that is good for 30 days and extendible for another 30 days. As with the visit visa, the application fee is US$35.

Journalists can apply for the journalist visa, which has the same restrictions and validity as the non-immigrant and visit visas except that the applicant must also fill in a biographical form.

Business visas, also good for 30 days, are relatively easy to obtain as long as you have a sponsoring agency in Laos. Many brokers in Vientiane (and a few in Thailand) can arrange such visas with one to two weeks notice. The visa fee itself costs 300B (US$12) at the Lao embassy in Bangkok, though brokers charge a fee on top of that to cover the cost of paperwork and the expense of contacting the Lao embassy in Bangkok.

Business visas can be extended from month to month indefinitely, although you will need a visa broker or travel agency to handle the extensions. After the first month's extension, the business visa can be converted to multiple-entry status, allowing you to leave and re-enter Laos as many times as you wish within the stated validity dates. Six month business visas are also available.

While non-immigrant and business visas may be collected in one's home country, the Lao embassy in Bangkok is a better place to pick them up since the staff are in daily contact with the appropriate ministries in Vientiane. Simply make sure that your sponsoring agency in Laos sends a confirmation telex or fax to the Bangkok embassy; if you can present the telex number or fax date to the embassy they can find your telex or fax and then issue your visa sooner.

Transit Visa The transit visa is intended for stopovers in Laos for people travelling between two other countries. It's common to ask for such a visa when travelling between Hanoi and Bangkok, for example. In Kunming, China, this is the only type of visa the Lao consulate will issue – at least so far. The visa is supposed to be granted only upon presentation of a visa for the country of final destination (eg Thailand), but often no-one asks to see such a visa. The maximum length of stay for the transit visa is 10 days, and no extensions are allowed. Some embassies and consulates abroad only offer five or seven days, in which case you may have to request the maximum 10 in advance. The fee for this visa is usually US$25 to US$30.

Visa Extensions
Rules surrounding the extension of tourist visas seem to change every six months or so in Laos. Of late they are very easy to obtain in Vientiane for US$3 per day. Legally only the immigration office in Vientiane is authorised to extend your visa, but we have heard of travellers getting the occasional extension in remote provinces such as Phongsali or Sainyabuli – usually for a good deal less than US$3 a day. Most immigration offices, however, are adamant about refusing to extend your visa – they will simply tell you you must go to Vientiane.

There no longer seems to be a limit on the number of times you can extend your visa, though we've never extended more than two times on the same trip. However if you anticipate needing to stay more than a month in Laos, you should investigate the possibility of obtaining a non-immigrant visa or a business visa.

Visit visas, non-immigrant visas, journalist visas and business visas have to be extended through the sponsoring person or organisation. In these cases the extension fee is also highly variable; for consulting agencies the fee may be comparable to the fees charged for tourist visa extensions, though for long-term visitors – those people ·staying more than a month – the fees are usually more reasonable.

The transit visa cannot be extended under any circumstances.

Overstaying Your Visa If you overstay your visa, you will have to pay a fine at the immigration checkpoint upon departure from Laos. The standard fine at the moment is US$5 for each day you've stayed beyond the visa's expiry date. There seems to be little fuss over this. We overstayed our visas twice on a recent trip (unavoidable because of delayed internal flights) and Vientiane immigration was quite understanding, to the point of not charging us for Sunday when the immigration office was closed.

Before intentionally overstaying your visa, however, be sure to check with immigration as to the latest regulations. Penalties could increase at any time.

Photocopies

It's a good idea to keep photocopies of all vital documents – passport data page, credit card numbers, airline tickets, travellers cheque serial numbers and so on – in a separate place from the originals. In case you lose the originals, replacement will be much easier to arrange if you can provide issuing agencies with copies. You might consider leaving extra copies of these documents with someone at home or in a safe place in Vientiane.

Travel Restrictions

For nearly 20 years following the 1975 revolution, the Lao government required travel permits (*bại anuyâat dọen tháang* in Lao or *laissez passer* in French) for all travel outside

Vientiane Prefecture. Both foreigners and Lao citizens were required to carry them. In March 1994 the permit system was abolished and foreigners are now theoretically free to travel throughout most of the country without any special permission other than a valid passport with a valid visa. Lao citizens, on the other hand, are still required to carry permits, along with their ID cards.

Recent travel experience suggests that local permits may still be required in areas where there's considerable unexploded ordnance (eg the Ho Chi Minh Trail) and in 'sensitive' areas like Sainyabuli (insurgents, opium), Hua Phan (re-education camps, the Pathet Lao caves) and most of all in the new Saisombun Special Zone – what used to be eastern Vientiane Province at the borders of Luang Prabang, Xieng Khuang and Bolikhamsai provinces. The latter area is still militarily insecure and has been plagued by attacks on vehicles passing through; for more details see the Dangers & Annoyances section in this chapter.

Some of the more remote provinces like Sekong, Attapeu and Hua Phan are run like independent fiefdoms by the local police, and in these areas travellers may occasionally come across officials who bar entry. In such cases it's best simply to obey the orders of the police and head in the opposite direction; it's no use arguing with people who have the power to incarcerate you indefinitely without trial.

Checkpoints The Lao government still has one major way of keeping track of your whereabouts. Each time you enter and leave a province – whether by land, air or water – you are supposed to stop at a customs or police office and get *jâeng khào* and *jâeng àwk* ('inform enter' and 'inform leave') rubber stamps on your departure card or on a slip of paper provided by the checkpoint officials. The police usually collect a charge for this service, anywhere from 100 to 200 kip per chop.

If you do a lot of interprovincial travel in Laos, the little paper slips fill up quickly with red and black visa stamps. Failing to get stamped in or out seems to be a fairly minor offence in most places. The main risk is being sent back to a place you've already been; for example, if you've just spent all day on a truck from Muang Xai (capital of Udomxai) to Pakbeng – an official exit point for boat travel from Udomxai to Luang Prabang or Bokeo – being sent back to Muang Xai would be a major inconvenience.

Every airport in the country has a desk or booth where officials check arriving and departing passengers in and out of the province, so if you're flying it's easy to comply with regulations. For road and river travel there are very few controls in most places and local officials don't seem to care whether you're stamped in or not. In fact it can be very difficult to locate anyone who will give you the necessary chops. A major exception is Luang Prabang where officials are quite strict about stamping you in and out of the province. In that province unstamped visitors may be subject to a 3000 kip penalty. See the Luang Prabang section of the Northern Laos chapter for details.

It's worth keeping abreast of the general trends regarding interprovincial stamps. As with visa extensions, it's an area which is remaining very fluid.

Onward Tickets
Unlike many countries, Laos makes no effort to ensure you possess onward flight tickets upon entry to the country. Most visitors arrive by land or river.

Travel Insurance
As when travelling anywhere in the world a good travel insurance policy is a wise idea. Travel insurance is a way to regain your money if your flights are cancelled, for example. Read the small print in any policy to see if hazardous activities are covered or if certain countries are not covered by the policy. Laos is generally considered a high-risk area.

If you undergo medical treatment in Laos or Thailand, be sure to collect all receipts and copies of the medical report, in English if possible, for your insurance company.

Driving Licence & Vehicle Insurance
An international driving permit is necessary for any visitor who intends to drive a motor vehicle in Laos. Anyone staying beyond 30 days is supposed to obtain a Lao driving licence issued by Vientiane Municipality's Vehicle Control Office, on the corner of Thanon Setthathirat and Thanon Sakkarin. Upon presentation of a valid driving licence from your home country or a valid international driving permit, plus filling out some papers and paying fees, the Lao licence will be issued automatically. If you don't already possess a valid driving licence or permit you'll have to take a written driving test; available in English, French, Chinese and Lao. A temporary three month licence will be followed by a permanent one which is valid indefinitely.

Third-party insurance is required for all vehicles, including motorcycles. Currently only one company in Laos is authorised to sell such insurance: Assurances Generales du Laos (☎ (021) 215903; fax 215904), That Dam Place, Vientiane. Other documents which should be carried with the vehicle include road tax papers and a current registration sticker, both issued twice yearly. These can be kept up to date at the Vehicle Control Office. For hired vehicles, these documents should be supplied by the owner.

Marriage Permits
No matter what type of visa they hold, foreign residents must have the approval of both the Ministry of Interior and Ministry of Foreign Affairs before they can legally marry a Lao citizen. Without such approval any foreigner who marries (or cohabits with) a Lao citizen is subject to arrest and confiscation of passport. Of late marriage permits have been very difficult to obtain.

EMBASSIES
Lao Embassies Abroad
Australia
  (☎ (02) 6286 4595; fax 6290 1910) 1 Dalman Crescent, O'Malley, Canberra, ACT 2606
Cambodia
  (☎ 26441) 15-17 Thanon Keomani, Phnom Penh

China
(☎ 6532 1224) 11 E 4th St, Sanlitun, Chao Yang, Beijing
Consulate: (☎ 317 6624) Room 3226, Camelia Hotel, 154 East Dong Feng Rd, 650041, Kunming
France
(☎ 45 53 02 98; fax 47 27 57 89) 74 Ave Raymond Poincare, 75116 Paris
Germany
(☎ 21501) Amlessing 6, 53639 Koenigswinter 1, Bonn
Indonesia
(☎ 520 2673; fax 522 9601) Jalan Kintamani Raya C15 No 33, Kuningan Timur, Jakarta 12950
Malaysia
(☎ 248 3895; fax 242 0344) 3 Loront Damai, 55000 Kuala Lumpur
Myanmar (Burma)
(☎ 22482; fax 227466) A1 Diplomatic Headquarters, Tawwin (Fraser) Rd, Yangon
Philippines
(☎ 833 5759) 34 Lapu-Lappu Street, Magallaness Village, Makati City, Manila
Singapore
(☎ 250 6044) 179-B Gold Hill Centre, Thomson Rd
Thailand
(☎ 538 3696, 539 6667) 520, 502/13 Soi Ramkhamhaeng 39, Bang Kapi, Bangkok
Consulate: (☎ 223473) 19/1-3 Thanon Phothisan, Khon Kaen
USA
(☎ 332 6416; fax 332 4923) 2222 S St NW, Washington, DC 20008
Vietnam
(☎ 8254576) 22 Tran Binh Trong, Hanoi
Consulate: (☎ 299275) 93 Pasteur St, District 3, Ho Chi Minh City
Consulate: (☎ 821208) 12 Tran Quy, Danang

Foreign Embassies in Laos

Seventy-five nations have diplomatic relations with Laos, of which around 25 maintain embassies and consulates in Vientiane (many of the remainder, for example Canada and UK, are served by their embassies in Bangkok, Hanoi or Beijing). The addresses and telephone numbers of the principal consular offices are listed below and several of the more important ones (embassies that Lonely Planet readers are likely to visit) are indicated on

the Vientiane map. The area code for Vientiane is 21.

Australia
(☎ 413600, 413805) Thanon Phonxay
Cambodia
(☎ 314952) Thanon Tha Deua, Ban That Khao
China
(☎ 315103) Thanon Wat Nak Nyai
France
(☎ 215258, 215259) Thanon Setthathirat
Germany
(☎ 312111, 312110) Thanon Sok Pa Luang 26
Indonesia
(☎ 413910) Thanon Phon Kheng
Malaysia
(☎ 414205) Thanon That Luang
Myanmar (Burma)
(☎ 314910) Thanon Sok Pa Luang
Philippines
(☎ 315179) Thanon Salakokthan
Singapore
(☎ 416860) Nong Bone Rd, Unit 12 Thanon Ban Naxay
Thailand
(☎ 214582, 214585) Thanon Phonkheng
USA
(☎ 212581, 212582) Thanon That Dam (Bartholomie)
Vietnam
(☎ 413400, 413403) Thanon That Luang

CUSTOMS

Customs inspections at ports of entry are very lax as long as you're not bringing in more than a moderate amount of luggage. You're not supposed to enter the country with more than 500 cigarettes or 1L of distilled spirits. All the usual prohibitions on drugs, weapons and pornography apply, otherwise you can bring in practically anything you want, including unlimited sums of Lao and foreign currency.

Border officials didn't start handing out customs declaration forms until 1993 – and typically no-one bothers to check them when you leave the country.

MONEY
Costs

Except for the high cost of the visa, Laos is a relatively inexpensive country to visit by most standards.

In the early 1990s hotel rates in Vientiane were among the highest in South-East Asia relative to the quality of rooms and service available. However, in the last few years a number of less expensive places to stay in the cities have become available, and even at the more expensive places rates have come down. In fact in larger towns and cities there is now an oversupply of rooms, which should keep rates low.

Nowadays even in Vientiane you can find rooms starting at around US$5 a night. Outside Vientiane basic local hotels and guesthouses typically charge 1500 to 3000 kip per bed, nicer places 6000 to 10,000 kip, single and double. Tourist hotels range from around US$22 a night to a high of US$65 or so.

The average meal in a Lao restaurant costs less than US$2 per person. A cup of coffee costs about US$0.16, a huge bowl of *fõe* (rice noodles) around US$0.40 upcountry or US$0.75 in Vientiane, and a large bottle of Beerlao US$0.75.

Bus transport is often priced according to road conditions; the more difficult the road, the more expensive the ride. Or to put it another way, the longer the trip takes – regardless of the distance – the higher the fare. Some typical fares out of Vientiane include: Savannakhet (nine hours) US$4, Luang Prabang (11 hours) US$5.40 and Pakse (15 hours) US$6.25. Flying cuts into your budget but saves time and thus hotel and food costs. Sample fares: Vientiane to Luang Prabang US$55; Luang Prabang to Xieng Khuang US$35; Vientiane to Pakse US$95.

Estimating a cost for Laos per day is difficult since it depends on how much you try to see, whether you travel by road, river or air and whether you choose to stay in hotels with air-conditioning and hot water. In Vientiane or Luang Prabang you can squeeze by on about US$10 a day if you stay in the cheaper guesthouses and eat local food; in remote areas where everything's less expensive you can whittle this figure down to around US$6 to US$8 a day. Budgets for those who need air-con, hot water and

falang (western) food leap to around US$25 per day minimum if you economise, as much as US$75 for top-end hotels and food. Of course you can spend even more if you stay in the best suites in the best hotels and eat at the most expensive restaurants in town, although such a scenario exists only in Vientiane and Luang Prabang for the moment.

Cash Strategies

As part of the 'baht bloc' (along with Thailand, Vietnam, Cambodia and Myanmar), Laos relies most heavily on the Thai baht for the domestic cash economy. An estimated one-third of all cash circulating in Vientiane, in fact, bears the portrait of the Thai king. This proportion has decreased slightly following the 1997-98 devaluation of the baht, which increased Lao demand for US dollars. The baht still finds favour for its availability and portability – a single 1000 baht note takes the place of 72,500 kip or 72 1000-kip notes plus change. Five 1000 baht notes – about US$125 worth – are quite a bit easier to carry around than 360 1000-kip notes, clumped in bundles of 10 by the bank!

Travelling in a country where the largest note amounts to only US$0.32 can be a major inconvenience (it's hard to believe the Lao government hasn't yet issued a larger note or at least whacked a few zeros off the value). Hence if you plan on making frequent transactions of over US$20 each, you can save luggage space by carrying most of your cash in baht, along with smaller amounts of kip and dollars. A workable plan would be to carry half your cash in baht and a quarter each in kip and US dollars. But if you plan to make only small purchases (under US$20 per transaction) and you won't be travelling more than a few days, carry kip.

Towards the end of a lengthy trip it's best to spend all your kip and put aside some baht for your return to Thailand. Once you cross the Mekong no-one – except perhaps other travellers on their way into Laos – will want your kip.

Credit Cards

Many hotels, upmarket restaurants and gift shops in Vientiane accept Visa and Master-Card credit cards. A few places also take American Express (Amex); the representative for Amex is Diethelm Travel Laos.

Banque pour le Commerce Extérieur Lao (BCEL) on Thanon Pangkham offers cash advances/withdrawals on Visa credit/debit cards for a 2.5% transaction fee if you take kip, or 3.5% for US dollars. As of 1998 cash advances on baht were not available. Other banks may charge more. The Lane Xang Bank in Luang Prabang, for example, charges 3% for cash advances on Visa. The Thai banks in Vientiane, including Thai Farmer's Bank, Siam Commercial Bank and Bangkok Bank, tend to collect up to US$5 per Visa or MasterCard exchange transaction as a 'communication charge' for this service. Depending on the amount you plan to exchange, you might save money by picking one of these schemes over another.

Outside of Vientiane credit cards are virtually useless. At the time of writing Luang Prabang's Phu Vao Hotel and Pakse's Champasak Palace were the only upcountry hotels which would accept Visa for room and restaurant charges. Also, the Lane Xang Bank in Luang Prabang and BCEL in Pakse accept Visa for cash advances.

Banking

Foreign residents of Laos are permitted to open US dollar, baht or kip accounts at several banks in Vientiane, including branches of six Thai banks. Unfortunately, if you already have an account at a Thailand-based branch of one of the latter banks, you won't be permitted to withdraw any money in Laos; you must open a new account. In 1998, typical savings account interest rates were 4% for US dollars, 7% for baht and 16% for kip.

Most banks in Laos are open from 8.30 am to 4 pm Monday to Friday.

A number of expatriates living in Vientiane maintain accounts at Thai banks across the river in Nong Khai because interest rates are higher (eg 10% to 12% for baht) and because more banking services – such as wire transfers – are available. Once a month or so they tuk-tuk down to the Friendship Bridge, hop on a bus to Nong Khai and take care of any financial chores. To do this, of course, you must have a multiple-entry visa.

Currency

The official national currency in the LPDR is the kip. Although only kip is legally negotiable in everyday transactions, in reality the people of Laos use three currencies for commerce: kip, Thai baht (B) and US dollars (US$). In cities such as Vientiane, Luang Prabang, Pakse and Savannakhet, baht and US dollars are readily acceptable at most businesses, including hotels, restaurants and shops.

In smaller towns and villages kip or baht may be preferred. The rule of thumb is that for everyday small purchases, prices are quoted in kip. More expensive goods and services (eg long-distance boat hire) may be quoted in baht, while just about anything costing US$100 or more (eg tours, long-term car rental) is usually quoted in US dollars. This is largely due to the relative portability of each currency.

In spite of the supposed illegality of foreign currency usage, a three-tier currency system remains firmly in place. In keeping with the local system, prices in this guidebook may be given in kip, baht or US dollars depending on how they were quoted at the source.

Kip notes come in denominations of one, five, 10, 20, 50, 100, 500 and 1000 kip. Notes smaller than 50 kip are almost never seen, however. Kip *aat* (coins) were once available but have been withdrawn from circulation since anything below one kip is virtually worthless. It's high time the government printed at least a 10,000 kip or 50,000 kip note.

Laos has no restrictions on the amount of money you can exchange upon entry.

Changing Money

Relative to most currencies, the kip held fairly steady after 1990, even increasing in value against the US dollar a bit between 1990 and 1993. During late 1994 an over-heated economy led to a surplus of hard currency, which resulted in a deflation of around 200 kip per dollar. Much more serious was the Asian economic collapse of 1997-98, which saw the kip lose 80% of its value against the US dollar and other hard currencies. At the time of writing the bank rate was fluctuating between 2400 and 2500 kip to the US dollar, with rates on the parallel market only slightly higher. At the moment no-one can safely predict what the kip rate will be even a month from today, much less six months or a year down the road. Hence all kip prices quoted in this book are unfortunately subject to extreme volatility, at least until the Asian economic situation stabilises.

Exchange Rates
Exchange rates at the time of going to press were:

Australia	A$1	=	1950 kip
Canada	C$1	=	2137 kip
Europe	€1	=	3412 kip
France	1FF	=	521 kip
Germany	DM1	=	1733 kip
Japan	¥100	=	2166 kip
Switzerland	SFr1	=	1617 kip
Thailand	100B	=	7256 kip
UK	£1	=	5114 kip
USA	US$1	=	3120 kip

With some exceptions the best exchange rates are available from banks rather than from moneychangers. At banks, travellers cheques receive a slightly better exchange rate than cash. The banks in Vientiane can change UK pounds, German marks, Canadian, US and Australian dollars, French francs, Thai baht and Japanese yen. Outside of Vientiane most provincial banks will accept only US dollars or baht.

In 1998 the best overall exchange rate was that offered at the BCEL (Thanaakhaan Kaan Khaa Daang Pathet Lao in Lao, or Lao Foreign Trade Bank in English). The BCEL takes a 0.09% commission on dollar-to-kip and baht-to-kip changes, and 0.04% com-mission in the reverse direction. By contrast, foreign banks may take up to a US$2 commission on each US$100 changed.

Licensed moneychangers also maintain booths around Vientiane (including the Talaat Sao or Morning Market) and at some border crossings. Without exception their rates and commissions are not as good as BCEL or other banks; their only advantage is being open longer hours.

Once outside of the major urban centres of Vientiane, Luang Prabang, Savannakhet and Pakse it can be difficult to change travellers cheques; even at Wattay international airport the moneychanger is sometimes short of kip (be sure to ask whether they can cover your cheques before signing). Hence visitors are advised to carry plenty of cash outside Vientiane. If you plan to carry baht and US dollars along for large purchases (as is the custom), be sure to arrange your cash stash in these currencies before you leave the capital. Even in Luang Prabang, the most touristed town in Laos after Vientiane, it is difficult to get anything but kip at the bank.

So far all banks outside Vientiane are government-owned. Exchange rates at these upcountry banks tend to be lower than what you'd get in Vientiane, despite the fact that the national bank mandates a single daily rate for all government banks. In a few cases we were able to bargain a better exchange rate by pointing this out. In Attapeu, the Phak Tai Bank split the difference with us, agreeing to pay the higher Pakse rate but not the official Vientiane rate.

Parallel Market Rates
Officially the kip is a free-floating currency but in reality higher rates than those offered by licensed banks are sometimes available from retail shops and unlicensed moneychangers in Vientiane. Typically these rates run about 25 kip more per dollar – with no commission – for crisp US$100 or 1000B notes. This represents a gain over the official rate of about 5000 kip for each US$100 changed – the price of a meal and a beer at most Lao (but not tourist) restaurants. On

some days when the rate is really fluctuating you may be able to gain as much as 50 kip to the dollar.

The row of unofficial moneychangers seen inside Vientiane's Morning Market (Talaat Sao) a few years ago are now gone, but near the market you will find a few moneychangers sitting on wooden stools beneath umbrellas. These generally offer the best rates for baht or US dollars. Once you've established an exchange rate with these moneychangers (beforehand you should have a thorough knowledge of the current bank rates), be sure to count your kip *before* handing over your dollars or baht. This way if there's any dispute or misunderstanding as to the count or the rate you can always back out of the deal. So far the sleight-of-hand short-changing scams practised in some other countries don't seem to be a problem in Laos, but you should be cautious. Occasionally the police crack down on the parallel market and arrest a few moneychangers but the crackdowns so far haven't lasted more than a few days or a week.

Tipping
Tipping is not customary in Laos except in upscale Vientiane restaurants where 10% of the bill is appreciated – but only if a service charge hasn't already been added to the bill.

Bargaining
Good bargaining, which takes practice, is one way to cut costs. Anything bought in a market should be bargained for; in some shops prices are fixed while in others bargaining is expected (the only way to find out is to try).

In general the Lao are gentle and very scrupulous in their bargaining practices. A fair price is usually arrived at quickly with little attempt to gouge the buyer (some tour operators are an exception to this rule). The amount they come down is usually less than what you see in neighbouring countries. Laos definitely has a 'two tier pricing system' when it comes to quoting prices to foreigners, but it's nowhere near as evident as in Vietnam.

Remember there's a fine line between bargaining and niggling – getting hot under the collar over 100 kip (about US$0.04) makes both seller and buyer lose face.

POST & COMMUNICATIONS
Postal Rates
Postage from Laos is reasonable in price, although most people who plan to send parcels overseas wait until they reach Thailand since the Thai postal service is more reliable.

Lao stamps are printed in Cuba and Vietnam – some come without glue so you may have to use your own or take advantage of the glue pots provided at every post office. Below are some sample letter and small parcel rates (in kip):

Weight	Thailand	Australia	Europe	USA
postcard	250	280	290	330
aerogram	400	400	400	400
10g	340	370	380	420
100g	550	850	950	1350
1kg	6680	10,120	11,120	15,120
2kg	7120	12,680	14,680	22,680

Add 250/600 kip for registered domestic or international mail.

Sending & Receiving Mail
Outgoing mail is fairly reliable and inexpensive. The arrival of incoming mail is not as certain, especially for packages. Express Mail Service or *páisánii duan phisèht* is available to 28 countries and is considered more reliable than regular mail. When posting any package you must leave it open for inspection by a postal officer. Incoming parcels must also be opened for inspection; there is a charge of around 800 kip for this mandatory 'service'.

The main post office in Vientiane has a poste restante service – be sure that those who write to you use the full name of the country, 'Lao People's Democratic Republic' or at least 'Lao PDR'.

The main post office is open Monday to Friday from 8 am to 5 pm, Saturday from 8 am to 4 pm and Sunday until noon. If you're moving to Vientiane, take note that there is no home mail delivery service. Post office boxes can be rented; the box areas are open Monday to Saturday from 8 am to 6 pm.

Throughout the country you can recognise post offices by the colour scheme: mustard yellow with white trim.

Telephone

Telephone service in Laos, both domestic and international, is on-again, off-again at best. In the towns and cities of the Mekong valley service has improved substantially in the last couple of years, and International Direct Dialling (IDD) finally became available for businesses and private residences in Vientiane in 1993. With the arrival of satellite telecommunications via IntelSat and AsiaSat, you can now dial 155 countries from Vientiane.

The best place to make international calls is from the Public Call Office on Thanon Setthathirat in Vientiane, which is open daily from 7.30 am to 10 pm. Operators still cannot place collect calls or reverse phone charges – you must pay for the call in cash kip when it is completed. All calls are operator-assisted. You can also make calls from the main post office opposite the Talaat Sao.

In provincial capitals, international telephone service is usually available at the main post office although some cities are now establishing separate telephone offices. Where a separate phone office exists, hours typically run from 7.30 am to 9.30 pm or 8 am to 10 pm.

Direct-dialled domestic long-distance calls cost from 150 to 250 kip per minute, while operator-assisted calls cost 450 to 750 kip for the first three minutes plus 150 to 250 kip for each additional minute.

International calls are also charged on a per minute basis, with a minimum charge of three minutes. In Vientiane the rates are now quoted in dollars according to a per-country system. Sample rates per minute:

Country	US$
Australia	1.15
China	3.00
France	2.65
Germany	3.00
Thailand	0.70
USA	3.00

Country, Access & Area Codes Until recently most cities in Laos could only be reached through a Vientiane operator. Nowadays it's possible to direct-dial to and from many places in Laos using IDD phone technology.

The country code for calling Laos is 856. For long-distance calls within the country, dial 0 first, then the area code and number. For international calls dial 00 first, then the country code, area code and number.

Telephone Cards Tholakham Lao (Lao Telecomm), a private company, issues telephone cards (*bát thóhlasáp*) that can be bought from any post or telephone office and used in special card phone booths in larger towns and cities. Cards are denominated in units which represent blocks of telephone time.

Although the cards are supposed to come in five different denominations from 50 to 500 units, the only ones that appear to be available are cards of 100 units (3000 kip) and 500 units (15,000 kip). Using the latest phone rates in 1998 as an example, 3000 kip

Laos Area Codes

Town	Area code
Attapeu	31
Huay Xai	84
Luang Nam Tha	86
Luang Prabang	71
Pakse	31
Pakxan	54
Phongsali	88
Sainyabuli	74
Salavan	31
Sam Neua	64
Savannakhet	41
Sekong	31
Tha Khaek	52
Udomxai	81
Vang Vieng	21
Vientiane	21
Xieng Khuang (Phonsavan)	61

was sufficient for a call lasting 13 minutes from Vientiane to Luang Prabang; while 15,000 kip would have paid for 4.1 minutes to France. In US dollar terms this was a good deal; an operator-assisted four minute call from the Public Call Office for the latter call would have cost US$10.86 as opposed to about US$6.25 using the phone card.

Be sure to compare pricing on your own. One reason the cards are in units of time rather than units of money is so that the company can raise the prices whenever it likes without having to manufacture new cards.

Fax, Telegraph & Email

At the Public Call Office in Vientiane fax, telex and telegraph services are available daily from 7.30 am to 9.30 pm. You can also send faxes from the main post office.

In provincial capitals fax, telex and telegraph services are handled at the main post office or at the separate telephone office, where they exist.

For a while some computer retail shops in Vientiane, such as V&T Computer, were offering email services but a government declaration against private commercial Internet use in 1998 forced them to stop. The government announced it would only be legal to access the Net through a government Internet service provider (ISP), as yet to be established, under the auspices of the government Science, Technology and Environment Organisation (STENO). For more details on this tightly controlled project, see the Online Services section later in this chapter.

However the government hasn't stopped private computer owners from logging onto LoxInfo and other ISPs in Thailand via long-distance dialling. Business centres in some hotels may be able to provide email via such systems, if you ask discreetly. It's also possible that the government will reverse its decision on this – just as they reversed the 1997 decision banning all foreign currency from Laos once it was clear the policy wasn't working and couldn't be enforced.

BOOKS

Books on Laos can be difficult to find. The government bookshops in Vientiane carry mostly Lao and Vietnamese books. One private bookshop in Vientiane (and soon in Luang Prabang), Raintrees, stocks new and used titles that include a number of books on Laos.

Overseas, the libraries of universities with Asian studies departments or faculties often carry some of the following English-language books. If you read French, you'll find others as well. Until recently very few books on Laos in any language had been published since the 1975 Revolution. Now that Laos is 'open', new books are beginning to reach the shelves in Bangkok and Singapore; a few even manage to find their way to Europe, Australia, the USA and Canada.

Most books are published in different editions by different publishers in different countries. As a result, a book might be a hardcover rarity in one country while it's readily available in paperback in another. Fortunately, bookshops and libraries search by title or author, so your local bookshop or library is best placed to advise you on the availability of the following titles.

Lonely Planet

Along with this travel guide to Laos, Lonely Planet publishes the *Lao travel atlas* and the *Lao phrasebook*, each of which is described in the Maps section of this chapter and the Language chapter.

Guidebooks

Several other contemporary publishers have followed Lonely Planet's lead in publishing a guidebook to post-1975 Laos (Lonely Planet has versions in English or French). We humbly believe that we have the best guidebook to the country but if we don't, we hope you'll let us know where we can improve.

The classic two-volume *Guide Madrolle* guide to Indochina, last updated in 1939, is worth reading in the original French if you can find it. The volume that includes Laos is entitled *Indochine du Nord*. Of course, many of the place names have changed several times since 1939 (and some places moved due to the nomadic nature of swidden agriculture or were bombed out of existence during the Indochina War), but for guidebook buffs it's a must-read.

An English edition of the *Guide Madrolle* entitled *Indochina* was issued in 1939, but the two volumes were condensed into one so it's not nearly as complete.

Travel

Several classic travel narratives written by 19th century French visitors to Laos have been translated into English and reprinted, including Henri Mouhot's famous *Travels in Siam, Cambodia, and Laos*. The book covers the 1858 to 1860 South-East Asia trip which resulted in the explorer's death in Luang Prabang. Mouhot shows his ambivalence about the Lao in such contradictory estimations as 'They appear to be more industrious than the Siamese and possess a more adventurous and mercantile spirit' while later on in the book he says, 'A race of children, heartless and unenergetic; the enervating climate makes them apathetic'.

Bangkok publisher White Lotus (GPO Box 1141, Bangkok 10501) has translated several other French travelogues, including *Travels in Upper Laos and Siam, with an Account of the Chinese Haw Invasion and Puan Resistance*, an 1884 volume by the Frenchman Dr P Neis and originally titled *Voyage dans le Haut Laos*. Originally published in 1912, and containing original photographs, *In Laos and Siam (Au Laos et Au Siam)* was written by Marthe Bassenne, one of the few French women of this era to have recorded her impressions of South-East Asia.

François Garnier's 1866 to 1868 Mekong River Commission expedition, which set out to explore trade routes through Indochina, is chronicled in the two volumes of *Travels in Cambodia and Part of Laos* and *Further Travels in Laos and in Yunnan*. A third volume containing the sumptuous illustrations – some of them in colour – created by

accompanying sketch artist Louis Delaporte, has been released under the title *A Pictorial Journey on the Old Mekong*. Another White Lotus reprint, *Travels in Laos: The Fate of the Sip Song Pana and Muong Sing*, covers an 1894 to 1896 journey by Emile Lefevre. Lefevre was a member of the infamous Misión Pavie, the colonial vanguard that managed not only to pull Laos into French Indochina but to vanquish the kingdoms of Muang Sing and Sipsongpanna.

In 1952 Norman Lewis narrated his trip through French Indochina in *A Dragon Apparent: Travels In Cambodia, Laos and Vietnam*, a book that contained this passage on Laos: 'Europeans who come here to live, soon acquire a certain recognisable manner. They develop quiet voices, and gentle, rapt expressions'.

The coffee-table-style book *The Mekong* by John Hoskins contains a multitude of photographs of Mekong River life as well as a compendium of fact and lore about the great river.

Art & Culture

The hard-to-find *L'Art du Laos*, a thick 1954 publication of the Ecole Française d'Extrême-Orient by Henri Parmentier, contains many rare photographs of early Lao architecture and sculpture. Unfortunately the overly judgmental and at times condescending text is not very informative. Perhaps even harder to find is the 1935, two-volume *Megalithes du Haut Laos*, by M Colani, an admirable research work that shows that the Plain of Jars of Xieng Khuang and megaliths of Hua Phan have received more scholarly attention than most people nowadays are aware of. Colani travelled overland from Hanoi to north-eastern Laos to complete her analysis.

Treasures from Laos, available in French as *Trésor du Laos*, a 1997 government-sponsored hardback book containing lots of historical photos from colonial Laos, is apparently available only in Vientiane and Luang Prabang. Both the English and French versions include accompanying Lao translation.

Visitors interested in Lao weaving should have a look at *Lao Textiles and Traditions* by Mary F Connors, the best overall introduction to the subject. Patricia Cheesman's *Lao Textiles: Ancient Symbols – Living Art* offers a thorough and well-illustrated explanation of the various weaving styles and techniques – old and new – found in Laos.

Atlas des ethnies et des sous-ethnies du Laos, written by Laurent Chazee, published in 1995 and sold in Bangkok and Vientiane, is based upon ethnographic research done from 1988 to 1994. This colour illustrated book also comes with an informative map tucked into a pocket in the back cover which shows the locations of 119 ethnic groups in Laos.

Traditional Recipes of Laos by Phia Sing, the former chef and master of ceremonies at the Luang Prabang royal palace, contains wonderful recipes for Lao dishes, including local Luang Prabang specialities.

Like other titles in the Culture Shock! series, *Laos Culture Shock!* by Stephen Mansfield serves as a useful introduction to Lao customs and etiquette. In spite of a few errors, such as describing *nâam paa* (fish sauce) as 'a thick paste' (it's actually quite thin, and not a paste at all), labelling a photo of an Iko or Akha as 'Ippo', and translating 'What is your name?' as *'Jao maa tae sai?'*, which really means 'Where do you come from?', the book's breezy and sometimes humorous style is engaging.

History & Politics

One of the classic histories of the French colonial period is Paul Le Boulanger's *Histoire du Laos français*. Jean Deuve's *Le Laos 1945-1949: Contribution à l'histoire du Lao Issala*, does an admirable job of covering the Lao Issara movement in that crucial period between the end of WWII and Lao independence from the French. Deuve extends his analysis into the American period with *Le Royaume du Laos 1949-1965: Histoire événementielle de l'indépendance à la guerre américaine*.

History of Laos by Maha Sila Viravong is a reasonably complete early (pre-War of Resistance) history written by a Thai. *A New History of Laos* by ML Manich Jumsai is basically a slight expansion and update of Viravong's work. A slight Thai bias can be detected though overall it seems fairly objective, if sketchy in places.

Historical Dictionary of Laos by Martin Stuart-Fox & Mary Kooyman contains a very detailed chronology of Laos dating from 500,000 BC to 1991. It lists key terms, people and events in Lao history and supplies lots of trivia you won't find elsewhere.

Notes on Lao History, a rather thin, self-published work by Lao author Somphavan Inthavong, attempts to present Lao history from a provocative 'new' point of view but distorts the work of earlier researchers by taking large chunks of Austro-Thai history out of context to support Lao nationalism. The author's conclusions have a decidedly anti-Thai bent.

The Haw: Traders of the Golden Triangle by Andrew Forbes & David Henley contains a chapter on the Haw wars in Laos as well as much well-researched information on Yunnanese caravan routes through northern Laos.

A collection of academic essays called *Contemporary Laos: Studies in the Politics & Society of the Lao People's Democratic Republic* edited by Martin Stuart-Fox includes detailed discussions of the history and workings of the Lao People's Party, minority politics, Buddhism since the 1975 Revolution, Lao-Thai and Lao-Vietnamese relations and Lao refugees. Some essays are quite well researched while others seem somewhat removed from reality.

Laos: Politics, Economics, & Society by the same author is a good overview of Laos during the early years of the Revolution, with some details on the post-1979 economic reforms. Stuart-Fox makes up for the shortcomings of the previous two titles in his 1995 *Buddhist Kingdom, Marxist State: The Making of Modern Laos* and his 1997 *A History of Laos*, both of which put post-1975 Lao politics into sharper focus.

Lao Peasants Under Socialism by Grant Evans presents a severe analysis of Lao communism backed by thorough empirical research. Evans concludes that the leadership has failed to move Laos out of feudalism towards anything like socialism.

The Politics of Ritual and Remembrance: Laos since 1975, also by Grant Evans, is an interesting work outlining how modern Lao historians have rewritten Lao history to boost nationalism while denying fratricide, and exalt monarchical succession while ignoring the fate of the last royal family. It also looks at the creation of a Kaysone Phomvihane personality cult while Lao historians discouraged the idea that the Revolution was anything but a collective enterprise.

Laos: Beyond the Revolution (edited by Joseph Zasloff & Leonard Unger) presents a collection of thoughtful essays on political and economic history through 1989.

Laos & the Indochina War

Laos: War & Revolution by Nina Adams & Alfred McCoy was commissioned by the Committee of Concerned Asian Scholars and represents the basic western academic left-wing view of pre-1975 Laos, a perspective that now seems out of date in the context of current developments in the country.

Readers interested in the politics, economics and history of opium in Laos should seek out Alfred McCoy's classic *The Politics of Heroin in Southeast Asia* and Dr Joseph Westermeyer's *Poppies, Pipes, and People: Opium and Its Use in Laos*. The former details the CIA-Mafia-Nationalist Chinese involvement in the global opium and heroin trade of the 1960s and 1970s, while the latter is a detailed study of opium production and addiction in Laos.

The Ravens: Pilots of the Secret War of Laos by Christopher Robbins is a very impressive work on the US-directed secret war, with plenty of historical context as well as tactical specifics. Robbins' earlier *Air America: The Story of the CIA's Secret Airlines*, which focuses on the infamous guns and drugs airline, was turned into an Hollywood comedy starring Mel Gibson. In the more recent *Back Fire*, author Roger Warner investigates declassified material from the US government and interviews key figures to uncover more on the secret war in Laos.

Codename Mule: Fighting the Secret War in Laos for the CIA by James E Parker Jr is a collection of war tales based on the author's experiences as a member of the CIA's special operations group in Laos. Like many war-adventure books of this nature, the general tone is 'War is hell, and hell makes men'. But for those searching for details on the US paramilitary presence, it has a few nuggets.

Tragic Mountains: The Hmong, the Americans and the Secret Wars for Laos, 1942-1992, by former Laos foreign correspondent, Jane Hamilton-Merritt, follows the Hmong struggle for freedom, from WWII, when the Hmong sided with the French against the Japanese, through their 1950s battles with the Viet Minh to the 1960s to 1970s war with the Pathet Lao and North Vietnamese armies.

Indochina's Refugees: Oral Histories from Laos, Cambodia and Vietnam by Joanna C Scott contains several personal stories describing events that prompted 10% of the population to leave after 1975. One essay, *Laos – Land of the Seminar Camps*, provides some sobering accounts of the PL's re-education camps.

General

Laos: A Country Study is one of the American University's Area Handbook Series, researched and written by the Foreign Area Studies Department. Probably the most comprehensive book available in English about Lao society, politics, history and economics, it's also remarkably objective considering it was commissioned by the US Army (and often erroneously credited to the CIA). You can sense the authors holding back, though, when recounting the events of the early 1960s leading to US involvement in Laos.

The out-of-print *Laos* by Tom Butcher & Dawn Ellis, has a well-written lay history of the country and many charming descriptions of Lao customs, marred only by a lot of linguistic errors (incorrectly applied terms, misspellings and mistranslations).

Travellers who have noticed that all the nicest cars and houses in Laos belong to NGOs and UN organisations may find a rationale for their angry resentment in *Tears of the White Man: Compassion as Contempt* by Pascal Bruckner, a translation of the original French *Le sanglot de l'homme blanc*. In this philosophical masterpiece, the author exposes the 'Third World-ism' that drives many aid and development projects, an attitude that may ultimately be 'the worst enemy of the people of the Third World, and the best friend of the dictatorships of the Third World'. Or as Jeanne Kirkpatrick, former US ambassador to the UN is quoted in the book, 'Much of what passes for sympathy today is as self-serving as yesterday's rationale for colonialism'.

ONLINE SERVICES

As mentioned in the Fax, Telegraph & Email section earlier in this chapter, the only Internet service provider (ISP) in Laos is the government. Actual service has yet to be established, but a project called PAN-Laos, created under the auspices of the government's Science, Technology and Environment Organisation (STENO) with help from Canada's International Development Research Centre (IRDC), promises to become the legal entity through which Laos will one day be able to access the Internet with a local phone call. For more details, check out their Web site (www. panasia.org.sg/netlaos/).

In the meantime, most people with computer modems get access to the Internet via long-distance calls to Thailand. The most popular and reliable service out of Thailand at the moment is LoxInfo, based in Bangkok but with 16 local access phone numbers around the country. From a private IDD phone in Laos, calls to Bangkok from Vientiane aren't terribly expensive. If PAN-Laos turns out to be as heavily regulated as some fear it will be, access through Thailand will probably remain the norm. For more information on LoxInfo, log onto their Web site (www.loxinfo.co.th). Temporary accounts may be purchased.

At the moment very little information on Laos worth mentioning can be found on the World Wide Web. Of course there's a Usenet group (soc.culture.laos) if you go in for free-for-all chats. A Yahoo! search for Internet categories and Web pages solely concerned with the country (rather than just mentioning the country in passing) scored just 36 sites. Most of the sites were linked to commercial entities such as tour agencies providing a little information on Laos in the hope of selling tours. Or linked to publishers like Lonely Planet doing much the same thing, though we like to think our site offers more meat than most commercial sites (www.lonelyplanet.com).

The Lao embassy in Washington, DC, has a Web site (www.laoembassy.com), containing up-to-date information on visa regulations and application processes, along with minimal travel info and a list of government departments and officials. The Web site of the US Library of Congress carries the lengthy *Laos: A Country Study* (lcweb2.loc.gov/frd/cs/latoc.html), prepared by the LOC's Federal Research Division. The current edition dates to July 1994 but features lots on geography, history, politics and economics.

NEWSPAPERS, MAGAZINES & JOURNALS

The *Vientiane Times*, launched the day before the opening of the Thai-Lao Friendship Bridge in April 1994, is a weekly English-language newspaper produced by the Ministry of Information & Culture. For the most part it's a business-oriented paper, with occasional articles on Lao culture and a short but useful list of ongoing cultural events and social activities in the capital. Since all the staff are government employees, the paper is careful not to print anything critical of the government or anyone in the government. Despite self-censorship it is still the best single source of news on Laos available anywhere.

The only other English periodical published in Laos is the skimpy, typewritten *Lao PDR News Bulletin*. Produced by Khao San

Pathet Lao (or KPL, the government's news service and successor to the pre-Revolutionary Agence Lao Presse), it's basically a list of announcements on the latest international trade agreements, National Assembly meetings and government policies.

The national Lao-language newspaper is *Pasason (The People)*, a somewhat propagandising government mouthpiece that is nonetheless widely read. *Wiangchan Mai (New Vientiane)* is a Vientiane daily with similar content. Other Lao-language newspapers include the *Khao Thulakit (Business News)* published by the Lao National Chamber of Commerce and *Sieng Khaen Lao (Sound of the Lao Khaen)*, a cultural organ for the Lao Writers' Association committed to literary endeavours and the maintenance of Lao language standards.

The *Lanxang Heritage Journal (Withayasaan Mawladok Lan Xang)*, published twice yearly by the Institute of Cultural Research, part of the Ministry of Information & Culture, contains scholarly articles on everything from linguistics to archaeology. Some articles are written in Lao, some in French and some in English. Articles seem to have been filtered to justify nationalist agendas and to remove any chance of any findings contrary to that agenda; none of the articles in the journal are dated.

A tourist-oriented periodical called *Discover Laos*, published six times yearly by Aerocontact Asia, appears to be almost entirely written by an unnamed editor whose ideas on the future of tourism in Laos fall into the category of 'Thailand is a tourist paradise lost'. Yet the magazine is a duplicate of similar ad-filled magazines found in Thailand – you won't read anything critical of the government or advertisers, at least some of whom would like nothing better than to reap the kind of tourism profits Thailand receives. But it contains a good map of Vientiane and the ads will give you an idea of what's new in Vientiane. Most of the magazine's content – both advertising and editorial – is oriented towards Vientiane.

The Lao government monopolises all distribution of the *Bangkok Post* and it is legally available only by subscription, ie it is illegal to buy or sell individual copies. The *Post* can be perused in some hotel lobbies and cafes but otherwise is rarely seen elsewhere in Laos except in government offices! Raintrees in Vientiane carries *Time, Newsweek, Asiaweek, Far Eastern Economic Review* and a few other news periodicals – but not the *Bangkok Post*.

Embassies are good sources of reading material in Vientiane. The French, US, UK and Australian posts are open to visitors, where slightly dated newspapers and magazines are available for perusal.

RADIO

The LPDR has one radio station, Lao National Radio (LNR). English-language news is broadcast twice daily on LNR but most expats prefer the English-language news available from the usual short-wave radio programming. With a short-wave radio you can easily pick up BBC, VOA, Radio Australia, Stockholm Radio, Radio Manila, Radio France International and others with transmitters in South-East Asia.

TELEVISION

Lao National Television sponsors two TV channels – 3 and 9 – which can only be received in the Mekong valley and are only broadcast from 7 to 11 pm daily. Typical fare includes Lao-dubbed episodes of *Alf* and Roadrunner cartoons. Most Lao watch Thai television, which can be received anywhere in the Mekong valley. Thailand's channels 5 and 9 broadcast a variety of English-language programmes.

Satellite TVs can pick up transmissions from CNN International, Star TV, BBC World Service, and various channels from India, Thailand, Japan, Hong Kong and Myanmar. No licence or special permit is necessary for the purchase and use of a satellite TV dish.

Most hotel satellite TV hook-ups are set to receive a minimal number of channels, usually around four or five – sometimes only one, which changes according to the whims of the staff.

PHOTOGRAPHY
Film & Processing
Film is reasonably priced (available in Vientiane, Luang Prabang, Savannakhet and Pakse), but the selection is generally limited to Fuji, Konica or Kodak colour print films in ASA 100 or 200. A few of the better photo shops in Vientiane and Luang Prabang carry slide films, typically Ekta-chrome Elite 50 or 100 or Fujichrome Sensia 100. Print film usually costs around 3000 to 4500 kip per roll, slide film 9000 to 10,000 kip. For B&W film or other slide films, you'd best stock up in Bangkok, where film is relatively cheap, before you come to Laos. A reasonable selection of film is available in Thailand in Nong Khai and Udon Thani as well.

Most of the shops that sell and process film in Vientiane can be found along Thanon Samsenthai and Thanon Khun Bulom. Processing is limited to negative and E-6 positive films. For Kodachrome you're better off waiting to process your film back home or in Bangkok.

Photography
As in other tropical countries, the best times of day for photography are early to mid-morning and late afternoon. A polarising filter would be helpful for cutting glare and improving contrast, especially when photographing temple ruins or shooting over water. If you'll be in Laos during the rainy season (June to October), pack some silica gel with your camera to prevent mould from growing on the inside of your lenses.

Camera batteries, especially lithium ones, can be difficult to find outside Vientiane and Luang Prabang. Bring spares or stock up in Vientiane before heading upcountry.

Restrictions
In rural areas people are often not used to having their photos taken, so be sure to smile and ask permission before snapping away. In tribal areas *always* ask permission before photographing people or religious totems; photography of people is taboo among several of the tribes. Use discretion when photographing villagers anywhere in the country as a camera can be a very intimidating instrument.

Lao officials are sensitive about photography of airports and military installations; when in doubt refrain.

Airport Security
So far only the airports in Vientiane and Luang Prabang use x-ray machines to view luggage, so employ the usual protective procedures (eg lead-lined bags, hand inspection) if you're flying in or out of these cities and are worried about x-ray damage to film.

TIME
Laos, like Thailand, is seven hours ahead of GMT/UTC. Thus noon in Vientiane is 10 pm the previous day in San Francisco, 1 am in New York, 5 am in London, 1 pm in Perth and 3 pm in Sydney.

ELECTRICITY
The LPDR uses 220V AC circuitry; power outlets most commonly feature two-prong round or flat sockets. Bring adapters and transformers as necessary for any appliances you're carrying. Adapters for the common European plugs are available at shops in Vientiane.

In smaller towns electricity generated by diminutive local power plants may be available only three or four hours per night. In many villages there is no power whatsoever.

Blackouts are common during the rainy season, so it's a good idea to bring a torch (flashlight).

WEIGHTS & MEASURES
The international metric system is the official system for weights and measures in the LPDR. Shops, markets and highway signs for the most part conform to the system. In the countryside distances are occasionally quoted in *meun*; one meun is equivalent to 12km. Gold and silver are sometimes weighed in *bàht*; one *bàht* is 15g.

HEALTH

Travel health depends on your predeparture preparations, your daily health care while travelling and how you handle any medical problem that does develop. While the potential dangers can seem quite frightening, in reality few travellers experience anything more than upset stomachs.

Predeparture planning

Immunisations There are no health requirements for Laos in terms of compulsory vaccinations unless you are coming from a yellow fever infected area. Be aware that there is often a greater risk of disease with children and in pregnancy.

Plan ahead for vaccinations: some of them require more than one injection, while some vaccinations should not be given together. It is recommended you seek medical advice at least six weeks before travel.

Record all vaccinations on an International Health Certificate, available from your doctor or government health department.

Discuss your requirements with your doctor, but the vaccinations that you should consider for this trip include:

- **Hepatitis A** The most common travel-acquired illness after diarrhoea which can put you out of action for weeks. Havrix 1440 and Vaqta are vaccinations which provide long term immunity (possibly more than 10 years) after an initial injection and a booster at six to 12 months.
  Gamma globulin is not a vaccination but is ready-made antibody collected from blood donations. It should be given close to departure because, depending on the dose, it only protects for two to six months.
  A combined hepatitis A and hepatitis B vaccination, Twinrix, is also available. This combined vaccination is recommended for people wanting protection against both types of viral hepatitis. Three injections over a six-month period are required.
- **Typhoid** This is an important vaccination to have where hygiene is a problem. Available either as an injection or oral capsules.
- **Diphtheria & Tetanus** Diphtheria can be a fatal throat infection and tetanus can be a fatal wound infection. Everyone should have these

Medical Kit Check List
Consider taking a medical kit including:

- ☐ **Aspirin** or **paracetamol** (acetaminophen in the USA) – for pain or fever.
- ☐ **Antihistamine** (such as Benadryl) – useful as a decongestant for colds and allergies, eases the itch from insect bites or stings and helps prevent motion sickness. Antihistamines may cause sedation and interact with alcohol, so care should be taken when using them; take one you know and have used before, if possible.
- ☐ **Antibiotics** – useful if you're travelling well off the beaten track, but they must be prescribed; carry the prescription with you.
- ☐ **Loperamide (eg Imodium)** or **diphenoxylate (eg Lomotil)** – to treat the symptoms of diarrhoea; prochlorperazine (eg Stemetil) or metaclopramide (eg Maxalon) is good for nausea and vomiting.
- ☐ **Rehydration mixture** – to treat severe diarrhoea; particularly important when travelling with children.
- ☐ **Antiseptic**, such as povidone-iodine (eg Betadine) – for cuts and grazes.
- ☐ **Multivitamins** – especially useful for long trips when dietary vitamin intake may be inadequate.
- ☐ **Calamine lotion** or **aluminium sulphate spray** (eg Stingose) – to ease irritation from bites or stings.
- ☐ **Bandages** and **Band-aids**
- ☐ **Scissors, tweezers** and **thermometer** – (note that mercury thermometers are prohibited by airlines).
- ☐ **Cold & flu tablets** and **throat lozenges** – Pseudoephedrine hydrochloride (eg Sudafed) may be useful if flying with a cold to avoid ear damage.
- ☐ **Insect repellent, sunscreen, lip salve** and **water purification tablets**
- ☐ **A couple of syringes** – in case you need injections in a country with medical hygiene problems. Ask your doctor for a note explaining why they have been prescribed.

vaccinations. After an initial course of three injections, boosters are necessary every 10 years.

- **Hepatitis B** This disease is spread by blood or by sexual activity. Travellers who should consider a hepatitis B vaccination include those who are visiting countries where there are known to be many carriers, where blood transfusions may not be adequately screened or where sexual contact is a possibility. It involves three injections, the quickest course being over three weeks with a booster at 12 months.

- **Polio** Polio is a serious, easily transmitted disease, still prevalent in many developing countries. Everyone should keep up to date with this vaccination. A booster every 10 years maintains immunity.

- **Rabies** Vaccination against rabies should be considered by those who will spend a month or longer in a country where rabies is common, especially if they are cycling, handling animals, caving or spelunking, travelling to remote areas, or for children (who may not report a bite). Predeparture rabies vaccination involves having three injections over 21 to 28 days. If someone who has been vaccinated is bitten or scratched by an animal they will require two booster injections of vaccine, those not vaccinated require more.

- **Japanese B Encephalitis** This mosquito-borne disease is not common in travellers, but it does occur in Asia. Consider having the vaccination if spending a month or longer in a high risk area, making repeated trips to a risk area or visiting during an epidemic. It involves three injections over 30 days. The vaccine is expensive and has been associated with serious allergic reactions so the decision to have it should be balanced against the risk of contracting the illness.

- **Tuberculosis** The risk to travellers of contracting tuberculosis (TB) is usually very low. For those who will be living with or closely associated with local people in high risk areas such as Asia, Africa and some parts of the Americas and the Pacific region, there may be some risk. As most healthy adults do not develop symptoms, a skin test before and after travel to determine whether exposure has occurred may be considered. A vaccination is recommended for children living in these areas for three months or more.

Malaria Medication Antimalarial drugs do not prevent you from being infected but kill the malaria parasites during a stage in their development and significantly reduce the risk of becoming very ill or dying. Expert advice on medication should be sought, as there are many factors to consider including the area to be visited, the risk of exposure to malaria-carrying mosquitoes, the side effects of medication, your medical history and whether you are a child or adult or pregnant. Travellers to isolated area in high risk countries may like to carry a treatment dose of medication for use if symptoms occur.

Health Insurance
Make sure that you have adequate health insurance. Look under Travel Insurance in the Visa & Documents section of this chapter for details.

Travel Health Guides If you are planning to be away or travelling in remote areas for a long period of time, you may like to consider taking a more detailed health guide.

Staying Healthy in Asia, Africa & Latin America
 Dirk Schroeder. Probably the best all-round guide to carry; it's compact, detailed and well organised.
Travellers' Health
 Dr Richard Dawood. Comprehensive, easy to read, authoritative and highly recommended, although it's rather large to lug around.
Where There is No Doctor
 David Werner. A very detailed guide intended for someone, such as a Peace Corps worker, going to work in an underdeveloped country.
Travel with Children
 Maureen Wheeler. Includes advice on travel health for younger children.

There are also a number of excellent travel health sites on the Internet. From the Lonely Planet home page there are links at www.lonelyplanet.com/weblinks/wlprep.htm to the World Health Organization and to the US Centers for Disease Control & Prevention.

Other Preparations Make sure you're healthy before you start travelling. If you are going on a long trip make sure your teeth are OK. If you wear glasses take a spare pair and your prescription.

If you require a particular medication be sure to take an adequate supply, as it may not be available in Laos, especially outside of the main cities. Take part of the packaging showing the generic name, rather than the brand, which will make getting replacements easier. It's a good idea to have a legible prescription or letter from your doctor to show that you legally use the medication to avoid any problems.

Basic Rules

Food There is an old colonial-era adage which says: 'If you can cook it, boil it or peel it you can eat it ... otherwise forget it'. Vegetables and fruit should be washed with purified water or peeled whenever possible. Beware of eating ice cream which is sold on the street or anywhere it might have been melted and refrozen; if there's any doubt (for example a power cut in the last day or two), it's best to steer well clear. Shellfish such as mussels should be avoided as well as undercooked meat, particularly in the form of mince. Steaming does not make shellfish safe for eating.

If a place looks clean and well run and the vendor also looks clean and healthy, then the food is probably safe. In general, places that are packed with travellers or locals will be fine, while empty restaurants are questionable. The food in busy restaurants is cooked and eaten quite quickly with little standing around and is probably not reheated.

Water The number-one rule is *be careful of the water* and especially ice. If you don't know for certain that the water is safe assume the worst. Reputable brands of bottled water or soft drinks are generally fine, although in some places bottles may be refilled with tap water. Only use water from containers with a serrated seal – not tops or corks. Take care with fruit juice, particularly if water may have been added. Milk should be treated with suspicion as it is often unpasteurised, though boiled milk is fine if it is kept hygienically. Tea or coffee should also be OK, since the water should have been boiled.

Water Purification The simplest way to purify water is to boil it thoroughly. A vigorous boiling should be satisfactory; however, at high altitude water boils at a lower temperature, so germs are less likely to be killed. Boil it for longer in these environments.

Consider purchasing a water filter for a long trip. There are two main kinds of filter. Total filters take out all parasites, bacteria and viruses, and make water safe to drink. They are often expensive, but they can be more cost effective than buying bottled water. Simple filters (which can even be a nylon mesh bag) take out dirt and larger foreign bodies from the water so that chemical solutions work much more effectively; if water is dirty, chemical solutions may not work at all. It's very important when buying a filter to read the specifications, so that you know exactly what it removes from the water and what it doesn't. Simple filtering will not remove all dangerous organisms, so if you cannot boil water it should be treated chemically.

Chlorine tablets (such as Puritabs, Steritabs or other brand names) will kill many pathogens, but not some parasites like giardia and amoebic cysts. Iodine is more effective in purifying water and is available in tablet form (such as Potable Aqua). Follow the directions carefully and remember that too much iodine can be harmful.

Medical Problems & Treatment

Self-diagnosis and treatment can be risky, so you should always seek medical help. Although we do give drug dosages in this section, they are for emergency use only. Correct diagnosis is vital.

In Laos an embassy, consulate or five-star hotel can usually recommend a good place to go for advice. In some places standards of medical attention are so low that for some ailments the best advice is to get on a plane and go somewhere else. Antibiotics should ideally be administered only under medical supervision. Take only the recommended dose at the prescribed intervals and use the whole course, even if the illness seems to be cured earlier. Stop immediately if there are any serious reactions

Nutrition

If your food is poor or limited in availability, if you're travelling hard and fast and therefore missing meals or if you simply lose your appetite, you can soon start to lose weight and place your health at risk.

Make sure your diet is well balanced. Cooked eggs, tofu, beans, lentils and nuts are all safe ways to get protein. Fruit you can peel (eg bananas, oranges or mandarins) is usually safe and a good source of vitamins, but melons are best avoided as they can harbour bacteria in their flesh. Try to eat plenty of grains (including rice) and bread. Remember that although food is generally safer if it is cooked well, overcooked food does lose much of its nutritional value. If your diet isn't well balanced or if your food intake is insufficient, it's a good idea to take vitamin and iron pills.

In hot climates make sure you drink enough – don't rely on feeling thirsty to indicate when you should drink. Not needing to urinate or small amounts of very dark yellow urine is a danger sign. Carry a water bottle with you on long trips. Excessive sweating can lead to loss of salt and therefore to muscle cramping. Salt tablets are not a good idea as a preventative, but in places where salt is not used much, adding salt to food can help.

and don't use the antibiotic at all if you are unsure that you have the correct one. Some people are allergic to commonly prescribed antibiotics such as penicillin or sulpha drugs; carry this information when travelling eg on a bracelet.

Laos has no facilities for major medical emergencies; the state-run hospitals and clinics are among the worst in South-East Asia in terms of the standards of hygiene, staff training, supplies and equipment, and the availability of medicines.

For any serious conditions, you're better off going to Thailand. If a medical problem can wait till you're in Bangkok, then all the

better, as there are excellent hospitals there (eg Seventh Day Adventist Hospital, 430 Phitsanulok Rd).

For medical emergencies that can't be delayed before reaching Bangkok and which can't be treated at one of the embassy clinics, you can arrange to have ambulances summoned from nearby Udon Thani or Khon Kaen in Thailand. The Wattana Private Hospital (☎ (66 42) 241031/3) in Udon Thani is the closest; Lao Westcoast Helicopter (☎ (021) 512023; fax 512055) at Hangar 703, Wattay airport, will fly emergency patients to Udon Thani for US$1200, subject to aircraft availability and government permission. Si Nakharin Hospital (☎ (66 43) 237602/6) is further away in Khon Kaen but this hospital is supposed to be the best medical facility in north-eastern Thailand. From either of these hospitals, the patient can be transferred to Bangkok if necessary.

Environmental Hazards

Fungal Infections Fungal infections occur more commonly in hot weather and are usually found on the scalp, between the toes or fingers, in the groin and on the body (ringworm). You get ringworm (which is a fungal infection, not a worm) from infected animals or other people. Moisture encourages these infections.

To prevent fungal infections wear loose, comfortable clothes, avoid artificial fibres, wash frequently and dry carefully. If you do get an infection, wash the infected area at least daily with a disinfectant or medicated soap and water, and rinse and dry well. Apply an antifungal cream or powder like tolnaftate (Tinaderm). Try to expose the infected area to air or sunlight as much as possible and wash all towels and underwear in hot water, change them often and let them dry in the sun.

Heat Exhaustion Dehydration and salt deficiency can cause heat exhaustion. Take time to acclimatise to high temperatures, drink sufficient liquids and do not do anything too physically demanding.

A deficiency in salt is characterised by fatigue, lethargy, headaches, giddiness and muscle cramps; salt tablets may help, but adding extra salt to your food is better.

Anhidrotic heat exhaustion, caused by an inability to sweat, is quite uncommon. It is more likely to strike people who have been in a hot climate for some time, rather than newcomers.

Heatstroke This serious, sometimes even fatal, condition can occur if the body's heat-regulating mechanism breaks down and body temperature rises to dangerous levels. Long, continuous periods of being exposed to high temperatures and insufficient fluids can leave you vulnerable to heatstroke.

The symptoms are feeling unwell, not sweating very much (or at all) and a high body temperature (39°C to 41°C or 102°F to 106°F). Where sweating has ceased the skin becomes flushed and red. Severe, throbbing headaches and a lack of coordination will also occur, and the sufferer may become confused or aggressive.

Eventually the victim will become delirious or convulse. Hospitalisation is essential, but in the interim be sure to get victims out of the sun, remove their clothing, cover them with a wet sheet or towel and then fan them continually. Give the person fluids if they are still conscious.

Jet Lag Jet lag is experienced when a person travels by air across more than three time zones (each time zone usually represents a one-hour time difference). It occurs because many of the functions of the human body (such as temperature, pulse rate and emptying of the bladder and bowels) are regulated by internal 24-hour cycles. When we travel long distances rapidly, our bodies take time to adjust to the 'new time' of our destination, and we may experience fatigue, disorientation, insomnia, anxiety, impaired concentration and loss of appetite. These effects will usually be gone within three days of arrival, but to minimise the impact of jet lag:

- Rest for a couple of days prior to departure.
- Try to select flight schedules that minimise sleep deprivation; arriving late in the day means you can go to sleep soon after you arrive. For very long flights, try to organise a stopover.
- Avoid excessive eating (which bloats the stomach) and alcohol (which causes dehydration) during the flight. Instead, drink plenty of non-carbonated, non-alcoholic drinks such as fruit juice or water.
- Avoid smoking.
- Make yourself comfortable by wearing loose-fitting clothes and perhaps bringing an eye mask and ear plugs to help you sleep.
- Try to sleep at the appropriate time for the time zone you are travelling to.

Motion Sickness Eating lightly before and during a trip will reduce the chances of motion sickness. If you are prone to motion sickness try to find a place that minimises movement – near the wing on aircraft, close to midships on boats, near the centre on buses. Fresh air usually helps to calm the stomach; reading and cigarette smoke don't. Commercial motion-sickness preparations, which can cause drowsiness, have to be taken before the trip commences. Ginger (available in capsule form) and peppermint are natural preventatives.

Prickly Heat Prickly heat is an itchy rash caused by excessive perspiration trapped under the skin. It usually strikes people who have just arrived in a hot climate. Keeping cool, bathing often, drying the skin and using a mild talcum or prickly heat powder or resorting to air-conditioning may help.

Sunburn In the tropics, the desert or at high altitude you can get sunburnt surprisingly quickly, even through cloud. Use a sunscreen, hat, and barrier cream for your nose and lips. Calamine lotion or stingose are good for mild sunburn. Protect your eyes with good quality sunglasses, particularly if you will be near water.

Infectious Diseases
Diarrhoea Simple things like a change of water, food or climate can all cause a mild

Everyday Health

The normal body temperature is 37°C (98.6°F); more than 2°C (4°F) higher indicates a high fever. The normal adult pulse rate is 60 to 100 per minute (children 80 to 100, babies 100 to 140). As a general rule the pulse increases about 20 beats per minute for each 1°C (2°F) rise in fever.

Respiration (breathing) rate is also an indicator of illness. Count the number of breaths per minute: between 12 and 20 is normal for adults and older children (up to 30 for younger children, 40 for babies). People with a high fever or serious respiratory illness breathe more quickly than normal. More than 40 shallow breaths a minute may indicate pneumonia.

attack of diarrhoea, but a few rushed trips to the toilet with no other symptoms is not indicative of a major problem.

Dehydration is the main danger with any diarrhoea, particularly in children and elderly people as dehydration can occur quite quickly. Under all circumstances *fluid replacement* (at least equal to the volume being lost) is the most important thing to remember. Weak black tea with a little sugar, soda water, or soft drinks allowed to go flat and diluted 50% with clean water are all good.

With a severe case of diarrhoea a rehydrating solution is preferable to replace the minerals and salts lost. Commercially available oral rehydration salts (ORS) are very useful; simply add them to boiled or bottled water. In an emergency you can make up a solution of six teaspoons of sugar and a half teaspoon of salt to a litre of boiled or bottled water.

You need to drink at least the same volume of fluid that you are losing in bowel movements and vomiting. Urine is the best guide to the adequacy of replacement – if you have small amounts of concentrated urine, you need to drink more. Keep drinking small amounts often. Stick to a bland diet such as plain rice or noodles as you recover.

Lomotil or Imodium can be used to bring relief from the symptoms, although they do not actually cure the problem. Only use these drugs if you do not have access to toilets eg if you *must* travel. For children under 12 years Lomotil and Imodium are not recommended. Do not use these drugs if the person has a high fever or is severely dehydrated.

In some situations antibiotics may be required: diarrhoea with blood or mucous (dysentery), fever, watery diarrhoea with fever and lethargy, persistent diarrhoea not improving after 48 hours and severe diarrhoea. In these situations gut-paralysing drugs like Imodium should be avoided.

A stool test is necessary to diagnose which kind of dysentery you have, so you should seek medical help urgently. Where this is not possible the recommended drugs for dysentery are norfloxacin 400mg twice daily for three days or ciprofloxacin 500mg twice daily for five days. These are not recommended for children or pregnant women. The drug of choice for children would be co-trimoxazole (Bactrim, Septrin, Resprim) with dosage dependent on weight. A five-day course is given. Ampicillin or amoxycillin may be given during pregnancy, but medical care is necessary.

Amoebic dysentery has a gradual onset of symptoms, and cramping abdominal pain and vomiting are less likely than with other diarrhoeas; fever may not be present. It will persist until treated and can recur and cause other health problems.

Giardiasis is another type of diarrhoea. The parasite causing this intestinal disorder is present in contaminated water. The symptoms are stomach cramps, nausea, a bloated stomach, watery, foul-smelling diarrhoea and frequent gas. Giardiasis can appear several weeks after you have been exposed to the parasite. The symptoms may disappear for a few days and then return; this can go on for several weeks. Tinidazole, known as Fasigyn, or metronidazole (Flagyl) are the recommended drugs. Treatment is a 2g single dose of Fasigyn or 250mg of Flagyl three times daily for five to 10 days.

Hepatitis Hepatitis is a general term for inflammation of the liver. It is a common disease worldwide. The symptoms are fever, chills, headache, fatigue, feelings of weakness and aches and pains, followed by loss of appetite, nausea, vomiting, abdominal pain, dark urine, light-coloured faeces, jaundiced (yellow) skin and the whites of the eyes may turn yellow. **Hepatitis A** is transmitted by contaminated food and drinking water. The disease poses a real threat to the western traveller. You should seek medical advice, but there is not much you can do apart from resting, drinking lots of fluids, eating lightly and avoiding fatty foods. People who have had hepatitis should avoid alcohol for some time after the illness, as the liver needs time to recover.

Hepatitis E is transmitted in the same way, and it can be very serious for pregnant women.

There are around 300 million chronic carriers of **Hepatitis B** in the world. The disease is spread through contact with infected blood, blood products or body fluids, for example through sexual contact, unsterilised needles and blood transfusions, or contact with blood via small breaks in the skin. Other risk situations include having a shave, tattoo, or having your body pierced with contaminated equipment. The symptoms of type B may be more severe and may lead to long term problems. **Hepatitis D** is spread in the same way, but the risk is mainly in shared needles.

Hepatitis C can lead to chronic liver disease. The virus is spread by contact with blood usually via contaminated transfusions or shared needles. Avoiding these is the only means of prevention.

HIV & AIDS HIV, the Human Immunodeficiency Virus, develops into AIDS, Acquired Immune Deficiency Syndrome, which is a fatal disease. HIV is a major problem in many countries. Any exposure to blood, blood products or body fluids may put the individual at risk. The disease is often transmitted through sexual contact or via dirty needles – vaccinations, acupuncture, tattooing and body piercing can be potentially as dangerous as intravenous drug use. HIV/AIDS can also be spread through infected blood transfusions; some developing countries cannot afford to screen blood used for transfusions.

If you do need an injection, ask to see the syringe unwrapped in front of you, or take a needle and syringe pack with you.

In Laos HIV is most commonly spread through intravenous drug use. Statistics on HIV/AIDS in Laos are devilishly hard to come by – not surprising given the lack of public health facilities and research in the country. As of late 1995 – the last year for which we were able to obtain data – the Ministry of Public Health had officially recorded 59 HIV-positive cases, along with 10 AIDS deaths. Since Laos has a relatively low ratio of doctors to citizens, and most people never visit a hospital or trained physician – even when deathly ill – most probably the actual numbers of infected individuals is significantly higher. Many observers think Laos is an 'AIDS time bomb' waiting to explode but to some extent the country is favoured by a low population density.

The use of condoms greatly decreases but does not eliminate the risk of STD infection. The Lao phrase for 'condom' is *thōng anáamái*. Condoms can be purchased at most *khāi yạa* (pharmacies). It is worth bringing your own condoms from home. Lao condoms may be of lesser quality and insufficient size for some.

The medical blood supply in Laos cannot be considered fully screened for HIV; if you need a transfusion the nearest safe supply is in neighbouring Thailand where adequate screening procedures are followed.

Fear of HIV infection should never preclude treatment for any serious medical condition.

Intestinal Worms These parasites are most commonly encountered in rural, tropical areas. The different worms have several ways of infecting people. Some may be ingested with food, including undercooked meat, and some enter through your skin. Infestations may not show up for some time, and although they are generally not serious, if left untreated some can cause severe health problems. Considering having a stool test when you return home to check for these and determine the appropriate treatment.

Liver Flukes One health warning specific to Laos is to be on guard against liver flukes or opisthorchiasis. These are tiny worms that are occasionally present in freshwater fish in Laos. The main risk comes from eating raw or undercooked fish. Travellers should in particular avoid eating uncooked *paa dàek* (an unpasteurised fermented fish used as an accompaniment for many Lao foods) when travelling in rural Laos. The paa dàek in Vientiane and Luang Prabang is said to be safe (or safer) simply because it is usually produced from noninfected fish, while the risk of infestation is greatest in the southern provinces.

Pathologists consider the overall risk of contracting liver flukes in Laos to be low. In neighbouring north-eastern Thailand, where liver flukes are endemic, the Thai government has a campaign to convince people not to eat the stuff.

In rural areas paa dàek is often carried around in bamboo tubes – slung over the shoulders of farmers. Since it's considered a great delicacy, it's often offered to guests – this is one case where you have to weigh carefully the possible health consequences against the risk of offending your hosts. I've eaten quite a bit of it without ill effect but I might just be lucky.

A much less common way to contract liver flukes is by swimming in rivers. According to a Czech parasitologist who spent several months researching opisthorchiasis in Laos, the only known area where the flukes might be contracted by swimming in contaminated waters is in the Mekong River around Don Khong (Khong Island) in the far south of Laos.

The intensity of the symptoms depends very much on how many of the flukes get into your body. At low levels, there are virtually no symptoms at all; at higher levels, an overall fatigue, a low-grade fever and swollen or tender liver (or general abdominal pain) are the usual symptoms, along with worms or worm eggs in the faeces.

If you suspect you have liver flukes, you should have a stool sample analysed by a competent doctor or clinic in Vientiane or Bangkok. Treatment is with 25mg per kg body weight of praziquantel (often sold as Biltricide) three times daily after meals for two days.

Schistosomiasis (Bilharzia) The overall risk for this disease is quite low in Laos, but highest in the southern reaches of the Mekong River – avoid swimming in this area.

Also known as bilharzia, this disease is carried in water by minute worms. They infect certain varieties of freshwater snails found in rivers, streams, lakes and particularly behind dams. The snails are generally found in still water close to the shore or bank. The worms multiply and are eventually discharged into the water.

The worm enters through the skin and attaches itself to your intestines or bladder. The first symptom may be a tingling and sometimes a light rash around the area where it entered. Weeks later a high fever may develop. A general feeling of being unwell may be the first symptom, or there may be no symptoms. Once the disease is established abdominal pain and blood in the urine are other signs. The infection often causes no symptoms until the disease is well established (several months to years after exposure) and damage to internal organs irreversible.

Avoiding swimming or bathing in fresh water where bilharzia is present is the main method of preventing the disease. Even deep water can be infected. If you do get wet, dry off quickly and dry your clothes as well.

A blood test is the most reliable test, but the test will not show positive in results until a number of weeks after exposure.

Sexually Transmitted Diseases In Laos the most common STD is gonorrhoea, followed by nonspecific urethritis. Gonorrhoea, herpes and syphilis are among these diseases; sores, blisters or rashes around the genitals, discharges or pain when urinating are common symptoms. In some STDs, such as wart virus or chlamydia, symptoms may be less marked or not observed at all especially in women. Syphilis symptoms eventually disappear completely but the disease continues and can cause severe problems in later years. While abstinence from sexual contact is the only 100% effective prevention, using condoms is also effective. The treatment of gonorrhoea and syphilis is with antibiotics. The different sexually transmitted diseases each require specific antibiotics. There is no cure for herpes or AIDS.

Typhoid Typhoid fever is a dangerous gut infection caused by contaminated water and food. Medical help must be sought.

In its early stages sufferers may feel they have a bad cold or flu on the way, as early symptoms are a headache, body aches and a fever which rises a little bit each day until it is around 40°C (104°F) or more. The victim's pulse is often slow relative to the degree of fever present – unlike a normal fever where the pulse increases. There may also be vomiting, abdominal pain, diarrhoea or constipation.

In the second week the high fever and slow pulse continue and a few pink spots may appear on the body; trembling, delirium, weakness, weight loss and dehydration may occur. Complications such as pneumonia, perforated bowel or meningitis may occur.

The fever should be treated by keeping the victim cool and giving them fluids, as dehydration should be watched for. Ciprofloxacin 750mg twice a day for 10 days is good for adults.

Chloramphenicol is recommended in many countries. The adult dosage is two 250mg capsules, four times a day. Children aged between eight and 12 years should have half the adult dose; and younger children one-third the adult dose.

Insect-Borne Diseases
Filariasis, leishmaniasis, sleeping sickness, lyme disease, typhus and yellow fever are all insect-borne diseases, but they do not pose a great risk to travellers. For more information on them see Less Common Diseases at the end of the Health section.

Malaria This serious and potentially fatal disease is spread by mosquito bites. Resistance to antimalarials is on the increase all over Asia, and most malaria in Laos is chloroquine resistant.

The highest risk area in Laos seems to be the Mekong valley south of Vientiane and the area in the north around Luang Nam Tha near the Chinese border. Both the *L Plasmodium vivax* and *falciparum* strains of malaria are present, although *LP. falciparum* is the dominant strain. In the southern provinces of Sekong and Attapeu people have been known to come down with both forms simultaneously.

If you are travelling in endemic areas it is extremely important to avoid mosquito bites and to take tablets to prevent this disease. Symptoms range from fever, chills and sweating, headache, diarrhoea and abdominal pains to a general, vague feeling of ill-health. Seek medical help immediately if malaria is suspected. Without treatment, malaria can rapidly become more serious and can be fatal.

For all practical purposes, Laos is considered to be completely chloroquine and Fansidar resistant. Mefloquine and doxycycline are the most commonly recommended prophylactics for Laos, though there is some mefloquine resistance.

If medical care is not available, malaria tablets can be used for treatment. You need to use a malaria tablet which is different to the one you were taking when you contracted malaria. The standard treatment dosage for Laos is mefloquine (three 250mg tablets and a further two six hours later). Alternatives are halofantrine (three doses of two 250mg tablets every six hours) or quinine sulphate (600mg every six hours). There is a greater risk of side effects with these dosages than in normal use if used with mefloquine, so medical advice is preferable.

Travellers are advised to prevent being bitten by mosquitoes at all times. The main precautions are:

- wear light coloured clothing
- wear long pants and long sleeved shirts
- use mosquito repellents containing the compound DEET on exposed areas (prolonged overuse of DEET may be harmful, especially to children, but its use is considered preferable to being bitten by disease-transmitting mosquitoes)
- avoid wearing perfume or aftershave
- use a mosquito net impregnated with mosquito repellent (permethrin) – it may be worth taking your own. The Australian Embassy Clinic in Vientiane sells light travel mosquito nets impregnated with permethrin for US$20.
- impregnating clothes with permethrin effectively deters mosquitoes and other insects

Dengue Fever In some areas of Laos there is a risk of contracting this mosquito-borne disease This time it's a day variety of mosquito *(Aedes aegypti)* that you have to worry about. Dengue is found in urban as well as rural areas of Laos, especially in areas where there is still water. A yearly outbreak occurs in Vientiane during the early rainy season, so take special care from May to July.

Dengue fever is caused by a virus and there is no chemical prophylactic or vaccination against it. In Laos there are four strains (serotypes) of dengue and once you've had one you usually develop an immunity specific to that strain. Symptoms come on suddenly and include high fever, severe headache and heavy joint and muscle pain (hence its older name 'breakbone fever'), followed a few days later by a rash that spreads from the torso to the arms, legs and face. Even when the basic symptoms are short-lived, it can take several weeks to fully recover from the resultant weakness.

In rare cases dengue may develop into a more severe condition known as dengue haemorrhagic fever (DHF), which can be fatal. The risk of DHF for most international travellers is very low.

The best way to prevent dengue, as with malaria, is to take care not to be bitten by mosquitoes.

The only treatment for dengue fever is symptomatic: rest in bed, rehydration and taking acetaminophen (Tylenol, Panadol) to reduce the fever. Avoid taking aspirin, which raises the chances of haemorrhaging. Hospital supervision is necessary in the most extreme cases.

Japanese B Encephalitis This viral brain infection is carried by mosquitoes. Most cases occur in rural areas, as the virus exists in pigs and some species of wading birds. Symptoms include fever, headache and alteration in consciousness. Hospitalisation is needed for correct diagnosis and treatment. There is a high mortality rate among those who have symptoms; of those that survive many are intellectually disabled.

Cuts, Bites & Stings
Rabies is passed through animal bites. See under Less Common Diseases further on for details of this disease.

Bedbugs & Lice Bedbugs live in various places, but particularly in dirty mattresses and bedding, evidenced by spots of blood on bedclothes or on the wall. Bedbugs leave itchy bites in neat rows. Calamine lotion or Stingose spray may help.

All lice cause itching and discomfort. They make themselves at home in your hair (head lice), your clothing (body lice) or in your pubic hair (crabs). You catch lice through direct contact with infected people or by sharing combs, clothing and the like. Powder or shampoo treatment will kill the lice and infected clothing should then be washed in very hot, soapy water and left in the sun to dry.

Cuts & Scratches Wash well and treat any cut with an antiseptic such as povidone-iodine. Where possible avoid bandages and Band-aids, which can keep wounds wet.

Insect Bites & Stings Bee and wasp stings are usually painful rather than dangerous. However in people who are allergic to them severe breathing difficulties may occur and require urgent medical attention. Calamine lotion or Stingose spray will give relief and ice packs will reduce the pain and swelling. There are some spiders with dangerous bites but antivenenes are usually available.

Leeches & Ticks Leeches may be present in damp rainforest conditions; they attach themselves to your skin to suck your blood. Trekkers often get them on their legs or in their boots. Salt or a lighted cigarette end will make them fall off. Do not pull them off, as the bite is then more likely to become infected. Clean and apply pressure if the point of attachment is bleeding. An insect repellent may keep them away.

You should always check all over your body if you have been walking through a potentially tick-infested area as ticks can cause skin infections and other more serious diseases. If a tick is found attached, press down around the tick's head with tweezers, grab the head and gently pull upwards. Try to avoid pulling the rear of the body as this may squeeze the tick's gut contents through the attached mouth parts into the skin, increasing the risk of infection and disease. Smearing chemicals on the tick will not make it let go and is not a recommended treatment.

Snakes To minimise your chances of being bitten always wear boots, socks and long trousers when walking through undergrowth where snakes may be present. Don't put your hands into holes and crevices, and be careful when collecting firewood.

Snake bites do not cause instantaneous death and antivenenes are usually available. Immediately wrap the bitten limb tightly, as you would for a sprained ankle, and then attach a splint to immobilise it. Keep the victim still and seek medical help, if possible with the dead snake for identification. Don't attempt to catch the snake if there is a possibility of being bitten again. Using tourniquets and sucking out the poison are now comprehensively discredited.

Women's Health
Gynaecological Problems Sexually transmitted diseases are a major cause of vaginal problems. Symptoms include a smelly discharge, painful intercourse and sometimes a burning sensation when urinating. Sexual partners must also be treated. Medical care should be sought and remember in addition to these diseases HIV or hepatitis B may also be acquired during exposure. Besides abstinence, the best thing is to practise safe sex using condoms.

Antibiotic use, synthetic underwear, sweating and contraceptive pills can lead to fungal vaginal infections when travelling in hot climates. Maintaining good personal hygiene, and loose-fitting clothes and cotton underwear will help to prevent these infections.

Fungal infections, characterised by a rash, itch and discharge, can be treated with a vinegar or lemon-juice douche, or yoghurt. Nystatin, miconazole or clotrimazole pessaries or vaginal creams are the typical treatment.

Pregnancy It is not advisable to travel to some places while pregnant as some vaccinations normally used to prevent serious diseases are not advisable in pregnancy eg yellow fever. In addition, some diseases are much more serious for the mother (and may increase the risk of a stillborn child) in pregnancy eg malaria.

Most miscarriages occur during the first three months of pregnancy. Miscarriage is not uncommon, and can occasionally lead to severe bleeding. The last three months should also be spent within reasonable distance of good medical care, so travel to Laos during this time is not really recommended. A baby born as early as 24 weeks stands a chance of survival, but only in a good modern hospital. Pregnant women should avoid all unnecessary medication, although vaccinations and malarial prophylactics should still be taken where needed. Additional care should be taken to prevent illness and particular attention should be paid to diet and nutrition. Alcohol and nicotine, for example, should be avoided.

Less Common Diseases

The following disease pose a small risk to travellers, and so are only mentioned in passing. It is important to seek medical advice if you think you may have any of these diseases.

Cholera This is the worst of the watery diarrhoeas and medical help should be sought. Outbreaks of cholera are generally widely reported, so you can avoid such problem areas. *Fluid replacement is the most vital treatment* – the risk of dehydration is severe as you may lose up to 20L a day. If there is a delay in getting to hospital then begin taking tetracycline. The adult dose is 250mg four times daily. It is not recommended for children under nine years nor for pregnant women. Tetracycline may help shorten the illness, but adequate fluids are required to save lives.

Filariasis This is a mosquito-transmitted parasitic infection found in many parts of Africa, Asia, Central and South America and the Pacific. Possible symptoms include fever, pain and swelling of the lymph glands; inflammation of lymph drainage areas; swelling of a limb or the scrotum; skin rashes and blindness. Treatment is available to eliminate the parasites from the body, but some of the damage already caused may not be reversible. Medical advice should be obtained promptly if the infection is suspected.

Lyme Disease Lyme disease is a tick-transmitted infection which can be acquired throughout North America, Europe and Asia. The illness usually begins with a spreading rash at the site of the tick bite and is accompanied by fever, headache, extreme fatigue, aching joints and muscles and mild neck stiffness. If untreated, these symptoms usually resolve over several weeks but over subsequent weeks or months disorders of the nervous system, heart and joints may develop. Treatment works best early in the illness. Medical help should be sought.

Rabies Rabies is a fatal viral infection found in many countries. Many animals can be infected (such as dogs, cats, bats and monkeys) and it is their saliva which is infectious. Any bite, scratch or even lick from a warm-blooded, furry animal should be cleaned immediately and thoroughly. Scrub with soap and running water, and then apply alcohol or iodine solution. Medical help should be sought promptly to receive a course of injections to prevent the onset of symptoms and death.

Tetanus Tetanus occurs when a wound becomes infected by a germ which lives in soil and in the faeces of horses and other animals. It enters the body via breaks in the skin. All wounds should be cleaned promptly and adequately and an antiseptic cream or solution applied. Use antibiotics if the wound becomes hot, throbs or pus is seen. The first symptom may be discomfort in swallowing, or stiffening of the jaw and neck; this is followed by painful convulsions of the jaw and whole body. The disease can be fatal.

Tuberculosis (TB) TB is a bacterial infection usually transmitted from person to person by coughing but may be transmitted through consumption of unpasteurised milk. Milk that has been boiled is safe to drink, and the souring of milk to make yoghurt or cheese also kills the bacilli. Travellers are usually not at great risk as close household contact with the infected person is usually required before the disease is passed on.

Typhus Typhus is spread by ticks, mites or lice. It begins with fever, chills, headache and muscle pains followed a few days later by a body rash. There is often a large painful sore at the site of the bite and nearby lymph nodes are painfully swollen. Typhus can be treated under medical supervision.

Seek local advice on areas where ticks pose a danger and always check your skin (including hair) carefully for ticks after walking in a danger area such as a tropical forest. A strong insect repellent can help, and serious walkers in tick-infested areas should consider having their trousers and boots impregnated with benzyl benzoate and dibutylphthalate.

TOILETS & SHOWERS

In Laos, as in many other Asian countries, the 'squat toilet' is the norm except in hotels and guesthouses geared towards tourists and international business travellers. Instead of trying to approximate a chair or stool like a modern sit-down toilet, a traditional Asian toilet sits more or less flush with the surface of the floor, with two footpads on either side of the porcelain abyss.

For persons who have never used a squat toilet it takes a bit of getting used to. If you find yourself feeling awkward the first couple of times you use one, you can console yourself with the knowledge that, according to those who study such matters, people who use squat toilets are much less likely to develop haemorrhoids than people who use sit toilets.

Next to the typical squat toilet is a bucket or cement reservoir filled with water. A plastic bowl or bucket usually floats on the water's surface or sits nearby. This supply of water has a two-fold function. Firstly, toilet-goers scoop water from the reservoir with the plastic bowl and use it to clean their nether regions while still squatting over the toilet. Secondly, since there is usually no mechanical flushing device attached to a squat toilet, a few extra scoops must be poured into the toilet basin to flush the waste into the septic system. The more rustic toilets in rural areas may simply consist of a few planks over a hole in the ground.

Even in places where sit-down toilets are installed, the plumbing may not be designed to take toilet paper. In such cases there will be the usual washing bucket nearby or there will be a waste basket where you're supposed to place used toilet paper – sometimes both.

Public toilets are uncommon outside hotel lobbies and airports. While you are on the road between towns and villages, it is perfectly acceptable to go behind a tree or even to use the roadside when nature calls.

Bathing

Most hotels and guesthouses in the country do not have hot water, though places in the larger cities will usually offer small electric shower heaters in their more expensive rooms. Very few boiler-style water heaters are available.

The vast majority of rural Lao bathe in rivers or streams. Those living in towns or cities may have washrooms where a large jar or cement trough is filled with water for bathing purposes. A plastic or metal bowl is used to sluice water from the jar or trough over the body. Even in homes where showers are installed, heated water is uncommon. Most Lao bathe at least twice a day.

If ever you find yourself bathing in a public place you should wear a *phàa salóng* or *phàa sìn* (cotton wraprounds for men and women respectively); nude bathing is not the norm.

WOMEN TRAVELLERS
Attitudes to Women

Laos is quite similar to Thailand with regard to women's social status in that Lao women have substantial gender parity in the workforce, inheritance, land ownership and so on, often more so than in many western countries. The bad news is that although women generally fare well in these areas, their cultural standing is a bit further from parity. An oft-repeated Lao saying reminds us that men form the front legs of the elephant, women the hind legs (at least they're pulling equal weight).

Lao Buddhism commonly holds that women must be reborn as men before they can attain nirvana, though many dhamma teachers point out that this presumption isn't supported by the suttas (discourses of the Buddha) or by the commentaries. But nevertheless it is a widespread belief, supported by the availability of a fully ordained Buddhist monastic status for men and a less prestigious eight-precept ordination for women.

One major difference between Laos and Thailand is that prostitution is much less common in Laos, where it is a very serious criminal offence. While a Thai woman who wants to preserve a 'proper' image usually won't associate with foreign males for fear of being perceived as a prostitute, in Laos this is not the case (although a Lao woman generally isn't seen alone with any male in public unless married). Lao women drink beer and *làa-láo* (rice liquor) in public, something 'proper' Thai females would rarely do, even in less conservative places such as Bangkok.

Hence a foreign woman seen drinking in a cafe or restaurant is not usually perceived as being 'loose' or available as she might be in Thailand. This in turn means that there are generally fewer problems with uninvited male solicitations.

Safety Precautions

Everyday incidents of sexual harassment are much less common in Laos than in virtually any other Asian country. In general all visitors to Laos are treated with the utmost respect and courtesy. Nevertheless women should exercise the usual cautions when travelling alone in remote areas of the country or when out late at night. Lao women almost never travel alone, so a foreign female without company is judged by most Lao – male and female – as being a bit strange. Marked behaviour raises the chance of being singled out.

What to Wear

The wearing of clothes that bare the thighs, shoulders or breasts is often perceived as improper or disrespectful behaviour in Laos. Long trousers and walking shorts (for men too), as well as skirts, are acceptable attire. Tank tops, sleeveless blouses and short skirts or shorts are not. Many visiting women find that the traditional Lao phàa sìn

or long patterned skirts make fine travel clothing. For Lao women such dress is mandatory for visits to government offices and museums.

GAY & LESBIAN TRAVELLERS

Lao culture is very tolerant of homosexuality although there is not as prominent a gay and lesbian scene as in neighbouring Thailand. The legal situation is unclear, and there are reports of several arrests in the early 1990s. Since homosexuals are free to meet wherever they wish without facing social prejudice, furtive encounters are much less common than in some western countries and other less liberated parts of the world. Public displays of affection – whether heterosexual or homosexual – are frowned upon.

Levels of Meaning

While many Lao taboos can be bent a little without creating a huge fuss, the following one cannot. Aboard transport such as trucks, buses or riverboats in Laos, women are expected to ride inside. Any attempt to ride on the roof will be immediately discouraged. When asked why women can't sit on the roof, the usual Lao answer is *'phít sąatsanǎa'* – 'it's against the religion', which is to say it's against Lao custom. Partially this is old-fashioned chivalry – 'it's too dangerous on the roof' – but mainly it's due to a deep-seated superstition that women's bodies should not intentionally occupy a physical space above a man's for fear of damaging men's spiritual status. Men wearing sacred tattoos or amulets often express the fear that such an arrangement will ruin the protection that these symbols are supposed to convey! The superstition runs to how laundry is hung out to dry. Women's clothing – especially underwear – is not to be hung above men's clothing.

DISABLED TRAVELLERS

With its lack of paved roads or footpaths (sidewalks) – even when present the latter are often uneven – Laos presents many physical obstacles for people with mobility impairments. Rarely do public buildings feature ramps or other access points for wheelchairs, nor do any hotels consistently make efforts to provide access for the handicapped (the single exception is the Lao Hotel Plaza in Vientiane, which has some ramping). Hence you're pretty much left to your own resources. Public transport is particularly crowded and difficult, even for the fully ambulatory.

For wheelchair travellers, any trip to Laos will require a good deal of advance planning. Fortunately a growing network of information sources can put you in touch with those who may have wheeled through Laos before. There is no better source of information than someone who has done it.

Three international organisations which act as clearing houses for information on world travel for the mobility-impaired are:

Access Foundation
    (☎ (516) 887-5798), PO Box 356, Malverne, NY 11565, USA
Mobility International USA
    (☎ (503) 343-1284; fax (541) 343-6812), PO Box 10767, Eugene, OR 97440, USA
Society for the Advancement of Travel for the Handicapped (SATH)
    (☎ (212) 447-0027; fax (212) 725-8253), 347 Fifth Ave, Suite 610, New York, NY 10016, USA. SATH publishes a good magazine called *Open World*.

Abilities magazine (☎ (416) 923-1885; fax 923-9829), 489 College St, Suite 501, Toronto, Ontario, Canada M6G 1A5, carries a column called 'Accessible Planet' which offers tips on foreign travel for people with disabilities. The magazine is also available online (indie.ca/abilities/magazine/magazine.html). The book *Exotic Destinations for Wheelchair Travelers* by Ed Hansen & Bruce Gordon has good information on South-East Asia, (including Thailand) though nothing specific on Laos.

If you're passing through Bangkok – as most people who visit Laos do – you might want to get in try contact with Disabled Peoples International, Council of Disabled People of Thailand (☎ (02) 255-1718; fax 252-3676) at 78/2 Thanon Tivanon, Pak Kret, Nonthaburi 11120, and Handicapped International at 87/2 Soi 15 Thanon Sukhumvit, Bangkok 10110.

SENIOR TRAVELLERS

Senior discounts aren't generally available in Laos, but the Lao more than make up for this in the respect they typically show for the elderly. In traditional Lao culture status comes with age; there isn't as heavy an emphasis on youth as in the western world. Deference for age manifests itself in the way Lao will go out of their way to help older persons in and out of vehicles or with luggage, and – usually but not always – in waiting on them first in shops and post offices.

Cross-generational entertainment is more common in Laos than in China, Vietnam or Thailand. Although there is some age stratification in Lao nightclubs, all ages are welcome. At traditional events such as rural temple fairs and other wat-centred events, young and old will dance and eat together.

TRAVEL WITH CHILDREN

Like many places in South-East Asia, travelling with children in Laos can be a lot of fun as long as you come well prepared with the right attitudes, physical requirements and the usual parental patience. Lonely Planet's *Travel with Children* by Maureen Wheeler contains a lot of useful advice on how to cope with kids on the road and what to bring along to make things go more smoothly, with special attention paid to travel in developing countries.

The Lao adore children and in many instances will shower attention on your offspring, who will readily find playmates among their Lao peers and temporary nanny service at practically every stop.

For the most part parents needn't worry too much about health concerns though it pays to lay down a few ground rules – such as regular hand-washing – to head off potential medical problems. All the usual health precautions apply (see the Health section earlier for details); children should especially be warned not to play with animals encountered along the way since rabies is very common in Laos.

DANGERS & ANNOYANCES
Road Travel

Until 1994 it was difficult to get permission to travel by road in Laos simply because the government was terrified of losing tourists to natural and not-so-natural mishaps, thus tarnishing the country's image. The natural risks are obvious – road conditions and the standard of vehicle maintenance outside the Mekong valley are quite inadequate, and if you were unlucky enough to be involved in a serious accident it might take days to reach a hospital.

Since the repeal of the travel permit requirement you can now travel almost anywhere in the country by road – that is, where you can find a road. The risk of breakdowns and accidents is as great as ever but the increased frequency and availability of interprovincial public transport over the last few years mean there's a better chance of getting help.

With a couple of exceptions most areas of the country are secure in the military sense. Route 13 has been paved all the way between Vientiane and Luang Prabang, an accomplishment that has brought troops to the area between Kasi and Muang Phu Khun previously troubled by Hmong bandits/guerrillas. This section of Route 13 is now considered as safe as any road in Laos – as proven by the fact that bus drivers have stopped carrying guns. Despite the apparent safety, I've heard rumours of some guerrilla attacks – none of them substantiated – so it might be a good idea to ask around in Luang Prabang or Vientiane before setting off. When I last travelled this road in 1998 it appeared safe and none of the Lao I talked to along the way had heard of any recent problems.

A section of road where ambushes are still frequent is the western portion of Route 7 in Xieng Khuang Province, between the road's westernmost terminus at Route 13 (Muang Phu Khun) and its crossing over the Nam Ngum river near Muang Sui (east of Phonsavan). An Australian engineer was killed in this area in early 1995 and several Lao have also died in attacks. At the time of writing checkpoints along this section of Route 7 were turning back anyone without a military escort. Just how many Lao have been killed in these attacks is not known since the government almost never allows the national press to report on them. When they do appear, official reports assign the blame to 'bandits' but rebels – most likely Hmong remnants from General Vang Pao's disbanded army or the Chao Fa band – may be responsible. Until this area is declared safe, you travel this road at your own risk; we recommend flying to Phonsavan or going by road from Nong Khiaw instead. Again, ask around in Vientiane or Luang Prabang to get the latest information.

To the south of Route 7 is the Saisombun Special Zone, a relatively new administrative district which was definitely *not* safe at the time of writing. Carved out of eastern Vientiane, south-western Xieng Khuang and north-western Bolikhamsai provinces in 1994, this 7105 sq km district (larger than the province of Bokeo) is considered a 'troubled' area. Four UN Drug Control Programme staff – all Lao – died in an attack here in 1994 and there have been some vicious attacks on local buses as well. The Lao government created the new zone with the intent of clearing up the guerrilla/bandit problem and have stationed two military battalions here to accomplish the task. The capital of this new zone is Long Chen, formerly a CIA/USAF/Hmong army base during the Indochina War; the town has been renamed Saisombun.

Route 6 north from Paksan through Saisombun Special Zone to just south of Muang Khun (Xieng Khuang Province) continues to be plagued with security problems. North of Muang Khun, all the way to

Sam Neua in Hua Phan Province, this road is relatively safe.

Another area in the north where attacks have occurred in the past – but not recently – is along the road between Luang Nam Tha and Huay Xai, especially in the vicinity of Vieng Phukha, a former Hmong guerrilla stronghold. Since 1995 this road has been considered secure and thousands of people have traversed it without any problem. In 1996 a Thai company started upgrading this road with the intent of sealing it all the way from Huay Xai to the Chinese border, but Thailand's economic crisis caused a substantial slowdown in the work.

While it might seem ironic that the former Liberated Zones are still the most insecure parts of Laos even though the war ended in 1975, the fact is that most of the Lao territory outside the Mekong valley was never secure. Even at the height of the Lan Xang Kingdom and later French colonial rule, the highland peoples retained a high degree of independence. The rugged mountains and upland valleys make as good a hiding place for anti-LPRP organisations and other unruly sorts today as for the PL during the war.

UXO

In the eastern portions of the country towards the Vietnamese border are large areas contaminated by unexploded ordnance (UXO) left behind by nearly a hundred years of warfare. The majority of UXO found today was left behind by ground battles and includes French, Chinese, American, Soviet and Vietnamese materials, among them mortar shells, munitions, white phosphorus canisters, land mines and cluster bombs. US-made cluster bombs (known as *bombi* to the Lao) pose by far the greatest potential danger to people living or travelling through these areas and account for most of the estimated 130 casualties per year (in Cambodia, by comparison, the UN estimates 800 people per year are killed by UXO). Most of those injured or killed are Lao citizens, roughly 40% of whom are children. Large bombs up

to 500kg dropped by US aircraft also lie undetonated in some areas, but it's very rare that one of these is accidentally detonated.

According to recent surveys undertaken by the Lao National UXO Programme (UXO Lao), financed by the UN under the auspices of the Ministry of Labour & Social Welfare, the provinces of Salavan, Savannakhet and Xieng Khuang are considered to be the most severely affected, followed by Champasak, Hua Phan, Khammuan, Luang Prabang and Sekong. In more exact human terms, about 11% of all villages in Laos fall into the first category, 15% in the second. A reported 61% of all villages are thought to be UXO-free (of this proportion 13% were formerly contaminated but have been cleared).

Statistically speaking, the UXO risk for the average foreign visitor is quite low, but travellers should exercise caution when considering off-road wilderness travel in the aforementioned provinces. Never touch an object on the ground that may be UXO, no matter how old, crusty and defunct it may appear.

Theft

On the whole, the Lao are trustworthy people and theft is not much of a problem. Still, it's best if you keep your hotel room locked when you're out and at night. If you ride a crowded bus, watch your luggage and don't keep money in your trouser pockets. If you ride a bicycle or motorcycle in Vientiane, it's best not to place anything of value in the basket – at night thieving duos on motorbikes have been known to ride by and snatch bags from baskets.

Queues

The Lao follow the usual South-East Asian method of queuing for services, which is to say they don't form a line at all but simply push en masse towards the point of distribution, whether it's ticket counters, post office windows or bus doors. It won't help to get angry and shout 'I was here first!' since first-come, first-served simply isn't the way things are done here. Rather it's 'first-seen, first-served'. Learn to play the game the Lao way, by pushing your money, passport, letters or whatever to the front of the crowd as best you can. Eventually you'll get through.

Paranoid Officials
Some of the more remote corners of eastern Laos, eg Hua Phan and Attapeu provinces, are renowned for the suspicious attitude of the local officials towards foreign visitors. In part this can be explained by the simple reality that some places see very few foreigners. It may also be due to the fact PL hardliners running the show in these areas haven't yet cottoned on to the liberalisation taking place elsewhere in the country.

In such police fiefdoms the typical scenario begins to unfold when you try to comply with the requirement that you check in with provincial immigration. Sometimes an official will spend a half hour – up to an hour in some cases, unbelievable as it may seem – thumbing through your passport, examining every visa two or three times. Occasionally they may want to hold onto your passport for safekeeping, to make sure you don't leave town for parts unknown without their knowledge.

In such instances the best thing to do is to stay patient and wait it out, as eventually you'll be sent on your way. Trying to speed things up by bribing officials isn't a good practice since it only contributes to corruption and will almost certainly result in future requests for bribes from every other foreigner who happens along.

If your papers aren't in order – in particular if your visa has expired – you could be in for a small hassle. Although in most places in Laos the penalty for overstaying your visa is a simple fine of US$5 per day, in the eyes of a hardliner you might be perceived as some sort of provocateur. Again it pays to remain patient and to comply with all requests for further explanation or documentation. Usually the worst that can happen is being sent back in the direction from which you came. On rare occasions you may be subject to a couple of days of questioning during which your passport is held at the police station and you're confined to town.

Incidents involving excessive suspicion such as described above are quite rare overall. As more foreigners travel to the far-flung corners of the country they should become even less frequent.

LEGAL MATTERS
Revolutionary Laos established its first national legal code in 1988, followed by a constitution two years later – the reverse order of how it's usually done in other nations. Although on paper certain rights are guaranteed, the reality is that you can be fined, detained or deported for any reason at any time, as has been demonstrated repeatedly in cases involving everything from marrying a Lao national without government permission to running a business that competes too efficiently with someone who has high government connections.

Your only consolation is that Lao officials generally don't come after foreigners for petty, concocted offences. In most cases you must truly have committed a crime to find yourself in trouble with the law. However, as documented by Amnesty International (and corroborated by local expats), you could easily find yourself railroaded through the system without any legal representation.

The message is clear: stay away from anything you know to be illegal, such as drug possession or prostitution. If detained, ask to call your embassy or consulate in Laos, if there is one. A meeting or phone conversation between Lao officers and someone from your embassy/consulate can result in quicker adjudication and release, though these are by no means guaranteed. On top of not wanting to hassle foreigners for misdemeanours, the Lao are not anxious to create international incidents by treating tourists unkindly.

BUSINESS HOURS
Government offices are generally open Monday to Friday from 8 am to 11.30 am or noon and from 1 pm to 5 pm. Some

Lao Festivals & Public Holidays
March
Lao Women's Day (8th) Public holiday for women only.

April
Pii Mai Lao The lunar new year begins in mid-April and practically the whole country celebrates. Houses are cleaned, people put on new clothes and Buddha images are washed with lustral water. In the wats, offerings of fruit and flowers are made at altars and votive mounds of sand or stone are set up in the courtyards. Later people take to the streets and douse one another with water, which is an appropriate activity as April is usually the hottest month of the year. This festival is particularly picturesque in Luang Prabang, where it includes elephant processions. The 15th, 16th, and 17th of April are official public holidays.

May
International Labour Day (1st) This public holiday honours workers all over the world. In Vientiane there are parades, but elsewhere not much happens.
Visakha Bu-saa (Visakha Puja, Full Moon) This falls on the 15th day of the 6th lunar month, which is considered the day of the Buddha's birth, enlightenment and *parinibbana* (passing away). Activities are centred around the wat, with much chanting, sermonising and, at night, beautiful candlelit processions.
Bun Bang Fai (Rocket Festival) This is a pre-Buddhist rain ceremony that is now celebrated alongside Visakha Puja in Laos and in north-eastern Thailand. This can be one of the wildest festivals in the whole country, with a great deal of music, dance and folk theatre (especially the irreverent *mǎw lǎm* performances), processions and general merrymaking, all culminating in the firing of bamboo rockets into the sky. In some places male participants blacken their bodies with lamp soot, while women wear sunglasses and carry carved wooden phalli to imitate men. The firing of the rockets is supposed to prompt the heavens to initiate the rainy season and bring much-needed water to the rice fields.

July
Khao Phansaa (also *Khao Watsa*, Full Moon) This is the beginning of the traditional three-month 'rains retreat', during which Buddhist monks are expected to station themselves in a single monastery. At other times of year they are allowed to travel from wat to wat or simply to wander the countryside, but during the rainy season they forego the wandering so as not to damage fields of rice or other crops. This is also the traditional time of year for men to enter the monkhood temporarily, hence many ordinations take place.

August/September
Haw Khao Padap Din (Full Moon) This is a sombre festival in which the living pay respect to the dead. Many cremations take place – bones being exhumed for the purpose – during this time, and gifts are presented to the Sangha so that monks will chant on behalf of the deceased.

offices may open for a half day on Saturday but this custom was generally abandoned in 1998 when the official two hour lunch break introduced by the French was reduced to one hour. Does this mean you can expect to find Lao officials back in their offices promptly at 1 pm? Probably not.

Shops and private businesses open and close a bit later and either stay open during lunch or close for just an hour. On Saturday some businesses are open all day, others only half day. Just about every business in Laos, except for restaurants, are closed on Sunday.

October/November

Awk Phansaa (Awk Watsa, Full Moon) This celebrates the end of the three-month rains retreat. Monks are allowed to leave the monasteries to travel and are presented with robes, alms-bowls and other requisites of the renunciative life. On the eve of Awk Phansaa many people fashion small banana-leaf boats carrying candles, incense and other offerings, and float them in rivers, a custom known as *lāi hūa fái*, similar to Loy Krathong in Thailand.

A second festival held in association with Awk Phansaa is *Bun Nam* (Water Festival). Boat races *(suang héua)* are commonly held in river towns, such as Vientiane, Luang Prabang and Savannakhet; in smaller towns these races are often postponed until National Day (2 December) so that residents aren't saddled with two costly festivals in two months.

November

That Luang Festival (Full Moon) This takes place at Pha That Luang In Vientiane. Hundreds of monks receive alms and floral offerings early in the morning on the first day of the festival. There is a procession between Pha That Luang and Wat Si Muang. The celebration lasts a week and includes fireworks and music, ending in a candlelit procession circling That Luang.

December

Lao National Day (2nd) This public holiday celebrates the 1975 victory over the monarchy with parades, speeches, etc. Lao national and Communist hammer-and-sickle flags are flown all over the country. Celebration is mandatory, hence many poorer communities postpone some of the traditional Awk Phansaa activities – usually practised roughly a month earlier – until National Day, thus saving themselves considerable expense (much to the detriment of Awk Phansaa).

December/January

Bun Pha Wet This is a temple-centred festival in which the *jataka* or birth tale of Prince Vessantara, the Buddha's penultimate life, is recited. This is also a favoured time (second to Khao Phansaa) for Lao males to be ordained into the monkhood. The scheduling of Bun Pha Wet is staggered so that it is held on different days in different villages. This is so that relatives and friends living in different villages can invite one another to their respective celebrations.

International New Year's Day 1-3 January, public holiday.

February

Magha Puja (Makkha Bu-saa, Full Moon) This commemorates a speech given by the Buddha to 1250 enlightened monks who came to hear him without prior summons. In the talk, the Buddha laid down the first monastic regulations and predicted his own death. Chanting and offerings mark the festival, culminating in the candlelit circumambulation of wats throughout the country (celebrated most fervently in Vientiane and at the Khmer ruins of Wat Phu, near Champasak).

Vietnamese Tet & Chinese New Year Celebrated in Vientiane, Pakse and Savannakhet with parties, fireworks and visits to Vietnamese and Chinese temples. Chinese and Vietnamese-run businesses usually close for three days.

PUBLIC HOLIDAYS & SPECIAL EVENTS

The traditional Lao calendar, like the calendars of China, Vietnam, Cambodia and Thailand, is a solar-lunar mix. The year itself is reckoned by solar phases, while the months are divided according to lunar phases (unlike the western calendar in which months as well as years are reckoned by the sun). The Buddhist Era (BE) calendar usually figures year one as 543 BC, which means that you must subtract 543 from the Lao calendar year to arrive at the Christian calendar familiar in the western world (eg 1999 AD is 2542 BE according to the Lao Buddhist calendar). An earlier Lao system – seen in some archaeological inscriptions – follows a scheme in which year one is 638 BC (eg 1999 AD = 2637 BE).

Festivals in Laos are mostly linked to the agricultural seasons or to Buddhist holidays. The general word for festival in Lao is *bun* (or *boun*). See the table on the previous pages for festival dates.

ACTIVITIES
Cycling

The overall lack of vehicular traffic makes cycling an attractive proposition in Laos, although this is somewhat offset by the general absence of roads in the first place. For any serious out-of-town cycling you're better off bringing your own bike, one that's geared to very rough road conditions.

In terms of road gradient and availability of food and accommodation, the easiest long-distance ride is along Route 13 from Luang Prabang south to the Cambodian border. In the dry season this road may become very dusty even in the paved sections, and trucks – though nowhere near as overwhelming as in Vietnam or Thailand – can be a nuisance. Other cycling routes of potential interest – all of them currently unpaved and rough but due to be upgraded over the next decade – include: Luang Prabang to Muang Khua; Huay Xai to Luang Nam Tha; Pakse to Attapeu; Muang Xai to Phonsavan; and Sam Neua to Phonsavan. The last two routes are quite remote and require that you be prepared to camp if necessary along the way.

For routes to avoid, see the Dangers & Annoyances section earlier.

Hiking & Trekking

The mountainous, forest-clad countryside makes Laos a potentially ideal destination for people who like to walk in the outdoors. All 13 provinces have plenty of hiking possibilities, although the cautious nature of the authorities means that overnight trips that involve camping or staying overnight in villages are viewed with suspicion. So far not a single travel agency in Laos has been

granted permission to lead overnight treks in any of the tribal areas, though several have tried to arrange such itineraries. Many visitors trekking on their own, however, have managed to spend the night in remote villages anyway. There doesn't appear to be any law forbidding this although it is somewhat frowned upon by the authorities in areas such as the provinces of Sekong and Attapeu.

Day hiking is another story and you're free to walk in the mountains and forests almost anywhere in the country except the Saisombun Special Zone. See the Dangers & Annoyances section earlier for more information on this new military-controlled district and for warnings on areas of eastern Laos contaminated by unexploded ordnance.

The provinces in Laos with the highest potential for relatively safe wilderness hikes include Bokeo, Luang Nam Tha, Luang Prabang, Vientiane, Khammuan and Champasak. In particular the 17 reserves known as National Biodiversity Conservation Areas (NBCAs) should be rewarding territory for exploration (see the Ecology & Environment section in the Facts about Laos chapter for more information).

Except at the occasional waterfall near towns or cities, recreation areas with public facilities are nonexistent in Laos.

Boating

The rivers and streams of Laos have potential for all sorts of recreational boating, particularly rafting, canoeing and kayaking. No modern equipment exists, however, so it's strictly bring-your-own. Nor are there any regular bamboo raft trips as in Thailand, though the country is prime territory for it.

As with bicycles, you shouldn't have any special customs difficulties in bringing your own small boat to Laos. Because of the difficulties of overland transport, however, the smaller and lighter your craft is, the more choices you'll have for places to paddle.

For trained paddlers almost any of the major waterways draining from the western slopes of the Annamite Chain towards the Mekong valley could be interesting. In the north, the Nam Ou, Nam Tha, Nam Khan, Nam Ngum and of course the Mekong River are navigable year-round. In central and southern Laos the Nam Theun, Se Don, Se Set and Se Kong as well as the Mekong are safe bets. The upstream areas of all these rivers can be accessed by road, so drop-offs and pick-ups are limited only by the availability of public or private vehicle travel.

In the area between Vientiane and Tha Khaek, several tributaries which feed into the Mekong are smaller and less known than the aforementioned but very scenic since they run through rugged limestone country. In particular the Nam Xan, Nam Kading and Nam Hin Bun seem to be wide and relatively clean rivers. The choices are somewhat limited by the availability of roads to take you upstream; see the Southern Laos chapter for details on which areas are accessible.

Between Champasak and the Cambodian border, the area of the Mekong known as Si Phan Don (Four Thousand Islands) is easily accessible and provides superior paddling possibilities among verdant islands and rapids.

There's one big caveat lurking behind reaching what could be paddler heaven: the legalities of floating down Lao waterways are a bit hard to discern. Local people do not need permits of any kind to launch self-propelled craft on any stream or river; technically foreigners aren't subject to any special regulations either, as long as they're not transporting commercial cargo or fee-paying passengers. You should be prepared to face the occasional suspicious government official along the way, simply because you're doing something that's out of the ordinary. The main thoroughfares such as the Mekong and Nam Ou have riverbank checkpoints at provincial borders where you'll need to have your papers stamped.

Should you want to navigate in the local Lao way, small new or used wooden canoes can be purchased for US$40 to US$100 without a motor; add US$40 to US$60 for motorised canoes. Small Japanese outboard motors of 5.5 horsepower to 11 horsepower can be purchased in any of the larger cities along the Mekong River. These sorts of boats are suitable only for well-navigated waterways as their weight and bulk prohibits portage around shallows or rapids.

COURSES
Language
Short-term courses in spoken and written Lao are available at the following study centres in Vientiane:

Centre de Langue Française
  (☎ (021) 215764), Thanon Lane Xang
Lao-American Language Center
  (☎ (021) 414321; fax 413760), 22 Phon Kheng, Ban Phon Sa-at
Saysettha Language Centre
  (☎ (021) 414480), Thanon Nong Bon, Ban Phonxai
Vientiane University College
  (☎ (021) 414873; fax 414346), Thanon That Luang, opposite the Ministry of Foreign Affairs

Mrs Kesone Sayasane at Burapha Development Consultants (☎ (021) 216708; fax 212981), 14 Thanon Fa Ngum, teaches Lao privately or can arrange custom-designed group courses. Mrs Kesone was a member of the short-lived Peace Corps Laos training staff and has worked with South-East Asian summer language courses given yearly at major university Asian studies departments in the US.

Meditation
If you can speak Lao or Thai, or can arrange an interpreter, you may be able to study *vipassana* (insight meditation) with Ajaan Sali, the abbot of Wat Sok Pa Luang in south-east Vientiane. See the Vientiane chapter for more details.

WORK
With Laos' expanding economy and the growing influx of aid organisations and foreign companies, the number of jobs available to foreigners increases slightly each year although one can't count on

finding employment immediately. By far
the greatest number of positions will be
found in Vientiane.

Possibilities include teaching English
privately or at one of the several language
centres in Vientiane, work which – in light
of kip deflation – is currently paying only
about US$8 an hour. Certificates or degrees
in English teaching aren't absolutely necessary, although they increase your chances
considerably.

If you possess technical expertise or international volunteer experience, you might
be able to find work with a UN-related
program or a non-governmental organisation involved with foreign aid or technical
assistance to Laos. For positions such as
these, your best bet is to visit the Vientiane
offices of each organisation and inquire
about personnel needs and vacancies.

*Liste du corps diplomatique et consulaire
à Vientiane*, published in French only by
the Ministry of Foreign Affairs, contains
the addresses of the main UN organisations
working in Laos. Another booklet entitled
*Directory of Non-Governmental Organisa-
tions in Laos* lists contact information as
well as programme descriptions for over 60
NGOs registered in Laos. Either publication
can be purchased at Raintrees or the State
Book Shop in Vientiane. If you're thinking
of launching your own aid project, note that
all projects, whether UN, bilateral or NGO,
must be approved by the government's
Committee of Investment & Cooperation
(CIC).

International companies hire locally on
the rare occasion. A list of such companies
in Laos is available from the Ministry of
Foreign Affairs.

Once you have a sponsoring employer, a
visa valid for working and residing in Laos
is relatively easy to obtain. The most time-
consuming part of the process is receiving
ministry approval in Vientiane; depending
on the sponsoring organisation and type of
work, permission from more than one ministry may be necessary.

If your sponsor takes care of all the pa-
perwork in Laos, however, this should

culminate in an order to a Lao embassy
abroad to issue you the appropriate visa in
a day or two.

ACCOMMODATION

Laos does not have a great number or variety
of hotels but, unlike in China or Myanmar,
foreigners aren't restricted to certain hotels,
except in the rare instance where a provincial
guesthouse is reserved for government officials. Tourist hotels are typically priced in
US dollars, while guesthouses and the less
expensive business hotels (commonly found
in Huay Xai, Luang Prabang, Savannakhet
and Pakse) are priced in baht or kip.

It is almost always cheaper to pay in the
requested currency rather than let the hotel
or guesthouse convert the price into another
currency. If the price is quoted in kip, you'll
do best to pay in kip; if priced in dollars,
pay in dollars. If you ask to pay a dollar-
quoted tariff in kip (or vice versa), you'll
lose out to the hotel's mandated lower exchange rate. Room rates in this book are
given in the currency medium quoted by
the particular establishment.

Outside the Mekong valley, most of the
provincial capitals have only two or three
basic hotels or guesthouses (some only one)
although the number and quality of places to
stay seems to be increasing every year. Hotel
rooms in Vientiane, Luang Prabang, Savannakhet and Pakse offer private bathrooms
and fans as standard features for around
US$10 to US$15 a night. Better rooms have
air-con, and sometimes hot water, for US$15
to US$25. Hot water is hardly a necessity in
lowland Laos (where it is most likely to be
available), but would be very pleasant in the
mountains (where it's almost never available). In this guidebook we have mentioned
the availability of hot water for each hotel or
guesthouse that offered it; when not mentioned you can assume it isn't available.

Small business hotels in Luang Prabang,
Muang Xai, Savannakhet and Pakse cost
around US$5 to US$8 per night for simple
double rooms. Vientiane has a few guesthouses now with rooms costing as low as
US$5 or US$6 a night with shared toilet and

bathing facilities. In the more far-flung areas of the country rustic guesthouses with shared facilities cost only 1500 to 3000 kip (about US$0.60 to US$1.25) per night per person. Although oriented towards the local market, these guesthouses are generally welcoming to foreigners.

Large hotels oriented towards Asian business and leisure travellers or the occasional tour group are beginning to multiply in the larger cities. At these, tariffs of US$25 to US$60 are common for rooms with air-con, hot water, TV and refrigerator. The government has plans to build more hotels of this nature over the next decade using foreign (mostly Thai, Singaporean and Taiwanese) capital. The only western chain that has so far entered the hotel market in Laos is Accor Australia Pacific, which took over The Belvedere in Vientiane.

FOOD

Lao cuisine is very similar to Thai cuisine in many ways. Like Thai food, almost all dishes are cooked with fresh ingredients, including *phák* (vegetables), *paa* (fish), *kai* (chicken), *pét* (duck), *mūu* (pork) and *sìn ngúa* (beef) or *sìn khwái* (water buffalo).

Because of Laos' distance from the sea, freshwater fish are more common than saltwater fish or shellfish. In rural areas wild rather than domestic animals – especially deer, wild pigs, squirrels, civets, monitor lizards, junglefowl/pheasants, dhole (wild dogs), rats and birds – provide most of the meat in local diets, though the eating of endangered species causes much consternation among international wildlife conservation agencies. In part this practice is due to the expense involved in animal husbandry, and partly due to the Lao preference for the taste of wild game. In the villages, domesticated animals such as pigs, chickens, ducks and cattle are reserved for ceremonial occasions.

Lime juice, lemon grass and fresh coriander leaf are added to give the food its characteristic tang. To salt the food, various fermented fish concoctions are used, most commonly *nâam paa*, which is a thin sauce of fermented anchovies (usually imported

from Thailand), and *paa dàek*, a coarser, native Lao preparation that includes chunks of fermented freshwater fish, rice husks and rice 'dust'. *Nâam paa dàek* is the sauce poured from *paa dàek*. (See the Health section earlier in this chapter for warnings on eating *paa dàek*.) *Phõng súu lot* – ajinomoto or MSG – is also a common seasoning, and in Laos you may even see it served as a table condiment in noodle restaurants. See the boxed text on the next page.

Other common seasonings include *khaa* (galingale), *màak phét* (hot chillies), *màak thua dįn* (ground peanuts – more often a condiment), *nâam màak khāam* (tamarind juice), *khįng* (ginger) and *nâam màak phâo* or *nâam kátí* (coconut milk). Chillies are sometimes served on the side in hot pepper sauces called *jaew*. In Luang Prabang, *nãng khwái hàeng* (dried skin of water buffalo) is quite a popular ingredient.

One of the most common Lao dishes is *làap*, which is a Lao-style salad of minced meat, fowl or fish tossed with lime juice, garlic, *khào khûa* (roasted, powdered sticky rice), green onions, mint leaves and chillies. It can be very hot or rather mild, depending on the cook. Meats mixed into *làap* are sometimes raw *(díp)* rather than cooked *(sùk)*. Làap is typically served with a large plate of lettuce, mint and steamed leaves of various sorts. Using your fingers you wrap a little làap in the lettuce and herbs and eat it with balls of sticky rice which you roll by hand.

Another dish you will often come across is *tam màak hung* (more commonly known as *tam sòm* in Vientiane), a spicy, tangy salad made by pounding shredded green papaya, lime juice, chillies, garlic, *paa dàek*, *nàam phàk-kàat* (a paste of boiled, fermented lettuce leaves) and various other ingredients together in a large mortar. This is a favourite market and street vendor food – customers typically inspect the array of possible *tam màak hung* ingredients the vendor has spread out on a table next to the mortar, then order a custom mix. For something different, ask the pounder to throw in a few *màak kàwk*, a sour, olive-shaped fruit. *Sàep lāi* (very delicious)!

Many Lao dishes are quite spicy because of the Lao penchant for màak phét. But the Lao also eat a lot of Chinese and Vietnamese food, which is generally less spicy. *Fõe* (rice noodle soup) is popular as a snack or even for breakfast, and is almost always served with a plate of fresh lettuce, mint, coriander, mung bean sprouts, lime wedges and sometimes basil to add to the soup as desired. Especially in the south, people mix their own fõe sauce of lime, crushed fresh chilli, *kápí* and sugar at the table using a little saucer provided for the purpose.

Another common noodle dish, especially in the morning, is *khào pɪak sèn*, a soft, round rice noodle served in a broth with pieces of chicken or occasionally pork. A popular condiment for this noodle soup is crushed fresh ginger. Many khào pɪak sèn vendors also sell *khào-nõm khuu*, small deep-fried, doughnut-like Chinese pastries. Some vendors even leave a pair of scissors on each table so that you can cut the pastries up and mix them into your soup. It may sound strange, but it's very tasty.

Khào pûn, flour noodles topped with a sweet and spicy *nâam kátí* (coconut sauce), is another popular noodle dish. These noodles are also eaten cold with various Vietnamese foods popular in urban Laos, particularly *nãem neûang* (barbecued pork meatballs) and *yáw* (spring rolls).

Rice is the foundation for all Lao meals (as opposed to snacks), as with elsewhere in South-East Asia. In general, the Lao eat *khào nĩaw* ('sticky' or glutinous rice), although *khào jâo* (ordinary white rice) is also common in the major towns.

Sticky rice is served up in lidded baskets called *típ khào* and eaten with the hands: the general practice is to grab a small fistful of rice from the típ khào, then roll it into a rough ball which you then use to dip into the various dishes. Watching others is the

MSG: Friend or Foe?

Monosodium glutamate (MSG, also known by its Japanese name *ajinomoto* or its Lao name *phõng súu lot)* is a simple compound of glutamate, water and about two-thirds less sodium by weight than table salt. Glutamate is an amino acid that occurs naturally in virtually every food, and is a major component of most natural protein sources such as meat, fish, milk and some vegetables. Like the flavour enhancers salt and sugar, MSG has been in use in Asia for centuries, originally as a distillate of seaweed. Today it's produced through a fermentation and evaporation process using molasses made from sugar cane or sugar beets. Despite its white, crystalline appearance, it is not, as many people mistakenly believe, a synthetic substance, nor does it necessarily compound one's intake of sodium. When small quantities of MSG are used in combination with table salt (or with fish sauce or soy sauce) during food preparation, the flavour-enhancing properties of MSG allow for far less salt to be used with food. Although often presumed to have no flavour of its own, MSG does in fact have an identifiable taste.

Contrary to much popular myth, the human body metabolises glutamate added to food the same way it metabolises glutamate found naturally in food. Although some people report physical reactions to MSG (the so-called 'Chinese restaurant syndrome'), every double-blind, placebo-controlled food research study on humans thus far published has concluded that such reactions can almost always be traced not to MSG but rather to psychological syndromes (a legacy of late 1960s media scares) or to food allergies triggered by ingredients other than MSG. If you're one of those few people who insist they have a direct allergy to MSG (despite your own everyday ingestion of glutamates present naturally in foods), just say *baw sai phõng súu lot* ('don't include MSG').

best way to learn. At the end of the meal it is considered bad luck not to replace the lid on top of the típ khào.

Khào jâo, on the other hand, is eaten with a fork and spoon. The fork (held in the left hand) is only used to prod food onto the spoon (in the right hand), which is the main utensil for eating this type of rice. *Mâi thuu* (chopsticks) are only used for eating fõe or other Chinese dishes served in bowls.

Where to Eat

Many restaurants or foodstalls, especially outside Vientiane, do not have menus, so it is useful to memorise a standard 'repertoire' of dishes. Those restaurants that do offer written menus don't always have an English version (in fact, it's rare when they do). Most provinces have their own local specialities in addition to the standards and you might try asking for *aahāan phi-sét* (special food), allowing the proprietors to choose for you. In remote areas of the north and south, choices can be rather limited.

The most economical places to eat and the most dependable are *hàan fõe* (noodle shops) and *talàat sâo* or morning markets. Most towns and villages have at least one morning market (which often lasts all day despite the name) and several hàan fõe. The next step up is the Lao-style cafe or *hàan kheûang deum* (drink shop) or *hàan kjn deum* (eat-drink shop), where a more varied selection of dishes is usually served. Most expensive is the *hàan aahāan* (food shop), where the menu is usually posted on the wall or on a blackboard (in Lao).

Many hàan aahāan serve mostly Chinese or Vietnamese food. The ones serving real Lao food can usually be distinguished by a large pan of water on a stool – or a modern lavatory – somewhere near the entrance for washing the hands before eating (Lao food is traditionally eaten with the hands).

What to Eat

Except for the 'rice plates' and the noodle dishes, Lao meals are typically ordered 'family style', which is to say that two or

more people order together, sharing different dishes. Traditionally, the party orders one of each kind of dish, for example, one chicken, one fish, one soup, etc. A few extras may be ordered for a large party. One dish is generally large enough for two people. If you come to eat at a Lao restaurant on your own and order one of these 'entrees', you had better be hungry or know enough Lao to order only a small portion. Eating alone is something the Lao generally consider to be rather unusual; but then as a falang you are an exception anyway. In Chinese or Thai restaurants a cheaper alternative is to order dishes *làat khào* (over rice).

In Vientiane, Savannakhet, Pakse and Luang Prabang, French bread is popular for breakfast. Sometimes it's eaten plain with *kạa-féh nóm hâwn* (hot milk coffee), sometimes it's eaten with *khai* (eggs) or in a baguette sandwich that contains Lao-style paté, and vegetables. Or you can order them *sai nâam nóm*, sliced in half lengthwise and drizzled with sweetened condensed milk. When they are fresh, Lao baguettes are superb. Croissants and other French-style pastries are also available in the bakeries of Vientiane.

A list of standard dishes with English, the Lao transliteration and Lao script is provided in the Language chapter.

DRINKS
Nonalcoholic Drinks

Water Water purified for drinking purposes is simply called *nâam deum* (drinking water), whether it is boiled or filtered. *All* water offered to customers in restaurants or hotels will be purified, so one needn't fret about the safety of taking a sip (for more information on water safety, see the Health section earlier in this chapter). In restaurants you can ask for *nâam pao* (plain water, which is always either boiled or taken from a purified source) served by the glass at no charge, or order by the bottle. A bottle of carbonated or soda water costs about the same as a bottle of plain purified water but the bottles are smaller.

Coffee Lao-grown coffee is known to be one of the world's best. Unlike the Thai, the Lao tend to brew coffee without adding ground tamarind seed as a flavouring or filler. Traditionally, pure Lao coffee is roasted by wholesalers, ground by vendors and filtered just before serving. On the other hand many Lao restaurants – especially in hotels, guesthouses and other tourist-oriented establishments – serve instant coffee with packets of artificial cream. On occasion, restaurants or vendors with the proper accoutrements for making traditional filtered coffee keep a supply of Nescafé just for foreigners. To get authentic Lao coffee ask for *kąa-féh thõng* (literally 'bag coffee'), which refers to the traditional method of preparing a cup of coffee by filtering the hot water through a bag-shaped cloth filter. Another phrase used on occasion is *kąa-féh tôm* (boiled coffee).

The usual brewed coffee is served mixed with sugar and sweetened condensed milk – if you don't want either be sure to specify *kąa-féh dąm* (black coffee) followed with *baw sai nâam-tąan* (without sugar). Coffee is often served in a glass instead of a ceramic cup – to pick up a glass of hot coffee, grasp it on the top rim.

In central and southern Laos coffee is almost always served with a chaser of hot *nâam sáa* (weak Chinese tea), while in the north it's typically served with a glass of plain hot water.

Tea Both Indian-style (black) and Chinese-style (green or semi-cured) teas are served in Laos. The latter predominates in Chinese restaurants and is also the usual ingredient in *nâam sáa*, the weak, often lukewarm, tea traditionally served in restaurants for free. The teapots commonly seen on tables in Chinese and Vietnamese restaurants are filled with nâam sáa; ask for a *jàwk pao* (plain glass) and you can drink as much as you'd like at no charge. For iced nâam sáa ask for a glass of ice *nâam kâwn* (which usually costs 50 kip to 100 kip) and pour your own; for stronger fresh Chinese tea, request *sáa jịin*.

Black tea, both imported and locally grown, is usually available in the same restaurants or foodstalls that serve real coffee. An order of *sáa hâwn* (hot tea) almost always results in a cup (or glass) of black tea with sugar and condensed milk. As with coffee you must specify beforehand if you want black tea without milk and/or sugar.

Alcoholic Drinks

Beer Lao Brewery Co (LBC), located on the outskirts of Vientiane, was established in 1973 by the government and is now the 13th largest company in Laos. LBC is currently a joint venture; 49% government-owned, and 51% held between two Thai companies, neither of which are involved with beer production in Thailand. Production is now 24 million litres per year, up from three million in 1973.

LBC's main product is the very drinkable Bia Lao, the romanised name for which is 'Beerlao' (sometimes spelt 'Beer Lao'). A draught version *(bịa sòt* or 'fresh beer') is so far available only in bars in Vientiane and like all Beerlao contains 5% alcohol. The price is standard at about 1300 kip per litre.

Beerlao also comes in glass bottles for a standard 1700 kip to 1800 kip for a 660mL bottle (prices can be much higher in tourist hotels or restaurants). Look for the tiger's head on the label. A 330mL can of Beerlao is also available. Heineken and Tiger beer from Singapore come in 330mL cans, whi costing the same as a 660mL bottle of Beerlao.

In the northern provinces bordering China, various Chinese brands of beer are available – these generally cost about 40% less than Beerlao (but are about 80% less drinkable!).

Distilled Spirits Rice whisky or *lào-láo* (Lao liquor) is a popular drink among lowland Lao. The best kinds of lào-láo come from Phongsali and Don Khong, the northern and southern extremes of the country, but are available virtually everywhere, at around 800 kip to 1000 kip per 750mL bottle. Strictly speaking, lào-láo is not legal but no-one seems to care. The government distils its own brand, Sticky Rice, which costs around 2000 kip for a bottle.

Lào-láo is usually drunk neat, with a plain water chaser. In a Lao home the pouring and drinking of lào-láo at evening meal takes on ritual characteristics. Usually towards the end of the meal, but occasionally beforehand, the hosts bring out a bottle of the stuff to treat their guests. The usual procedure is for the host to pour one jigger of lào-láo onto the floor or a used dinner plate first, to appease the house spirits. The host then pours another jigger and downs it in one gulp. Jiggers for each guest are poured in turn; guests must take at least one offered drink or risk offending the house spirits.

Three brands of lower-alcohol sticky rice liquor similar in taste to Thailand's famous Mekong whisky are also available as Phan Thong (the label reads Chevreuil d'Or), Sing Thong (Gold Tiger) and Mae Khong – each costing around 2500 kip for a 750mL bottle. These are best taken over ice with a splash of soda and a squeeze of lime,

though some prefer to mix them with Coke (imported from Thailand) or Pepsi (made in Laos). The Lao Winery Co also makes Highlander Whiskey (4400 kip per bottle), Five Star Brandy (3800 kip), Hercules Herbal Wine (3000 kip) and Black 99 (4300 kip); the latter is an imitation Scotch.

In rural provinces, a weaker version of lào-láo known as *lào-hái* (jar liquor) is fermented by households or villages. Lào-hái is usually drunk from a communal jar using long reed straws. It's not always safe to drink, however, since unboiled water is often added to it during and after the fermentation process.

Tourist hotel bars in the larger cities carry the standard variety of liquors.

Wine In Vientiane there are decent French and Italian wines abundantly available at restaurants, in shops specialising in imported foods and in a few shops which sell nothing but wine. You will also find a limited selection in Luang Prabang, Savannakhet and Pakse. Wines of Australian, American, South African, Chilean and other origins are so far sadly neglected.

Luang Prabang is famous for a type of light rice wine called *khào kam*, a red-tinted, somewhat sweet beverage made from sticky rice. It can be quite tasty when properly prepared and stored, but rather mouldy-tasting if not.

ENTERTAINMENT
Music & Dancing

In most of rural Laos, entertainment means sitting around with friends over a few jiggers of lào-láo, telling jokes or recounting the events of the day, and singing *phéng phêun múang* (folk songs).

Religious and seasonal festivals are an important venue for Lao folk and pop music performances – see the Public Holidays & Special Events section earlier in this chapter for details.

Almost every provincial capital has a couple of dance halls or *banthóeng* (roughly 'nightclub') – called 'discos' by the Lao in English in spite of the fact that they usually host live bands nightly and play no recorded music. Food as well as drinks are always available at Lao dance halls, though most people drink rather than eat. By government decree, the music is mostly Lao, though in the north and north-east you'll also hear Chinese and Vietnamese songs mixed into the repertoire.

Western pop songs are expressly forbidden but bands will slip them in occasionally or improvise Lao lyrics to make them more acceptable to the music police. Fortunately there is no prohibition on dance styles, which in any given place may vary from the traditional *lam wong* to American country-style line dancing to wiggle-your-hips-and-dangle-your-fingertips pop styles – all in one night. You'll even see a foxtrot now and then.

In Vientiane foreign embassies (particularly the French and US) sponsor occasional pop, rock or classical concerts.

Cinema & Video

At one time several movie houses thrived in the Big Three (Vientiane, Savannakhet and Luang Prabang), but the arrival of video in the late 1980s completely killed off local cinema. Video shops in the larger cities rent pirated versions of all the latest Chinese, Thai and western videos.

See the Entertainment section of the Vientiane chapter for information on other film venues.

SPECTATOR SPORT

Football (soccer) and other stadium sports can occasionally be seen at the National Stadium in Vientiane. Admission fees are inexpensive. Interprovincial matches take place on fields or stadiums in each provincial capital. Laos participated in the 1995 South-East Asian Games in Chiang Mai, Thailand, where the team took bronze medals in running and boxing.

Boxing

Many Lao sports fans living in the western part of the country are glued to their TV sets during the Sunday afternoon *muay thai*

(Thai kickboxing) matches that are televised from Ratchadamnoen Stadium in Bangkok. Though very popular, kickboxing is not nearly as developed a sport in Laos as in Thailand and is mostly confined to amateur fights at upcountry festivals. It's not uncommon for the better Lao pugilists to drift across the Mekong to compete in Thai boxing rings, where there's more money to be made.

As in muay thai, in the Lao version of kickboxing all surfaces of the body are considered fair targets and any part of the body except the head may be used to strike an opponent (one small concession to safety). Common blows include high kicks to the neck, elbow thrusts to the face and head, knee hooks to the ribs and low crescent kicks to the calf. A contestant may even grasp an opponent's head between his hands and pull it down to meet an upward knee thrust. Punching is considered the weakest of all the blows and kicking as merely a way to 'soften up' one's opponent; knee and elbow strikes are decisive in most matches.

International boxing *(múay sãak̦n)* is gaining popularity in Laos and is encouraged by the government in spite of the obvious Lao preference for the bang-up South-East Asian version. At local festival programmes, an eight-match line-up might include three matches in the international style and five in the Lao-Thai style.

Kátâw

Kátâw, a contest in which a woven rattan – or sometimes plastic – ball around 12cm in diameter is kicked around, is almost as popular in Laos as it is in Thailand and Malaysia. It was introduced to the South-East Asian Games by Thailand but the Malaysians seem to win more often.

The traditional way to play kátâw is for players to stand in a circle (the size of the circle depends on the number of players) and simply try to keep the ball airborne by kicking it soccer-style. Points are scored for style, difficulty and variety of kicking manoeuvres.

A popular variation on kátâw – and the one used in local or international competitions – is played with a volleyball net, using all the same rules as in volleyball except that only the feet and head are permitted to touch the ball. It's amazing to see the players perform aerial pirouettes, spiking the ball over the net with their feet.

THINGS TO BUY

Shopping in Laos continues to improve. Many of the handicrafts and arts available in Laos are easily obtainable in Thailand too, but some items – as noted below – are unique to Laos. Hill tribe crafts can be less expensive in Laos, but only if you bargain.

Like elsewhere in South-East Asia, bargaining is a tradition (introduced by early Arab and Indian traders). Though most shops have fixed prices, fabric, carvings and jewellery are usually subject to bargaining.

Warning – there is a *total* ban on the export of antiques and Buddha images from Laos, though the enforcement of this ban appears to be very slack.

Fabric (Textiles)

Silk and cotton fabrics are woven in many different styles according to the geographic provenance and ethnicity of the weavers. Although Lao textiles do have similarities with other South-East Asian textiles, Lao weaving techniques are unique in both loom design and weaving styles, generating fabrics that are very recognisably Lao. See the special Weaving section starting on page 311 for more information.

Generally speaking, the fabrics of the north feature a mix of solid colours with complex geometric patterns – stripes, diamonds, zigzags, animal and plant shapes – usually in the form of a *phàa nung* (a women's wraparound skirt). Sometimes gold or silver thread is woven in along the borders. Another form the cloth takes is the *phàa bìang*, a narrow Lao-Thai shawl that men and women wear singly or in pairs over the shoulders during weddings and festivals.

The southern weaving styles are often marked by the *mat-mîi* technique, which involves 'tie-dyeing' the threads before weaving. The result is a soft, spotted pattern similar to Indonesian *ikat*. Mat-mîi cloth can be used for different types of clothing or for wall-hangings. Among Lao Theung and Mon-Khmer communities in the southern provinces there is a mat-mîi weaving tradition which features pictographic story lines, sometimes with a few Khmer words, numerals or other nonrepresentational symbols woven into the pattern. In Sekong and Attapeu provinces some fabrics mix beadwork with weaving and embroidery.

Among the Hmong and Mien tribes, square pieces of cloth are embroidered and quilted to produce strikingly colourful fabrics in apparently abstract patterns that contain ritual meanings. In Hmong these are called *pa ndau* (flower cloth). Some larger quilts feature scenes that represent village life, including both animal and human figures.

Many tribes among both the Lao Sung and Lao Theung groups produce woven shoulder bags in the Austro-Thai and Tibetan-Bumese traditions, like those seen all across the mountains of South Asia and South-East Asia. In Laos, these are called *nyaam*. Among the most popular nyaam nowadays are those made with older pieces of fabric from 'antique' phàa nung or from pieces of hill tribe clothing. Vientiane's Morning Market is one of the best places to shop for this kind of accessory.

In general the best place to buy fabric is in the weaving villages themselves, where you can watch how it's made and get 'wholesale' prices. Failing this, you can find a pretty good selection and reasonable prices at open markets in provincial towns, including Vientiane's Talaat Sao (Morning Market). The most expensive places to buy fabric are in tailor shops and handicraft stores.

Carvings

The Lao produce well-crafted carvings in wood, bone and stone. The subject can be anything from Hindu or Buddhist mythology to themes from everyday life. Unlike in Thailand, authentic opium pipes seem to be plentiful in Laos and sometimes have intricately carved bone or bamboo shafts, along with engraved ceramic bowls. I've noticed, though, that the selection gets thinner every year.

To shop for carvings, look in antique or handicraft stores. Don't buy anything made from ivory; quite apart from the elephant slaughter caused by the ivory trade, many countries will confiscate any ivory items found in your luggage.

Jewellery
Gold and silver jewellery are good buys in Laos, although you must search hard for well-made pieces. Some of the best silverwork is done by the hill tribes. Gems are also sometimes available, but you can get better prices in Thailand.

Most provincial towns have a few shops specialising in jewellery. You can also find jewellery in antique and handicraft shops.

Antiques
Vientiane, Luang Prabang and Savannakhet each have a sprinkling of antique shops. Anything that looks old could be up for sale in these shops, including Asian pottery (especially porcelain from the Ming dynasty of China), old jewellery, clothes, carved wood, musical instruments, coins and bronze statuettes. Because of the government's lax enforcement of the ban on the export of antiques, due to an overall lack of funds and personnel, you might be tempted to buy these objects. However, bear in mind not only that it is illegal to take them out of the country but that if you do so you will be robbing the country of its precious and limited heritage.

Getting There & Away

AIR
Airports & Airlines
At the moment Vientiane is the only legal port of disembarkation in Laos for foreign air passengers. However, the government has designated the newly expanded Luang Prabang airport as 'international', and in 1998 Lao Aviation announced plans to begin a Chiang Mai to Luang Prabang service. As we went to press those plans had not yet come to fruition, most likely due to the company's chronic shortage of aircraft. A few years ago Lao Aviation also had flights between Pakse in southern Laos and Phnom Penh, but these have been indefinitely discontinued.

So at the time of writing Vientiane is the only way in by air, with regularly scheduled international air links to/from Bangkok, Chiang Mai, Phnom Penh, Hanoi, Ho Chi Minh City (Saigon) and Kunming.

Lao Aviation uses a Boeing 737 leased from an American company for all international flights except those to Chiang Mai, for which it employs a French ATR-72.

Bangkok
Flights to Vientiane leave from Bangkok's international airport daily, a service which alternates between Thai Airways International (Thai) and Lao Aviation, depending on the day of the week.

Thai often fills up because it has more cachet among international business travellers, so it's usually easier to get a seat on Lao Aviation. On either airline you should book early to make sure you have a seat. For Lao Aviation especially, it's imperative you arrive at check-in well in advance of departure, as the airline staff have a tendency to bump confirmed passengers for VIPs. Flights departing on Saturday and Sunday are usually less in demand than weekday flights.

The flight takes about an hour to reach Wattay international airport on the outskirts of Vientiane. The fare is the same for both airlines – US$100 one way in economy class, US$120 in business class; return fares are double. Weekend specials as low as US$75 one way are sometimes available on Thai. Both Lao Aviation (for international flights only) and Thai accept major credit cards for ticket purchases. With the Thai baht in extreme flux it may be less expensive to purchase tickets in Bangkok rather than abroad; in early 1998, for example, the US$100 fare to Vientiane worked out to just US$78 if purchased in Bangkok using baht – that's assuming you purchased the baht with US dollars. Either airline can issue tickets for the other. The smaller discount agencies that sell cheap international tickets can't do a better fare than the two airlines. Some agencies add a surcharge over and above the listed ticket price.

Some people save money by flying from Bangkok to Udon Thani in Thailand first, then carrying on by road to Nong Khai and over the Friendship Bridge to Vientiane. Udon Thani is 55km south of Nong Khai and a Bangkok-Udon air ticket on Thai costs US$52. Thai Airways operates an express van direct from Udon airport to Nong Khai for 100B per person or you can take a local bus for 20B; count on around 35 minutes for the former, a bit over an hour for the latter.

Chiang Mai
Lao Aviation flies between Vientiane and Chiang Mai every Thursday and Sunday. The one hour flight costs US$70 one way (less if paid for with baht).

Hanoi
Direct flights between Hanoi and Vientiane leave Wednesday, Thursday, Saturday and Sunday aboard Vietnam Airlines, and on Monday, Tuesday and Friday with Lao Aviation. Flights take approximately an hour and cost US$90 one way.

Ho Chi Minh City (Saigon)

Lao Aviation flies between Ho Chi Minh City (Saigon) and Vientiane every Friday for US$170 one way; the flight takes about three hours. In addition Vietnam Airlines has four Vientiane-bound flights a week to/from Ho Chi Minh City via Hanoi for the same fare. Either airline can issue tickets for the other.

Kunming

Lao Aviation flies between Kunming and Vientiane on Sunday, while China Yunnan Airlines (CYA) does the job on Wednesday, Thursday and Friday. Both airlines usually charge US$155 one way but special fares as low as US$100 are occasionally available. Flights take 80 minutes. Lao Aviation and CYA can issue tickets for either

Air Travel Glossary

Baggage Allowance This will be written on your ticket and usually includes one 20kg item to go in the hold, plus one item of hand luggage.

Bucket Shops These are unbonded travel agencies specialising in discounted airline tickets.

Bumped Just because you have a confirmed seat doesn't mean you're going to get on the plane (see Overbooking).

Cancellation Penalties If you have to cancel or change a discounted ticket, there are often heavy penalties involved; insurance can sometimes be taken out against these penalties. Some airlines impose penalties on regular tickets as well, particularly against 'no-show' passengers.

Check-In Airlines ask you to check in a certain time ahead of the flight departure (usually one to two hours on international flights). If you fail to check in on time and the flight is overbooked, the airline can cancel your booking and give your seat to somebody else.

Confirmation Having a ticket written out with the flight and date you want doesn't mean you have a seat until the agent has checked with the airline that your status is 'OK' or confirmed. Meanwhile you could just be 'on request'.

Courier Fares Businesses often need to send urgent documents or freight securely and quickly. Courier companies hire people to accompany the package through customs and, in return, offer a discount ticket, sometimes a phenomenal bargain. In effect, what the companies do is ship their freight as your luggage on regular commercial flights. This is a legitimate operation, but there are two shortcomings – the short turnaround time of the ticket (usually not longer than a month) and the limitation on your luggage allowance. You may have to surrender all your allowance and take only carry-on luggage.

ITX An ITX, or 'independent inclusive tour excursion', is often available on tickets to popular holiday destinations. Officially it's a package deal combined with hotel accommodation, but many agents will sell you one of these for the flight only and give you phoney hotel vouchers in the unlikely event that you're challenged at the airport.

Lost Tickets If you lose your airline ticket an airline will usually treat it like a travellers cheque and, after inquiries, issue you with another one. Legally, however, an airline is entitled to treat it like cash and if you lose it then it's gone forever. Take good care of your tickets.

MCO An MCO, or 'miscellaneous charge order', is a voucher that looks like an airline ticket but carries no destination or date. It can be exchanged through any International Association of Travel Agents (IATA) airline for a ticket on a specific flight. It's a useful alternative to an onward ticket in those countries that demand one, and is more flexible than an ordinary ticket if you're unsure of your route.

airline (CYA actually owns 60% of Lao Aviation) on this route.

Phnom Penh

Lao Aviation flies between Phnom Penh and Vientiane Monday and Friday. The flight takes about 90 minutes and costs US$133 one way. Royal Air Cambodge flies to Vientiane and back Tuesday and Thursday.

Singapore

Silk Air flies between Singapore and Vientiane twice weekly for US$355 each way.

Lao Aviation Offices & Agents Abroad

Lao Aviation (☎ (021) 212058, 212051; fax 212056) has its headquarters in Vientiane; see the Getting There & Away section of the Vientiane chapter for details.

No-Shows No-shows are passengers who fail to show up for their flight. Full-fare passengers who fail to turn up are sometimes entitled to travel on a later flight. The rest are penalised (see Cancellation Penalties).

On Request This is an unconfirmed booking for a flight.

Onward Tickets An entry requirement for many countries is that you have a ticket out of the country. If you're unsure of your next move, the easiest solution is to buy the cheapest onward ticket to a neighbouring country or a ticket from a reliable airline which can later be refunded if you do not use it.

Open Jaw Tickets These are return tickets where you fly out to one place but return from another. If available, this can save you backtracking to your arrival point.

Overbooking Airlines hate to fly empty seats and since every flight has some passengers who fail to show up, airlines often book more passengers than they have seats. Usually excess passengers make up for the no-shows, but occasionally somebody gets bumped. Guess who it is most likely to be? The passengers who check in late.

Point-to-Point Tickets These are discount tickets that can be bought on some routes in return for passengers waiving their rights to a stopover.

Reconfirmation At least 72 hours prior to departure time of an onward or return flight, you must contact the airline and 'reconfirm' that you intend to be on the flight. If you don't do this, the airline can delete your name from the passenger list and you could lose your seat.

Restrictions Discounted tickets often have various restrictions on them – such as needing to be paid for in advance and incurring a penalty to be altered. Others are restrictions on the minimum and maximum period you must be away, such as a minimum of 14 days or a maximum of one year.

Round-the-World Tickets RTW tickets give you a limited period (usually a year) in which to circumnavigate the globe. You can go anywhere the carrying airlines go, as long as you don't backtrack. The number of stopovers or total number of separate flights is decided before you set off and they usually cost a bit more than a basic return flight.

Stand-by This is a discounted ticket where you only fly if there is a seat free at the last moment. Stand-by fares are usually available only on domestic routes.

Transferred Tickets Airline tickets cannot be transferred from one person to another. Travellers sometimes try to sell the return half of their ticket, but officials can ask you to prove that you are the person named on the ticket. This is less likely to happen on domestic flights, but on an international flight tickets are compared with passports.

Travel Periods Ticket prices vary with the time of year. There is a low (off-peak) season and a high (peak) season, and often a low-shoulder season and a high-shoulder season as well. Usually the fare depends on your outward flight – if you depart in the high season and return in the low season, you pay the high-season fare.

Following are the international offices and agents for Lao Aviation:

Australia
   Orbitours (☎ (02) 9954 1399; fax 9954 1655), Suite 17, 7th floor, Dymocks Bldg, 428 George St, Sydney, NSW
Cambodia
   Lao Aviation (☎/fax (21) 26563), 58B Sihanouk Ave, Phnom Penh
   Royal Air du Cambodge (☎ (21) 25887), 62 Tou Sarmuth St, Phnom Penh
Canada
   Skyplan Business Development (☎ (403) 250 1605), 200-35 McTavish Pl NE, Calgary, Alberta
Germany
   Muller & Partner (☎ (30) 282 3262; fax 282 3686), Friedrichstrasse 130C, Berlin
Hong Kong
   China Travel Air Service (☎ 2853 3488; fax 2544 6174), 5/F CTS House, 78-83 Connaught Rd, Central
Italy
   Vivitours (☎ (02) 657 0441; fax 657 1943), Via A Volta 10, Milan
Japan
   Transindo Japan (☎ (3) 3453 3391; fax 3454 3350), Mita Sanshin Bldg 2-7-16, Mita Minkoku, Tokyo
Thailand
   Lao Aviation (☎ (02) 236-9822), ground floor, 491/17 Silom Plaza, Thanon Silom,Bangkok
   Lao Aviation (☎ (053) 418258), 240 Prapokklao Rd, Chiang Mai
USA
   Lao-American (☎ (708) 742 2159), 338 South Hancock Ave, South Elgin, IL 60177
Vietnam
   Vietnam Veterans Tourism Services (☎ (4) 236789; fax 237467), 21 Phan Din Phung St, Ba Dinh, Hanoi
   39/3 Tran Nhat Duat, District 1, Ho Chi Minh City (☎ (8) 442807; fax 442723)

Airport Arrival

Arrivals at Wattay international airport in Vientiane tend to be a rather casual event. The customs and immigration procedures are much less cumbersome than in most other countries, especially Communist ones, Carry-on bags are not usually inspected if that's all that you have brought; checked baggage, when claimed at the baggage counter, sometimes is.

The government bank has a foreign exchange counter in the terminal but if you have Thai baht and US dollars – which are just as acceptable as kip in Vientiane – there's no need to rush out and change money. If you're hoping for a visa on arrival, you'd better have US$50 ready as the exchange counter does not sell dollars.

A Japanese grant is paying for a large new airport terminal, complete with a Japanese-looking roof line.

LAND

Laos shares land borders with Thailand, Myanmar, Cambodia, China and Vietnam, all of which permit overland crossings for locals living on either side of the border but not necessarily for foreigners. Legalities change from month to month so it's worth checking with a Lao embassy or consulate abroad for the latest.

Thailand

Nong Khai The Thai-Lao Friendship Bridge (Saphan Mittaphap Thai-Lao) spans the Mekong River from Nong Khai Province (specifically Hat Jommani) on the Thai side and Vientiane Province (Tha Na Leng) on the Lao side and is currently the main land crossing into Laos. The 1240m Australian-financed bridge opened in 1994 with much hoopla about how it would improve transport and communications between the two countries. It is only the second bridge to have been erected over the Mekong (the first is in China).

In spite of its two 3.5m-wide traffic lanes, two 1.5m-wide footpaths and space for a railway line down the centre, the bridge has had done little to fulfil its potential. Shuttle buses ferry passengers back and forth across the bridge from designated terminals nearby for 10B per person; there are departures every 20 minutes from 8 am to 5.30 pm. You must arrange your own transport to the bridge bus terminal from Nong Khai. The bus stops at Thai immigration control on the bridge, where you pay 10B to have your passport stamped with an exit visa. Passengers then reboard the bus and after crossing the bridge stop at Lao immigrations and customs, where you will pay a fee of 20B to have your passport stamped (40B between noon and 2 pm and on weekends).

From the bridge it's 100B by jumbo (three-wheeled taxi) or 150B by car taxi to Vientiane, about 20km away. You can also catch a No 14 bus into town for 400 kip; around fifteen buses a day (from 6.30 am to 5 pm) pass the bridge area on their way from Tha Deua (the old ferry pier) to Vientiane's Morning Market.

The Lao government has made it very difficult for foreign-registered vehicles to get permission to cross the bridge even for temporary visits, and so far there are no private transport services across the Friendship Bridge other than the shuttle.

Rail A joint venture agreement between the Lao government and a new company called Lao Railways Transportation was signed in 1998 to establish a railway line along the middle of the Friendship Bridge. After a two year feasibility study is completed the line, which will reportedly extend to Vientiane and Luang Prabang, is supposed to become operational in four years. Like most other transport projects in Laos, however, it will probably take much longer – if it happens at all.

Chong Mek A crossing from Chong Mek in Thailand's Ubon Ratchathani Province to Champasak has been open for use by foreign visitors since 1993. You no longer need a specially endorsed visa to use this crossing – any visa will do.

To get to Chong Mek from Ubon, take a bus first to Phibun Mangsahan (15B), then switch to a Phibun to Chong Mek *songthaew* (18B). At Chong Mek you simply walk across the border (Lao immigration and customs are open from 8 am to noon and from 1 to 4.30 pm) and proceed from Ban Mai Sing Amphon – the village on the Lao side of the border – to Pakse. It is about an hour from the border via bus or taxi and ferry. See under Pakse in the Champasak Province section in the Southern Laos chapter for details on transport to Pakse.

Chiang Khong In 1996 a Thai company announced plans to construct a bridge over the Mekong between Chiang Khong and Huay Xai but so far nothing has materialised. If built, this bridge will connect with the 250km road running north-east to the Chinese border via Bokeo and Luang Nam Tha provinces. The same company also has plans – currently stalled due to the Thai economic downturn – to upgrade and pave this entire stretch.

From Huay Xai the only way to head south to Luang Prabang or Vientiane – at the moment – is via long-distance river ferry, speedboat or aeroplane. For details see the Getting There & Away sections for each of these destinations.

Train to Nong Khai & Ubon Trains from Bangkok's Hualamphong railway station run express daily to Nong Khai (11 hours) and Ubon Ratchathani (10 hours). Both lines offer sleeping carriages on overnight trains, a very convenient way to get an early morning start across the border while saving money on a hotel room. Basic one way fares are 238B (Nong Khai) and 219B (Ubon) 2nd class or 497B (Nong Khai) and 457B (Ubon) 1st class respectively, not including surcharges for express service or sleeping berths. These fares will probably increase if the State Railway of Thailand is privatised.

Vietnam

Lao Bao Border officials at the border-post opposite Lao Bao, a small town on the Vietnam side of the Lao-Vietnamese border near Sepon (250km east from Savannakhet) will permit visitors holding Laos visas to enter the country overland from Vietnam. Lao Bao lies 80km west of Dong Ha and 3km east of the border. There is an international bus which runs between Danang (Vietnam) and Savannakhet. In Vietnam, you can catch this bus in Danang, Dong Ha or Lao Bao. In Laos, the only place you are likely to board is Savannakhet. This bus is supposed to make its run every Sunday, Tuesday and Thursday, but this schedule is hardly engraved in stone and will probably increase in frequency.

Dong Ha to Savannakhet on this bus costs US$15 for foreigners. From the Vietnamese side, departure from Danang is at 4 am, from Dong Ha at 10 am and from Lao Bao at 2 pm. Arrival in Savannakhet is at 7 pm. Border guards (both Lao and Vietnamese) have been known to ask for bribes.

There are also local buses which just go to the border from either side. It's cheaper to go by local bus rather than to take the cross-border express, but more of a hassle. For one thing, there is a 1km walk between the Vietnamese and Lao checkpoints. Furthermore, the bus from Dong Ha terminates at Lao Bao, which is 3km from the actual border checkpoint (though you can cover this 3km by motorbike taxi). The bus from Dong Ha to Lao Bao costs US$1 to US$4 depending on whether it's a standard service or a 'deluxe' one. These buses normally depart twice daily (early morning and noon), but departure times are variable because the buses won't leave until they're full.

There is a restaurant on the Lao side of the border, 500m back from the border-post. You might be able to sleep in the restaurant if you ask nicely, as there are no hotels. To say that the facilities around the border are primitive is an understatement.

From the Lao side there's only one local bus a day to Savannakhet. It leaves around 1 pm but this could change (two years ago the sole bus left around 8 am) and the trip takes six hours. If you miss the bus your best bet is to arrange transport to Sepon and spend the night there. In the reverse direction – from Laos to Vietnam – you'll also need a visa from a Vietnamese embassy or consulate in Laos. For more information see the Savannakhet Getting There & Away section in the Southern Laos chapter.

Visas for Laos can be obtained in Ho Chi Minh City, Hanoi or Danang. If you are departing or entering Vietnam via this route, your Vietnamese visa must indicate the Lao Bao border crossing. If you have a Vietnamese re-entry visa, it can be amended at the Vietnamese consulate in Savannakhet.

Kaew Neua A relatively new crossing at Kaew Neua (also called Nam Phao) in Bolikhamsai Province, adjacent to Cau Treo in Vietnam, connects with the Vietnamese town of Vinh, 2½ hours by bus from the border. Recent reports say it can be difficult to find a bus from Vinh to the border but this will undoubtedly change as the crossing becomes more established. From Nam Phao/Kaew Neua it's a 40km jumbo ride along Route 8 to Kham Keut. From the latter there are frequent buses to Paksan and to Tha Khaek, both of which are on Route 13, with connections north to Vientiane or south to Savannakhet.

Other Crossings Another border crossing between Laos and Vietnam at Sop Hun in Phongsali Province just across from Tay Trang (32km west of Dien Bien Phu) is open only to Lao and Vietnamese citizens at the moment. Stay tuned.

China
From Mengla district in China's Yunnan Province it is legal to enter Laos via Boten, Luang Nam Tha Province, if you possess a valid Lao visa. From Boten there are morning and afternoon buses to Luang Nam Tha and Muang Xai, three and four hours away respectively.

The Lao consulate in Kunming, China, issues only seven-day transit visas. It costs from US$25 to US$28 and takes three to five days to process. You must bring *four* photos and already have a visa from a third country (such as Thailand) stamped in your passport. Most travellers from Kunming go via Jinghong to Mengla and thence to the border at Mohan. As the bus journey from Jinghong will take the better part of the day, you will probably have to stay overnight in Mengla.

A second China-Laos crossing from the same area of Yunnan may be possible via Bun Neua district in Phongsali Province. Lao and Chinese citizens regularly use this crossing as a short cut from north-western Laos, travelling across a narrow section of Yunnan Province that juts down between the Lao provinces of Luang Nam Tha and

Phongsali. Although it's an official border crossing for Chinese and Lao citizens only, in 1995 we met some Japanese visitors who managed to cross at Bun Neua with advance written permission from a Lao consulate in China. It's worth inquiring.

Cambodia
Lao and Cambodian citizens are permitted to cross back and forth at Voen Kham, Champasak Province. Rumours say this crossing will be open to foreigners as soon as the highway from Pakse to Voen Kham is finished. If you want to try this one, inquire at the Lao embassy in Phnom Penh first – they will know whether it's open yet or not.

Myanmar
We've heard rumours – balanced by denials from the Lao government – regarding entry from Myanmar at the Lao town of Xieng Kok, on the Mekong River in Luang Nam Tha Province. Travellers who want to try this crossing will increase their chances of success if they arrive with a valid visa.

RIVER
Thailand
Since the opening of the Friendship Bridge, the Tha Deua ferry in Nong Khai has been closed to non-Thai and non-Lao citizens. However it is still legal for non-Thai foreigners to cross the Mekong River by ferry from Thailand into Laos at the following points: Nakhon Phanom (opposite Tha Khaek), Chiang Khong (opposite Huay Xai) and Mukdahan (opposite Savanna-khet). You no longer require any special permission attached to your visa for any of these crossings. Regular Lao tourist visas can be obtained from travel agencies in each of these towns if you haven't already

got one. If the bridge between Chiang Khong and Huay Xai is ever constructed, passenger ferry service at this crossing will probably be discontinued.

Thais are permitted to cross at all of the above checkpoints plus at least six others from Thailand's Loei and Nong Khai provinces, including Pak Chom, Chiang Khan, Beung Kan, Ban Pak Huay, Ban Nong Pheu and Ban Khok Phai. In the future one or more of these may become available for entry by foreign visitors as well, particularly those crossings along the Sainyabuli Province border.

DEPARTURE TAX
The international departure tax is US$5, which can be paid in kip, baht or dollars only.

WARNING
The information in this chapter is particularly vulnerable to change: prices for international travel are volatile, routes are introduced and cancelled, schedules change, special deals come and go, and rules and visa requirements are amended. Airlines and governments almost seem to take a perverse pleasure in making price structures and regulations as complicated as possible. You should check directly with the airline or a travel agent to make sure you understand how a fare (and ticket you may buy) works. In addition, the travel industry is highly competitive and there are many lurks and perks.

The upshot of this is that you should get opinions, quotes and advice from as many airlines and travel agents as possible before you part with your hard-earned cash. The details given in this chapter should be regarded as pointers and are not a substitute for your own careful, up-to-date research.

Getting Around

AIR

Lao Aviation handles all of the domestic flights in Laos with Vientiane as the main hub – all flights originate and terminate at Wattay international airport with the exception of one plane kept in Pakse for certain southern routes.

Lao Aviation does not accept credit cards for domestic ticket purchases – all payments must be made in cash. Prices for foreigners are quoted in dollars and you can only pay in cash dollars. You can, however, purchase tickets with credit cards through a travel agency rather than directly from Lao Aviation. Diethelm Travel and Lao Air Booking are conveniently located just a block or so away from Lao Aviation on Thanon Setthathirat.

Since January 1995 Lao Aviation has been 60% owned by China Yunnan Airlines. The main aircraft used for Lao Aviation's domestic flights are the 15-passenger Chinese Yun-12 and the 50-passenger Yun-7, both copies of Russian Antonov aircraft with upgraded features. Lao Aviation also has one ATR-72 for international and Luang Prabang flights. When Lao Aviation finds itself short of Chinese planes, an old Antonov 24 may be pulled from retirement and used instead. In 1998 the entire domestic fleet amounted to 10 aircraft: one ATR-72, one Antonov 24, four Yun-12s (of which only one is fully operational – the other three are used for parts), four Yun-7s, and one 25-person ME-8 helicopter (used when one of the regular aircraft is grounded).

Booking seats can be tricky on domestic flights since the number of air passengers in Laos has grown faster than the number of functioning aircraft. Because of this shortage of planes, the company has to scramble to maintain a schedule and it's sometimes impossible to know whether a particular flight will be going at a particular time on a particular date until a day or two before the flight.

Booking far in advance, therefore, doesn't help. If you buy a ticket in Vientiane for a Luang Nam Tha to Huay Xai flight you may get a date but not a departure time; the staff will tell you to check with the Lao Aviation office in Luang Nam Tha the day before the hoped-for departure. Don't be surprised if you're told in Luang Nam Tha that the flight has been postponed a day – or has left a day early! In other words if you plan to fly domestically, you must be flexible. All of the departure and arrival times given throughout this guide are *scheduled* flight times. In practice, flights are often delayed an hour or two due to weather conditions in the mountains – which includes all destinations except Vientiane, Savannakhet and Pakse.

Basically the airline is run exactly like most ground transportation in Laos, that is maximising profit by running the minimum number of aircraft at full capacity rather than many aircraft at less than full capacity. Several of the routes and fares listed by Lao Aviation – such as flights to Attapeu, Muang Khong or Phongsali – hardly ever happen. If you have a group of six or more you can sometimes charter a Lao Aviation plane to these destinations, but with the current aircraft shortage even this is difficult.

Safety records for Lao Aviation aren't made public. At the moment pilots must rely on visual flying techniques except when flying the ATR-72 to Luang Prabang. When heavy cloud cover is present they are forced to circle the area searching for a hole through which to descend; if none is found within the time allotted by fuel capacity, the pilots either return to the departure point or land at another airport in the same region. After refuelling, they give it another go! A Yun-12 crashed into a cloud-obscured mountain near Phonsavan in December 1993, killing all aboard, so this method has its shortcomings. The new airport at Luang Prabang has radar, and a rumour persists that radar equipment will be installed at Attapeu and Sam Neua. It

CHINA

Phongsali

VIETNAM

MYANMAR
(BURMA)

HANOI

Luang
Nam Tha
46
Muang Xai
(Udomxai)
41
37
37
Sam Neua
Huay Xai
46
28
47
Kunming
155
80
36
Possible
future route to
Chiang Mai
25
Luang
Prabang
35
Phonsavan
90
71
Sainyabuli
THAILAND
88
55
Gulf
of
Tonkin
42
44
70
Chiang Mai
70
VIENTIANE
Lak Sao
50
57
Tha Khaek
61
44
78
Savannakhet
91
44
95
44
THAILAND
Salavan
VIETNAM
33
Pakse

Airfares Chart

0   100   200 km

All fares in $US
Prices for international fares
are intended as a guide only

Bangkok
75-100

Phnom
Penh
133

Ho Chi
Minh City
170

Singapore
355

CAMBODIA

is unlikely that instrument landings are going to become the norm throughout the country anytime soon.

Fares & Taxes

Air fares for Lao citizens are subsidised at less than half what a foreigner must pay. Children aged five to 12 are charged half the adult fare, infants pay only 10%. See the Airfares chart above for the regular adult fares.

The departure tax for domestic flights is 300 kip. Passengers must also pay 100 kip to immigration officers at each domestic airport for the privilege of checking in or out of the province each time they arrive or depart by air.

Offices

The offices of Lao Aviation are in Vientiane; see the Getting There and Away section of the Vientiane chapter.

Helicopter

The Lao Westcoast Helicopter Co (☎ (021) 512023; fax 512055), Hangar 703, Wattay

Fares
More than just about any other type of pricing, passenger fares in Laos were in a state of extreme flux while this edition was being updated due to the fluctuation of the kip's value against hard currencies like the US dollar and Japanese yen. This is because most vehicle parts, tyres and most especially fuel must be imported using such currencies for payment. The baht to kip ratio also affects such purchases. As import costs rose, so did fares for all types of transport – boat, bus, jumbo, taxi and so on. At one point we watched fares bobbing up nearly every week for a period of three months. Thus all passenger fares quoted in this book must be considered very tentative.

airport, charters out five-passenger French AS 350B Squirrel helicopters with expatriate pilots for aerial surveys, photography or passenger transport to just about anywhere in Laos (but subject to government permission obtained by the passengers). The usual rate is US$1110 per airborne hour, including all taxes.

BUS & TRUCK
The availability of interprovincial public transport continues to increase. It is now possible to travel to at least part of every province in Laos by some form of public road conveyance. Regular buses – mostly Japanese or Korean-made – ply Route 13 between Vientiane and Savannakhet an average of two or three times daily. Other routes in the south, eg Pakse to Sekong, typically use large flat-bed trucks mounted with a heavy wooden carriage containing seats in bus-like rows. Other routes, such as Vientiane to Luang Prabang, use a mix of the Japanese buses, trucks and pick-ups.

In the northern provinces, Chinese, Vietnamese, Russian and Japanese trucks are often converted into passenger carriers by adding two long benches in the back. These

passenger trucks are called *thaek-sii* (taxi) or in some areas *sǎwng-thâew*, which means 'two rows' in reference to the two facing benches in the back.

Because of road conditions, the frequency of intercity bus service is for the most part limited to one or two vehicles per day. As each of the major highway projects is completed, public transport options will continue to multiply and the frequency of bus departures will increase.

TRAIN
Nothing yet – but a Thai-Lao joint venture is currently studying the feasibility of constructing a 1400km railway through Laos. If such a railway becomes a reality, it will connect with the Thai railhead in Nong Khai as well as rail networks in China and Vietnam.

CAR & MOTORCYCLE
Visitors with valid International Driving Permits are permitted to drive cars in Laos, though a car and driver can be hired for less than the cost of a rental car in most towns (see the Taxi section later in this chapter for information on car-and-driver hire, or under Vehicle Hire below for 4WD rental).

The number of vehicles in the country – including cars, motorcycles, trucks, buses and jeeps – is less than 250,000. Estimates say there are nearly four times as many motorcycles as cars. In spite of this, bringing your own vehicle into the country is nearly impossible unless you work for a company or other organisation doing business in Laos (even then it's a major bureaucratic headache). It is much easier to buy or rent a vehicle in Laos than import one.

Small motorbikes – under 150cc – can be rented from some motorcycle dealers in Vientiane as well as in Luang Prabang and Savannakhet. The going rate is from US$10 to US$12 a day. A new Honda Dream II 100cc motorbike (assembled in Laos) costs from US$900 to US$1000.

Petrol costs around 700 kip per litre at stations in the Mekong valley, up to 900 or 1000 kip in remote provinces.

Siam Bike Travel (fax (66 53) 495987) in Chiang Mai, Thailand, arranges two week, 1500km overland motorbike trips through Laos from Thailand to China and back.

Vehicle Hire

Small Japanese pick-ups can be chartered between towns or provinces. Because Lao roadways generate a high degree of wear and tear on these vehicles, hire charges run as high as US$100 a day. In Vientiane you can hire a 4WD vehicle – and driver – for upcountry trips for US$120 to US$160 a day; prices are kept high by the tendency for UN organisations to shell out up to US$300 a day for the same vehicles. Long-term 4WD rentals of around US$65 per day are possible. One of the more reliable places to hire vehicles and drivers is Asia Vehicle Rental (☎ (021) 217493), at 8/3 Thanon Lan Xang, in Vientiane.

Road System

The road system in Laos remains very un-developed. Although the French installed full highway systems in Vietnam and Cambodia, they built only one road of any significance in Laos, Route Coloniale 13 along the lower Mekong River, plus the less impressive Routes Coloniales 7 and 9 through two Annamite mountain passes.

Later contributors to the road system include the Chinese and North Vietnamese, who constructed a number of all-weather roads in northern Laos (all of them, of course, within the former liberated zone) in the 1960s and early 1970s. In return for their labour, the Chinese were allowed to cut and export as much timber as they liked. Most of these roads radiate out from Muang Xai and Xieng Khuang, often only as far as provincial borders. From Phonsavan (the capital of Xieng Khuang Province), for example, the road is in a fair condition until it reaches the Hua Phan Province border, then it's lousy as far as Sam Neua, then good again all the way to the Vietnamese border.

As of 1996 Laos had 22,321km of classi-fied roads (8350km more than the previous year), the bulk of which can be charitably described as 'in a deteriorated condition'. An estimated 16% are tarred; 38% are graded and sometimes covered with gravel; the remaining 46% are ungraded dirt tracks. The roads around Vientiane Prefecture, as far as Vang Vieng, are surfaced and ade-quate for just about any type of vehicle. Route 13 going north to Luang Prabang and south to Savannakhet has also been paved. Bridge construction over rivers bisecting this highway has yet to catch up with road construction, so these routes aren't quite as fast as one might otherwise think.

Elsewhere in the country, unsurfaced roads are the rule. Since Laos is 70% moun-tains, even relatively short road trips involve incredibly long intervals; a typical 200km upcountry trip can take as much as 10 to 18 hours to accomplish, depending on conditions.

A number of international aid projects continue to promise to upgrade the current system and build new roads by the end of the decade. From Luang Prabang the road (Route 13) will continue to Pak Mong in northern Luang Prabang province, where it will connect with the Chinese-built Xieng Khuang to Muang Xai highway. The Pakse to Salavan road has already been upgraded and is now one of the best roads in Laos. The sealing of Route 13 from Savannakhet to the Cambodian border lags behind its scheduled 1998 completion date but should be fully sealed by 2000. To follow that

Road Warning

All road travel times quoted in this book are best estimates based on personal ex-periences of the author (who has done most routes in this book himself) or someone the author trusts. Still, they are estimates only. Road conditions and the condition of the vehicles you're travelling in will greatly affect actual travel time. In Laos there is no such thing as a perfect road schedule.

Bad Roads, Good People

When a scheduled three hour ride in a mega-crowded Lao 'bus' crafted from a Soviet truck cab mated with a hand-sawn wooden carriage open to dust and diesel fumes turns into a 12 hour ordeal; when the road is so rough and the vehicle so poorly maintained that you have two breakdowns and a flat tyre; or when you wait by the side of the road for the 8 am bus that everyone says will arrive any minute and the sun is shining its high-noon rays right into your skull; you might have occasion to wonder: is it worth all this?

Was it more gratifying to travel through Sumatra before the highway had been paved? Some people would answer, yes, Sumatra was more of a journey, more of a challenge and more of a travel experience in those days. It's 'those days' now in much of Laos. I think the real difference, though, lies not in the masochistic road trips themselves but in the people who travel those roads. A woman who ran a cafe alongside a newly sealed highway in Mexico once told me, when I asked about how things had changed since the sealing: 'Bad roads, good people. Good roads, all kinds of people'.

Joe Cummings

project are three sealed east-west thoroughfares along Routes 1, 9 and 18.

The Thais have offered to assist in the construction of roads that would link Thailand with Vietnam via Savannakhet (for Danang), Tha Khaek (for Vinh) and Pakse (for Ho Chi Minh City), but so far nothing has emerged from the offer. Thailand, Myanmar, China and Laos also agreed in May 1993 to develop road links in the area bordering the upper reaches of the Mekong River, thus linking Thailand's Chiang Rai Province with Xishuangbanna District (Yunnan) in southern China via Laos' Bokeo and Luang Nam Tha provinces. As of 1998 a Thai company had graded about a third of 220km Route 3, which stretches from Huay Xai to Boten. For the time being, however, this project has been stalled by the economic downturn in South-East Asia and no-one seems to know when it will see fruition.

Road Rules

Watch carefully for vehicles making left turns from a side road. Lao drivers typically turn into the left lane before moving over to the right – a potentially dangerous situation if you're not ready for it. Rather than stop and wait for traffic to pass, motorists typically merge into the oncoming traffic without bothering to look to the rear, reasoning that any big or fast-moving vehicle approaching from behind will sound a horn.

Like many places in Asia, every two-lane road has an invisible third lane in the middle that drivers feel free to use at any time. Passing on hills and curves is common – as long as you've got the proper Buddhist altar on the dashboard, what could happen?

BICYCLE

Bicycles are a popular form of transport throughout urban Laos and can be hired in Vientiane, Luang Prabang, Savannakhet, Muang Sing and Don Khong for around 2000 kip to 3000 kip per day – some hotels and guesthouses even loan them out for free. These Thai or Chinese-made street bikes come in varying degrees of usability; you can buy a new one for US$70 to US$90. The Chinese bikes are sturdier, the Thai bikes more comfortable. Low-quality Chinese or Taiwanese mountain bikes are available for US$90 to US$140.

Lao customs doesn't object to visitors bringing bicycles into the country. If you plan to do any extensive interprovincial cycling, consider taking along the following items:

- pump
- tyre patch kit
- bike wrench
- chainbreaker
- spoke wrench
- spare spokes
- allen wrenches as necessary

- toothbrush (for cleaning bike parts)
- chain oil
- brake pads
- booting material for tyres
- spare seat & stem bolts
- light raingear
- hammock, space blanket, portable mosquito net

HITCHING
Hitching rides on cargo trucks presents another transport option. Smaller vehicles will sometimes stop as well. Remember, though, that hitching is never entirely safe in any country in the world, and therefore we don't recommend it. Travellers, especially women, should be aware that they are taking a small but potentially serious risk by hitching.

If you're waiting by the side of the road for a ride, it helps to know whether approaching vehicles are likely to take on passengers. You can identify the ownership by looking at the licence tags – black tags with yellow letters mean the vehicle is licensed to carry paying passengers; red on yellow means it's a privately owned vehicle; red is military-owned (not likely to pick up passengers); white on blue is civil service, UN or NGO; and blue-on-white tags belong to embassies or international organisations (who will sometimes pick up foreign passengers). White tags with red lettering mean the vehicle has right-hand drive!

RIVER
Navigable waterways totalling 4600km of rivers are the traditional highways and byways of Laos, the main thoroughfares being the Mekong, Nam Ou, Nam Khan, Nam Tha, Nam Ngum and Se Kong. At 2030km, the Mekong is the longest and most important route and is navigable year-round between Luang Prabang in the north and Savannakhet in the south (about 70% of its length in Laos). Depending on the season this stretch of the Mekong can carry boats of between 15 tonnes and 140 tonnes. Smaller rivers accommodate traditional dugout pirogues used for fishing and transport.

With the increase in road travel, passenger services are declining year by year. In the south, for example, only a handful of long-distance ferry services still operate – all of them below Pakse – and these will probably fall by the wayside once Route 13 is sealed all the way to Cambodia. Likewise the river ferry and speedboat service between Luang Prabang and Nong Khiaw has almost totally been replaced by road travel.

River Ferries
Large diesel river ferries designed for cargo transport are still used between Huay Xai and Vientiane, but the boats see few passengers south of Luang Prabang now that the Luang Prabang to Vientiane road is sealed. Huay Xai to Luang Prabang is now the main long-distance river trip. From Vientiane to Pakse nowadays one sees cargo traffic only. South of Pakse smaller passenger ferries still ply routes to Champasak and Don Khong though we are probably seeing the final days of this traffic. At the moment, however, boat transport is still preferable to road transport along these latter routes.

Some of the long-distance ferries between Huay Xai and Vientiane have two decks, with sleeping areas and on-board kitchens. For overnight trips, it's a good idea to bring food along. Ferry facilities are quite basic; passengers sit, eat and sleep on wooden decks. The toilet – when one exists – is an enclosed hole in the deck. Women are expected to ride inside and to the back of the boat; men are permitted to sit on the front and top decks, including the roof.

For boats running along the Mekong between Huay Xai and Vientiane, foreigners are charged 50% more than locals.

River Taxis
For shorter river trips, from Luang Prabang to the Pak Ou caves for example, it's usually best to hire a river taxi since the large river ferries only ply their routes once a day at most, sometimes only a couple of times a week. The *héua hãng nyáo* (longtail boats) with engines mounted on the stern are the most typical, though for a really short trip, say crossing a river, a *héua phái* (rowing boat) can be hired. The héua hãng

nyáo are not as cheap to hire as you might think – figure on around 6000 kip an hour for a boat with a capacity for eight to 10 people. Larger boats that carry up to 20 passengers are sometimes available for around 8000 kip per hour.

Along the upper Mekong River between Huay Xai and Vientiane, and on the Nam Ou between Luang Prabang and Hat Sa (Phongsali), Thai-built *héua wái* (speedboats) – shallow, 5m-long skiffs with 40 horsepower Toyota outboard engines – are common. These are able to cover a distance in six hours that might take a ferry two days or more. They're not cheap – charters cost about US$20 per hour – but some ply regular routes so the cost can be shared among passengers.

LOCAL TRANSPORT
Taxi
Each of the four largest towns – Vientiane, Luang Prabang, Savannakhet and Pakse – has a handful of car taxis that are used by foreign businesspeople and the occasional tourist. The only place you'll find these are at the airports (arrival times only) and in front of the larger hotels. Until the mid-1990s the cars were mostly of Eastern European or Russian origin, with the occasional older US car turning up, but these days Japanese cars are more common. Taxis like these can be hired by the trip, by the hour or by the day. Typical all-day hires within a town or city cost US$20 to US$40 depending on the vehicle and your negotiating powers. By the trip, you shouldn't pay more than US$0.50 per kilometre.

Three-wheeled taxis are common in these same cities as well as in some smaller ones. This type of vehicle can be called *thaek-sii* (taxi) or *sāam-lâw* (samlor or three-wheels). The larger ones made in Thailand are called *jamboh* (jumbo) and can hold four to six passengers. In Vientiane they are sometimes called *túk-túk* as in Thailand (though in Laos this usually refers to a slightly larger vehicle than the jumbo), while in the south (Pakse, Savannakhet) they may be called *sakai-làep* ('Skylab') because of the

perceived resemblance to a space capsule! Fares vary according to the city you're in and on your bargaining skills. Locals generally pay about 500 kip per kilometre. They can go anywhere a regular taxi can go, but aren't usually hired for distances greater than 20km or so.

Pedicab
The bicycle *samlor*, once the mainstay of local transport for hire throughout urban Laos, has nearly become extinct. These used to be commonly called *cyclo (sii-khlo)* following the French, but this term is used much less frequently than samlor (actually *sāam-lâw*, which means 'three wheels') nowadays. If you can to find a samlor, fares are about the same as motorcycle taxis but are generally used only for distances less than 2km or so. Bargaining is sometimes necessary to get the correct fare, though the ageing pedicab drivers seem to be more honest than the motorcycle taxi drivers.

ORGANISED TOURS
All tours in Laos are handled by agencies authorised by the National Tourism Authority of Laos (NTAL). Such authorisation isn't easy to obtain as the NTAL requires that each agency maintain a US$50,000 bond, two minivans and telex, fax and phone numbers.

In 1998 there were 16 agencies operating in Vientiane, some of which have branches in other cities such as Luang Prabang, Pakse and Phonsavan. For the most part, each agency has a standard set of packages, ranging from two nights in Vientiane only to 14 days in Vientiane, Luang Prabang, the Plain of Jars (Xieng Khuang), Savannakhet, Salavan and Champasak. Some agencies advertise tours which they can't actually deliver, while better ones can go almost anywhere and can create custom itineraries.

Standard prices vary little from company to company; the main difference is linked to the number of people signing up for a package. Per-person rates drop – typically by around US$50 to US$100 per person –

for each person added to the group. Costs for travelling solo can be as much as US$200 or more per day, while four to six people travelling together can arrange packages for under US$50 per person per day. If you don't mind travelling with other people, ask if you can join a group already scheduled to depart – some agencies will allow this while others try to keep the groups as small as possible in order to collect the most loot.

It is also possible to bargain in some cases. Several readers have written to describe how they shopped around from agency to agency and were able to get at least a few tour operators to lower their asking rates.

If you book a tour outside Laos, you must deal with an authorised agent of one of these Lao agencies. This means additional cost to you, as the tour operators have to pay a wholesale price to the agencies in Laos.

The costs can vary widely from agency to agency, but in general it's a bit cheaper to book upcountry tours in Vientiane rather than outside the country. In some cases the difference in price between tours booked in Vientiane and those booked in the outer provinces represents another layer of markups. One Vientiane agency, for example, charged US$250 for a Xieng Khuang tour add-on operated by a local Xieng Khuang company that only charged US$60 if it was booked locally.

In general, tours arranged by the Vientiane agencies are not bad value as far as package tours go. Except for the obvious inconvenience of having to put up with a group (although sometimes the group is as small as two to four people) and follow a guide around, the tours are generally well planned and genuinely informative. Guides are usually flexible when it comes to the itinerary, adding or deleting bits (within obvious time, distance and cost limits), according to your needs.

At each destination, the agencies arrange all accommodation (double occupancy) and a tour guide. In more expensive packages in-country transport and meals are included. Prices for packages without meals are much lower, and eating out is often more fun than prearranged hotel meals anyway.

Meals, where they are included, are plentiful if a bit on the bland side, but you can sometimes request local specialities. Or simply inform your guide that you want to eat real Lao food during the tour, not the ersatz version usually offered to westerners.

Unlike some early China tours in which visitors were herded from factory to agricultural collective, Laos itineraries do not try to present visitors with a proletarian paradise – political rhetoric is relatively absent from guide commentary.

Vientiane Tour Operators

The following are some reputable tour operators in Vientiane:

Diethelm Travel Laos
(☎ (021) 215920; fax 217151), Namphu Square, Thanon Setthathirat, PO Box 2657
Inter-Lao Tourisme
(☎ (021) 214832; fax 216306), corner of Thanon Pangkham and Thanon Setthathirat, PO Box 2912
Lane Xang Travel
(☎ (021) 212469; fax 215804), Thanon Pangkham, PO Box 4452
Lao Travel Service
(☎ (021) 216603; fax 216150), 8/3 Thanon Lan Xang, PO Box 2553
SODETOUR (Société de Développement Touristique)
(☎ (021) 216314; fax 216313), 16 Thanon Fa Ngum, PO Box 70
That Luang Tour
(☎ (021) 215809; fax 215346), 28 Thanon Kamkhong, PO Box 3619

Rate structures among these companies are similar though That Luang and Lane Xang seem to try harder to keep their prices down.

Vientiane

HISTORY

Set on a bend in the Mekong River, Vientiane was originally one of the early Lao valley fiefdoms or *meuang* that were consolidated around the time that Europe was leaving the Dark Ages. The Lao who settled here chose the area because the surrounding alluvial plains are so incredibly fertile. Early on, the Vientiane meuang prospered and enjoyed a fragile sovereignty.

At various times over the 10 or so centuries of its history, however, Vientiane lost its standing as an independent kingdom and was controlled by the Vietnamese, Burmese, Siamese and Khmers. When the kingdom of Lan Xang (Million Elephants) was founded in the 14th century by the Khmer-supported conqueror Fa Ngum, it was at first centred in Muang Sawa (Luang Prabang), but by the mid-16th century the capital had shifted to Vientiane.

When Laos became a French protectorate in the late 19th and early 20th centuries, Vientiane was named as the capital city, and it has remained so under Communist rule today.

Vientiane's name is translated as Sandalwood City, and is actually pronounced Wieng Chan (Wieng means 'city' or 'place with walls' in Lao; Chan is the Lao pronunciation of the Sanskrit 'Chandana'). The French gave the city its common romanised spelling.

It is one of the three classic Indochinese cities (the others being Saigon/Ho Chi Minh City and Phnom Penh) that most strongly conjure up images of exotic Eurasian settings. For the most part, Vientiane lives up to these images, with its intriguing mix of Lao, Thai, Chinese, Vietnamese, French, US and Soviet influences. Of the three capitals, Vientiane is by far the most laid-back in atmosphere.

Modern Vientiane is actually three separate entities: province (with a population of around 528,000), prefecture (260,000) and

HIGHLIGHTS

- **Pha That Luang**, Laos' national symbol, and one of its most sacred sites

- **Wat Si Saket**, one of the oldest and most interesting wats in Vientiane

- **Wat Ong Teu**, with its huge bronze Buddha

- **Buddha Park (Xieng Khuan)**, a riverside collection of whimsical Hindu and Buddhist sculptures

city (133,000). Even though Vientiane is the largest city in the country, it's still small enough to get to know easily. Parts of the town are really quite attractive, particularly the older section along the Mekong River. The tree-lined boulevards and many old temples impart an atmosphere of timelessness to the city, in spite of passing traffic (which is growing year by year but is never very heavy) and new construction on the outskirts.

Vientiane's Monarchs

During the last 150-odd years of the Lan Xang Kingdom's history (1548-1707), the royal seat was situated in Vientiane. In 1707 Lan Xang divided into the three separate kingdoms of Vientiane, Luang Prabang and Champasak. The kingdom of Vientiane was ruled by the following monarchs:

Sai Ong Hue	1707-35
Ong Long	1735-60
Ong Boun	1760-78
interregnum	1778-82
Nan	1782-92
In	1792-1805
Chao Anou (Anouvong)	1805-28

ORIENTATION

The city curves along the Mekong River following a bent north-west to south-east axis, with the central district of Muang Chanthabuli at the centre of the bend. Most of the government offices, hotels, restaurants and historic temples are in Chanthabuli, near the river. Some old French colonial buildings and Vietnamese-Chinese shophouses remain, set alongside newer structures built according to the rather boxy Social Realist school of architecture.

In this district street signs in Lao and English make life easier for foreigners, though outside Chanthabuli the street signs are mostly written in Lao script, and only rarely in French. The English and French designations for street names vary (eg route, rue, road and avenue) but the Lao script always reads *thanŏn*. Therefore, when asking directions it's always best to avoid possible confusion and just use the Lao word thanŏn.

The main streets in the downtown district are Thanon Samsenthai, which is the pre-eminent shopping area; Thanon Setthathirat (pronounced Setthathilat since there is no 'r' sound in modern Lao), where several of the most famous temples are located; and Thanon Fa Ngum, which runs along the river and is lined with eucalyptus, pipal and teak trees. Branching off to the north-east, out of Muang Chanthabuli and into Muang Saisettha, is Thanon Lan Xang, Vientiane's widest street.

The main portion of Thanon Lan Xang is a divided boulevard that leads from the presidential palace past Talaat Sao (the Morning Market) to the Patuxai or Victory Gate. After the Patuxai, it splits into two roads, Thanon Phon Kheng and Thanon That Luang. Thanon Phon Kheng leads to the Unknown Soldiers Memorial. Thanon That Luang leads to Pha That Luang.

To the north-east of Muang Chanthabuli is Muang Saisettha, where Pha That Luang and several embassies are located. This is also a residential area of newer French and US-style mansions inhabited by expatriates working for aid programs or multinational companies.

To the south-east of central Vientiane is the mostly local residential meuang of Sisattanak and to the west is the similarly residential Muang Sikhottabong.

The meuangs of Vientiane are broken up into *bâan*, which are neighbourhoods or villages associated with local wats. Wattay airport, for example, is in Ban Wattai, a village in the southern part of Muang Sikhottabong centred around Wat Tai.

Maps & Guides

The *Vientiane Tourist Map*, published by the National Tourism Authority of Laos in 1993, is a fairly useful street map of the city featuring major sites and the mostly unlabelled locations of many hotels and public services. It is available through the National Geographic Service, Raintrees, Phimphone Market and several other shops in the city.

The three pages of fold-out maps at the back of the Women International Group's *Vientiane Guide* are more detailed and feature a useful index. This helpful book, last published in 1995, contains over 190 pages of practical information on what you can see and do in Vientiane. It is oriented

VIENTIANE

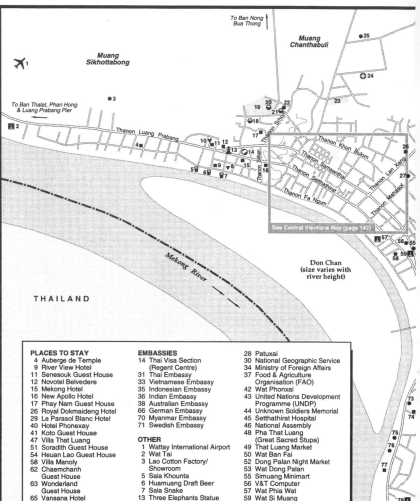

To Ban Nong Bua Thong

Muang Chanthabuli

Muang Sikhottabong

To Ban Thalat, Phan Hong & Luang Prabang Pier

Thanon Luang Prabang

Thanon Khun Bulom
Thanon Samsenthai
Thanon Setthathirat
Thanon Fa Ngum

See Central Vientiane Map (page 142)

Mekong River

THAILAND

Don Chan (size varies with river height)

PLACES TO STAY
4 Auberge de Temple
9 River View Hotel
11 Senesouk Guest House
12 Novotel Belvedere
15 Mekong Hotel
16 New Apollo Hotel
17 Phay Nam Guest House
26 Royal Dokmaideng Hotel
29 Le Parasol Blanc Hotel
40 Hotel Phonexay
41 Koto Guest House
47 Villa That Luang
51 Soradith Guest House
54 Heuan Lao Guest House
58 Villa Manoly
62 Chaemchanh
   Guest House
63 Wonderland
   Guest House
65 Vansana Hotel
74 Thieng Thong
   Guest House
77 Muang Lao-China Hotel

PLACES TO EAT
8 Bar Brasserie Anousone
10 Sakura Japanese
   Restaurant
32 Lao Residence
39 Nazim Restaurant
61 Nang Bunmala

EMBASSIES
14 Thai Visa Section
   (Regent Centre)
31 Thai Embassy
33 Vietnamese Embassy
35 Indonesian Embassy
36 Indian Embassy
38 Australian Embassy
66 German Embassy
70 Myanmar Embassy
71 Swedish Embassy

OTHER
1 Wattay International Airport
2 Wat Tai
3 Lao Cotton Factory/
   Showroom
5 Sala Khounta
6 Huamuang Draft Beer
7 Sala Snake
13 Three Elephants Statue
18 Buses to Luang Prabang
19 Talaat Laeng (Khua Luang)
20 Buses to the North
21 Senesabay Bus Co
22 Vientiane Theatre
   (Odeon Rama)
23 Thong Khan Kham Market
24 Hôpital de l'Amitié
25 National Circus
   (Hong Kanyasin)
27 Ministry of Interior

28 Patuxai
30 National Geographic Service
34 Ministry of Foreign Affairs
37 Food & Agriculture
   Organisation (FAO)
42 Wat Phonxai
43 United Nations Development
   Programme (UNDP)
44 Unknown Soldiers Memorial
45 Setthathirat Hospital
46 National Assembly
48 Pha That Luang
   (Great Sacred Stupa)
49 That Luang Market
50 Wat Ban Fai
52 Dong Palan Night Market
53 Wat Dong Palan
55 Simuang Minimart
56 V&T Computer
57 Wat Phia Wat
59 Wat Si Muang
60 Hospital 109
64 Water Tower
67 Wat Sok Pa Luang
68 Sokpaluang Swimming Pool
69 Hôpital de Medicine
   Traditionnelle
72 Wat Si Amphon
73 China Yunnan Airlines
75 Australian Club (AERC)
76 UNICEF
78 Wat Ammon

Vientiane

| 0 | 0.5 | 1 km |

To Xieng Khuan
& Tha Deua

towards the newly arrived expatriate who is setting up house in Vientiane, so not all of the information (eg hiring domestic staff, electrical repair) is useful for travellers who are just passing through. The guide costs US$12 and can be purchased at Raintrees, Phimphone Market and various other shops around the city.

INFORMATION
Tourist Office

The National Tourism Authority of Laos (NTAL) – also known as the Lao National Tourist Authority – maintains its national office (☎/fax 212013) on Thanon Lan Xang between Talaat Sao and the Patuxai. As an information source on where to go, or even on official tourism policy, this office is nearly worthless (see the Tourist Offices entry in the Facts for the Visitor chapter) and you're better off relying on this guidebook or on tourist information material which is available from various souvenir shops downtown.

The NTAL office is supposed to be open Monday to Friday from 8 am to 5 pm, but as in other government offices you'll rarely find anyone around between 11.30 am and 2.30 pm.

Foreign Embassies

See Foreign Embassies in Laos in the Facts for the Visitor chapter for a list of embassies in Vientiane.

Immigration

Vientiane's immigration office, on Thanon Hatsady near the Morning Market, is open Monday, Wednesday, Thursday, Friday and Saturday from 8 to 11.30 am and from 2 to 4.30 pm. If you need a visa extension, bring a couple of photocopies of the information page of your passport to speed up the process. Photos aren't necessary. Tourist visa extensions cost US$3 per day. You can usually obtain an extension while you wait, and if you get bored you can always make use of the Ping-Pong table at the back of the waiting room, but be sure to bring your own ball and paddles.

Money

La Banque pour le Commerce Extérieur Lao (BCEL; Lao Foreign Trade Bank) at Thanon Pangkham and Thanon Fa Ngum, near the Lane Xang Hotel, has the best foreign exchange rate of any bank in Vientiane. It's open from 8.30 am to 4.30 pm Monday to Friday, and until 11 am Saturday. Several other banks, mostly Thai, can be found along Thanon Lan Xang between Thanon Setthathirat and Thanon Saylom. Both BCEL and Thai Farmer's Bank (80/4 Thanon Lan Xang) can issue cash advances and debits for Visa and MasterCard.

Other banks equipped to handle foreign exchange include:

Bangkok Bank
    28/13-15 Thanon Hatsady
Bank of Ayudhya
    Thanon Lan Xang
Joint Development Bank
    31-33 Thanon Lan Xang
Krung Thai Bank
    Thanon Lan Xang
Nakhornluang Bank
    39 Thanon Pangkham
Siam Commercial Bank
    602/4-5 Thanon Nong Bon, east of Talaat Sao
    Thanon Samsenthai and Thanon Lan Xang
Thai Farmers Bank
    80/4 Thanon Lan Xang
Thai Military Bank
    69 Thanon Khun Bulom

Licensed moneychanging booths can also be found in Talaat Sao and a few other locations around town. The one opposite the Asian Pavilion Hotel on Thanon Samsenthai accepts Visa, travellers cheques and cash – for a sizeable commission. You can also change on the 'parallel market' at various shops in town for no commission or from the unofficial moneychangers hanging out near Talaat Sao. The latter usually offer the best rates in Vientiane but it helps to be on your toes as far as knowing what the going rates are; count your money carefully. See the Money section of the Facts for the Visitor chapter for details on exchange restrictions, bank accounts and credit/debit card cash advances.

Post

The Post, Telephone & Telegraph office (PTT) is on the corner of Thanon Lan Xang and Thanon Khu Vieng, across the road from Talaat Sao. Business hours are from 8 am to 5 pm Monday to Friday, till 4 pm Saturday and until noon Sunday.

Telephone & Fax

The PTT office is only for calls and faxes within Laos. Overseas calls and fax transmissions can be arranged at the Public Call Office on Thanon Setthathirat. It's open daily from 7.30 am to 10 pm. Fax services are available in a separate room in the same building from 7.30 am to 9.30 pm. There are also a couple of Cardphone booths right in front of the building; cards may be purchased inside or at the PTT office.

Local calls can be made from any hotel lobby – usually there is no charge. The area code for Vientiane is 21.

Couriers

International courier services in Vientiane include DHL Worldwide Express (☎ 216 830, 214868), 52 Thanon Nokeo Khumman; TNT Express Worldwide (☎/fax 214 361), 8/3 Thanon Lan Xang; and United Parcel Service (☎ 414392), 12/26 Thanon Nong Bon, Ban Nong Bon.

Travel Agencies

See the Organised Tours section in the Getting Around chapter for a list of authorised tour operators in Vientiane.

Bookshops

Vientiane does not offer much in the way of books in English. Laos' first and largest bookseller, Raintrees (☎ 213060), 52 Thanon Nokeo Khumman, stocks a selection of new and used paperbacks, guidebooks, magazines and other periodicals. Most of their stock is in English, though the shop also maintains smaller selections of French and German material. It is open Monday to Saturday from 8.30 am to 5 pm. Raintrees also has three smaller branches: 54/1 Thanon Pangkham (next to the THAI office); in the

Lao Hotel Plaza on Thanon Samsenthai; and in the Novotel Belvedere on Thanon Luang Prabang.

The State Book Shop on the north-east corner of Thanon Setthathirat and Thanon Manthatulat carries books and magazines in Lao and English, along with Lao handicrafts, political comic books and posters. According to the saleswoman, 'Lenin sells well; nobody buys Marx or Engels'. It's open Monday to Saturday from 8 to 11.30 am and 2 to 4.30 pm.

The gift shop at the Lane Xang Hotel has a few books in English for sale, and some rather expensive maps of Vientiane and Laos. Phimphone Market and Phimphone Minimart, on opposite sides of Thanon Samsenthai near the Hotel Ekalath Metropole, also sell a few English and French-language materials.

Cultural Centres

The Centre de Langue Française (☎ 215 764), on Thanon Lan Xang directly opposite the NTAL office, offers French and Lao language classes, weekly French films and has a small French library (open from Monday to Saturday).

The Russian Cultural Centre (☎ 212030) on the corner of Thanon Luang Prabang and Thanon Khun Bulom offers similar services oriented towards Russian language and culture.

Laundry

Most hotels and guesthouses offer laundry services. Several laundries and dry cleaners can be found in Vientiane's Chinatown area, especially along Thanon Heng Boun and Thanon Samsenthai just east of Thanon Chao Anou. Typical laundry rates run at about 500 kip per piece, and same-day service is usually available if you drop off your clothes in the morning.

Medical Services

Medical facilities in Vientiane are quite limited. The two state hospitals, Setthathirat (☎ 413783) and Mahasot (☎ 214018), operate at levels of skill and hygiene quite

below those available next door in Thailand. Mahasot Hospital has a Diplomatic Clinic (also called the International Clinic) 'especially for foreigners' that is open 24 hours, but the reality is that very few foreigners use this clinic. A friend hospitalised there with acute falciparum malaria was treated well – and she recovered fine.

The Australian embassy maintains a clinic that can treat minor problems for Australian residents (but not travellers).

The 150-bed Friendship Hospital, or Hôpital de l'Amitié (☎ 413306), is a centre for trauma and orthopaedics run by the Association Médicale Franco Asiatique (AMFA), and is located at the site of the old Soviet Hospital north of the city on the road to Tha Ngon. For emergencies you're supposed to be able to call for a radio-dispatched ambulance, but reports from Vientiane residents indicate this may not be a reliable procedure. At night the hospital is closed and locked, with no staff on duty.

Finally, there are Hospital 103 (☎ 312 127) and Hospital 109, military facilities on Thanon Sok Pa Luang and Thanon Khu Vieng respectively, which have reasonable reputations but rarely take foreigners.

If a medical problem can wait till you're in Bangkok, all the better, since there are some excellent hospitals available there. For medical emergencies, it is possible to arrange to have an ambulance summoned from nearby Udon Thani or Khon Kaen in Thailand, or to use the services of Lao West coast Helicopter. Look under the Health section in the Facts for the Visitor chapter for details.

Vientiane's better pharmacies are found on Thanon Nong Bon or Thanon Mahasot near Talaat Sao. Pharmacie Kamsaat (☎ 212 940, closed Sunday) and Pharmacie Sengthong Osoth (☎ 213732, open daily), both on Thanon Nong Bon in this vicinity, have a greater selection than most pharmacies in the city.

Traditional Medicine A state-sponsored traditional Lao medical clinic (Hong Maw Pin Pua Duay Yaa Pheun Meuang, or

Hôpital de Medicine Traditionnelle; ☎ 313 584) can be found in the Ban Wat Naak neighbourhood of Muang Sisattanak. The clinic offers herbal saunas (600 kip per visit) and traditional massage (600 kip for 15 minutes or 2500 kip for an hour) as well as acupuncture. Other than 'Ban Wat Naak', the clinic has no street address – see the Vientiane map for the location. If coming by jumbo, ask the driver to take you to Wat Si Amphon – it's a short walk from the latter (look for small red signs that read 'Hôpital de Medicine Traditionnelle').

Emergency

The six districts within Vientiane each have a police station, but you're unlikely to have contact with them unless you're involved in an accident. The emergency phone numbers below are supposed to summon immediate help:

Ambulance	☎ 195 or ☎ 13360
Fire	☎ 190
Police	☎ 191

Dangers & Annoyances

Vientiane has a very low crime rate, but the city is not as innocent as it might appear. We have heard a few reports of people having had a purse, shoulder bag or backpack snatched at night by teams of two men (presumed, by their appearance, to be Lao) riding on motorcycles.

The one location most of the reports had in common was the dark and relatively empty area near the Lao Revolutionary Museum – either on Thanon Samsenthai in front of the museum or on the two roads on either side of the open area across from the museum. As a precaution, avoid walking in this area late at night (say after 9 pm when the traffic thins out). If you rent a bicycle or motorbike, don't carry anything valuable in the basket, as this makes an easy target for the motorcycle thieves.

Vientiane has an unofficial curfew that's applied to all parts of the city outside the downtown area. Anyone out after midnight or so may be hassled by military types.

These incidents seem to be most common in the north-eastern and north-western edges of town; in the typical scenario, a foreigner or group of foreigners is stopped by two or three armed men – often not wearing a uniform – and firmly escorted back to their homes or hotels with no explanation. This kind of occurrence happens to foreign residents as well as to visiting foreigners. The expat grapevine suggests this is a public security force acting to 'protect' you from unsavoury elements that might be out and about. If you stick to well-trafficked areas after midnight you're unlikely to have such an encounter.

WAT SI SAKET

Less well-known by its full name, Wat Sisaketsata Sahatsaham, this temple sits opposite the Presidential Palace at the eastern corner of Thanon Lan Xang and Thanon Setthathirat. Built in 1818 by King Anouvong (Chao Anou), it is perhaps the oldest temple still standing in Vientiane – all the others were either built after Wat Si Saket or were rebuilt after destruction by the Siamese in 1828. King Anouvong, who was educated in the Bangkok court and was more or less a vassal of the Siamese state, had Wat Si Saket constructed in the early Bangkok style but surrounded it with a thick-walled cloister similar to – but much smaller than – the one that surrounds Pha That Luang.

The stylistic similarity to their own wats may have motivated the Siamese to spare this wat when they crushed King Anouvong's rebellion against Siamese rule. According to a new sign outside the temple, however, this temple *was* destroyed in 1828, and the current monastery was built in 1935. Whatever the truth is, the temple is a favoured spot for Lao art students making sketches.

In spite of the Siamese influence, Wat Si Saket has several unique features. The interior walls of the cloister are riddled with small niches that contain over 2000 silver and ceramic Buddha images. Over 300 seated and standing Buddhas of varying

Bone Shrines

Most wats in Laos contain at least a few *thâat kádụuk* (literally 'bone element' or 'bone stupa'), small stupa-shaped reliquaries containing the cremated remains – a mixture of ash and bone remnants – of temple-goers. Usually these will be erected in a line along the inside of a monastery wall, or sometimes scattered in a less orderly fashion in a wooded area within the wat compound. The construction of such thâat is usually commissioned by the deceased's family, sometimes well in advance of death but more typically afterward. A plaque on the front of the thâat will be inscribed with the dead person's name (*seu*), date of birth (*kpet*), death date (*mawrana*) and, for those who aren't good at maths, *lúam aanyu* or age at death. Following the death date, the inscriptions may also feature the day of the week and time of death.

A photo of the deceased is sometimes placed behind a glass pane and embedded in marble or cement above the inscription. Sometimes the ashes of more than one person may be kept inside – on occasion a whole family – in which case there's often a little wooden door with a padlock on it so that more ashes can be added later.

Relatives of the person whose remains are enshrined may drop by the wat at any time to pay their respects to the memory of the deceased by lighting candles and leaving flowers. *Wán pha*, the twice-monthly full moon and new moon worship days, are popular occasions for such visits. The Haw Khao Padap Din festival, held on the full moon day of August/September, is considered a particularly auspicious time to visit thâat kádụuk.

---

sizes and materials (wood, stone, silver and bronze) rest on long shelves below the niches, most of them sculpted or cast in the characteristic Lao style (see the Arts section in the Facts about Laos chapter for details on Lao religious sculpture). Most of the images are from 16th to 19th century Vientiane but a few hail from 15th to 16th century Luang Prabang. A slightly damaged Khmer-style Naga Buddha – in which the Buddha is seated on a coiled cobra deity whose multiheaded hood shelters the image – is also on display; it was brought from a Khmer site at nearby Hat Sai Fong. Along the western side of the cloister is a pile of broken and half-melted Buddhas from the 1828 Siamese-Lao war.

The *sim* (ordination hall) is surrounded by a colonnaded terrace in the Bangkok style and topped by a five-tiered roof. The interior walls bear hundreds of Buddha niches similar to those in the cloister, as well as beautiful – but decaying – *jataka* murals depicting the Buddha's life story. Portions of the Bangkok-style murals are unrestored 1820s originals, while others are a 1913 restoration. UNESCO announced it would fund a restoration in 1991 but so far the murals are still fading.

The flowered ceiling was inspired by Siamese temples in Ayuthaya, which were in turn inspired by floral designs from Versailles. At the rear interior of the sim is an altar with several Buddha images, bringing the total number of Buddhas at Wat Si Saket to 6840! The standing Buddha to the left on the upper altar is said to have been cast to the same physical proportions as King Anouvong. The large gilt wood candlestand in front of the altar is an original, carved in 1819.

On the veranda at the rear of the sim is a 5m-long wooden trough carved to resemble a *naga* or snake deity. This is the *láang song nâam pha* (image-watering rail), which is used during Pii Mai Lao (Lao New Year) to pour water over Buddha images for ritual cleansing.

To the far left of the entrance to the cloister, facing Thanon Lan Xang, is a raised

VIENTIANE

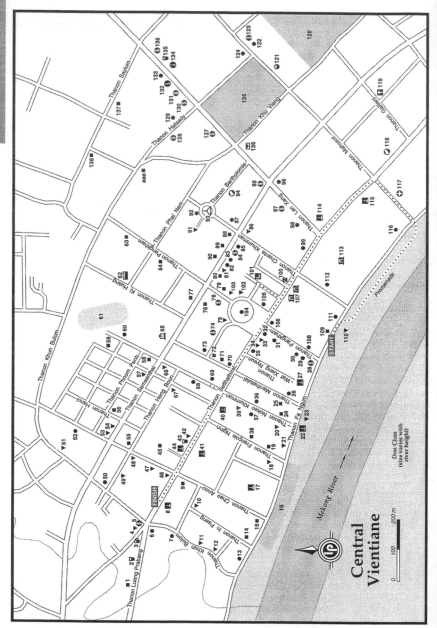

Central Vientiane

Mekong River

Promenade

Don Chan
(size varies with
river height)

0   100   200 m

PLACES TO STAY
1 Vientiane Hotel
9 Saysana Hotel
14 Phornthip Guest House
15 Inter Hotel
19 Tai-Pan Hotel
24 Douang Deuane Hotel
25 Samsenthai Hotel
38 Lao International Guest House
45 Lani I Guest House
55 Anou Hotel
56 Vannasinh Guest House
58 Santisouk Guest House & Restaurant
59 Syri Guest House
63 Belmont Settha Palace Hotel (Under Construction)
64 Day Inn Hotel
71 MIC Guest House
72 Phantavong Guest House
76 Settha Guest House
77 Lao Hotel Plaza
79 Pangkham Guest House
80 Lao-Paris Hotel
88 Hotel Ekalath Metropole; Phimphone Market
89 Asian Pavilion Hotel
90 Hua Guo Guest House
109 Lane Xang Hotel
137 Lani II Guest House
138 Lao Elysee Guest House
139 Saylomyen Guest House

PLACES TO EAT
4 Phikun Restaurant
10 Le Vendôme
11 Xang Coffee House
12 Nang Kham Bang
16 Night Market
18 Le Bistrot Snack Bar
20 Le Safran
21 Nazim Restaurant
23 John Reataurant
33 Healthy & Fresh Bakery & Eatery
34 Lo Stivale Deli Café

39 La Terrasse
42 Le Bayou Bar Brasserie
46 Nai Xieng Chai Yene; Guangdong Restaurant
47 Sweet Home & Liang Xiang Bakeries
48 Le Chanthy (Nang Janti)
49 Nang Suli & Vieng Sawan Restaurants
51 Vegetarian Food
53 Moey Chin
54 Samsenthai Fried Noodle
57 Phikun Restaurant
66 Uncle Fred's
67 Restaurant Ha-Wai
75 Scandinavian Bakery; Restaurant Le Provençal
81 PVO
86 Kua Lao
91 Soukvimane Lao Food
102 Restaurant-Bar Namphu; L'Opera Italian Restaurant
103 The Taj Restaurant
110 Salongxay Restaurant

TEMPLES
8 Wat In Paeng
17 Wat Chanthabuli
27 Wat Xieng Nyeun
40 Wat Mixai
41 Wat Ong Teu Mahawihan
44 Wat Hai Sok
114 Wat Si Saket
115 Haw Pha Kaew

OTHER
2 Win West Pub (Bane Saysana)
3 Shell Station
5 Thai Military Bank
6 Russian Cultural Centre
7 Couleur d'Asie
13 SODETOUR
22 Haw Kang (Chinese Shrine)
26 The Art of Silk

28 La Banque pour le Commerce Extérieur Lao (BCEL; Lao Foreign Trade Bank)
29 Thai Airways International
30 Raintrees Bookstore
31 Lane Xang Travel
32 Inter-Lao Tourisme
35 Lao Air Booking
36 Mixay Massage
37 Raintrees Bookstore
43 Samlo Pub
50 Maningom Supermarket
52 Vietnamese Association
60 Vientiane Tennis Club
61 National Stadium
62 Public Pool
65 Lao Revolutionary Museum
68 Lao Gallery
69 Lao Textiles
70 State Book Shop
73 IMF
74 Bank of Lao PDR
78 Nakhornluang Bank
82 Souvenir & Handicraft Shops
83 Vins de France
84 Money Exchange
85 Phimphone Minimart
87 Kanchana Boutique
92 Champa Gallery
93 That Dam ('Black Stupa')
94 US Embassy
95 Siam Commercial Bank
96 EDL (Électricité du Laos)
97 Krung Thai Bank
98 Ministry of Education
99 Ministry of Information and Culture
100 Public Call Office
101 Mosque
104 Fountain Circle
105 Diethelm Travel
106 National Library
107 Colonial Villas
108 Lao Aviation
111 Former National Treasury
112 Presidential Cabinet

An Architectural Walking Tour of Vientiane

This 1.6km walk will take you past some of the city's most historic attractions as well as a few lesser known spots of interest. Starting at the **Lane Xang Hotel**, Vientiane's premier hotel during the 1975-89 socialist era (and until 1994 its largest single source of foreign currency), begin strolling south-east along Thanon Fa Ngum parallel to the Mekong River. Almost immediately on your left stands a very large, rambling colonial-style administration building that served as the **National Treasury** until the revolution. The neglected and decaying structure holds great architectural potential; a Thai company supposedly has plans to develop the derelict building as a hotel.

On the opposite side of Thanon Fa Ngum, just east of the tourist-oriented Salongxay Restaurant, begins a modest, brick-paved **riverside promenade**. A few concrete benches offer support for the weary or the romantic and, during the rainy season, views of the river. During dry months the river recedes hundreds of metres towards Thailand and the emerging flood plains are planted with vegetable crops. Walking along the promenade, or along the pavement opposite, you'll pass two very old banyan trees and farther on over 25 tall, wide-girthed teak trees – each of them at least 200 years old – standing on either side of the street. A few coconut palms and acacias are mixed in. If you like banyans, turn the corner left onto Thanon Chanta Khumman, where you can't miss an extremely large banyan threatening to overturn a brick wall surrounding the ex-National Treasury.

Back on Thanon Fa Ngum heading south-east, on your left you'll see a high iron fence that surrounds the **Presidential Palace**, a vast Beaux Arts-style chateau originally built to house the French colonial governor. After independence King Sisavang Vong (and later his son Sisavang Vatthana) of Luang Prabang used it as a residence when visiting Vientiane. Since the banishment and death of the royal family in the late 1970s it has been used for hosting guests of the Lao government and for ceremonial government occasions. The Presidential Cabinet meets in a smaller building towards the north-western end of the compound. Neither building is open to the public. Next on the left, and housed in another old French colonial on Thanon Fa Ngum, is the headquarters for the **Lao Revolutionary Youth Union**, the Communist Party's equivalent of the Boy Scouts.

Starting near the foot of Thanon Mahasot and running along the riverbank opposite Mahosot Hospital, a string of vendors sell food and drinks beneath colourful umbrellas. Turn left at Thanon Mahasot and after one block turn left again onto Thanon Setthathirat; almost immediately on your left you'll come to the entrance for the **Haw Pha Kaew**, a former royal temple that now serves as a national museum for religious objects. It's the *hāw tại* (Tripitaka library) with a Burmese-style roof. The scriptures that were once contained here are now in Bangkok. Only one of the four doors is original: the other three were restored in 1913.

The grounds of the wat are planted with coconut, banana and mango trees, plus pots of bougainvillaea along the eastern wall of the wat. *Thâat kádụuk* – small stupa-shaped monuments containing the cremated remains of temple devotees – line the northern and western walls of the wat compound.

Wat Si Saket is open Tuesday to Sunday from 8 to 11.30 am and 2 to 4.30 pm, closed on public holidays; admission 500 kip. A Lao guide who speaks French and English is usually on hand to describe the temple and answer questions. There is no charge for the services of the guide.

HAW PHA KAEW

About 100m from Wat Si Saket, just down Thanon Setthathirat, is the former royal temple of the Lao monarchy, Haw Pha

---

only temple in Vientiane with a veranda around the entire perimeter of the building. Continuing north-west along Thanon Setthathirat, look for the ochre-painted **Wat Si Saket** on the opposite side of the street on your right. Considered the oldest surviving Buddhist monastery in Vientiane, Wat Si Saket contains many older Buddha figures and some fading temple murals.

Continue walking north-west along Thanon Setthathirat, past the northern side of the Presidential Palace and across Thanon Chanta Khumman. On your left you will pass two sizeable **former French colonial homes** that have been used on and off by various commercial concerns as offices since 1989. These are among the best restored two-storey colonials you'll see in central Vientiane (to see five more restored colonial homes nearby, make a detour north to Thanon Samsenthai between Thanon Chanta Khumman and Thanon Lane Xang). Farther along, on the opposite side of the street, an alley leads not quite a hundred metres to the **Jamé Mosque**, a pseudo-Moghul prayer hall where you can hear the daily calls to prayer in Tamil, Arabic, Lao and English.

A little farther ahead on the corner of Thanon Pangkham and Thanon Setthathirat stands the French-built and recently French-restored **National Library**. The large **fountain** or *nâam phu* diagonally opposite is partially surrounded by restored colonial shophouses now housing the Vietnamese Cultural Centre, Restaurant-Bar Namphu, and other businesses. The tall abandoned building looming over the fountain's west side was

once the French Cultural Centre. The top three floors were reportedly never used, as the building had no lift. Vientiane's original Morning Market once flanked Thanon Pangkham north of the fountain. The former market area is now occupied by newer shophouses, several of them tailoring businesses.

Thanon Setthathirat continues north-west into the heart of central Vientiane's temple district. Along the way, turn right onto Thanon Nokeo Khumman and walk a few dozen metres to **Lao Textiles**, housed in another well-restored colonial home. Back on Thanon Setthathirat, a short walk north-east will take you past four of central Vientiane's major wats: **Wat Mixai**, **Wat Ong Teu**, **Wat Hai Sok** and **Wat In Paeng**.

JULIET COOMBE\LA BELLE AURORE

A guardian giant or *nyak* at Wat Mixai

Kaew. It has been converted into a museum and is no longer a place of worship.

According to the Lao, the temple was originally built in 1565 by command of King Setthathirat. Setthathirat had been a ruler of the nearby Lanna Kingdom in northern Thailand while his father King Phothisarat reigned over Lan Xang. After his father died, he inherited the Lan Xang throne and moved the capital of Lan Xang to Vientiane. From Lanna he brought with him the so-called Emerald Buddha (Pha Kaew in Lao, which means Jewel Buddha Image – the image is actually made of a type of jade). Wat Pha Kaew was built to house this image and to serve as the King's personal place of worship. Following a skirmish with the Lao in 1779, the Siamese stole the Emerald Buddha and installed it in Bangkok's own Wat Phra Kaew (Phra is the Thai word for Buddha image; Pha is Lao). Later, during the Siamese-Lao war of 1828, Vientiane's Wat Pha Kaew was razed.

Between 1936 and 1942, the temple was rebuilt, supposedly following the original plan exactly. Herein lies the problem in dating the original temple. If the currently standing structure was restored in the original style, it doesn't seem likely that the original could have been built in the mid-16th century, as it doesn't resemble any known structure in Siam, Laos, Myanmar or Cambodia from that period. In fact it looks very much like a 19th century Bangkok-style sim. On the other hand, if the restoration's architects chose to use the more common 19th century style (as exemplified by Wat Si Saket) because they didn't have the original plans after all, then it's possible the original was constructed in 1565 as claimed (if it wasn't, it casts the whole Emerald Buddha story into doubt).

At any rate, today's Haw Pha Kaew (Hall of the Jewel Buddha Image) is not particularly impressive, except in size. The rococo ornamentation that runs up and down every door, window and base looks unfinished. But some of the best examples of Buddhist sculpture found in Laos are kept here, so it's worth visiting for that reason alone. A dozen or so

prominent sculptures are displayed along the surrounding terrace. These include a 6th to 9th century Dvaravati-style stone Buddha; several bronze standing and sitting Lao-style Buddhas – including the 'Calling for Rain' (standing with hands at his sides), 'Offering Protection' (palms stretched out in front) and 'Contemplating the Tree of Enlightenment' (hands crossed at the wrist in front) poses; and a collection of inscribed Lao and Mon stelae. Most of the Lao bronzes are missing their *usnisa* or flame finial.

Inside the sim are royal requisites such as a gilded throne, more Buddhist sculpture (mostly smaller pieces, including a wooden copy of the Pha Bang, the original of which is in Luang Prabang), some Khmer stelae, various wooden carvings (candlestands, door panels, lintels), palm-leaf manuscripts and bronze frog drums. A bronze 'Calling for Rain' Buddha, tall and lithe, is particularly beautiful; also unique is a 17th century Vientiane-style bronze Buddha in the 'European pose', ie with the legs hanging down as if seated on a chair or bench.

A stone Khmer Buddha, a marble Mandalay Buddha and several other figures stand at the front altar. Visiting Thais worship here and, although the place is no longer used as a wat, they lay offerings of money on a small platform atop the wooden naga image (from Xieng Khuang) after worship.

The sim is surrounded by a nicely landscaped garden. At the back of the building is a large reconstructed stone jar from Xieng Khuang's Plain of Jars.

Haw Pha Kaew is open Tuesday to Sunday from 8 to 11.30 am and from 2 to 4.30 pm, and is closed Monday and public holidays; admission is 500 kip. A French and English-speaking guide is occasionally available.

WAT ONG TEU MAHAWIHAN

Called Wat Ong Teu (Temple of the Heavy Buddha) for short, this temple is one of the most important in all of Laos. It was originally built in the mid-16th century by King Setthathirat and as such is a contemporary

continued on page 150

PHA THAT LUANG

Pha That Luang (Great Sacred Reliquary or Great Stupa) is the most important national monument in Laos, a symbol of both the Buddhist religion and Lao sovereignty. Its full official name, Pha Jedi Lokajulamani, means World-Precious Sacred Stupa, and an image of the main stupa appears on the national seal. Legend has it that Ashokan missionaries from India erected a *thâat* or reliquary stupa here to enclose a breastbone of the Buddha as early as the 3rd century BC, but there is no evidence to confirm this. However, excavations suggest that a Khmer monastery may have been built near here between the 11th and 13th centuries AD.

When King Setthathirat moved the Lan Xang capital from Luang Prabang to Vientiane in the mid-16th century, he ordered the construction of That Luang in its current form on the site of the Khmer temple. Construction began in 1566 AD and in succeeding years four wats were built around the stupa, one on each side. Only two remain today, Wat That Luang Neua to the north and Wat That Luang Tai to the south. Wat That Luang Neua is the residence of the Supreme Patriarch (Pha Sangkhalat) of Lao Buddhism. The main building, in its present form, is a reconstruction from the early years of this century.

The monument looks almost like a missile cluster from a distance. Surrounding it is a high-walled cloister with tiny windows, added by King Anouvong in the early 19th century as a defence against invaders. Even more aggressive looking than the thick walls are the pointed stupas themselves, which are built in three levels. From a closer perspective, however, the Great Stupa opens up and looks much more like a religious monument.

The neglected and overgrown Pha That Luang, seen here as it looked in the middle of last century, when Louis Delaporte visited.

An aerial plan shows the rigid geometry of Laos' national symbol; the encircling cloister contains various Buddha images.

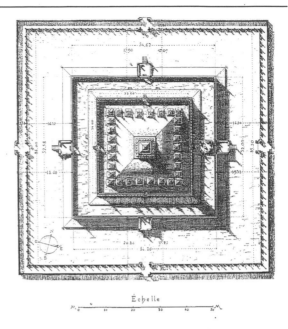

Échelle

The Great Stupa is designed to be mounted by the faithful, so there are walkways around each level, with stairways between. Each level of the monument has different architectural features in which Buddhist doctrine is encoded; visitors are supposed to contemplate the meaning of these features as they walk round. The first level is a square base measuring 68m by 69m that supports 323 *sima* (ordination stones). There are also four arched *haw wái* (prayer gates), one on each side, with short stairways leading up to and beyond them to the second level. The second level is 48m by 48m and is surrounded by 120 lotus petals. There are 288 simas on this level, as well as 30 small stupas symbolising the 30 Buddhist perfections *(pálamíi sãam-síp thàat)*, beginning with alms-giving and ending with equanimity. These stupas at one time contained smaller gold stupas and gold leaves, but these were taken by Chinese bandits while That Luang was abandoned in the 19th century.

Arched gates again lead to the next level, which is 30m along each side. The tall central stupa, which has a brick core that has been stuccoed over, is supported here by a bowl-shaped base reminiscent of India's first Buddhist stupa at Sanchi. At the top of this mound the superstructure, surrounded by lotus petals, begins.

The curvilinear, four-sided spire resembles an elongated lotus bud and is said to symbolise the growth of a lotus from a seed in a muddy lake bottom to a bloom over the lake's surface, a

metaphor for human advancement from ignorance to enlightenment in Buddhism. The stupa is crowned by a stylised banana
flower and parasol; the entire thâat was regilded in 1995 to celebrate the LPDR's 20th anniversary. From ground to pinnacle, That
Luang measures 45m tall.

The encircling cloister (85m on each side) contains various
Buddha images. Both classic Lao sculpture and Khmer figures are
displayed on either side of the front entrance (inside). Worshippers
sometimes stick balls of rice to the walls (especially during the That
Luang Festival) to pay their respects to the spirit of King Setthathirat.

In 1641, Gerrit van Wuystoff, an envoy of the Dutch East Indies
Company, visited Vientiane and was received by King Sulinya
Vongsa at That Luang in a reportedly magnificent ceremony. The
Lan Xang Kingdom was at the peak of its glory and Van Wuystoff
wrote that he was deeply impressed by the 'enormous pyramid,
the top of which was covered with gold leaf weighing about a thousand pounds'.

Unfortunately, the glory of Lan Xang and That Luang was only
to last another 60 years or so. The stupa and the temples were
damaged considerably during the 18th and 19th centuries by
invading Burmese and Siamese armies. During a Siamese invasion in 1828, Vientiane was ransacked and depopulated to such
an extent that That Luang remained abandoned until it was badly
restored under French rule in 1900.

Thirty-three years prior to the restoration of 1900, the French
explorer and architect Louis Delaporte had stumbled on the abandoned and overgrown That Luang and made a number of detailed
sketches of the monument. Between 1931 and 1935, a French university department reconstructed That Luang according to Delaporte's sketches. Or so say the French; the Lao today claim the
French carried out the reconstruction because they didn't like the
way their predecessors had botched the job in 1900. Records to
confirm or refute either story are somewhat scarce, though a 1910
report says detractors of the original French restoration called the
angular, modern central stupa the 'Morin spike' after its designer.
The 1931-35 restoration replaced the Morin spike with the original
Lao-style lotus-bud shape as depicted in Delaporte's sketches.

Pha That Luang is about 4km north-east of the centre of
Vientiane at the end of Thanon That Luang. Facing the compound
is a statue of King Setthathirat.

A small booklet on the temple's history costs 200 kip at the
entrance. A well-illustrated, 56 page book (in French) called *Le
That Luang de Vientiane* has a history and description of the monument, and is available at the *Vientiane Times* office on Thanon
Pangkham and at the State Book Shop for 5800 kip.

The temple is the site of a major festival in early November; see
the Festivals section later in this chapter.

Pha That Luang is open to visitors from Tuesday to Sunday
from 8 to 11.30 am and 2 to 4.30 pm, closed Monday and public
holidays. Admission is 500 kip per person.

continued from page 146

of Pha That Luang, but like every temple in Vientiane except possibly Wat Si Saket, it was destroyed in later wars with the Siamese, then rebuilt in the 19th and 20th centuries. The Hawng Sangkhalat (Deputy Patriarch) of the Lao monastic order has his official residence at Wat Ong Teu and presides over the Buddhist Institute, a school for monks who come from all over the country to study *dhamma* in the capital.

The temple's namesake is a large 16th century bronze Buddha of several tonnes that sits in the rear of the sim, flanked by two standing Buddhas. This sim is deservedly famous for the wooden façade over the front terrace, a masterpiece of Lao carving. The carved wooden window shutters are also impressive.

Wat Ong Teu is on a shady stretch of Thanon Setthathirat between Thanon Chao Anou and Thanon François Nginn.

WAT HAI SOK

Across Thanon Setthathirat from Wat Ong Teu is the less acclaimed Wat Hai Sok, which recently underwent restoration. It's worth a quick look because of the impressive five-tiered roof (nine if you count the lower terrace roofs), which is topped by an elaborate set of *nyâwt jâo fâa* (roof-ridge spires).

WAT MIXAI

Wat Mixai is in the next block east from Wat Ong Teu and Wat Hai Sok, on the same street. The sim is in the Bangkok style, with a surrounding veranda. The heavy gates, flanked by two *nyak* (guardian giants), are also Bangkok style. An elementary school shares the compound.

WAT IN PAENG

A rough translation of this monastery's name is 'Assembled by Indra', a tribute to the artistry displayed in the sim's stucco relief. Over the front veranda gable hangs an impressive wood and mosaic façade. The temple occupies the block west of Wat Ong Teu.

WAT CHANTHABULI (WAT CHAN)

This wat is on Thanon Fa Ngum near the river, a block south of Wat Ong Teu. The carved wooden panels on the rebuilt sim are typically Lao and well executed. Inside the sim is a large bronze seated Buddha from the original temple that stood on this site (the Buddha was never moved). In the courtyard are the remains of a stupa that once had Buddha images in the 'Calling for Rain' pose on all four sides; one image remains.

WAT SI MUANG

These temple grounds – the most frequently used in all of Vientiane – are the site of the *lák meúang* (city pillar/phallus) and are considered the home of the guardian spirit of Vientiane. Legend has it that the spot was selected in 1563 as the site for a new wat by a group of sages when King Setthathirat moved his capital to Vientiane. Once the spot was chosen, a large hole was dug to receive the heavy stone pillar (probably taken from an ancient Khmer site nearby), which was suspended over the hole with ropes. Drums and gongs were sounded to summon the townspeople to the area and everyone waited for a volunteer to jump in the hole as a sacrifice to the spirit. A pregnant woman finally leapt in and the ropes were released, establishing the town guardianship. Some people mistakenly believe the name of the wat is somehow related to the name of the legendary human sacrifice, but in fact *wat sīi meúang* simply means 'holy city monastery' in Pali-Lao.

The sim (destroyed in 1828 and rebuilt in 1915) was constructed around the lák meúang, which forms the centre of the altar. The stone pillar is wrapped in sacred cloth, and in front of it is a carved wooden stele with a seated Buddha in relief. The stele is wrapped in blinking red and green lights.

Several other Buddha images surround the pillar. One worth noting is kept on a cushion a little to the left and in front of the altar. The rather crude, partially damaged stone Buddha survived the 1828 destruction in one of the original thâat (stupa) in the wat grounds. The locals believe this image has the power to grant wishes or answer troubling questions – the practice is to lift the image off the pillow three times (alternatively two sets of three) while mentally phrasing a question or request. If your request is granted, then you are supposed to return to Wat Si Muang at a later date with an offering of bananas, young coconuts, flowers, incense and candles (usually two of each). This is why so many platters of fruit, flowers and incense are sitting around the sim!

Behind the sim is a crumbling laterite *jedi* (stupa), probably of Khmer origin. Devotees deposit broken deity images and pottery around the jedi's base in the belief that the spirits of the jedi will 'heal' the bad luck created by the breaking of these items. In front of the sim is a little public park with an unlabelled statue of King Sisavang Vong (1904-59) – the identifying plaque taken off after the 1975 Revolution. In his hand, the king holds a palm-leaf manuscript representing the country's first legal code.

Wat Si Muang is located at a three-way intersection where Thanon Setthathirat and Thanon Samsenthai converge to become Thanon Tha Deua.

WAT SOK PA LUANG

Wat Mahaphutthawongsa Pa Luang Pa Yai is the full name for this *wat paa* (forest temple) in south Vientiane's Sisattanak district. It's famous for its herbal saunas, which are usually administered by lay people who reside at the temple. The small sauna hut sits on a platform. After the relaxing sauna, you can take herbal tea on the veranda while cooling off; expert massage is also available. For optimum medicinal results you're not supposed to wash away your accumulated perspiration for two or three hours afterwards. Apparently this allows the herbs to soak into your pores. The temple charges 1000 kip for use of the sauna, 3000 kip for a 40 minute massage. Nearby **Wat Si Amphon** also does herbal saunas (see the Getting There & Away section following).

Wat Sok Pa Luang is known for its course of instruction in *vipassana*, which is a type

of Buddhist meditation that involves careful mind-body analysis. The abbot and teacher is Ajaan Sali Kantasilo, who was born in Yasothon, Thailand, in 1932. Ajaan Sali came to Laos in 1953 at the request of monks and laity in Vientiane who wanted to study vipassana. He accepts foreign students but only speaks Lao and Thai, so interested people will have to arrange for an interpreter if they don't speak either of these languages. Before 1975 he had many western students; since then he's taught only Lao followers and a small trickle of interested westerners (look under Vipassana Meditation in the Activities section later in this chapter).

Getting There & Away

Taxi, jumbo and tuk-tuk drivers all know how to get to Wat Sok Pa Luang. If you're travelling by car or bicycle, take Thanon Khu Vieng south past Talaat Sao for about 2.5km until you come to a fairly major road on the left (this is Thanon Sok Pa Luang, but it's unmarked). Turn left here; the entrance to the wat is about 500m on the left. The temple buildings are back in the woods so all you can see from the road is the tall, ornamented gate.

Wat Si Amphon is farther south off Thanon Si Amphon. A few hundred metres past Thanon Sok Pa Luang, turn right on Thanon Si Amphon; Wat Si Amphon is on the left.

THAT DAM

The so-called 'Black Stupa' or That Dam is on Thanon Bartholomie, between the Hotel Ekalath Metropole and the US embassy. Local mythology says the stupa is the abode of a dormant seven-headed dragon that came to life during the 1828 Siamese-Lao war and protected local citizens. The stupa appears to date from the Lanna or early Lan Xang period and is very similar to stupas in Chiang Saen, Thailand. Until recently That Dam was overgrown with weeds sprouting through cracks in its brick and stucco structure; a 1995 renovation sealed the cracks but it still looks old and atmospheric.

XIENG KHUAN

Often called 'Buddha Park' (Suan Phut), this collection of Buddhist (and Hindu) sculpture lies in a meadow by the side of the Mekong River 24km south of the town centre off Thanon Tha Deua.

The park was designed and built in 1958 by Luang Pu (Venerable Grandfather) Bunleua Sulilat, a yogi-priest-shaman who merged Hindu and Buddhist philosophy, mythology and iconography into a cryptic whole. He developed a very large following in Laos and north-eastern Thailand, and moved to Thailand around the time of the 1975 Revolution. In 1978, he established the similarly inspired Wat Khaek in Nong Khai, Thailand, where he now resides. Originally, Bunleua is supposed to have studied under a Hindu *rishi* (sage) who lived in Vietnam. According to legend he was walking in the mountains when he fell through a sinkhole and landed in the rishi's lap! He remained in the cave, called Kaew Ku (Jewel Grotto), for several years.

The concrete sculptures at Xieng Khuan (Spirit City) are bizarre but compelling in their naive confidence. They includes statues of Shiva, Vishnu, Arjuna, Buddha and every other Hindu or Buddhist deity imaginable, as well as a few secular figures, all supposedly cast by unskilled artists under Luang Pu's direction. The style of the figures is remarkably uniform. Children will enjoy cavorting around some of the more fantastic shapes, such as the deity with tentacles.

There is one building on the grounds, a large pumpkin-shaped concrete monument with three levels joined by interior spiral stairways. It is said that the three levels represent hell, earth and heaven. The rooms on the inside have been filled with small sculptures and are designed so that you can either enter them for viewing or merely look in through windows from an outer hallway at each level. The last spiral stairway leads onto the top of the structure, from where you can view the gigantic sculptures outside.

A few food vendors in the park offer fresh coconuts, soft drinks, beer, *pîng kai*

(grilled chicken) and *tạm màak-hung* (spicy green papaya salad).

Since Luang Pu abandoned the site, the municipality has turned it into a public park. It's open daily from 7.30 am to 6 pm; entry is 800 kip, plus 400 kip for cameras, 600 kip for camcorders.

Getting There & Away

To reach Xieng Khuan by bus take Nos 14 or 49, which leave Talaat Sao terminal every 40 minutes or so throughout the day for 600 kip per person. Alternatively, a chartered jumbo costs around 5000 kip one way, 8000 kip return. Or hop on a shared jumbo (800 kip) as far as the ferry pier at Tha Deua and then walk or take a samlor for the final 4km to the park. You could also pedal a bicycle here fairly easily – assuming you don't find 24km a daunting distance – as the road is relatively flat all the way.

PATUXAI

The Patuxai, a large monument reminiscent of the Arc de Triomphe in Paris, is known by a variety of names. The official Lao name, Patuxai, is approximately equivalent to Arch (*pátuu*, also translated as door or gate) of Triumph (*xái*, from the Sanskrit *jaya* or victory). Begun in the early 1960s, it was finished in 1969 with US-purchased cement that was supposed to have been used for the construction of a new airport. Hence residents sometimes refer to it as 'the vertical runway'.

Since its purpose was to commemorate the Lao who had died in pre-Revolutionary wars, current Lao maps typically label it 'Old Monument' in contrast to the newer Unknown Soldiers Memorial.

Whatever you call it, this huge arch at the end of Thanon Lan Xang is within walking distance of the town centre and is worth a quick visit if the weather's agreeable. From a distance, it looks very much like its French source of inspiration. Up close, however, the Lao design starts to come out. The bas-relief on the sides and the temple-like ornamentation along the top and cornices are typically Lao. A stairway leads to the top levels of the monument, where for a 200 kip fee you can look out over the city. The stairs are open daily from 8 am to 5 pm.

LAO REVOLUTIONARY MUSEUM

The Lao Revolutionary Museum (Phiphittaphan Patiwat Lao) is housed in a well-worn mansion on Thanon Samsenthai. Originally built in 1925 as the French governor's residence, in independent Laos the building has been used as a royal residence, a state guesthouse and as various ministerial offices before becoming a museum in 1985. For the most part, the museum contains artefacts and photos from the Pathet Lao's lengthy struggle for power. Many of the displays consist of historic weaponry; some labels are in English as well as Lao.

The rooms near the entrance feature small cultural and geographical exhibits, as if these were incidental to the Revolution rather than vice versa. The more interesting items include several Khmer sandstone sculptures of Hindu deities and a display of traditional musical instruments.

Inner rooms are dedicated to the 1893-1945 French colonial period, the 1945-54 struggle for independence, the 1954-63 resistance to American imperialism, the 1964-69 provisional government and the 1975 Communist victory. Labels often employ the 'capitalist running dog'-style vocabulary commonly used by Asian Communists; a picture of a road crew tamping earth during the French era is labelled 'barbarous slavery'.

No mention is made of the thousands of Vietnamese troops who occupied eastern Laos during the Indochinese War, although in one room a bust of Ho Chi Minh stands next to one of Lenin. An interesting diorama of the Pathet Lao caves at Vieng Xai is labelled in Lao only. One of the more curious items on display is a chest expander, enshrined in a glass cabinet, used by Kaysone Phomvihane 'in the gymnastic session during the elaboration of the plan to seize power'.

Posted hours (which are not scrupulously followed) for the museum are from 8 to 11.30 am and 2 to 4.30 pm weekdays; entry is 200 kip.

UNKNOWN SOLDIERS MEMORIAL

This white thâat-like structure was built to commemorate the Pathet Lao who died during the 1964-73 War of Resistance. It's north of Pha That Luang off Thanon Phon Kheng.

KAYSONE PHOMVIHANE MEMORIAL & MUSEUM

Opened in late 1995 to celebrate the late president's 75th birthday, this new facility serves as a tribute to Indochina's most pragmatic Communist leader. It's worth visiting only if you are interested in the history of the Lao revolution. A bronze bust of Kaysone, fashioned by a North Korean sculptor, stands in the central entrance hall, around which the various exhibiting rooms are arranged. The first room displays pictures of Laos' most important cultural and historic sites. Another contains a mock-up of Kaysone's childhood home in Ban Na Seng, Savannakhet Province, while another exhibit evokes his youth and includes a desk from the French school he attended at Ban Tai, surmounted by family pictures.

Other exhibits of historic photography and minor artefacts chronicle the founding of the Lao Issara and the Indochinese Communist Party. A model of a portion of 'Kaysone Cave' in Hua Phan Province contains a revolver, binoculars, radio and other personal effects; given the difficulties in receiving permission to view the real thing in Vieng Xai, this may be your only chance to see what it looks like. This is followed by minor exhibits covering events in the 1950s and 1960s, ending with a summary of the 1975 Revolution and subsequent nation-building.

The museum-memorial is inside the former USAID/CIA compound off Route 13 south near Km 6. The self-contained headquarters that Americans called 'Six Clicks City' (and less commonly 'Silver City') once featured bars, restaurants, tennis courts, swimming pools, a commissary and assorted offices from where the Secret War was orchestrated. During the 1975 takeover of Vientiane, the Pathet Lao forces ejected the Americans and occupied the compound themselves. Kaysone lived here until his death in 1992. If you're coming by private transport, turn left about 300m before the new Children's Home; follow the road for about 300m and turn left again just before the gate to the army post. Follow this road for 800m; you'll round a curve to the right and then see the museum (signed 'Area of Memorial Museum of Former President Kaysone Phomvihane') on your right. It's open daily, except Monday and holidays, from 8 to 11.30 am and 2 to 4.30 pm; admission is 200 kip.

NATIONAL ETHNIC CULTURAL PARK
This relatively new facility on the Mekong River at Km 18, Thanon Tha Deua, has yet to live up to its name. So far the only attractions are a small zoo with monkeys, bears and birds, a children's playground, statues of dinosaurs, a few souvenir shops and a long-distance view of the Friendship Bridge.

A stage occasionally hosts cultural shows. Lao-style buildings under construction will one day contain exhibits on Lao culture. Kids would probably like this place in spite of its obvious shortcomings. It's open daily 8 am to 6 pm; 500 kip entry.

DONG DOK UNIVERSITY
Travellers who'd like to meet Lao university students might want to visit Dong Dok University, known as Sisavangvong University before the 1975 Revolution. It's about 9km north of the city off the road to Tha Ngon (Route 10). Students at the university's Foreign Language Institute are usually delighted to meet someone who speaks the language they're studying (Vietnamese, French, Japanese and English are common languages of study).

ACTIVITIES
Swimming Pools
There are now several places in Vientiane where you can work on your strokes or simply take a cooling dip. Sokpaluang Swimming Pool on Thanon Sok Pa Luang in south-eastern Vientiane offers a large

pool with marked swimming lanes, a shallow kids' pool, a snack bar with Lao and *falang* (foreign, usually western) food, and lockers and changing rooms for the reasonable rate of 1500 kip per person per day. It's open daily from 9 am to 8 pm.

Not far from the south-east corner of the National Stadium is a public pool open from Tuesday to Sunday that costs only 500 kip a day, but cleanliness is not always up to par; most of the girls who swim here wear their street clothes rather than bathing suits (at the Sokpaluang pool, these are compulsory).

The simple, clean pool at the Royal Dokmaideng Hotel on Thanon Lan Xang is open to the public for US$2.50 per visit. The kidney-shaped swimming pool (and pool bar) at the Lane Xang Hotel may be used by non-guests for US$2 per day. The Novotel and Lao Hotel Plaza pools are also open to non-guests for a steep US$5 per visit.

See also Recreation Clubs, under Entertainment, in this chapter for information on the pool at the Australian Embassy Recreation Club (AERC).

Tennis & Squash
The Vientiane Tennis Club, just next to the National Stadium off Thanon Samsenthai, has three decent illuminated courts available to members only. Memberships cost 1000 kip per month (plus a 3000 kip application fee), plus 500 kip for 45 minutes of playing time. Foreigners may apply but memberships are limited.

The AERC maintains a squash court which is open to members only. See Recreation Clubs under Entertainment for more details.

Table Tennis
The Vietnamese Association of Vientiane, at 167 Thanon Chao Anou, has a Ping-Pong table that is open to the general public. Even if you're not excited by table tennis you might be interested in the building, a Franco-Chinese mansion – complete with Chinese stucco relief – constructed in 1933.

VIENTIANE

Golf
The Santisuk Lane Xang Golf Club (☎ 812022) at Km 14, Thanon Tha Deua, offers a 2800 yard, nine hole course, par 35. It's open to the public and green fees are a reasonable 7000 kip to 9000 kip, plus a 3000 kip caddie fee. Open from 7 am to 6 pm; no flip-flops (thongs) allowed.

The Vientiane Golf Club (☎ (020) 515 820) at Km 6, south along Route 13, is a members-only club with a fair nine hole course, clubhouse and pro shop.

Exercise
The AERC holds three types of exercise classes for members: step and water aerobics as well as regular aerobics. The notice board at the AERC has dates and times. See Recreation Clubs under Entertainment for details.

Non-guests may use the sauna and fitness room at the Tai-Pan Hotel for US$4 per visit. L'Arlequin, in the Si Muang area, has aerobics and African dance classes. Call Muriel (☎ 215594) or Laurence (☎ 217627) for more information.

Massage/Sauna
Mixay Massage (☎ 213576) on Thanon Nokeo Khumman is a legitimate massage clinic. It's open daily from 2 to 9 pm; a Lao massage costs US$5 per hour.

See the entry on Wat Sok Pa Luang earlier in this chapter for a description of massage and sauna possibilities there. Also see Traditional Medicine under Medical Services for information on massage at Hong Maw Pin Pua Duay Yaa Pheun Meuang.

Hash House Harriers
This is one expat organisation that doesn't charge a membership fee. The Vientiane Harriers have a blackboard at the AERC (see Recreation Clubs in the Entertainment section) which announces the location of the weekly hash run, held every Monday at 5.30 pm (5 pm December to February). Postings may also be seen at the Fountain Circle, Scandinavian Bakery, Tai-Pan Hotel and at Phimphone Market. To participate in the 4km to 5km race, you contribute US$5,

which pays for the beer, soft drinks and food at the end of the run. Newcomers are usually coerced into downing quite a lot of Beerlao.

A second club known as the Vientiane Bush Hash meets every Saturday at 4 pm at the Fountain Circle, where transport is provided to a 'bush' site outside the city for a more challenging race.

Language Courses
See Courses in the Facts for the Visitor chapter for details on Vientiane language schools which teach Lao.

Vipassana Meditation
On Saturday from 4 to 5 pm, the Buddhist abbot Ajaan Sali and nun Mae Kakeo lead an hour of sitting and walking meditation at Wat Sok Pa Luang. The session is held in a small pavilion (to the left of the sim) and garden dedicated to Ajaan Paan, the previous abbot. All are welcome – about half the participants are Lao, the other half foreigners – and there is no charge. A question period occurs after the meditation session when there's someone around to translate.

Twice a year, once in February or March and again in September or October, Ajaan Sali holds intensive meditation workshops at the monastery.

Festivals
If you happen to be in Vientiane in early November, don't miss the That Luang Festival (Bun That Luang), the largest temple fair in Laos. Along with religious fervour comes a trade show and a number of carnival games. The festivities begin with a *wíen thíen* (circumambulation) around Wat Si Muang, followed by a procession to Pha That Luang, which is illuminated all night for a week or so. The festival climaxes on the morning of the full moon with the *tàak bàat* ceremony, in which several thousand monks from across the country receive food alms from Lao Buddhists. That evening there's a final *wíen thíen* around Pha That Luang, when devotees carry *paasàat*, miniature temples made from banana stems and decorated with flowers and other offerings.

Fireworks cap off the evening and everyone makes merit or merry till dawn.

Another huge annual event is Bun Nam or River Festival at the end of Phansaa in October, during which boat races are held on the Mekong River. Rowing teams from all over the country as well as Thailand, China and Myanmar compete, and Vientiane's riverbank is lined with food stalls, temporary discos, carnival games and beer gardens for three nights.

PLACES TO STAY

Vientiane has a choice of over 60 hotels and guesthouses to accommodate all of the tourists, travellers, business people, spies and other visitors who come to town.

Many hotels and guesthouses in Vientiane quote US dollar or Thai baht rates and some of the more expensive require payment in US currency, despite a 'ban' on currencies other than kip. At less expensive places you can usually pay with any of the three currencies, though if the rate is established in dollars or baht and you want to pay in kip you'll be at the mercy of the management's sometimes arbitrary exchange rate. All offer 5% to 20% discounts for long-term stays. The difference between a 'guesthouse' and a 'hotel' is the array of services provided; the former don't usually have dining rooms or bars.

PLACES TO STAY – BUDGET

Over the last couple of years the selection of budget-priced accommodation in Vientiane has broadened considerably, making the city a relatively inexpensive place to spend a few days or weeks.

Guesthouses

The multistorey *Ministry of Information & Culture (MIC) Guest House* (☎ 212362), 67 Thanon Manthatulat, is still the cheapest place in town. Large, three-bed rooms with fan cost 9000 kip per person, all with attached toilet/bath; add 3000 kip for air-con. Rates are payable in kip, baht or dollars. The rooms are reasonably clean and it's good value if you share with others. MIC also offers laundry and visa extension services. There's a small coffee shop two doors up the street that rents bicycles for 2000 kip per day.

Just up Thanon Manthatulat from the MIC Guest House, at 69/5 Thanon Manthatulat, the private *Phantavong Guest House* (☎ 214738) offers 19 basic rooms for US$6 with shared bath and fan, US$8 with private bath and fan, and US$12 with private bath and air-con. The dining area offers breakfast all day. Cleanliness is not a strength of this place and some of the rooms are rather stuffy, but some people like it.

The *Santisouk Guest House* (☎ 215303), above the Restaurant Santisouk at 77-79 Thanon Nokeo Khumman, has nine plain but clean rooms with wooden floors, high ceilings and air-con for US$10 with shared bath, US$12 with attached bath. The restaurant downstairs is quite a good spot to have breakfast.

A little out from the centre, the friendly *Senesouk Guest House* (☎ 215567; fax 217449), near the Novotel off Thanon Luang Prabang (Km 2 Ban Khounta), offers a rabbit warren of rooms for 300B for a double with shared bath, 300/400B single/double with attached bath and 500B for TV and fridge. The small to medium rooms all have air-con. It's next to a nightclub that probably feeds the night-time influx of guests – not always a good sign.

The *Saylomyen Guest House* (☎ 214246), a two storey shophouse-style establishment on Thanon Saylom, has eight simple, clean rooms for US$5 with fan and shared toilet/cold shower, US$6 with fan and shared toilet/attached bath, US$7 with fan and attached toilet/bath and US$10 for air-con with attached toilet and hot bath. There's some street noise so take a room towards the back.

One centrally located place that bridges the gap between budget and middle is the friendly *Vannasinh Guest House* (☎/fax 222020) at 51 Thanon Phnom Penh on the edge of Chinatown (a block north of Thanon Samsenthai). The small but clean rooms with high ceilings and fans cost

US$8 single/double with shared toilet and hot shower or US$10 with private toilet and shower, while much larger rooms with air-con and hot shower cost US$20 (or US$16 if you stay three nights or more). There are also a couple of family units with two bed-rooms and similar prices; discounts can be negotiated for long-term stays. Breakfast is available in a small dining room. Propri-etors Somphone and Mayulee speak very good French and English. The popular Van-nasinh tends to fill up by noon.

Another place in a good position is the friendly *Syri Guest House* (☎ 212682; fax 219 191) in a large house in the old Chao Anou residential quarter. Spacious rooms with fan are US$10 single/double/triple with shared hot bath, US$15 double with hot bath and US$20 double/triple for air-con rooms with attached hot bath, TV, fridge and phone. Bikes are available for US$2 per day.

Half a block north of the Fountain Circle, at 72/6 Thanon Pangkham, a narrow four storey building houses the new *Pangkham Guest House* (☎ 216382). Small window-less rooms with fan, attached toilet and hot shower cost US$10 while similar rooms with air-con cost US$12. Slightly larger rooms with windows are available for US$16. Rooms at the back are quieter than those facing Thanon Pangkham. Decent bikes are available for rent for 2200 kip per day. The manager speaks good English.

Around the corner in a new shophouse at 359 Thanon Samsenthai, the Chinese-run *Hua Guo Guest House* (☎ 216612; fax 222505) has some rather unexceptional and slightly cramped rooms with air-con and TV for US$10 single with shared shower, US$15/20 double/triple with attached hot shower.

Downtown towards the river, the *Lao In-ternational Guest House* (☎/fax 216571) at 15/2 Thanon François Nginn, north of the Tai-Pan Hotel, has 11 rooms. A room with fan and attached bath on the unimpressive 2nd floor costs US$10/12 single/double – not such a good deal. Up on the nicer 3rd floor, smaller air-con rooms with hot showers go for US$20; two of these rooms have TV and fridge. A restaurant on the ground floor serves Vietnamese food at medium to high prices. Bikes are available for US$1 per day, motorcycles for US$10 per day.

Three blocks west, tucked away on par-allel Thanon In Paeng at No 72, is the similar but better-designed *Phornthip Guest House* (☎ 217239). Spacious, clean, basic single rooms with fan and shared bath cost US$6.50 to US$9, double rooms with fan and attached bath are US$10 to US$11, while air-con rooms with attached bath go for US$14/16 single/double. The guest-house enforces a 11.30 pm curfew, after which the front door is locked.

Conveniently located near the Talaat Laeng (Khua Luang) bus terminal for buses heading north to Vang Vieng and Luang Prabang, *Phay Nam Guest House* (☎ 216 768), Thanon Khua Luang, offers rooms in a large 1960s-vintage house set back off the road. All of the rooms come with private bath, air-con and fridge; depending on the size of the room, prices run from 300B to 400B single/double.

The unimpressive *Lao Elysée Guest House* (☎ 213619; fax 215628), at 168/5 Thanon Khun Bulom close to the immigra-tion office, has noisy motel-like rooms in a multistorey shophouse for US$7 with one bed, fan, private toilet and hot shower, US$10 for the same with air-con and $13 with two beds, air-con and TV. A grubby restaurant downstairs serves breakfast. We wouldn't mention it except that it's conve-nient to the immigration office.

The *Soradith Guest House* (☎ 412233; fax 413651), at 150 Thanon Dong Palan Thong (near the Dong Palan night market), offers 20 well-appointed, spotless rooms in a converted modern family home for US$10 a night single/double, US$15 with satellite TV and fridge, US$20 for a larger room, all with air-con and hot water. A relatively pricey restaurant serving European food is attached, as well as a simpler Lao/Thai restaurant. The MVT Music Vientiane Café is also on the premises. The relatively low rates may simply be a factor of the deflated kip – the guesthouse seems like an anomaly given the sophistication of the restaurant and club.

There are plenty of other guesthouses in this price range scattered around Vientiane in all directions, but none that we thought worth mentioning here. Either the location was poor, the room conditions were lacking or the rates were way out of line with the going market.

Hotels

Hotel Ekalath Metropole (☎ 213420, 213 421; fax 222307) on the corner of Thanon Samsenthai and Thanon Chantha Khumman has gone through at least three incarnations, starting with the pre-1975 Imperial Hotel. The latest version is basically a middle-price hotel, but an annexe contains cheap, plain rooms with fan for US$5.50 to US$6.60 single and US$7.70 to US$8.80 double with shared cold shower, or US$12 single and US$14 double with fan and attached cold shower (but shared toilet).

Inter Hotel (☎ 215137) at the corner of Thanon Chao Anou and Thanon Fa Ngum (24-25 Thanon Fa Ngum) is near the river. The Lao pronunciation of the hotel's name is 'Aengtaek'. Rates here are US$12 to US$16 single/double, depending on the size of the room; all rooms come with air-con and hot water. Larger two-room units with TV, fridge and bath cost US$18. This hotel is well located and often full, although the rooms are nothing special. One definite drawback is the hotel disco, which when active causes the whole building to shake.

Saysana Hotel (☎ 213580) on Thanon Chao Anou between Thanon Setthathirat and Thanon Fa Ngum has single/double rooms with air-con and hot water for US$10 and seems to serve mainly as a place to spend the night for people who can't (or don't want to) find their way home from the neon-lit Victory Nightclub downstairs. One gets the impression that foreigners are not welcome.

Samsenthai Hotel (☎ 212166, 216287) at 15 Thanon Manthatulat near the river has gone through its ups and downs and at last check was looking OK again. Simple single rooms with fan and shared bath go for US$6, double rooms with fan and attached toilet/bath are US$8, while for US$12/15 you get air-con, private toilet and hot shower. Downstairs is a restaurant serving Chinese and European food.

The long-running *Vientiane Hotel* (☎ 212 928), at 8/3 Thanon Luang Prabang, could use a total renovation – with this level of decrepitude it surely must be government-owned. Rooms with fan cost 9000/10,000 kip single/double, while air-con rooms are 10,800/14,000 kip. All rooms have attached toilet/bath. There's a Lao restaurant in the lobby. The rooms aren't good value by local standards. Beware: some low-end package tour operators outside Laos use this hotel.

The spooky *Hotel Phonexay* at the corner of Thanon Saylom and Thanon Nong Bon near Wat Phonxai is a large, dilapidated hotel that serves as a holding place for South Asians – Indians, Pakistanis, Bangladeshis – waiting for visas to Thailand. Large rooms with attached bath and fan cost 6000/8000/ 9500 kip double/triple/quadruple a night, 15,000 kip quadruple with air-con, but are hardly worth it (unless you want to practise your Bengali or Punjabi) considering the better deals downtown.

PLACES TO STAY – MIDDLE
Guesthouses

Vientiane has an abundance of mid-range guesthouses catering to NGO staffers and long-term visitors who prefer the family-like atmosphere these places provide rather than the typical hotel ambience. Discounts for long-term stays are usually available. Many places in this category stood half-empty even during the tourist miniboom of 1997-98, when more people visited Vientiane than ever before, so discounts may be available.

One of the more centrally located places is *Lani I Guest House* (☎ 216103; fax 215639) at 281 Thanon Setthathirat, near Wat Hai Sok. Twelve large, comfortable air-con rooms in an old house cost US$25 single and US$30 to US$35 double. Each room comes with phone and hot shower, and there is a pleasant terrace dining area attached. These prices do not include 10% tax. A second branch, *Lani II* (☎ 213022; fax 215639) at 268 Thanon Saylom, is also located well off the street in a large house – if anything it's quieter than Lani I. Seven large and pleasantly decorated rooms start at US$15/20 single/double with air-con, fan and phone, with toilet and hot shower down the hall. Add private toilet, hot shower and fridge for US$20/25; one larger room is available at the same rate. At either place bicycles are available for US$2 per day.

Down Thanon Samsenthai in an easterly direction at No 80/4, just opposite the new Lao Hotel Plaza, the Chinese-owned *Settha Guest House* (☎ 213241; fax 215995) is in a modern four storey building set back from the road. Six air-con suites with hot water and separate sitting rooms cost US$16 single/double, but it's a bit sterile overall. As it's often empty or near-empty, offers of discounts are forthcoming. On the ground floor is the banquet-style Hong Kong Restaurant, serving Chinese food of course.

The *Koto Guest House* (☎ 412849; fax 415323), at 229 Thanon Nong Bon near Wat Phonxai, features seven air-con rooms done in a vaguely Japanese style (some rooms have sliding shojis). All cost US$15/17 single/double, which includes the choice of western or Japanese breakfast in a Japanese restaurant on the ground floor.

Villa That Luang (also called That Luang Guest House; ☎ 413370; fax 412953) is at 307 Thanon That Luang, not far from Pha That Luang. It's clean, and the staff seem eager to please. Large, air-con rooms with hot water and fridge are US$20, including daily laundry service; add US$10 for TV and IDD phone. A restaurant and snack bar are located next door. Also quite close to Pha That Luang, but on Thanon Sisangvone, the friendly *Sisangvone Guest House* (☎ 414 753) offers quiet rooms in an older house about 500m from the monument. Rates are 400B for a single with air-con and private hot shower, or 500/600B single/double with air-con, TV and fridge.

The French-owned *Auberge de Temple* (☎/fax 214844), at 184/1 Thanon Sikhotabang, is a large house 20m off Thanon Luang Prabang opposite the Blue Star nightclub. The eight rooms are tastefully decorated with furniture of the owner's design. There are two air-con rooms with one large bed each and shared hot bath for US$10, another two rooms with two beds and shared bath for US$15 and four double rooms with attached bath for US$20. They also offer a four-bed dorm with fan and shared hot bath for US$7 per bed; 10% discount for long-term stays. Breakfast is served in a small dining room downstairs. The rooms with windows facing Thanon Luang Prabang catch some street noise, so choose a room at the back if you prefer quiet.

Next to Honour International School, very near Wat Si Muang and a short stroll from the river, the friendly *Villa Manoly* (☎ 212282; fax 218907) is a very large villa sitting on quiet, nicely landscaped grounds. The house is furnished with antiques, there's a sitting terrace on the 2nd floor and service is generally excellent. The twelve high-ceilinged rooms come with attached hot shower and cost US$20 single, US$25 double. In the same area but closer to Wat Si Muang (almost across the street, opposite the park with Sisavang Vong's statue), *Heuan Lao Guest House* (☎/fax 216258) at 55 Ban Si Muang – actually in a *soi* (alley) off Thanon Samsenthai – has OK rooms with private bath for US$7 single/double with fan, US$13 single/double with air-con and hot water, US$15 air-con triple with hot water or US$25 air-con triple with TV and fridge.

East and south of the centre of town in leafy residential areas near Wat Sok Pa Luang are a number of other mid-priced guesthouses. In this area it can be hard to find taxis or jumbos into town at night, though it's within easy pedalling distance if you have a bike. The quiet and friendly *Chaemchanh Guest House* (☎/fax 312700) at 73 Thanon Khu Vieng (actually 50m north-east of Thanon Khu Vieng) offers eight large rooms with air-con and hot water for US$20; room sizes tend to vary widely, so it pays to look first. The beautiful garden surrounding the house is an attractive addition. The proprietors offer plants for sale as well as rattan furniture from their factory on Thanon Tha Deua, Km 6.

The brick-and-tile *Thieng Thong Guest House* (☎ 313782; fax 312125), off Thanon Sok Pa Luang in Ban Wat Naak near the Myanmar embassy, has 13 air-con rooms with hot water and fridge for US$20 single/double, US$17 for long-term stays. Price includes breakfast or laundry (guests must choose). If you make your request in advance, a small restaurant on the premises can prepare Lao and European food.

The *Wonderland Guest House* (☎/fax 314 682), about 200m north-east of Thanon Khu Vieng in peaceful Ban Phonsavan Tai, Muang Sisattanak, has 10 clean rooms furnished with rattan in a two storey brick building, all with hot shower and air-con, ranging from 500B single/double (some rooms with TV and fridge) to 700B for a 'family' room with one large bed and bunks, TV and fridge. Half the rooms have small balconies. There's a restaurant downstairs and a 2nd floor veranda with a sitting area. Discounts are available.

Situated in the northern part of town near the Talaat Thong Khan Kham, *Sisavad Guest House* (☎/fax 212719) at 93/12 Ban Sisawat Neua offers modern bungalows with large, clean air-con rooms for US$20 single/double. It's possible to negotiate a lower rate, especially for long-term stays. All rooms have private hot showers, and there's a pool on the premises – a real plus for people travelling with children. In a shophouse opposite, at 161/16 Ban Sisawat Kang, relatives of the family who own the original Sisavad run *Sisavad Guest House II* (☎ 212560; fax 216586). All rooms come with air-con, starting at US$8 single with shared toilet/shower and phone, US$12 single with attached toilet/shower and no phone, US$15/20 single/double with hot shower, phone and TV. The original Sisavad is better.

Hotels

The *Asian Pavilion Hotel* (☎ 213430; fax 213432), at 379 Thanon Samsenthai, is a good mid-priced choice with a bit of history behind it. In its pre-Revolutionary incarnation, this was the Hotel Constellation (immortalised in the John Le Carré novel *The Honourable Schoolboy*). The original owner, a former Royal Lao Army colonel who had been trained in the USA, was sent to a re-education camp from 1975 until 1988; he reopened the hotel under the name of the Vieng Vilay Hotel in 1989. After a 1991 renovation the hotel changed names yet again. 'Standard' (read 'old') rooms in the back of the hotel are a reasonable US$18 single/double and include fan, air-con, telephone and private hot bath, while more modern and slightly larger 'superior' rooms with TV, fridge and bathtub are US$25. An even larger room is available for US$35. Add 10% service charge and 10% tax to all rates. Rooms are relatively well kept and the staff is helpful and efficient, which is why a lot of business people stay here. It's also relatively quiet since there is no disco. Credit cards accepted.

On the opposite side of Thanon Samsenthai, a bit farther west towards Thanon Pangkham, stands the Vietnamese-owned *Lao-Paris Hotel* (☎ 222229, 213440; fax 216382). It is a modern building where rooms with air-con and private hot bath go for US$10 single, US$15 single/double or US$20 triple with TV, telephone and fridge. Downstairs is a restaurant serving Lao, Thai, French and Vietnamese food.

The *Hotel Ekalath Metropole* (☎ 213420, 213421; fax 222307) has large but decaying air-con rooms ranging from US$11/15.40 single/double for fan rooms with bath and shared toilet to US$36.30/44 for 'deluxe' air-con rooms with private hot bath, satellite TV, fridge and phone. These rates include breakfast in the dining room. Discounts of up to 50% are available for long-term stays. Try to get a room away from the disco if you seek quiet. All in all there are better deals available in the mid-range guesthouses.

The newly renovated *Anou Hotel* (☎ 213 630; fax 213635) at the corner of Thanon Heng Boun and Thanon Chao Anou has smallish rooms for US$30/45 single/double (including breakfast), all with air-con, hot water, satellite TV, fridge and operator-assisted phone. Although it's not bad value, given the current Vientiane hotel market I'd expect the rates to come down in the next year or two. Credit cards accepted.

Douang Deuane Hotel (☎ 222301; fax 222300), on Thanon Nokeo Khumman near the river, is a four storey place with simple but clean, medium-sized rooms with fridge, TV, air-con, soft beds and hot showers with tubs for US$22 single/double. There is no lift (elevator), Visa accepted.

Two blocks west of the New Apollo Hotel (see Places to Stay – top end), on the same side of Thanon Luang Prabang, a large apartment building that once housed many of Vientiane's Russian and Eastern European residents in the 1970s and 1980s has been converted into the *Mekong Hotel* (☎ 212938; fax 212822). All rooms in this Chinese-owned hotel feature air-con, hot showers, telephone, refridgerator and TV for US$20 single/double standard, US$25 single/double deluxe (with slightly nicer amenities) or US$30 for a room with one queen-size bed and one twin. Long-term rentals are available. The clientele is mostly Chinese. The facilities include a medical clinic, Chinese restaurant, Thai-Lao restaurant/bar with karaoke lounge, and a disco.

Next to the river in the quiet Thai-owned *River View Hotel* (☎ 216231; fax 216232) at the corner of Thanon Sithan Neua and Thanon Fa Ngum. Spacious, clean rooms cost US$15 single, US$20 to US$35 double and US$40 for a five-bed room with a view. All 32 rooms have air-con, hot water and phone. TVs may be rented separately.

North-east of the town centre at 263 Thanon Si Bun Heuang (a bit north of the Patuxai monument) is *Le Parasol Blanc Hotel* (☎ 216091, 215090; fax 222290), where modern air-con rooms with attached hot bath, IDD phone, satellite TV plus a pool and garden cost US$33 single/double.

Laundry service is included in the rates. A restaurant/piano bar serves French, Lao and Thai cuisine. The manager speaks French, and many of the guests are French.

Similar, but a bit more out of the way on Thanon Phon Than east of Wat Sok Pa Luang, the quiet, well-run *Vansana Hotel* (☎ 413894, 414189; fax 413171) has large, clean rooms with fan, air-con, hot water, satellite TV, fridge and phone for US$25/30 single/double. Facilities include a sauna, massage service, swimming pool, restaurant and nightclub. Visa and Amex cards are accepted. Jumbos and samlors seem to be scarce in this area, so the Vansana is best used by visitors with their own transport.

The Chinese-owned *Muang Lao-China Hotel* (☎ 313325; fax 312380), Thanon Tha Deua, Km 4, is a bit out of town, on the way to the Tha Deua ferry, and is on the Mekong River near the AERC. Large, clean, air-con rooms with bath, hot water, satellite TV, IDD phone and fridge cost from US$25 double to US$50 for a two-room suite. There's a cafe downstairs. Most of the guests are Chinese.

Vientiane's original luxury hotel, the *Lane Xang Hotel* (☎ 214102; fax 214108) faces the Mekong on Thanon Fa Ngum, around the corner from Lao Aviation, THAI and BCEL. This four storey wonder was until very recently Laos' classiest digs and the hotel of choice for visiting VIPs. The 109 clean and spacious rooms at the Lane Xang have a socialist-era feel – some of the spacious bathrooms still feature funky Russian water heaters (but state-of-the-art Japanese air-con) as well as huge lavatories with bidets. The executive suite we looked at even had a full-sized beauty parlour-style hair dryer attached to one wall, plus a formal dining room with place settings. All rooms have satellite TV, air-con and mini-bars. Other amenities include a lift (or elevator, the second one installed in all of Laos), restaurant, bar, nightclub, business office, swimming pool, putting green, snooker club, two badminton courts, gift shop and a fitness centre out the back with sauna and exercise equipment. At the time

VIENTIANE

we visited, the Lane Xang was a great deal with rooms costing just US$22/25 single/double, spacious junior suites for US$45 and huge apartment-sized executive suites for US$55; all rates include breakfast, service charge, tax and free taxi service to and from the airport. Visa and Amex credit cards are accepted. About the only drawback to this place is that it frequently hosts large outdoor wedding parties on weekends – complete with live bands. Sometimes two receptions are held on the same weekend night so that you're bombarded from both sides of the hotel! However, the parties always end promptly between 11.15 and 11.30 pm, so unless you're an early-to-bed person it shouldn't be a problem.

Around the corner from the plush Lao Hotel Plaza, the *Day Inn Hotel* (☎ 214792; fax 222984) at 059/3 Thanon Pangkham is a tidy three storey building that once housed the Indian embassy. The completely renovated building contains large, sunny, airy rooms decorated with rattan furniture and pastel colours, and furnished with TV, stocked fridge, air-con and large hot-water bathrooms with bathtubs. Rates run from 65,000 kip for a one-bed room to 75,000 kip for two beds or 87,500 kip for three beds. There's a relatively inexpensive coffee shop downstairs.

PLACES TO STAY – TOP END

Due to a glut in top-end hotel rooms in the city, coupled with the depreciation of the kip, almost all room rates at this end of the spectrum have dropped since the last edition of this book.

One of the best deals in the over US$50 realm is the very clean and sedate *Tai-Pan Hotel* (☎ 216906; fax 216223, or in Bangkok (02) 260-9888; fax 259-7908) at 2-12 Thanon François Nginn, half a block from the river. All rooms in this modern four storey hotel feature individual balconies, TV with satellite and video, fridge, IDD phone and polished wooden floors. Prices start at US$49/64 single/double, while deluxe rooms are US$54/68, junior suites US$65/79, two-room suites US$75/89 and

three-room suites US$125/138/152 double/triple/quadruple. These rates include an American breakfast, a free airport pick-up, tax and service. There is also an email service, but for guests only. A 5% discount is offered for long-term stays; Visa and Amex are accepted.

Vientiane's largest international-class hotel is the four storey *Novotel Belvedere Vientiane* (☎ 213570; fax 213572), a 206 room establishment at Km 2 on Thanon Luang Prabang (just west of the western end of Thanon Samsenthai near the three-headed elephant statue). The hotel boasts an airport reservation desk and free airport shuttle, a 24 hour business centre, Chinese restaurant, coffee shop, bar, pool, sauna, tennis courts, Lao massage, fitness centre, snooker, game room, beer garden and disco. All rooms come with IDD telephone with dataport, cable TV, central air-con, minibar, hairdryer and electric thermos for making coffee. Rates are US$150 for a superior room, US$180 for a deluxe room, US$250 for a junior suite, US$280 for an executive suite and US$400 for a presidential suite (plus tax); lower corporate rates are casually dispensed. Major credit cards accepted. There's a branch of the Raintrees book store in the lobby.

Also in the high-class category is the huge and imposing *Royal Dokmaideng Hotel* (☎ 214455; fax 214454), on Thanon Lan Xang near the Patuxai monument. This five storey hotel features lots of wood and marble in the public areas; large rooms with all mod cons cost US$50/55 single/double and US$91 for a suite, not including tax and service. Facilities and services include a pool, herbal sauna, massage centre, Chinese nightclub, lobby bar, business centre and email service for guests only. Among Lao residents – including jumbo drivers – the hotel is more commonly known as the 'Royal Hotel' or simply the 'Royan' (the Lao pronunciation of Royal).

The *New Apollo Hotel* (☎ 213244, 213343; fax 213245) at 69A Thanon Luang Prabang (formerly the Apollo Hotel and before that the Santiphap Hotel) has rather ordinary rooms by international standards. All come with air-con, hot water, TV and fridge and cost US$45/50 single/double for standard rooms, while deluxe rooms go for US$50/55. Suites are available for US$65. These rates include breakfast, service charge and tax. Visa and Amex cards are accepted. The hotel's hostess-style nightclub makes it popular with Thai, Japanese and Chinese business travellers. A bit of hotel trivia: in its first life as the Santiphap Hotel, this was the first building in Vientiane with a lift.

The multistorey *Lao Hotel Plaza* (☎ 218 800; fax 218808, or in Bangkok (☎ (02) 255-3410; fax 225-3457), at 63 Thanon Samsenthai near the Lao Revolutionary Museum, is the nation's newest and biggest hotel, a sprawling 142-room complex managed by Thailand's Felix Hotels & Resorts chain. Ample-sized rooms feature air-con, hot water, IDD phone, satellite TV and fridge. Walk-in rates are US$100/120 single/double for a standard room, US$130/ 140 for 'executive', US$200 for a deluxe suite, US$300 for an executive suite and US$400 for a presidential suite with private jacuzzi. Add 10% tax to all rates. The executive standard rooms include free airport transfer, free local phone calls, complimentary drinks at the piano bar between 6 and 7 pm and a complimentary fruit basket every day. When we looked at the rooms, the front desk was offering executive standard rooms for half the rack rate; this may have been their 'soft opening' rate but it's worth asking for a discount if it looks as empty as when we visited. Some of the other amenities include a swimming pool, sauna and jacuzzi, fitness centre, rest-aurants, nightclub, business centre and a branch of Raintrees bookshop. All major credit cards are accepted.

An old colonial structure on the upper end of Thanon Pangkham between Thanon Phai Nam and Thanon Khun Bulom is slowly being reconstructed by a Lao company with plans to eventually open the *Belmont Settha Palace Hotel*. Progress has been so slow that it's impossible to say when the place will actually open or even whether it will properly belong in the top-end bracket – but making a guess from its appearance, it looks like it might run in the US$65 to US$100 range.

PLACES TO EAT

Vientiane is a good town for food, with a wide variety of cafes, street vendors, beer gardens and restaurants offering everything from rice noodles to filet mignon.

Breakfast

Most of the hotels in Vientiane offer set 'American' breakfasts (two eggs, toast and ham or bacon) for around 1500 to 3000 kip. Or you could get out on the streets and eat where the locals do. One popular breakfast is khào jii pá-têh, a split French baguette stuffed with Lao-style pâté (which is more like English or American luncheon meat than French pâté) and various dressings. Vendors who sell these breakfast sandwiches also sell plain baguettes (khào jii) – there are several regular bread vendors around town, but especially on Thanon Heng Boun between Thanon Chao Anou and Thanon Khun Bulom.

At the north-west corner of Thanon Pangkham and Thanon Samsenthai, a no-name *coffee shop* serves very good kaa-féh nóm hàwn (Lao-style milk coffee) and khào jii khai dạo (two fried eggs with sliced baguette). You can also eat Chinese doughnuts (pá-kôh or khào-nõm *khuu*) or plain French bread with coffee.

Another good spot for breakfast is the *Restaurant Santisouk* (also known by its pre-Revolutionary name, *Café La Pagode)* on Thanon Nokeo Khumman, near the Lao Revolutionary Museum. The menu has a variety of western breakfasts (including tasty potato omelettes) as well as pastry plates and good coffee, and the prices are very reasonable.

Bakeries

The expat-owned *Scandinavian Bakery* (☎ 215199), on the Fountain Circle, sells fresh bread, pies, sandwiches, croissants, cakes and ice cream; there are a few tables inside and out. It's open Monday to Saturday from 7 am to 7 pm, Sunday 9 am to 7 pm. *Healthy & Fresh Bakery & Eatery* (☎ 215265), two doors east of Lo Stivale Deli Café on Thanon Setthathirat, features yoghurts, sandwiches, fruit and a large selection of baked goods; it's good, if a little expensive, and open Monday to Saturday from 7 am to 7 pm.

Two side-by-side cafes on Thanon Chao Anou, *Liang Xiang Bakery House* and *Sweet Home Bakery*, sell decent croissants and other pastries – at about half the price of the fare at the falang bakeries (though the quality is completely different) – from around 7 am till 9 pm; each has a couple of tables out front where you can eat with a view of street life, as well as a row of inside tables. Breakfasts of khào jịi khai dạo and other egg dishes are available at each. The Sweet Home has ice cream sundaes.

There's a string of at least half a dozen *cake shops* along Thanon Saylom, just off Thanon Lan Xang, all with selections of inexpensive Lao interpretations of European cakes and pastries.

Noodles, Chinese & Vietnamese

Noodles of all kinds are popular in Vientiane, especially along Thanon Heng Boun, Thanon Chao Anou, Thanon Khun Bulom and the west end of Thanon Samsenthai, which outline the unofficial Chinatown. In the noodle department, the basic choice is fõe, a rice noodle that's popular throughout mainland South-East Asia (known as kwethio or kuaytiaw in Thailand, Malaysia and Singapore), mii, the traditional Chinese egg noodle, and khào pûn, very thin wheat noodles with a spicy Lao sauce. Fõe and mii can be ordered as soup (eg fõe nâam), dry-mixed in a bowl (eg fõe hàeng) or fried (eg fõe khùa), among other variations.

Samsenthai Fried Noodle on Thanon Samsenthai, around the corner from Vannasinh Guest House, specialises in large plates of delicious fõe khùa (fried rice noodles), with your choice of chicken, pork or shrimp. Order phii-sẹht (special) and

they'll add more green vegies to the mix. It's open Monday to Saturday from 10 am to around 9 pm. A few doors west along the same street at No 201 (on the corner of Thanon Chao Anou) is *Moey Chin* (no English sign), a small place with delicious roast duck on rice (khào pét). It's open from 10 am to 2 pm and from 5 to 10 pm daily.

The spotlessly clean, air-con *Guangdong Restaurant*, on Thanon Chao Anou near the two bakeries, offers a few varieties of inexpensive dim sum, fresh mii, and a 70-item menu of various Chinese specialities.

One of my favourite Lao-Vietnamese noodle dishes is khào pịak sèn, a bowl of toothy, round rice noodles served in chicken broth with strips of chicken. The best place in downtown Vientiane to sample khào pịak sèn is from a couple of sidewalk vendors on the eastern side of Thanon Pangkham about midway between Thanon Samsenthai and the Fountain Circle amid a row of tailor shops. One vendor commands an area next to Adam Tailleur, the other next to Saigon Tailor. The scissors standing in the chopsticks jar are used to cut khào-nõm khuu into bite-sized pieces to be added to the soup, along with dollops of fresh crushed ginger, chilli jam and a possible medley of other condiments found on each table.

Le Chanthy (Nang Janti) Cuisine Vietnamienne, a small shop on Thanon Chao Anou, one door south of the corner with Thanon Heng Boun, makes very good Lao-style khào pûn with a selection of three toppings – it's probably the best place downtown to try this dish. Janti also offers Vietnamese nãem neŭang (barbecued pork meatballs) and yáw (spring rolls), usually sold in 'sets' (sut) with cold khào pûn, fresh lettuce leaves, mint, basil, various dipping sauces, sliced starfruit and green plantain.

Right around the corner on Thanon Heng Boun west of Thanon Chao Anou are two more popular Chinese-Vietnamese places with similar fare – *Nang Suli* (also known as *Lao Chaloen*, or to local expats, 'Green Hole in the Wall') and, next door, *Vieng Sawan* (no English signs for either). Both specialise in nãem neŭang and yáw; the

Vieng Sawan is the better of the two. You can also order sìn jæm, thinly sliced pieces of raw beef which customers boil in small cauldrons of coconut water placed on the table and eat with dipping sauces.

Several óp pét restaurants (serving roast duck) can be found along the east side of Thanon Khun Bulom towards the river, while farther north on the west side of this same street are four fõe places in a row. This is the best area in town for fõe, especially at night when it's very busy.

For all-round quality, one of the better – and more expensive – Chinese-Vietnamese places in Vientiane is the casual but clean Restaurant Ha-Wai at 75 Thanon Chao Anou. The lengthy menu features Vietnamese, Cantonese and a few Lao and French dishes; almost everything is made from scratch, so it may take a while to get served.

The relative newcomer PVO, on Thanon Samsenthai opposite the Hua Guo Guest House, is a modest garage-style place that serves good, inexpensive Vietnamese and Lao food.

Lao
For authentic, cheap Lao meals, Vientiane's night markets and street vendors are your overall best source. Most extensive is the Dong Palan night market, off Thanon Ban Fai (marked as Thanon Dong Palan on some maps), at the back of the Nong Chan ponds near Wat Ban Fai. Vendors sell all the Lao standards, including làap and pîng kai.

In the central downtown area, the best pîng kai vendors are found in a spot opposite the Maningom Supermarket near the corner of Thanon Khun Bulom and Thanon Heng Boun from around 5.30 till around 8 or 9 pm. A set of tables behind the vendors allows you to eat on the premises, though most people do takeaways. Towards the northern end of Thanon Chao Anou, on the right-hand side before it crosses Thanon Khun Bulom, a slightly smaller group of vendors also offer slightly less expensive pîng kai, along with tạm (spicy mortar-pounded salads) made with shredded green papaya or green beans, all for takeaway

The Mixay
Throughout the latter half of 1997 there was major construction work on Thanon Fa Ngum along the Mekong riverfront, during which one of the city's classic drinking and eating spots, the infamous Mixay Restaurant, was completely razed. As we went to press we heard that this and other cafes may be permitted to build along the new promenade, once completed. If this historic cafe does reopen, one hopes the original casual style and location will be preserved. The old Mixay was in a weather-worn wooden building open on three sides, overlooking the river near the intersection of Thanon Fa Ngum and Thanon Nokeo Khumman. From 1975 to 1989 when aid from the Soviet Union and eastern Europe was part of the national budget, this was one of the few nightspots Russian expats could afford – hence many non-Russian expats referred to it as 'the Russian club'.

As for the Mixay's menu, the làap (the English menu always read 'lard') was very tasty and could be ordered with chicken, pork, beef or fish. But the Mixay's main draw was draught Beerlao sold in plastic pitchers. If it reopens, this is a great spot to watch the sun set over the Mekong River, with the Thai town of Si Chiengmai visible on the other side.

only. If tạm màak hung (spicy green papaya salad) is a particular favourite, seek out the famous stall belonging to Thim Manivong, in front of Wat Phoxai at Km 4, Thanon Tha Deua. Thim reputedly makes the best tạm màak hung in Vientiane.

A small, open-air night market of sorts convenes along the high levee beside the Mekong River; look for a string of well-spaced bamboo tables and chairs which begins just west of the Inter Hotel and extends south a hundred metres or so. Some of the vendors here offer cold beer and soft drinks only, others prepare pîng kai, tạm màak hung or nãem (minced sausage mixed with rice, herbs and roasted chillies with a plate of greens on the side). This is a peaceful spot to watch Mekong sunsets or full moons (some of the vendors stay open late) while enjoying cheap snacks.

If you're looking to eat pîng kai with a roof over your head, the clean, popular and inexpensive *Nang Bunmala* (no sign in English) on Thanon Khu Vieng is your best choice. The chickens cooked here are much plumper than the Lao norm and roasted to perfection for 3000 kip per half, 5000 kip for a whole chicken. Also available are pîng pét (grilled duck), pîng pạa (grilled fish), tam màak hung (spicy papaya salad), sticky rice and draught beer. It's open daily from 11 am to 10 pm.

Along Thanon Fa Ngum, facing the river between Wat Xieng Nyeun and Wat Chanthabuli, is a sprinkling of Lao food shops specialising in làap as well as nãem, fried rice and other simple dishes. *John Restaurant* on Thanon Fa Ngum looks indistinguishable from the other little shops in the area but features an English-language menu offering Lao dishes and rice plates alongside American breakfasts, salads and sandwiches.

Serious connoisseurs of Lao food should seek out *Soukvimane Lao Food* (☎ 214 441), a restaurant at the end of an alley next to That Dam off Thanon That Dam. Among the house specialities (which vary from day to day) are kạeng pạa khai mot (fish soup with ant larvae) and làap pạa (spicy minced fish salad).

Another very good place for traditional Lao dishes is the friendly and inexpensive *Nang Kham Bang*, at 97 Thanon Khun Bulom in a little house not far from the river. This one also has a bilingual menu; specialities include stuffed frogs (kóp yat sài), roast quail (thàwt nok), roast fish (pîng pạa), pickled lettuce (sòm pákàat), beef or chicken làap and yám sìn ngúa. It's open daily for dinner.

Compared to the foregoing, *Kua Lao* (☎ 215777) on the corner of Thanon Samsenthai and Thanon Chantha Khumman seems tame and pricey, though the food is quite OK. Housed in a large, renovated French colonial mansion, the menu consists of a mix of Lao and Thai standards, which makes it popular among Thai tourists. It's open daily for lunch and dinner.

Even more touristy is the grandiose *Lao Residence* (Tamnak Lao) on Thanon That Luang, north-east of the Patuxai monument on the way to Pha That Luang. The menu here is more Thai than Lao, but neither cuisine is prepared authentically as the chefs seem bent on creating bland dishes oriented towards their mostly package tour clientele.

Dinner Show *Salongxay Restaurant*, opposite the Lane Xang Hotel on Thanon Fa Ngum, offers Lao food accompanied by Lao classical dancing (evenings only). It's open daily from 11 am to 2 pm and 5 to 10 pm. A set menu costing 15,000 kip includes a multicourse Lao dinner, beverages and dessert. A small attached beer garden offers outdoor dining.

Western
The number of restaurants and cafes serving western food in Vientiane continues to grow as Laos becomes the darling of the aid-and-development set. Most are quite expensive by local standards but good value compared with continental cuisine just about anywhere else in the world.

French At the cheap end of the spectrum and of particularly good value is *Restaurant Santisouk* (known once as Café La Pagode; ☎ 215303) on Thanon Nokeo Khumman, near the Lao Revolutionary Museum. Although the bland, slightly tatty decor does nothing to engage the senses – the cuisine is of the simple 'French grill' type and quite tasty. A filling plate of steak or filet mignon – served on a sizzling platter – or filleted fish or roast chicken with roast potatoes and vegetbales costs less than 5000 kip. Their breakfasts are also very good. The restaurant is open every day from 7 am to 10 pm. Look under Santisouk Guest House on the Central Vientiane map.

Le Bistrot Snack Bar (☎ 215972), opposite the Tai-Pan Hotel on Thanon François Nginn, is owned by an older Lao couple who spent most of their lives in Paris. The fare includes good, relatively inexpensive French dishes such as poulet provençal and boeuf bourguignon (both of which come with vegetables and potatoes or rice), along with a spicy salade chinoise made with bean-thread noodles and chicken, and a variety of couscous meals offered with chicken, mutton or merguez (spicy Moroccan lamb sausage). Open daily from 8.30 am to 11.30 pm.

Popular with diplomats, UN staff and other expats on large salaries is the intimate and tastefully decorated *Restaurant-Bar Namphu* (☎ 216248) on the Fountain Circle off Thanon Pangkham. The food and service are impeccable and the menu includes a number of German and Lao dishes as well as French – the popular blue-cheese hamburger adds an American touch; there's also a well-stocked bar. Prices per entree average roughly one-tenth of a Lao's average annual income. It's open daily from 10.30 am to 3 pm and 6.30 to 11.30 pm.

Also on the Fountain Circle, look for the *Restaurant Le Provençal* (☎ 217251, (020) 513412), nicely decorated in brick and wood. The complimentary appetisers start things off; there's a good French wine list and a fully stocked bar. The cuisine tends towards the more rustic southern French style with dishes such as salade niçoise and poulet moutarde, along with various daily specials. Prices are lower than at the Namphu. It's open Monday to Saturday for lunch and dinner.

The cosy, French-owned *Le Vendôme* (☎ 216402) is tucked away in an old house on a small street behind Wat In Paeng. The restaurant has a very pleasant candle-lit, bamboo-curtained outdoor seating area plus an air-con indoor section. The menu offers a selection of salads, French and Lao food, wood-fired pizza and desserts. Prices are moderate; it's open Monday to Friday for lunch and dinner, Saturday and Sunday for dinner only.

Le Bayou Bar Brasserie on Thanon Setthathirat, diagonally opposite Wat Ong Teu and under the same ownership as Le Vendôme, is a simple but charming spot with a choice of seating in the air-con dining room or narrow beer garden alongside. Prices are very reasonable – among the lowest of any European restaurant outside the Santisouk and Le Bistrot – and the fare includes breakfasts, pasta, pizza, sandwiches, salads, fondue, brochettes, fruit shakes, wine and Lao beer on tap. The salad with chevre (goat cheese), watercress, lettuce leaves, cashews and croutons is especially delicious. It has similar hours to Le Vendôme.

Two inexpensive French-inspired eateries have opened up along Thanon Nokeo Khumman, not far from Raintrees. French-owned *La Terrasse* serves soups, omelettes, sandwiches, salads, quiche and barbecued seafood, plus Tex-Mex food (burritos, tacos, nachos, enchiladas), pizzas and vegetarian, fish or chicken burgers in a garden setting. *La Safran*, a little farther down Nokeo Khumman towards the river (opposite the Douang Deuane Hotel), is similar in ambience but more focused on French cuisine.

Italian Vientiane nowadays has two Italian restaurants, both of high standard. Opposite the Restaurant-Bar Namphu on the Fountain Circle is the older and very popular *L'Opera Italian Restaurant* (☎ 215099), a branch of a restaurant of the same name in Bangkok. The mostly Italian menu includes pizzas (served with fresh ground chili and oregano on the side), pasta, antipasti, seafood and salads, plus a selection of Italian coffees and wines. Big spenders are occasionally offered complimentary liqueurs. The gelati bar offers takeaway gelati. Overall, the quality of the food is consistent, and the prices are moderately high.

The newer *Lo Stivale Deli Café* (☎ 215 561) at 44/2 Thanon Setthathirat takes the prize for the best pizza and gnocchi in town. An array of pasta dishes, soups, salads, coffees, wines and tasty desserts, including home-made ice cream, are also available.

The prices are a bit higher than is normal for Vientiane, even for European cuisine. It is open from 10 am to 10 pm every day; credit cards accepted.

Other The *Xang Coffee House* (☎ 223173), on the east side of Thanon Khun Bulom towards the river, takes the prize for the most innovative restaurant decor with its vibrant colour scheme and vaguely Tex-Mex theme. The menu covers a broad range of light international fare, European and American breakfasts, burgers, sandwiches, salads, ice cream, pastries, espresso coffee drinks, fruit juices, cocktails and prices averaging 1500 to 3000 kip. Lots of English-language magazines and newspapers – including the *Bangkok Post* – are available to read, and an upstairs room features a TV tuned to CNN or BBC. It's open Wednesday to Monday from 9 am to 9 pm.

American-owned *Uncle Fred's* (☎ 222 964), on Thanon Samsenthai close to the Lao Revolutionary Museum, is a casual fast food-style place. The lengthy menu includes grilled chicken, seafood, burgers, fries, sandwiches, spaghetti, salads and American breakfasts (the latter are served all day). Beerlao is served in chilled mugs. Other specialities include home-made ice cream, milkshakes and yoghurt shakes. Prices range from 1800 kip for a one-egg sandwich (though there's an extra charge if you want mayonnaise) to 5300 kip for steak and eggs.

Europe Restaurant, attached to the Soradith Guest House (☎/fax 413651) at 150 Ban Dong Palan Thong (near the Dong Palan night market), offers the most elegant atmosphere of any restaurant in Vientiane. The changing menu offers the full range of Swiss cuisine, mixing German, French and Italian influences. Prices are similar to those at the Restaurant-Bar Namphu.

Every Friday and Saturday from 3 to 5 pm the *Lao Hotel Plaza* hosts high tea (afternoon tea, with pastries and tiny sandwiches) with live piano accompaniment in the lobby lounge for 5600 kip per person.

Thai

With all the Thais visiting Vientiane for business and pleasure these days, Thai restaurants are not uncommon. On Thanon Samsenthai just past the Lao Revolutionary Museum, the *Phikun* (English sign reads 'Thai Food') has all the Thai standards, including tôm yam kûng (prawn and lemon grass soup) and kài phàt bai kàphrao (chicken fried in holy basil). The curries are good here – something you don't see much of in Lao cuisine. A second branch of the Phikun can be found on Thanon Luang Prabang, near the Thai Military Bank just west of Thanon Khun Bulom. It's open daily from 11 am to 9 pm.

The *Vientiane Department Store* (part of Talaat Sao) has a small but very popular food centre with an extensive variety of Thai, Lao and western dishes in the 1500 to 2000 kip range.

Indian

The Taj (☎ 212890) on Thanon Pangkham opposite Nakhornluang Bank (just north of the Fountain Circle) has an extensive menu of well-prepared dishes from North India, including tandoor dishes, curries, vegetarian plates and many different types of Indian breads. Service is good and the place is very clean, though à la carte prices are a bit high by Vientiane standards. The Taj also has a sizeable daily lunch buffet and fixed-price evening dinners. It's open daily from 11 am to 2.30 pm and 6 to 10.30 pm. Visa cards are accepted.

Cheaper Indian food can be found at *Nazim Restaurant* (☎ 223480) on Thanon Fa Ngum between Thanon François Nginn and Thanon Nokeo Khumman. The large menu has mostly North Indian dishes such as tandoori chicken, along with a few spicier items from South Indian such as masala dosa, plus a page of Malaysian specialities. It's open daily from 11 am to 11 pm. An older branch (☎ 413671) of the same restaurant can be found on Thanon Phonexay near the Australian embassy and opposite the Phonexay Hotel. This one opens daily from 11 am to 2 pm and 5.30 to 11 pm.

Japanese

The *Sakura Japanese Restaurant* (☎ 212 274), at Soi 3 Khounta Thong (off Thanon Luang Prabang near the Novotel), serves good Japanese cuisine, including sushi and teishokus.

Vegetarian

Vegetarianism hasn't caught on in Laos as much as it has in Thailand. *Aahaan Pheua Sukhaphaap* ('Food for Health', but the English sign reads 'Vegetarian Food') is a stall on the east side of Thanon Khun Bulom just north of the Thanon Samsenthai intersection. Not surprisingly it's owned and operated by a Thai woman (from Songkhla). The food is 100% vegan, with tofu, gluten and mushrooms sitting in for meat. It's very inexpensive and open daily from 7 am to around 2 pm.

Just for Fun, a small shop on Thanon Pangkham next to Raintrees bookshop, has a few vegetarian dishes inspired by Thai, Lao and Indian cuisine, plus Lao coffee and lots of herbal teas. It's open Monday to Saturday from 9 am to 10 pm.

For fresh fruit shakes – solo or mixed – one of the best and least expensive places is *Nai Xiang Chai Yene* on Thanon Chao Anou, just a few shops down from the Liang Xiang and Sweet Home bakeries towards the river and next door to the Guangdong Restaurant.

Beer Gardens

Vientiane abounds in casual outdoor places built of bamboo and thatch where patrons while away the hours drinking beer and eating traditional snacks or káp kâem.

A lengthy string of tiny, bamboo-thatch places right on the river can be found in the vicinity of the River View Hotel, the most distinguished of which is *Sala Khounta* about 120m upstream from the hotel. Also known as the 'Sunset Bar' among those who can't remember the name, it's basically a small bamboo platform over the Mekong, decorated with orchids, fishtraps and basketry. Beerlao is the main attraction, but the friendly and enterprising proprietors

also offer an array of Lao and Vietnamese snacks that vary from week to week or season to season. One of the occasional specialities here is delicious yám màak klûay, a tangy and spicy salad made by pounding green bananas (with the skins), chillies, màak khēua (pea eggplants), fish sauce, garlic and lime all together in a mortar. Savoury yáw jęun (fried Vietnamese spring rolls) – sliced into sections and served with khào pûn, lettuce, mint, coriander and steamed mango leaves – sell out fast here. The Sala Khounta usually closes after sunset, though it may stay open longer in hot weather.

A bit downriver on the same side of the road and south of the River View Hotel, *Sala Snake* has a similar ambience with the addition of recorded traditional Lao music; owner Sanit Maniphon is a musician from Luang Prabang. On Saturday evenings from around 6 pm an ensemble of student musicians sometimes perform live. In the same general vicinity *Huamuang Draft Beer Restaurant*, another bamboo affair on the riverside, is popular with Lao youth for its cheap beer and Lao food, and because it plays foreign rock and roll on the sound system in defiance of government bans (which means, of course, the restaurant may not last long!).

Farther downriver stands the much more substantial *Bar Brasserie Anousone* (☎ 222 347), a wooden *sala* on the west side of the road. In the evening, and during cooler weather during the day, the proprietors place tables on the riverbank opposite. The food and service are good, prices reasonable. The clientele is a mix of falang expats and Lao over 30. It's open on Monday from 5 to 11.30 pm, Tuesday to Sunday from 9.30 am to 11.30 pm. Nearby, the *Mekong Riverside* (Lao name: *Sala Khaem Khong*) is popular with Lao youth who have some money to spend on enjoying Thai pop music and mood lighting. Right around the corner on a dirt road leading to Thanon Luang Prabang, an enterprising group of young Lao operate an outdoor cafe called *Casper* on the grounds of the illuminated ruins of an old French mansion. This one could be temporary, but if it lasts it's a very atmospheric spot.

Right in the centre of town stands the Croatian-owned *Namphou Garden*, a set of tables and chairs encircling the renovated fountain (lit with coloured lights in the evening) where you can get Lao, European and Indian food, beer and cocktails till around 11 pm. When the weather's hot, this place can be packed with patrons seeking the cooling effects of the large fountain.

South-east of town on Thanon Tha Deua at Km 12, the Lao Government Brewery has its own thatched *Salakham Beer Garden* where you can drink inexpensive Lao draught beer (bia sót, literally fresh beer – and it doesn't get any fresher than this) and eat Lao snacks.

Minimarkets

For the largest selection of fresh groceries and the best prices, you should stick to the markets (see the Things to Buy section later in this chapter). But if there's something 'western' you're yearning for, an increasing number of minimarkets catering to the foreign community have opened.

Among the most popular is the *Phimphone Market* on the corner of Thanon Samsenthai and Thanon Chantha Khumman, attached to the Hotel Ekalath Metropole. Phimphone carries an expensive selection of biscuits, canned and frozen foods as well as toiletries. The original but smaller *Phimphone Minimart* across the street at 94/6 Thanon Samsenthai is still open. Both are open daily from 7.30 am to 10 pm.

Maningom Supermarket (☎ 216050), at the corner of Thanon Heng Boun and Thanon Khun Bulom, carries dairy products, breakfast cereals, biscuits, canned foods and imported chocolate; it's open daily from 7.30 am to 9.30 pm.

Simuang Minimart (☎ 214295), at 51 Thanon Samsenthai near the statue of King Sisavang Vong at Wat Si Muang, stocks a very good selection of imported foods and wines, credit cards are accepted. *Vins de France* (*Vinothèque la Cave*; ☎ 217700) at

354 Thanon Samsenthai has one of the best French wine cellars in South-East Asia.

The *Vientiane Department Store* at the Talaat Sao has Asian foods imported from Thailand and Singapore.

ENTERTAINMENT

Vientiane is no longer the illicit pleasure palace it was when Paul Theroux described it in his 1975 book *The Great Railway Bazaar* as a place in which 'The brothels are cleaner than the hotels, marijuana is cheaper than pipe tobacco and opium easier to find than a cold glass of beer'. Nowadays, brothels are strictly prohibited, Talaat Sao's marijuana stands have been removed from prominent display and cold beer has definitely replaced opium as the nightly drug of choice. Most of the bars, restaurants and discos close by midnight.

Dancing

Vientiane has at least six 'discos', though the term is rather a misnomer (it's what the Lao call these places), because often the music is live. Although a younger Lao crowd tends to predominate, there is usually a mix of generations and the bands or disc jockeys play everything from electrified Lao folk (for *lam wong* dancing) to quasi-western pop. By law all entertainment places are supposed to close by 11.30 pm and most of the clubs seem scrupulous about obeying.

Still the most popular place in town is the large *Nightclub Vienglatry* on Thanon Lan Xang, a bit north of Talaat Sao on the same side of the street. Basically a dance floor surrounded on three sides by padded sofas and tables, the Vienglatry features live Lao bands nightly and also serves food and liquor (no Beerlao, only Carlsberg); by 10.30 pm the cavernous room is packed. It closes by midnight.

Other Lao nightclubs with live bands, whirling lights and romantically dark sitting areas include the *Nokkeo Latry*, *Blue Star* and *Marina*, all out on Thanon Luang Prabang past the Novotel between Km 2 and Km 5.

Hotel Clubs

The *Anou Hotel, Saysana Hotel, Ekalath Metropole* and *Inter Hotel* all have nightly Lao-style discos which are a bit smaller in scale than the Nightclub Vienglatry; the Anou Cabaret is again the most popular after its reopening following more than a year of renovations. At some of these places a charge will be tacked onto your bill if you are male and one of the female staff comes and sits at your table (the Inter, for example, charges 3500 kip per sit).

Big, flashy Hong Kong-style nightclubs can be found in the *New Apollo Hotel* and the *Royal Dokmaideng Hotel. Lao Hotel Plaza*'s Le Club Disco is the most modern in all of Laos but it hasn't really taken off yet. The disco at the *Novotel* is the only one likely to stay open beyond the legal 11.30 pm closing time.

Bars

Outside of the hotels, Vientiane doesn't have many bars. Until four or five years ago the ones that did exist seemed semi-clandestine, perhaps semi-legal, but today several operate more or less within Lao law. All serve beer, along with a colonial history of other alcoholic beverages – French champagne, Johnny Walker and Stolichnaya – and the newer arrivals carry a great deal more, including various liqueurs. Still, for a city its size Vientiane seems to have fewer bars than you'd expect.

Samlo Pub, on Thanon Setthathirat (opposite Wat In Paeng), is a well-stocked bar that recently doubled its seating capacity. Draught Beerlao is available on tap.

Other watering holes worth checking out include the tiny but well-serviced bar at *Restaurant-Bar Namphu*. On hot nights *Namphou Garden*, the collection of outdoor tables around the fountain, is also quite popular.

If you're looking for something with more of a local flavour, and less expensive than the expat bars, your best bet is one of the many *bja sót bars* (selling draught beer) around town. These are usually nondescript rooms filled with wooden tables at the bottom of a shophouse – look for plastic jugs of beer on the tables.

Bane Saysana, also known as the *Win West Pub*, follows the Thai model in providing an ersatz Wild West atmosphere; it's near the Shell station at the intersection of Thanon Luang Prabang, Thanon Setthathirat and Thanon Khun Bulom.

Cinema & Video

Lao cinema houses have all died out in the video shop tidal wave of recent years. Thais with videos were able to copy new releases in Thailand and distribute them to video rental shops in Vientiane before movie houses ever received the films.

The *Centre de Langue Française* (☎ 215 764) on Thanon Lan Xang screens French films (subtitled in English) each Thursday at 7.15 pm. Admission is 500 kip and the screenings are open to the public. Film titles for the following week are usually listed in the weekly *Vientiane Times* or you can call the centre for information. They also have a video rental library – but you need your own VCR to see them!

The *Australian Embassy Recreation Club* shows videos on a wide-screen TV every Sunday at 7 pm (kid's movies are shown at 6.30 pm).

Russian films are presented on video at the *Russian Cultural Centre* (☎ 212030), at the corner of Thanon Luang Prabang and Thanon Khun Bulom, every Saturday at 4 pm. Admission is free.

There are various private video shops around town that hire out Thai and English-language videos for 500 to 800 kip per night. *Settha Video* on Thanon Setthathirat opposite Wat Ong Teu has a good selection of English-language videos. A couple of doors down, *OK Video* has a smaller selection of the same.

National Circus

The old Russian Circus established during the time of Soviet influence in Laos, now known as Hong Kanyasin or the National Circus, continues to present performances of the Lao national circus troupe from time to time. Keep an eye out for announcements listed in the *Vientiane Times*. The National Circus venue also occasionally plays host to pop and classical music performances sponsored by the French embassy; such musical events are usually widely advertised well in advance.

Recreation Clubs

The *Australian Embassy Recreation Club* (AERC; ☎ 314921), or the *Australian Club* for short, is out of town on the way to the Thailand ferry pier at Thanon Tha Deua, Km 3. The club has a brilliant pool, right next to the Mekong River, and at sunset quite a few expats (mostly non-Australian!) gather here for an impromptu social hour. On Friday from 6 to 7 pm there is an official Happy Hour at the snack bar. There are also squash courts, a Ping-Pong table, billiards and darts. Memberships are usually purchased by the year, but short-term memberships can be arranged for US$10 per day. Or perhaps you could find someone who is already a member and go along as their guest. The club is open daily from 10 am to 10 pm, though members may use the swimming pool from 7 am.

On Thanon Lan Xang the *Centre de Langue Française* has a French library with over 20,000 books, and it also has a small selection of videos.

The *Australian Embassy Library* at the Australian embassy on Thanon Phonexay is open to the public on Tuesday and Thursday from 1 to 4 pm, Saturday 9 am to 1 pm. The *British Trade Office*, opposite the Australian embassy, offers UK newspapers and magazines.

THINGS TO BUY

Just about anything made in Laos is available for purchase in Vientiane, including hill tribe crafts, jewellery, traditional textiles and carvings. The main shopping areas in town are Talaat Sao (Morning Market), the eastern end of Thanon Samsenthai (near the Asian Pavilion and Ekalath Metropole hotels) and Thanon Setthathirat, and on Thanon Pangkham.

Computer Supplies

It's not easy finding places to buy hardware and/or software for computers. If you're using DOS/Windows your best bet is Microtec Computer Shop (☎ 213836; fax 212 933) at 168-169 Thanon Luang Prabang, next to the Mekong Hotel. Alice Computer (☎ 314999) on Thanon Tha Deua, Km 2, is also good.

Other smaller shops include:

Intercom Computers
    (☎ 219222), Thanon Samsenthai (opposite the Lao-Paris Hotel)
KPC
    (☎ 215709), 34/3 Thanon Chao Anou
V & T Computer
    (☎ 215803; fax 214064), 482/2-3 Thanon Samsenthai (near Wat Si Muang)

Fishing Equipment

A shop at 275/1 Thanon Setthathirat carries a complete inventory of fishing rods, lines, nets, lures and all the other supplies needed to land a big one.

Furniture & Interior Design

Several workshops around town produce inexpensive custom-designed furniture of bamboo, rattan and wood (eg teak and Asian rosewood). Couleur d'Asie (☎ 223 008), Thanon Khun Bulom (opposite the western side of Wat In Paeng), carries some beautifully designed, Asian-accented furniture, along with a number of interior design accessories, including some household linens. After browsing, you can enjoy Lao coffee or tea and snacks in the shop's tea corner.

Phai Exclusive (☎ 214804) at 3 Thanon Thong Tum makes both furniture and accessories of bamboo (plus some interesting cards depicting historic Vientiane architecture).

For rattan furniture, visit the Saylom Rattan Furniture Co (☎ 215860) on Thanon Khun Bulom. Bamboo and Rattan Handicraft (☎ 412606) at 257 Ban Jommani Tai, south on Route 13, offers a large selection of both bamboo and rattan. Furniture can be made to order from their catalogue or from custom designs.

Many shops make wood furniture but the quality can be highly variable. One shop with a good reputation is Lao Wood Industry, Thanon Tha Deua Km 10.

Handicrafts, Antiques & Art

Several shops along Thanon Samsenthai and Thanon Pangkham sell Lao and Thai tribal and hill tribe crafts. Hmong-Lao Handicrafts (☎ 212220) on Thanon Samsenthai specialises in Hmong embroidery, including large squares with village scenes. A few also carry carved opium pipes (the real thing, not the misrepresented tobacco pipes sold in northern Thailand) – try the no-name shop at 350 Thanon Samsenthai.

The Kanchana Boutique (☎ 213467) opposite the Hotel Ekalath Metropole on Thanon That Dam carries an extensive selection of crafts. Lao Phattana Art and Handicrafts Co-operative (☎ 212363) at 53 Thanon Pangkham has a fair selection of antique and new hand-woven silks and cottons, antique silver, wood carvings and other crafts.

T'Shop Lai Galerie (☎ 223178), to be found on Thanon In Paeng next to Restaurant Le Vendôme, has a range of modern and traditional art in all media.

Nikone Handicraft Centre (☎ 212191), 1B Thanon Dong Mieng, near the National Circus, specialises in quality handicrafts oriented towards interior decoration.

Champa Gallery (☎ 216299), just northwest of That Dam, features the colourful, well-crafted collages of Monique Mottahedeh as well as works by other local artists. Lao Gallery (☎ 212943), opposite Lao Textiles at 92/2 Thanon Nokeo Khumman, displays contemporary art by Lao and Vietnamese artists.

Hammer-and-sickle flags and Lao national flags can be purchased in varying sizes at a stationery and office supplies shop at 268-270 Thanon Samsenthai, near the Vannasinh Guest House.

Jewellery

Most of the jewellery shops in Vientiane are along Thanon Samsenthai. Gold and silver are usually the best deals. Saigon Bijoux (☎ 214783) at No 367-369 is supposedly reputable – it sells and repairs gold and silver jewellery and can also make new pieces on request. This shop accepts Visa, MasterCard and Amex.

The Indian-owned Bari Jewellers (☎ 212 680) at 366-368 Thanon Samsenthai is one of the few stores which deals in precious stones as well as gold and silver.

The Talaat Sao is also a good place to buy gold and silver jewellery.

Tailors & Cobblers

The tailor shops along Thanon Pangkham also sell fabric and can design and cut clothes to fit. Queen's Beauty Tailor (☎ 214191) at No 21 (on the Fountain Circle) has quite a good reputation and fair prices, but they take a while to make clothes (two to three weeks). Mai Tailleur (☎ 215 616) at 77/5 Thanon Pangkham and Nova Tailleur around the corner at 64 Thanon Samsenthai can cut and sew a pattern in a week.

Teng Liang Ky at 78/2 Thanon Pangkham makes inexpensive leather shoes for men and can also repair shoes and luggage. There are a few cobblers at Talaat Thong Khan Kham and along Thanon Khu Vieng near Talaat Sao.

Textiles & Clothing

Talaat Sao (the Morning Market, though it runs all day) is a good place to look for fabrics; the stalls with modern styles of fabric are run by Indians and Pakistanis while traditional Lao-style textiles are sold by Lao vendors. Many carry antique as well as modern fabrics, plus utilitarian items such as shoulder bags (some artfully constructed around squares of antique fabric), cushions and pillows. Lao Antique Textiles (☎ 212381) in stall A2-4 has a good selection, though her competitors in the market are improving. The proprietor, Mrs Chanthone Thattanakham, also maintains a textile gallery in her home at 72/08 Thanon Tha Deua (near Km 2) in Ban Suanmon (she also offers ceramics and silver). If you're interested in building your own Lao loom or collecting the loom components, a booth diagonally opposite from Lao Antique Textiles everything you will need for sale, except the frame itself (which is normally made from scratch), including hand-carved wooden shuttles.

On Thanon Nokeo Khumman (look for an old two storey French-Lao house), Lao Textiles (☎ 212123) sells high-end contemporary, original-design fabrics inspired by older Lao weaving patterns, motifs and techniques. The American designer, Carol Cassidy, employs Lao weavers who use modified Swedish looms to produce wider pieces of fabric than those made on traditional Lao looms. Her textiles mix tapestry, brocade, *ikat* and weft ikat techniques, applied only to silk fabrics and completely hand-dyed using natural dyes. Items for sale include scarves, shawls, wall hangings and home-furnishing accessories. The prices are what you might expect from a weaving house that has exhibited in galleries and museums in major cities around the world. It's open Monday to Friday, from 8 am to noon and 2 to 5 pm, Saturday from 8 am to noon, or by appointment.

Hai Ngeun Mai Kham (☎ 313223), a small shop in the Lane Xang Hotel, specialises in old Lao textiles, along with new clothing that use old fabrics, especially silk. Also for sale are a few well-chosen artefacts, paintings and silverwork.

Supported by the Lao Women's Union, UNICEF and SIDA, The Art of Silk (☎ 214 308), just opposite the Samsenthai Hotel on Thanon Manthatulat, carries a selection of silk and cotton weavings in both traditional and modern designs. There is also a small textile museum above the shop.

To see Lao weaving in action, seek out the weaving district of Ban Nong Bua Thong, north-east of the town centre in Muang Chanthabuli. About 20 families (many originally from Sam Neua in Hua Phan Province) live and work here, including a couple of households which sell textiles directly to the public and welcome visitors who want to observe the weaving process. The Nanthavongduangsy family's Phaeng Mai Gallery (☎ 217341) is the most equipped for visitors; their large, white, two storey house is in the centre of the neighbourhood.

Yani (☎ 212918), in the Mixay Arcade on Thanon Setthathirat, is a small shop owned by a French-Vietnamese dress designer with Paris fashion school experience; some of the women's clothing designs here are very becoming, with an eye towards ethnic chic, Lao-style.

The Lao Women's Pilot Textile Project, a UN-sponsored programme, has a clothing factory called Lao Cotton (☎ 215840) in Ban Khunta, off Thanon Luang Prabang around 2.5km west of the centre of Vientiane. It specialises in hand-woven Lao cotton products in both modern and traditional designs, including shirts, dresses, handbags, place mats, table linen etc. Simple short-sleeved men's shirts are a great buy. It's open from 9 am to 5 pm Monday to Saturday.

Talaat Sao

The Morning Market is on the eastern corner of the intersection of Thanon Lan Xang and Thanon Khu Vieng. It actually runs all day, from 6 am to 6 pm. The sprawling collection of stalls offer fabric, ready-made clothes, jewellery, cutlery, toiletries, bedding, hardware and watches, as well as electronic goods and just about anything else imaginable.

In the centre of the area is a large building that houses the Vientiane Department Store, which carries mostly imported goods (canned foods, clothes, appliances, handicrafts, cassette tapes) from Thailand, China, Vietnam and Singapore. One section of the department store features a small supermarket that sells soap, local and imported foodstuffs and beer. Some departments now accept Visa cards.

Other Markets

East of Talaat Sao and beyond the bus terminal on Thanon Khua Vieng, the Khua Din Market (Talaat Khua Din) offers fresh produce and fresh meats, as well as flowers, tobacco and assorted other goods. For three years now it has been rumoured this market would move but so far it has stayed put.

A bigger fresh market is Thong Khan Kham Market (Talaat Thong Khan Kham). Like Talaat Sao, it's open all day, but is best in the morning. It's the biggest market in Vientiane and has virtually everything. You'll find it north of the town centre in Ban Thong Khan Kham (Gold Bowl Fields Village) at the intersection of Thanon Khan Kham and Thanon Dong Miang.

Near this market are a number of basket and pottery vendors. The old Talaat Nong Duang, more commonly known as Talaat Laeng (Evening Market), still has a few vendors but it's rather dull.

The That Luang Market is a little southeast of Pha That Luang on Thanon Talaat That Luang. One of the specialities here is exotic wildlife foods such as bear paws and snakes.

GETTING THERE & AWAY
Air
Departures from Vientiane are perfectly straightforward. Upstairs in the airport is a restaurant/lounge area with decent enough food. Departure tax is US$5.

See the introductory Getting There & Away chapter earlier in this book for details on air transport to Laos.

Airline Offices Lao Aviation (☎ 212058) has its main office at 2 Thanon Pangkham around the corner from the Lane Xang Hotel. This office handles international bookings for Lao Aviation and is also an agent for China Southern Airlines, Royal Air du Cambodge and Air France (Air France does not fly out of Vientiane, but bookings can be made here for flights out of Bangkok). Lao Aviation is open weekdays from 8 am to noon and 2 to 5 pm, and Saturday from 8 am to noon. The office for domestic bookings is in a smaller building to one side of the main building. Lao Aviation's phone number at Wattay airport is (☎ 512028, 512000).

Directly across the street from Lao Aviation is the Thai Airways International (THAI) office (☎ 216143), open weekdays from 8 am to 5 pm, and Saturday until noon. Other airlines with offices in town include Malaysia Airlines (☎ 218816), 1st floor, Lao Hotel Plaza; Silk Air (☎ 217492), 2nd floor, Royal Dokmaideng Hotel; and Vietnam Airlines (☎ 217562) on Thanon Dong Palan near the Dong Palan night market.

Lao Air Booking (☎ 215560) at 43/1 Thanon Setthathirat also handles ticketing for Lao Aviation (international only), Royal Air du Cambodge and Vietnam Airlines. Lao Air Service (☎ 213372; fax 215694) at 77 Thanon Fa Ngum can sell tickets for Lao Aviation, Malaysia Airlines, Silk Air and Thai Airways International.

Road
Buses South The main provincial bus terminal, built with Japanese aid in 1990, stands next to Talaat Sao on Thanon Khu Vieng. This one handles bus transport to nearby towns in Vientiane Province as well as points south.

A second terminal on Route 13 near Km 6 also has buses to the south, eg to Tha Khaek, Savannakhet and Pakse. Fares and departure frequencies are the same. If you plan to travel by interprovincial bus out of Vientiane, it's a good idea to visit the terminal the day before your anticipated departure to confirm departure times, which seem to change every few months. For some of the long-distance buses, eg Savan and Pakse, it may be possible to purchase tickets in advance.

Senesabay Bus Co (☎ 218052) runs a higher-class bus from Vientiane to Savannakhet, advertising on-board beverage and snack service, air-con, assigned seats and an eight hour trip duration with stops in Paksan and Tha Khaek only. It leaves each morning at 7 am from the Senesabay office opposite the Vientiane Theatre (Odeon Rama) near Talaat Laeng (Talaat Thong Khan Kham) or at 7.15 am from the Talaat Sao terminal. Tickets cost 10,000 kip (the same as the government bus) and can be

Leaving Vientiane by Bus		
Destination	*No of Daily Departures**	*Fare (kip)*
Ban Keun	every 20 minutes	1500
Luang Prabang	3	13,000
Paksan	6	2500
Pakse	3	15,000
Savannakhet	2	10,000
Thalat	every 20 minutes	1500
Tha Deua & Wat Xieng Khuan (Buddha Park)	every 40 minutes	600+
Tha Khaek	2	5000*
Vang Vieng	every 20 minutes	5000*

*from Talaat Sao terminal
+from Talaat Laeng (Khua Luang) terminal

purchased either at the Senesabay office or at the Talaat Sao terminal. Another private company, Angkham Bus Co (☎ 414848), maintains an office at Km 5 south on Route 13 (next to Angkham Toyota). Angkham operates two air-con buses per day to Savannakhet, at 7 am and 8 am respectively, also for 10,000 kip per person.

Buses North Another terminal recently started up inside the parking lot of the Talaat Laeng off Thanon Khua Luang with buses heading north along Route 13 to Thalat, Vang Vieng and Kasi. Jumbo drivers most often refer to this station as the *kíw lot khua lūang* or 'Khua Luang Bus Queue'.

Buses heading north to Luang Prabang leave from just around the corner from the market, on Thanon Khua Luang near its T-junction with Thanon Nong Duang. There are three departures every day, at 6.30 and 7.30 am and 11 pm; each costs 13,000 kip. These buses take around 11 hours to reach Luang Prabang; many travellers make an overnight stop in Vang Vieng to break up the trip.

Friendship Bridge For travel across the Thai-Lao Friendship Bridge, see the introductory Getting There & Away chapter. For fare details to and from Vientiane, see taxi and motorcycle taxi details in the Getting Around section farther on in this chapter.

Train
See the introductory Getting There & Away chapter for information on using Thai trains to reach the Lao-Thai border.

River
Long-Distance Ferry A single river route runs north to Luang Prabang along the Mekong River from Vientiane. Passenger boat service to Luang Prabang has become extremely irregular following improvements to Route 13 north to Vang Vieng and Luang Prabang; most Lao nowadays use road transport since it's faster and cheaper.

Cargo boats to Luang Prabang usually take four or five days upriver, three or four days down, depending on the type of boat, the cargo load and the river height. During the peak dry season ferries can slow considerably, taking as long as a week in either direction. When the river is low, the direct Vientiane-Luang Prabang service on the large, two-deck ferries can be suspended and passengers must take smaller craft, changing boats at the halfway point at Pak Lai.

Luang Prabang ferries leave from the Kao Liaw Boat Landing (Tha Heua Kao Liaw), which is 7.7km west of the Novotel (3.5km west of the fork in the road where Route 13 heads north) in Ban Kao Liaw. The usual departure time is between 8 and 9 am and the maximum passenger load for most boats is 20 people. You should go to Kao Liaw the day before your intended departure to make sure a boat is going and to reserve deck space.

As there is no longer a regular passenger ferry to Luang Prabang, rates are negotiable. Most boat owners will want at least 35,000 kip for the trip. The boats make several stops along the way. Passengers typically sleep on the boat except in Pak Lai, where there are a couple of small guesthouses. If you want to get off in Pak Lai, you would pay less – around 15,000 kip.

Frankly, few people take the slow cargo boats between Vientiane and Luang Prabang any more, especially in this direction. Note that women customarily ride inside the ferries – the outside, front and top decks are considered 'improper' places to sit.

Speedboats Faster boat service is available on six-passenger *héua wái* (speedboats), which cost 25,000 kip per person to Pak Lai, 42,000 kip to Tha Deua and 51,000 kip to Luang Prabang. Count on a full day to reach Tha Deua or Luang Prabang, four or five hours for Pak Lai. To charter a speedboat you'd have to pay a fee roughly equal to six passenger fares. Speedboats leave from the Kao Liaw Boat Landing.

GETTING AROUND

Central Vientiane is entirely accessible on foot. For exploring neighbouring districts, however, you'll need vehicular support.

Although traffic in Vientiane has grown steadily along with the ability of residents to afford vehicles, the expected explosion in numbers of vehicles crossing the Friendship Bridge still hasn't occurred. Privately owned Thai-registered vehicles face many bureaucratic obstacles in entering Laos; new, unregistered vehicles meant for sale in Vientiane, however, can enter more easily.

Mixed in with the Japanese imports you'll see a greying fleet of Citroens, Peugeots and Renaults from the 1940s, American Chevrolets and Fords from the 1960s and early 1970s, and Soviet Volgas and Ladas from the late 1970s and early 1980s.

To/From the Airport

Wattay international airport is only a 10 minute taxi ride north-west of the city centre. Taxis wait in front of the airport for passengers going into town. The going rate for a jumbo (motorcycle taxi) to the centre of town is 4000 kip, for a car taxi 5000 kip

or 100B; drivers may ask for more. Since the kip – and the baht – are on a roller-coaster ride these days, you'd best figure on paying no more than the kip or baht equivalent of US$2 to US$3.

You can also hop a shared jumbo with other passengers for 1000 kip per person – just follow the Lao who have arrived at the airport.

If you're heading farther – say to eastern Vientiane past Wat Si Muang – you'll have to pay around 1500 kip per person for a jumbo, 6000 kip for a car.

There are no public buses direct from the airport, but if you walk 100m south of the terminal to Thanon Luang Prabang, you can catch a bus into town for 300 kip.

Going to the airport from the centre of town, a jumbo costs 2000 kip, a car 2500 to 3500 kip. You can also catch a Phon Hong bus from the Talaat Sao for 300 kip.

Bus

There is a city bus system but it's not oriented towards the central Chanthabuli district where most of the hotels, restaurants, sightseeing and shopping are. Rather, it's for transport to outlying districts to the north, east and west of the centre. Fares for any distance within Vientiane Prefecture are low – about 300 kip for a 20km ride.

Taxi

A small fleet of car taxis operate in Vientiane, mostly stationed in front of the larger hotels as well as at the airport during flight arrival times. Most taxis in town are old Toyotas, 20-year-old leftovers from Bangkok's taxi services. You might also see a new taxi with a 'Taxi Meter' sign on it but in reality the meters are never used and these are the most expensive type of taxi.

For most short trips within town a pedicab or jumbo is cheaper since car taxis are usually reserved for longer trips and for hourly or daily hire. In Vientiane, an older car and driver for the day costs US$20 to US$25 as long as the vehicle doesn't leave town. If you want to go farther afield, eg to Ang Nam Ngum or Vang Vieng, you may have to pay US$30 to US$40 a day.

The standard car taxi fare from the Friendship Bridge to the centre of Vientiane is 200B or up to 10,000 kip. This is reasonable considering that drivers charge half that amount from Wattay airport into town, though the bridge is about five times farther away.

Motorcycle Taxi

Motorcycle taxis usually hold two or three passengers; the larger ones (called jumbos or tuk-tuks) have two short benches in the back and can hold four or five, even six passengers. Fares are similar to pedicabs but of course they're much speedier.

A motorcycle taxi driver will be glad to take passengers on journeys as short as half a kilometre or as far as 20km. Although the common fare for tourists seems to be 1000 kip per person, the fare for a chartered jumbo should be 500 kip per person for distances of 2km or less, plus 200 or 300 kip for each kilometre beyond two; bargaining is mandatory. Share jumbos which run regular routes around town (eg Thanon Luang Prabang to Thanon Setthathirat or Thanon Lan Xang to That Luang) cost 400 kip per person, no bargaining necessary.

From the Thai-Lao Friendship Bridge to the centre of Vientiane the standard jumbo fare is 2000 kip, though many drivers will ask new arrivals from Thailand for 200B (which is what a car taxi should cost). A shared jumbo between the bridge and Talaat Sao is only 600 kip.

You can flag down empty jumbos on the street or pick them up at one of the two main jumbo stands, one on Thanon Khu Vieng near Talaat Sao and the other on Thanon Chao Anou at the Thanon Heng Boun intersection.

Motorcycle Hire

Vientiane Motor, opposite the fountain on Thanon Setthathirat, rents motorbikes from US$10 (Chinese-built 80cc bikes) to US$12 (Thai-assembled 100cc Japanese bikes) per day.

Pedicab

Of late, *sāam-lâw* (samlor) have almost become extinct. Charges are about 800 kip per kilometre (but don't hire a samlor for any distance greater than 2km or so).

Bicycle

This is the most convenient and economical way to get around the city, besides walking. Several guesthouses rent bikes on a regular basis for around 2000 kip per day. Kanchana Boutique (opposite the Hotel Ekalath Metropole on Thanon That Dam) and Queen's Beauty Tailor (on the Fountain Circle) also offer a few bikes for rent for around $2 per day.

Around Vientiane

VIENTIANE TO ANG NAM NGUM

Route 13 leads north from Vientiane to Luang Prabang. While road trips all the way to Luang Prabang were once plagued by security problems around Kasi, the road has been sealed the entire distance and is now generally considered safe due to the heavy presence of Lao military just north of Kasi. Whether the highway is 100% safe from future Hmong bandit/guerrilla attacks in this area, only time will tell. Although we heard rumours of incidents occurring along this road in 1997 and 1998, whenever we tried tracking the stories nothing could be confirmed. Certainly there have been no incidents, however, between Vientiane and Vang Vieng in recent years.

Along the way to Ang Nam Ngum (Nam Ngum Reservoir) are a number of interesting stopover possibilities. **Ban Ilai**, in the district of Muang Naxaithong, has a good market for basketry, pottery and other daily utensils. Three waterfalls can also be visited in Muang Naxaithong. The first, **Nam Tok Tat Khu Khana** (also called Hin Khana), is easy to reach via a 10km turn-off west from the village of Ban Naxaithong near Km 17. The unsigned turn-off for **Nam Tok Tat Son** is near Ban Hua Khua, 25km from Vientiane and 100m past the bridge at Ban Hua Khua. The falls here aren't much, really a stepped set of rapids, but there's a picnic area and trails that lead to nearby limestone caves. To reach **Nam Tok Tat Nam Suang**, take the turn-off west off Route 13 near Km 40 (follow the sign for the Lao-Australian Project Centre), which is between Ban Nakha and Ban Nong Sa. Turn left 3km from the highway before a steel bridge; the falls are around 500m from the bridge. A bit farther north along the river is a set of *kâeng* (rapids) and a picnic area with tables.

At Km 52 along the highway is **Talaat Lak Haa-Sip Sawng** (Km 52 Market), a large daily market which is often visited by

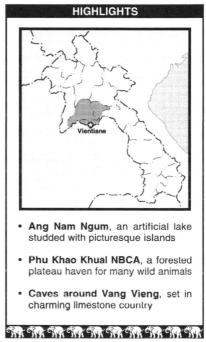

HIGHLIGHTS

• **Ang Nam Ngum**, an artificial lake studded with picturesque islands

• **Phu Khao Khual NBCA**, a forested plateau haven for many wild animals

• **Caves around Vang Vieng**, set in charming limestone country

Hmong and other local ethnic minorities. A bit farther north is the prosperous town of **Phon Hong** at the junction of the turn-off for Thalat and Ang Nam Ngum; Route 13 continues north from here to Vang Vieng. If you're looking for somewhere to eat lunch, Phon Hong is the best bet anywhere between Vientiane and Vang Vieng.

Vientiane Zoological Gardens, also known as Thulakhom Zoo, stands alongside Route 10, 60km from Vientiane. Although this new facility hasn't collected too many different animals yet (with the exception of plenty of deer), the landscaping is good and the zoo seems fairly humane. Entry is 1000 kip, and hours are 8 am to 4.30 pm daily. To

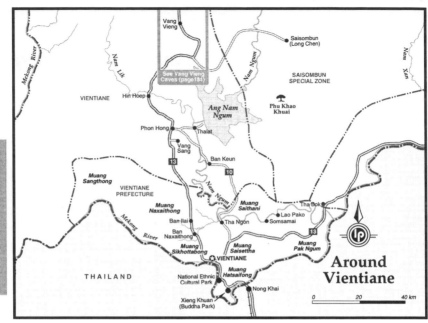

AROUND VIENTIANE

reach here by public transport, take a Ban Keun-bound bus (800 kip) and ask to get off at 'Suan Sat Vieng Chan'.

At **Vang Sang**, 65km north of Vientiane via Route 13, a cluster of 10 high-relief Buddha sculptures on cliffs is thought to date from the 16th century, although there are some local scholars who have assigned it an 11th century Mon provenance. Although this is not likely, given the absence of any other Mon sites in the area, no-one can say for sure that this might not have been some kind of stopover for Buddhist travellers from Mon-Khmer city-states in southern Laos or northern Thailand. Two of the Buddhas reach over 4m in height. The name means Elephant Palace, a reference to an elephant graveyard once found in the vicinity. About 20m farther on from the main sculptures is another cluster with one large and four smaller images. To reach Vang Sang, take the signed turn-off at Km

62 near Ban Huay Thon, and follow a dirt road 1.8km to the sanctuary.

Thalat (Thaa Laat), a little more than halfway between Phon Hong and Ang Nam Ngum, is known for its environmentally incorrect market, which sells all kinds of forest creatures – deer, spiny anteaters, rats and so on – for local consumption.

Between the Route 13 turn-off for Thalat and Ang Nam Ngum are a number of pleasant picnic areas along the river.

ANG NAM NGUM

Situated about 90km from Vientiane, Ang Nam Ngum is a huge artificial lake created by the damming of the Nam Ngum river. A hydroelectric plant here generates most of the power used in the Vientiane area as well as power that's sold to Thailand.

About 250 sq km of forest were flooded when the river was dammed. Several logging rigs – most of them joint Thai-Lao ventures

– are using hydraulic underwater saws to cut submerged teak trees. A Swiss-financed fishing co-operative also harvests fish from the lake.

The lake is dotted with picturesque little islands and a cruise is well worth arranging. Boats holding up to 20 people can be hired from the main pier in Nakheun at the southern end of the lake for 15,000 kip per hour.

Following the 1975 Pathet Lao conquest of Vientiane, an estimated 3000 prostitutes and petty criminals were rounded up from the capital and banished to islands on Ang Nam Ngum – men on separate islands from the women – for several years.

Places to Stay & Eat

A trip to Ang Nam Ngum and back could be done in a day, but if you want to spend a night or two, accommodation is available. *Nam Ngum Tour Co* operates a floating hotel with large, clean rooms complete with private hot baths and air-con for 15,000 kip per night. The boat is fairly pleasant but rarely leaves the pier except when groups book the entire boat; the dock location is not very scenic owing to the grubby lumber operations nearby.

Away from the lake towards the dam itself is a set of solid, Japanese-built *EDL Bungalows* that formerly housed the Japanese engineers who helped design the dam. These are now open to the public as tourist accommodation for US$15/20 single/double per night. Each room has hot water and air-conditioning.

A modest *hotel* on Don Dok Khon Kham, an island only 10 minutes by boat from the harbour, charges 12,000 kip single/double; food is available but running water and electricity only come on in the evening. A shuttle boat out to Don Dok Khon Kham costs 2000 kip.

An older *hotel* on Don Santiphap – Peace Island, quite a bit farther out in the lake – offers basic bungalows for 5000 kip per person. It's badly decaying, and there is no power or running water. The 30 minute boat ride out to this island costs 2500 kip per person.

Next to the floating hotel is a pleasant *floating restaurant* where fish are kept on tethers beneath the deck. When there's an order, the cook lifts a grill in the deck and yanks a flapping fish directly into the galley.

Getting There & Away

Reaching Ang Nam Ngum by public transport is a fairly simple matter. From the Talaat Sao bus terminal you can catch the 7 am bus all the way to Kheuan Nam Ngum (Nam Ngum Dam) for 1000 kip. This trip takes about three hours and proceeds along Route 13 through Thalat. If you don't make the 7 am bus, you'll have to take a bus to Thalat (84km from Vientiane, 1500 kip, 2½ hours by bus) and then get a pick-up or jumbo to the lake for 400 kip. From Vientiane there are four or five buses daily to Thalat.

Taxis in Vientiane usually charge US$35 to US$40 round trip to go to the lake. If you hire one, ask the driver to take the more scenic Route 10 through Ban Keun for the return trip, completing a circle that avoids backtracking. Route 10 is about the same distance as via Thalat.

PHU KHAO KHUAI NBCA

Off Route 13, west of Tha Bok, a gravel road leads to Water Buffalo Mountain, a partially pine-forested plateau at around 670m elevation (rising to 1026m at its highest point). It is surrounded by 2000m peaks and was off-limits to foreigners for many years following the 1975 Revolution because of the presence of a 'secret' Lao army/air force base. Phu Khao Khuai NBCA (National Biodiversity Conservation Area) offers a cool retreat from the furnace-like heat of Vientiane during the March to May hot season. At other times of the year it can be misty and cold.

Surveys in 1994 confirmed the presence of wild elephants and gibbons in the area; locals also report such rare species as the gaur, Asiatic black bear, tiger, clouded leopard, Siamese fireback pheasant and green peafowl. About 88% of Phu Khao Khuai NBCA is forested, though only 32% has been classified as dense, mature forest. The total NBCA covers 2000 sq km, though a section of 710 sq km towards the west – which contains the army base and several villages – may soon be excised to make conservation decrees easier to enforce.

Despite a 600 kip entry fee, there are as yet no visitor facilities. Snacks can be purchased from villages – some of which have been inhabited by resettled Hmong – along the way, but it is better to come prepared with your own picnic.

Getting There & Away

Public transport to Phu Khao Khuai is unavailable. It takes around two hours to reach the NBCA from Vientiane via paved Route 13 south and an all-weather gravel road that heads east from Tha Bok.

The western edge of the NBCA – and the namesake mountain peak itself – can be approached from the south via a winding dirt road from Route 10 east of the Tha Ngon bridge over the Nam Ngum. This route is sometimes impassable in the rainy season; any time of year you'd need a sturdy, high-clearance vehicle to negotiate the road. There are still lots of men in green about in this section – along the way you'll pass a couple of Lao military checkpoints.

LAO PAKO

This rustic bamboo thatch ecological resort on the banks of the Nam Ngum river offers a relaxing getaway from Vientiane. Built and operated by an Austrian-German couple in a secluded corner of Vientiane Prefecture (about 55km from the capital), Lao Pako offers quiet country nights along with opportunities for swimming and boating in the river, volleyball and badminton on the property or hiking to nearby villages, wats and waterfalls. The community-oriented proprietors were instrumental in creating a 40 hectare forest preserve on the river's opposite bank; they've also donated money to local village schools.

Lodgings on the landscaped property are built of native materials. A bamboo and wood longhouse contains a seven-bed dorm that costs 14,000 kip per person, plus three rooms for 45,000 kip single/double. Sepa-

rate bungalows with private bath are also available for 60,000 kip. There is also an open-air *sala* where you can sleep on the floor for 6000 kip a night. Lao-style buffet meals are served in a separate open-air shelter. Each month the resort puts on a full-moon party with a barbecue and the sharing of *lào-hái* (Lao-style jar liquor). The latter comes from a nearby village, Ban Kok Hai, which is only 15 minutes away by river. Another riverbank village worth visiting is Tha Sang (Elephant Landing), where a local wat houses a large reclining Buddha and classic central Lao-style *chedi*.

For reservations (advisable on weekends and holidays), call or fax ☎ (021) 312234.

Getting There & Away

The best way to reach Lao Pako is to drive or take the 1½ hour bus trip to Somsamai (bus No 19 from Talaat Sao, 500 kip, three times daily at 6.30 and 11.30 am and 3 pm) on the Nam Ngum river, where a motorised canoe will take you on to the lodge, a 25 minute journey, for 3000 kip.

VANG VIENG

This small town 160km north of Vientiane, or 230km south of Luang Prabang via Route 13, nestles along a scenic bend in the Nam Song river. The town (population 25,000) itself is not without charm, but the main attraction is the karst topography lining the west bank of the river. Honeycombed with unexplored tunnels and caverns, the limestone cliffs here are a spelunker's heaven. Several of the caves are named and play small roles in local mythology – all are said to be inhabited by spirits.

Even if you don't plan on exploring any caves, a walk along the river can be rewarding. Most of the local fishing pirogues are poled along the river, so the scenery is unmarred by noisy motors.

Other than the Chinese-built cement factory 7km south of town and a little-used 1500m American-built airstrip (known as 'Lima Site 6' during the Indochina War) between Route 13 and the town, Vang Vieng is well removed from modernisation and there are lots of tropical birds in the vicinity. Several monasteries in Vang Vieng district date to the 16th and 17th centuries, among them Wat Si Vieng Song (Wat That), Wat Kang, Wat Khua Phan, Wat Si Suman and Wat Phong Phen. Outside of town are a number of Hmong villages, including two which are just 7km and 13km west of town across the Nam Song.

Services in town include a post office, central market, bus station and provincial hospital.

Caves

Tham Jang The most famous of the Vang Vieng caves, this large cavern was used as a bunker in defence against marauding Jiin Haw (Yunnanese Chinese) in the early 19th century; *thàm* means cave, *jang* is steadfast. A set of stairs leads up to the main cavern entrance.

Until recently the only method for lighting your way through the cave was by ignited brush or torch (flashlight), but lights have since been installed which the caretakers will turn on once you've paid the 2500 kip entry fee. The fee is payable at the entrance to Vang Vieng Resort before you are allowed to walk through the resort to the hanging footbridge across the river. On top of the entrance fee there are also fees for crossing the resort grounds – 400 kip per car or large vehicle, 200 kip for a motorcycle, 100 kip for bicycles and 200 kip for pedestrians. You could also try reaching the cave by pirogue from town, although chances are someone from the resort would find you and collect the fee anyway.

From the main cave chamber you can look out over the river valley through an opening in the limestone wall; a cool spring at the foot of the cave feeds into the river. You can swim upstream via this spring around 80m into the cave. We have heard reports of muggings or attempted muggings inside Tham Jang. Don't take valuables or lots of cash, and consider visiting this cave in a small group rather than alone or as a couple.

Another cave in the vicinity, **Tham Baat** (Begging Bowl Cave), contains a rusting iron

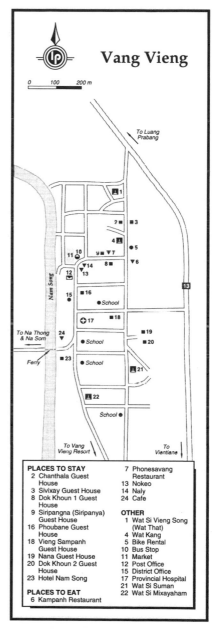

Vang Vieng

0   100   200 m

To Luang Prabang

Nam Song

To Na Thong & Na Som

Ferry

To Vang Vieng Resort

To Vientiane

PLACES TO STAY	
2	Chanthala Guest House
3	Sivixay Guest House
8	Dok Khoun 1 Guest House
9	Siripangna (Siripanya) Guest House
16	Phoubane Guest House
18	Vieng Sampanh Guest House
19	Nana Guest House
20	Dok Khoun 2 Guest House
23	Hotel Nam Song

PLACES TO EAT	
6	Kampanh Restaurant
7	Phonesavang Restaurant
13	Nokeo
14	Naly
24	Cafe

OTHER	
1	Wat Si Vieng Song (Wat That)
4	Wat Kang
5	Bike Rental
10	Bus Stop
11	Market
12	Post Office
15	District Office
17	Provincial Hospital
21	Wat Si Suman
22	Wat Si Mixayaham

AROUND VIENTIANE

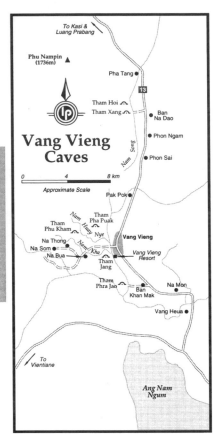

rice fields towards the formation. There are various smaller caves in the vicinity, all of them with entrances high in the limestone cliffs. Getting there is half the fun.

Tham Phu Kham To reach this one, ford the river at the Nam Song Hotel crossing, then walk 6km along an unpaved road to Na Thong village, passing Na Bua village on the way. The same tractor-taxis that ford the river usually continue on to Na Thong for a few hundred kip. From Na Thong follow the path another kilometre to a hill on the north side of the village, following signs to Phu Kham cave. Someone is usually around to collect a 1000 kip entrance fee when you cross the turquoise stream at the base of the formation holding the cave. It's a stiff 200m climb through some interesting scrub forest to the cave, whose cavernous hall contains a recently donated Thai bronze reclining Buddha. Deeper galleries branch off the main cavern formation.

Tham Phra Jao This one takes a little more effort to reach, and although the cave itself is not spectacular, the pleasant walk and natural setting make it worthwhile if you have the time. Follow Route 13 south 6km to Ban Khan Mak village, then take a side road down to the Nam Song. Hire a pirogue to ford the river (or wade across in the driest months), and then follow a path on the opposite bank till it breaks right into a banana grove. At this point head for the giant lone dipterocarp tree (note the huge bees nests hanging high above, and the steps added to the trunk for easy honey collection) standing sentinel near the cave. Soon you'll see the heart-shaped entrance to the medium-size cavern, which contains a Buddha figure but little else.

Tham Xang To reach 'Elephant Cave', head 8km north on Route 13 to Ban Na Dao, then walk west down a wide lane immediately after Km 165 till you meet the river. Cross the footbridge here, or if it's down, hail a pirogue. Walk towards the isolated outcropping on the other bank marked

begging bowl that supposedly belonged to a hermit who lived and died in the caves; you must be fairly nimble to wriggle into this one.

Tham Pha Puak A little farther north of Tham Jang, you can climb to this cave in a karst outcropping surrounded by the aptly named Phaa Daeng (Red Cliffs). To reach it, first ford the Nam Song next to the Nam Song Hotel (by pirogue in high water, or by a Chinese minitractor pulling a wheeled wooden cart in low water), then cross the by tall dipterocarp trees and a small rustic temple. The small cavern contains a few Buddha images and a Buddha 'footprint', plus the elephant-shaped stalactite which gives the cave its name. It's best visited in the morning when light enters the cave.

Tham Hoi If you've already found yourself at Tham Xang you can hike a short distance farther north-west to this cave. Cross a small footbridge over a stream, then traverse some rice fields towards the nearby limestone cliff in which you should be able to see the cave opening. The entrance is guarded by a large Buddha figure; reportedly the cave continues several kilometres into the limestone.

Guides & Maps To find these caves and others, ask an angler or boatman along the river to show you the way – most will be glad to guide you to two or three caves for a couple of thousand kip. Except in the drier months, when you can easily wade across the river, you may also need to hire a boatman to ferry you across the river by pirogue. The section of the river where most of the caves are found is within walking distance (about 2km south-west) of the town centre.

For more extensive cave tours, most guesthouses can arrange a cave guide. A young Lao man called Puk, who can be contacted through the Siripangna (Siripanya) Guest House, can speak some English and is experienced in taking small groups on half-day tours of the caves. He charges 23,000 kip for two people, negotiable for more.

You can buy a sketch map to some of the caves from small restaurants near the market for a few hundred kip.

Places to Stay

With so many travellers spending a few nights here on their way to or from Luang Prabang, Vang Vieng has experienced a minor boom in guesthouses over the last couple of years. On the main road through town, *Sivixay Guesthouse* has very basic rooms for truckers in an older building next

to the road for 3000 kip per room; shared bath and toilet facilities are at the rear. Farther back from the road towards the quieter rear of the property are two newer buildings with four clean rooms for 5000 kip single/double. Each contains two beds, attached toilet and cold shower. Across the street from the Sivixay, the rougher *Chanthala Guest House* is a two storey block building even more oriented towards truckers. Rates are 3000 kip for not-very-clean rooms with shared facilities; the proprietors don't seem very keen on taking foreigners.

Farther south but still in the middle of town, a short road leads east to *Nana Guest House*, a clean and modern two storey house with a curving staircase leading to the 2nd floor and a little parking area in front. Five very clean, ample-sized rooms with attached toilet and hot shower, two beds and ceiling fan cost a reasonable 10,000 kip. Just a few metres farther along the same lane stands the larger two storey *Dok Khoun 2 Guest House*, where all rooms cost 5000 kip single/double. Some rooms contain one large bed, others two twin beds. It's clean and friendly; rooms downstairs offer only shared facilities, while those upstairs have attached toilet and shower.

Off the main road near the main market are several other choices. *Siripangna (Siripanya) Guest House*, next to Phonesavang Restaurant, features basic rooms with attached bath in a one storey building for 4000 kip. The rooms are nothing special, but the staff are friendly and can help with cave explorations. The *Dok Khoun 1 Guest House* on the other side of the street is a bit better but costs 5000 kip.

A little south of the market, almost opposite the District Office, *Phoubane Guest House* offers several slightly dank rooms in a concrete house with shared facilities for 3000/4000 kip single/double. The garden restaurant/sitting area in front might be pleasant if it weren't for the sluggish service and indifferent attitude of the staff. Around the corner on a road leading back to the highway, the *Vieng Samphanh Guest House* has rows of rooms with bamboo walls for 2000/3000

AROUND VIENTIANE

kip single/double. It's the cheapest place in town but not very well kept.

The French-owned *Hotel Nam Song* sits on a slight bluff facing the Nam Song river, with a number of very clean and comfortable rooms with fan, minifridge, attached toilet and hot shower; air-con may be added in the near future. Corner rooms cost US$25, others facing the river are US$20 and rooms around the back are US$16. There's a pleasant veranda sitting area in front with river views, plus a spacious garden. Breakfast is 3000 kip per person.

Vang Vieng Resort (☎ (021) 214743, radio phone 130440), slightly out of town but near the river and opposite Tham Jang, features quiet, comfortable red-tiled cottages (some in duplexes, others separate) for US$20 per room. All rooms come equipped with private toilet and hot shower. The resort also has some dark bamboo rooms in a row house with shared cold shower for 8000 kip. The cottages aren't as nice as the rooms at the Hotel Nam Song, however. Although the location is good, the staff display a somewhat hostile attitude. As we were going to press we heard from a fairly reliable source that a Canadian-Lao had taken over the management of the resort with the intention of lowering prices and making it a better place to stay all around.

Places to Eat
A number of small noodle shops can be found in the vicinity of the market. The *Kampanh Restaurant* is a reliable noodle place on the main road. *Nokeo* and *Naly* on the curve in the road near the market serve standard Lao rice and noodle dishes. Nokeo adds lots of vegies to its foe and also to its khào lâat nàa (stir-fried whatever over rice – your choice of beef, chicken or pork) – not just for fussy foreigners worried about maintaining a high vitamin intake but for all their customers. During the day there are also several food vendors in the market.

The large and relatively clean *Phonesa-vang Restaurant* next to Siripangna Guest House tries hard to meet the idiosyncratic needs of western travellers with vegie versions of noodle and rice dishes and a reduction in the use of chillies and other seasonings too pungent for some visitor's palates. Although the staff seems to get orders wrong about half the time, they try hard and service will undoubtedly improve with experience.

Another spot popular with backpackers is a no-name outdoor *cafe* overlooking the river next to the Hotel Nam Song, near the main river crossing. The food is just OK, and the beer only mildly chilled, but sunsets from this little restaurant can be splendid and it's a good vantage point to watch locals crossing the river, fishing, collecting snails, doing laundry and bathing.

Getting There & Away
Route 13 has been paved all the way to Vang Vieng. From Vientiane's Talaat Laeng (Khua Luang) terminal songthaews leave every 20 minutes in the early part of the day, thinning out a little at night. Departure frequency is similar out of Vang Vieng and vehicles leave from the market area. The fare either way is 5000 kip and the trip takes about three hours. A good place to break the journey along the way to/from Vientiane, if you're travelling by private transport, is at the scenic Hin Hoep river junction. The Pathet Lao, Prince Souvannaphouma and Prince Bounome signed a short-lived peace treaty in the middle of the bridge at Hin Hoep in 1962.

Large buses – usually the heavy wooden kind but occasionally a nicer bus with real seats – to/from Luang Prabang cost 11,000 kip per person and take around six hours. If for any reason you want to get off at Kasi on the way to Vang Vieng you'll only have to pay 10,000 kip and ride for four hours. Buses depart thrice daily – twice in the morning and once in the mid-afternoon.

You can charter a songthaew from Vang Vieng to Luang Prabang for 130,000 kip (or US$50 or 2600B); this means if you could get a group of 12 together you could ride to Luang Prabang with a little more room to stretch out and without having to make frequent stops along the way – for the same individual fare (11,000 kip each). Or pay a bit more and take fewer passengers.

Getting Around

You can easily walk anywhere in town on foot. A shop on the main road between Sivixay Guesthouse and Kampanh Restaurant rents bicycles for US$2 a day. Some people ferry these across the river and ride to villages and caves west of the Nam Song. For cave sites out of town you can charter songthaews in the market – expect to pay around US$10 per trip up to 20km north or south of town.

KASI

This town is little more than a lunch stop for bus passengers and truck drivers travelling on Route 13 between Luang Prabang and Vientiane. About 40km north of town, next to the T-junction between Route 13

and Route 7 going east into Xieng Khuang Province, is Muang Phu Khun, site of a former French fort. The brick and stucco ruins of what may have been an officers quarters (some dispute this, saying it was merely an administration office for the construction of Route 13 early this century) are still visible, overlooking a deep valley. Each room had its own fireplace, a testimony to the area's often chilly cool season temperatures.

The section of highway between Kasi and Muang Phu Khun, which runs along a mountain ridge with excellent views, is an area where rebel attacks have been known to take place. Two army posts in this sector have supposedly secured the highway from such assaults but with the national news blackout on anything having to do with insurgency, it's impossible to know just how secure this district really is.

How Safe is Safe?

Until as recently as 1995, vehicles plying Route 13 just north of Kasi experienced occasional Hmong guerrilla attacks. I've heard unconfirmed rumours that there have been additional incidents since the final sealing in 1996, but none of these were first-hand accounts so it's difficult to know what to believe. A German friend living in Luang Prabang told me that he heard the army had blocked off the highway in the vicinity of Kasi for a few hours in March 1998, and that people living nearby heard automatic weapons fire. Whether these were 'exercises' as alleged, or a more troubling incident, he was unable to ascertain.

The Lao army have established a base north of Kasi and have soldiers and their families living permanently alongside the highway in thatched huts. Another security measure has been cutting down the thick stands of tall grass that once lined the highway here, allowing guerrillas to reach the road quickly and then escape virtually unseen.

I myself would not hesitate to travel the road by public or private transport – I last did so in early 1998 – but with the government's penchant for secrecy regarding military matters it's virtually impossible to say whether the highway can be considered completely secure or not. One thing is certain – it is much, much safer than it was during the 1980s, when estimates said around 10 to 15 people a year were killed along this road.

It's your choice. Hundreds, perhaps thousands of foreigners have traversed the entire stretch between Luang Prabang and Vientiane without any problem. If you count the Lao who travel this road on a daily basis, then millions can be said to have travelled this highway safely. Alternatives include flying with Lao Aviation (whose last crash in 1993 killed more passengers than died in the troubled Kasi area that year) or going by boat from Vientiane, an alternative not without its own safety concerns.

Joe Cummings

Farther north towards Luang Prabang the scenery becomes even more spectacular, with lots of craggy mountain peaks and among the highest limestone formations in South-East Asia – a remote and desolate landscape tailor-made for rebels. Beginning around Km 228, you'll start getting views of **Phu Phra**, a craggy limestone peak considered holy to animist hill tribes and Buddhists alike, on your right (on your left going south).

Places to Stay & Eat
Should you find yourself in Kasi overnight, *Somchith (Nang Som Jit) Guest House*, above a shophouse restaurant on the highway in the middle of town, offers decent two-bed rooms with shared bath for 5000 kip per room.

All the buses, songthaews and trucks stop in the vicinity of several restaurants on the main drag. One is as good as another for basic rice and noodle fare.

Getting There & Away
Kasi is about two hours north of Vang Vieng via paved Route 13. Buses – actually huge truck flatbeds mounted with heavy wooden carriages – cost 1500 kip from Vang Vieng.

From here onward to Luang Prabang along the much improved highway takes four to six hours (depending on vehicle and driver) and costs 10,000 kip.

Northern Laos

Luang Prabang Province

According to the 1995 census the mountainous northern province of Luang Prabang had a total population of 365,000 (down from 434,000 in 1960 – mostly because of refugee emigration) divided among 12 ethnicities, of whom 46% are classified Lao Theung, 40% Lao Loum and 14% Lao Sung. Over 80% of the population are engaged in farming – mostly rice – and of the remaining 17%, who are involved in commerce, most live in the Luang Prabang capital district. For centuries cut off from major markets by a lack of reliable surface transport (even the Mekong is not navigable year-round), the province has developed a small, fragile and largely insular economy of local production and services on a traditional subsistence foundation.

Now that Route 13 from Vientiane is fully sealed and the province can be reached in a single day's drive, this will probably change quite quickly.

History

In the area that now encompasses Luang Prabang Province archaeologists have found large stone drum-shaped objects bearing engraved motifs that are very similar to those of north Vietnam's Dongson bronze drums. Conclusions as to whether they are related to the Dongson culture – and if so whether they are pre or post-Dongson (a culture generally considered to have thrived from 500 BC to 100 AD) – have yet to be drawn. There is also the possibility of a prehistoric or proto-historic connection with the stone jars of Xieng Khuang Province's Plain of Jars.

What is certain is that early Thai-Lao *meuang* established themselves in the high

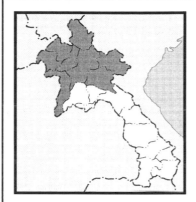

HIGHLIGHTS

- **Luang Prabang**, with its many historic temples, hill tribes and dramatic scenery

- **Pak Ou Caves**, filled with antique Buddha images

- **Boat trips** on the Mekong and Nam Ou rivers

- The enigmatic **Plain of Jars**, littered with mysterious stone vessels

river valleys along the Mekong River and its major tributaries, the Nam Khan, the Nam Ou and the Nam Seuang (Xeuang) sometime between the 8th and 13th centuries. The first Lao kingdom, Lan Xang, was consolidated here in 1353 by the Khmer-supported conqueror Fa Ngum. At that time it was known as Muang Sawa (named after Java, possibly relating to the Javanese invasion of Chenla, centred in southern Laos and northern Cambodia, between the 6th and 8th centuries).

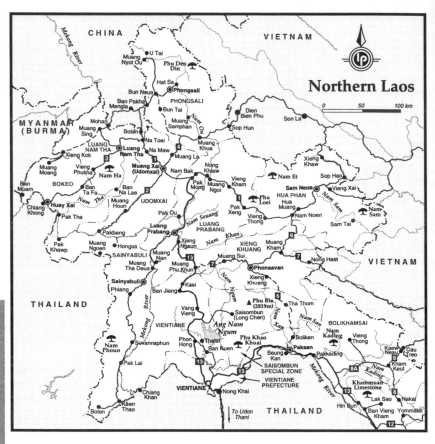

In 1357 the name was changed to Muang Xieng Thong (Gold City District), but some time after King Fa Ngum accepted a Sinhalese Buddha image called Pha Bang (Large Holy Image) as a gift from the Khmer monarchy, the city-state became known as Luang (Great or Royal) Prabang. Luang Prabang remained the capital of Lan Xang until King Phothisarat moved the administrative seat to Vientiane in 1545.

But throughout the Lan Xang period, Luang Prabang was considered the main source of monarchical power. When Lan Xang broke up following the death of King Sulinya Vongsa in 1694, one of Sulinya's grandsons set up an independent kingdom in Luang Prabang which competed with kingdoms in Vientiane and Champasak.

From then on, the Luang Prabang monarchy was so weak that it was forced to pay tribute at various times to the Siamese, Burmese and Vietnamese. After a particularly destructive attack by the Black Flag wing of the Chinese Haw in 1887, the Luang Prabang kingdom chose to accept French protection, and a French Commissariat was established in the royal capital. The French allowed Laos to retain the Luang Prabang monarchy, however, as did the fledgling independent governments that followed; it wasn't until the Pathet Lao took over in 1975 that the monarchy was finally dissolved.

The last king, queen and prince of Luang Prabang were imprisoned in a cave in northeastern Laos where they died, one by one, from lack of adequate food and medical care between 1977 and 1981. The Lao PDR government has yet to issue a full report on the royal family's whereabouts following the Revolution.

LUANG PRABANG

The city of Luang Prabang (officially titled 'Nakhon Luang Prabang', but more commonly known locally as 'Muang Luang') is barely starting to wake up from a long slumber brought on by decades of war and revolution. The population for the entire capital district is 63,000 but the municipality itself has only around 16,000 residents, which is not much of an increase over the 10,000 residents registered when August Pavie governed the city under the French. Only a few concessions have been made to the modern world save for electricity and growing numbers of cars, trucks and motorcycles; rush hour occurs when school lets out and the streets are filled with bicycles.

Luang Prabang has become a tourist attraction because of its historic temples – around 32 of the original 66 built before the era of French colonisation are still standing – and because of its delightful mountain-encircled setting, about 700m above sea level at the confluence of the Khan and Mekong rivers. As well as famous wats as Wat Xieng Thong and Wat Mai Suwannaphumaham, Luang Prabang is also home to the magnificent Royal Palace Museum.

The city's mix of gleaming temple roofs, crumbling French provincial architecture and the multi-ethnic population (Hmong, Mien and Thai tribal people can often be seen walking around town on their way to and from the markets) tends to enthral even the most jaded travellers. The availability of

Luang Prabang's Monarchs

Until the reign of King Sai Setthathirat, the Lan Xang Kingdom was based in Luang Prabang, after which the Lan Xang royal seat moved to Vientiane. In 1707 Lan Xang split into the separate kingdoms of Vientiane, Luang Prabang and Champasak. The separate kingdom of Luang Prabang had the following monarchs:

Kitsalat	1707-25
Khamon Noi	1726-27
Inta Som	1727-76
Sotika Kuman	1776-81
Suryavong	1781-87
interregnum	1787-91
Anulat	1791-1817
Manthatulat	1817-36
Sukaseum	1836-51
Tiantha	1851-72
Oun Kham	1872-87
interregnum	1887-94
Sakkalin	1894-1904
Sisavang Vong	1904-59
Sisavang Vatthana	1959-75*

*Official Lao histories claim Sisavang Vatthana was never crowned.

reasonably priced accommodation keeps many visitors staying on longer than they had planned.

Much of this may change now that Route 13 has been paved all the way through to Luang Prabang from Vientiane, allowing same-day road travel between the two cities for the first time in Lao history. Another paved highway will eventually link Luang Prabang with the Chinese border, turning the city into a relay point for China-Laos-Thailand commerce. One can only hope that some sort of highway bypass will be constructed so that the highway doesn't run straight through the city – as has so far been proposed. The city's fairly recent ascension to UNESCO World Heritage status may yet save the golden goose.

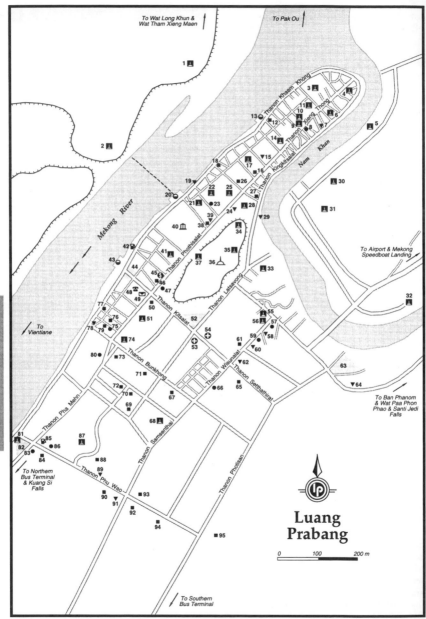

NORTHERN LAOS

To Wat Long Khun &
Wat Tham Xieng Maen

To Pak Ou

1

Thanon Khaem Khong

3

13

12

11
10
9

Xieng Thong

Thanon

14

6

8

7

5

2

To Vientiane

Mekong River

18

15

17

16

19

26

22

25

27

Thanon Kingkitsalat

Nam Khan

30

20

21

23

24

28

39

29

31

40

38

34

42

41

37

35

36

To Airport & Mekong
Speedboat Landing

33

44

45

46

47

Thanon Phothisalat

43

48

49

50

Thanon

Thanon Latsavong

77

76

52

54

55

56

57

32

78

79

75

51

53

Thanon Kitsalat

59

58

60

80

73

74

61

63

Thanon Bunkhong

71

Thanon Wisunalat

62

64

72

70

69

67

66

65

Thanon Setthathirat

To Ban Phanom
& Wat Paa Phon
Phao & Santi Jedi
Falls

68

Thanon Samsenthai

81

82

83

85

86

87

84

To Northern
Bus Terminal
& Kuang Si
Falls

88

89

Thanon Phu Wao

Thanon Pha Mehn

90

91

93

Thanon Photisan

92

94

95

**Luang
Prabang**

0   100   200 m

To Southern
Bus Terminal

PLACES TO STAY
12 Auberge Calao
16 Villa Santi
18 Mekong Guest House
26 Pa Phai Guest House
27 Saynamkhan Guest House
38 Phoun Sab Guest House
46 New Luang Prabang Hotel
50 Phousi Hotel
61 Rama Hotel
65 Viengkeo Hotel
67 Mouang Luang Hotel
69 Somchith Guest House
70 Boun Gning Guest House
71 Souan Savan Guest House
72 Vannida Guest House
73 Hotel Souvannaphoum
76 Viradessa Guest House
77 Vinnida 2 Guest House
79 Vanvisa Guest House
84 Sirivongvanh Hotel
88 Suan Phao Guest House
90 Keopathoum Guest House
92 Muangsua Hotel
93 Maniphone Guest House
94 Manoluck Hotel
95 Phou Vao Hotel

PLACES TO EAT
7 Bar-Restaurant Duang Champa
15 Lao Food Vegetarian

19 Bane Hous; View Khaem Khong
24 Le Saladier
29 Khem Karn Food Garden
39 Luang Prabang Bakery
44 Night Market
58 Luang Prabang Restaurant
60 Visoun Restaurant
62 Yoongkhun Restaurant
64 Vieng Mai Restaurant
78 Nang Somchan Restaurant
89 Villa Sinxay
91 Malee Lao Food

TEMPLES
1 Wat Chom Phet
2 Wat Xieng Maen
3 Wat Xieng Thong
4 Wat Pakkhan
5 Wat Sa-at
6 Wat Khili
9 Wat Sop
10 Wat Sirimungkhun
11 Wat Si Bun Heuang
14 Wat Saen
17 Wat Nong Sikhunmeuang
21 Wat Chum Khong
22 Wat Xieng Muan
25 Wat Paa Phai
28 Wat Pha Phutthabaat
30 Wat Paa Khaa
31 Wat Phon Song
32 Wat Tao Hai
33 Wat Aphai
34 Wat Thammo

35 Wat Tham Phu Si
37 Wat Paa Huak
41 Wat Mai Suwannaphumaham
51 Wat Ho Siang
55 Wat Aham
56 Wat Wisunalat
68 Wat Manolom
74 Wat Pha Mahathat (Wat That)
81 Wat Pha Baat Tai
87 Wat That Luang

OTHER
8 Ban Khily
13 Boats to Pak Ou
20 Ferry Pier
23 Ban Xieng Muan (future Heritage House)
36 That Chomsi
40 Royal Palace Museum
42 Petrol Station
43 Long-Distance Ferries
45 Lane Xang Bank
47 UNESCO Office
48 Telephone Office
49 Post Office
52 Talaat Dala
53 Provincial Hospital
54 Chinese Clinic
57 Lao Red Cross
59 Immigration
63 Talaat Vieng Mai
66 Lao Aviation
75 Silversmiths
80 Provincial Office
82 Talaat That Luang
83 Provincial Treasury
85 Petrol Station
86 Finance Department

NORTHERN LAOS

Orientation

The town nestles in the bent junction of the Mekong and Khan rivers. A large hill called Phu Si (sometimes spelt Phousi) dominates the town skyline towards the middle of the peninsula formed by the confluence of the two rivers. Most of the historic temples are located between Phu Si and the Mekong, while the trading district lies to the south of the hill. Virtually the whole town can be seen on foot in a day or two, though many visitors extend their stay here in order to soak up more atmosphere.

Street names vary widely on city maps and address cards: the main street heading north-east up the peninsula is sometimes called Thanon Phothisalat at its south-west end, and Thanon Xieng Thong towards its north-east end, and yet may be alternatively known as Thanon Sisavang Vong, Thanon Navang or Thanon Sakkarin! Thanon Sisavang Vong (named after the penultimate

The Preservation of Luang Prabang
Marthe Bassene, a French woman married to a colonial doctor, wrote in her published journal of 1909: 'Oh! What a delightful paradise of *far niente* this country protects, by the fierce barrier of the stream, against progress and ambition for which it has no need! Will Luang Prabang be, in our century of exact sciences, of quick profits, of victory by money, the refuge of the last dreamers, the last lovers, the last troubadours?'

As if to answer Bassene's rhetorical question with a resounding affirmative, UNESCO's World Heritage programme and its many independent supporters began lobbying in the early 1990s to have the city added to the World Heritage list. In a preliminary survey UNESCO pronounced Luang Prabang 'the best preserved city in South-East Asia' and on 2 December 1995 the organisation placed the city's name on the register, which makes the city eligible for UN funds for preservation, and Luang Prabang's future now seems to be relatively assured.

The historical and cultural heart of the city straddles a peninsula measuring 1km long by 250m wide inside the confluence of the Nam Khan and Mekong rivers. Here are found the city's most important religious edifices along with the residences of the former nobility and trading aristocracy. It is a graceful neighbourhood of ponds, coconut palms, old wooden or colombage (bamboo lattice daubed with natural mortar) homes in the traditional Lao style, brick and stucco colonial buildings with tiled roofs and neocolonial houses that mix Lao and French motifs with ground-floor walls of brick and plaster and upper-floor walls of wood. Although a few French administrative buildings near the junction of Thanon Phothisalat and Thanon Kitsalat date to between 1909 and 1920, most of the old colonial buildings now standing were constructed between 1920 and 1925.

UNESCO has two French architects and five Lao architects working full-time in Luang Prabang. So far they have identified 679 historic structures in the city and classified them by construction methods and materials. In the next phase, pending approval from the Lao government, the project will develop an architectural typology and each edifice will be granted some degree of legal protection according to its perceived importance to world heritage. In addition to the preservation and restoration of local architecture, the programme calls for a careful review of any new construction and for the restoration and conservation of natural wetlands within the city limits.

If the UNESCO team is successful in their endeavours to preserve and even enhance Luang Prabang's current charm, they will have helped Laos' most important tourist attraction attain a level of sustainability that few places in Asia have been able to maintain. In this the city can truly be called a 'refuge of the last dreamers'.

king) has definitely gone out of government favour but they seem ambivalent about Thanon Sakkarin, named for another king and the last pre-1975 name for the northeastern end (official Lao PDR maps never use this name, however). If UNESCO had its way it might restore the name to Avenue Auguste Pavie, the street's original French colonial name! When giving directions, the locals fortunately almost never quote street names, using landmarks instead.

Easy-to-reach attractions outside of town include the Pak Ou caves to the north, which are reached by river, and the waterfalls of Kuang Si and Taat Sae to the south, reached by road.

Guides & Maps A particularly good French guidebook to the town, if you can find it, is *Louang Prabang* by Thao Boun Souk (pen name for Pierre-Marie Gagneaux), which was published in 1974 by the now defunct

Bulletin des Amis du Royaume Lao. Local tour guides rely heavily on this little book, though local historians question some of its dates in light of new research.

The National Tourism Authority of Laos (NTAL) and National Geographic Service released a good bilingual colour map of the city, *Louang Prabang Tourist Map No 2*, in 1994 – it's available at the main tourist hotels for around US$2.

Information

Tourist Office The NTAL (☎ 212092) maintains an office in the Provincial Offices building on Thanon Pha Mehn (labelled as Thanon Phalanxai on some maps). Aside from the Luang Prabang tourist map and a few other government-printed brochures, there is little printed information available but the staff seem to be reasonably well informed. However, the opening hours are unposted and erratic.

UNESCO World Heritage Information

The UNESCO project maintains an office and information centre in the old customs house on Thanon Navang/Phothisalat. A more public exhibit and information centre called Heritage House (La Maison de Patrimonie) will eventually open in an old wooden Lao house on teak pillars currently undergoing restoration in Ban Xieng Muan. At the moment there is only a little printed information available at the office but the staff say they will soon be printing a map of historical Luang Prabang for distribution.

Immigration Luang Prabang immigration is the strictest in the country when it comes to checking in and out of the province. If you fly into the city, the *jâeng khào/jâeng àwk* procedure is efficiently taken care of at Luang Prabang airport, as it is at most other Lao airports. There are also small immigration police posts at the ferry and speedboat landings, and one at each bus terminal as well.

If you arrive by private vehicle, be sure to check in with immigration on the day of arrival if possible. Officials in Luang Prabang

are quick to levy fines – in fact they do so with great gusto – if you delay the procedure for checking in. The main immigration office (☎ 212435) is on Thanon Wisunalat. Here you'll find a list of all the potential fines you must pay for neglecting to check in or for overstaying your visa; they are the highest in Laos and it's no use arguing that other provincial offices charge less.

Some local guesthouses still post notices warning travellers they must check in at the main immigration office even if they have already been stamped in at an official port of entry. But as of 1998, this was no longer necessary.

Money The Lane Xang Bank, at 65 Thanon Phothisalat near the New Luang Prabang Hotel, will exchange Thai baht, US, Australian and Canadian dollars, French and Swiss francs, German marks and British pounds – cash or travellers cheques – for kip. The bank normally won't change in the other direction because of a claimed shortage of these currencies. They also take Visa credit cards for kip only (same exchange rate as dollars) with a US$100 minimum, charging a 3% commission fee for this service. The bank is open Monday to Saturday from 8.30 am to 3.30 pm. Lane Xang Bank also has an exchange booth inside the post office.

Post The old French-built post office was vacated in favour of a gleaming modern edifice on the corner of Thanon Phothisalat and Thanon Kitsalat, opposite the Phousi Hotel. Domestic and international phone calls can be made at a phonecard booth in front of the post office; cards may be purchased inside. The post office is open weekdays from 8.30 am to 5 pm.

Telephone A new telephone office around the corner from the post office offers both domestic and international calls. It is open from 7.30 am to 10 pm. As elsewhere in Laos, it is cash only and collect (reverse-charge) calls can't be made. On our last visit to Luang Prabang the phone office was closed and a sign in Lao read 'Out of Service'. We checked at the post office and were able to make calls there.

Luang Prabang's area code is 71.

Travel Agencies Although the Luang Prabang Tourism Company (☎ 212199), on Thanon Navang, would like you to think they still have a monopoly on tourism services in the city (as in the pre-privatisation days), they're just one of several tour agencies in town; others include SODETOUR (☎/fax 212092) on Thanon Khaem Khong, Diethelm (☎ 212277) on Thanon Phothisalat, Inter-Lao Tourism (☎ 212034) on Thanon Khingkitsalat, Lane Xang Travel (☎/fax 212753) on Thanon Wisunalat and Lao Travel Service (☎ 212317) on Thanon Navang.

All basically offer the same sorts of one to three-day tours around the province, including visits to hill tribe villages (though none is permitted to provide overnight village treks). Lane Xang Travel seems to be the most receptive to individual travellers looking for something different in the way of itineraries.

Medical Services The Provincial Hospital, on the western side of Thanon Kitsalat, and a Chinese-funded clinic opposite are the only public medical facilities in Luang Prabang to speak of. Neither receive high or even average marks from foreign medical observers. Foreign visitors with serious injuries or illnesses are almost always flown back to Vientiane for emergency transit to hospitals in north-eastern Thailand. If flight services between Luang Prabang and Chiang Mai, Thailand, are initiated (rumour has that it will happen within the next two years), a direct flight to Chiang Mai would be quicker.

Dangers & Annoyances During the late dry season, roughly from February to May, the air over Luang Prabang can become very smoky due to slash-and-burn agriculture in the hills and mountains around the city. It becomes so bad in March and April

that even local residents will complain of red, watery eyes and breathing difficulties. Landscape photography is hopeless, except on the rare day when a strong breeze flushes out the valley. With the arrival of rain in late May or June, the air clears and generally stays that way till the following year. One hopes the authorities will get a handle on the situation before all the forests are gone, and extensive erosion and flooding result.

Walking Tour
If you're in Luang Prabang on your own, a simple walking circuit around the north-east quarter of town will take you to most of the historic and sightseeing spots. You might want to do this circuit in two stages – one part in the coolness of early morning and another in the late afternoon – with time off in between for lunch and a rest. Most of the highlighted sights mentioned below are described in detail later in this chapter.

An easy morning walk might start at the bustling **Talaat Dala** *(tálàat dạláa* or 'Dara Market') at the corner of Thanon Kitsalat and Thanon Latsavong. The area surrounding this market is Luang Prabang's commercial nerve centre and you'll find all sorts of interesting and not-so-interesting shops and vendors here. From the market, head south-east along Thanon Kitsalat, passing the Provincial Hospital on the right and more shops on the left.

At the next big crossroads, and turn left and continue past the Rama Hotel. On the left about 150m past the hotel stands **Wat Wisunalat**, one of the city's oldest temples. At the eastern end of the temple compound is the bulbous **That Makmo** – the Watermelon Stupa. Adjacent to the northern side of the temple is another older temple, **Wat Aham**, which is known for its two large and venerable banyan trees.

Exiting from the east entrance to Wat Aham, bear left (north-west) onto the somewhat busy road that connects central Luang Prabang with the airport. Continue north-west until this road terminates and bear right, following the road that winds its way between the Nam Khan below on the right and Phu Si above on the left. As you continue north-east along this road you'll pass several views of river life below. If you are hungry, look out for the scenic Khem Karn Food Garden on the right overlooking the river; there are also several other informal eating places along the riverbank nearby. Or you can walk up the steep, zigzagging *naga* (water dragon) stairs to **Wat Thammothayalan** (opposite Khem Karn), one of the few active monasteries on Phu Si, for good views of the Nam Khan.

For the second half of this walking circuit, start at the **Royal Palace Museum** on Thanon Phothisalat. (If you would like to tour the museum, note that it's only open Monday to Friday from 8.30 to 10.30 am). From the museum, go north-east on Thanon Phothisalat towards the eastern end of the peninsula formed by the confluence of the Mekong and Khan rivers. Along this road you'll pass several temples of minor note, including **Wat Saen, Wat Sop, Wat Si Muang Khun** and **Wat Si Bun Heuang**, all lined up along the left (north) side of the street. These are interspersed with a number of charming brick-and-stucco **French colonial buildings** on both sides of the street, along with some of the traditional wood-and-mortar houses and hybrid French-Lao brick dwellings. Most of the colonial buildings were built during the 1920s and 1930s.

When you reach the end of the road, bear left and follow the river bend round to **Wat Xieng Thong**, one of the town's premier temples and one well worth spending some time at. After you've had your fill of this wat, exit towards the river and head west (left) on the river road. On your left you'll pass side streets that lead to small, older temples that the usual guided tour itineraries don't include – **Wat Paa Phai, Wat Xieng Muan** and **Wat Chum Khong**.

When you pass the rear side of the Royal Palace Museum on your left, take the next left turn and follow the short road south back to Thanon Phothisalat, where you'll come to **Wat Mai Suwannaphumaham** – noted for its exterior gilded relief – on your

right. On the other side of the street, opposite the front of the Royal Palace Museum, are a set of steps that lead up the north-west side of Phu Si. To the right of the steps above the road is the abandoned *sim* (ordination hall) of one of Luang Prabang's oldest temples, **Wat Paa Huak**, whose interior murals are not to be missed – if you can find someone with a key.

If you're ready for a climb, ascend the steps to the summit of **Phu Si**, where you'll find good views of the town. Sunset vistas from the west side of the hill next to the 19th century **That Chomsi** (Large Stupa) can be superb, except in the late dry season when even the sun's intensity is strongly muted.

Royal Palace Museum (Haw Kham)

This is a good place to start a tour of Luang Prabang since the displays convey some sense of local history. The palace (known locally as Haw Kham or Golden Hall) was built in 1904 – during the early French colonial era – as a residence for King Sisavang Vong and his family. The site for the palace was chosen so that official visitors to Luang Prabang could disembark from their river journeys directly below the palace and be received there.

When Sisavang Vong died in 1959, his son Sisavang Vatthana ascended the throne. According to official Pathet Lao history the 1975 Revolution prevented the prince's actual coronation, though foreign diplomats tell a different story. At any rate, after two years as 'Supreme Advisor to the President', King (or rather Crown Prince) Sisavang Vatthana and his wife were exiled to northern Laos – where they soon expired in a cave – and the palace was converted into a museum. A brochure made by the Ministry of Information & Culture and until recently given out at the museum read, 'On his return to Luang Prabang, Sisavang Vatthana moved to his private residence close to Xieng Thong temple and offered the royal palace to the Government'.

Architecturally, the building features a blend of traditional Lao motifs and French Beaux Arts styles, and has been laid out in

NORTHERN LAOS

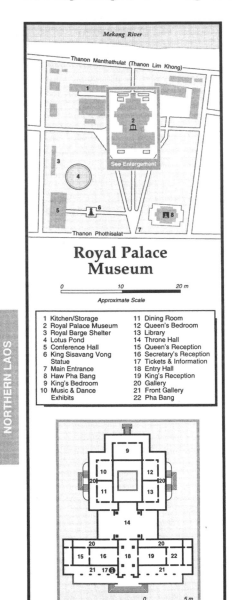

Royal Palace Museum

0   10   20 m

Approximate Scale

1 Kitchen/Storage
2 Royal Palace Museum
3 Royal Barge Shelter
4 Lotus Pond
5 Conference Hall
6 King Sisavang Vong Statue
7 Main Entrance
8 Haw Pha Bang
9 King's Bedroom
10 Music & Dance Exhibits
11 Dining Room
12 Queen's Bedroom
13 Library
14 Throne Hall
15 Queen's Reception
16 Secretary's Reception
17 Tickets & Information
18 Entry Hall
19 King's Reception
20 Gallery
21 Front Gallery
22 Pha Bang

0   5 m

Approximate Scale

a double-cruciform shape with the entrance on one side of the lower crossbar. The steps leading to the entrance are Italian marble. Various royal religious objects are displayed in the large entry hall, including the dais of the former Supreme Patriarch of Lao Buddhism, a venerable Buddha head presented to the king as a gift from India, a reclining Buddha with the unusual added feature of sculpted mourners at his side, an equally uncommon Buddha seated with a begging bowl (the bowl is usually only depicted with a standing figure) and a Luang Prabang-style standing Buddha sculpted of marble in the 'Contemplating the Bodhi Tree' pose.

To the right of the entry hall is the king's reception room, where busts of the Lao monarchy are displayed along with two large gilded and lacquered Ramayana screens crafted by local artisan Thit Tanh. The walls of the room are covered with murals that depict scenes from traditional Lao life. They were painted in 1930 by French artist Alix de Fautereau; each wall is meant to be viewed at a different time of day – according to the light that enters the windows on one side of the room – which corresponds to the time of day depicted.

In the right front corner room of the palace, which opens to the outside, is a collection of the museum's most prized art, including the Pha Bang. Cast of a gold, silver and bronze alloy, this Buddha stands 83cm tall and is said to weigh either 53.4kg or 43kg. Legend says the image was cast around the 1st century AD in Sri Lanka and later presented to the Khmer King Phaya Sirichantha, who in turn gave it to King Fa Ngum in 1359 as a Buddhist legitimizer of Lao sovereignty. Since stylistically it is obviously of Khmer origin, most likely its casting took place nearer to the latter date. The Siamese twice carried the image off to Thailand (1779 and 1827) but it was finally restored to Lao hands by King Mongkut (Rama IV) in 1867. Persistent rumours claim that the actual image on display is a copy and that the original is stored in a vault either in Vientiane or Moscow. The 'real' one supposedly features a bit of gold leaf over the eyes and a hole drilled through one ankle.

Also in this room are large elephant tusks engraved with Buddhas, Khmer-crafted sitting Buddhas and Luang Prabang-style standing Buddhas, an excellent Lao frieze taken from a local temple and three beautiful *saew mâi khán* (embroidered silk screens with religious imagery) that were crafted by the queen.

To the left of the entry hall, the secretary's reception room is filled with paintings, silver and china that have been presented to Laos as diplomatic gifts from Myanmar, Cambodia, Thailand, Poland, Hungary, Russia, Japan, Vietnam, China, Nepal, USA, Canada and Australia. The objects are grouped according to whether they're from 'socialist' or 'capitalist' countries.

The next room to the left was once the queen's reception room. Large royal portraits of King Sisavang Vatthana, Queen Kham Phouy and Crown Prince Vong Savang, painted by the Russian artist Ilya Glazunov in 1967, are hung on the walls. Also on display in this room are friendship flags from China and Vietnam, and replicas of sculpture from New Delhi's Indian National Museum.

Behind the entry hall is the throne hall where royal vestments, gold and silver sabres, and the king's elephant chair (or saddle) are exhibited. Glass cases hold a collection of small Buddhas made of crystal and gold that were found inside the That Makmo stupa. Intricate wall mosaics, placed on a deep red background, took eight craftsmen 3½ years to complete and are a highlight of the palace's art.

Beyond the throne room are the halls or galleries that lead to the royal family's residential quarters. The royal bedrooms have been preserved as they were when the king departed, as have the dining hall and a room that contains royal seals and medals. One of the more interesting displays in the museum is a room in the residential section that now contains Lao classical musical instruments and masks for the performance of Ramayana dance-drama – just about the only

place in the country where you see these kinds of objects on display.

A highly ornate religious pavilion called the Haw Pha Bang – a project planned before the monarchy was abolished – has almost completed construction in the northeast corner of the museum compound. Eventually the Pha Bang will be moved from the museum proper to this pavilion.

Towards the south-east corner of compound stands a large, unlabelled bronze statue of King Sisavang Vong.

Visiting the Museum The Royal Palace Museum (☎ 212470) is open Monday to Friday from 8.30 to 10.30 am and admission is 1100 kip, except during Pii Mai Lao in mid-April when it's upped to 2100 kip. Shoes and other footwear (socks OK) can't be worn inside the museum, there is no photography permitted and you must leave all bags with the attendants. A dress code declares that foreigners must not wear shorts, T-shirts or 'sundresses'. For Lao men the dress is the same, but for Lao women pants, shorts and skirts are forbidden and *phàa sìn* or 'ethnic costume' must be worn.

Wat Xieng Thong

Near the northern tip of the peninsula formed by the Mekong and Khan rivers is Luang Prabang's most magnificent temple, Wat Xieng Thong (Golden City Monastery). King Saisetthathirat built Wat Xieng Thong's sim in 1560, and the compound remained under royal patronage until 1975. Like the royal palace, Wat Xieng Thong was placed within reach of the Mekong. The *hǎw tại* (Tripitaka library) was added in 1828, the *hǎw kạwng* (drum tower) in 1961.

Along with Wat Mai Suwannaphumaham this was the only Luang Prabang wat spared by the Black Flag Haw sacking of the city in 1887. The Black Flag's leader, Deo Van Tri (a Thai Khao or White Thai from the north Vietnamese province of Lai Chau), had studied here as a monk earlier in his life, and he used the desecrated, if not destroyed, temple as his headquarters during the invasion.

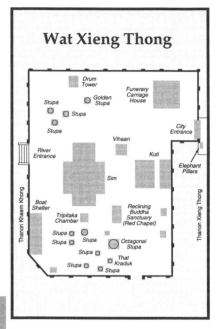

Wat Xieng Thong

Drum Tower

Funerary Carriage House

Golden Stupa

Stupa

Stupa

Stupa

City Entrance

Vihaan

River Entrance

Kuti

Elephant Pillars

Sim

Boat Shelter

Reclining Buddha Sanctuary (Red Chapel)

Tripitaka Chamber

Stupa

Stupa Stupa

Octagonal Stupa

Stupa

That Kraduk

Stupa Stupa

Thanon Khaem Khong

Thanon Xieng Thong

The sim represents what is considered classic Luang Prabang temple architecture, with roofs that sweep low to the ground (the same style – part of the Lan Xang-Lanna legacy – is found in northern Thailand as well). The rear wall of the sim features an impressive 'tree of life' mosaic set in a red background. Inside, the elaborately decorated wooden columns support a ceiling that is vested with *dhammachakkas* (dharma wheels). Other gold-stencilled designs on the interior walls depict the exploits of legendary King Chanthaphanit, about whom there exists no verifiable written history.

To one side of the sim, towards the east, are several small chapels (actually *hǎw*, or hall/building in Lao) and stupas containing Buddha images of the period. The *hǎw tại pha sǎi-nyàat* or reclining Buddha sanctuary (dubbed La Chapelle Rouge or Red Chapel by the French) contains an especially rare reclining Buddha that dates from

the construction of the temple. This one-of-a-kind figure is exquisitely proportioned in classic Lao style (most Lao recliners imitate Thai or Lanna styles), with the monastic robes curling outward at the ankle like rocket fumes. Instead of merely supporting the head, the unique right-hand position extends away from the head in a simple but graceful gesture. In 1931 this image was taken to Paris and displayed at the Paris Exhibition, after which it was kept in Vientiane until its return to Luang Prabang in 1964.

Gold leaf votives line the upper walls of the sanctuary on either side of the reclining image. In front of the image are several seated bronze Buddhas of different styles and ages, and on either side of the altar are small embroidered tapestries depicting a stupa and a standing Buddha. A mosaic on the back exterior wall of this chapel was done in the late 1950s in commemoration of the 2500th anniversary of the Buddha's attainment of *parinibbana* (post-death nirvana). The mosaic is unique in that it relates the exploits of Siaw Sawat, a hero from a famous Lao novel, along with scenes of local village life, rather than a religious scene.

Near the compound's east gate stands the *hóhng kép mîen* (royal funerary carriage house). Inside is an impressive 12m-high funeral carriage (crafted by local artisan Thit Tanh) and various funeral urns for each member of the royal family. (The ashes of King Sisavang Vong, the queen and the king's brother, however, are interred at Wat That Luang at the southern end of Luang Prabang.) Glass cabinets hold royal puppets that were once used for performances of *la-kháwn lek*. Gilt panels on the exterior of the chapel depict semi-erotic episodes from the Ramayana.

Admission to Wat Xieng Thong is 250 kip.

Wat Wisunalat (Wat Vixoun)

This temple to the east of the town centre was originally built in 1513 during the reign of Chao Wisunalat, making it the oldest operating temple in Luang Prabang, but was rebuilt in 1896 to 1898 following an 1887 fire set by the marauding Black Flag Haw.

NORTHERN LAOS

The original was wooden, and in the brick and stucco restoration the builders tried to make the balustraded windows of the sim appear to be fashioned of lathed wood (an old south Indian and Khmer contrivance that is uncommon in Lao architecture). The front roof that slopes sideways over the terrace is another unique feature. Inside the high-ceilinged sim is a collection of gilded wooden 'Calling for Rain' Buddhas and 15th to 16th century Luang Prabang *sima* (ordination stones). These were placed here by Prince Phetsalat after the Haw invasion. The Pha Bang was kept here from 1507 to 1715 and from 1867 to 1894.

In front of the sim is the 34.5m That Pathum (Lotus Stupa), which was started in 1503 by order of Nang Phantin Xieng, wife of King Wisun, and took 19 months to complete. Workmen filled the interior of the stupa with small Buddha images made of precious materials and other sacred items; many of these were stolen when the Haw destroyed the temple (the remainder are on display in the Royal Palace Museum). The stupa underwent reconstruction in 1895 and again in 1932 after a partial collapse due to rain. It is more commonly known as That Makmo or 'Watermelon Stupa' because of its semi-spherical shape.

Admission costs 400 kip.

Wat Aham

Between Wat Wisunalat and the Nam Khan is Wat Aham, which was formerly the residence of the Sangkhalat (Supreme Patriarch of Lao Buddhism). Two large bodhi trees grace the grounds, which are semi-deserted except for the occasional devotee who comes to make offerings to the town's most important spirit shrine at the base of the trees.

Wat Mai Suwannaphumaham

Close to the Phousi Hotel and the post office is Wat Mai (New Temple), which was inaugurated in 1821 (some sources claim it was built in 1797) and was at one time a residence of the Sangkhalat (succeeding Wat Aham). The five-tiered roof of the wooden sim is in the standard Luang

Prabang style. The front veranda is remarkable for its decorated columns and the sumptuous gold relief walls that recount the tale of Vessantara (Pha Wet), the Buddha's penultimate incarnation, as well as scenes from the *Ramayana* and village life. To one side of the sim is a shelter where two long racing boats are kept. These slender, graceful craft are brought out during Lao New Year in April and again in October during the Water Festival. Heavily decorated with flower garlands, each boat will hold up to 50 rowers, plus a coxswain.

Like Wat Xieng Thong, Wat Mai was spared destruction by the Chinese Haw, who reportedly found the sim too beautiful to harm. Most of the other 20 or so buildings are newer.

The Pha Bang, which is usually housed in the Royal Palace Museum, is put on public display at Wat Mai during the Lao New Year celebrations.

A 200 kip admission fee is charged.

Wat That Luang

Legend has it that Wat That Luang was originally established by Ashokan missionaries from India in the 3rd century BC. However, there is no evidence to confirm this and the currently standing sim was built in 1818 under the reign of King Manthatulat. The ashes of King Sisavang Vong are interred inside the large central stupa, which was erected in 1910. A smaller *thâat* (stupa) in front of the sim dates to 1820. Inside the huge sim are a few Luang Prabang Buddha images and other artefacts. This temple appears to have the largest contingent of monks in Luang Prabang.

Wat Manolom

Although its outer appearance isn't very impressive, Wat Mano stands just outside the barely visible city walls and occupies possibly the oldest temple site in Luang Prabang. City annals say it was founded in 1375 on the site of a smaller temple established by King Fa Ngum himself. The decaying sim held the Pha Bang from 1502 to 1513 and still contains a huge sitting bronze Buddha cast in 1372. This image is approximately 6m high and weighs an estimated two tonnes – some parts of the bronze are 15mm thick. Considered an important city talisman, the image would probably have been moved to another temple by now if anyone could figure out how to move it!

The Buddha's arms reportedly came off during a battle between French and Thai armies in the late 19th century. After the battle the colonialists allegedly made off with the appendages except for a portion of one forearm now placed beside one of the feet. Near the sim are the scant remains of an older temple, Wat Xieng Kang, allegedly constructed in 1363.

Wat Mano is west of the Lao Aviation office on Thanon Samsenthai, south-east of the Boun Gning and Vannida guesthouses.

Phu Si

The temples on the upper slopes of 100m-high Phu Si were recently constructed, but it is likely there were other temples previously located on this important hill site. There is an excellent view of the town from the top of the hill.

On the lower slopes of the hill are two of the oldest (and now abandoned) temples in Luang Prabang. The decaying sim at **Wat Paa Huak** – on the lower northern slope near the Royal Palace Museum – has a splendid carved wood and mosaic façade showing Buddha riding Erawan, the three-headed elephant of Hindu mythology (who is usually depicted as Lord Indra's mount). The gilded and carved front doors are often locked, but during the day there's usually an attendant nearby who will open the doors for a tip of a couple of hundred kip. Inside, the original 19th century murals have excellent colour, considering the lack of any restoration. The murals show historic scenes along the Mekong River, including visits by Chinese diplomats and warriors arriving by river and horse caravans. Three large seated Buddhas and several smaller standing and seated images date from the same time as the murals or possibly earlier.

Around on the north-eastern flank of the hill are the ruins of **Wat Pha Phutthabaat**, originally constructed in 1395 during the reign of Phaya Samsenthai on the site of a 'Buddha footprint'. The ruins are of mixed style but are said to show a definite Lanna or Chiang Mai influence, as well as some later Vietnamese augmentation.

To climb to the summit of the hill you must pay a 650 kip fee, collected at the northern entrance near Wat Paa Huak (you do not have to pay the fee to reach the latter temple, however).

At the summit is the 24m-high **That Chomsi**, which was originally erected in 1804 and restored in 1914. This stupa is the starting point for a colourful Lao New Year procession in mid-April. If you continue over the summit and start down the path on the other side you'll come to a small cave shrine called **Wat Tham Phu Si**. Since it's really nothing more than one large, fat Buddha image (a form called Pha Kachai in Lao) and a sheltered area for worshippers, it hardly lives up to its designation as a wat. On a nearby crest is a Russian anti-aircraft cannon which children use as a makeshift merry-go-round.

Other Temples

In the north-east corner of town near the meeting of the Khan and Mekong rivers is a string of historic, still active temples. Facing Thanon Phothisalat just north-east of Villa Santi (see Places to Stay later in this section) is **Wat Saen** (the name, 100,000 Temple, refers to its founding on an initial 100,000 kip donation), a Thai-style wat built in 1718 and restored in 1932 and 1957. The abbot, Ajaan Khamjan, who ordained here in 1940, is one of the most revered monks in Luang Prabang, perhaps in all of Laos. Behind Villa Santi near the river road, the simple **Wat Nong Sikhunmeuang** was built in 1729, burned in 1774 and rebuilt in 1804.

South-west of Villa Santi and set back off the street is **Wat Paa Phai** (Bamboo Forest Temple), whose classic Thai-Lao fresco over the gilded and carved wooden façade

continued on page 209

TEMPLE ARCHITECTURE

Laos never really distinguished itself architecturally. Partially, this is because many structures were built of wood: fire, weather, invasions and B-52 saturation bombing have left few wooden structures in Laos that hail from the pre-eminent 16th to 18th centuries.

The most emblematic edifice in Laos is the Pha That Luang (Great Sacred Stupa) in Vientiane (see the Vientiane chapter earlier for more detail). A *thâat* (from the Pali-Sanskrit *dhatu*, meaning element or component part – usually a sacred relic) is a spire or dome-like structure that commemorates the life of the Buddha. The distinctive shape may have been inspired by the staff and begging bowl of the wandering Buddha, or may be related to pre-Buddhist burial mounds. Many thâat are said to contain dhatu – parts of the Buddha's body, for example, a hair, nail or piece of bone. Considering the number of thâat throughout Buddhist Asia, it is very unlikely that all those which claim to contain Buddha relics actually do.

The curvilinear, four-cornered superstructure on the Pha That Luang is the Lao standard – most stupas of truly Lao origin are modelled on this one (you'll also see Lao stupas in north-eastern Thailand, which is mostly populated by ethnic Lao). It's often said to symbolise an unfurled lotus bud, representing the cooling effect of Buddhism on human passions. Other types of stupas in Laos are either Siamese or Khmer-inspired. An exception is That Makmo, or Watermelon Stupa, in Luang Prabang, which is hemispherical in shape – of possible Sinhalese influence, but still distinctive.

Previous page: The blanket bombing of northern and eastern Laos only decades ago was particularly destructive of the Lao architectural heritage, but earlier skirmishes also took their toll. Haw Pha Kaew, the Jewel (or Emerald) Buddha Temple, in Vientiane was ransacked and plundered of its namesake in 1828 by the Siamese, and remained overgrown until it was rebuilt this century.

Right: The intricate façades of Lao temples are topped by equally impressive roofs. Apart from distinctive layering, they also feature elements such as jâo fâa *(the corner 'hooks') and* nyâwt jâo fâa *(on the central roof ridge), all imbued with spiritual meaning and purpose.*

What's a Wat?

Technically speaking, a *wat* or *vat* is a Buddhist compound where monks reside; without monks it isn't a wat. The word derives from the Pali-Sanskrit term *avasa* which means dwelling. Anywhere in Laos, a typical wat will contain the following structures: *uposatha* or *sim*, a chapel where monks are ordained; a *hāw tại* (Tripitaka library) where Buddhist scriptures are stored; *kuti* (monastic quarters); a *hāw kạwng* (drum tower); a *sāaláa lóng thám* (open-air meeting place where monks and laity listen to *thám* (from the Sanskrit *dharma* or Buddhist doctrine); and various *thâat* (stupas). The smaller stupas are *thâat kádúuk* (bone stupas), where the ashes of worshippers are interred; on *wán pha* (twice-monthly worship days), many people place lighted candles around the thâat kádúuk of their relatives.

Many wats also have a *hāw phīi khún wat* (spirit house), for the temple's reigning earth spirit – in spite of the fact that spirit worship is illegal in Laos today. Various other buildings may be added as needed for wat administration, but these structures are the basics.

The *uposatha* (or in Lao *sim)*, the building in which new monks are ordained, is always the most important structure in any Theravada Buddhist wat. In Laos, there are basically three architectural styles for such buildings – the Vientiane, Luang Prabang and Xieng Khuang styles. In Vientiane, sim are large rectangular buildings constructed of brick and covered with stucco, much like their counterparts in Thailand. The whole structure is mounted on a multilevel platform or pediment.

The high-peaked roofs are layered to represent several levels (always odd in number – three, five, or seven, occasionally nine) corresponding to various Buddhist doctrines which have been codified into groups of these numbers (the three characteristics of existence, the seven levels of enlightenment etc). The edges of the roofs almost always feature a repeated flame motif, with long, finger-like hooks at the corners called jâo fâa (sky lords). Legend has it that these hooks are for catching evil spirits that descend on the sim from above. Umbrella-like spires along the central roof-ridge of a sim, called *nyâwt jâo fâa* or 'topmost jao faa', sometimes bear small pavilions or nagas (mythic water serpents) in a double-stepped arrangement meant to be a representation of Mount Meru, the mythical centre of the Hindu-Buddhist cosmos.

Vientiane Style

The front of a sim in the Vientiane style usually features a large veranda with heavy columns which support an ornamented, over-hanging roof. Some Lao sim will also have a less-ornamented rear veranda, while those that have a surrounding terrace are Bangkok-influenced.

One of the best features of the Vientiane style is the carved wooden shade that often appears along the top portion of the front veranda. Usually the carving depicts a mythical figure such as the half-bird, half-human *kinnari*, or sometimes the Buddha himself, against a background of dense, stylised foliage. The artisans of Lan Xang were extremely adept at this type of woodcarving. Carved porticoes like these represent one of the highlights of Lao art and provide links to sculptural and musical motifs that are seen throughout South-East Asia, from Myanmar to Bali.

Top: The Vientiane style of wat often features an elaborately carved wooden shade over the front veranda.

Right: A bronze cast buddha resting on the veranda of Haw Pha Kaew in Vientiane.

BERNARD NAPTHINE

Luang Prabang Style

In Luang Prabang, the architectural style of the city's temples is akin to the northern Siamese or Lanna style, which is hardly surprising as for several centuries Laos and northern Thailand were part of the same kingdoms. As with the Vientiane style, the roofs are layered, but in Luang Prabang they sweep very low, almost reaching the ground in some instances. The over-all effect is quite dramatic, as if the sim were about to take flight. The Lao are fond of saying that the roofline resembles the wings of a mother hen guarding her chicks.

The temples of the Luang Prabang style are also admired for the gold relief on the doors and the outside walls of some temple structures. Wat Xieng Thong is the prime example. The building's foundation features a much more modest pediment than the Vientiane version.

BETHUNE CARMICHAEL

Above: Detail of a door carving from Wat Xieng Thong in Luang Prabang.

Left: The temples of Luang Prabang have broad sweeping eaves influenced by styles from northern Thailand.

Decades of war has spared only a handful of temples in the Xieng Khuang style.

Xieng Khuang Style

Very little remains of the Xieng Khuang style of sim architecture simply because the province of Xieng Khuang was so heavily bombed during the Indochina War. Fortunately for admirers of temple art, a few examples of the Xieng Khuang style remain in Luang Prabang. As in the Vientiane style, the sim is raised on a multilevel platform; the roof sweeps wide and low, as in the Luang Prabang style, but isn't usually tiered. Cantilevered roof supports play a much more prominent role in the building's overall aesthetics, giving the sim's front profile an almost pentagonal shape. The pediment is curved, adding a grace beyond that of the pediments of the typical Luang Prabang and Vientiane styles.

A fourth, less common style of temple architecture in Laos has been supplied by the Thai Lü, who like the lowland Lao are Theravada Buddhists. Thai Lü temples are typified by thick, whitewashed stucco walls with small windows, two or three-tiered roofs, curved pediments and naga lintels over the doors and steps. Stupas that accompany the Thai Lü style are typically octagonal and gilded, and are often swathed with Thai Lü fabrics embroidered with beads and bits of foil. Though there are examples of Thai Lü influence in a few Luang Prabang and Muang Sing temples, their main location is in Sainyabuli Province, where road travel is rather difficult. Thai Lü temples can be seen in abundance in Thailand's Nan and Phrae provinces.

The Royal Funeral Chapel at Luang Prabang's most magnificent temple, Wat Xieng Thong, which was under royal patronage until 1975.

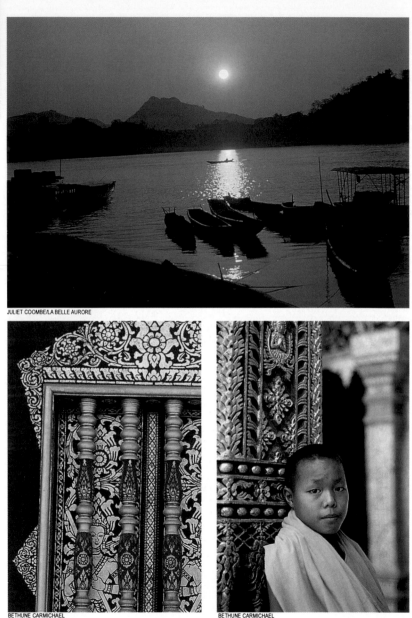

JULIET COOMBE/LA BELLE AURORE

BETHUNE CARMICHAEL

BETHUNE CARMICHAEL

Luang Prabang
Top: A golden sunset over the Mekong River, once the country's prime transport route.
Bottom Left: Ornate window at Wat Saen – Luang Prabang is Laos' capital of traditional arts.
Bottom Right: Young monk at another of the city's richly decorated temples, Wat Long Khun.

continued from page 202

is at least a hundred years old; the pictures depicts scenes from everyday Lao life from the era in which it was painted. Just west of Wat Paa Phai are **Wat Chum Khong** and the older **Wat Xieng Muan**, whose sim dates to 1879. The sculpture inside Wat Xieng Muan is better than average and the ceiling is painted with gold nagas (water dragons), an uncommon motif in this position – possibly a Thai Lü influence. Both of these wats are known for their elaborate *háang thíen* (candle rails) with nagas at either end.

Wat Pha Mahathat, two wats southwest of the Phousi Hotel, is named for a venerable Lanna-style thâat erected in 1548. The sim in front – built in 1910 – is quite ornate, with carved wooden windows and portico, rosette-gilded pillars, exterior jataka (stories of Buddha's life) reliefs and roof in the Luang Prabang style lined with temple bells. The massive nagas along the steps, also Lanna in style, resemble those at Wat Pha That Doi Suthep in Chiang Mai, Thailand.

An easy 3km walk or bicycle ride southeast of town is **Wat Paa Phon Phao**, a forest meditation wat famous for the teachings of Ajaan Saisamut. Saisamut died in 1992 and his funeral was the largest and most well attended monk's funeral Laos has seen in decades. The temple's Santi Jedi (Peace Pagoda), built in 1988, has become something of a tourist attraction. This large yellow stupa contains three floors inside plus an outside terrace near the top with a view of the surrounding plains. The inside walls are painted with all manner of Buddhist stories and moral admonitions. Santi Jedi is open daily from 8 to 10 am and 1 to 4.30 pm.

Behind Talaat That Luang (That Luang Market) in town is a modern Vietnamese-Lao temple, **Wat Pha Baat Tai** (Southern Buddha-Foot Temple). The temple itself is rather garish but behind the temple is a shady terrace overlooking the Mekong; on a hot afternoon this a good place to cool off and watch the sunset.

Across the Mekong River

Across the Mekong from central Luang Prabang are several notable temples in the Xieng Maen district. Xieng Maen itself played an important role as the terminus of the historic road between Luang Prabang and various northern Thai kingdoms (eg Nan and Phayao).

Wat Long Khun, almost directly across the river from Wat Xieng Thong, is the best place to disembark by boat for Xieng Maen explorations. This wat features a nicely decorated portico of 1937 vintage, plus older sections from the 18th century and a few fading jataka murals. When the coronation of a Luang Prabang king was pending, it was customary for him to spend three days in retreat at Wat Long Khun before ascending the throne. A restoration project, which was finished in January 1995 by the Department of Museums & Archaeology with the assistance of the Ecole Française d'Extrême Orient, has brought new life and beauty to the monastery buildings.

Founded in 1889 and since abandoned, **Wat Tham Xieng Maen** is in a 100m-deep limestone cave (known as Tham Sakkalin Savannakuha) a little to the north-west of Wat Long Khun. Many Buddha images from temples that have fallen into decay are kept here; during Pii Mai Lao (Lao New Year) many local worshippers come to Wat Tham to pay homage and cleanse the images. The large stone-block entrance built around the mouth of the cave displays well-done relief work on stair pedestals, and is flanked by two large ruined spirit houses and a couple of champa trees. An iron grate across the cave mouth is usually locked; inquire at Wat Long Khun for someone to come and unlock the gate and guide you through the cave. A donation of 500 kip is requested for this service; the cave is very long and dark, and parts of the cave floor are slippery, so it's a good idea to go with a guide. Bring a torch (flashlight). There are several other caves nearby that are easily found and explored with local help, though none is quite as extensive as Tham Sakkalin Savannakuha.

NORTHERN LAOS

Pii Mai Lao (Lao New Year)

In the middle of April the three day Songkan or 'water festival' celebrates the start of Lao New Year. Songkan, from the Sanskrit *samkranta* (fully passed over), signifies the passage of the sun from the sign of Pisces into the sign of Aries in the zodiac. All of Laos observes this festival, but it is particularly well celebrated in Luang Prabang, where many people dress in traditional clothes for the major events.

On a spiritual level, the Lao traditionally believe that during this three day period the old Songkan spirit departs and the new one arrives. On the first day of the festival, when the old spirit departs, people give their homes a thorough cleaning. The Pha Bang leaves the Royal Palace Museum and is taken to Wat Mai Suwannaphumaham in a solemn procession. The second day is a 'rest day', while on the third the new spirit arrives. This day is considered especially crucial and cleansing rituals extend to the bathing of Buddhist holy images by pouring water onto them through naga-ornamented wooden sluice pipes on raised stands. Senior monks receive a similar treatment, and younger Lao will also pour water over the hands (held palms together) of their elderly relatives in a gesture of respect. A final procession takes place in which three figures wear large red-hued wooden heads with thick hair-like material draped over the rest of their bodies.

Two of the wooden heads are round and display big teeth and heavy eyebrows, features meant to portray the Lao Theung who lived in Luang Prabang before the Lao arrived. Although from one perspective the exaggerated features would appear to be disrespectful of Luang Prabang's Lao Theung antecedents (thought to have been Khamu), the lowland Lao consider these Lao Theung spirits – called Grandfather Nyeu and Grandmother Nyeu – to be guardians of the environment and thus worthy of veneration. A third figure, Sing Kaew Sing Kham (Jewel Lion/Gold Lion), wears the same hairy robe but is topped by a stylised lion head and is possibly a representation of a Khamu king. The three figures receive offerings at Wat Aham and then begin their procession to Wat That Luang, Wat Wisunalat and Wat Xieng Thong, stopping to dance at each. The festival – or at least its spiritual aspect – ends when the Pha Bang is returned to the palace museum. A hundred years ago the festivities used to include an elephant procession and even an elephant basi ceremony but Laos' elephant population has become too small (a study published in 1997 estimated there were only 15 domesticated elephants living in Luang Prabang Province, no doubt all of them engaged full time in logging).

Although the true meaning of the festival is kept alive by ceremonies such as these, nowadays it's mainly a festival of fun. As in Thailand and Myanmar, this is the height of the hot and dry season, and the locals revel in being able to douse one another with cold water to cool off. Activities don't usually get quite as rowdy as in these neighbouring countries but you still have groups of teenagers standing along the roadside and dousing every person or vehicle that passes by with bowls or buckets of water. Foreigners are not exempt from the soaking, so watch out!

At the top of a hill above Wat Long Khun and Wat Tham is peaceful **Wat Chom Phet** (established 1888), from where there is an undisturbed view of the town and river. A small thâat here contains the bones of Chao Thong Di (wife of King Sakkalin), who died in 1929.

Nearby **Wat Xieng Maen** was founded in 1592 by Chao Naw Kaewkumman, son of Setthathirat, but it fell into ruin and had to be rebuilt in 1927. The newer sim contains a few artefacts dating from the original temple, including the original doors. This spot is especially sacred to Xieng Maen residents because it once housed the Pha Bang – on its way back to Luang Prabang in 1867 following a lengthy stay in Vientiane – for seven days and seven nights.

Getting There & Away You can charter boats from Luang Prabang's northern ferry pier to Wat Long Khun for 3000 kip round trip, or you can wait for the infrequent ferry boats which charge a mere 100 kip per passenger.

Markets
Luang Prabang's main market, the **Talaat Dala**, stands at the intersection of Thanon Kitsalat and Thanon Latsavong. Although not enormous by Vientiane standards, it does have an impressive array of hardware, cookware, dried and preserved foodstuffs, textiles and handicrafts.

The main fresh food market, **Talaat That Luang** (also known as Talaat Sao) is at the intersection of Thanon Pha Mehn and Thanon Phu Wao near the river and Wat Pha Baat Tai. Also important for fresh produce is **Talaat Vieng Mai** at the north-eastern end of Thanon Photisan. There is also a small morning vegetable and fruit market where Thanon Kitsalat terminates at the Mekong River, which turns into a night market with food stalls after 5 pm.

Massage & Sauna
At the Lao Red Cross on Thanon Wisunalat, which is housed in a nicely preserved Lao-French building with half-timbered walls, you can take a traditional herbal sauna for 4000 kip and/or an hour-long Swedish-Lao massage for 8000 kip. It is open from Monday to Saturday from 5 to 7.30 pm, Sunday 9 to 11 am (no saunas on Sunday morning, only massage).

Festivals
The two most important annual events in Luang Prabang are Pii Mai Lao (Lao New Year) in April (see the Lao New Year aside) and the boat races during Bun Awk Phansaa in October.

Places to Stay – budget
A boom in accommodation has brought at least a dozen new guesthouses since the last edition of this guide, with more on the way.

Near the Mekong The old silversmithing district near the Mekong, a neighbourhood known as Ban Wat That (named for nearby Wat Pha Mahathat, or 'Wat That' for short), has become a centre for a cluster of modest guesthouses. Facing the river on Thanon Mahin Ounkham (also called Thanon Lim Khong), *Vannida 2 Guest House* is in a white, two storey, flat-roofed house of 1960s vintage. Rooms with high ceilings cost 6000 kip single/double/triple with shared toilet and shower.

Right around the corner in the heart of Ban Wat Thai, another post-independence house contains the friendly *Viradessa Guest House*, where beds in a simple dorm cost 2000 kip or two-bed rooms cost 3500/4000 kip single/double.

Vanvisa Guest House (☎/fax 212925) features six rooms at the back of a shop selling textiles, antiques and handicrafts. Rates are US$5 with shared bath, US$8 with attached bath. The owner, a cultured Lao lady, sometimes makes family-style dinners for guests and can even arrange an informal cooking workshop.

Khem Karn Food Garden (see Places to Eat) on the Nam Khan has three basic huts behind the restaurant area for rent for 15,000 kip. Toilet and bathing facilities are shared.

Historic Temple District In the most concentrated area of colonial architecture and historic monasteries on and off Thanon Photisalat are a few new places with cheap rooms. In an old shophouse between the Royal Palace Museum and the Luang Prabang Bakery, *Phoun Sab Guest House* offers simple but clean two-bed rooms for US$5 with shared hot shower or US$8 with attached hot shower. There's a basic cafe downstairs and rental bikes are available.

Opposite Wat Paa Phai, the friendly *Pa Phai Guest House* (☎ 212752) occupies an historic two storey French-Lao house with a small garden in front. Bamboo walls separate the rooms, which cost 8000 kip single, 15,000 kip double with shared bath. The same family runs the *Mekong Guest House* (same phone number), a larger two storey, post-independence house a couple of blocks away towards the Mekong, where a large two-bed room with shared bath costs 7000 kip, or 13,000 kip with attached bath.

In an old, partially restored colonial-era building two houses up from Villa Santi on Thanon Xieng Thong, the Lao Food Vegetarian restaurant is opening six rooms with outside bath for 20,000 kip per double. The owners said that the tentative name is *Le Marche Guest House*.

Thanon Wisunalat This area is centrally located for trips to Talaat Dala, the immigration office, Lao Red Cross and several restaurants but is otherwise uninspiring. One of the first nongovernment hotels to open following the 1975 Revolution was the *Rama Hotel* (☎ 212247) on Thanon Wisunalat, a basic but well-run hotel where 27 large, clean rooms with fan and private cold bath cost 10,000/15,000 kip single/double a night. The restaurant next door turns into a disco at night – for maximum quiet be sure to request a room at the back and top of the hotel. Or wait it out – the band stops at 11.30 pm.

Viengkeo Hotel (☎ 212271) around the corner on Thanon Setthathirat is a funky two storey house that has seven not-so-clean two and three-bed rooms with shared bath for US$4 per room. Some newer rooms in a row house in back are better at US$6 single/double with private cold shower, US$7 with hot shower. The staff seem a little indifferent and virtually no English or French is spoken. An upstairs veranda sitting area overlooks the street. There are better places to stay.

Ban Wat That This mostly residential neighbourhood extending roughly between Wat Manolom and Wat That Luang and is leafy and quiet. The *Vannida Guest House* (☎ 212374), 87/4 Thanon Noranarai (also

known as Thanon Souvannaphouma), is a atmospheric 80-year-old mansion that once belonged to Chao Khamtan Ounkham, the younger brother of King Sisavang Vatthana. Once governor of Luang Prabang Province, Chao Khamtan died in a 1953 plane crash in Sainyabuli. Most rooms cost 8,000/10,000/ 12,000 kip single/double/ triple with shared toilet and hot showers. Room No 1 downstairs is larger than the rest and comes with hot shower for 15,000 kip. Breakfasts may be ordered in the large downstairs dining area, which is decorated with historic photos of various Luang Prabang personages. The manager speaks good English and French, but since he is also in charge of the Vannida 2 down on the Mekong, he is not always around.

Just 50m south-east along the same street, *Boun Gning Guest House* (☎ 212274) offers 16 rooms with screened windows in a rambling, one storey house for 5000/7000 kip single/double, with shared facilities. All the rooms come with fans. Breakfast is available in the small reception area at the front of the house.

A block to the north-east at 132 Thanon Bunkhong, the *Souan Savan Guest House* (☎ 213020), is a big two storey, cruciform-shaped modern building where ample rooms cost 10,000 kip single/double with shared bath, 12,000 kip with attached bath. There's a pleasant sitting area with chairs and tables downstairs. The owners say they plan to add hot water and air-con without raising rates. If so it will become one of the best value places in town.

Somchith Guest House (☎ 212522), on Thanon Jittalat (the south-westernmost extension of Thanon Latsawong), features several nice-looking rooms in a modern two storey wooden house for 7000/10,000 kip single/double with shared toilet and hot showers.

Thanon Phu Wao This relatively major thoroughfare towards the south end of town features a string of restaurants, guesthouses and hotels, most of which straddle the line between budget and middle range places.

One that falls firmly into the budget end is *Suan Phao Guest House*, which actually lies well off Thanon Phu Wao on a side street behind Wat That Luang. It's really nothing special, a small modern house with only two rooms – a two-bed room for 7000 kip and a three-bed room for 12,000 kip. Bathroom facilities are shared; one of the shower rooms has hot water.

Keopathoum Guest House (☎212978), towards the middle of Thanon Phu Wao, is a modern two storey house which has well-appointed rooms with private toilet and shower for 20,000 kip, not a bad deal. Farther south-east along this street, *Maniphone Guest House* (☎ (071) 212636) is a large hotel-like place run with hotel efficiency. Plain but well-maintained rooms cost 10,000 to 20,000 kip, all with private toilet and shower.

Places to Stay – middle

Historic Temple District The new *Saynamkhan Guest House* (☎ 212976; fax 213009) is housed in a restored two storey colonial near the banks of the Nam Khan, right opposite Wat Phu Phutthabaat, on the street that wraps around the peninsula parallel to the river (as usual the street has more than one name, including Lim Khong, Khaem Khong and Khingkitsalat). The exterior of the building is very attractive, but the interior restoration could have been better. Instead of restoring the original wooden floors the proprietors installed cheap, thin carpet and fake linoleum upstairs. Downstairs looks better, with a cosy bar and slim outdoor terrace. Clean rooms with air-con, TV and small fridge cost US$20/25 single/double, or US$30 for a large corner room with a bathtub.

Farther north-east on the same street, the *Bar-Restaurant Duang Champa* rents four spacious, clean, high-ceilinged rooms, each with four beds and attached hot shower for US$20.

The 40-room *Phousi Hotel* (☎ 212292; fax 212719) is well located at the corner of Thanon Kitsalat and Thanon Phothisalat, on the site of the former French Commissariat.

Standard one-bed rooms are US$28 single/double, while standard two-bed rooms cost US$35 single/double; larger rooms with slightly better furnishings go for US$40 single/double. Tax and service charge are included. All of the rooms are equipped with air-con, hot bath, TV, fridge, minibar and phone. The Phousi has a restaurant inside, as well as a garden snack bar out front. It is a quiet place to stay in spite of its location; during the cool season small tour groups often use this hotel. Credit cards are accepted.

Near the same intersection, the *New Luang Prabang Hotel* (☎ 212264), next to the office of Luang Prabang Tourism Company, offers 15 medium-size rooms on three floors, all with air-con, fridge and hot water, for US$30 single/double. The attached restaurant is open for breakfast, lunch and dinner. It's an OK place, if a bit sterile.

Thanon Phu Wao The *Muangsua Hotel* (☎ 212263) on Thanon Phu Wao has economy rooms with fan for US$15, one-bed air-con rooms for US$20 and two-bed air-con rooms for US$25. All of the 17 rooms come with toilet and hot shower. There's a weekend disco at the back, but like the Rama Hotel it shuts by 11.30 pm.

The nearby *Manoluck Hotel* (☎ 212250; fax 212508) at 121/3 Thanon Phu Wao, constructed in the modern Lao style (classic motifs melded with modern function), offers 30 rooms with fridge, satellite TV, air-con, phone and private hot bath for US$30 to US$40 depending on the number of beds. Most guest rooms are at the back of the building, hence they're protected from street noise, while the restaurant and reception are at the front. The restaurant serves Lao, Chinese, Thai, Vietnamese and European food. Amenities include laundry service, car, motorcycle and bicycle rental and airport transfer. Credit cards accepted.

The *Sirivongvanh Hotel* (☎ 212278), a large cement place on Thanon Phu Wao opposite Wat That Luang, has rooms with private facilities for 25,000/27,000 kip single/double. The entrance to the hotel is around the back, facing away from the street – leading one to suspect this may be a no-tell motel.

Places to Stay – top end

Historic Temple District *Villa Santi* (☎/fax 212267) on Thanon Xieng Thong, about midway between the Royal Palace Museum and Wat Xieng Thong, was the first place in Luang Prabang to take advantage of the abundant French-Lao colonial architecture. Formerly the residence of King Sisavong Vong's wife, then inherited by Princess Manilai, the villa was taken over by the government in 1976, but finally returned to the princess and her family in 1991. Her son-in-law extensively remodelled the 120-year-old residence and decorated it with Lao art and antiques.

In 1992 they opened as an 11-room guesthouse, where comfortable air-con rooms with private bath cost US$45 single/double. A new 14-room wing which was opened in 1995 closely mimics the classic French-Lao architecture of Luang Prabang; standard rooms here also cost US$45, while larger suites are available for US$70 to US$85. Regional cuisine is served in separate upstairs dining rooms in each building; in the old wing there are a few tables and chairs on an adjacent terrace overlooking the street. Traditional massage and sauna are offered. During the high season (December to February) the Villa Santi is often booked out.

A beautifully restored 1930-vintage colonial house facing the Mekong close to Wat Xieng Thong contains the friendly and welcoming *Auberge Calao* (*Heuan Phak Le Ca-Lao Guest House*) (☎ 212100). A Canadian-Lao joint venture, this stately mansion built in a Sino-Portuguese-style has five capacious rooms, all with air-con, private facilities, and verandas overlooking Thanon Lim Khong and the river. Originally built by a Chinese-Lao, the house was occupied by a French merchant from 1936 to 1968. It deserves praise for one of the best architectural renovations – both interior and exterior – in Luang Prabang. A terrace restaurant in front serves Lao and western food. Rooms cost a reasonable US$45 in low season, US$55 in high season.

Ban Wat That Once the official residence of Prince Souvannaphouma, the rambling *Hotel Souvannaphoum* (☎ 212200) opposite the Provincial Office on Thanon Phothisalat had its renovations finished under French supervision in 1995. The government required the owners to drop the final 'a' from the name so as not to evoke the monarchy. Spacious, well-decorated air-con rooms cost US$54/60 single/double, larger suites go for US$70/80 and there are a couple of smaller rooms for US$50/55. A large parlour downstairs is a perfect place to do some quiet reading or postcard writing; an adjacent dining room serves French and Lao cuisine. A new two storey wing added to the property has large air-con rooms with attached bath and private terraces which face a garden for US$50/55 single/double.

Thanon Phu Wao The *Mouang Luang Hotel* (☎/fax 212790) on Thanon Bunkhong is a large two storey, palace-like building with an intricate Lao-style roof and polished dark wood floors throughout. The 35 spacious high-ceilinged rooms have air-con, minibar and marble bathrooms with bathtubs. The two suites feature sitting areas. Rates are US$45 for the regular rooms, US$60 for the suites. Their open-air restaurant offers a menu of Lao and European dishes. The swimming pool was under repair when we visited. Credit cards accepted.

Sitting on the crest of Phu Wao (Kite Hill) on the southern edge of town, the *Phou Vao Hotel* (☎/fax 212194; fax 212534) has gone by several names, including Ratchathirat, Luang Prabang and Mittaphap. Now under European management, the hotel features 57 modern rooms and two suites, all with air-con, private bath and telephone. There is also a pool, landscaped gardens, a piano bar and large restaurant serving Lao and French dishes. Rates are US$45 to US$60 depending on room location (those with city views cost more).

Places to Eat

Regional Luang Prabang has a cuisine all its own. One of the local specialities is *jaew bong*, a jam-like condiment made with chillies and dried buffalo skin. A soup called *áw lám*, made with dried meat, mushrooms, eggplant and a special bitter-spicy root, is also a typical Luang Prabang dish (roots and herbs with bitter-hot effects are a force in Luang Prabang cuisine). Other local delicacies include *phák nâam*, a delicious watercress that's rarely found outside the Luang Prabang area, and *khái pâen*, dried river moss fried in seasoned oil, topped with sesame seeds and served with jaew bong. *Khào kam*, a local red, sweet, slightly fizzy wine made from sticky rice, is abundantly and inexpensively available by the bottle in Luang Prabang. It can be good or bad depending on the brand.

Very good and authentic Lao food is available at *Malee Lao Food*, a casual eatery run by Malee Khevalat on Thanon Phu Wao. Her house specialities include áw lám, khái pâen, phák nâam, làap (mixed with eggplant in the local style) made with water buffalo, deer or fish, áw pǎa-dàek (fish-sauce curry), tǎm-sòm (green papaya salad), pîng nâam-tók (marinated meat barbecued on skewers), tôm jaew pǎa (spicy fish and eggplant soup), kǎeng awm (a very bitter and hot stew) and sáa (minced fish or chicken salad with lemon grass and ginger).

Also on hand at Malee is lào-láo, home-distilled liquor darkened with la-sá-bǐi (a herb that's said to be an appetite-sharpener), khào kam (local rice wine) and Lao beer. The prices are very reasonable; three or four people could sit down to a Lao feast and share four or five dishes with ample beer or lào-láo for under 10,000 kip. Malee is open daily from 10 am to 10 pm.

Another good spot for local cuisine is *Nang Somchan Restaurant* (☎ 252021), a simple but pleasant outdoor place near the cluster of guesthouses in Ban Wat That. The menu features a large selection of Lao and Luang Prabang dishes, including the best choice of vegetarian Lao food in town. It's open daily for lunch and dinner.

Lao, Thai & Chinese Smaller and more basic but also quite good is the *Vieng Mai Restaurant* (an English sign reads 'Lao Restaurant'), a small, wooden local place near Talaat Vieng Mai with very tasty làap, tôm yám pǎa (fish and lemon grass soup), jeun pǎa (fried fish) and sticky rice.

A couple of doors down from Villa Santi, *Lao Food Vegetarian* is a small garden cafe in front of an old colonial house. Vegetarian versions of various traditional Lao dishes, including a làap made from tofu, are available, plus Thai curries, salads, noodles, soups, fruit shakes and Lao beer. A few meat and fish dishes also appear on the menu. Service can be very slow.

Yoongkhun Restaurant, across the street from the Rama Hotel, makes a good 'Salad Luang Prabang', a savoury arrangement of watercress, sliced boiled eggs, tomatoes and onions with a unique dressing. The stir-fried long beans here are also good, as are their egg sandwiches made with baguettes, the chicken curry with potatoes and the fruit smoothies. Tôm yám (lemon grass soup with fish or chicken) is a house speciality. Two or three doors east of the Yoongkhun is the equally good *Visoun Restaurant*, which serves mostly Chinese food. Both restaurants are open from early in the morning till late at night and have fairly extensive bilingual menus; the Visoun also serves Chinese khào-nǒm khuu and other pastries in the early morning.

Farther north-east along the same road, the *Luang Prabang Restaurant* caters to a mostly western clientele with consistent if relatively toned-down Lao and Chinese dishes.

Run by a Frenchman and his Lao wife, the very clean *Villa Sinxay*, on Thanon Phu Wao across the street from the Keopathoum Guest House, serves good, moderately priced Lao and Thai food for breakfast, lunch and dinner.

Riverfront Along the Mekong are several small thatched, open-air restaurants with passable Lao food, including the *View Khaem Khong* and *Bane Hous*. Around the bend on the west bank of the Nam Khan is the *Khem Karn Food Garden* (also called Sala Khem Kane), a larger thatched place with good river views.

A small night market sets up along the river on Thanon Kitsalat close to the long-distance ferry landing, beginning at 5 pm. Illuminating their wares with candles, the vendors offer delicious màak dẹn yat sài (stuffed tomatoes) among many other delights; also look out for khào-nõm bạ-pîng (pancakes made with rice and shredded coconut).

European The new *Luang Prabang Bakery* (☎ 212617) on Thanon Phothisalat offers all kinds of home-made pastries, yoghurt, cheese, sandwiches, ice cream and coffee drinks at moderate prices. There are tables inside as well as a few on the pavement. It's open daily 7 am to 7 pm and is especially popular for breakfast.

Luang Prabang's first independently owned falang eatery, *Bar-Restaurant Duang Champa*, is housed in a white two storey colonial building near the Nam Khan. The extensive menu includes set meals such as steak frites or poulet grillé et frites, along with ice cream, pâté, sandwiches, a few Lao dishes and French wines by the glass or bottle. It's open daily from 9 am to 11 pm.

Bo Ben Nyang, a cafe contained in the gallery/bookshop Baan Khily (☎ 212611) on Thanon Xieng Thong, offers a selection of teas, coffees and snacks with a view of the four temples across the street.

Le Saladier on Thanon Phothisalat one block north-east of Luang Prabang Bakery and Phoun Sab Guest House (on the opposite side of the street) proffers a long list of salads, burgers, French grill, risotto, soups, spaghetti, omelettes, sandwiches, buffalo steak, fruit shakes, wine, beer, cocktails and desserts in an old colonial shophouse. Next door to Le Saladier, the opening of the pizza restaurant *Le Potiron* created a small controversy; what was a pizza joint doing in the historical district?

Hotels Of the main tourist hotels in town, the *Villa Santi* offers the best and most

authentic cuisine – primarily because the chef is the daughter of Phia Sing, who was the last king's personal chef (and author of the only book on Lao cuisine to be published in English). Breakfast at the Santi is usually a western-style egg-and-toast affair (though fõe is available), while lunch and dinner are Lao or French. The Lao food at Villa Santi is much better than the French. French wines are available, but don't miss the house drink called 'Return of the Dragon', a blend of banana liqueur and khào kam.

The restaurant at *Auberge Calao* features a Lao and western menu, but it's the latter food that's best – burgers, fries, sandwiches, salads, omelettes and pancakes.

The dining room at the *Hotel Souvannaphoum* is reported to serve good French food and the decor is superior. The restaurants in the *Phousi* and *Phou Vao* hotels are decent for Lao and international food, though like the Luang Prabang Restaurant the Lao food served here is formulated for falang palates. The Phou Vao has the better service and is also a bit of a nightspot – the poolside tables are a popular gathering place and on weekends there is sometimes a live band.

Entertainment

Most of Luang Prabang is sound asleep or at least nodding off behind a bottle of khào kam by 10 pm.

The only regular nightclub in town is attached to the *Rama Hotel* – it's a very low-key affair with a live band and a loyal Lao clientele who shift easily from dancing the lam wong to the electric slide. The band stops playing promptly at 11.30 pm and it's amazing how fast the crowd clears out after. The *Muangsua Hotel* operates a dance club on weekends.

Things to Buy

The central Talaat Dala market has the best overall selection of textiles and handicrafts, including silver vendors who sell a variety of old and new pieces at fair prices. For quality silver, visit the workshop of silversmith Thithpeng Maniphone, in Ban Wat That (follow the signs opposite the Hotel

Souvannaphoum). Thithpeng crafted silverware for Luang Prabang royalty before 1975 (Thailand's royal family are now some of his best customers). He has 15 apprentice silversmiths working under him to create his designs, but still does the most delicate work himself, including ceremonial swords and spears.

Baan Khily (☎ 212611), on Thanon Xieng Thong, carries a collection of unique and carefully selected Lao crafts, including handmade saa paper. Also on hand are books on Laos and South-East Asia, local and international artwork and an upstairs gallery with rotating exhibits. The German owner is very knowledgeable about the area and is happy to answer questions.

The Villa Santi and Phou Vao Hotel each hold small gift shops with Lao textiles and other handicrafts. Luang Prabang Gallery, just south of the Provincial Hospital, sells T-shirts, postcards and handicrafts.

Sakura Photo on Thanon Setthathirat near the Rama and Viengkeo hotels has the best selection of films, including Fujichrome 100 slide film.

Getting There & Away

Air The US$2 million Thai-assisted up grading of Luang Prabang airport (☎ 212 173) has been completed. The new runway and control tower can now receive larger planes from Vientiane and Chiang Mai, Thailand. The new terminal was designed by Lao architect Hongkad Souvannavong, who also designed the new Lao embassy in Bangkok and the National Assembly in Vientiane, and features a restaurant, phonecard telephone, post office, exchange booth, a branch of the Lane Xang Bank, a National Tourism Authority of Laos booth (which wasn't staffed when we visited), an air-con departure lounge and modern toilets.

Lao Aviation has daily flights to Luang Prabang from Vientiane – sometimes two a day. The flight takes only 40 minutes and the fare is US$55 one way. There are four flights per week to/from Phonsavan (35 minutes, US$35) and three flights per week from Huay Xai (50 minutes, US$46), plus one or two flights per week to/from Luang Nam Tha (30 minutes, US$37) and Muang Xai (35 minutes, US$28). Flight frequency to/from Luang Nam Tha and Muang Xai depends largely on passenger load and the availability of aircraft; the only way to find out for sure is to ask at Lao Aviation a day in advance of scheduled departures.

When flying into Luang Prabang, try to get a window seat – the view of the town as the plane descends over the mountains in preparation for landing is excellent.

Airline Offices Lao Aviation (☎ 212172) is on the same road as the Rama Hotel (but west of Thanon Kitsalat/Thanon Setthathirat) on the way to Wat Manolom on the south side of the street. Even if you have a return reservation from Luang Prabang, you should confirm it the day before your departure.

Road See Dangers & Annoyances in the Facts for the Visitor chapter for important information on bandit/rebel attacks between Kasi and Luang Prabang.

To/From Vientiane Travel between Vientiane and Luang Prabang (420km) has got a lot easier with the sealing of Route 13.

Direct buses to Luang Prabang leave Vientiane from a spot on Thanon Khua Luang near the Talaat Laeng bus terminal – see the Vientiane Getting There & Away section for details. Many visitors break the trip in Vang Vieng.

From Luang Prabang, buses leave from the new southern terminal on Route 13 a few kilometres out of town and go all the way to Vientiane for 13,000 kip (10 hours). To Kasi costs 10,000 kip (four hours) and to Vang Vieng costs 11,000 kip (six hours). Buses leave three times a day at 7 and 8.30 am and noon; the earliest departure is a real bus while the second and third use Soviet trucks with handmade wooden carriages. As bus travel to/from Vientiane increases no doubt the wooden truck-buses will become extinct. It's also possible to charter songthaews to Vang Vieng for 130,000 kip – ask around the southern terminal or in town. The terminal is just a dirt lot with a small covered waiting area and some food vendors.

To/From Muang Xai & Luang Nam Tha

Luang Prabang is linked with Muang Xai Province by road via Pak Mong and via Muang Xai to Luang Nam Tha Province. Songthaews to Pak Mong leave Luang Prabang's northern bus terminal once or twice a day in the morning. The fare is 3000 kip and the trip takes about two hours. From Pak Mong it's another 3000 kip and two hours to Muang Xai. These travel times are only estimates – in Laos such factors as number of passengers, number of stops, weather and road conditions affect travel times.

See the Getting There & Away section for Muang Xai in Udomxai Province later in this chapter for further details.

To/From Nong Khiaw, Xieng Khuang & Sam Neua

It's possible to reach Xieng Khuang via Route 7 (which continues east into northern Vietnam), but this road is beset with hazards both natural and political. For the present the only way to reach Xieng Khuang safely by road from Luang Prabang is to bus north to Pak Mong (3000 kip, two hours), then catch a songthaew to Nong Khiaw and connect to another bus heading south-east along Route 1 until it reaches Route 6 at Nam Noen in southern Hua Phan Province. From Nam Noen you'll have to change to another bus heading south to Phonsavan. Sometimes in either Pak Mong or Nong Khiaw you can intercept the occasional direct Muang Xai-Phonsavan bus. There are also daily direct songthaews to Nong Khiaw for 4000 to 4500 kip per person; the trip takes about four hours. See the Nong Khiaw and Phonsavan sections further on for details.

From Nam Noen you can connect with buses north-east to Sam Neua in Hua Phan Province; see the Sam Neua section for more. From Luang Prabang it's also possible to get buses to the following towns in Luang Prabang Province that lie next to Route 7 between Nong Khiaw and Nam Noen: Vieng Kham (5500 kip, five to six hours, leaves twice daily) and Vieng Thong (10,000 kip, 10 hours, leaves every other day). The trouble with bussing to these towns is that you'll end up waiting for the same Nong Khiaw-Nam Noen connections as you would have in Nong Khiaw. Some people may find the districts of Vieng Kham and Vieng Thong – both of which are heavily populated with Blue Hmong – interesting in themselves.

River Ferries are a major form of transport between Luang Prabang and Huay Xai on the Thai border to the north-west, less so to other towns. In Luang Prabang the main landing for long-distance Mekong River boats, at the north-west end of Thanon Kitsalat, is called Tha Heua Meh. A blackboard at the Navigation Office announces long-distance boat departures, eg to Nong Khiaw and Vientiane – it's all in Lao. A second pier near the Royal Palace Museum is sometimes used when the river level is too low for the main pier.

Speedboats use a landing at Ban Don, 6km north of Luang Prabang. A jumbo to Ban Don from Talaat Dala can be chartered for 3500 kip. From Ban Don into town foreigners are charged a standard 1000 kip for a shared jumbo; to charter one you must pay 6000 kip.

To/From Pakbeng & Huay Xai

As there is no direct road between Huay Xai and Luang Prabang, this is a popular route, especially for visitors doing a north to south Laos itinerary. The Mekong River border crossing at Huay Xai (300km) in Bokeo Province is now open to foreigners carrying valid visas for Laos. Pakbeng (160km) on provincial border of Sainyabuli andUdomxai is a place to break your trip in either direction or to use as a starting point for road trips north-east to Muang Xai.

By slow river ferry the trip to Huay Xai takes two days, with an overnight stay in Pakbeng. The passenger fare is 28,000 kip from Luang Prabang, only 14,000 kip as far as Pakbeng.

The faster and smaller speedboats reach Pakbeng in three hours, Huay Xai in six or seven. The fares are 19,000 kip and 38,000 kip respectively. To charter a speedboat the pilots usually ask that you pay the equivalent of six passenger fares but they'll usually go if you pay for four spaces – often they have paid cargo to carry, too. If you want to share the cost of hiring a boat with other passengers it's best to show up at the northern pier the day before you want to leave and see what your prospects are. Then show up again around 6 am on the morning of your intended departure to queue up. Speedboat passengers have been required to wear life vests and helmets since a Thai passenger was killed in a mishap just south of Pakbeng in 1992.

Speedboat fares are often quoted in Thai baht, though either kip or US dollars are acceptable payment.

To/From Vientiane Several times a week cargo boats leave Vientiane's Kao Liaw jetty for the 430km trip to Luang Prabang. The duration of the voyage depends on the river height, but is typically four or five days upriver, three days down. Passenger travel on these boats, except for merchants accompanying fragile cargo, is rare now that Route 13 is relatively safe and fast. See the Getting There & Away section of the Vientiane chapter for further details.

Speedboat trips downriver to Vientiane take eight or nine hours and cost 51,000 kip for foreigners. To charter a speedboat costs 315,000 kip. Other possible stops along the way include Muang Tha Deua (9000 kip or 60,000 kip for a charter) and Pak Lai (25,000 kip, 105,000 kip charter).

To/From Nong Khiaw & Muang Khua An alternate way to Luang Prabang from Muang Xai in Udomxai Province is via Nong Khiaw in northern Luang Prabang Province, along the Nam Ou river. The Nong Khiaw landing is sometimes referred to as Muang Ngoi, the village on the opposite bank of the Nam Ou, or as Nam Bak, a larger village to the west.

Nowadays speedboat departures north to Nong Khiaw are infrequent due to improved road travel. If you insist on going to Nong Khiaw by boat you may have to charter. In Nong Khiaw it will be easier to find boats farther north to Muang Khua and Hat Sa.

Speedboats between Luang Prabang and Nong Khiaw cost 15,000 kip and take about 2½ hours when the water is high enough; during the dry season some stretches of the upper Nam Ou can be treacherous and most pilots won't attempt the trip. From Nong Khiaw it is an hour west to Nam Bak by passenger truck.

Farther upriver from Nong Khiaw are the riverbank villages of Muang Khua (205km from Luang Prabang) and Hat Sa (265km), both jumping-off points for excursions into Phongsali Province. When available, speedboats to Muang Khua cost 27,000 kip per person from Luang Prabang and take four to five hours.

Be sure to inquire thoroughly as to river conditions before embarking on a Nam Ou trip; from mid-February on it's not unusual for speedboat pilots to get stranded in Nong Khiaw, unable to bring their boats back till the rains arrive in May or June.

You can also sometimes get on a slow cargo ferry from Luang Prabang to Nong Khiaw (7500 kip per person) and Muang Khua (15,000 kip), but given the fact that songthaews to Nong Khiaw cost only 4000 to 4500 kip and take only four hours, you'd have to love river travel for its own sake to spend two days on a cargo boat.

Getting Around
To/From the Airport Shared jumbos or minitrucks charge a uniform 2000 kip per foreigner (less for Lao) from the airport into town; in the reverse direction you can usually charter an entire jumbo for 2500 to 3000 kip.

Local Transport Most of the town is accessible on foot. Jumbos and motor samlors charge around 800 kip for the first kilometre, and 500 kip per additional kilometre.

Several guesthouses rent out bicycles for 2000 to 3000 kip per day.

AROUND LUANG PRABANG
Pak Ou Caves
About 25km by boat from Luang Prabang along the Mekong River, at the mouth of the Nam Ou, are the famous Pak Ou caves (Pak Ou means Mouth of the Ou). Two caves in the lower part of a limestone cliff facing the river are stuffed with Buddha images of all styles and sizes (but mostly classic Luang Prabang standing Buddhas). The lower cave, known as Tham Ting, is entered from the river by a series of steps and can easily be seen in daylight. Stairs to the left of Tham Ting lead round to the upper cave, Tham Phum, which is deeper and requires artificial light for viewing – be sure to bring a torch (flashlight) if you want to see both caves. Entry to the caves costs 2000 kip.

On the way to Pak Ou, you can have the boat stop at the small villages on the banks of the Mekong. Opposite the caves at the mouth of the Nam Ou, in front of an impressive limestone cliff called Phaa Hen, is a favourite spot for local fishers.

Villages near Pak Ou The most common village stop on the way to the caves is **Ban Xang Hai**, which means Jar-Maker Village because at one time that was the cottage industry here. Nowadays the jars come from elsewhere, and the community of around 70 fills them with lào-láo made in the village. Australian archaeologists have excavated pots beneath the village that may be 2000 or more years old.

At **Ban Thin Hong**, opposite the jar village and close to Pak Ou, a recently excavated cave has yielded artefacts dating back 8000 years, including stone, bronze and metal tools, pottery, skeletons and fabrics.

Opposite Pak Ou on the north bank of the Nam Ou, an arduous path over the limestone ridge leads to a rarely visited **Hmong village**.

During the late dry season (January to April) villagers paddle out to sand bars in the middle of the Mekong and pan for gold using large wooden platters.

Getting There & Away You can hire boats to Pak Ou from the pier at the back of the Royal Palace Museum. A longtail boat holding up to 10 passengers should go for 20,000 to 25,000 kip for the day, including petrol. The trip takes 1½ to two hours upriver, and one hour down, not including optional stops at villages. Speedboats from Ban Don can cover the distance in 30 minutes upstream, 20 to 25 minutes down; for one of these you'll have to pay 30,000 kip for a trip of two hours or less. Speedboats can take up to six passengers.

If you go to Pak Ou as part of a guided tour, the guide will most likely stop in at least one village along the way. A picnic lunch is usually brought along to be eaten at the sala (shelter) between the caves.

Ban Phanom & Mouhot's Tomb
This Thai Lü village east of Luang Prabang, around 4km past the airport, is well known for cotton and silk hand-weaving. On weekends, a small market is set up in the village for the trading of hand-woven cloth, but you can turn up at any time and the villagers will bring out cloth for inspection and purchase. Even if you don't expect to buy anything, it's worth visiting to see villagers working on their hand looms. Pieces range from around 3000 to 50,000 kip each. Some of these women are quite wealthy by Lao standards; earning 80,000 kip per day on average.

Between Ban Phanom and the river is the tomb of the French explorer Henri Mouhot, best known as the person who 'discovered' Angkor Wat. Mouhot perished of malaria in Luang Prabang on 10 November 1861. The last entry in his journal was 'Have pity on me, O my God' and his engraved tomb was neglected until found by foreign aid staff in 1990. Mouhot's simple tomb can be found about 4km along the Nam Khan from Ban Phanom; follow the road along the river till you see a wooden bench on the left, descend a track opposite towards the river, then walk about 300m along an overgrown path (upriver from the bench) to reach the whitewashed tomb. If this sounds too complicated, ask someone from the village to guide you to the grave for a tip of 500 kip.

Getting There & Away Songthaews from Luang Prabang to Ban Phanom leave from Talaat Dala several times a day for 300 kip. You can walk here from town in 30 minutes or so.

Kuang Si Falls

This beautiful spot 32km south of town has a wide, many tiered waterfall tumbling over limestone formations into a series of cool, turquoise pools. The lower level of the falls has been turned into a public park with shelters and picnic tables. Vendors sell drinks and snacks.

A trail ascends through the forest along the left side of the falls to a second tier which is more private (most visitors stay below) and has a pool large enough for swimming and splashing around. A cave behind the falls here goes back 10m. You can continue along a more slippery extension of the trail to the top of the falls for a view of the stream that feeds into it. The best time to visit the falls is between the end of the monsoon in November and the peak of the dry season in April.

On the way to Kuang Si you'll pass Ban Tha Baen, a scenic Khamu village with a cool stream, rustic dam and several miniature waterfalls. The owners of the Vanvisa Guest House in Luang Prabang say they have plans to open a Lao-style guesthouse in this village soon.

Getting There & Away Guided tours to the falls booked through a local agency cost US$50 to US$60 and include transport and lunch at the falls. Freelance guides in Luang Prabang offer trips by jumbo for 18,000 kip for two persons, four persons for 26,000 kip. An alternative to going by jumbo all the way would be to take a boat an hour (25km) down the Mekong and do a shorter jumbo ride over to the falls. Freelancers can arrange the latter trip for about the same cost as a straight jumbo trip.

Taat Sae

A conjunction of the Huay Sae and the Nam Khan, the falls at Taat Sae feature multi-level limestone formations similar to those at Kuang Si except that the resulting pools are more numerous, the falls are shorter in height, and the site is much closer to Luang Prabang. Popular with local picnickers on weekends, this place is almost empty during the week.

A 35 minute jumbo ride south of town will take you to the turn-off from Route 13, then to the pristine Lao village of Ban Aen on the Nam Khan river. Jumbo drivers will travel to Ban Aen for 16,000 kip for two persons, 20,000 kip for four, including waiting time in the village while you visit the falls for a few hours. You could also easily reach Ban Aen by bicycle – there's a sign reading 'Tat Se' at the Route 13 turn-off.

From the riverbanks at Ban Aen you can hire a boat to the falls – only five minutes upstream – for 2000 kip each way.

The falls are best visited from August to November when there is still an abundance water in the pools.

NONG KHIAW (MUANG NGOI)

Anyone going by road or river between Luang Prabang, Muang Xai, Xieng Khuang, Phongsali or Hua Phan provinces stands a good chance of spending some time in Nong Khiaw, a village on the west bank of the Nam Ou in northern Luang Prabang Province. Route 1, which extends west to east from Boten to Nam Noen (at the junction with Route 6 in Hua Phan Province), crosses the river here via a steel bridge. Route 13 north from Luang Prabang meets Route 1 about 33km west of town at Pak Mong.

As road travel along these roads has improved over the last few years, the village of Nong Khiaw (Green Pond) has grown considerably, but it is still not much more than a haphazard collection of houses, guesthouses and noodle shops. The village has not yet been hooked into the power grid, though some of the locals run their own generators in the evening.

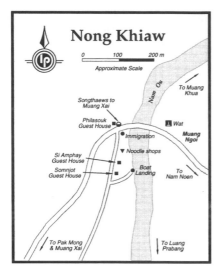

As a few intrepid travellers have found, the wooded karst around Nong Khiaw means there's more to do in the area than just waiting for the next boat or bus out of town. A one day trek into the surrounding forest will take you to Tham Pha Tok, a limestone cave where villagers lived during the Indochina War, and to a nearby waterfall. There are other caves as well, and a few Hmong villages nearby. Loi, owner of Somnjot Guest House, will lead hikes to these and other choice spots for 10,000 kip per person.

Sometimes Nong Khiaw is referred to as Muang Ngoi, which is actually the group of houses on the east bank, and sometimes it's called Nam Bak, which is actually 23km west of Nong Khiaw by road.

Places to Stay & Eat

Near the bridge and river landing are a number of rustic but charming and cheap guesthouses, a big improvement over the old bamboo shack by the landing of years past. Crossing the bridge on Route 1 coming from Xieng Khuang or Hua Phan provinces, the first place you'll come to on your right is the *Philasouk Guest House*, a new two storey wooden house with rooms for 3000 kip per person, though you could probably negotiate to 5000 kip for two. Simple clean rooms have mosquito nets and hard mattresses. Clean bucket baths and toilets are in back of the house. Philasouk is the only guesthouse in Nong Khiaw so far to have its own generator, which runs from sunset till about 10 pm. There is an eating area in front downstairs and the food is good.

Turning left coming from the bridge into town, the first place you'll see is *Si Amphay Guest House*, which is considerably smaller and charges just 1000 kip per person for basic rooms in a slightly cramped house. Candles provide evening lighting.

A little farther on the left, the friendly *Somnjot Guest House* features an unusual row of cubicle-like rooms on stilts inside a small building for 1000 kip per person. Candles again, for now.

A couple of very simple outdoor *noodle shops* opposite Philasouk Guest House offer fish soup, sticky rice and noodles. The Philasouk itself has a large menu.

Getting There & Away

With improved road conditions along Route 13, more people arrive by bus than by boat from Luang Prabang. Speedboats are still available but the price is steep for a charter and it seems there are rarely enough locals travelling by boat these days to count on sharing one. It's also cheaper to charter a songthaew to Luang Prabang than it is to charter a boat.

Road Songthaews bound for Muang Xai leave from in front of Philasouk Guest House two or three times each morning – it's best to check with one of the guesthouses the night before you want to leave to make sure. A vehicle straight through to Muang Xai costs 4000 kip per person. You can also take one of the more frequent songthaews southwest to Pak Mong (the junction of Route 1 and Route 13) for 1,500 kip, then change to another songthaew (3000 kip) to Muang Xai. It takes around four or five hours to reach

Muang Xai depending on the number of passengers and number of stops.

Songthaews or buses going to or from Luang Prabang take four hours and cost 4000 to 4500 kip per person.

For information on getting to Nong Khiaw from points east of the Nam Ou see the Phonsavan or Sam Neua sections.

River Boat travel along the Nam Ou south of Nong Khiaw has been eclipsed by travel along the improved Route 13. Speedboats are still available, however, and they are (for the time being) faster than public buses and songthaews. If you can find people to share a boat to/from Luang Prabang, the going rate is 15,000 kip for a 2½ hour ride, or a steep 100,000 for a charter (some pilots in Nong Khiaw ask even more).

Speedboats going north to Muang Khua in the south of Phongsali Province are more common since the river route is still much faster than road travel if you're coming from Luang Prabang. You can charter a speedboat for 60,000 kip or share with five other passengers for 11,000 kip per person. The trip takes four hours. In Muang Khua you can get another boat farther north to Hat Sa, near Phongsali.

NAM BAK & PAK MONG

These two towns, respectively 23km and 33km west of Nong Khiaw, are little more than supply depots along Route 1 between the Nam Ou river and Muang Xai. Pak Mong (also called Ban Pak Mong) at the junction of Routes 1 and 13 has eclipsed Nam Bak since the sealing of Route 13 north from Luang Prabang. Both towns have post offices, guesthouses and noodle shops, but Pak Mong is the place to make bus connections (west to Muang Xai and Luang Nam Tha, east to Hua Phan and Phonsavan provinces, and south to Luang Prabang).

From Pak Mong you can catch a songthaew to Muang Xai for 3000 kip or to Luang Prabang for the same amount. Either trip takes around two hours or so. To Nong Khiaw, an hour away, it's 1500 kip.

Xieng Khuang Province

Flying into Xieng Khuang Province, one is first struck by the awesome beauty of high green mountains, rugged karst formations and verdant valleys. But as the plane begins to descend, you notice how much of the province is pockmarked with bomb craters in which little or no vegetation grows. Along with Hua Phan, Xieng Khuang is one of the northern provinces that was most devastated by the war. Virtually every town and village in the province was bombed at some point between 1964 and 1973. It has also been the site of numerous ground battles fought over the last 150 years.

The province has a total population of around 200,000 (a surprising increase since the Revolution, probably due to the influx of Vietnamese), mostly comprised of lowland Lao, Vietnamese, Thai Dam, Hmong and Phuan. The original capital, Xieng Khuang, was almost totally bombed out, so the capital was moved to Phonsavan (often spelt Phonsavanh due to Vietnamese influence) after the 1975 change of government. Near Phonsavan is the mysterious Plain of Jars (Thong Hai Hin).

The altitude (average 1200m) in central Xieng Khuang, including Phonsavan and the Plain of Jars, means an excellent climate – not too hot in the hot season, not too cold in the cool season and not too wet in the rainy season. The coldest months are December and January, when visitors should come with sweaters or pullovers, plus a light jacket for nights and early mornings.

History

Although briefly a part of the Lan Xang Kingdom in the 1500s, Xieng Khuang has more often than not been an independent principality or a vassal state of Vietnam called Tran Ninh. From the early 1800s until 1975, central Xieng Khuang – including the Plain of Jars – has been a recurring battle zone. In 1832 the Vietnamese captured the Phuan king of Xieng Khuang, publicly executed him in Hué and made the kingdom a prefecture of Annam, in which the people were forced to adopt Vietnamese dress and customs. Chinese Haw also ravaged Xieng Khuang in the late 19th century, which is one of the reasons that Xieng Khuang accepted Siamese and later French protection later that century.

Major skirmishes between the Free Lao and the Viet Minh took place in 1945 to 1946, and as soon as the French left Indochina the North Vietnamese commenced a build-up of troops to protect Hanoi's rear flank. By 1964 the North Vietnamese and Pathet Lao had at least 16 anti-aircraft emplacements on the Plain of Jars, along with a vast underground arsenal. By the end of the 1960s this major battlefield was undergoing almost daily bombing by American planes as well as ground combat between the US-trained and supplied Hmong army and the forces of the North Vietnamese and Pathet Lao. Among the US military in Laos the area was known as 'PDJ', an acronym for the French term Plaine de Jarres.

A single 1969 air campaign – part of the secret war waged in Laos by the US Air Force and the CIA – annihilated at least 1500 buildings in the town of Xieng Khuang, along with some 2000 more on the Plain of Jars, erasing many small towns and villages off the map permanently. Continuous saturation bombing forced virtually the entire population to live in caves; 'The bombs fell like a man sowing seed' according to one surviving villager.

North Vietnamese troops did their share of damage on the ground, destroying nearby Muang Sui, a city famous for its temples, and towns or villages held by the Royal Lao Army (RLA) in the west of the province.

Now that eastern Xieng Khuang is peaceful, village life has returned to a semblance of normality, although the enormous amount of war debris and unexploded bombs (UXO) spread across the central and eastern areas of the province are a deadly legacy that will remain for generations.

PHONSAVAN

Xieng Khuang's new capital district (population 57,000) has grown tremendously in the 1990s – there are now several semipaved main streets lined with tin-roofed wooden shops, a sprinkling of new concrete structures, two markets, a few government buildings, a bank and several modest hotels and guesthouses. The government has recently added a Lao-Vietnamese Friendship Monument (erected over the buried remains of unidentified war dead) and the Kaysone bust beneath a Buddhist-style pavilion, the latter now mandatory in every district of the country.

Traditionally, the area surrounding Phonsavan and the former capital of Xieng Khuang has been a centre of Phuan language and culture (part of the Thai-Kadai family, like Lao, Siamese and Thai tribals). The local Vietnamese presence continues to increase and you'll hear Vietnamese in the streets almost as frequently as Lao and Phuan.

On some current Lao maps, Phonsavan is labelled 'Muang Pek' (pronounced *meúang paek)*; outside the province most Lao (including Lao Aviation) still call the capital 'Xieng Khuang'.

Information

The staff at the Muang Phuan and Phu Doi hotels and the Auberge de Plaine de Jarres can answer questions on local sights and travel logistics, as well as provide guide services. Sousath Tourism (☎ 312031; fax 312003), at the Maly Hotel, is also a good source of information.

Except for those establishments with their own generators, Phonsavan has electricity from 6 to 11 pm only.

Money Opposite the Phu Doi Hotel is a branch of Aloun May Bank but it doesn't seem to keep regular hours. Don't count on cashing any travellers cheques here – bring plenty of cash to tide you over. The bank also has an exchange desk at the airport.

Post & Communications There is a post office on the main road near the two markets.

Limestone formations, caves and waterfalls are natural features of northern Laos, and can all be seen at Kuang Si Falls, a short distance from Luang Prabang.

BERNARD NAPTHINE

JULIET COOMBE/LA BELLE AURORE

The tranquil image of Muang Khua (top) belies the tragedy of the USA's saturation bombing of northern and eastern Laos during the Indochina War; it remains in the form of war scrap used by villagers (such as the bomb casing fence, bottom), and more sadly in the injuries and deaths from unexploded ordnance.

Domestic phone service here has improved greatly since a satellite connection was established. Phonsavan's area code is 61.

Medical Services The Lao-Mongolian Hospital, on the road to the new airport, isn't too bad as far as Lao provincial hospitals go, although for any major trauma it's quite handicapped.

Dangers & Annoyances Take care when walking in the fields around Phonsavan as undetonated live bombs are not uncommon. Muddy areas are sometimes dotted with 'bomblets' – fist-sized explosives that are left over from cluster bombs dropped in the 1970s.

The western third or so of Xieng Khuang province – more or less west of the Nam Ngum river – remains one of the nation's few hotspots of Hmong guerrilla activity. Other than truck drivers carrying beer, cement and other goods, relatively few residents use Route 7 west of Muang Sui for long-distance travel. The last confirmed attack occurred in February 1998 about 10 to 20km west of Muang Sui on Route 7.

As long as you aren't travelling west of Muang Sui you should be OK. The rainy season is considered the riskiest time of year for attacks. On rare occasions trouble has erupted east of Muang Sui. For example, in early 1997 a 9 pm curfew was imposed in Phonsavan because Hmong terrorists from the western areas of Xieng Khuang threatened to extort local hotel and restaurant owners. Virtually every business owner in town is said to keep a couple of guns to guard against such incidents.

Places to Stay – budget
The simple but friendly *Hay Hin Hotel*, a wooden place on the main street near the market, has basic two-bed rooms with mosquito nets and shared cold bath for 5000 kip per night. The mattresses and walls are thin but the bathrooms are clean. Farther east along the same street, the *Dokkhoun Guest House* (☎ 312189), a two storey white building with a balcony offers OK rooms

with mosquito nets and better quality mattresses for 5000 kip with shared facilities, or 7000 kip with private shower and toilet.

Continuing east along the same street, the *Muang Phuan Hotel* (☎ 312046) has similar but more numerous rooms with shared bath for 5000 kip single/double, attached bath for 6000 kip single/double and four-bed rooms with shared bath for 8000 kip per room. Those in the rear annexe are quietest. This hotel also has its own restaurant.

Next door to the Mouang Phouan, the *Vinh Thong Guest House* (☎ 212622) looks OK from the outside but it's not that well kept inside. Another drawback is the unhelpful all-male staff, who sit around drinking in the lobby nightly. Simple two-bed rooms with shared facilities cost 7000 kip single/double.

The new three storey *Phonsavanh Hotel* (☎ 312206) has a fancy marble front, but ordinary rooms with attached cold shower cost 10,000 kip single, 13,000 kip double. There's a clean restaurant area downstairs.

Back towards the market is the two storey *Vanhaloun (Vanearoune) Hotel* (☎ 312070). It charges 5000 kip for simple rooms with shared bath, 8000 to 10,000 kip for larger rooms with private shower and toilet. It's very clean and food can be arranged.

Places to Stay – middle & top end
A couple of kilometres south-west of the market-bus terminal area, towards the airport and the Plain of Jars (Site 1), the well-run *Maly Hotel* (☎ 312031; fax 312003) offers 11 comfortable rooms (with plans to expand to 21) ranging from US$8 to US$20 a night, all with private toilets and hot showers. A cozy restaurant downstairs has some of the best cooking in town, especially if you order in advance. The owner speaks good English and French, and can arrange tours to the Plain of Jars, local villages, Tham Piu and places farther afield (including Sam Neua and Vieng Xai in neighbouring Hua Phan Province).

The nearby military-owned *Phu Doi Hotel* is housed in a two storey, V-shaped building opposite Aloun May Bank. Ordinary rooms with shared toilet and cold shower facilities

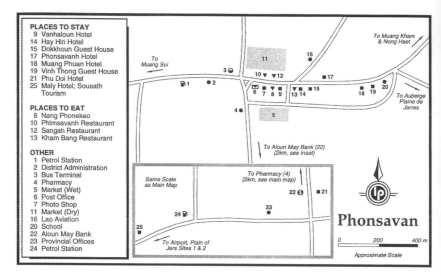

PLACES TO STAY
9 Vanhaloun Hotel
14 Hay Hin Hotel
15 Dokkhoun Guest House
17 Phonsavanh Hotel
18 Muang Phuan Hotel
19 Vinh Thong Guest House
21 Phu Doi Hotel
25 Maly Hotel; Sousath
     Tourism

PLACES TO EAT
8 Nang Phonekeo
10 Phimsavanh Restaurant
12 Sangah Restaurant
13 Kham Bang Restaurant

OTHER
1 Petrol Station
2 District Administration
3 Bus Terminal
4 Pharmacy
5 Market (Wet)
6 Post Office
7 Photo Shop
11 Market (Dry)
16 Lao Aviation
20 School
22 Aloun May Bank
23 Provincial Offices
24 Petrol Station

To Muang Kham & Nong Haet
To Muang Sui
To Auberge Plaine de Jarres
To Aloun May Bank (22) (2km, see inset)
Same Scale as Main Map
To Pharmacy (4) (2km, see main map)
To Airport, Plain of Jars Sites 1 & 2

Phonsavan

0   200   400 m
Approximate Scale

are overpriced at US$8; some better rooms costing from US$12 to US$30 come with hot showers and good mattresses.

On a ridge above the town and surrounding valley is the *Auberge de Plaine de Jarres* (also known locally as the Phu Pha Daeng Hotel), a quiet resort with several two-room cabins with fireplace and hot baths. There is also a separate dining/sitting area with a fireplace and windows which overlook the valley. The cabins are owned by a Vientiane travel agency, which usually books them as part of their Xieng Khuang packages. When not part of a package deal, the cabins cost US$40 to US$50 a night. During the cool season, when the night-time temperatures hover near freezing, the fireplaces and hot baths are very attractive. On the downside the road up the hill can be almost impassable in the rainy season, forcing guests to eat in the overpriced restaurant.

Places to Eat

Besides the hotels with restaurants (Auberge de Plaine de Jarres, Muang Phuan Hotel, Maly Hotel), along the main street through town are several noodle shops and two

places regularly serving rice. You can also get noodles in the early morning at the daily *wet market* behind the post office. This is also the place to come for fresh produce.

The clean and well-run *Sangah (Sa-Nga) Restaurant* near the market and post office offers an extensive menu of Chinese, Thai and Lao food, including good yám, tôm yám, khào khùa and fõe, plus a few western food items. Some expats working in Phonsavan have been known to survive on a nightly diet of steak and chips here. *Phimsavanh Restaurant* next door to the Sangah is similar. Exactly opposite the Sangah, the friendly *Nang Phonekeo (Phonkaew)* serves the best fõe in town.

The newer *Kham Bang Restaurant* on the main street near the Vanhaloun Hotel is a large open-air place with an extensive Lao and Chinese menu. It's one of the few places in town open for breakfast.

Entertainment

A new nightclub called the *Xieng Khuang Mai* can be found just off the road behind the bus terminal. This is where those with a little money – military types and business owners – hang out. Heading west past the petrol station near the bus terminal are a couple of more plebeian *banthóeng* (night-clubs), the *Savanh Raty* and, a little farther west on the opposite side of the street, the *Chitavan Club*. Lao bands play a mixture of Lao, Chinese and Vietnamese pop at all three.

The warehouse-like *Pilot Club* (there is no sign, this is what the locals call it in English) near the Phu Doi Hotel, on the road that leads to the Plain of Jars, provides live music for the entertainment of the Lao airmen stationed nearby and anyone else who should happen along. It is open only on weekends.

Things to Buy
At the dry-goods market near the bus stop you'll find a small but sometimes interesting selection of textiles and other handicrafts, particularly silver, much of it turned out by the Hmong.

Noi Xok Khai, a handicraft shop near the Maly Hotel on the way to the Plain of Jars, sells textiles, silver, woodcarvings and various other locally made items.

Getting There & Away
Air The Soviet ME-8 helicopters that used to fly to Phonsavan have been replaced by Chinese Yun-12 turboprops, and the old Vietnamese airstrip has been replaced by a Russian-built one. Planes fly to/from Vientiane one or two times a day (40 minutes, US$44), and to/from Luang Prabang four times weekly (35 minutes, US$35). Delays are common on the latter flight. The Lao Aviation office (☎ 312027), a wooden shed off the main street in town, is open daily from 7 to 11 am and 1.30 to 3.30 pm; these hours are not strictly followed.

Road Xieng Khuang Province can best be reached by road from the north, ie from Udomxai, northern Luang Prabang (but not southern Luang Prabang) and Hua Phan provinces.

To/From Udomxai & Sam Neua The pot-holed Route 1 carries passengers east across

Udomxai and northern Luang Prabang till the road terminates at Route 6, where a change of buses at the village of Nam Noen continues southward to Phonsavan. It's best to break this journey up by spending the night in Nong Khiaw in northern Luang Prabang so that you can get an early start and make it straight to Phonsavan in one day – a journey of about 12 hours, including a change of bus in Nam Noen. You're also more likely to find public transport in the early morning; afternoon buses are rare in this part of the country. The alternative is to spend the night in the dismal guesthouse in Nam Noen. Expect to pay about 9000 kip from Nong Khiaw to Nam Noen (eight to nine hours), another 5000 kip from the latter to Phonsavan (four hours).

To/from Sam Neua, capital of Hua Phan Province, it's a 12 hour, 238km road trip to Phonsavan via Routes 6 and 7. You must change buses at Nam Noen. Logistically one of the best ways to do this trip is to fly to Sam Neua from Vientiane, then head south by road to Phonsavan. For details see the Sam Neua section.

To/From Vientiane & Luang Prabang It is also possible to reach Xieng Khuang by road from Vientiane or southern Luang Prabang via Routes 13 and 7 (the junction for the two roads is at Muang Phu Khun, about 38km north of Kasi). However, it is a gruelling two or three day trip along a high mountain road, and western Route 7 is considered unsafe – due to rebel attacks – as far east as Muang Sui. This stretch passes military checkpoints which you are highly unlikely to pass without special permission from the Department of Defence.

To/From Pakxan Route 6 connects Phonsavan with Pakxan in Bolikhamsai Province but the road is in a deplorable condition – especially south of Tha Thom (102km from Phonsavan), where it's only passable in the dry season. Route 6 south also goes through the 'insecure' Saisombun Special Zone.

From February to June it's possible to go by road to Tha Thom, then boat to Pakxan (three days down, five or six up) along the Nam Xan. Although this road-river combination is more feasible than trying to travel all the way on Route 6, the danger of guerrilla attacks in Saisombun preclude either journey as a sensible travel choice until security improves.

Other From the bus terminal opposite the dry-goods market, there are public buses to Muang Kham (51km, two hours, 3000 kip, four times a day) and Nong Haet (117km, three hours, 3500 kip, twice a day), plus Russian or Chinese trucks to Muang Sui (51km, two or three hours, 3000 kip, once a day) and Nam Noen (138km, four hours, 5000 kip, once a day).

There are also share taxis – mostly old Volgas or Toyotas – to/from Muang Kham, for 4000 kip per person. All of these prices fluctuate with the availability of petrol from Vietnam, on which Phonsavan depends.

Getting Around
Jumbos are the main form of public transport in town. The standard foreigner price anywhere within a 3km radius is 1000 kip. You can hire a jumbo out to Thong Hai Hin (Plain of Jars, Site 1) for 10,000 kip round trip, including waiting time, for up to six people.

Cars and jeeps can also be hired through the guide services at Sousath Tourism at the Maly Hotel or through just about any guesthouse or hotel for jaunts outside of town.

PLAIN OF JARS
The Plain of Jars is a large area extending around Phonsavan from the south-west to the north-east where huge jars of unknown origin are scattered about in at least a dozen groupings. Site 1 or **Thong Hai Hin** (Stone Jar Plain), 15km southwest of Phonsavan and the largest of the various sites, features 250 jars which weigh mostly from 600kg to one tonne each; the biggest of them weighs as much as six tonnes. Despite local myth, the jars have been fashioned from solid stone, most from a tertiary conglomerate

known as *molasse* akin to sandstone, and a few from granite. The stone doesn't seem to have come from the area; a visiting geologist told me he thought it may have come from the mountains dividing Xieng Khuang and Luang Prabang provinces.

Many of the smaller jars have been taken away by various collectors, but there are still several hundred or so on the plain in the five major sites considered worth visiting. Site 1, the biggest and most accessible, has two pavilions and restrooms that were built for a visit by Thailand's crown prince. This is also where you'll find the largest jar on the plain – it's said to have been the victory cup of mythical King Jeuam and so it's called Hai Jeuam. There's an entrance fee of 1000 kip.

Near Site 1 is a Lao air force base which, along with the new pavilions, somewhat mars the atmosphere. Large bottle-shaped clearings on surrounding hill slopes have traps as the 'bottle top' for snaring swallows – the birds are apparently attracted by the opportunity to take dust baths.

Two other jar sites are readily accessible by road from Phonsavan. Site 2, about 25km south of town, is known locally as **Hai Hin Phu Salato** and features 90 jars spread across two adjacent hillsides. Vehicles can reach the base of the hills, so it's only a short if steep walk to the jars.

More impressive is 150-jar Site 3, also known as **Hai Hin Laat Khai**. It's about 10km further south from Site 2 (or 35km from Phonsavan) on a scenic hilltop near the charming Lao village of Ban Sieng Dii in Muang Kham district, south-east of Phonsavan. Ban Sieng Dii contains a small monastery where the remains of Buddha images that were damaged in the war have been displayed. The villagers, who live in unusually large houses compared with those of the average lowland Lao, grow rice, sugar cane, avocado and banana. To reach the jar site you must hike around 2km along rice paddy dikes and up the hill.

Many smaller sites can also be seen in Muang Kham district, but none of them contain more than 40 or so jars. Only Sites

Plain of Jars

Among the most enigmatic sights in Laos are several meadow-like areas close to Phonsavan littered with large stone jars. Quite a few theories have been advanced as to the functions of the stone jars – they were used as sarcophagi, or used as wine fermenters or for rice storage – but no evidence confirming one theory over the other has been uncovered. Stone lids for a few of the jars can be seen lying around. White quartzite rocks have also been found lying next to some of the jars, along with vases that may have contained human remains.

M Colani, a noted French archaeologist who spent three years studying the Plain of Jars in the 1930s, found a human-shaped bronze figure in one of the jars at Site 1, as well as tiny stone beads. The current whereabouts of these cultural artefacts and

JOE CUMMINGS

One of the largest of the 2000-year-old 'jars', the purpose of which is still a lasting mystery to archaeologists.

other Colani discoveries – photographs of which exist in her 1935 *Megalithes du Haut Laos* – are unknown. You can see the relief of a human figure carved onto jar No 217 at Site 1 – a feature Colani missed. Aerial photographic evidence suggests that a thin 'track' of jars may link the various jar sites in Xieng Khuang, and some researchers hope future excavations will uncover sealed jars whose contents may be relatively intact.

The jars are commonly said to be 2000 years old, but in the absence of any organic material associated with the jars – eg bones or food remains – there is no reliable way to date them. The jars may be associated with the equally mysterious stone megaliths ('menhirs' in Colani's words) found off Route 6 on the way north to Sam Neua, and/or with large Dongson drum-shaped stone objects discovered in Luang Prabang Province. All of the unanswered questions regarding the Plain of Jars make this area ripe for archaeological investigation, a proceeding that has been slowed by years of war and by the presence of UXO. Laos' chief government archaeologist is now studying for an advanced degree at an Australian university in preparation for a renewed, in-depth investigation of the jars. In a few years time we should know much more about them.

Meanwhile local legend says that in the 6th century a cruel chieftain named Chao Angka ruled the area as part of Muang Pakan. Sensitive to the plight of Pakan villagers, the Lao-Thai hero Khun Jeuam supposedly came down from southern China and deposed Angka. To celebrate his victory, Khun Jeuam had the jars constructed for the fermentation of rice wine. According to this version, the jars were cast from a type of cement that was made from buffalo skin, sand, water and sugar cane and fired in a nearby cave kiln. A limestone cave on the Plain of Jars that has smoke holes in the top is said to have been this kiln (the Pathet Lao used this same cave as a shelter during the war).

NORTHERN LAOS

UXO in Xieng Khuang

Left behind by nearly a hundred years of warfare, unexploded munitions, mortar shells, white phosphorous canisters (used to mark bomb targets), land mines and cluster bombs of French, Chinese, American, Soviet and Vietnamese manufacture have affected up to half the population in terms of land deprivation and accidental injury or death. A preponderance of the reported unexploded ordnance (UXO) accidents that have occurred in Xieng Khuang happened during the first five years immediately following the end of the war, when many villagers returned to areas of the province they had evacuated years earlier. In 1974 UXO caused an average of three to four accidents per day nationwide. Today about 40% of the estimated 60 to 80 casualties per year are children, who continue to play with found UXO – especially the harmless-looking, ball-shaped 'bomb light units' (BLUs) or *bombis* left behind by cluster bombs – in spite of public warnings.

Hunters also open or attempt to open UXO to extract gunpowder and steel pellets for their long-barrelled muskets – a risky activity that has claimed many casualties. Several groups are working steadily to clear the province of UXO, including the relatively new Lao National UXO Programme (UXO Lao), financed by a UN trust fund that has significantly increased the availability of multilateral aid for this purpose.

1, 2 and 3 are considered to be reasonably free of UXO. Even at these sites you should take care to stay within the jar areas and stick to worn footpaths.

Getting There & Away

You can charter a jumbo from Phonsavan to Site 1, 15km from the Phonsavan market, for 10,000 kip round trip. For Sites 2 and 3 your best bet is to arrange a jeep and driver through one of the guesthouses or hotels.

Sousath at the Maly Hotel in Phonsavan-charges US$50 for all-day transport and guiding to Sites 2 and 3 for up to four people, with stops along the way at Ban Sieng Dii near Site 3 and a Hmong village in the area of Muang Kham.

PHONSAVAN TO NONG HAET

The best road in the province at the moment is Route 7, linking Xieng Khuang Province with north Vietnam via Muang Kham and Nong Haet.

Near Km 27 on the way to Muang Kham (north side of the road) is **Nong Pet**, a large picturesque spring surrounded by rice fields which is said to be the source of the Nam Ngum river.

A sizeable **Hmong market** is held at 7 am on Sunday about 30km east of Phonsavan on the way to Muang Kham. Between Muang Kham and Nong Haet it's not unusual to see small poppy fields – which typically bloom in January – along the side of the road next to Hmong villages. You may also see Thai Dam funerary shrines on this journey – large white tombs with prayer flags, offerings of food and a pile of the departed's worldly possessions.

Muang Kham is little more than a rustic highway trading post but there are several jar sites in the vicinity (see the Plain of Jars section earlier). A simple eatery called *Nang Kham Pui* next to the bus terminal area offers noodles and sticky rice.

About 56km from Phonsavan on the way to Nong Haet, the large Hmong village of **Ban Na Sala** lies on a hillside 2km off the road. Farther east along Route 7, 120km from Phonsavan, is the market town of **Nong Haet**, which is only about 25km short of the Vietnamese border.

See the Getting There & Away section under Phonsavan, above, for information on bus and share taxi travel to Muang Kham and Nong Haet.

Mineral Springs

Two hot mineral springs can be visited near Muang Kham. **Baw Yai** (Big Spring) is the larger of the two and lies 18km from Muang Kham, 51km from Phonsavan. It has been developed as a resort with bungalows and bathing facilities, and was originally built by Kaysone Phomvihane's wife for visiting politicians. The spring source is in a heavily wooded area where several bamboo pipes have been rigged so that you can bathe nearby.

In a large cleared area farther from the source are a couple of private bathing rooms where hot water is piped in from the spring into American-style tubs; a soak in one of these costs 800 kip. Nearby bungalows cost 2500 kip per night per person. Baw Yai is now open to the public; entry is 1000 kip for foreigners, 1500 kip for vehicles.

Baw Noi (Little Spring) is the smaller of the two and feeds into a stream just a few hundred metres off Route 7, a couple of kilometres before Baw Yai on the way from Muang Kham. You can sit in the stream where the hot spring water mixes with the cool stream water and 'adjust' the temperature by moving from one area to another.

Tham Piu

When we first visited this cave in 1989 local guides had trouble finding it, but it has since become a standard on Xieng Khuang tour itineraries. The cave is near the former village of Ban Na Meun where an estimated 200 to 400 villagers were killed by a single rocket fired into the cave (most likely from a Nomad T-28 fighter plane manned by a Royal Lao Air Force pilot, although some versions of the story identify an American pilot) in 1969. The floor of the large cave, in the side of a limestone cliff, is littered with rubble from the partial cave-in caused by the rocket as well as minor debris left from the two storey shelter built into the cave. Near the entrance are a few human bones that have been unearthed. Government propaganda says many of those who died in the bombing were Lao women and children, but another version of events say

that it was a makeshift Vietnamese hospital where troop casualties were treated. Adding credence to the latter story is the fact that Vietnamese officials visited the cave in the 1980s, removed virtually all of the human remains and artefacts, and took them back to Vietnam.

Although Tham Piu is certainly a moving sight, the journey to the cave is the main attraction, since it passes several Hmong and Thai Dam villages along the way and involves a bit of hiking in the forest. From the cave mouth is a view of the forest and the plains below. A stream and small irrigation dam at the base of the cliff is picturesque. Another cave known as Tham Piu Sawng (Tham Piu 2) can be found a little higher up on the same cliff. This one has a small entrance that opens up into a large cavern; since it wasn't bombed, the cave formations can be seen in their original state. Don't forget your torch (flashlight).

Tham Piu is just a few kilometres east of Muang Kham on Route 7.

Getting There & Away You can hire a jeep and driver in Phonsavan for around US$20 to US$30 a day for trips to Tham Piu and back.

To get to Tham Piu by public transport, you'd have to take a Nong Haet bus and ask to be let out at the turn off for Tham Piu. From the turn-off, start walking towards the limestone cliff north of the road until you're within a kilometre of the cliff. At this point you have to plunge into the woods and make your way along a honeycomb of trails to the bottom of the cliff and then mount a steep, narrow trail that leads up to the mouth of the cave. It would be best to ask for directions from villagers along the way or you're liable to get lost; live ordnance is another danger. Better still, find someone in Phonsavan who knows the way and invite them to come along for an afternoon hike.

OLD XIENG KHUANG (MUANG KHUN)

Xieng Khuang's ancient capital was so heavily bombarded during the Indochina War (and ravaged in the 19th century by Chinese and Vietnamese invaders) that it

War Scrap

War junk has become an important part of the local architecture and economy in Xieng Khuang. Torpedo-shaped bomb casings are collected, stored, refashioned into items of everyday use or sold as scrap. Among the most valuable are the 1.5m-long casings from US-made cluster bomb units (CBUs), which split lengthways when released and scattered 600 to 700 tennis-ball-size bomblets (each containing around 250 steel pellets) over 5000 sq metre areas.

Turned on its side, a CBU casing becomes a planter; upright they are used as fence posts or as substitutes for the traditional wooden stilts used to support rice barns and thatched houses. Hundreds of casings used like this can be seen in Xieng Khuang villages along Route 7, which stretches north-east all the way from Phonsavan to Hanoi, or in villages in the vicinity of the old capital. Aluminium spoons sold in local markets are said to be fashioned from the remains of downed American aircraft.

Farmers from around the province keep piles of war junk – including pieces of F-105 Thunderchiefs, A-1 Skyraiders and other US planes downed during the war – beneath their stilt houses or in an unused corner of their fields, using bits and pieces as needed around the farm or selling pieces to itinerant scrap dealers who drive their trucks from village to village. These trucks bring the scrap to small warehouses in Phonsavan, where it is sold to larger dealers from Vientiane. Eventually the scrap is melted down in Vientiane or across the Mekong River in Thailand as a source of cheap metal.

Recently the Lao government made it illegal to trade in leftover war weaponry – bombs, bullets, arms – of any kind. According to National Law Chapters 71 and 72, the illegal purchase, sale, or theft of these can result in a prison term of between six months and five years.

was almost completely abandoned by 1975. Twenty years after war's end the old capital is once again inhabited (population 14,000), though only one of French colonial building still stands, a former commissariat which is now used as a social centre. The rubble that was once some quaint provincial French-Lao architecture has been replaced by a long row of plain wooden buildings with slanted metal roofs on either side of the dirt road from Phonsavan. Officially the town has been renamed Muang Khun. Many of the residents are Phuan, Thai Dam or Thai Neua, along with a smattering of lowland Lao and Vietnamese.

Several Buddhist temples built between the 16th and 19th centuries lie in ruins. The foundation and columns, along with a large seated Buddha, of **Wat Si Phum** are still standing at the east end of town.

That Phuan (also called That Chomsi), a tall 25m to 30m *jedi* constructed in the Lan Xang/Lanna style, and a few isolated Buddha statues, are all of **Wat Phia Wat** that managed to survive the bombing. Sadly the only intact Xieng Khuang-style temples left in Laos today – characterised by striking pentagonal silhouettes when viewed from the front – are in Luang Prabang.

Ban Naa Sii, near Wat Phia Wat, is a sizeable Thai Dam village.

Places to Stay & Eat

The town has one funky wooden *hotel* with rooms for 2000 kip. Near the market in the centre of town are a couple of noodle shops. *Haan Khai Foe* (the sign reads 'Restaurant') opposite the market is the best choice for lunch.

Things to Buy

If you ask around you may be able to buy Thai tribal textiles (especially Phuan, Thai Dam or Thai Neua) in town, though forget about buying antique Xieng Khuang styles – these were picked over long ago by collectors from Vientiane and abroad.

Getting There & Away

Four buses a day ply the bumpy, tortuous 36km route between Phonsavan and Xieng Khuang for 2500 kip per person. The going rate for a guide and car between the two towns is around US$50.

MUANG SUI

Once a city of antique Buddhist temples and quaint provincial architecture, Muang Sui became a headquaters of the Neutralist faction and 'Lima Site 108' (a landing site used by US planes) during the Indochina War. The North Vietnamese Army totally wrecked Muang Sui late in the war after running the Royal Lao Army out of Xieng Khuang Province.

Like Xieng Khuang, the town is now rebuilding and is part of a new district called Muang Phu Kut (population 20,200), and on government maps the town is called Ban Nong Tang.

Ruins of several older temples can be seen; **Wat Ban Phong**, which still has resident monks, once contained a beautiful bronze Xieng Khuang-style Buddha called Pha Ong, said to hail from the 14th century. Lao Communists reportedly transferred the image to Vieng Xai in Hua Phan Province, though it's not on display there. Adjacent to the town, a large natural lake called **Nong Tang** is another attraction.

There are no public lodgings in Muang Sui. Keep in mind that there's still lots of UXO around Muang Sui and that it's dangerous to continue east of town along Route 7 due to Hmong insurgents. The most insecure region is about 10 to 20km west of Muang Sui after the road crosses the Nam Jat river.

Getting There & Away

Route 7 to Muang Sui from Phonsavan is in a very poor state of repair most of the way. Large passenger trucks leave Phonsavan's bus terminal daily around 7 am; occasionally

there's a second departure around 1 pm. Depending on the road conditions and the number of stops along the way, this 51km trip can take anywhere from two to four hours. The fare is 3000 kip. The Nam Ngum river crosses the road just east of Muang Sui and during the rainy season you'll have to cross by boat.

In Phonsavan you can hire a jeep, driver and English-speaking guide to Muang Sui and back for US$50 to US$80 through Sousath Tourism or through other sources. Given the lack of accommodation in Muang Sui, you'll get the most out of a visit there in the company of a guide.

Hua Phan Province

The mountainous north-eastern province of Hua Phan, enclosed by Vietnam to the north, east and south-east, Xieng Khuang to the south-west and Luang Prabang to the west, has a total population of 246,000, of whom around 46,800 live in the provincial capital of Sam Neua ('Northern Sam', a reference to its position towards the north end of the Nam Sam river). Twenty-two ethnic groups make the province their home, predominantly the Thai Khao, Thai Daeng, Thai Meuay, Thai Neua, Phu Noi, Hmong, Khamu, Yunnanese and Vietnamese. The Vietnamese influence is very strong here as Sam Neua is closer to (and more accessible from) Hanoi than Vientiane; because the province falls on the eastern side of the Annamite Chain, Thai TV and radio broadcasts don't reach here either.

For much of the last 500 years Hua Phan has been either an independent Thai Neua kingdom or part of an Annamese vassal state known as Ai Lao. It also came briefly under Siamese protectorship as a state called Chao Thai Neua in the 1880s. Except for a two year interval (1891 to 1893) when the state was under Luang Prabang suzerainty, Hua Phan really only became a Lao entity under French colonial rule. During the colonial era the French commissariat at Sam Neua gave a great deal of autonomy to the Thai Neua chiefs and village headmen. By the end of the Indochina War, all traces of the French presence had been erased.

Since 1989 the US and Lao governments have operated a heavily funded joint anti-narcotics program in Hua Phan Province. The USA has contributed more than US$14 million to date for crop substitution projects and to build roads, schools, clinics, dams, irrigation and electrical power systems. The Lao government news service in 1998 reported that 'With more than 460 hectares of new irrigated paddy land, villagers happily give up opium production'.

As a tourist attraction the province's main claim to fame is that Vieng Xai served as the headquarters for the Pathet Lao throughout most of the war years. Textiles in the 'Sam Neua' style – of tribal Thai origins – are another draw. The best textiles are said to come from the areas around Muang Xon and Sop Hao.

SAM NEUA (XAM NEUA)

Tucked away in a long, narrow valley formed by the Nam Sam at about 1200m above sea level, Sam Neua is so far one of the country's least visited provincial capitals. Verdant hills, including the pointy Phu Luang, overlook the town but other than the natural setting there's not a lot to write home about. Residents are mostly Lao, Vietnamese and Hmong, along with some Thai Dam, Thai Daeng and Thai Lü.

On a rise to one side of town sit the town hall, post office and police station. The latter can be found at the back of a newer building with peaked rooflines and blue trim; this is where you must check in and out of the province. Hua Phan Province has its own tourist office in Sam Neua and a new English-speaking staff member who seems more eager than his predecessor to help with information.

Things to See & Do

For local residents, Sam Neua boasts what is perhaps the largest and fastest-growing market in the region. Products from China and Vietnam line up beside fresh produce and domestic goods. Sam Neua-style textiles can be found inside the main market building; prices can be very good although quality is generally not up to the standard of markets in Vientiane. Local Hmong, Thai Dam, Thai Daeng and Thai Lü frequent this market. Most connoisseurs agree that the Thai Daeng weave the most attractive textiles. Along with textiles you'll find field rats (live ones for 3500 kip, skinned a bit more), banana leaves stuffed with squirming insects and forks and spoons made with aluminium salvaged from war debris. One vendor can make and custom-fit a silver ring in about 10 minutes.

A 1979 **independence monument** mounted by a red star sits on a hill at the north-west edge of town; it's an easy climb, worthwhile for the modest view. From this hill you can continue walking to **Wat Pho Xai**, a distance of around 2km from the market. The only monastery in town, with only five monks in residence (the minimum needed for holding the monastic ordination ceremonies), the wat features a small sim

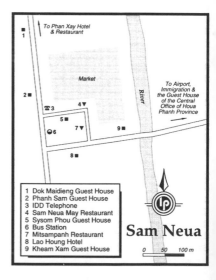

1 Dok Maidieng Guest House
2 Phanh Sam Guest House
3 IDD Telephone
4 Sam Neua May Restaurant
5 Sysom Phou Guest House
6 Bus Station
7 Mitsampanh Restaurant
8 Lao Houng Hotel
9 Kheam Xam Guest House

Sam Neua

0   50   100 m

that was destroyed in the war and rebuilt in 1983. Two small **thâat** to be seen on the way to the independence monument are the last remnants of local prewar temples.

Places to Stay

Welcome to Laos' rat capital. *Lao Houng Hotel*, near the western end of a bridge that spans the Nam Sam near the market, is a crumbling Chinese/Vietnamese-style place built around a couple of courtyards by the Vietnamese in 1975 – though it looks much older. Until recently under government management, the hotel is now privately managed but is still pretty basic. Ordinary rooms with two beds, mosquito nets and shared facilities cost US$8, while the same with private shower and toilet costs US$10. Larger rooms with hot showers cost US$12, while suites with spacious sitting rooms, one large bed, private toilet and hot shower are US$15. The Lao Houng has a major rat problem – at night rats running about in the ceiling sound like children playing football on the roof. An attached beer garden serves cold Beerlao, and the hotel hosts dances on Sunday nights until midnight.

In front of the market, diagonally across from the Lao Houng Hotel, the *Kheam Xam Guest House* is a new three storey cement place and the tallest building in town. On the ground floor is a cafe with TV and VCR, while the 2nd and 3rd floors hold three rooms each. Each room contains two or three twin beds with mosquito nets and shared, clean bathrooms for 6,000 kip. Apparently the rats haven't made a home here – yet.

In the same area but a little closer to the bus stop, *Sysom Phou Guest House* has dingy dorm beds, separated from the main kitchen and sitting area by a thin curtain, for 1,500 kip. There are also private rooms with shared facilities for 4,000 kip single/double or 5,000 kip triple. Experience suggests this place probably has more rats than the other places to stay in town simply because of the dirt level and proximity to the unhygienic market.

Around the corner from Lao Houng on a street up from the market, the new *Phanh Sam Guest House* is a two storey cement

building with a balcony on the upper floor. The 20 small rooms are bare save for a few sticks of wooden furniture, and they cost 5000 kip single/double. The staff are friendly and meals can be arranged here.

Next down this street, the *Dokmaidieng Guest House* is a three storey cube with rooms with shared facilities for 5000 kip. Rats, yes, but not as many as the Lao Houng or the Sysom. About 500m along the same road is the *Phanxay Hotel*, a business-like two storey place similar to the Sysom. Rates are 3000 kip per person in the dorm, 7000 kip in a room with attached bath; the rats are free. There is a restaurant in a separate but adjacent building.

Closer to the airport, a government-run place with *The Guest House of the Central Office of Houa Phanh Province* written in bold script across the front offers large dusty rooms in a former office building, each with two narrow wooden beds and a spacious sitting area, for 6000 kip. While every place else in town is full, this one may be empty save for a chicken or two running through the lower floors.

Places to Eat

Since we've been talking up the rats in Sam Neua we should mention right up front that the first bowl of fŏe we were served on this trip – at the friendly *Kheam Xam Restaurant*, attached to the guesthouse of the same name – contained rat meat in the broth. This gives you some idea of both the prevalence of rats in the area and the general culinary sphere of the town.

Better fŏe is available at the clean and new *Sam Neua May Restaurant* near the market. For a variety of Lao dishes try the *Mitsampanh Restaurant* about 20m down a side lane opposite the Sam Neua May.

Two eating establishments inside the market compound can do simple rice and noodle dishes, though for anything other than fŏe you must order in advance. *Joy's Place* is the better of the two and is open daily 6.30 am to 9 pm. *Hin Restaurant* is similar but it's not as clean and service is a little slack.

Getting There & Away
Air Lao Aviation has daily flights between Vientiane and the renovated airport at Sam Neua (75 minutes, US$70 one way). Flight scheduling is irregular due to the shortage of available aircraft – only the Yun-12 can safely make the impressive descent through the narrow Sam Neua valley. During our most recent visit to Sam Neua a Yun-12 lost one wing during a rough landing, thus reducing Lao Aviation's tiny fleet by yet one more craft.

The airport lies around 3km from the area of town where the market and most of the guesthouses and hotels can be found. A shared jumbo from the airport to any lodgings in town costs 1000 kip per person.

Road Sam Neua can be reached by road from both Xieng Khuang and Udomxai provinces. Route 6 from Xieng Khuang is quite good by Lao standards between Phonsavan and Nam Noen, a small truck stop at the junction of Routes 6 and 1 just north of the Hua Phan Province border. Between Nam Noen and Sam Neua it's a steep, winding and rough but highly scenic dirt road that passes through numerous Lao, Hmong and Khamu villages. It's usually necessary to change buses (actually large converted Russian or Chinese diesel trucks) in Nam Noen. From Phonsavan to Nam Noen takes four to five hours and costs 5000 kip, while from Nam Noen to Sam Neua takes six hours and costs 6000 kip. Occasionally – perhaps once a week – there's a direct passenger truck between Sam Neua and Phonsavan for 12,000 kip, but total travel time still involves at least 11 hours.

South-east of Sam Neua, Route 6 joins Route 1 from Nong Khiaw (Luang Prabang Province) and Muang Xai (Udomxai Province). To/from Nong Khiaw also involves changing buses in Nam Noen. The Nong Khiaw to Nam Noen leg costs 8000 kip and takes eight to nine hours (longer with breakdowns, which are normal) along winding roads and brilliant scenery, passing many Blue Hmong villages along the way and an international narcotics control project in the

district of Meuang Hiam. In Nam Noen you must switch to a Sam Neua-bound truck – often this means spending a night in Nam Noen.

The Vietnamese border at Sop Hao is open to Vietnamese and Lao nationals, and it is not likely that a foreigner would be allowed to cross here – travel in this area is restricted probably because it's the one of the last surviving nodes in the Lao PDR's post-Revolution gulag. The road from Sam Neua to Sop Hao is reportedly quite good, so if the border opens to foreigners Hanoi would become a logical Hua Phan gateway.

AROUND SAM NEUA
A 580 sq km area of forested hills along the Nam Sam near Sam Tai in the south-eastern section of the province was declared the **Nam Sam National Biodiversity Conser- vation Area** in 1993. Nam Sam NBCA is thought to be a habitat for wild elephant, various gibbons, gaur, banteng, tiger, clouded leopard, Asiatic black bear and Malayan sun bear. Despite the NBCA designation – and even though the area can only be reached by a 4WD track from Vieng Xai – shifting cultivation by hill tribes and cedar logging by a Yunnanese company threatens the forests.

Taat Saloei, about 37km south of Sam Neua off the road to Nam Noen, is a waterfall said to be very beautiful just after the rainy season.

The road north-east from Sam Neua to **Sop Hao** on the Vietnamese border passes by several Hmong and tribal Thai villages. A former French army camp in Sop Hao now serves as one of Laos' last remaining political prisons or 're-education camps'. Officials in this area can be very touchy about foreigners.

Suan Hin
This 'stone garden', far more interesting than its name makes it sound, was first described in print by French archaeologist M Colani in her 1935 thesis *Megalithes du Haut Laos* (Megaliths of Highland Laos). Often likened to Britain's Stonehenge because of the site's

Samana

Hua Phan is perhaps most infamous for the re-education camps established around the eastern half of the province immediately following the 1975 Revolution. Inspired by Vietnamese examples (several in Hua Phan were actually designed and constructed by Vietnamese architects and labourers), such camps, called *samana* in Lao, mixed forced labour with political indoctrination to 'rehabilitate' thousands of civil servants from the old regime.

Though most of the camps were closed by 1989, Re-education Camp No 7 is believed to remain in operation somewhere near the Vietnamese border; another camp near the village of Sop Hao also reportedly still retains captives.

According to Amnesty International (AI) in London, three political prisoners (all former senior officials in the Lao PDR government) were sentenced to 14 years imprisonment in Hua Phan for peacefully advocating a multiparty political system in 1992. There were no defence lawyers at their trial. All three subsequently became very ill and one of the prisoners, 59-year-old Thongsouk Saysangkhi (former deputy minister of science & technology), died of alleged maltreatment in February 1998. Three more political prisoners received life sentences in 1992 after having been held without trial for 17 years. AI also reports that at Sop Hao at least two camp inductees held since 1975 were only released in 1994.

According to AI, the conditions in these camps are 'extremely harsh and fall well short of international minimum standards'. Prisoners are denied medical treatment, visits and all access to reading or writing material.

Although as many as 30,000 people were thought to have been interned by 1978 to 1979 – the samana's numeric peak – the Lao government has never issued a statement either confirming or denying the existence of the camps.

rough-hewn, 2m stone uprights, Suan Hin is as much of a mystery as the Plain of Jars; indeed they may be historically related. The stone chosen for the megaliths coincides with that used to fashion the jars; beneath some of the pillars are tunnel-like ditches whose purpose is as enigmatic as the pillars and jars themselves – current speculation suggests a funerary function.

The pillars are a 4km hike off Route 6 beginning at a point roughly 45km south-east of Sam Neua. They aren't that easy to find, so your best bet would be to hire a vehicle to Hua Muang on Route 6 about two-thirds of the way between Sam Neua and Nam Noen. Once in Hua Muang, you can arrange for a local person to lead you to the pillars. Or you could take a public conveyance from either Sam Neua or Nam Noen (you'll arrive earlier in the day if you start from the latter) and ask to get off at the turn-off for Ban Pakha near Hua Muang. Then ask on

the road to Ban Pakha for directions to Suan Hin. This of course leaves much to chance – if you don't meet anyone or cannot communicate because of language differences, you're on your own.

Sousath Travel in Phonsavan, the capital of Xieng Khuang Province, can provide transport and guidance to Suan Hin for US$80 a day. You could also try asking for assistance from the tourist office in Sam Neua.

SAM NEUA TO VIENG XAI

Even if you aren't able to arrange prior admission to the caves at Vieng Xai (see the following section), the district is still worth wandering about for its scenic beauty. Between Kms 11 and 12, coming from Sam Neua, is a fairly big Hmong Lai (Striped Hmong) village called **Ban Hua Khang**. You'll start seeing **karst formations**, many with cave entrances, after Km 13 along with pretty little valleys terraced in rice. At Km 20 is an intersection; the right fork reaches Vieng Xai after 9km, then continues to Nam Maew on the Vietnamese border (87km from Sam Neua), while the other road goes to Sop Hao.

Six km before the Vieng Xai turn-off, coming from Sam Neua, is the 80m-high **Taat Nam Neua**. You can walk to the top of the falls straight from a bridge where the road crosses the Nam Neua just after the road forks towards Vieng Xai. For an all-in-one view from the bottom, take the left fork and proceed for 2km till you see some terraced rice fields on the right-hand side of the road. A trail winds for a kilometre or so through the fields, along and across a stream and through bamboo thickets before reaching the bottom. You may have to ask locally for directions as the trail isn't particularly obvious. Be sure to apply insect repellent to your feet and ankles in order to keep leeches at bay. As usual, the falls are most beautiful just after the rainy season, when you can swim in the lower pools.

VIENG XAI

Originally called Thong Na Kai (Chicken Field) because of the abundance of wild jungle fowl in the area, the postwar name for this former Pathet Lao (PL) revolutionary headquarters means Walled City of Victory. The district (population 32,800) sits in a striking valley of verdant hills and limestone cliffs riddled with caves, several of which were used to shelter PL officers during the Indochina War.

The district capital itself is a small town that seems to be getting smaller as Sam Neua grows larger. The central market is a poor collection of vendors who can't afford transport to the provincial capital, 29km away.

Caves

There are 102 known caves in the district, around a dozen with war history. The Vieng Xai caves are supposed to be open to the public as a revolutionary memorial and tourist attraction, but in practice the local authorities have been known to treat them

as if they're a military secret. The book *Stalking the Elephant Kings* by Christopher Kremmer contains an enlightening chapter on the author's experiences attempting and finally succeeding in entering the caves in the mid-1990s. The book also contains some background on the royal family's short stay here during the late 1970s.

The setting of the caves – inside a narrow and precipitous limestone-walled valley surrounding the town of Vieng Xai – is quite impressive. The PL leadership first started using them in 1964 because the caves are virtually unassailable by land or air. Today the caves considered the most historically important are named after the figures who once occupied them. They are within easy walking distance of town.

High in the side of a limestone cliff, **Tham Thaan Souphanouvong** (called Tham Phaa Bong before the war) was deemed fit for royalty and housed Prince Souphanouvong, the so-called 'Red Prince'. Wooden walls and floors, as well as natural cave formations, divided the cavern into bedrooms, meeting rooms, artillery and weapons storage areas and various other spaces. Souphanouvong eventually built a house in front of the cave entrance and today the house is treated with the same mix of fear and respect as the cave.

Tham Thaan Kaysone, the office and residence of the PL chief – who served as prime minister and president from 1975 till his death in 1992 – extends 140m into a cliff that was scaled by rope before steps were added. A bust of Kaysone sits inside the entry. The cave's various rooms included a political party centre, reception room, bedroom, recreation room, meeting room and a library. The rear of the cave opens onto a clearing that was used as an outdoor meeting place and kitchen. Kaysone also built a handsome two storey house in front of his cave. **Tham Thaan Khamtay**, named after the current president Khamtay Siphandone, is an artificial cave dug out of a limestone cliff, similarly divided into various rooms, with a Franco-Chinese-style house out front. Of the three main caves open to tourists, this is the only one without electric lights; labels appear in Lao only.

One of the deepest caves (200m) is **Tham Xieng Muang**, which was used for hospital facilities. Other caves housed weaving mills, printing presses and other facilities needed by the PL to remain self-sufficient.

Visiting the Caves Before entering any of the caves, visitors must report to a mustard-coloured building in front of Tham Thaan Souphanouvong, where a fee of 1500 kip per person will be collected. A local Lao guide assigned by the government must accompany all visits. So far none of the guides speak English or French; perhaps they're 'minders' rather than guides. The officials have been known to ask the question 'Are you a journalist or writer?' before giving permission to enter the caves; if you answer in the affirmative you may be refused.

Only the Souphanouvong, Kaysone and Khamtay caves were open at the time of writing, and at these three you are free to take photographs inside and out. A sign in Lao only in front of the Souphanouvong cave, forbids visitors from entering the caves without first reporting to the administrative office, and from bringing food or flowers inside.

Places to Stay & Eat
At the moment you'd do better to stay in Sam Neua rather than in Vieng Xai as there's more choice of accommodation and food.

The *Vieng Xai Hotel* (also known as Hotel No 2), originally built by the Vietnamese in 1973 as a 're-education' facility, sits at the edge of town near a large pond. It's even more decrepit than its Sam Neua counterpart, the Lao Houng. Though less than 30 years old, the hotel's windows mostly have no glass or bear only a few broken shards, and many of the doors have no latches or locks. A room costs 3500 kip single/double; toilet and shower facilities are shared.

Two *fŏe shops* in the market are the only places to eat. Rice isn't normally available unless you buy it in the market and cook it yourself.

Getting There & Away
The military-owned Air Lao flies between Vieng Xai and Vientiane a couple of times a week but it's impossible to pin down the schedule except by showing up at Vieng Xai's tiny airfield in the morning and asking.

The 29km journey from Sam Neua to Vieng Xai takes around 45 minutes by private vehicle or about an hour by public truck. The road is in horrendous condition, with large patches of crumbling asphalt alternating with patches of dirt. Passenger trucks run between Sam Neua and Vieng Xai two or three times a day depending on passenger demand; the fare is 1500 kip. If you go by truck you should be prepared to spend the night in Vieng Xai in case there are no return departures later in the day.

You can hire a motorcycle to take you from Sam Neua to Vieng Xai and back for 18,000 kip or US$7, assuming a half day's charter.

NAM NOEN
Anyone travelling between Nong Khiaw and Phonsavan or Sam Neua and Phonsavan by road must pass through this settlement at the junction of Routes 6 and 7. *Nam Noen Guesthouse*, a low wooden building with iron-barred windows, offers beds with mosquito nets in dorm-like rooms for 2000 kip per person. *Nang Lam Phon*, across from the Nam Noen Guesthouse, provides sticky rice and instant noodles. There are a couple of other noodle shops as well.

Buses to and from Nong Khiaw, Phonsavan and Sam Neua tend to reach Nam Noen around noon or 1 pm so if you're looking for a connection to any of these towns you'd best arrive in Nam Noen by midday. Early morning is another good time to get a passenger vehicle. After 2 pm it's almost impossible unless an incoming vehicle has been delayed by a breakdown.

NONG KHIAW TO NAM NOEN
Route 7 between Nong Khiaw and Nam Noen passes through bits of beautiful scenery with lots of green mountains – even in the dry months when everywhere looks

brown – rivers, fern-covered cliffs and villages of Striped and Blue Hmong. The districts of **Muang Vieng Kham** and **Muang Vieng Thong** are populated with Blue Hmong and other ethnicities. Vieng Kham, about 50km east of Muang Ngoi, is a fairly substantial village with a couple of wats and a couple of places to eat. **Ban Wang Way**, the next town west after Vieng Kham, is more prosperous than many others along the road and a little bigger than Vieng Kham itself. Besides Hmong, you'll see plenty of lowland Lao here, many of whom keep fabric looms beneath their stilted houses.

Phongsali Province

Enclosed on three sides by China and Vietnam, Phongsali is northern Laos' most inaccessible province. Twenty-two ethnicities make up the province's population of approximately 152,000, among them Kheu, Sila, Lolo, Hanyi, Hmong, Pala, Oma, Eupa, Loma, Pusang, Mien, Akha, Haw, Thai Dam, Thai Khao, Thai Lü, Phuan, Khamu, Phai, Vietnamese and Yunnanese. The Phu Noi (recognisable by their white leggings) are the most numerous ethnicity, followed by the Thai Lü, Haw, Akha and Khamu. Prior to the Sino-French Treaty of 1895, Phongsali was an independent Thai Lü principality attached to Xishuangbanna in southern Yunnan.

Phongsali's population density is 9.4 per square kilometre, the lowest in the country after Sekong and Attapeu provinces. Opium poppy cultivation is widespread among the Hmong, Mien and Lolo in this province. As in Udomxai and Luang Nam Tha the Chinese presence has increased steeply with recent road and construction development.

Phu Den Din NBCA covers 1310 sq km in the north-eastern corner of the province along the Lao-Vietnamese border, adjacent to Vietnam's Muong Nhe Nature Reserve. Mountains in this area reach up to 1948m and bear 77% primary forest cover. Many threatened or endangered mammals live in the area, including elephant, tiger, clouded leopard, banteng, gaur and Asiatic black bear.

PHONGSALI

Built on the steep slopes of Phu Fa (1625m) at an elevation of around 1400m, Phongsali possesses a year-round cool climate that comes as a welcome relief during the hotter (March to May) season. In fact the climate has more of an affinity for what you would find in northern Vietnam than much of Laos. It can be quite cold during the cool season with temperatures as low as 5°C at night, 10°C during the day. Fog and low clouds are common in the morning at any time of year. Rainfall can be intense and cold. Be sure to bring a pullover, jacket and waterproofs, even in March, April and May, just in case.

The capital district (population 25,000) is surrounded by rolling, deforested hills. If you've come expecting to see lots of colourfully garbed minorities in the market or around town, you'll be disappointed unless you arrive during a major holiday like Lao New Year in April, when residents from all around the province visit the capital. The best areas for hill tribe village exploration are found in the extreme north-west corner of the province, where there are no roads. Reaching this area involves walking two or more days.

Phongsali does boast some colonial architecture, and wandering about the town's back streets and alleys can be interesting.

Information

Electric power is available from 6 to 9 pm only. There is a post office 200m southwest of the Phongsali Hotel and across the street from the card phone.

Immigration At the Hat Sa boat landing to the east of town, no-one seems particularly anxious to provide the jâeng khào/jâeng àwk stamps that you are legally supposed to collect when entering and leaving each province. The immigration office in town occupies a two storey building with a blue

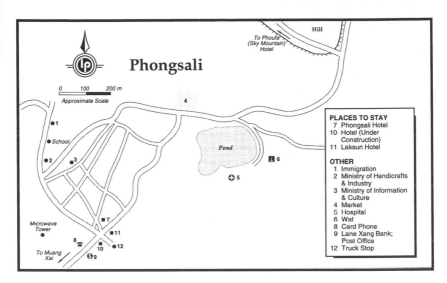

Phongsali

PLACES TO STAY
7 Phongsali Hotel
10 Hotel (Under
     Construction)
11 Laksun Hotel

OTHER
1 Immigration
2 Ministry of Handicrafts
    & Industry
3 Ministry of Information
    & Culture
4 Market
5 Hospital
6 Wat
8 Card Phone
9 Lane Xang Bank;
    Post Office
12 Truck Stop

tile front, just up the hill from the school and north-west of the hotel area. If the front door is locked, go around to the back of the building as all the offices have doors that open to the back, and these are usually open during government working hours.

Money A branch of Lane Xang Bank next to the post office, south-west of the Phongsali Hotel, can change US dollars, Thai baht or Chinese yuan (but no travellers cheques) for kip.

Dangers & Annoyances We have had a letter about an English-speaking con man masquerading as a guide in Phongsali who first agrees to lead a trek, takes passports for safekeeping and then charges ridiculous sums using the passports as blackmail. The letter notes that the local police were no help.

If you want to go trekking with anyone in Phongsali (and this should hold for anywhere in Laos), be sure to come to a clear understanding of all costs beforehand. An informal written statement of costs should be drawn up, and copies retained by both parties. Under no circumstances should you

surrender your passport to anyone except an immigration or police officer. Of course if the latter are in on a scam there's little you can do. This is the first such scam of this nature we've heard of in Laos, so chances are you won't run into anything like this. But it pays to be cautious.

Places to Stay

Phongsali has three places to stay now. Best is the Chinese-built *Phongsali Hotel*, a centrally located four storey building that's the highest structure in the province. The hotel offers 28 plain rooms, most with three beds (good mattresses), all with shared bath and toilet facilities, for 6000 kip per room. The staff speak Lao, Phu Noi and Chinese.

Opposite the Phongsali Hotel, the rustic *Laksun Hotel* is a two storey, metal-roofed wooden structure with a few basic rooms with mosquito nets for 2000 kip per bed in a three bed room. There's a decent restaurant downstairs.

The wooden *Phoufa Hotel*, on the hill of the same name (Phu Fa), was a Chinese consulate and military base in the 1960s. It's another basic place with three beds per room (hard mattresses), mosquito nets and shared facilities for 2000 kip per person. The hotel commands a good view of the area; downstairs is a spartan restaurant. Just before going to press we heard that this hotel was being upgraded to a US$10 to US$15 a night place, and the name may change to Sky Mountain Hotel (the English translation of Phu Fa).

A new hotel is under construction next to the main bus stop and diagonally opposite the Phongsali Hotel.

Hat Sa Hat Sa has a *guesthouse* with multi-bed rooms for 1500 kip per person.

Places to Eat
The three hotel restaurants are reasonably priced. *Phongsali Hotel* offers the largest menu, mostly Chinese food plus a few Lao dishes. It's best to order in advance so that the cooks can pick up the necessary ingredients – the hotel has no refrigeration. There are several *noodle shops* on the main street through town towards the market; bowls of fõe are among the cheapest in the country, mostly 500 to 800 kip. Chinese beer is cheap all over town, while Beerlao is relatively expensive. The local lào-láo is tinted green with herbs and is quite a smooth tipple.

Getting There & Away
Air Lao Aviation lists a fare of US$87 for flights to Phongsali, though there are no regularly scheduled flights at this time; official visitors from Vientiane generally arrive by helicopter.

Road From Muang Xai in Udomxai Province it is now possible to travel by road along Route 4 north-east to a junction about 30km west of Muang Khua in southern Phongsali, and then head north on a relatively new graded, unsealed road all the way to Phongsali. Buses leave once a day (early morning) from either end as long as there are enough passengers; the 10 hour, 280km trip costs 11,000 kip per person. Route 4 has been plagued by rockslides and is currently undergoing substantial repairs –

hence travel time may shrink when the project is finished. The new road north (as yet unnumbered) is in relatively good condition despite its lack of sealing.

From Hat Sa From the boat landing at the small town of Hat Sa, passengers can share a 4WD vehicle for the 20km journey to Phongsali. Originally built by the French, this rutted and rough dirt track is locally known as the 'buffalo road' since it seems more fit for beast than vehicle. The trip takes 1½ hours and costs 3000 kip per person, although repairs to the road should shorten the trip.

From China Another way to reach Phongsali is from Luang Nam Tha Province via Yunnan. If the Yunnan-Phongsali border should open to foreign travellers in the near future (it is currently open to Chinese and Lao nationals) it will be easier to reach Phongsali from Mengla, Yunnan, than from most points in Laos. Rumours say negotiations between the provincial governments of Yunnan and Luang Nam Tha will eventually allow foreigners to travel across this stretch of China. The road from the Lao settlement of Ban Pakha (a village of Akha refugees who fled the Communist takeover of China in the 1940s) near the Chinese border to Phongsali is relatively good; local buses cost around 2000 kip per person and take about two hours to reach Bun Neua, where you must change to another bus (another two hours, 2000 kip) for the final leg to Phongsali. There is a guesthouse in Bun Neua should you get stranded.

River Another way to reach Phongsali is via the Nam Ou river from Muang Khua. You can reach Muang Khua by road from Muang Xai (four to six hours, 4500 kip) or by boat from Nong Khiaw (see the Nong Khiaw section for details). Boats end up in Hat Sa, a short distance by road from Phongsali. When the level of the river is low, however, the boat service may be cancelled; lately this doesn't seem to happen till March or April though in previous years it has stopped much earlier – much depends on the annual monsoon.

From Muang Khua boats leave irregularly (in the mornings only) for Hat Sa. The slow boat costs 15,000 kip per passenger and takes five to six hours, while speedboats cost just 18,000 kip per person and take a comfortable 1½ to two hours.

Muang Khua and Hat Sa can also be reached by river from Luang Prabang along the Nam Ou (except when the river is low). See the Luang Prabang Getting There & Away section for further details.

MUANG KHUA

This small town sits at the junction of the Nam Ou river – the major north-south transport artery in and out of the province – and Route 4, which connects Udomxai and Phongsali provinces with Dien Bien Phu in Vietnam.

The Lane Xang Bank in Muang Khua can change dollars, baht and yuan – cash only – for kip. There's no electricity in town but individual generators power the town's hotels at night.

Places to Stay & Eat

The four storey *Muang Khua Guesthouse*, without an English sign (look for '1989' incorporated into the 3rd floor balcony), is the friendliest of the town's three lodgings and keeps its generator running longer. Rates are 2000 kip per person in clean three and four-bed rooms. Toilets and bathing facilities are shared.

Nang Aen Kaew Hotel (there no sign in English), named for the friendly Lao lady who runs the place, offers five dark but relatively clean rooms for 3000 kip per room. The shared bathing facilities aren't so clean. It's opposite the bus stop.

The top-end place in town is the *Muang Khoua Hotel*, a single storey white building with a parking area for the self-propelled and fair lodgings for 4000 kip per room. The facilities are shared.

The Muang Khoua has its own *Chinese restaurant*. There's one other *restaurant* in town near the Muang Khua Guesthouse.

Getting There & Away

See the earlier Getting There & Away section for Phongsali, Muang Xai and Nong Khiaw for details on transport to Muang Khua. The port master in Muang Khua speaks English relatively well.

Udomxai Province

This rugged province is wedged between Luang Prabang to the east, Phongsali to the north-east, Luang Nam Tha to the north-west and Sainyabuli to the south, with a small northern section that shares a border with China's Yunnan Province (less than 60km from Mengla in Yunnan's Xishuangbanna District). Most of the provincial population of 211,000 is a mixture of some 23 ethnic minorities, mostly Hmong, Akha, Mien, Phu Thai, Thai Dam, Thai Khao, Thai Lü, Thai Neua, Phuan, Khamu, Lamet, Lao Huay and Yunnanese Chinese (Haw).

The Yunnanese presence has intensified recently with the influx of Chinese skilled labourers working in construction, as well as tradespeople from Kunming, the capital of Yunnan. In the 1960s and early 1970s the Chinese were appreciated in Udomxai because they donated a network of two-lane paved roads radiating throughout the far north, using Udomxai as the hub. These roads were very important in moving Pathet Lao and NVA troops and supplies around the north during the war. Following the 1979 ideological split over Cambodia (China sided with the Khmer Rouge, Laos with Vietnam), the Chinese withdrew all support until the early 1990s.

The new Chinese influx is regarded by many Udomxai inhabitants as economic infiltration, since the construction and road building is no longer foreign aid but paid work for hire, using plenty of imported Chinese materials and labour.

Because Udomxai has a road system of sorts (it has deteriorated considerably since the 1970s but is still the best in the north),

NORTHERN LAOS

this province is the most accessible of the country's far northern provinces.

MUANG XAI (UDOMXAI)

The capital of Udomxai is most commonly called Muang Xai, though some maps label it Udomxai. Before the Indochina War there wasn't much here but the district became a centre for Chinese troops during the war and today it's a boom town riding on imported Chinese wealth.

After roughing it through some beautiful countryside along the Mekong River and along Route 2 from Pakbeng (or from the east via Nong Khiaw and the Nam Ou) to get here, the town can be something of a disappointment. Basically Muang Xai consists of two long strips of asphalt and dirt where Routes 1 and 2 intersect, flanked by wooden shacks, cement boxes and construction sites, set in the middle of a deforested valley.

More traditional thatched houses spread across the rim of the valley towards the base of the surrounding mountain range. If you get off the main street you can find some very picturesque village-like sections.

The town is roughly 60% Lao Theung and Lao Sung, 25% Chinese and 15% Lao Loum. Some 4000 Chinese workers may be in the area at any one time, and the Yunnanese dialect is often heard more than Lao in the cafes and hotels. Most of the vehicles in town bear Vietnamese or Chinese licence plates; the town is also a conduit for caravans of Japanese vehicles assembled in Thailand and driven to China for sale.

About the only sight of interest is the large day **market** in the centre of town. A polyglot mix of people from around the province – including many Hmong and tribal Thai – come to buy and sell; the bulk of the products on sale are Chinese or Vietnamese. The most interesting part of

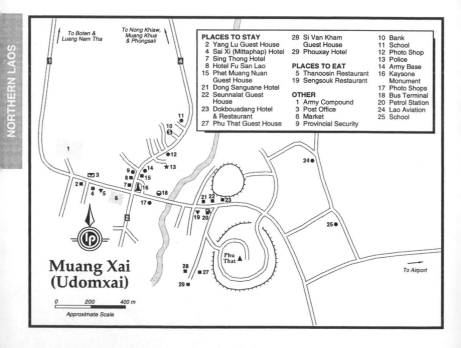

PLACES TO STAY
2 Yang Lu Guest House
4 Sai Xi (Mittaphap) Hotel
7 Sing Thong Hotel
8 Hotel Fu San Lao
15 Phet Muang Nuan Guest House
21 Dong Sanguane Hotel
22 Seunnalat Guest House
23 Dokbouadang Hotel & Restaurant
27 Phu That Guest House

28 Si Van Kham Guest House
29 Phouxay Hotel

PLACES TO EAT
5 Thanoosin Restaurant
19 Sengsouk Restaurant

OTHER
1 Army Compound
3 Post Office
6 Market
9 Provincial Security

10 Bank
11 School
12 Photo Shop
13 Police
14 Army Base
16 Kaysone Monument
17 Photo Shops
18 Bus Terminal
20 Petrol Station
24 Lao Aviation
25 School

To Boten & Luang Nam Tha
To Nong Khiaw, Muang Khua & Phongsali

Muang Xai (Udomxai)

Phu That ▲

To Airport

0   200   400 m
Approximate Scale

the market is at the rear where fresh produce and herbs – brought to market by small farmers – are sold.

Muang Xai now has electricity all day.

Information

Immigration Except at Muang Xai airport, no-one in Udomxai seems interested in stamping your papers in or out of the province – perhaps they're too busy processing all the Chinese migrants. If you want to try, go to the police office, which is about 500m north-east of the main intersection. You'll find the immigration department in room No 9.

Money In town you can spend yuan, dollars, baht or kip. Lane Xang Bank, on the edge of town on the road to Phongsali, can give you kip for dollars, baht or yuan but not vice versa. Nor are travellers cheques accepted. Bring cash.

Post & Communications The post office, a large white and mustard-coloured building with a telecom tower about 400m west of the bus terminal, is open Monday to Friday from 8 am to 4 pm, Saturday from 8 am to noon. A telephone office in the same building is open daily from 8 to 11.30 am, 2 to 4.30 pm and 6.30 to 9 pm. Phone cards are available there for use in the international and domestic phone booth out front. Muang Xai's area code is 81.

Places to Stay

The number of places to stay in Muang Xai has expanded rapidly over the last two or three years. Most places in town cost 10,000 kip or less. Nearly all of the hotels and guesthouses are owned and operated by Chinese immigrants. Several are operating mainly as brothels for Chinese workers.

Perhaps the best place to stay in Muang Xai, at least for those who would like to get off the noisy, dusty main streets, are two places at the end of a dirt road towards the eastern edge of town – the street entrance can be found about 400m east of the bus terminal. The Lao Petroleum-owned *Phouxay*

(Phuxai) Hotel (☎ 312140), in the former Chinese consulate compound off the main street near the south end of town, offers clean two and three-bed rooms with mosquito nets, ceiling fans and shared bath and toilet facilities for 3500 kip per room. There are also a couple of rooms with private bath and toilet for 4500 kip, or with a sitting room for 5500 kip. The rooms are set around a courtyard; there is a dining room that seems to open only for groups.

Near the Phouxay the friendly, family-run *Si Van Kham Guest House* (☎ 312253) – only the words 'guesthouse' are signed in English – has simple rooms in a two storey house with shared bath for 4000 kip single/double and rooms with attached bath for 6000 kip. There's a sitting area upstairs, a yard at the back where you can wash and dry clothes, and a restaurant.

Opposite the Si Van Kham, the new one storey *Phu That Guest House* has only six ordinary rooms – nothing special, in fact a little smelly – for 6000 kip with two beds and attached cold shower. There's also one small room with one bed only for 5000 kip, and a shared bath – a little overpriced for the market. Bargaining is definitely in order.

Just east of and opposite the road that leads to the Phouxay Hotel and Si Van Kham Guest House are a string of three inexpensive guesthouses in a row of shophouses, with restaurants downstairs. From the west, the first is the *Dong Sanguane Hotel*, which has very basic two-bed rooms with shared bath for 3000 kip per person, plus a three bed room with sitting room and attached bath for 5000 kip per person.

A few doors east, the newer and cleaner *Seunnalat Guest House* (☎ 312384) offers a couple of five and seven-bed rooms with shared cold shower for 2000 kip per bed. Or for a minor splurge, get a three bed room with ceiling fan, and private hot shower and mosquito nets for 15,000 kip. There are also two-bed rooms with similar amenities for 12,000 kip. Cheaper rooms with attached cold shower and two beds are available for 8000 kip. A good-sized restaurant can be found downstairs in the back, though hardly anyone seems to eat there. A little farther east along the same row of shophouses is the similar *Dokbouadang Hotel & Restaurant* (☎ 312142).

At the north-west corner of the main intersection of Route 1 and Route 2/4 (Route 2 changes to Route 4 north of Route 1), the Chinese-owned and operated *Sing Thong Hotel* asks US$15 for very plain rooms with cold bath in a three storey, L-shaped building attached to a nightclub. Such rates can only be designed to deter ordinary visitors with no intention of patronising the prostitutes working the nightclub.

Just north of the Sing Thong on Route 4, the dingy, three storey *Hotel Fu San Lao* (☎ 312198) refused to quote prices for its rooms. The dimly lit nightclub downstairs supplies male guests with young Yunnanese girls. As usual at the Chinese-owned places in town, very little English or Lao is spoken. Across the street is a three storey cube called *Phet Muang Nuan Guest House* (☎ 212214), which claimed to be full in the middle of the day but quoted rates of 6000 kip with shared bath, 8000 kip with attached bath.

Continuing towards the west end of town near the post office, about 200m west of the main intersection, stands the Chinese-run *Yang Lu Guest House*. The two storey white building contains dank rooms with hard beds for 5000 kip, plus five-bed dorms for 1500 per bed, all with shared toilet and shower. This place does not seem to be a brothel but the dorms are often full with Chinese workers.

Next door to the Yang Lu, opposite the post office, is the *Mittaphap Hotel* (the Chinese name is Xai Si Hotel), a four storey place where not-so-clean three, four and five-bed rooms with hard mattresses and shared facilities cost 3500 kip per bed. Nicer two-bed rooms with good mattresses, fan, TV and hot shower cost 10,000 kip per room; add 5000 kip for air-con. A 4th floor patio offers good views of town; downstairs are a restaurant and snooker hall. Very little English or Lao is spoken. Choose a room that doesn't face the noisy main street, although things do quieten down between 10 pm and 5.30 am.

Places to Eat

The relatively clean and popular *Thanoosin Restaurant*, between the market and the Mittaphap (Xai Si) Hotel, offers a four page English menu of reasonably priced Lao, Thai and Chinese dishes. Portions are large given the prices.

Though it's not particularly clean, the simple, wooden *Sengsouk Restaurant* opposite the Dong Sanguane Hotel offers the best fŏe in town as well as an English menu. They also serve fried rice, curried chicken, steamed fish, roast chicken and some vegetable dishes.

There are six or seven other ramshackle wooden cafes along the main road in the vicinity of the market. The restaurants at the guesthouses are OK but it helps to order in advance. The *Si Van Kham Guest House* has possibly the best cooking in town, but only if you order ahead.

Getting There & Away

Air Lao Aviation flies between Vientiane and Muang Xai twice a week; the flight takes an hour and 20 minutes and costs US$71 one way for foreigners. Flights to/from Luang Prabang are more frequent – five times a week (one hour, 35 minutes; US$28) – and there are also twice-weekly flights to/from Huay Xai (50 minutes, US$37).

The friendly Lao Aviation office (☎ 312 130) is in a small wooden building on the road to the airfield.

Road The Chinese-built bitumen roads that radiate from Muang Xai are still in fair condition, except for the road to Pakbeng on the Mekong River. Japanese pick-ups handle most of the public interprovincial transport; they park at a dirt area about 250m east of the main crossroad in the centre of town. Each truck parks at its own signed (Lao only) stand and waits for a full load of passengers before leaving. The best time to catch a pick-up out of town is between 7 and 8 am.

Pakbeng & Luang Nam Tha Route 2, the 144km road between Pakbeng and Muang Xai, takes seven hours by public transport.

See the Pakbeng section later in this chapter for details.

Luang Nam Tha is 117km north-west of Muang Xai via the all-weather Route 1, a five hour truck ride for 3000 kip per person (40,000 kip charter).

Nong Khiaw & Luang Prabang Running eastwards from Muang Xai to Nong Khiaw (129km) on the banks of the Nam Ou in northern Luang Prabang Province is Route 1, a decent all-weather road with regular transport for 4500 kip per person, charters for 50,000 kip. The trip to Nong Khiaw takes three or four hours.

It's also now possible to go on by road to Luang Prabang from Muang Xai via Pak Mong, which is about 48km west of Nong Khiaw. Songthaews to Pak Mong cost 3000 kip per person, leave around six times a day and only take around two hours (as always, this depends on road conditions). From Pak Mong it's relatively easy to connect with a songthaew heading south to Luang Prabang for another 3000 kip, two hour investment. Direct songthaews to Luang Prabang from Muang Xai are also available three times a day. These cost 6000 kip and take roughly five hours.

Muang Khua & Phongsali Another road, Route 4, heads north-east from Muang Xai to Muang Khua in southern Phongsali Province, then continues eastward to the Vietnamese border. Passenger trucks to Muang Khua cost 4000 kip per person and take four hours – as soon as the current roadwork is finished this will likely drop to two hours and the fare may drop with it. From Muang Khua you can reach Hat Sa near Phongsali by boat along the Nam Ou. See the Phongsali section earlier in this chapter for more details. Another way to reach Phongsali is on a direct songthaew from Muang Xai; these cost 11,000 kip and takes 10 hours, including a two hour break near Km 70 on the way.

Boten This border crossing between Laos and China can be reached in four hours by pick-up for 4000 kip. There are usually three or four departures every day from the Muang Xai bus stop.

River See Getting There & Away under Pakbeng later in this chapter for details on transport along the Mekong River from Luang Prabang.

When the Nam Ou is high enough (from June to early January usally, but some years much later), you can take a speedboat to Nong Khiaw from Luang Prabang. Nowadays this is strictly a novelty trip for most travellers, as the road to Luang Prabang via Pak Mong (see Road above) is cheaper and quicker. See the Nong Khiaw section earlier in this chapter for details on this route.

AROUND MUANG XAI
North and south of town are a string of Hmong villages where the tribespeople have come down from higher elevations – either because of mountaintop deforestation due to swidden agriculture, or because they have been pressured by the government to integrate into lowland society.

East of town off Route 1 at Km 11 is **Taat Lak Sip-Et** (Km 11 Waterfall), a slender cataract that cascades over a limestone cliff into a Nam Beng tributary. *Baw nāam hàwn* or **hot springs** can be found 28km from Muang Xai near Muang La, off the road to Phongsali near the banks of the Nam Pak river.

TO MUANG XAI VIA PAKBENG
The river-and-road trip from Huay Xai or Luang Prabang to Muang Xai is an experience in itself. Three hours by speedboat, or a day's travel by river ferry, the Mekong River journey to Pakbeng (jumping-off point for the road to Muang Xai) passes craggy stone cliffs, sandy shores, undulating mountains, fishing villages and expanses of both primary and secondary forest.

Pakbeng itself is worth an overnight stay if time allows (see the Pakbeng section following), then it's on to Muang Xai via Route 2, an old Chinese-built road that runs parallel to the Nam Beng most of the way.

The mostly sealed road is very rough in spots but is supposed to be resealed in the next few years. Along the way you'll pass Phu Thai, Thai Lü, Hmong, Thai Dam, Lao and Khamu villages, plus primary monsoon forest alternating with secondary growth and slash-and-burn plots.

At Km 90 (about one third of the way to Muang Xai) is **Muang Houn,** the largest village between Pakbeng and Muang Xai and a convenient rest stop. Muang Houn has a few basic guesthouses with rooms in the 1500 to 3000 kip range, plus plenty of places to eat or stock up on food supplies. Around Km 18 to Km 21 (counting south from Muang Xai) are at least a dozen Hmong villages cultivating opium poppies. From Muang Houn to Pakbeng is 52km.

There are a couple of scenic waterfalls not far from the main road. **Taat Yong** is said to be the largest and is a 12km hike from Km 87. There are plans for a road to the falls. A more fanciful plan is for a series of 'model' villages showing Lao Loum, Lao Theung and Lao Sung culture near Pakbeng (the National Tourism Authority of Laos' idea of 'cultural' tourism). So far the plan has thankfully not borne fruit.

PAKBENG

This rustic town-village at the junction of the Mekong River and the smaller Nam Beng river (Pakbeng means Mouth of the Beng) lies about halfway between Luang Prabang and Huay Xai (Bokeo Province). The Mekong here forms the border between Udomxai and Sainyabuli provinces; Pakbeng is on the northern bank and so belongs to the former.

Basically a market town and transit point for travel to Muang Xai, Huay Xai and Luang Nam Tha, Pakbeng's 500 or so wooden houses sit along a steep hillside. Close to the ferry and speedboat piers is a collection of makeshift shops and cafes that get more interesting the farther away from the river you go. Hmong and tribal Thais are frequently seen on the main street. A few vendors along the street sell local textiles and handicrafts.

Two wats of mild interest can be visited in town, both of which are off the left side of the road north, overlooking the Nam Beng. **Wat Khok Kho** is the newer of the two, with a sim of rather recent construction and a wooden *kuti* (monks' quarters).

Farther up the road, a series of stairs on the right-hand side lead past a small school to **Wat Sin Jong Jaeng**, an older temple that dates to the early French colonial period or possibly earlier. On the front exterior wall of the small but classic Lao sim is a mural that includes figures with moustaches and big noses – presumably early Dutch or French visitors. Inside there are a number of Buddha images of varying ages. A new Lao-style thâat on the premises was constructed in 1991; it's gilded at the top, and the base is said to contain a cache of *sáksít* (sacred) material (probably small Buddha images of crystal or silver, prayer cloths and rosaries from revered monks). The 82-year-old abbot of Wat Sin Jong Jaeng is highly respected.

Nearby villages might be worth visiting if you can find a guide – ask at any of the guesthouses.

Places to Stay & Eat

The all-wood *Soukchareun Sarika Hotel* burned down just after the previous edition of this guide was released and is now undergoing reconstruction in concrete. Its best feature will be its location overlooking the river.

A virtual explosion of small, inexpensive wooden guesthouses have opened along the main sloped street leading away from the boat landing. Most cost around 3000 kip single and 4000 or 5000 kip double for small rooms with one or two beds with hard mattresses and mosquito nets, and shared facilities around the back or downstairs.

First on the left coming from the landing is *Xai Khong Pattana Guest House*, with nothing to recommend it except that it's easy to find and next door to two restaurants. Next on the left is the nicest place in town so far, the well-kept *Monsavan Guest House*, a two storey place with bamboo walls, friendly proprietors and a very clean toilet and bathing area. Monsavan charges 5000 kip per person.

Phanh Thavong is next on the left, with several rooms in the back of a restaurant for 4500 kip. Immediately on the right after that is *Monhmany Guest House*, only 4000 kip and very basic. Next on the right is the government-run *Puvien (Phu Vieng) Hotel*, beside the agricultural office, which costs 4000 kip for a very basic and not so clean room, your choice of wooden upstairs or cement downstairs.

The *Mime Guest House*, coming next on the right, has a similar layout but uses it to better potential with an upstairs veranda. Small tour groups sometimes use this one. It's 3000 kip single, 5000 kip double.

There are several simple *restaurants* along the street leading from the pier, most serving fõe and a few basic Chinese dishes. Two places with large English-language menus are *Bounmy* and *Kham Niaw*. A day *market* in the centre of town on the left has a few vendors with prepared Lao food.

Getting There & Away
Road Two songthaews a day ply Route 2 between Pakbeng and Muang Xai for 5500 kip per person – around 8 am and 10am are the most sure departure times in either direction. At last try the trip took seven hours. You can usually charter a truck for 45,000 to 55,000 kip – with no stops along the way a light vehicle can cover the distance in about five hours. Some travellers have chartered jumbos along this road, but because of the lack of any decent suspension or shock absorbers on these machines, doing it by jumbo is only for masochists.

If you miss one of the direct songthaews to Pakbeng from Muang Xai you can catch one of the more frequent songthaews to Muang Houn, 92km south-west of Muang Xai on the way to Pakbeng. These leave about 10 times a day between dawn and dusk, cost 3500 kip, and take about four or five hours. In Muang Houn it's easy to pick up another songthaew on to Pakbeng, two hours away, for 2000 kip. The same is true in reverse; you can take a bus from Pakbeng to Muang Houn, then pick

up a Muang Xai-bound vehicle fairly easily. There are two or three basic guesthouses in Muang Houn if you get stuck.

At the moment Route 2 is in deplorable condition – more pothole than road – but a World Bank-funded road upgrading project claims it will reseal the entire road by 2002.

River The slow boat from either Luang Prabang or Huay Xai costs 14,000 kip per person. The trip takes eight to 10 hours downriver, 11 to 14 hours upriver.

Speedboat taxis from Luang Prabang or Huay Xai take around three hours upriver, 2½ hours downriver and cost 19,000 kip per person to either Huay Xai or Luang Prabang. These powerful craft can take up to six passengers; if you want to share one you'll have to wait at the pier until five other passengers turn up. Sometimes when only five passengers show up one of the more affluent passengers will chip in an extra fare – which should buy a little extra sitting space.

Or you can charter a speedboat for the Luang Prabang to Pakbeng or Huay Xai to Pakbeng routes for 120,000 kip; baht or US dollars are acceptable.

The speedboat ride can be quite thrilling as the shallow craft skip along sections of rapids at 80km/h or more. A Thai passenger was killed in a collision with an unseen rock near Pakbeng in 1992; since then safety helmets and life vests have been required and the Lao authorities are very strict about enforcing this rule.

Luang Nam Tha Province

Bordered by Myanmar to the north-west, China to the north, Udomxai to the south and east and Bokeo to the south-west, Luang Nam Tha (Nam Tha for short) is a mountainous province, with quite a substantial number of Lao Sung and other minorities.

The provincial population totals 114,500, made up of 39 classified ethnicities (the largest number in the nation), including Hmong, Akha, Mien, Samtao, Thai Daeng, Thai Lü, Thai Neua, Thai Khao, Thai Kalom, Khamu, Lamet, Lao Loum, Shan and Yunnanese. As in Udomxai Province, the Chinese presence is increasing rapidly with the arrival of skilled labourers from Yunnan to work in construction and road building.

In the early 1960s the western half of the province became a hotbed of CIA activity; the infamous William Young, a missionary's son raised in Lahu and Shan villages in northern Myanmar and northern Thailand, built a small CIA-financed, pan-tribal anti-Communist army in Ban Thuay, Nam Yu and Vieng Phukha (Lima Sites 118A, 118 and 109). Much of the opium and heroin transported by the CIA's Air America and other air services either originated in or came through Luang Nam Tha. Westerners still seem to carry a romance for Nam Tha and there is a higher than average number of World Bank, UN, NGO and commercial projects underway in the province.

South of the provincial capital, a 445 sq km area of monsoon forest wedged between the Nam Ha and Nam Tha rivers was declared the Nam Ha NBCA in 1993. Containing some of the most densely forested regions (96% primary forest cover) in Laos, the Nam Ha NBCA protects a number of rare mammal species. A second, larger piece of land to the west of the Nam Ha is under consideration for similar status.

The Chinese and Lao governments recently opened the border crossing at Boten (pronounced Baw Taen) to foreign travellers, making Luang Nam Tha a new gateway into Laos and ushering in a new era of overland travel between China, Laos and Thailand.

LUANG NAM THA

Rising from the ashes of war, Luang Nam Tha's capital is expanding rapidly in its role as entrepôt for commerce between China, Thailand and Laos. There are two town centres, one in the older, southern section of the district near the airfield and boat landing, and the second 7km to the north where the highways come in from Muang Sing, Boten and Muang Xai. The main market is located in the latter section.

Both centres are little more than large clusters of wood, breeze block and cement buildings centred around the airfield and market respectively. Like Muang Xai, this is a town best appreciated by walking well away from the bustling main streets. Near the airfield are two 50-year-old wats, **Wat Ban Wing Neua** and **Wat Ban Luang Khon**, both of mild interest. Across the Nam Tha river from this area is a Thai Dam village of around 50 families; there's also a large Thai Kalom village in the same area.

Luang Nam Tha has two **markets**, a modest dry goods market near the main north-south street through town, and a huge morning market several blocks west opposite the main bus terminal. The latter opens around 5 am and is finished by 8 am; this is the only market in Laos where I've seen fruit bats for sale. The dry goods market is open from 8 am to 4 pm.

Information

Immigration Except at the airport (departure and arrival times only), it's even harder to get stamped in Luang Nam Tha than in Muang Xai. Although there's a small police post next to the dry goods market, the police there don't seem interested in seeing your papers. If you insist on adhering to the letter of the law, officers on the military post at the southern edge of town will apply the appropriate red or black stamps.

Money Lane Xang Bank, roughly opposite the dry goods market, is open Monday to Friday from 8 am to 3.30 pm, Saturday from 8 am to 11.30 pm. Travellers cheques (US dollars only) can be exchanged for kip. Cash dollars, baht and yuan are also accepted. For both travellers cheques and cash, the rates here are a little lower than in Vientiane. Lane Xang also has an exchange booth in the dry goods market, open daily from 8.30 am to 3.30 pm.

PLACES TO STAY
2 Sinsavanh Guest House
4 Hongthaxay Somboune Hotel
8 Oudomsin Hotel
13 Kikham Guest House
16 Xaichaleun Guest House & Restaurant
18 Many Chan Guest House
21 Lao-Jiin Hotel
24 Darasavath Guest House
29 Houa Khong Hotel

PLACES TO EAT
11 Saikhonglongsack Restaurant
15 Phone Xai Restaurant

OTHER
1 Petrol Station
3 School
5 Radio Station
6 Provincial Offices
7 Paseutsin Shop
9 Dongsavang Video
10 Kaysone Monument
12 Post Office
14 Police
17 Lane Xang Bank
19 Bus Stop
20 Dry Goods Market
22 Nit Phasa Beer Garden
23 Lao Aviation
25 Military Post
26 Hospital
27 Bus Terminal
28 Morning Market
30 Wat Ban Luang Khon
31 Boat Landing

NORTHERN LAOS

Places to Stay

North Four new guesthouses have opened in Luang Nam Tha since the last edition of this guide and they are much better places to stay than the town's three hotels. Conveniently located three doors down from the bank and across from the dry goods market, *Many Chan Guest House* is a two storey wooden place with simple but good rooms for 2000 kip single, 4000 kip double or 6000 kip for a big corner room with three beds and wash basin. In a sitting area, a pitcher of *nâam sáa* awaits guests throughout the day.

The friendly owner, a former Royal Lao Government pilot and regional head of Lao Aviation, speaks English.

Farther north up the road is another new one, *Sinsavanh Guest House*, in a brightly painted two storey wooden house. Rooms with two beds and mosquito nets cost just 2500 kip, making this the cheapest place in town. The family proprietors are friendly, the shared bathroom facilities are large and clean and there's a pleasant sitting area on the upper terrace.

Moving a little upscale, the *Darasavath*

Guest House, opposite the road leading to the provincial hospital, offers OK rooms behind a very nice outdoor restaurant for 4000 to 8000 kip, with bathrooms out the back.

Three Chinese-run guesthouses in town can only be recommended for the desperate. Best of the three is *Kikham Guest House*, roughly opposite the post office, which has scruffy upstairs rooms over a restaurant for 5000 kip. Nearer the market, the *Xaichaleun Guest House & Restaurant* looks very unsavoury, with groups of drunk, card-playing Chinese downstairs much of the day. When we asked about rooms the staff refused to quote prices or show us a room.

The small *Lao Jiin (Lao-Chinese) Hotel* (the English sign reads 'Hotel-Restaurant-Video') on a side street next to the dry goods market contains a video parlour, grubby restaurant and bare clapboard cubicles for only 1000 kip per bed.

About 250m north of the dry goods market, a dirt road leads east off the main street to the 16-room, wooden *Oudomsin Hotel*. Basic two-bed rooms with mosquito nets cost 5000 kip with shared shower and toilet, while three-bed rooms with private facilities are 8000 kip. Compared with rooms available at the better guesthouses in town, these are clearly overpriced. There is a restaurant (not always open) and nightclub on the premises; the latter shuts down around 11 pm. A reader reports that rats in the roof and walls can be noisy at night.

Significantly more upscale – for Luang Nam Tha – is the 28 room *Hongthaxay Somboune Hotel* (☎ (086) 312078; fax 312 079), another 500m north of the Oudomsin Hotel turn-off and then 150m west of the main street. Two-bed air-con rooms with private hot shower are 10,000 kip single/double, while rooms with better mattresses are 12,000 kip single/double. There is a nicely landscaped garden area and a small shop selling hand-woven Luang Nam Tha fabrics and garments made of silk and cotton. A nightclub in the compound, which is especially popular on weekends, stops by 11.30 pm, after which it's a reasonably quiet place.

South (Airfield) *Houa Khong Hotel*, right across from the airfield, features separate bungalows with two or three rooms per unit, some with private bath and fan, some with shared bath, for 3500 kip per person. The bungalows feature large sitting areas with rattan furniture. There's a restaurant on the premises. No-one ever seems to eat or stay at this place.

Na Maw Roughly halfway between Muang Xai and Luang Nam Tha you can stay at a wooden *hotel* over a shop in the small town of Na Maw for 2000 kip.

Places to Eat

The *Darasavath Restaurant*, in front of the guesthouse of the same name, offers the best breakfasts in town, whether it's khào jii khai dạo (French bread and eggs) or khào piạak (rice soup). Their other meals – Lao, Thai and western – are also good, as is the service.

The *Phone Xai Restaurant* (formerly the Luang Nam Tha Restaurant), just a simple wooden place around the corner from the dry goods market, serves passable Lao and Chinese fare. It's generally open from early morning till 8 or 9 pm.

Better Lao fare is available next to the post office at *Saikhonglongsack Restaurant*, a simple but clean and friendly eatery with both sticky rice and 'normal' white rice.

The restaurant at the *Hongthaxay Somboune Hotel* serves decent Lao and Chinese food. There are a couple of very good fõe places in the morning market next to the main bus stop.

Down towards the Nam Tha river, *Nit Phasa* (formerly Jampa Thong Restaurant) is now a beer garden overlooking a fish pond; no food is served. Wear mosquito repellent.

Despite its impressively long menu, the restaurant at the *Houa Khong Hotel* opposite the airfield only serves noodles and fried rice. It's a good place to eat or have a cup of tea while waiting for Lao Aviation pilots to find a hole in the clouds.

Things to Buy

On a side street of the main road through the new part of town, Paseutsin Shop sells local silk textiles. A small shop at the Hongthaxay Somboune Hotel has a very good selection of textiles and clothing, as well as some jewellery.

Two kilometres from Luang Nam Tha on the right-hand side of the road to Muang Sing, the Luang Nam Tha Handicraft Centre is funded by the European Union and overseen by a British woman. It's a pleasant walk to the newly constructed riverside centre, where a good range of handicrafts are offered for sale at fixed US dollar prices. Some travellers will find the prices to be high compared with the markets or bargaining directly with villagers, but the project is dedicated to establishing a higher profit margin on behalf of village-based artisans. Refreshments are also available.

Getting There & Away

Air Lao Aviation flies a Yun-12 to Luang Nam Tha from Vientiane thrice weekly (one hour and 10 minutes, US$80). Flights to/from Luang Prabang are supposed to depart twice weekly (35 minutes, US$37), but in reality the schedule varies with passenger demand. There are also twice-weekly flights to/from Huay Xai (40 minutes, US$41). The flights to/from Muang Xai have fallen victim to Lao Aviation's plane shortage.

For the less regular flights, ie to Luang Prabang and Huay Xai, you should make inquiries at the Lao Aviation office (☎ (086) 312080, 312053) near the Darasavath Guest House a couple of days before your departure date. It's open Monday to Friday from 8 am to 4 pm. Your reservation might make the difference between the company's cancelling or operating a scheduled flight.

Road There are a couple of options for heading north from Luang Nam Tha, and a southward route to Huay Xai. A new bus terminal – as usual just a large square of gravel and dirt with a wooden shack alongside – has been established opposite the new morning market. All buses out of Luang

Nam Tha leave from there. Coming into Luang Nam Tha, a few buses stop at the old station (opposite Many Chan Guest House).

To/From Muang Xai Luang Nam Tha can be reached via the all-weather Route 1 from Muang Xai (117km south-east) in four or five hours. Passenger trucks cost 5000 kip (60,000 kip charter) and leave five times a day, early morning to early afternoon, from either end.

To/From Huay Xai See under Huay Xai in the Bokeo Province section later in this chapter for details of this road.

To/From Boten A side road going north off Route 1 about one-third of the way to Muang Xai leads directly to Boten on the Lao-Chinese border. Passenger trucks for Boten leave four times a day from Luang Nam Tha (3000 kip, two to three hours on a very poor road).

To/From Muang Sing Four or five large trucks a day ply between Luang Nam Tha and Muang Sing, a journey of around two hours (3000 kip).

River When the water is high enough, passenger boats occasionally run down the Nam Tha river to Pak Tha on the Mekong River for 15,000 kip per person. Pak Tha is about 36km downstream from Huay Xai. If there aren't enough passengers around for a regular service, you can charter boats to Pak Tha for US$50 to US$100, depending on the size and condition of the boat. It's reportedly a beautiful trip, but one that will be terminated forever if the damming of the river goes ahead. On the way you can stop at Ban Na Lae, a charming village with one guesthouse and a noodle shop.

Getting Around

From the new bus terminal to the main street a jumbo costs 800 kip. Jumbos from the main street to the airport, 7km away, cost 3000 kip. Shared pick-ups also ply this route several times a day for just 400 kip per person.

MUANG SING

Lying on the broad river plains of the Nam La north-west of Luang Nam Tha, Muang Sing is a traditional Thai Lü cultural nexus as well as a trade centre for Thai Dam, Lao Huay (Lenten), Akha, Hmong, Mien, Lolo and Yunnanese. The entire district numbers 23,500 inhabitants, making it the second most populous district in the province after Luang Nam Tha itself.

From at least the late 16th century until 1803 Muang Sing belonged to the principality of Chiang Khong, after which it came

under control of the Nan Kingdom. After a number of Shan princes took refuge from the British Raj here (and in southern Yunnan) in 1885, the British laid claim to the area but finally relinquished pretensions to all lands on the east bank of the Mekong in an 1896 agreement with the French.

One of the arms of the 'China Road' passes through Muang Sing on its way to Mengla, Yunnan, and the area has come under a lot of Chinese influence since the 1960s. Visiting Chinese soldiers can be seen strutting around the streets and even some local hill tribe men wear olive-drab Mao hats. Most telling is the presence of Chinese tractors (called *khabuan* by the Lao), often bearing Chinese licence tags and transporting goods and people back and forth from the Chinese border – sugar cane to China, garlic and onions to Muang Sing.

Information

Muang Sing has no bank as yet, so bring whatever cash is necessary for the duration of your stay. There is a tiny post office opposite the market.

Electricity service is available from 6.30 to 9.30 pm nightly. Most guesthouses give guests a thermos of hot water which can be used to heat up cold-water scoop showers on chilly nights.

Things to See & Do

Among the buildings left standing from the French era is a 75-year-old brick and plaster **garrison** which once housed Moroccan and Senegalese troops. It's now used as a small Lao army outpost and some of the buildings are under restoration, others in ruins. Along the town's main street you'll also see hybrid Lao-French architecture where the ground floor walls are brick and stucco and the upstairs walls are wooden. One of the better examples has been restored to contain the **Muang Sing Exhibitions**, a collection of cultural artefacts from the area. At the time of writing it hadn't yet opened.

Two Buddhist temples in town show Thai Lü architectural influence. At **Wat Sing Jai (Wat Luang Ban Xieng Jai)** on the main

Muang Sing

0   100   200 m
Approximate Scale

To Chinese Border (10km)
To Xieng Kok
To Luang Nam Tha

PLACES TO STAY
1 Sangdaeone Hotel
2 Noy Vanasay Guest House
5 Singthong Guest House
6 Hotel (Under Renovation)
7 Vieng Phon Guest House
8 Viengxay Guest House
9 Senkhatiyavong Guest House
10 Blue House
14 Singxai Hotel
17 Boua Chan Guest House

OTHER
3 Wat Luang Ban Xieng Jai
4 Muang Sing Exhibitions
11 Post Office
12 Bus Stop
13 Market
15 French Garrison
16 Kaysone Monument
18 Petrol Station
19 Wat Nam Kaew Luang

NORTHERN LAOS

street, you can see this mainly in the monastic quarters, with the massive steps and tiny windows, while in the less typical, rustic *wihāan* (main Buddha sanctuary) you'll see classic Thai Lü-style *thong* – long vertical prayer flags woven of colourful patterned cloth and bamboo. Red and silver-lacquered pillars are also a Thai Lü temple design characteristic. Farther north near the beginning of the road to Xieng Kok, **Wat Nam Kaew Luang** also has monastic quarters in the Thai Lü style, actually converted from a former wihāan. Mud-brick antechambers before a wooden passageway leading to the wihāan are unusual and may be a Yunnanese addition.

The northern end of town is the best place to see thatched Thai Lü houses known as *heuan hong* or 'swan houses'.

The main market at Muang Sing – called *talàat nyai* in Lao, *kaat long* in Thai Lü – was once the biggest opium market in the Golden Triangle, a function officially sanctioned by the French. Perhaps the most colourful market in northern Laos, today

it's a venue for fresh produce and clothing staples bought and sold by a polyglot crowd mainly consisting of Thai Dam, Thai Lü, Thai Neua, Hmong, Akha, Yunnanese, Shan and Mien. Traditional textiles – especially the simple, naturally dyed silks and cottons of the Thai Lü – are also sold in the market. Villagers come in to town to sell textiles to foreign visitors hanging out in guesthouse restaurants.

A number of Lao Theung and Lao Sung **villages** in the vicinity – particularly those of the Akha – can be visited on foot from Muang Sing. In general you'll find Hmong and Akha villages to the west and north-west of Muang Sing in the hills, repatriated Mien to the north-east and Thai Dam to the south. The Thai Dam are doing the best weaving in the district these days. One of the closest Thai Dam villages is **Nong Bua**. Ask around the guesthouses if you'd like a guide.

There's little to see at the Lao-Chinese border, 10km from Muang Sing. Along the way the narrow, paved road passes through

The Story of O

According to 1996 statistics, Muang Sing district produced 4.5 tonnes of opium, about 3% of all opium produced in Laos that year. Over two-thirds of that opium is thought to have been consumed in the district itself, where it is used as medicine, as food, in exchange for hired labour, for the hosting of guests and for spiritual ceremonies. A darker statistic estimates there are 1400 opium addicts in Muang Sing, whose addiction rate as a district ranks fifth in all of Laos. As elsewhere in South-East Asia the hill tribes appear to be most susceptible; nearly one in every 10 Akha tribespeople in the district, for example, are said to be addicted. Negative effects of such high addiction rates include a reduced male labour force and corresponding increase in women's workloads (most addicts are men) and reduced overall agricultural production.

Opium is traditionally a condoned vice of the elderly, yet an increasing number of young people in the villages are now taking opium and even heroin. In the town of Muang Sing local Yunnanese and hill tribe addicts sometimes peddle opium openly to falang visitors, setting a poor example for unaddicted local youth, and everyone knows where the local 'dens' are. This potentially explosive situation will sooner or later lead to police bribery, arrests or both. If you're tempted to experiment with a little 'O', keep in mind the effect your behaviour may have on the local sociocultural situation – you may smoke once and a few weeks later be hundreds of kilometres away while the villagers continue to face the temptation every day.

Thai Lü

Thai Lü dominate local culture and commerce in Muang Sing district. Keen traders, they have been unusually successful in maintaining their traditions despite the pressures of outside Lao and Chinese influence, while at the same time enjoying the relative prosperity their district has developed as a Thailand-Laos-China trade centre.

The matrilineal Thai Lü practise a mix of Theravada Buddhism and animism; though traditionally endogamic (tending to marry within one's own clan) they've recently begun marrying outsiders – usually Thai Lü or Thai Neua from other districts. Women are said to enjoy greater political freedom and power than in most ethnic groups in Laos.

Typical Thai Lü villages are on the eastern bank of a stream or river, with at least one wat at the northern end and a cemetery at the west. An important folk tale says a swan deity flew down from heaven and showed the Thai Lü how to build their houses on stilts as protection from animals and flooding, and with long sloping roofs to shield the inhabitants from sun, wind and rain. Small shuttered windows known as *pong liem* allow residents to see out but restrict outsiders from seeing in. In reference to this bit of folklore, they call their traditional homes *heuan hong* or 'swan houses'.

One of their more distinctive customs includes *su khwan khuay*, a *basi* (string-tying) ceremony performed for hard-working water buffaloes.

three villages, including one called **Ban Nakham** at Km 100 (about 4km or 5km from the Chinese border) whose mud-brick homes suggest a Yunnanese population. The minuscule Lao village at the crossing, called **Pang Hai**, is little more than a cluster of wooden buildings.

That Muang Sing Festival

During the full moon of the 12th lunar month, which usually occurs between late October and mid-November, all of Muang Sing and half of the province turns out for the That Muang Sing Festival *(bun thâat meúang sĭng)*. Centred around a Thai Lü stupa on a sacred hill south of town, the festival combines Theravada Buddhism and animistic elements of worship and includes many of the ceremonies associated with the That Luang Festival in Vientiane (which occurs at the same time).

The thâat itself stands around 10m high and is constructed in the Lanna-Lan Xang style, with a stepped, whitewashed octagonal base and gilded spire. A shrine building off to one side contains a row of Buddha images mounted on a sarcophagus-like Thai Lü altar.

The festival begins a few days before the official full moon day as merit-makers climb a broad winding path to the thâat grounds atop the hill and pay their respects by carrying offerings of candles, flowers and incense around the base of the stupa – a tradition called *wíen thíen*. The morning of the full moon Buddhist monks from around the province gather at the stupa for *tàak bàat*, the collection of alms-food. There are also traditional dance performances, carnival-style game booths and plenty of food vendors selling khào lăam (sweetened sticky rice baked in bamboo), noodles and other snacks. Many Chinese vendors cross over from Yunnan during the festival to sell cheap Chinese cigarettes, beer and apples. Festival activities spill over into town, where there are nightly outdoor Lao pop music performances with lots of drinking and dancing. Food vendors line the main street at night with candlelit tables.

In spite of its Thai Lü origins, the That Muang Sing Festival is celebrated by virtually all ethnic groups in the area, as much for its social and entertainment value as anything else. This is the biggest event of the year, and one of the best times to visit Muang Sing.

Places to Stay

Several new guesthouses have opened to fill the demand created by backpackers who have taken a liking to Muang Sing. All of them bar two (the Singxai and Boua Chan behind and beside the market) are strung out along the main street and are easy to find, and all except one (the Singxai) are in two storey houses.

The most popular place in town is the *Viengxay Guest House*, a large place on the main street not far from the market. Large upstairs rooms cost 3000 kip for two beds, 5000 kip for three beds. There's an upstairs veranda that is good for reading, relaxing or viewing the passing scene. Clean showers and toilets are found at the rear of the building. Evening power lasts a little longer here as the guesthouse has a generator. There is a sizable restaurant downstairs. The *Vieng Phon Guest House* and *Senkhatiyavong Guest House* on either side of the Viengsay are quite similar.

Opposite the Viengxay and Senkhatiya vong is the newest guesthouse in town, so new in fact it had no name when we stayed there. It's the only house painted blue on this street so travellers were calling it the *blue house*. Clean rooms come with two or three beds, mosquito nets and mirrors for 4000 kip per room. The main feature that sets the blue house apart from all the other guesthouses in town is the fact that the bathrooms are conveniently located on the second floor (on a back veranda) where most of the rooms are. The proprietors are quite friendly.

The *Singxai Hotel* is a concrete establishment behind the market with three-bed rooms for 6000 kip; each room has attached toilet and bathing facilities. Food is served in a separate building but service is lacking and the quality is poor. This hotel is quieter than the others as it's set back from the main street.

Singthong Guest House, in a large two storey white Chinese-style house, features basic rooms with two beds and mosquito nets for 5000 kip per room. The bathrooms are larger than in many places, and there's a sink for a change.

On a dirt street that runs east off the main street along the south side of the market, *Boua Chan Guest House* looks much the same as the other two storey guesthouses in town except that the rooms are a little larger than average. All rooms have three beds, mosquito nets, towels, mirrors and cans of bug spray. Clean bathrooms are downstairs.

Farther to the north along the main street, across a stream towards the north edge of town, is *Noy Vanasay Guest House*. Run by a very friendly Lao family, it offers three basic but clean two-bed rooms for 4000 kip, with bathrooms downstairs. There are a few tables downstairs with food service.

Farther north still is the larger and well-run *Sangdaeone Hotel*. This new concrete/plaster rectangular building offers six upstairs rooms and a balcony along the front for 6000 kip each. There are good views across to the mountains from the balcony, and even better views from the accessible rooftop. There's a restaurant downstairs, and toilets and showers out back.

Places to Eat

Most of the guesthouses have small dining areas downstairs. The *Viengxay* and *Vieng Phon* have long menus featuring omelettes, tofu, french fries, Lao and Chinese food (the Viengxay even labels the condiments in Lao, French and English) and are quite popular. The *Sangdaeone Hotel* has very good food as well.

Aside from the guesthouses, the only places to eat are a few simple *föe shops* along the main street and in the market.

Getting There & Away

The winding, partially sealed 58km road from Luang Nam Tha to Muang Sing parallels the Nam Tha, Nam Luang and Nam Sing rivers, crossing them at various points along the way, and passes through strikingly beautiful monsoon forest and several hill tribe villages. During the rainy season this road can be difficult, even impassable, due to high water and rockslides.

To Luang Nam Tha there are usually three or four trucks a day, at 8, 9, 10 and 11 am, although it could be less often depending on passengers, and a truck may leave early if it's really full. The fare is 3000 kip per person and the trip takes around two hours. These are large Russian or Chinese trucks with two bench rows in back – every inch of available space between is usually taken up with cargo, often from China.

In Muang Sing all passenger vehicles depart from in front of the market.

A dirt road near the southern end of town leads 70km to Xieng Kok, a Lao village on the Mekong River opposite Myanmar. Trucks to Xieng Kok leave Muang Sing early in the morning several times a week, cost 15,000 kip per person, and take all day. When road conditions are bad it may even be necessary to spend the night in a village along the way.

To/From China Although Muang Sing is only 10km from the Chinese border, you can't legally cross into China here without permission arranged through the NTAL in Vientiane or some other travel agency. Lao border officials will usually allow foreigners to cross for a few hours if you leave your passport with them at the border, but there's really nothing to see on the Chinese side for several kilometres, till you come to a large gleaming customs building at the end of a smooth-topped dual carriageway at Zaho.

Getting Around

Several places on the main north-south road through Muang Sing rent bicycles for 2000 kip per day; just look for the signs. Some of the bikes are in bad condition, so check in early for a decent selection.

XIENG KOK

Roughly 75km from Muang Sing via a tortuous road that parallels the Nam Ma river much of the way, this Lao village on the Mekong River is Laos' only official border crossing with Myanmar. Although ostensibly this crossing is open only to Lao and Burmese nationals, we have heard of foreigners who were able to get 28-day tourist visas at the border for US$30. You might do better to arrange a visa in advance from the Myanmar embassies in Vientiane or Bangkok before attempting to cross here.

It is reported that Xieng Kok is a major smuggling conduit for opium and heroin in both directions, depending on market destination.

Most visitors to Xieng Kok are more interested in taking a boat down the Mekong to Huay Xai. See Getting There & Away below for details.

Places to Stay & Eat

A new, as yet unnamed *guesthouse* at the edge of town – look for a blue-painted cement building – offers clean rooms for 2000 kip per bed, with shared toilet/bath facilities. Two restaurants in Xieng Kok serve simple but remarkably good Lao food – for the location.

Getting There & Away

Trucks from Muang Sing to Xieng Kok run three or four times a week; inquire at the truck stop area in front of the Muang Sing market. The 75km trip takes all day – up to a day and a half under certain road conditions – but the road may be upgraded in the near future. The fare is 15,000 kip.

If you're successful in entering Myanmar, you can catch a Japanese pick-up south-west to meet with the road which runs between Thachilek (on the Thai-Burmese border opposite Mae Sai) and Kengtung in Shan State. From Kengtung you can continue into the interior of Myanmar by plane or by bus. The latter mode of transport still isn't legal for foreigners due to fighting between the Mong Tai Army, a large Shan guerrilla army, and Myanmar's government.

More commonly, foreigners that do make it to Xieng Kok end up taking six-passenger speedboats going down the Mekong River to Huay Xai. This takes three to four hours and costs US$15 to US$20 per person or US$120 for the whole boat. It may be possible to board a slower boat but you will have to bargain hard to get a reasonable price.

Via Ban Muam You can get better rates by asking for a speedboat to Ban Muam rather than Huay Xai. Ban Muam, about two hours downriver, is a large speedboat depot near the point where the borders of Thailand, Myanmar and Laos meet. All boats must stop here anyway to allow Lao immigration and customs officers to check everyone's papers.

A speedboat from Xieng Kok to Ban Muam costs around 15,000 kip per person (assuming there are six passengers), and another speedboat on to Huay Xai – just 1½ hours farther downriver – will cost 12,000 kip per person. This works out to be about half the per-person cost of a charter all the way from Xieng Kok to Huay Xai.

In the upriver direction boat fares should be about the same but travel time is longer by up to a half hour.

BOTEN
This village on the Chinese border in the north-eastern corner of Luang Nam Tha Province is a major exit point for Japanese cars being smuggled from Thailand to China via Laos. Other than the lines of parked cars, thick with dust, waiting to get into China, there's virtually nothing else to see here.

Now that Boten is a legal border crossing for all nationalities, and with the upgrading of the road to Luang Nam Tha, the village is growing into a town of sorts, complete with basic guesthouses and noodle shops. Better facilities are available in Mengla on the Chinese side.

The Lao border crossing is open from 8 am to noon and 2 to 4 pm, while the Chinese crossing is open from 8 am to 5 pm. The best time of day to cross into Laos from China is the early morning when public transport onward to Luang Nam Tha and Muang Xai is most frequently available. See the Luang Nam Tha and Muang Xai Getting There & Away sections for details on transport to/from Boten.

Going in either direction you will need a visa in advance before being allowed to cross into China or Laos. In Kunming you can obtain only a seven day transit visa from the Lao consulate.

Bokeo Province

Laos' smallest and second least populous province, wedged between the Mekong River border with Thailand and Luang Nam Tha Province, has a population of 113,500. In earlier times Bokeo was known as Hua Khong (Head of the Mekong); its current name means Gem Mine, a reference to minor sapphire deposits in Huay Xai district. The province borders both Thailand and Myanmar, and is less than 100km from China, and so it has become a focus of the much-ballyhooed 'Economic Quadrangle', a four-nation trade zone envisioned mainly by corporate entities in Thailand and China.

Despite its diminutive size Bokeo harbours 34 ethnicities, the second-highest number of ethnic groups per province (after Luang Nam Tha) in the country. They include Lao Huay (Lenten), Khamu, Akha, Hmong, Mien, Kui, Phai, Lamet, Samtao, Tahoy, Shan, Phu Thai, Thai Dam, Thai Khao, Thai Daeng, Thai Lü, Phuan, Thai Nai, Ngo, Kalom, Phuvan, Musoe (Lahu) and Chinese. Bokeo is the only province with a significant population of Lahu, a hill tribe common in northern Myanmar and Thailand.

For years the tourist industry in Laos has been pushing a circular overland itinerary that takes in Luang Prabang, Muang Xai, Luang Nam Tha and Bokeo. With the re-opening and upgrading of the road between Huay Xai and Luang Nam Tha, this notion is getting closer to reality. A Thai company won the bid for an aid-financed road project which will eventually produce a direct land route from Thailand to China

NORTHERN LAOS

Lao Huay

Also known as Lene Tene, Lenten or Laen Taen (Dressed in Blue), the Lao Huay or 'Stream Lao' are classified by the government as Lao Sung despite the fact they do not – and never have – lived anywhere other than lower river valleys. Ethnolinguistically they fall within the Hmong-Mien family, most of whom live at higher elevations.

The Lao Huay build their homes – multifamily longhouses of palm and bamboo thatch – alongside rivers or streams from which they irrigate rice fields using simple wooden hydraulic pumps. Unlike the closely related Mien, they do not cultivate opium poppy for trade, only for smoking. Lao Huay women can be identified by the single large coin (usually an old Indochina piastre, sometimes accompanied by several smaller coins) suspended over the part in their long, straight hair and by their lack of eyebrows, which are completely depilated at age 15 according to custom. Both sexes favour dark blue or black clothes – baggy shirts and trousers – trimmed in red.

The Lao Huay use Chinese characters to write their language, often on handmade bamboo paper. Their belief system encompasses a mix of Taoism, ancestor worship and animism, with spirits attached to the family, father house, village, sky, forest, earth, water and birds. Around 5000 Lao Huay live in Laos; in Bokeo Province they're mostly concentrated in Nam Nyun district. This ethnolinguistic group isn't found in Myanmar or Thailand though there are some Lao Huay villages in Yunnan (China) and northern Vietnam.

through Laos – including a new bridge over the Mekong between Chiang Khong and Huay Xai. The 1998 economic slump put the brakes on some aspects of the project (including the bridge), although work is continuing on the road.

HUAY XAI

For centuries Huay Xai was a disembarkation point for Yunnanese caravans led by the Hui (Chinese Muslims) on their way to Chiang Rai and Chiang Mai in ancient Siam; today Chinese barges from Yunnan are able to navigate this far, so there is still a brisk trade in Chinese goods. Thailand's Chiang Khong, on the opposite river bank, is also a significant source of trade. Speedboats seen along Laos' northern rivers are imported from Chiang Khong, for example.

Nowadays Huay Xai is a bustling riverside town where the biggest commercial district is centred around the vehicle and passenger ferry landings for boats to Chiang Khong. Many new shophouses are being constructed along the main street, which curves along the base of a hill overlooking the river.

A set of naga stairs ascends this hillside to **Wat Jawm Khao Manilat**, a thriving temple that overlooks the town and river. Constructed in 1880, the teak Shan-style temple houses a 1458 stele donated by a former Chiang Khong prince. Many of the brightly coloured jataka paintings that decorate the exterior of the sim were sponsored by Lao refugees who had been repatriated from the US.

Fort Carnot, built by the French and also on the hill, is now occupied by Lao troops and is off limits to visitors.

Huay Xai's main morning market, **Talaat Muang Bokeo Huay Xai,** or simply Talaat Sao, can be found in the southern part of town. This is also the main road transport depot.

For most ferry arrivals from Chiang Khong, Huay Xai is just a stopover before boarding a boat south-east to Pakbeng or Luang Prabang, or catching a truck northeast to Luang Nam Tha.

Information

Immigration Huay Xai is a valid border entry/exit point for any visitor. You no longer need special permission to cross into Laos here, just a valid visa. Lao visas are available at several agencies in Chiang Khong; the most reliable is Ann Tour, housed in a small booth just north of Ban Tammila Guest House. A regular 15 day tourist visa costs US$60. If you leave your passport (no accompanying photos necessary) here at 8.30 am, you can pick it up at 3 pm.

Bokeo Travel, on the main street south of the pier, can arrange trips to nearby villages – including Lao Huay villages – or to a sapphire mining area 12km south. The agency charges a basic rate of US$30 a day including car, driver and English-speaking guide.

Money Lane Xang Bank, in a new location opposite the Arimid Guest House, is open Monday to Friday from 8 am to 3.30 pm. Lane Xang also has an exchange booth at the immigration and customs office near the ferry pier. US dollars, travellers cheques, or cash in baht and Japanese yen can be changed for kip at either location, but not vice versa.

Post & Communications A post and telephone office, a few hundred metres south of the main hotel area, is open daily from 8 am to 4 pm; you can make phone calls here till 10 pm. The area code in Huay Xai is 84.

Places to Stay

Immediately on your right coming up from the passenger ferry landing is the well-run *Manilat Hotel* with basic but clean rooms with fan and private hot showers for 8000 kip or 200B single/double. There's a very good, inexpensive restaurant downstairs.

The *Hotel Houei Sai*, a little farther south on the same side of the street, is similar in appearance and rates but is significantly shabbier. Head north on this street and you'll come to a new place on your right called *Thaveesinh Hotel*, a clean three storey hotel where rooms with one large bed and fan cost 10,000 kip, two beds with

Huay Xai

0   100   200 m

To Speedboat Landing, Morning Market, Bus Terminal, Airport & Keo Oudomphone Hotel

PLACES TO STAY	
6	Amirid Guest House
11	Thaveesinh Hotel
13	Hotel Houei Sai
14	Manilat Hotel

PLACES TO EAT	
9	Khaem Khong Restaurant
15	Noodle Shops

OTHER	
1	Slow Boat Landing
2	Market
3	Customs & Immigration
4	Petrol Station
5	School
7	Lane Xang Bank
8	Drinking Water Factory
10	Photo Shop
12	Customs & Immigration
16	Bokeo Travel
17	Wat Jawm Khao Manilat
18	Lao Aviation
19	School
20	Post Office
21	Telecom Tower

NORTHERN LAOS

fan 12,000 kip. Air-con rooms cost 16,000 kip with one large bed or 20,000 kip with two beds. All rooms have hot showers.

Continue north another 400m or so to reach the friendly *Arimid (Aalimit) Guest House*, a collection of thatched bamboo bungalows opposite a petrol station. All bungalows have attached bathrooms with small electric hot-water heaters but when we visited the water supply was intermittent. The rates are 8000/10,000 kip single/double. The husband-and-wife owners speak French and English. The pier for slow boats going to Pakbeng and Luang Prabang is only about 200m away.

In the opposite direction, about halfway between the town centre and the speedboat landing, the efficient three storey *Keo Oudomphone Hotel* (☎ 312002; fax 312 006) offers very clean rooms for 10,000/12,000 kip single/double with fan, 16,000 kip single/double for a 'special room' with air-con and fan. All the rooms have attached hot showers.

Places to Eat

The *Khaem Khong Restaurant*, a cluster of wooden tables under a thatch roof which overlooks the Mekong passenger ferry landing, makes decent fried rice, fried noodles and tôm yám. *Arimid Guest House* has good food and cold beer but very slow service. The downstairs cafe at the *Manilat Hotel* is more reliable and more authentic, though it closes early in the evening.

Cheap noodle and rice plates are available in open-air shops in the vicinity of the Manilat and Houei Sai hotels.

Getting There & Away

Air The airfield, of US construction, lies a few kilometres south of town. Lao Aviation flies between Huay Xai and Vientiane twice weekly for US$88. The trip takes an hour and 20 minutes. Flights to/from Luang Prabang operate once or twice daily for US$46 each way and take 50 minutes.

There are also weekly flights scheduled to/from Luang Nam Tha (US$41) and Muang Xai (US$37). All flights in and out of Huay Xai use Yun-12 aircraft.

Lao Aviation (☎ 312022) has an office in the centre of town off the main street; it's open Monday to Saturday from 8 am to 4 pm.

Road The road north-east to Luang Nam Tha used to be extremely difficult because of its poor surface, but upgrading is underway. Hmong guerrilla activity in the Vieng Phukha area seems to be a thing of the past, although heroin production and trafficking along the Burmese border means that areas off the highway can be touchy.

Passenger trucks to Luang Nam Tha, 217km north-east, cost 20,000 kip and take 10 hours under good road conditions, though during the rainy season it's often impassable. A bandanna would be handy for dust protection in the dry season. When the upgrading project is done, the road will be traversable year-round and buses should be able to make the trip in four to six hours (depending on the number of stops). You can stop off in Vieng Phukha (120km from Huay Xai) for 6000 kip. There is a guesthouse there.

In Huay Xai the passenger truck terminal can be found next to the main morning market near the provincial stadium, about 2km south of the Chiang Khong passenger ferry pier. Buses – one a day in both directions – leave from Luang Nam Tha and Huay Xai at around 7 am.

River

To/From Thailand The short longtail ferry ride from Chiang Khong on the Thai side costs 20B one way. In the other direction it's the same cost for the ferry (or its kip equivalent) but you must also pay an 'exit tax' of 1000 kip. On the Huay Xai side, the ferry landing is just below the Manilat Hotel.

Plans to construct a bridge from Chiang Khong to Huay Xai by late 1997 were derailed by the economic crash.

Slow Boats South Long-distance ferries – the 'slow boat' *(héua sáa)* – going down the Mekong to Pakbeng and Luang Prabang leave daily around 9 am. These are cargo boats with space for passengers – locals working for the speedboat mafia will often say there are no slow boats or in some other way try and steer you towards the speedboats. The best way to get on one of the slow boats is to go to the landing yourself the afternoon before you want to go and make arrangements. Or just show up around 7 am and be persistent.

If you're going to Luang Prabang the slow boat takes two nights, one spent in Pakbeng and the second moored next to a village called Ban Khok Kaat (this may change depending on seasonal river flows).

The slow boat passenger fare to Pakbeng is 14,000 kip or 300B. On the way to Pakbeng the boat stops in Pak Tha (5000 kip or 100B per person) and Pak Khawp (9500 kip or 300B). A stop at Pak Tha is in order if you want to try and get a boat to Luang Nam Tha, though strategically it's better to do that trip in the downstream direction. As for Pak Khawp we haven't discovered a reason to stop there – all the more to check it out for yourself (and let us know)!

You can charter one of the smaller slow boats with capacity for around 20 people (many more if you cram in) for 125,000 kip as far as Pakbeng. To Pakbeng it's an all-day trip (roughly 9 am to 6 pm, depending on water levels).

All the way to Luang Prabang a slow boat costs 28,000 kip or 600B (250,000 kip or 4000B to charter). All of these rates depend upon the price of diesel – which depends on the dollar-baht and baht-kip exchange rations, so prices can be rather volatile.

The Mekong slow boat landing is located north of the town centre next to the vehicle ferry crossing to Thailand. You can walk up the hill about 100m to a market area to buy supplies.

Fast Boats Six-passenger fast boats or speedboats *(héua wái* in Lao) to Pakbeng and Luang Prabang cost 19,000 kip or 400B and 38,000 kip or 800B respectively per person (you can pay in kip or dollars but baht are preferred). By speedboat it's only three hours to Pakbeng, six hours to Luang Prabang. You can hire a whole boat for 114,000 kip and 228,000 kip respectively.

Paa Béuk

The Mekong River stretch that passes Huay Xai is an important fishing ground for the giant Mekong catfish (paa béuk in Lao, *Pangasianodon gigas* to ichthyologists), probably the largest freshwater fish in the world. A paa béuk takes at least six and possibly 12 years (no-one's really sure) to reach full size, when it will measure two to 3m in length and weigh up to 300kg. Locals say these fish swim all the way from Qinghai Province (where the Mekong originates) in northern China. In Thailand and Laos its flesh is considered a major delicacy; the texture is very meaty but has a delicate flavour, similar to tuna or swordfish, only whiter in colour.

These fish are only taken between mid-April and May when the river depth is just three to 4m and the fish are swimming upriver to spawn in Lake Tali, Yunnan Province, China. Before netting them, Thai and Lao fishermen hold a special annual ceremony to propitiate Chao Mae Paa Beuk, a female deity thought to preside over the giant Mekong catfish. Among the rituals comprising the ceremony are chicken sacrifices performed aboard the fishing boats. After the ceremony is completed fishing teams draw lots to see who casts the first net, and then take turns casting.

Around 40 to 60 catfish are captured in a typical season. Fishermen sell the meat on the spot for around US$20 per kg (a single fish can bring up to US$4500 in Bangkok), most of which ends up in Bangkok or Chiang Mai restaurants, since local restaurants in Huay Xai and Chiang Khong can't afford such prices; transport to Vientiane is considered too costly.

Because of the danger of extinction, Thailand's Inland Fisheries Department has been taking protective measures since 1983, including a breed-and-release programme. Every time a female is caught, it's kept alive until a male is netted, then the eggs are removed (by massaging the female's ovaries) and put into a pan; the male is then milked for sperm and the eggs are fertilised in the pan. In this fashion over a million paa béuk have been released into the Mekong since 1983.

NORTHERN LAOS

The speedboat landing is about 2km south of the town centre. Snacks and drinks can be bought from vendors there.

AROUND HUAY XAI

Various hill tribe villages can be visited from Huay Xai, some of them within walking distance and others a short drive north or south of town. One that everyone seems to know about is the Lao Huay village of **Ban Nam Sang**. It's less than an hour away by songthaew – 17km to be exact – and you can either charter a pick-up truck from the morning market in Huay Xai for about 200 baht each way, or catch the regular morning songthaew from the same market around 8 or 8.30 am for 1000 kip per person. If you go it's best to check in with the *phùu nyai bâan* or village headman first. He's a relatively young man who doesn't mind showing visitors around.

A reminder: do not bring candy, T-shirts, pharmaceuticals or any other such items to give away to the villagers as such 'generosity' threatens to interfere with the traditional way of life, and worse, threatens to foster a culture of dependency and turn Ban Nam Sang into a village of beggars.

When we visited Ban Nam Sang the villagers seemed to have a strong sense of cultural identity and no-one asked for handouts. If you feel strongly about contributing to the community you might offer the headman a small monetary contribution to be used for the village school (all you need say is *sǎmláp hóng hían* – 'for school'. If you truly feel compassion for the Lao Huay, do not under any circumstances give directly to the villagers.

Sainyabuli Province

This upside-down-L-shaped province lying between Thailand to the west and Vientiane and Luang Prabang provinces to the east is one of the most remote provinces in Laos despite its proximity to the nation's capital.

The province is quite mountainous (with several peaks higher than 1000m and one as high as 2150m) and devoid of vehicle roads except for one north-south route extending from the provincial capital to the Thai border opposite Thailand's Loei Province. The population totals around 292,000, including Lao, Thai Dam, Thai Lü, Khamu, Htin, Phai, Kri, Akha and Mabri; many of these groups migrate between Sainyabuli and Thailand, since the border is fairly unpoliced.

Sainyabuli (also spelt Xaignabouri and Sayaburi) shares a 645km border with six different Thai provinces. The north-western section of the province is considered to be of major military and commercial importance because Pakbeng – the start of a road link (Route 2) with northern Udomxai and the Chinese border at Boten – lies less than 50km from the Thai border.

The province is rich in timber (including teak) and lignite (brown coal), and is considered the 'rice basket' of northern Laos, since most other northern provinces are too mountainous to grow enough rice. Other important crops include maize, oranges, cotton, peanuts and sesame.

The southern reach of the province was the site of a brief but heated border skirmish between the Thai and Lao in 1988. The Lao, using a 1960 American map, claimed the border followed one tributary of the Nam Heuang while the Thai said the border should follow another branch of the river according to a 1908 Siam-France treaty. Laos sent in troops to occupy the disputed 77 sq km territory, and in response Thailand launched air strikes against Laos – a daring move considering that 50,000 Vietnamese troops were deployed in Laos at the time. Over a hundred Thai and Lao soldiers died in battle before an agreement was reached and a compromise border was fixed.

Today pockets of the longtime Hmong insurgency, particularly the 2000-strong Chao Fa (Lords of the Sky) under Hmong chieftain Zhong Zhua Her, remain in the province and threaten to cause trouble for the government.

A string of rocky limestone precipices known as **Pha Xang** or Elephant Cliffs (so named because from a distance the grey-white cliffs resemble walking elephants) parallels the Mekong River on the eastern side of the province. Along the western edge of the province is the newly declared **Nam Phoun NBCA**, a 1150 sq km tract of rugged, forested hills thought to sustain elephant, Sumatran rhino, gaur, gibbon, dhole, Asiatic black bear, Malayan sun bear and tiger.

The southern part of the province harbours several scenic waterfalls, including 150m **Nam Tok Na Kha** (3km from Ban Nakha), 105m **Nam Tok Ban Kum** (5km from Ban Kum) and 35m **Taat Heuang** (40km from Ban Meuang Phae). Unfortunately, none of these villages are easily accessible by road as yet, and this corner of the province is reputed to be a hang-out for smugglers and possibly insurgents. The Lao government considers much of the province insecure due to difficulties along the Thai border (specifically eastern Nan Province), including bandits and smuggling (drugs and timber, especially teak).

The 30m **Taat Jaew**, a 1km walk northwest of Muang Tha Deua, is a popular local picnic spot.

Other than the fine mountain scenery and waterfalls, there are few attractions for the tourist since the province never prospered under the Lan Xang or Vientiane kingdoms, nor did the Khmers reach this to leave behind any ruins or sculpture. The French had a minor presence in the capital but left little infrastructure behind.

More visitors make it to Pak Lai, a stop on the Mekong River trip between Vientiane and Luang Prabang, than to the capital of Sainyabuli itself.

SAINYABULI

The capital stands on the banks of the Nam Hung, a tributary of the Mekong River towards the northern end of the province. The district (population 60,000) contains a large number of Mien tribals, who control the main market and several successful businesses in town.

Because of the security situation it's not unusual to see soldiers in town.

Other than a couple of wats there is little of interest. The grounds of **Wat Si Bun Huang**, south of town past the police station in an adjacent village, contain the brick foundations of Buddhist monuments which are rumoured to be over 500 years old. In town **Wat Si Savang Vong**, reportedly built by King Sisavang Vong on an older temple site, displays a colourful version of Buddhist hell on its front walls.

Sainyabuli Province has more elephants than any other province in Laos and there is a working **elephant camp** about 45 minutes drive south of Sainyabuli in Phiang district.

Very little English is spoken in Sainyabuli so be sure to pack your phrasebook.

Information
Immigration In the not-so-distant past Sainyabuli officials were quite suspicious of foreigners, understandably so in light of the Thai border difficulties and problems with smugglers and insurgents. Nowadays they seem to have loosened up considerably, although travel to the southern end of the province is still discouraged. The only place interested in checking and stamping your papers is the police station at the south end of town.

Money The Lane Xang Bank, 50m west of Sayaboury Guest House on the opposite side of the street, is open Monday to Friday from 8 to 11 am and 2 to 4 pm. The bank accepts only cash – Thai baht or US dollars – at a lower rate than in Vientiane.

Post & Communications The post office is open Monday to Friday from 8 am to 4 pm. Telephone services are available from 8 am to 8 pm daily.

Places to Stay & Eat
The friendly *Pha Xang Hotel*, a two storey building next door to the post office, has two-bed rooms with cold bath for 7000 kip per person. There's a pleasant balcony sitting area upstairs and a restaurant and nightclub at the back. The band stops playing promptly at 11.30 pm.

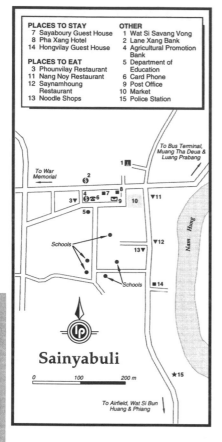

PLACES TO STAY
7 Sayaboury Guest House
8 Pha Xang Hotel
14 Hongvilay Guest House

PLACES TO EAT
3 Phounvilay Restaurant
11 Nang Noy Restaurant
12 Saynamhoung Restaurant
13 Noodle Shops

OTHER
1 Wat Si Savang Vong
2 Lane Xang Bank
4 Agricultural Promotion Bank
5 Department of Education
6 Card Phone
9 Post Office
10 Market
15 Police Station

Sainyabuli

Lao-Chinese food is good and reasonably priced. The English-speaking owner says he may soon build a guesthouse behind the restaurant. Another new place, the *Saynamhoung Restaurant*, also features a menu in English. Although the food is nothing to get excited about, portions are large.

Nang Noy Restaurant, east of the market near the market's main gate, serves a variety of fish, fowl, meat and vegetable dishes – it's the only true restaurant in town outside the hotels and guesthouses.

There are several simple *noodle shops* along the main road, some with rice dishes as well. You can also buy takeaway food from the market.

Getting There & Away

Air Lao Aviation shows a thrice weekly flight to Sainyabuli from Vientiane in their schedule, but when we tried to book a flight we were told they were unavailable for the foreseeable future. When it operates, the fare is US$42 and flights take 45 minutes each way.

Road There is still no direct road running between Vientiane and Sainyabuli. An all-weather, partially paved road runs south-west from Luang Prabang to Muang Nan on the Mekong's eastern bank, then connects by ferry with Muang Tha Deua on the western bank and then continues on to the provincial capital. There is a regular passenger ferry to either side of the Mekong for 200 kip.

There is also a road running north to Sainyabuli from Kaen Thao, which is on the Nam Heuang opposite the Thai villages of Ban Pak Huay and Ban Nong Pheu – both are legal crossing points for Thai and Lao, but not for foreigners.

Buses from Luang Prabang to Muang Tha Deua leave around 7 or 8 am for 3000 kip per person and take around 3½ hours. On the way you'll stop at Muang Nan, about 20 minutes before Muang Tha Deua. The fare includes the ferry ride. From Muang Tha Deua to Sainyabuli takes one hour and costs 1000 kip.

The *Hongvilay Guest House*, south of the market next to the Nam Hung river, has 10 rooms with good mattresses and shared toilet and bath for 10,000 kip single/ double. Out the back is a restaurant and good river views.

The marble-floored *Sayaboury Guest House*, 100m west of the main road, has 10 very nice rooms, a large dining room downstairs and an upstairs tea room. It's still reserved for Lao government officials only.

The relatively new *Phounvilay Restaurant* offers an English-language menu, and the

Sainyabuli Province – Around Sainyabuli 267

Mabri

Along the Thai-Lao border in Sainyabuli Province survives a single village of around 60 Mabri (sometimes spelt Mrabri or Mlabri), whom the Lao call *khàa tạwng leūang* (Slaves of the Yellow Banana Leaves). The men wear very little clothing, preferring nothing more than a small piece of cloth to cover the groin, while the women tend to wear castoffs from other hill tribes or from lowlanders. The most nomadic and endangered of all the minorities in Laos or Thailand, the Mabri customarily move on when the leaves of their temporary huts turn yellow – about every two weeks – hence their Lao name. Their numbers have been greatly reduced (possibly to as few as 250 – around 150 of whom live in Thailand) and experts suspect that few of the Mabri still migrate in the traditional way.

In the past the Mabri were strict hunter-gatherers but many now work as field labourers for the Lao, or for other hill tribe groups such as the Hmong, in exchange for pigs and clothing. Little is known about the tribe's belief system except that they are animists who believe they are not entitled to cultivate the land for themselves. Their matrilineal social organisation allows serial monogamy; a Mabri woman typically changes mates every five or six years, taking any children from the previous union with her. The Mabri knowledge of medicinal plants is said to be enormous, encompassing the effective use of herbs for fertility and contraception, and for the treatment of snake or centipede poisoning. When a member of the tribe dies, the body is put in a tree top to be eaten by birds.

Unlike in Thailand, where government and nongovernment agencies are attempting to help the Mabri integrate into the modern social milieu, no-one in Laos has come forth to try and protect the Mabri from becoming an enslaved community within an increasingly capitalist rural economy. Because of their antimaterialist beliefs, the Mabri perform menial labour for the Hmong and other hill tribes for little or no compensation.

In Sainyabuli the main bus terminal is 2km north-east of town.

River Since long-distance passenger ferries between Vientiane and Luang Prabang are now relatively rare, few people stop at Pak Lai. If you do manage to get a boat to Pak Lai it will cost around half the going fare to Vientiane (or to Luang Prabang, depending on which end you're starting from). From Pak Lai passenger trucks continue the journey to Sainyabuli for 5000 kip. The road trip takes five to six hours under good conditions; during the rainy season it may be impassable.

AROUND SAINYABULI
Pak Lai

There isn't much to this small town, though more travellers end up staying here than in Sainyabuli because it's an overnight stop for Mekong River ferries between Vientiane and Luang Prabang.

A branch of the Lane Xang Bank may be able to change dollars to kip.

Places to Stay & Eat Pak Lai has two government-run *guesthouses*, but the nicer one is reserved for government employees only. The other has no name or sign; it's about a kilometre upriver from the boat landing, just before a sawmill. Look for the last house at the end of the road on the left; it's a two storey building, constructed of wood on top of cement. The simple two-bed rooms with mosquito nets cost 3000 kip per person. The toilet and shower facilities are downstairs. The manager speaks decent English; food can be arranged with advance notice.

Just south of the ferry landing and across from the athletic field are a couple of *restaurants* which serve soups, fried rice and a few

NORTHERN LAOS

Lao dishes. There are also a couple of *noodle shops* in the market 500m north of the landing.

Getting There & Away Pak Lai is inaccessible by road for several months out of the year due to swollen stream and river crossings. Passenger trucks to/from Sainyabuli run from late November to May; the fare is 5000 kip and the trip takes five or six hours. Eventually this road will be upgraded to an all-weather route.

The slow boat to Pak Lai from Vientiane (216km) takes 1½ days. Speedboats do the same stretch in four hours. Figure on paying about half the standard Vientiane-Luang Prabang passenger fare for either boat.

Muang Ngoen

This remote village in the extreme north of the province, near the Thai border, is a traditional Thai Lü settlement. Houses on stilts with high-pitched roofs sloping low to the ground resemble those found in Muang Sing and in China's Xishuangbanna District. Farming is the main activity, and one made more profitable by the open Thai-Lao border at nearby Ban Huay Kon – a crossing permitted for Thai and Lao nationals only. **Wat Ban Kon** is a traditional Thai Lü-style temple where the monks still use palm leaves for the preservation of Buddhist texts.

The district of Muang Ngoen is home to more than hundred domesticated elephants, used for logging and agriculture. So important are the pachyderms to daily life here that the Thai Lü perform yearly *basi* ceremonies on their behalf.

Places to Stay There are no guesthouses in Muang Ngoen, but politely dressed visitors might be permitted to stay at the wat.

Getting There & Away The easiest way to each Muang Ngoen is via a dirt road from the bank of the Mekong River opposite Pakbeng in Luang Prabang Province, a distance of roughly 35km. Ask in Pakbeng about the availability of transport – your best bet may be to hitch a ride with someone coming from Pakbeng.

Southern Laos

While Vientiane is modernising bit by bit and Northern Laos is almost a country apart with its predominantly hill tribe and tribal Thai culture, in many ways Southern Laos remains the most traditionally 'Lao' region of the country. This half of the country also claims the most forest cover and highest concentrations of wildlife.

Only two southern provinces, Savannakhet and Champasak, are regularly visited by tourists. The rural areas of the Mekong Valley are mostly inhabited by lowland Lao who still weave their own cloth, grow their own food and devoutly practise Buddhism. The southern highlands are populated by a mixture of Thai tribal groups and various Mon-Khmer groups. Perhaps because the ethnic groups of the south aren't as colourfully garbed as those in the north, the south receives fewer 'hill tribe gawkers'. Traditions are strong, however, and in the rural south people can still say they do things the way their parents taught them, and the way their parents in turn learned from *their* parents, and so on for many generations.

HIGHLIGHTS

- Ancient **Angkor-period ruins** at Wat Phu Champasak

- Idyllic **islands** and **rapids** of the Mekong River, Si Phan Don

- The scenic **Bolaven Plateau** with its waterfalls and wildlife

Bolikhamsai & Khammuan Provinces

Bolikhamsai and Khammuan straddle the narrow, central 'neck' of the country, an area of moderately high mountains sloping south-west to meet the Mekong Valley. Lowland Lao, who speak a dialect peculiar to these two provinces, dominate the population followed by lesser numbers of tribal Thais, Phuan, Ta-oy (Tahoy), Kri, Katang, Maling, Tri and Hmong.

Khammuan Limestone NBCA, a huge wilderness area (1580 sq km) of turquoise streams, monsoon forests and striking karst topography across central Khammuan, was made a National Biodiversity Conservation Area in 1993. Although much of the NBCA is inaccessible by road, the local people have nonetheless managed to reduce key forest-dependent species to very small numbers through hunting, mining and logging. The area is home to the endangered Douc langur, François' langur and several other primate species. If its protected status is properly enforced, Khammuan Limestone NBCA has great potential for wildlife conservation.

Nakai-Nam Theun, the largest NBCA in Laos at 3710 sq km, covers a large area of east Khammuan on the Vietnamese border, as well as a smaller section of Bolikhamsai. Forest – including extensive stands of wet

and dry evergreen, old growth pine, cypress and riverside forest – covers an estimated 93% of the area, hence Nakai-Nam Theun NBCA is an incredibly important habitat for the country's wildlife heritage. Over a dozen threatened species live in the area, including elephant (one of the country's largest herds), giant muntjac (endemic to this region), gaur, banteng, Asiatic black bear, Malayan sun bear, clouded leopard, tiger and the saola (Vu Quang ox), a horned animal unknown to scientists before its discovery in 1992 in Vietnam's neighbouring Vu Quang Nature Reserve. The saola has since been sighted on Laos' Nakai plateau, only a third of which falls within the protection of the Nakai-Nam Theun NBCA.

PAKSAN

The capital of Bolikhamsai Province, a town of 35,000 at the mouth of the Nam San where it feeds into the Mekong River, functions as a commercial centre and army base but is of little interest to the visitor. On the opposite bank of the Mekong from Paksan is the Thai town of **Beung Kan**, but the border crossing is for Lao and Thai citizens only.

Until the mid-1990s foreigners were discouraged from staying in Paksan because of guerrilla activity linked to the Thai Isaan Liberation Party, an anti-Communist group led by Thai-Lao trade union activists and two former Thai MPs. In the last five or six years, however, there have been no threats of violence. The local population is predominantly Phuan, a tribal Thai group; many are Christian, which makes them doubly suspicious in the eyes of Lao authorities. The area has become considerably more secure since the upgrading of the highway between Vientiane and Paksan.

Places to Stay

The *Paksan Phattana Hotel* (also known as the Phudoi Phathana Hotel) has a row of peephole-ridden rooms at the back of the property for 7000 kip a single/double, while rooms in the main building go for 8000 kip. All the rooms have two beds, fan and shared

facilities. It can be noisy due to the nightclub on the premises.

The *Phonxay Guest House* looks bleak from the outside but the rooms are bigger than at the Paksan Phattana and don't seem to have as many peepholes. The rate is 6000 kip a single/double with fan and shared toilet/shower.

Places to Eat

There are several *noodle stands* near the Paksan Phattana Hotel as well as a couple of regular Lao restaurants. The *Sainamsan Restaurant* on the river and *Nang Daet* (the sign says 'Nang Deth') on the main drag have similar food, though Sainamsan is a bit pricier.

Getting There & Away

From the Talaat Sao bus terminal in Vientiane, bus No 18 leaves twice a day (7.30 and 10 am) for Paksan costing 2500 kip per person; the trip takes two to three hours. Buses are also available from a small terminal near Km 6 outside Vientiane. Once the Vientiane-Paksan section of Route 13 is completely sealed and the various bridges along the way are finished, it shouldn't take any longer than 1½ hours to reach Paksan.

If you are just visiting Wat Pha Baat Phonsan, you won't need to go all the way to Paksan, as the wat is just over the Vientiane Prefecture border, before Paksan. Under current road conditions it's one hour from Vientiane by private vehicle, 1½ hours by public bus – hop on any Paksan-bound bus and ask to get off at the wat; catch any Vientiane-bound bus later in the day if you don't intend to stay in Paksan or continue south.

AROUND PAKSAN
Wat Pha Baat Phonsan

Eighty kilometres north-east of Vientiane via Route 13, on the way to Paksan, is a large *pha bàat* (Buddha footprint) shrine, an important pilgrimage place for lowland Lao from Bolikhamsai and Vientiane. The highly stylised 'print' – along with a substantial reclining Buddha figure – sits on a sandstone

SOUTHERN LAOS

Horns of a Dilemma

The 1992 discovery of the *saola* or spindlehorn (*Pseudoryx nghetinhensis*) in Vietnam's Vu Quang Nature Reserve in west-central Vietnam – very near the Laos-Vietnam border – stimulated intense international interest in the potential for finding other large, undiscovered mammals in the area. Surveys in 1993 and 1994 confirmed the existence of the spindlehorn in Laos in the northern reaches of the newly decreed Nakai-Nam Theun National Biodiversity Conservation Area (NNTNBCA), a reserve that runs along the eastern portions of Bolikhamsai and Khammuan provinces in the Annamite Chain. Its range is now thought to encompass some 4000 sq km of montane evergreen broad-leaved forest between 200m and 2000m above sea level – most frequently at 500m to 1000m – along both sides of the central Laos-Vietnam border.

Researchers from the Vientiane office of the Wildlife Conservation Society examined a live saola – captured in Khammuan Province – for the first time in early 1996. This encounter, along with physical evidence left behind by local hunts and horn collections, indicates the antelope-like animal stands 80cm to 90cm at the shoulder and weighs up to 100kg. Its distinctively long, slender horns have a slight backwards curve and measure 40cm to 50cm. At the moment there is some disagreement among zoologists as to whether the saola properly belongs in the Bovinae subfamily – which includes wild cattle, spiral-horned antelopes and nilgai – or to the goat-related Caprinae. The spindlehorn has already become one of only three land mammals to earn its own genus in this century; most likely the animal will be assigned its own zoological subfamily very soon. Total numbers for the saola are difficult to estimate; the infrequency with which it's encountered even by local hunters confirms the belief that it is an endangered species. In 1994 it was added to the UN Convention on International Trade in Endangered Species (CITES), Appendix 1.

Hunting in the area poses a continual threat, as virtually every Lao and Vietnamese household in the Annamite Chain possesses at least one home-fashioned hunting rifle and a set of snare lines; automatic rifles aren't unknown and ammunition is cheap. Logging poses additional threats in the form of further habitat loss in the Nam Theun highlands where the saola makes its home. In spite of the legal protection afforded to the area con-tiguously covered by the NNTNBCA and by Vietnam's Vu Quang Nature Reserve, most of the human activity traditionally practised in the region will continue to degrade the primary forest and its endemic wildlife, unless some steps are taken to enforce protection of a core area. The saola can be viewed as an indicator species for the region's environmental health; if allowed, its disappearance would darken the outlook for biodiversity in Laos.

The first live *saola* (spindlehorn) was caught in Khammuan Province in 1996.

bluff along with older monastic structures and stands of bamboo. A well-ornamented 1933-vintage stupa is reminiscent of That Ing Hang in Savannakhet, and the drum tower contains a drum whose head measures 2m in diameter, one of the largest in the country. Unfortunately, recent construction has not added to the temple's charm. Wat Pha Baat Phonsan hosts a large festival on the full moon of the third lunar month (around July).

Nam Kading

The Nam Kading river, which feeds into the Mekong River about 50km east of Paksan, is one of the most pristine rivers in Laos. Flowing through a forested valley surrounded by high hills and limestone formations, this broad, turquoise-tinted river has tremendous potential for wilderness recreation. Confirmed animal rarities in the area include elephant, giant muntjac, pygmy slow loris, François' langur, Douc langur, gibbon, dhole, Asiatic black bear, tiger and a large variety of birds.

Unpaved roads parallel the Nam Kading upriver some distance, so launching places for canoes, rafts or kayaks are available. **Taat Wang Fong**, about 60km from Route 13 by road along the river, is a small waterfall in a very picturesque setting.

Ban Nape

The area around Ban Nape, roughly 200km south-east of Vientiane via Routes 13 and 8 near the Vietnamese border, is well known for its scenic limestone formations. You'll have to have your own vehicle to reach Ban Nape, as there is no regular public transport from Route 13.

THA KHAEK

Once an outpost of the Mon-Khmer Funan and Chenla empires, when it was known as Sri Gotabura (Sii Khotabun in Lao), the capital of Khammuan Province traces its present-day roots to French colonial construction in 1911-12. The town name means Guest Landing, a reference to its earlier role as a boat landing for foreign traders. Before

the Indochina War (and during the war until the North Vietnamese Army and Pathet Lao cut the road to Vientiane), Tha Khaek was a thriving gambling town for day-tripping Thais.

Until the Revolution the population was 85% Vietnamese, many of whom had come with the French and/or had fled the Viet Minh movement in North Vietnam. Their numbers dipped drastically as many Vietnamese left in the late 1970s to seek their fortunes in more favourable climes. Today Tha Khaek is a quiet transport and trade outpost of 68,300 – mostly lowland Lao, Vietnamese and Thai.

The surviving Franco-Chinese architecture, mixed with newer structures, is similar to that found in Vientiane and Savannakhet. At the western end of Thanon Kuvoravong near the river is a modest fountain square. Save for the occasional highway project engineer, only a few foreigners stop over here; for those people seeking urban Mekong Valley culture, this laid-back, friendly town is worth a couple of days.

Opposite Tha Khaek on the Thai side is Nakhon Phanom, which is a legal border crossing for foreigners. Thai investors have offered to finance a new highway from Tha Khaek to the Vietnamese border to facilitate trade between Thailand, Laos and Vietnam (and beyond via the Gulf of Tonkin). There has even been talk of building an international bridge across the Mekong River between Nakhon Phanom and Tha Khaek. Both proposals are on hold at the moment due to the current parlous state of the Thai economy.

Information

Money A branch of Banque pour le Commerce Extérieur Lao (BCEL), on the north side of Thanon Kuvoravong, about 200m east of the post office, changes Thai baht, US dollars and Lao kip. Both cash and travellers cheques are accepted, and the bank can also arrange a cash advance on Visa. There's also the Lao May Bank at the corner of Thanon Kuvoravong and Route 13, with cash-only services.

SOUTHERN LAOS

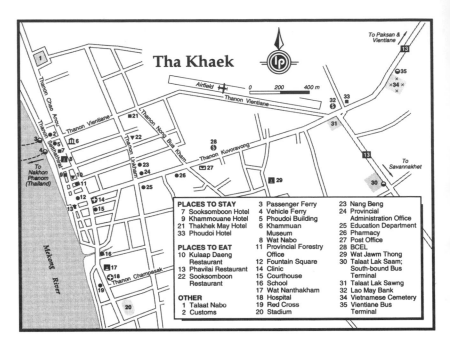

Tha Khaek

PLACES TO STAY
7 Sooksomboon Hotel
9 Khammouane Hotel
21 Thakhek May Hotel
33 Phoudoi Hotel

PLACES TO EAT
10 Kulaap Daeng
   Restaurant
13 Phavilai Restaurant
22 Sooksomboon
   Restaurant

OTHER
1 Talaat Nabo
2 Customs

3 Passenger Ferry
4 Vehicle Ferry
5 Phoudoi Building
6 Khammuan
   Museum
8 Wat Nabo
11 Provincial Forestry
   Office
12 Fountain Square
14 Clinic
15 Courthouse
16 School
17 Wat Nanthakham
18 Hospital
19 Red Cross
20 Stadium

23 Nang Beng
24 Provincial
   Administration Office
25 Education Department
26 Pharmacy
27 Post Office
28 BCEL
29 Wat Jawm Thong
30 Talaat Lak Saam;
   South-bound Bus
   Terminal
31 Talaat Lak Sawng
32 Lao May Bank
34 Vietnamese Cemetery
35 Vientiane Bus
   Terminal

Post & Communications You can post letters and arrange long-distance phone calls at the main post office on Thanon Kuvo-ravong. The area code for Tha Khaek is 52.

Things to See & Do
In town the large **Talaat Lak Sawng** (Km 2 Market) purveys hardware, clothes, fresh produce and just about everything else the people of Tha Khaek use in daily life. In addition to the usual gold shops there are a large number of vendors selling silverwork.

The **Khammuan Museum** close to Wat Nabo occupies one room in a government building with no other apparent function. Items on display – some labelled in Lao, some unlabelled – include pottery said to be 2000 years old, basketry, captured French and Japanese rifles, a few antique textiles, pictures of tourist sites in the province and an endless series of snapshots showing provincial officials at various meetings.

Places to Stay
The *Khammouane Hotel* (☎ 212216), a big four storey, white building with a curved front facing the Mekong, is still the best deal in town. Landscaped with palm trees, it was probably pretty impressive when it first opened but is now a bit faded; at least the sunset views over the river are tremendous. Large, plain, clean rooms with TV, fridge, air-con, hot water and good mattresses cost 10,000/15,000/17,000 kip a single/double/triple. The Lao name for this hotel is 'Khammuan Sai Khong', while most samlor drivers know it as 'Sii San' (Four Floors). The staff are friendly and the restaurant next door will deliver to your room.

If you are looking to economise, then the *Thakhek May Hotel* (☎ 212043) a couple of blocks away from the river on Thanon Vientiane offers simple rooms in a two storey building for 8000 kip a single/double with a fan and shared bath. For 10,000 kip a single/double there is a choice of a room with shared bath and air-con or private bath and fan. The outside of the building doesn't look like much but the rooms are quite OK.

A little upriver from the Khammouane Hotel stands the *Sooksomboon Hotel* (☎ 212 254, 212225), housed in a former police station from the French era. The interior of the hotel has been redone in a surreal Art Deco style; the staff are friendly but there's the general feeling that rooms here are used for assignations with women from the adjacent nightclub. Large, clean rooms in the main building feature high ceilings, air-con, hot water and TV for 20,000 kip. A motel-like new building around the back has some less expensive rooms which cost 10,000 kip a single/double with fan and hot water. A 10% service charge will be tacked onto these rates.

The *Phoudoi Hotel* (☎ 212048), near the main junction for Route 13 on the east side of town, is a more modern place where small rooms with two twin beds, TV, air-con, fan and hot shower cost 16,500 kip. But it's not as good as the Khammouane Hotel, and service is slack. Just behind the Phoudoi you can find the Baw Phaw Daw Discotheque; the name stands for 'Bolisat Phattanakhet Phu Doi', the name of the military-backed company that owns the hotel and dominates the economy and politics of Khammuan Province.

Lak Sao In Lak Sao (see the Around Tha Khaek section later) you can stay at the Baw Pha Daw's second *Phoudoi Hotel* for 15,000 kip a night. There's also a *guesthouse* about 3km west of the town centre with very basic rooms for 10,000 kip.

Places to Eat
Although there is no shortage of small restaurants and noodle shops, none of them are culinary stand-outs. The *Kulaap Daeng (Red Rose) Restaurant*, behind the Khammouane Hotel on Thanon Chao Anou, has good Thai, Lao and Chinese aahãan taam sang (food according to order). The rather

more fancy *Sooksomboon Restaurant* on Thanon Unkham appears to be open only in the evenings.

The *Phavilai Restaurant*, on Thanon Kuvoravong not far from the river landing and the fountain square, serves up standard Lao-Chinese rice and noodle dishes; it's open from morning till evening. You'll also find several khào jii vendors on the fountain square in the morning.

Just upriver from the fountain square is a small, unnamed *noodle shop* run by two women who make delicious fõe hàeng, dry rice noodles served in a bowl with various herbs and seasonings but no broth; regular fõe is also available.

There are lots of noodle vendors at Talaat Lak Sawng, plus a smaller cluster of noodle and rice shops near Talaat Lak Saam (Talaat Suksombun) and near the Vientiane bus terminal on Route 13. Look for sweet Tha Khaek watermelons.

Things to Buy
Nang Beng and her daughters weave made-to-order *phàa bɪang* (traditional shoulder wraps) and *phàa nung* (sarong skirts) on traditional central Laos looms in front of their home on Thanon Unkham.

Getting There & Away
Air Lao Aviation has had an on-again off-again flight between Vientiane and Tha Khaek costing US$57 each way for foreigners. Now that road travel between the capital and Tha Khaek has improved, it's doubtful Tha Khaek has much priority over other routes strained by Lao Aviation's chronic aircraft shortage.

The Lao Aviation schedule also lists a weekly flight between Vientiane and Lak Sao but in reality the flights go only when at least six passengers make advance bookings – which isn't very often. The flight takes an hour and 10 minutes and costs US$50.

Road Two direct buses a day leave Vientiane's bus terminal for the 360km, six to seven hour trip to Tha Khaek; the fare is 5000 kip. You can also catch Savannakhet

SOUTHERN LAOS

or Pakse-bound buses and get off in Tha Khaek for the same fare.

In Tha Khaek the main terminal for Vientiane and other north-bound buses stands next to a Vietnamese cemetery on Route 13 at the north-eastern edge of town. Savannakhet and other south-bound buses depart from Talaat Lak Saam (Talaat Suksombun).

The bus to Savannakhet takes two hours and costs 3500 kip; there are five departures per day from 6 am to noon.

Trucks with wooden carriages ply two basic routes into the Khammuan Province interior, one going to Mahaxai (towards the Nakai-Nam Theun NBCA) and the other to Nyommalat (in the vicinity of Khammuan Limestone NBCA). There are only two departures per day along both lines, one at 7.30 am and another at noon from the Vientiane terminal near the cemetery. Mahaxai and Nyommalat cost 1000 kip; intermediate points are 400 to 500 kip.

River The long-distance river ferry service from Vientiane has been discontinued. If reinstated – not likely except if massive flooding occurs along Route 13 – the trip from Vientiane will take around eight to 10 hours to reach Tha Khaek, depending on the number of stops along the way.

To/From Nakhon Phanom Ferries cross the Mekong frequently from 8 am to 5 pm weekdays, and to 12.20 pm Saturday. The fare is 35B each way. In Tha Khaek, the passenger ferry landing is about 300m north of the Khammouane Hotel; the vehicle ferry landing is between the two.

From Bangkok, Nakhon Phanom is served by express bus.

Getting Around
Jumbos cost 700 kip to the bus terminals.

AROUND THA KHAEK
Wat Pha That Si Khotabong, also known as Wat Sikhotabun and Pha That Meuang Ka, is 8km south of town. This temple dates from the 19th century and features a large seated Buddha, constructed by the order of King Anouvong (Chao Anou). According to local lore this temple was erected on the site of a 10th century *thâat* built by King Nanthasen during a time when Tha Khaek was part of a principality called Sii Khotabun. Considered one of the most important thâat in Laos, Si Khotabong was restored in the 1950s and later augmented in the 1970s. It's visible from the Thai side of the river and is the site of a major festival on the full moon of the third lunar month (usually in July).

Striking limestone formations, especially along the Se Bang Fai river near **Mahaxai**, 50km east via Route 12, are the province's drawing card for future tourism. Water-sculpted rocks at **Tha Falang** are reachable by pirogue along the scenic Nam Don, 14km east of Tha Khaek via Route 12. Also known as Wang Santiphap, Tha Falang (French Landing) features a wooded area on a stream where colonials used to picnic.

The well-known limestone caves nearby include **Tham Xieng Liap**, a tunnel intersected by a perennial stream beneath a 300m cliff; **Tham Phaa Baan Tham**, a Buddhist shrine cave; **Tham Naang Aen**, a favoured weekend destination for the natural air-conditioning provided by a constant breeze issuing from the cave; and **Tham Phaa Xang**, a large cave complex with separate floors connected by ladders. These caves, as well as hundreds of other unnamed caves, are an important habitat for an extensive variety of bat species. All are accessible from Route 12 between Km 8 and Km 16 on the way from Tha Khaek to Mahaxai; to reach them you need your own transport and directions from Tha Khaek.

A road heads east to **Lak Sao** (also spelt Lak Xao) at Ban Vieng Kham, around 30km north of town on Route 13 halfway between Hin Bun and Tha Khaek. Until five years ago a fairly undistinguished village, Lak Sao (Km 20) has become the pet development project of Phattanakhet Phu Doi Co, an enterprise headed by a Lao general involved in logging, hotels, construction and cargo transport. The district now boasts a population of 24,000 and is set to become an industrial zone servicing the Vietnam-

Laos-Thailand trade along Routes 8 and 12. A market at Lak Sao is known for the sale of wildlife, mostly birds, squirrels, rats, rabbits and reptiles, but also several more threatened species.

Savannakhet Province

Savannakhet is the country's most populous province (671,000 – around 15% of the country's population) and is a very active junction for trade between Thailand and Vietnam. The population consists of lowland Lao, Thai Dam, several small Mon-Khmer groups (Lave, Katang, Pako, Suay, Bru, Mangtong, Kaleung, Chali), Vietnamese and Chinese. The villages of Savannakhet are among the most typically Lao, especially those in the Jamphon Valley near Ban Kengkok (south-east of the capital).

Savannakhet is the best place in Laos for seeing the flotsam of the Ho Chi Minh Trail, the primary supply route to South Vietnam for the North Vietnamese Army during the Indochina War. It is also the main gateway for visitors arriving from Vietnam via Lao Bao.

About 85km north of Savannakhet, the 1050 sq km **Phu Xang He NBCA** covers a hilly area of dense evergreen and deciduous forest. Surveys have suggested the presence of 17 bird species deemed of conservation importance (such as the Siamese fireback and red-collared woodpecker), along with animals like elephant, giant muntjac, gaur, lesser slow loris, Douc langur and tiger.

SAVANNAKHET

Officially known as Muang Khanthabuli (but more commonly called Muang Savan or simply Savan), this growing district of 124,000 just across the Mekong River from Mukdahan, Thailand, has become a major relay point for trade between Thailand and Vietnam. From Savan, Route 9 extends east

all the way to the Vietnamese border at Lao Bao, where it continues eastward to the port of Dong Ha on the lower Gulf of Tonkin. Savan is also a lumber centre and there are several lumberyards on the outskirts of town.

Information
Foreign Consulates The Thai consulate (☎ 212261) maintains a temporary office at the Nanhai Hotel. There is also a Vietnamese consulate (☎ 212182) on Thanon Sisavangvong. Both consulates can issue visas.

Money You can change money (cash) at the Lao May Bank on Thanon Khanthabuli or at the BCEL on Thanon Udomsin.

Post & Communications There is a post office on Thanon Khanthabuli just south of the town centre. Savan's area code is 41.

Travel Agencies Savannakhet Tourism Co (☎ 212733), housed in the Savanbanhao Hotel on Thanon Saenna, has information on local attractions and can arrange tours to Sepon, the Ho Chi Minh Trail, Heuan Hin and other spots outside the city. SODE-TOUR (☎ 212260) has a branch in the Auberge du Paradis.

Town Centre
The Vietnamese presence in Savan grew during the French era and, while it shrank during the Indochina War, a Vietnamese school, Mahayana Buddhist temple and a Catholic church testify to a continued Vietnamese influence.

Like Vientiane and Luang Prabang, Savan has a number of French colonial and Franco-Chinese buildings, most of which are found in the small **business district** near the intersection of Thanon Khanthabuli and Thanon Si Muang. Daily activity centres around the cargo and passenger piers for ferries across the river to Mukdahan. Boats are loaded to the gunwales with Chinese and Vietnamese-made goods – particularly ceramics – on their way to Thailand.

Another centre of activity is the **Talaat Savan Xai**, a substantial new market area

PLACES TO STAY
3 Nanhai Hotel; Thai Consulate
5 Phonepaseut Hotel
8 Hoongtip Hotel
16 Savanbanhao Hotel
23 Sayamungkhun Guest House
27 Auberge du Paradis
   (Sala Savanh Guest House)
32 Mekong Hotel
34 Santyphab Hotel
37 Phonevilay Hotel

PLACES TO EAT
9 Nang Bin
17 Savanbanhao Restaurant
21 Nang Iam Foe
28 Savanhlaty Food Garden
29 Nang Khamweung
30 Lung Taam
33 Haan Aahaan Lao-Paris

OTHER
1 Petrol Station
2 Wat Chom Kaew
4 Petrol Station
6 Pier for Boats to Vientiane
   & Tha Khaek
7 Boat Ticket Office
10 BCEL
11 Pier for Vehicle Ferry
   to Thailand
12 Night Market
13 Wat Sainyaphum
14 Kuvoravong Statue
15 Chinese Temple
18 Vietnamese School
19 Vietnamese Consulate
20 Wat Lattanalangsi
22 St Theresa's Catholic Church
24 Wat Sainyamungkhun
25 Petrol Station
26 Savannakhet Chinese School
31 Lao May Bank
35 Pier for Passenger Ferry to
   Mukdahan (Thailand);
   Customs Building
36 Post Office
38 Airport

Savannakhet

off Thanon Sisavangvong near the bus terminal. The market runs all day and is visited by a fascinating variety of people.

Along Thanon Phetsalat downtown, in the vicinity of Wat Sainyamungkhun, are two dirt *pétanque* grounds where older Lao and Vietnamese men toss metal balls back and forth in the French game.

Wat Sainyaphum
This temple on the river is Savan's largest and oldest. An unrestored *sim* (ordination hall) dates to the 1896 founding of the

temple. Also on the grounds is a large, elegantly designed secondary school for monks, which brings the number of monks to over 200.

Wat Lattanalangsi
Nearly as large as Wat Sainyaphum, this wat was built in 1951 and houses a monks' primary school. The sim is unique in that it has glass windows (most windows in Lao temples are unglazed). Other structures include a rather gaudy Brahma shrine, a new *sáaláa lóng thám* (sermon hall), and a

shelter containing a 15m reclining Buddha backed by *jataka* (Buddha's life story) paintings.

Places to Stay – budget

Savan's cheaper hotels were once clustered in the older part of town towards the ferry piers. Only one is still open, the run-down but OK *Santyphab Hotel* (☎ 212277) on Thanon Tha Dan, two blocks east of the passenger ferry pier to Thailand. Basic rooms cost 4500 kip a single/double with fan or 6500 kip with air-con, both with shared bath.

On the river in an old French colonial villa is the Vietnamese-owned *Mekong Hotel* (☎ 212249), with large, high-ceilinged rooms, fans, air-con, tile floors and lots of wood panelling. The musty rooms are in poor condition, however, and the place seems deserted most of the time, except at night when the downstairs nightclub is filled with Vietnamese men and hostesses. Rates are 8000 kip per single/double.

A slightly more upscale budget place can be found on Thanon Saenna in the middle of town. Consisting of four two-storey houses built around a series of courtyards, the *Savanbanhao Hotel* (☎ 212202) has the largest variety of rooms in town. Spacious one-bed fan rooms with outside cold bath cost 4500 kip (7000 kip with air-con), one or two-bed rooms with air-con and attached cold bath cost 7500 kip, and one or two-bed rooms with air-con and hot bath are 9000 kip (12,000 kip with TV). The mid-price rooms are very good value. This is also the headquarters for Savannakhet Tourism Co.

Towards the south end of town are two other places worth considering. The very friendly *Sayamungkhun Guest House* (☎ 212 426) offers big, spotlessly clean rooms in a big house on Thanon Latsavongseuk for 6000 kip with fan, 8000 to 12,000 kip with air-con, all with private toilet and shower. The rooms at the back are much quieter than those at the front.

The *Phonevilay Hotel* (☎ 212284) at 137 Thanon Phetsalat consists of one and two-storey cottages built around a small courtyard. Rooms come in varying sizes. As the rates climb the rooms get bigger and the mattresses get softer. Simple 5000 kip rooms come with two beds, fan and shared cold shower, while 7000 kip buys two beds with air-con and private shower. Three-bed rooms with air-con and hot shower cost 14,000 per single/double/triple. Slightly larger rooms with TV, fridge and all the rest are 14,000 kip per single/double.

The proprietors of the Phonevilay also operate the newer *Riverside Resort* (☎ 212 775), a cluster of bungalows on quiet, landscaped grounds overlooking the Mekong about 1km south of town on the road to the hospital. Rates run 5500 kip for a fan room with private toilet/shower, 9000 kip for an air-con room, and 12,000 kip for a 'special' room with air-con, TV, refridgerator and hot water.

The *Fuangphet Guest House* (☎ 212517), near Talaat Savan Xai and the bus terminal, offers seven clean rooms in a two storey house for 12,000 kip with air-con and private bath, 15,000 kip with fridge and hot water. There's a restaurant downstairs and a small terrace upstairs.

If you have an early bus to catch, or if you simply want to stay in the cheapest place in town, there is a one storey Vietnamese-owned *hotel* built along one side of the bus terminal north of town with bare two and three-bed rooms for just 1500 kip per person.

Places to Stay – middle & top end

The centrally located *Auberge du Paradis* (*Sala Savanh Guest House*; ☎ 212445), on Thanon Kuvoravong near the main square, is housed in a restored 1926 French villa. Spacious rooms with air-con, hot water, fan and mosquito nets cost US\$20 a single/double. There's a garden at the back with a sitting area where meals can be arranged in advance. SODETOUR has a branch office here.

Two blocks north of Thanon Udomsin and off Thanon Sisavangvong, the *Phonepaseut Hotel* (☎ 212158) offers some clean, modern rooms around a small courtyard and a 25m-long pool across the street – probably the best pool in all of Laos, though the

SOUTHERN LAOS

dressing facilities have gone downhill; it's free for guests or 800 kip for visitors. All rooms come with fridge, TV, air-con and private hot showers, and cost US$25 a single/double, sometimes discounted down to US$20. This is where UN staff and employees of other international aid agencies usually stay. There is also a nightclub on the premises, so it may get noisy at night.

The *Hoongtip Hotel* (☎ 212262; fax 213 230), a four storey neogothic place on the corner of Thanon Phetsalat and Thanon Udomsin, charges US$21 for large modern rooms with air-con and hot water. Built from the cheapest materials, this is the kind of hotel that will probably look run-down in a few years. There is a restaurant and nightclub, but no lift.

Farther north at the edge of town off Thanon Latsavongseuk is the huge six storey *Nanhai Hotel* (☎ 212371; fax 212 381). Built by a company from Guangzhou, China, the standards are fairly high; air-con rooms with phone and private bath range from US$20 for very small singles to US$32/34 for singles/doubles with much larger rooms and the same amenities plus satellite TV and breakfast. Suites are available with added fridge for US$52/54. Some of the facilities on the premises include a swimming pool, lift, karaoke lounge, coffee shop and a restaurant that serves Chinese, Thai and French dishes. In typical Chinese fashion, the hotel provides a thermos of hot water and lidded ceramic tea mugs for each room.

Places to Eat

Savan isn't exactly a culinary capital but there are plenty of opportunities to sample Thai, Chinese and Vietnamese food. Local specialities include sìn sawǎn (a slightly sweet, dried, roasted beef) and jaew pạadàek, a thick sauce of mashed chilli, onion, fish sauce and lotus bulb.

Along the Mekong riverbank, opposite the Mekong Hotel and Wat Sainyaphum, a small *night market* convenes each evening. Most of the vendors offer only bagged snacks and cold beverages, but a few make fresh tạm màak hung (spicy green papaya salad), grilled chicken and kebabs. This can be a nice breezy spot for watching the sun set over Mukdahan.

In the customs/immigration building which overlooks the ferry pier, a restaurant called *Say Chai* serves simple Lao fare and cold beer.

In the centre of town are many small Chinese-Vietnamese restaurants, none of them particularly outstanding. Lao food can be difficult to find, but *Nang Khamweung*, a very humble two-table place on Thanon Phetsalat (a block north of Thanon Si Muang), is famous for beef or buffalo làap and of course sticky rice; it's generally open from noon to 11 pm daily. Two doors down from Nang Khamweung on the side street is another authentic Lao restaurant, *Lung Taam*.

Of the many places offering fõe, local consensus says the best is an unmarked hâan khǎi fõe called *Nang Iam* east of the Catholic church near Huay Longkong (third house on the left from Thanon Latsavongseuk). A huge bowl of steaming beef fõe here comes with a table full of condiments – including saucers of small but incendiary yellow-and-purple-streaked chillies.

The *Nang Bin* cafe and noodle shop opposite Hoongtip Hotel is good. There are a few more *noodle shops* in the next block north along Thanon Phetsalat.

A small night market called *Savanhlaty Food Garden*, towards the river from the Catholic church in the small town plaza, serves good, inexpensive Lao, Chinese and Thai food. Two side-by-side, hole-in-the-wall *Vietnamese restaurants* half a block north of the square serve Thai dishes as well as Vietnamese standards. It's 1300 kip for any dish over rice and soup, or 2000 kip for a set menu.

The *Haan Aahaan Lao-Paris (Lao & French Food Restaurant*; ☎ 212792), formerly the Four Seasons Restaurant, is in an old Chinese shophouse near the river. Run by a friendly Lao-Vietnamese couple who spent many years in France and Thailand, this spot features Lao, Vietnamese and French dishes, including nãem néuang, tuna baguettes, Korean beef, spaghetti, steak, french fries, good breakfasts, Lao coffee and French wine by the glass. Prices are reasonable. It is open from 8 am to 10 pm daily.

One block north of the Lao May Bank is an ice cream shop called *Nang Bunliem*.

The *Phonepaseut*, *Savanbanhao*, *Hoongtip* and *Nanhai* hotels have restaurants. The Savanbanhao (whose restaurant is actually across the street from the hotel) has quite decent food. The Hoongtip and Nanhai are a bit expensive.

There are several OK noodle and rice shops at the bus terminal; *Khiw Lot* is a little bit better than the others.

Entertainment
The *Savanbanhao*, *Phonepaseut* and *Mekong* hotels all have popular nightclubs with Lao bands.

Getting There & Away
Air Lao Aviation (☎ 212140) flies Yun-12 planes from Vientiane to Savannakhet daily except Friday. The fare for foreigners is US$61 one way; the trip takes 65 minutes.

Flights between Savan and Pakse are listed on Lao Aviation's latest fare sheet but in reality this flight almost never happens unless requested by a tour group. When operating, this leg costs US$44 per person and takes 50 minutes.

Road Three or four buses a day leave Vientiane's Talaat Sao bus terminal for the eight to nine hour ride to Savannakhet. The fare is 10,000 kip. In both directions, buses leave at around 7.30 am and 10 or 11 am. The road between Vientiane and Savan has improved greatly in the last couple of years.

To/from Pakse the bus costs 5000 kip and takes around six hours; departure is usually around 6 am. This trip will be much quicker when Route 13 is finished; for the moment it's a gruelling ride.

Savan's bus terminal – usually referred to as the *khíw lot* or bus queue – is near the Talaat Savan Xai at the northern edge of town. Vendors sell coffee and noodles to early morning bus passengers; there's even an attached motel with cheap rooms – the only such arrangement in Laos.

To/From Lao Bao, Vietnam It is legal to enter or exit Laos via Lao Bao on the Lao-Vietnamese border. From the Savan end, one bus a day goes to the border along Route 9 at 5.30 am, arriving around noon for 5000 kip. In the reverse direction the bus leaves around 1 pm and arrives around 7 pm. The 250km road is rough and buses tend to be very crowded. Travel can be very difficult during the June to October rainy season.

Dong Ha, on Vietnam's main north-south highway and railway, is only 75km east of Lao Bao. At Savan's bus terminal you can book buses straight through to Danang (28,000 kip, 508km), Hué (18,000 kip, 409km), Dong Ha (14,000 kip, 329km), Vinh (27,000 kip, 629km) and to Hanoi (39,000 kip, 916km).

If you don't already have a visa for Vietnam, you can get one at the Vietnamese consulates in Savannakhet or Pakse.

To/From Mukdahan, Thailand There are ferries crossing the Mekong River between Savan and Mukdahan frequently between 8.30 am and 5 pm weekdays and 8.30 am to 12.30 pm Saturday, for 30B from Thailand, 1100 kip from Laos.

It's legal for foreigners to enter and exit the country via Savannakhet. Most nationalities receive an automatic 30 day visa on arrival in Thailand. If you want a longer visa, go to the Thai consulate at the Nanhai Hotel in Savannakhet.

Getting Around
Savan is just big enough that you might want to resort to samlor on occasion. Fares run around 800 kip for trips of up to 2km. The Savan equivalent to Vientiane's jumbo is the *sakai-laep* or 'Skylab' – like the famed space station that fell to earth. You can usually find lots of these parked in front of the passenger ferry pier.

You can rent bicycles for 3000 kip a day at the Santyphab Hotel.

SOUTHERN LAOS

AROUND SAVANNAKHET
That Ing Hang
Thought to have been built in the mid-16th century (about the same time as Vientiane's Pha That Luang), this well-proportioned, 9m-high thâat is the second holiest religious edifice in southern Laos after Wat Phu Champasak. Built on or near the spot where Chao Fa Ngum's forces were based during the takeover of Muang Sawa in the mid-14th century, That Ing Hang may occupy an earlier site sacred to the Sii Khotabun Kingdom.

Not including the Mon-inspired cubical base, That Ing Hang was substantially rebuilt during the reign of King Sai Setthathirat (1548-71) and now features three terraced bases topped by a traditional Lao stupa and a gold umbrella weighing 40 *baht* (450g). A hollow chamber in the lower section contains a fairly undistinguished collection of Buddha images (by religious custom, women are not permitted to enter the chamber). The French restored That Ing Hang in 1930. Some original stucco decoration on the exterior remains intact but the sculpture in the outside niches is new and not very well executed.

The grounds are surrounded by high cloister walls on three sides and a low wall in front, with ornate gates on all four sides. Some older standing Buddha images in a small sim next to the main thâat are worth seeing if you can get someone to unlock the door.

Behind the That Ing Hang cloister are several wooden temple buildings used by a handful of resident monks.

On the full moon of February or March there is a big festival featuring processions and fireworks.

Getting There & Away That Ing Hang is 12km north-east of Savan via Route 13, then 3km east on a dirt road. Any northbound bus passes this turn-off.

Heuan Hin
On the Mekong River south of Savan is this set of Cham or Khmer ruins (the name means Stone House), built between 553 and 700 AD. Of interest mainly to pre-Angkor art fanatics, the unrestored ruins are little more than a few walls and piles of laterite rubble. No carvings remain; the only known lintel from the site is in Paris.

The best way to get to Heuan Hin is by boat along the Mekong – when the water's high enough it's a 70km, three hour trip by chartered longtail boat. By road you must first travel 75km south via Route 13, then 15km west along a rough road. The Savannakhet Tourism Co at the Savanbanhao Hotel says they can provide a van, driver and guide to Heuan Hin (and to That Phon – see below) and back for US$70.

That Phon
Said to date from the 16th century, this large, rounded white stupa is quite similar to Luang Prabang's That Makmo (and like That Makmo, That Phon is said to contain a cache of valuable Buddha images) is 65km south of Savan off Route 13 on the way to Heuan Hin.

SEPON (XEPON) & THE HO CHI MINH TRAIL
One of the nearest towns to the Ho Chi Minh Trail is Sepon (often spelt 'Xepon', population 35,600), about 170km east of Savannakhet via Route 9. Sepon was destroyed during the war and is now just one of many makeshift wooden towns that mark the long-term legacy of the bombing of eastern Laos during the Indochina War.

Sepon is a starting point for visits to the Ho Chi Minh Trail, the outer edges of which begin some 15 to 20km to the east of the town. Although there is plenty of war debris around, much of it is in the bush covered by the undergrowth. Unless you are prepared to go on a hike for some distance from the road (because of the risk of encountering UXO – unexploded ordnance – you'll need a guide), it is hardly worth your while going to Sepon.

A few kilometres east of Sepon stands the small village of Ban Dong, and 34km farther on is the Vietnamese border itself,

Ho Chi Minh Trail

The infamous Ho Chi Minh Trail – actually a complex network of dirt paths and gravel roads – runs parallel to the Laos-Vietnam border beginning at a point directly east of Savannakhet.

Though mostly associated with the 1963-74 Indochina War, the road network was originally used by the Viet Minh against the French in the 1950s as an infiltration route to the south. The trail's heaviest use occurred between 1966 and 1971 when over 600,000 North Vietnamese Army (NVA) troops – along with 100 tonnes of provisions and 500,000 tonnes of trucks, tanks, weapons and ordnance – passed along the route in direct violation of the 1962 Geneva accords. At any one time around 25,000 NVA troops guarded the trail, which was honeycombed with underground barracks, fuel and vehicle repair depots as well as anti-aircraft emplacements.

The North Vietnamese denied the existence of the trail throughout most of the war. The USA, on their part, denied bombing it. In spite of 1.1 million tonnes of saturation bombing (begun in 1965 and reaching up to 900 sorties per day by 1969, including outings by B-52 behemoths), traffic along the route was never interrupted for more than a few days. Like a column of ants parted with a stick, the Vietnamese soldiers and supplies poured southward with only an estimated 15% to 20% of the cargo affected by heavy bombardment. One estimate says that 300 bombs were dropped for every NVA casualty. The Yanks even tried bombing the trail with canned Budweiser beer (incapacitation through intoxication!), Calgonite dishwasher detergent (to make the trail too slippery for travel) and massive quantities of defoliants and herbicides.

The nearest sizeable town to the Ho Chi Minh Trail is Sepon, approximately 170km east of Savannakhet via Route 9. From Sepon the outer edges of the Ho Chi Minh Trail are another 15 to 20km. The trail is even more accessible from the village of Pa-am, in Attapeu Province, which sits almost right on the main thoroughfare. South of here the trail enters Cambodia, where (until March 1970 when a coup toppled Prince Sihanouk in Phnom Penh) it met up with the 'Sihanouk Trail', another Communist supply route running up from the Gulf of Thailand.

Along the more remote parts of the trail, anti-aircraft emplacements, Soviet tanks and bits of other war junk can sometimes be seen. Because of the area's remoteness from scrap metal markets, a lot of the debris in more remote sections of the trail lies untouched. However, near population centres the only visible remains are a few bomb craters and a tank wreck or two.

Ban Dong, 34km west of the Vietnam border near Route 9, has a few houses partially built from scrap metal. Eastern Savannakhet Province (along with Salavan, Sekong and Attapeu provinces farther south) is also one of the primary areas where joint Lao-American teams – under the direction of a US colonel in Vientiane – are searching for the remains of American MIAs. Eighty percent of the American servicemen not yet accounted for in Laos are thought to have gone down somewhere along the Ho Chi Minh Trail.

---

where there is a small market offering Vietnamese and Chinese goods.

Places to Stay

Some rustic guesthouse accommodation is available in Sepon.

Getting There & Away

The bus from Savan to the Vietnamese border stops in Sepon for 4000 kip. Savannakhet Tourism Co at the Savanbanhao Hotel can arrange car and driver for up to five passengers for around US$100.

Salavan Province

The big attraction in Salavan (also spelt Saravan or Saravane) is the Bolaven Plateau, which actually straddles Salavan, Sekong, Champasak and Attapeu provinces. On the Se Set (Set river, a tributary of the Se Don) are several waterfalls and traditional Lao villages. Like the Plain of Jars in Xieng Khuang Province, the Bolaven Plateau has an excellent climate. On the Champasak side of the plateau there is some tourist accommodation available (refer to the Champasak Province section later in this chapter for more information).

Among the province's approximately 256,000 inhabitants are a number of relatively obscure Mon-Khmer groups, such as the Ta-oy (Tahoy), Lavai, Katang, Alak, Laven, Ngai, Tong, Pako, Kanay, Katu and Kado. There are no Lao Sung native to the area.

The province boasts 51% natural forest cover though only one section has thus far received protected status. The **Phu Xieng Thong NBCA** covers 995 sq km adjacent to the Mekong River in the western part of the province (about 40km north of Pakse), the only NBCA in Laos that encompasses the river's typical flats and sandbanks. The opposite bank is protected by Thailand's Pha Taem National Park; both sides are characterised by exposed sandstone ridges and outcroppings (some of which contain rock shelters with prehistoric paintings), interspersed with scrub and mixed monsoon deciduous forest. Rare beasts thought to inhabit this area include elephant, gaur, banteng, Douc langur, gibbon, Asiatic black bear, clouded leopard, tiger and Siamese crocodile.

In the far north-eastern corner of the province is **Samouy**, a district that was once part of Savannakhet Province. Bordering Vietnam, it is remote and difficult to access, but a 162km road (dry season only) will soon be cut to Samouy (and Tahoy) via Route 23, north of the provincial capital.

Samouy is an official border crossing – for Lao and Vietnamese only – between Da Lai in Vietnam and this district.

SALAVAN

Before it was renamed Salavan (Sarawan in Thai) by the Siamese in 1828, this area was a Champasak Kingdom outpost known as Muang Mam and inhabited mostly by Mon-Khmer minorities. The provincial capital of Salavan was all but destroyed in the Indochina War, when it bounced back and forth between Royal Lao Army and Pathet Lao occupation. The rebuilt town is a collection of brick and wood buildings with a population of around 40,000. Only the post office shows evidence of the French era.

The town market was until recently famous for its wildlife products, but this notorious trade seems to have shifted to Lak Sao farther north in Khammuan Province. For the most part Salavan serves as a supply centre for farmers in surrounding districts. A large sheet metal plant recently opened on the southern outskirts of Salavan, providing the town's first manufacturing jobs.

Information

You can change US dollars or Thai baht for kip (cash only) at the Phak Tai Bank a little west of the market.

In front of the post and telecommunications office is a card phone. The area code in Salavan is 31.

Places to Stay & Eat

The government-owned *Saise Guest House* (☎ 3171) is a cluster of three buildings about 2km from the bus terminal. Saise offers five-bed rooms with fan and shared bath for 8000 kip per bed, three-bed rooms with fan and shared bath for 9000 kip per bed, rooms with one double bed, air-con and shared bath for 11,000 kip, and one room with two double beds, air-con and attached bath for 14,000 kip.

The best restaurant in town is *Nong Vilaivone* (☎ 3209), a nicely maintained place with bamboo walls and ceiling fans, across the street from the Finance Department.

The menu includes Lao, Vietnamese and Chinese dishes, most of which cost around 5000 kip.

There are several *noodle shops* in the vicinity of the market, plus a small night market along a side street near the main market with pre-cooked Lao food.

Bouavan Ratree is a restaurant and nightclub with Lao food, live Lao music and dancing.

Getting There & Away
Air Lao Aviation lists a fare of US$91 to Salavan from Vientiane or US$44 from Savannakhet. In reality service was suspended in 1995 for the upgrading of Salavan's airstrip and has yet to resume.

Road There are regular passenger trucks to Salavan from Pakse in Champasak Province via Khong Sedon between 6 and 11 am. The road (Route 20) between these two towns is one of the best interprovincial routes in the country. The 150km trip takes 2½ hours and costs 2500 kip per person.

Trucks to/from Sekong (90km) along Route 16 cost 3000 kip and take three or four hours; see the Sekong section later in this chapter for details. From Sekong you can continue on to Attapeu.

If you're coming from the north along Route 13, get off in Khong Sedon to connect with the bus to Salavan instead of riding all the way to Pakse.

During the dry season you can take Route 23 north via Tumlan to Route 9 in the Sepon area. For those thinking that Salavan might be a shortcut for reaching Lao Bao from farther south, it may look shorter on a map but Route 23 north from Salavan is in very poor condition; the fords are a particular problem as the French-built concrete bridges were all bombed out during the Indochina War. It is, however, a very interesting route from the perspective of those interested in the local Austro-Asiatic tribes.

AROUND SALAVAN
The lake of **Nong Bua**, 14km east of town near the source of the Don river (Se Don), is famous for its dwindling population of Siamese crocodiles (*khàe* in Lao), which are most likely to be seen during the rainy season. **Phu Katae**, a 1588m peak, is visible nearby.

Nong Kangdong, a lake in Khong Sedon district south-west of the capital, also reportedly has crocs. In this same district stands a decaying 300-year-old stupa, the 10m **That Kadaotuk**, which is an important regional pilgrimage spot.

In **Tumlan**, a Katang village around 40km north of the capital via Route 23, you can see a 100m-long longhouse for 30 families and see the local weaving techniques. Katang textiles differ substantially from textiles made in northern Laos, and feature more numerous, narrow bands of colours and patterns.

The **Tahoy** (Ta-oy) district, to the east of Tumlan, is a centre for the Ta-oy ethnic group, who number around 26,000 spread across the eastern areas of Salavan and Sekong provinces. The Ta-oy live in forested mountain valleys at 300m to 1000m, often in areas shared with the Katu and other Mon-Khmer groups. Like many of the Mon-Khmer groups in southern Laos, they practice a combination of animism and shamanism; during village ceremonies, the Ta-oy put up diamond-patterned bamboo totems outside the village to warn outsiders not to enter. The Ta-oy's textiles are valued locally and by collectors in Vientiane. Visitors are only permitted to stay in the house of the district chief.

Champasak Province

The Champasak area has a long history that began with participation in the Funan and Chenla empires between the 1st and 9th centuries AD. Between the 10th and 13th centuries, Champasak was a part of the Cambodian Angkor Empire. Following the decline of Angkor between the 15th and late 17th centuries, it was enfolded into the Lan

SOUTHERN LAOS

Xang Kingdom but then broke away to become an independent Lao kingdom at the beginning of the 18th century. The short-lived Champasak Kingdom had only three monarchs: Soi Sisamut (nephew of Sulinya Vongsa, 1713-37), Sainyakuman (1737-91) and Fai Na (1791-1811). During the French era, it was sometimes known as Bassac or Pasak, a shortening of 'Champasak'.

Today Champasak Province (three separate provinces prior to 1975 – Champasak, Sedon and Sithandon) has a population of around 500,000 that includes lowland Lao (including many Phu Thai), Khmers and a host of small Mon-Khmer groups – Suay, Ta-oy (Tahoy), Lavai, Chieng, Nyaheun, Laven, Kaseng, Katang, Nge, Inthi, Oung, Katu, Kien, Salao, Tahang and Kate – most of whom live in the Bolaven Plateau region.

Timber is the province's main source of income, followed by coffee, tea, cardamom, rattan and other agricultural products. The province is also well known for *mat-mìi* silks and cottons that are hand-woven with tie-dyed threads.

PAKSE

Founded by the French as an administrative outpost in 1905, Pakse (population 64,000) is a relatively new town at the confluence of the Mekong and Se Don rivers. It is now the capital of Champasak Province but the town is mainly of interest to the traveller as a point of departure for the Bolaven Plateau, the Khmer ruins at Wat Phu Champasak, Si Phan Don (Four Thousand Islands) or Ubon Ratchathani, Thailand. There are only a few colonial-era buildings left standing, most of Franco-Chinese design. One of the better examples is the elaborately ornamented **Chinese Society** building on Thanon 10 in the centre of town.

The large and lively **central market** features a very good selection of produce due to Pakse's proximity to the fertile Bolaven Plateau. The enclosed market building was gutted by fire in 1997 and now stands empty, so the vendors have moved outside to sell clothes, household goods and preserved foods. Presumably the building will

be repaired and will reopen. Trade with Thailand is brisk and the economy is also boosted by the presence of a large pharmaceutical factory 4km south of town.

Opposite the ferry pier on the Mekong River's west bank is **Ban Muang Kao**, the beginning of the road journey to Chong Mek on the Thai border. You'll see lots of Thailand-bound timber being loaded onto barges here.

Short day trips from Pakse can be made to **Taat Sae** waterfall at Km 8, south off Route 13. **Ban Saphai**, a weaving village 15km north of town, produces distinctive silk and cotton *phàa sálóng*, long sarongs for men.

Many of the town's population are of Chinese or Vietnamese descent – you might want to avoid Pakse during Tet (Chinese and Vietnamese New Year), during which the whole town becomes a fireworks battlefield for three days.

Information

Tourist Office The Tourism Authority of Champasak Province (☎ 212021) has an office on the banks of the Se Don river near the town centre. The staff are helpful and can arrange vehicles for anyone looking for private transport.

Vietnamese Consulate Visas for travel to Vietnam can be arranged at the Vietnamese consulate (☎ 212058, 212827), which is just off Route 13 in a neighbourhood known as Ban Wat Pha Bat.

Money You can change Thai baht or US dollars (cash) for kip at the BCEL branch near the central market and Pakse Hotel. It's open weekdays from 8.30 am to 3.30 pm, Saturday from 8.30 to 10 am. Phak Tai Bank on Route 13 also changes money, albeit at a lower rate than BCEL.

Post & Communications The main post office stands on the corner of Thanon 8 and Thanon 1, south-west of the town centre. Also on Thanon 1 there is a telephone/fax/telegraph office. The area code for Pakse is 31.

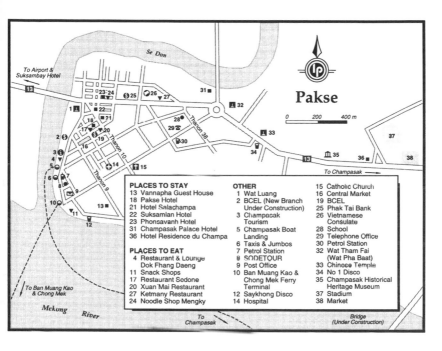

Pakse

0   200   400 m

PLACES TO STAY
13 Vannapha Guest House
18 Pakse Hotel
21 Hotel Salachampa
22 Suksamlan Hotel
23 Phonsavanh Hotel
31 Champasak Palace Hotel
36 Hotel Residence du Champa

PLACES TO EAT
4 Restaurant & Lounge
  Dok Fhang Daeng
11 Snack Shops
17 Restaurant Sedone
20 Xuan Mai Restaurant
27 Ketmany Restaurant
24 Noodle Shop Mengky

OTHER
1 Wat Luang
2 BCEL (New Branch
  Under Construction)
3 Champasak
  Tourism
5 Champasak Boat
  Landing
6 Taxis & Jumbos
7 Petrol Station
8 SODETOUR
9 Post Office
10 Ban Muang Kao &
   Chong Mek Ferry
   Terminal
12 Saykhong Disco
14 Hospital

15 Catholic Church
16 Central Market
19 BCEL
25 Phak Tai Bank
26 Vietnamese
   Consulate
28 School
29 Telephone Office
30 Petrol Station
32 Wat Tham Fai
   (Wat Pha Baat)
33 Chinese Temple
34 No 1 Disco
35 Champasak Historical
   Heritage Museum
37 Stadium
38 Market

To Airport &
Suksambay Hotel

Se Don

To Ban Muang Kao
& Chong Mek

Mekong River

To
Champasak

Bridge
(Under Construction)

To Champasak

Travel Agencies You can arrange tours to the Bolaven Plateau, Wat Phu Champasak or Don Khong (Khong Island) from SODE-TOUR (☎ 212122), near the ferry pier on Thanon Thasala Kham; Lane Xang Travel & Tours (☎ 212281), next to the Suksamlan Hotel on Thanon Wat Luang; Inter-Lao Tourisme (☎ 212226), on Route 13 near the Phak Tai Bank; DAFI Travel & Tours (☎ 212329), 146-148 Route 13; or the Lao Travel Service (☎ 212503), on Route 13.

These agencies can arrange private boats holding up to 20 persons to Wat Phu Champasak for US$40 or to Don Khong for US$200.

Medical Services Pakse has a provincial hospital (☎ 212018, 212041).

Champasak Historical Heritage Museum This museum on Route 13 near the Hotel Residence du Champa gathers together all kinds of artefacts and documents to chronicle the history of the province. Once past the Lao national flag and the Communist hammer-and-sickle flag at the entrance, you'll come to not-so-exciting historical photos of cultural events, foreign meetings and portraits of political figures Kaysone Phomvihane, Nouhak Phoumsavan and Khamtay Siphandone, all of whom hail from the south. There is also a small collection of minerals, some black and white photos of Wat Phu Champasak and a couple of very beautiful 7th century sandstone lintels found at Um Tomo near the town of Champasak.

The other exhibits on the ground floor include musical instruments, stelae in the Tham script dating from the 15th to 18th centuries, a water jar from the 11th or 12th centuries, a small *lingam* (Shiva phallus), stucco decoration and pottery from around the province plus a model of Wat Phu Champasak.

The upstairs room has more of an ethnological focus, including mannequin-like figures displaying different ethnic clothing styles, along with textile and jewellery collections from the Nyaheun, Suay and Laven. The large iron ankle bracelets and ivory ear plugs are of particular interest since these are only rarely worn nowadays. The textile exhibit is quite educational; you can tell the sometimes highly similar southern Lao ethnicities apart by the designs of their *phàa sìn*. Other exhibits include bamboo implements, ceramics, basketry, bronze Buddha figures, a tiny bronze Ganesha figure, various sandstone deities, farming implements, hunting traps and an elephant saddle. War buffs will see a telling photo of Neo Lao Issara (Lao Freedom Front) meetings with Vietnamese volunteers present, along with a photo of French prisoners of war in Sam Neua after the defeat of the French at Dien Bien Phu.

Most of the exhibits bear captions in Lao and French or Lao and English. In a final display of Revolutionary-era artefacts, the captions to photos of Communist Party history and decorated Lao officials aren't translated.

The museum is open daily from 7.30 to 11.30 am, except during parts of March when it's open from 8 am to 4 pm. Admission is 200 kip.

Temples

There are about 20 wats in the city, of which **Wat Luang** and **Wat Tham Fai** (both founded in 1935) are the largest. A monastic school at Wat Luang features highly ornate concrete pillars, heavy carved wooden doors, and murals; the artist's whimsy departs from canonical art without losing the traditional effect. Behind the sim is an older monks' school in an original wooden building. A thâat on the grounds contains the ashes of Khamtai Loun Sasothith, a prime minister in the Royal Lao Government before his death in 1959.

Wat Tham Fai, near the Champasak Palace Hotel, is undistinguished except for its spacious grounds, which make it a prime site for temple festivals. It's also known as Wat Pha Baat because there is a small Buddha footprint shrine on the premises.

Places to Stay – budget

The five storey *Phonsavanh Hotel* (☎ 212 842), on Route 13 close to the bridge over the Se Don, offers 18 very basic rooms for 5000/6000/7000 kip a single/double/triple, all with shared toilet and cold bath. There's a spartan sitting area downstairs and a bulletin board where travellers sometimes post travel information or leave messages.

Near the central market, the large *Pakse Hotel* (☎ 212131) has 38 slightly better rooms starting at 8000 kip for a single/double with fan and shared bath at the front of the hotel, 9500 kip for a quieter single/double of the same sort towards the back, or 12,000 kip for a single/double with air-con and private cold bath. Singles with bath and air-con towards the front cost 11,500 kip. There are also some three-bed rooms with bath and fan for 11,500 kip, or with air-con for 15,000 kip.

The clean and friendly *Suksamlan Hotel* (☎ 212002) on Thanon 14 in the downtown area has 24 decent air-con rooms with comfortable beds and private hot bath for US$10 a single, US$12 a double. Many of the guests at the Suksamlan are Thais doing business in Pakse. The associated *Suksambay Hotel* out near the airport is similar.

Vannapha Guest House (☎ 212502), on Thanon 9 past the hospital and next to Nam Pa Pa Lao (Lao Water Co), is a quiet two storey house where rooms on the ground floor go for 8000/10,000 kip with one bed/two beds, fan and shared bath, while rooms on the upper floor are 15,000 kip with air-con and attached bath. In a separate house rooms with fan and attached bath cost 10,000 kip. A small outdoor restaurant in front serves good fõe and khào pı̨ak sèn.

Places to Stay – middle & top end

The *Hotel Salachampa* (☎ 212273), two blocks south-east of the Suksamlan Hotel on Thanon 14 in a restored French villa, offers huge rooms with wooden floors (tiled downstairs), high ceilings and private hot bath for US$25 a single/double. Breakfast is served on a pleasant terrace overlooking the courtyard. A set of newer rooms alongside the original building lack the charm of the old house and cost US$20. All rooms have air-con and hot shower.

Hotel Residence du Champa (Baan Phak Champa in Lao; ☎ 212120; fax 212765) at the eastern edge of town, on Route 13 near the bus terminal, consists of three separate modern houses decorated in marble and teak. All 35 rooms come with satellite TV, air-con and hot water; some have bathtubs, some showers only. The rate is US$30 a single/double. The dining room serves very good breakfasts, lunches and dinners; also on the premises is a small gift shop with some tribal crafts from Attapeu and Sekong. French and English is spoken. The hotel will pay your tuk-tuk fare from the bus terminal, boat landing or airport. It's good value, though it's a bit of a hike from town.

The largest hotel in Pakse is the Thai-owned *Champasak Palace Hotel* (☎ 212 263; fax 212781), on Route 13 about 1km east of the town centre. Formerly known in Lao as Wang Nyai Chao Bounome (Prince Bounome Palace), this five storey palace on the Se Don served as the former residence of Chao Bounome na Champasak, the last prince of Champasak and the prime minister of the Kingdom of Laos between 1960 and 1962. Bounome started building the palace in 1968, fled to Paris in 1974 and died in 1978. The Thai renovation isn't bad – it's worth seeing the tile floors and intact teak fittings on the bottom floor, though most of the interior has been completely redone. Plastic furniture spoils the atmosphere in the dining room and bar – bamboo or rattan would have been better. There are nice views of the Se Don from the terrace and garden at the back. Next to the hotel is a steel bridge built by the Soviets in 1990.

Rates for large standard rooms at the Champasak Palace are US$25/27 a single/double; larger superior rooms are US$35/37 and palatial VIP suites reach US$75; these rates include American breakfast, tax and service. All rooms have air-con, private hot bath, colour TV, phone and refrigerator. The facilities include a coffee shop, lounge, restaurant serving Lao, Thai, Chinese and western dishes, a snooker club and fitness centre. This is the only place in town that accepts credit cards (Visa only).

Places to Stay – out of town
Alongside the Huay Nyang Kham, a pretty stream south of town near Km 5, stands the *Houyyangkham (Huay Nyang Kham) Guest House* (☎ 212755; fax 212756), a quiet spot with mountain and river scenery. There are 20 rooms in five well-kept cottages, each 15,000 kip with fan and private hot shower, 25,000 kip with air-con. There is a nightclub on the premises and thatched pavilions along the stream bank. This would be a good place to stay if you were stuck in Pakse and wanted to get out of town.

The owners of the Hotel Residence du Champa are building a hotel on the Mekong south of town near the new bridge, to be called either *Champa Residence II* or *La Boucle du Mekong*. The property will feature five houses for rent by the night or long-term at top-end rates, plus some rooms in a motel-like building in the middle range. Contact the *Hotel Residence du Champa* (☎ 212120; fax 212765) for more information.

Places to Eat
Most of the restaurants and cafes in Pakse serve Chinese and Vietnamese food. Take-away Lao food is available in the central market.

Restaurant Sedone, opposite the market area and near the Pakse Hotel, serves decent noodle soups, rice dishes, breakfast, Lao coffee, stir-fried dishes, tasty french fries and ice cream. It's open early till late and its Lao/English menu caters somewhat to foreigners.

The *Xuan Mai Restaurant*, on the corner opposite the Pakse Hotel, serves good fõe and khào pûn. Excellent mii pét (duck noodles) are available at a nondescript *restaurant* directly opposite the Hotel Salachampa. *Noodle Shop Mengky*, a little north of the

SOUTHERN LAOS

Phonsavanh Hotel on the same side of the street, is a basic but clean noodle shop.

The *Paliane* and *Suksamlan* restaurants next door to the Suksamlan Hotel are good and serve mostly Chinese food. The restaurant at the *Champasak Palace Hotel* serves decent Lao, Thai and Chinese food; prices are surprisingly moderate. This hotel also has the only fully stocked bar in Pakse.

Restaurant & Lounge Dok Fhang Daeng, on Thanon 11 west of the market towards the river junction, serves Lao, Thai, Vietnamese and Chinese food. It's open nightly except when reserved by groups – and seems to be empty except when groups come.

Better Vietnamese food can be found at *Mai Kham* on Thanon 35, though if you don't smoke you may well find the lack of ventilation irritating. *Ketmany Restaurant*, east of the Phak Tai Bank on the north side of Route 13, is a relatively clean Chinese place with Chinese and European food, plus ice cream.

A row of thatched umbrellas and tables overlooking the main ferry landing offer cold drinks and snacks. On the street in front of the Hotel Salachampa, two *baguette vendors* purvey various sizes of khào jii in the morning, your choice of plain with sweetened condensed milk or Lao paté.

Nang Manisuk Restaurant, next to the airport, has good, inexpensive food and is a good place to hang out while waiting for a flight.

Entertainment

For a night of modern Lao live music and dancing, check out the *Sop Sengtavan Cabaret* (behind SODETOUR near the ferry pier), *Saykhong Disco* (farther south-east along the Mekong) or the new and popular *No 1 Disco* on Route 13 opposite Wat Tham Fai.

Getting There & Away

Air Lao Aviation flies Yun-7 turboprops (or occasionally the fleet's single Antonov 24) to Pakse from Vientiane daily. The flight takes an hour and 20 minutes and costs US$95 one way.

Other flights to/from Pakse appear on the schedule, including Savannakhet (US$44), Don Khong (US$29), Salavan (US$33) and Attapeu (US$26), but in practice these flights are available only on a charter basis at this time.

In Pakse the Lao Aviation office (☎ 212 252) is next to the airport, a couple of kilometres north-west of town off Route 13.

Road The intercity bus terminal has split into two separate parts, one 7km north of town and the other 8km south. At the northern terminal *(khíw lot lák jét* or 'Km 7 bus queue')* you'll find buses to Vientiane, Savannakhet and Tha Khaek. Direct buses between Vientiane and Pakse ply Route 13 once a day for 15,000 kip per person. These leave from either end around 6 am and take a gruelling 13 or 14 hours. The bus going north stops at Tha Khaek for 9000 kip; figure on around 10 hours. Two buses a day go to/from Savannakhet at around 5 and 10 am. These cost 5000 kip per person and take about six hours.

For buses south, head to the southern terminal *(khíw lot lák baet* or 'Km 8 bus queue')*. To/from Champasak there are truck departures at 9 and 11 am, and at 1 pm. The journey takes two hours and costs 2000 kip. You can also hop on a passenger truck bound for Ban Don Talaat, since these stop off in Champasak, for the same fare.

Other departures include: Taat Lo (7 and 9 am, 2½ hours, 1500 kip); Salavan (8 am and 1 pm, three hours, 2000 kip); Sekong (6 am, five to six hours, 5000 kip); Attapeu (5 or 6 am, five hours, 5000 kip); and Paksong (frequent departures between 6 am and 2 pm, 90 minutes, 2000 kip).

For information on land transport from Pakse to Don Khong, see the Si Phan Don section later in this chapter.

Only a few proper buses leave out of Pakse; most of the public conveyances here are large flatbed trucks with heavy wooden carriages. Generally they are extremely crowded, with cargo piled 2m high on the roof so they barely move at 15km/h at most. From Km 8 south of town all the way to the

Cambodian border, the road is in very bad condition. You should consider taking boats south instead; even though they're much slower than passenger trucks, the level of comfort is much higher.

The Asian Development Bank is funding two major roadways through Pakse and across the south to facilitate trade and travel between Thailand, Laos, Vietnam and Cambodia. ADB 6 will go from Chong Mek to Pakse, then on to Attapeu and Yalakhountum on the Vietnamese border; ADB 7 will stretch from Pakse to Voen Kham on the Cambodian border (basically replacing or enhancing Route 13). Construction is expected to be completed by 1999.

River Boats to Champasak take about 1½ hours down, 2½ hours up, and cost 1000 kip per person. One or two boats leave from the Pakse landing between 7 and 8 am, and again between noon and 1 pm. Most boats hold around 30 people and can be chartered for 50,000 kip.

Boats to Don Khong cost 5000 kip and take around eight hours. Service has increased as road construction on Route 13 south of Pakse has slowed traffic. Boats currently run daily during the dry season, and every two days during the monsoon (because the river's current is so strong at this time). For further details on boat travel to Don Khong, see the Si Phan Don section later in this chapter. Once Route 13 has been sealed all the way to Hat Xai Khun, opposite Don Khong, the boat services will probably evaporate entirely.

To/From Chong Mek, Thailand Ferries run back and forth between the pier at the junction of the Se Don and Mekong rivers and Ban Muang Kao on the west bank of the Mekong throughout the day. The ferry costs 500 kip per person (minimum four people) or you can charter a boat across for 2000 kip. The ferry service will become obsolete once the bridge crossing the Mekong a few kilometres south of town is open. Construction is expected to be finished by March 2001.

From Ban Muang Kao to the Lao-Thai border you can queue up for a shared taxi that carries six passengers for 2000 kip each or hire a whole taxi for 9000 kip. The 40km journey to Ban Mai Sing Amphon on the Lao side of the border takes about 45 minutes and operates from 4 am to 6 pm daily. At the border you simply check out through Lao immigration, walk across the line and catch a songthaew on the Thai side to Ubon Ratchathani via Phibun Mangsahan. When we last crossed we had no problem checking in with Thai immigration at the border, but we've since heard rumours that you must now check in with Thai immigration in Phibun Mangsahan, not at the border. If the Thais won't stamp you in at the border, head for Phibun.

Getting Around
There are four kinds of local transport around Pakse; samlor, motorised samlor, jumbo and tuk-tuk. The latter differs from the usual jumbo in that it has two rows of bench seats facing forward. Riding any of these vehicles on a shared basis costs 500 kip to anywhere in town. For charter, the standard fares are 1000 kip (samlor or motorised samlor), 2000 kip (jumbo) and 3000 kip (tuk-tuk).

BOLAVEN PLATEAU
Centred on the north-east of Champasak Province, the fertile Bolaven Plateau (sometimes spelt Bolovens, known in Lao as Phu Phieng Bolaven) wasn't farmed intensively until the French planted coffee, rubber and bananas in the early 20th century. Many of the French planters left following independence in the 1950s and the rest followed as US bombardment intensified in the 1960s.

Today the Lao have revived the cultivation of coffee beans, and both *arabica* and *robusta* are grown in village plots throughout the region. The workers on the coffee plantations tend to come from the Laven tribe, one of the largest ethnic groups native to the plateau (which is named after them – Bolaven means Place of the Laven). Alak and Katu farmers also grow coffee, drying the harvested beans on the ground or on large platforms next to their villages. The villagers sell it in units of 20L (the volume of a used vegetable oil can) to wholesalers who come by pick-up from Pakse. Soft world coffee prices have kept production low, although Lao coffee fetches among the highest prices in the world. Other local products include fruits, cardamom and rattan.

Along with the Laven, the plateau is a centre for several other Mon-Khmer ethnic groups, including the Alak, Katu, Ta-oy (Tahoy) and Suay tribes. The Katu and Alak arrange their palm-and-thatch houses in a circle and are well known in Laos for a water buffalo sacrifice which they perform yearly (usually on a full moon in March) in homage to the village spirit. The number of buffaloes sacrificed – typically one to four animals – depends on their availability and the bounty of the previous year's agricultural harvest. During the ceremony, the men of the village don wooden masks, hoist spears and wooden shields, and dance around the buffaloes in the centre of the circle formed by their houses. After a prescribed period of dancing the men converge on the buffaloes and spear them to death. The meat is divided among the villagers and each household places a piece in a basket on a pole in front of their house as a spirit offering.

One unique Katu custom is the carving of wooden caskets for each member of the household well in advance of an expected death; the caskets are stored beneath rice sheds until needed.

Among the other tribes, the animistic-shamanistic Suay (who call themselves Kui) are said to be the best elephant handlers. Elephants are used extensively in the forests for clearing land and moving timber.

The Alak, Katu and Laven are distinctive for the face tattoos of their women, a custom that is slowly dying out as the Lao influence in the area increases. The Lao government now provides free electricity to many Bolaven villages.

Several **Katu** and **Alak villages** can be visited along the road between Pakse and Paksong at the western edge of the plateau.

There are also a few within walking distance of the Tadlo Resort (see the following Places to Stay section). In Lao Ngam (not to be confused with Muang Lao Ngam on the road to Salavan), around 40km east of Pakse, is a large day market frequented by many tribal groups. Other villages can be found by following the dirt road that runs between Paksong and Salavan to the north, notably in the vicinity of Muang Tha Taeng on the border of Sekong and Salavan provinces.

Several waterfalls are linked with the Set river (Se Set). The most commonly visited are Taat Lo and Taat Fan, both just a few kilometres west of Paksong. **Taat Lo** (pronounced tàat láw) is only about 10m high but is quite wide; the large and deep pool at its base is suitable for swimming, while the Tadlo Resort close by offers comfortable accommodation. During the dry season, dam authorities release river water in the evening, more than doubling the waterfall volume – it's worth checking out what time the release occurs (usually just after sunset) so that you're not standing at the top of the waterfall then – a potentially fatal error.

Kạa-féh Láo (Lao Coffee)

Good coffee, both arabica and robusta, is grown in the Bolaven Plateau area of southern Laos, particularly in the district of Paksong. Bolaven Coffee Plantation, one of the country's biggest companies, produces over 6000 tonnes per year, while smaller enterprises add another 4000 tonnes. Ninety percent of the beans produced are exported; the largest share – about 14% – is sent to France and another 10% is consumed in Vietnam, despite the fact that Lao coffee costs more per tonne than almost any coffee in the world.

In Vientiane you can buy quality Lao coffee, either whole bean or ground, in brown bags labelled as 'Pakxong Lao Coffee'.

Originating from Huay Bang Lieng, **Taat Fan** drops in two parallel streams over 120m and is best viewed from a distance – take the turn-off north on Route 16 at Km 38 till it ends and walk down a path to the edge of the small canyon to see the falls.

Elephant Rides
Tadlo Resort offers rides on their two elephants for 5000 kip per hour. The typical elephant ride lasts about two hours, plodding through streams, forests and villages; a longer ride to an Alak village can be arranged. The ride is actually quite fun as it crosses terrain you wouldn't dream of crossing on foot (eg streams full of slippery rocks), and you will be giving these domesticated elephants needed work. If you've booked a Bolaven Plateau package through SODETOUR, the elephant ride is included in the deal. You can buy your own elephant for about the same price as a new Honda motorbike.

Places to Stay
Tadlo Resort next to the Taat Lo waterfall, is a modest complex of privately owned thatched bungalows. Simple rooms with shared cold bath cost US$15/20 a single/double, while rooms with private cold bath cost US$20/25. At the top end are a couple of well-appointed bungalows with fan and private hot bath that overlook the falls for US$35 a night. The resort has a large and very pleasant open-air dining room and sitting areas.

To reserve a room at Tadlo Resort in advance (a good idea at any time of year except the rainy season), contact SODETOUR in Vientiane or Pakse, or you can write to Tadlo Resort, PO Box 04, Salavan, attention 'Nhonh'.

A less expensive alternative at Taat Lo is *Saise Guest House*, a small government-run operation a couple of hundred metres downstream from Tadlo Resort. The guesthouse consists of two sections. One section is set back from the river in a large white house. This part is rather run-down and unattractive and costs 8000 kip a single, 10,000 kip a double with shared toilet and shower facilities. Much better is the so-called 'Green House' or *heûan khĩaw* section farther upstream and directly opposite the Tadlo Resort restaurant. Officially called *Heuan Mittaphap Lao-Thai (Lao-Thai Friendship House)*, this larger house overlooking the river contains six rooms, all but two of which have attached facilities. VIP rooms with balconies overlooking the falls cost 10,000 kip while the rest of the rooms are 8000 kip. To obtain a room at the Green House, check in at the white house section of Saise Guest House.

Places to Eat
Whether they're staying at Saise or Tadlo Resort, everyone ends up eating at the resort's atmospheric, open-air *restaurant*. The food – Lao, Thai and European – is quite good and prices aren't too bad. The alternative is to bring your own food from Pakse or Salavan.

Getting There & Away
Passenger trucks going between Pakse and Salavan (which pass the entrance to Tadlo Resort) depart at 7 and 9 am, cost 1500 kip per person and take about 2½ hours. Tadlo Resort is 100km north-east of Pakse and about 1.5km east of the road to Salavan. The turn-off for Tadlo comes after Muang Lao Ngam, about 30km before Salavan; you should get off the bus at the small village of Ban Saen Wang Nyai, next to a bridge over the Se Set. Ask at the pharmacy near this stop for help with your luggage if you can't make the 1.5km walk.

If you're heading for Paksong, the main centre for the local coffee trade, buses from Pakse cost 2000 kip and take about 1½ hours. There are also one or two trucks a day between Salavan and Paksong; these take about two or three hours and cost 2500 kip.

CHAMPASAK
This small district of 38,000 people on the western bank of the Mekong is a ghost of its former colonial self. An ambitious fountain circle in the middle of the main street

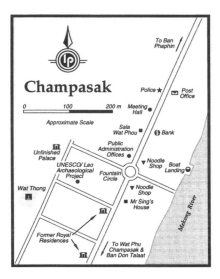

looks almost absurd, while both sides of the street are lined with French colonial homes in various states of disrepair (including one that once belonged to Chao Bounome na Champasak and another to his father Chao Ratsadanai, who was the last king of Champasak), along with a couple of noodle shops, a wooden bank building and a single hotel.

The Angkor-period ruins of Wat Phu Champasak lie 8km south-west of town; to reach them you must pass through Champasak. A UNESCO office in town, open only part of the year, directs a survey and restoration project at Wat Phu. A collection of religious art dating back nearly 1500 years is sitting in a warehouse next to the UNESCO office, awaiting the possible establishment of a museum. A corner of the same building contains the office of the Projet de Recherches en Archéologie Lao (Lao Archaeological Research Project), associated with the Musée Guimet in Paris and the Ministry of Information and Culture in Vientiane.

On Don Daeng, the large island opposite Champasak, the villages of Si Mungkhun,

Xieng Vang, Bung and Sisuk support themselves by growing coconuts and fishing in the Mekong.

Temples

Champasak has a couple of mildly interesting temples. In town, west of the UNESCO office on a dirt road parallel to the main north-south street, is the turn-of-the-century Wat Nyutthitham, more commonly known as **Wat Thong**. An old sim features an arched and colonnaded veranda, and has a washed pastel stucco relief on the front. This has been the wat used by Champasak's royal family, and the *thâat kádụuk* (bone reliquaries) here contain the ashes of King Nyutthitham (died in 1885), Chao Ratsadanai (1946) and Chao Bounome (1975) as well as an assortment of other princes and princesses.

About 8km south of town on the Mekong stands the oldest active temple in Champasak, Wat Phuthawanaram, more popularly known as **Wat Muang Kang**. Like the sim at Wat Thong, the intriguing *hǎw tại* (Tripitaka library) at Wat Muang Kang combines elements of French colonial and Lao Buddhist architecture. A large sim is surrounded by a roofed veranda in the Thai style, and there's a semi-open air *sǎaláa lóng thám* (chanting hall) made of plastered thick brick walls. The inside is little more than an expansive, bare wooden floor, with one big *thammat* or dhamma throne at one end. The three-tiered roofs of the sim and hǎw tại have coloured mosaic at the corners, and a small box with coloured crystal windows at the centre of the top roof ridge – reminiscent of Burmese architecture.

Ostensibly these crystal-sided boxes hold Buddha images, but local legend ascribes a more magical purpose to the one atop the hǎw tại. Supposedly at a certain moment in the annual lunar calendar (most say it's during the Wat Phu Festival), in the middle of the night, a mystic light beam comes from across the river, bounces through the *kâew* (crystal) and alights atop Sri Lingaparvata, the holy mountain on which Wat Phu Champasak is situated.

Champasak in Antiquity

Although you wouldn't know it from looking at today's Champasak, the town once served as the centre for a major pre-Angkor culture. The original city site – usually referred to locally as Muang Kao (Old City) – actually lies about 4km south of the current town centre, where the Huay Sawa feeds into the Mekong.

Aerial photographs show the remains of a rectangular city measuring 2.3km by 1.8km, surrounded by double earthen walls on three sides and protected on the east by the Mekong River. Other traces of the old city include a few small *baray* (a Khmer word meaning 'pond', usually used for ritual purposes), the foundations for circular brick monuments of unknown proportions, evidence of an advanced system of irrigation, various Hindu statuary and stone carvings (including a lintel in the style of 12th century Sambor Prei Kuk), stone implements and ceramics.

The rectangular city layout bears similarities with Muang Fa Daet in north-eastern Thailand and Sambor Prei Kuk in north-western Cambodia and may have begun as either a Mon or Cham state during the first centuries of the Christian era. A very important 5th century stele discovered in the old city bears a Sanskrit inscription saying the city was founded by King Devanika and was called Kuruksetra. The oldest surviving Sanskrit inscription in South-East Asia, the stele mentions the auspicious Sri Lingaparvata mountain nearby, a clear reference to the mountain on which Wat Phu Champasak is found. 'Honoured since antiquity', the mountain was said to represent the phallus of the Hindu god Shiva (even today many Lao call the peak Phu Khuai or Mount Penis). An association with the Mon-Khmer kingdoms of Funan and Chenla has also been suggested.

The city took on other names as well. Two Nandi (Shiva's bull mount) sculptures discovered in 1990-91 bear inscriptions calling it Sri Citrasena, and placing the city under the rule of the Khmer King Mahendravarman. It is clear that by the 8th century Champasak was under Khmer rule, and that it remained so until the 13th or 14th century. Over time the city was also known as Samapura, Champa Nakhon and Nakhon Champasak.

Because the 'skeletal remains' of the old city are extremely fragile, and because the Angkor-style restoration of Wat Phu Champasak threatens to obscure or even destroy the pre-Angkor elements that are associated with the site, UNESCO, through its office in Champasak, is attempting to create a preservation zone to include all the archaeological remains of the province. If UNESCO is successful, this Zoning Environmental Management Project (ZEMP) will be the only such programme dedicated to any pre-Angkor city site in South-East Asia, and may become an important source of archaeological research for understanding the links between pre-Angkor, classic Angkor and post-Angkor urban development.

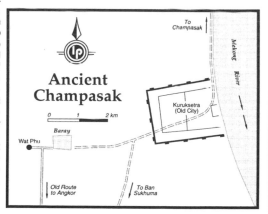

Ancient Champasak

0   1   2 km

To Champasak

Mekong River

Kuruksetra (Old City)

Baray

Wat Phu

Old Route to Angkor

To Ban Sukhuma

SOUTHERN LAOS

You can reach Wat Muang Kang by boat from the landing in Champasak for a few thousand kip, or come by bicycle (or motorbike) on the narrow dirt road along the riverbank. You might consider combining a boat trip to Wat Muang Kang with a visit to Um Muang across the river. See the Um Muang section later in this chapter for details.

Places to Stay & Eat

The *Sala Wat Phou*, a reincarnation of the former Champasak Hotel, is housed in a renovated two storey building near the main boat landing and the fountain circle. Nine medium-sized rooms with high ceilings, fan and hot water are priced at US$22/25 per single/double or with air-con are US$30 a single/double. In back there is also a five bed dorm room that costs US$5 per person. Meals are available in the hotel dining room – it's best if you order in advance. Rooms can be booked in advance through SODE-TOUR in Pakse (☎ 212175, 212122) or Vientiane (☎ (021) 216314).

If you are looking for a less expensive place to stay in Champasak, try *Mr Sing's House*, actually a rice and noodle shop just south of the fountain circle with a couple of basic rooms at the back for 5000 kip per person.

We've heard rumours that someone will be opening a guesthouse on the small, wooded island of Don Pha Kham. Chao Bounome na Champasak once kept a weekend house here and it's possible that the ruins of the house may be used for the proposed guesthouse.

Another rumour indicates someone may be opening a guesthouse in Ban Thong Khop, at the junction of the road to Ban Don Talaat and Wat Phu Champasak south of Champasak.

Besides Sala Wat Phou and Mr Sing's, there are very few places to eat in town. Between the boat landing and the traffic circle on the east side of the street are three *fõe shops* usually open from 7 am till around 9 pm. We thought the *tin-roofed stand* next to the traffic circle had the best fõe, especially when ordering chicken; sticky rice is

also available. Mr Sing's also does rice dishes and offers cold beer. The morning market in front of the boat landing burned down in 1997 and has yet to be rebuilt.

During the annual Wat Phu Festival (usually in February) every room in Champasak is usually taken, so be sure to arrive a few days in advance. Some foreigners have managed to sleep on the ground at Wat Phu Champasak during the festival. If you plan to try this, it's best to ask at one of the food tents for a safe place to sleep after all the nightly hubbub dies down. During the most recent festival we met a British traveller who lost all his travellers cheques from the pouch under his shirt while sleeping on the floor of one of the sanctuaries at Wat Phu Champasak.

Getting There & Away

Ferries from Ban Muang on the east side of the Mekong River to Ban Phaphin (5km north of Champasak) and Champasak on the west side run regularly throughout daylight hours and cost 750 kip per person, with a minimum of two people or 1500 kip. During the three day Wat Phu Festival in February ferries run 24 hours a day. From Ban Phaphin to Champasak a songthaew or any vehicle including a motorised three-wheeler costs another 500 kip per person. Chartering a vehicle between Champasak and Ban Phaphin costs 3000 to 4000 kip.

You can also charter a ferry – actually two canoes lashed together with a few planks across the top to create a rustic catamaran – from Ban Muang straight across to the Champasak market landing (near the Sala Wat Phou and fõe shops) for 3000 to 4000 kip.

Buses to Ban Muang from Pakse run regularly throughout the day for 1500 kip per person. You can also take a bus bound for Hat Xai Khun or other points south along Route 13 and get off at the Ban Thang Beng T-junction. From Thang Beng it's 3500 kip by jumbo to the landing at Ban Muang. Jumbos from Thang Bang can be few and far between, so you may have to resort to hitchhiking.

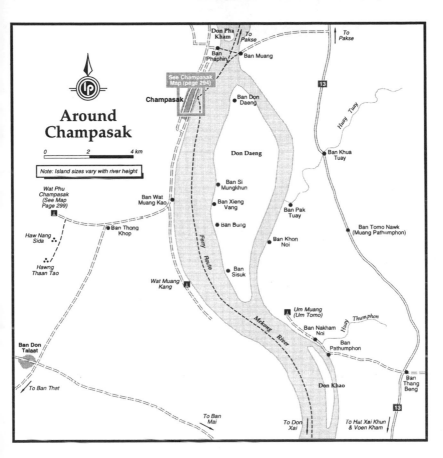

Around Champasak

0   2   4 km

Note: Island sizes vary with river height

Getting Around

Bicycles can be rented from Sala Wat Phou for 2500 kip per day. Jumbos around town are available for about 500 kip per kilometre. If you want to ride in more comfort, Sala Wat Phou will hire out its 4WD to Wat Phu Champasak (US$11), Phu Asa (US$30), Pakse (US$30) or Taat Lo (US$60).

WAT PHU CHAMPASAK

Literally Mountain Temple, this Khmer temple site spreads over the lower slopes of Phu Pasak (also known more colloquially as Phu Khuai), 8km south-east of Champasak. Though small compared with the Angkor-era sites in Siem Reap, Cambodia, or with Buriram, Thailand, Wat Phu is charged with atmosphere. The surviving structures date from as early as the Chenla Kingdom (6th to 8th centuries) to as late as the Angkor period (9th to 13th centuries), though exact dating is still in question.

The government supposedly has plans to restore the site and establish a museum in Champasak with international aid. Archaeological surveys were being conducted with

Wat Phu Champasak

The site of Wat Phu Champasak was probably chosen by the Hindu Khmers of Angkor because of a spring that flows from near the top of the 607m hill (approximately 75m above the surrounding plain), and because the peak is shaped like a *lingam* or Shiva phallus.

Historians say that Wat Phu Champasak was in fact sacred to the pre-Angkor kingdom of Chenla and may have been the site of human sacrifices; some scholars believe that Champasak may have been the capital of Chenla or even the earlier Funan kingdom. Whatever its provenance, the temple is known to have been the site of a cult closely associated with the Indianised monarchies of ancient Indochina, particularly with the vast Khmer empire that 200 years later made Angkor its capital.

The layout of the site forms a logical progression through three levels, with a long promenade connecting them; a harmonious ascendance from river to plain to mountain that must have provided a powerful set of symbols for the cult.

the assistance of the Musée Guimet in Paris and UNESCO at the time of writing; some restoration work has already been carried out, mainly to slow the damage caused by water erosion.

The mountain itself was sacred to local peoples centuries before the construction of any of the ruins now visible. Undoubtedly the original Austro-Asiatic tribes living in this area paid respect to animist spirits associated with the mountain and its rock shelter spring. Before it became an Angkor site associated with the Hindu god Shiva there is some speculation that under a 4th century Cham ruler called Bhadravarman, worship of the mountain was dedicated to Bhadresvara (a minor Indian deity related to Shiva).

The archaeological site itself is divided into three main levels which are joined by a long, stepped promenade flanked here and there by statues of lions and *nagas* (water dragons). The lowest part consists of ruined palace buildings of 20th century origin – used by recent Lao monarchs to observe the annual Wat Phu Festival – at the edge of a large rectangular pond used for ritual ablutions and boat races. A second pond nearby to the west and north has dried up; such ponds are known as *baray* in Khmer or *nãwng sá* in Lao. The naga stairway leading to the sanctuary probably dates from the 11th century and is lined with *dàwk jampaa* (plumeria), the Lao national tree.

The middle section features two exquisitely carved, rectangular **pavilions** built of sandstone, thought to have been used for gender-segregated worship. The pavilion on the right is in better condition with regard to sculpture. Wat Phu was converted into a Buddhist temple in later centuries but much of the original Hindu sculpture remains in the lintels, which feature various forms of Vishnu and Shiva as well as Kali, the Hindu goddess of time and death. The rear third of this structure reportedly dates to the 6th century Chenla era while the front two-thirds were probably constructed during the late Angkor period (11th to 13th centuries). Over the main entrance is a relief of Shiva and Parvati sitting on Nandi, Shiva's bull mount, with what seems to be Lakulisa (an obscure, Buddha-like Shiva deity) below. This entrance is flanked by well-executed reliefs of Parvati.

The remains of a **Nandi pavilion** (dedicated to Shiva's mount) and two galleries flanking another set of laterite steps lead to the next level. Six ruined brick pavilions – only their bases remain – separate the lower two levels from the final and holiest level. Roots and mosses hold the bricks together in some places, and drive them apart in others.

Along the north edge of the next promenade level stands an impressive Khmer statue that some people believe to be a representation of an Angkor-era monarch, though it could just as well be a simple *dvarapala* or sentinel figure. If you step down off the walkway and onto the grassy area just north you'll come to the remains of a *yoni*, the cosmic vagina-womb symbol associated with Shaivism. Offerings of flowers and incense indicate it is now considered one of the primary worship points for Wat Phu pilgrims. Very near the yoni lie two prone, headless and armless **Khmer statues** half-buried in the grass. Local Lao tell various tall tales about what these figures mean, none of which coincide with their original functions as probable Hindu deities. Off the east side of the walkway, sitting on a ruined wall, are the remains of a large **Ganesha** (Shiva's elephant-headed son).

On the uppermost level is the main temple **sanctuary** itself, which once enclosed a large Shiva phallus (lingam) that was bathed – via a system of stone pipes – by the sacred spring above and behind the complex. A lintel inside the south entrance depicts the story of Krishnavatara in which Krishna kills his uncle Kamsa; this same subject was used for lintels at Prasat Muang Khaek in Nakhon Ratchasima Province and Prasat Phanom Rung in Buriram Province, Thailand, suggesting these three temples were ritually linked. The archaeological evidence

also indicates that Wat Phu was linked to Khao Phra Wihaan (130km east on the Thai-Cambodian border), the personal temple of Khmer monarch Suryavarman I in the early 11th century. Reportedly the lingam at Wat Phu was used in ceremonies to 'release' the sacred power of the lingam at Khao Phra Wihaan.

This sanctuary now contains a set of crude, almost clown-faced Buddha images on an altar at one end. Local worshippers have returned pieces of sculpture – mostly stone window balustrades – that had been taken from the ruins, believing that anyone who takes a piece of Wat Phu away is in for a run of bad luck.

The upper platform affords a high, wide-angle view of the surrounding plains, and in the evening monkeys cavort in the trees nearby. Behind the upper level is a shallow cave from which the sacred spring flows. Sections of stone pipe that carried the water from the cave to the sanctuary are lying in or near the cave. The spring is still considered sacred – for good luck Lao visitors always dunk their heads under a blue plastic spout leading from the spring.

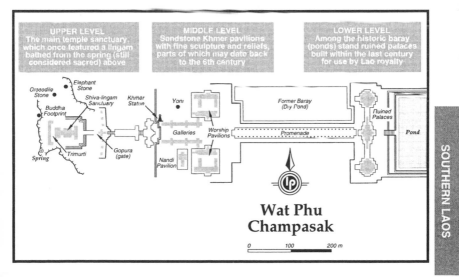

Sculpted into a large boulder behind the topmost sanctuary is a Khmer-style **trimurti**, the Hindu triumvirate of Shiva, Vishnu and Brahma. A few monks reside at a rustic Theravada Buddhist wat nearby. The best view of the plains below are from this wat; the cool, shady grounds are a good spot for a picnic.

East of the sanctuary and the newer wat on the upper level a winding path leads north to the so-called **crocodile stone**, a boulder with a deep, highly stylised carving of a croc. This sculpture may have been the site of Chenla human sacrifices. Farther on along the same path stands a huge boulder with the likeness of an **elephant** carved onto one side. Both the croc and elephant carvings are important stops on the Wat Phu pilgrimage route.

Hours & Admission
The Wat Phu complex is open daily from 8 am to 4.30 pm. Admission is 400 kip per person, plus 800 kip for a camera permit or 3000 kip for camcorders. During the Wat Phu Festival the entry fee is waived for everyone.

Other Sites Associated with Wat Phu
South of Wat Phu are three smaller Angkor-era sites in very poor condition – probably not worth the trouble unless you're a die-hard fan of Khmer architecture and have a vivid imagination. Each of the three stands alongside an ancient route that once linked Wat Phu Champasak with Angkor Wat in Siem Reap, Cambodia.

An easy 1km walk south of Wat Phu – use the trail heading south from the terraced promenade – stands **Haw Nang Sida**, a pile of sandstone and laterite rubble that may have served as a 'hospital' for Angkor pilgrims. Little has been published about Haw Nang Sida ('Lady Sida Hall', a reference to a local legend bearing no relation to the monument's original function), although a UNESCO survey may soon be disseminated to the public. Another kilometre south of Haw Nang Sida along the same axis stands another rubble pile, **Hawng Thaan Tao** ('Lord Turtle Room'), said to have been a

Vishnu shrine built under King Jayavarman VII in the 13th century. Another few kilometres on, close to the village of **Ban That**, stand three Khmer stupas reminiscent of similar tripartite monuments in Thailand's Lopburi and Sukhothai. No doubt symbolic of the Hindu trimurti of Shiva, Brahma and Vishnu, the three *prang* or Khmer-style towers are in poor condition; the northernmost one has collapsed entirely. This site, too, is said to be a 13th century construction by King Jayavarman VII. A large, dried-up baray (water reservoir) can be seen nearby.

During times of heavy rain, stream crossings may make these sites unapproachable on foot from Wat Phu. Ban That can be reached by jumbo from Champasak or Ban Thong Khop.

Festivals
The most important local festival is the three day **Bun Wat Phu Champasak** (Wat Phu Champasak Festival), held as part of Magha Puja (Makkha Bu-saa) during the full moon of the third lunar month – usually in February. Thousands of pilgrims from throughout southern Laos, north-eastern Thailand and farther afield come to worship at Wat Phu during this event. The central ceremonies performed are Buddhist, culminating on the third day (the full moon day of that lunar month) with the early morning file of monks receiving alms food from the faithful, followed that evening by a candle-lit circumambulation *(wíen thíen)* of the lower shrines.

Throughout the three days of the festival Lao visitors wind their way up and around the hillside, stopping to pray and to leave offerings of flowers and incense at various places through the complex – including at the feet of Hindu deities, next to lingam and yoni and other non-Buddhist entities. In some years a water buffalo may be quietly sacrificed in a corner of the complex. Other events include daily boat races on the large pond at the foot of the hill, Thai boxing matches, cockfights (sometimes substituted with bullfights), comedy shows, music and dancing. A long row of vendor stalls lining the road from Ban Thong Khop to the foot of the hill sells all manner of food, toys and cheap household items. Three or four larger areas are cordoned off for open-air night-clubs featuring bands from as far away as Vientiane. After dark the beer and *lào-láo* flow freely, and the atmosphere becomes rather rowdy.

Each June the locals perform a **water buffalo sacrifice** to the ruling earth spirit for Champasak, Chao Tengkham. The blood of the buffalo is, offered to a local shaman serving as a trance medium for the appearance of the spirit, who is believed to preside over the rice-growing season.

Getting There & Away
Wat Phu Champasak is 46km from Pakse, 13km from Ban Phaphin and 8km from Champasak. A shared jumbo from Champasak to Ban Thong Khop, the village opposite Wat Phu, should cost 500 kip per person. You can charter a jumbo direct to Wat Phu or Muang Kao (Old City) for around 4000 kip each way (or 10,000 kip round trip, including waiting time at the site). You can also hop on a passenger truck or bus bound for Ban Don Talaat (500 kip) farther south and ask to be let off at Ban Thong Khop.

UM MUANG
Um Muang (more commonly called either Muang Tomo or Um Tomo) is a Khmer temple ruin thought to have been built late in the 9th century during the reign of the Khmer King Yasovarman I and dedicated to Rudani, an aspect of Shiva's consort. It's about 45km south of Pakse off Route 13, in a forest on a small tributary of the Mekong. The ruins include an esplanade bordered by lingams and two crumbling laterite sanctuaries. The more intact of the sanctuaries contains a large vestibule and lintel sculpted with various Vaishnava motifs, along with a *mukhalinga* – a lingam or Shiva phallus onto which four faces (mukha) have been carved. A number of other sandstone lintels are displayed on rocks beneath towering

dipterocarp trees. A large tin shed at the site contains a bronze Sukhothai-style Buddha from Thailand.

Getting There & Away
From Ban Muang (the village on the far side of the Mekong from Champasak) or from Champasak you can charter a boat to Ban Nakham Noi (the riverbank village nearest the ruins) for 10,000 kip round trip (or 5000 kip one way), including waiting time of an hour or so while you locate and tour the ruins. The village is about 1km south of the ruins. Climb the bank next to the mouth of a tributary stream (Huay Thumphon) to the village, then turn left and walk north along a smaller stream into the forest. When the path forks, stay right and walk for about 10 minutes till you see some metal-roofed sheds in the forest on your right, then leave the trail and head for the sheds, which shelter parts of the ruins. If you'd rather not test your orienteering skills, children from the village are usually glad to lead you to the ruins.

The ruins can also be reached by vehicle from Pakse by turning west at Km 30 at Ban Thang Beng and heading to Ban Nakham Noi by road and foot via Ban Pathumphon (just south of Nakham Noi).

If you are travelling by boat, you could combine a trip to Um Muang with a stop at Wat Muang Kang on the west bank of the Mekong. A half day's use of a boat from Champasak or Ban Muang to both sites will cost about 20,000 kip or US$8.

BAN PHAPHO & KIET NYONG
At the Suay village of Ban Phapho (27km east of Route 13) in Pathumphon district is an elephant training complex, where at any one time around 100 young elephants may be in training for timber and agricultural work. Many villages in the area keep as many as 15 to 20 working elephants, which are mostly used for carrying bags of rice and other cargo.

In nearby Kiet Nyong, you can contact headman Thaan Nu to arrange half-day elephant treks (overnight trips aren't presently permitted by the government). The going

SOUTHERN LAOS

rate is 10,000 kip or US$4 per elephant for the half-day, and each elephant can take two people.

The elephant trek typically goes to the summit of a hill called **Phu Asa**, named for a 19th century war hero who fought against the Siamese. From the flat hill crest there is a good view of the village, pond and rice fields below. You can also explore the remains of a bizarre assemblage of stone on the top of the hill. The slate-brick columns, mounted by lipped slabs, stand about 2m high and are arranged in a semi-circle. Some locals say the pillars date from the 19th century, and were possibly built in defence of the area; if so there are a lot missing. Others have suggested they're some sort of ritual megaliths. Like so many other archaeological sites in Laos, the origins of the site are clouded by legend, speculation and many years of war.

Getting There & Away
Ban Phapho and Kiet Nyong can be reached by vehicle via a 27km road that branches east off Route 13 near Ban Thang Beng.

SI PHAN DON (FOUR THOUSAND ISLANDS)
During the rainy season this scenic 50km-long section of the Mekong River just north of the Cambodian border reaches a breadth of 14km, the river's widest girth along its 4350km journey from the Tibetan Plateau to the South China Sea. During the dry months between monsoons the river recedes and leaves behind hundreds (or thousands if you count every sand bar) of islands and islets. The largest of the permanent islands are inhabited year-round and offer fascinating glimpses of tranquil river-oriented village life – 'more detached from time than from the riverbank' as one source described it. Communities tend to be self-sufficient, growing most of their own rice, sugar cane, coconut and vegetables, harvesting fish from the Mekong and weaving textiles as needed.

The villages of Si Phan Don are often named for their position at the upriver or downriver ends. The upriver – usually the northern – end of the island is called *hŭa* or head, the downriver or south end is called *hăang* or tail. Hence Ban Hua Khong would be a village at the northern end of Don Khong, while Ban Hang Khong is a village at the southern end.

The French left behind a defunct short railway (the only railway ever built in Laos), a couple of river piers and a few colonial villas on the islands of Don Khong, Don Det and Don Khon. Other attractions include some impressive rapids and waterfalls, where the Mekong suddenly drops in elevation at the Cambodian border, and a rare species of freshwater dolphin.

The best time to visit Si Phan Don is between November and January when the weather is cool and dry. March to May can be very hot, most of the rice fields will be dried out and the monsoon forest will have turned brown or shed leaves. During the rainy season from June to October, smaller unsealed roads are frequently washed out.

Don Khong (Khong Island)
Named for the surrounding river (using the Thai pronunciation *'khŏng'* rather than the Lao 'khãwng'), this large island measures 18km along its north-south axis and 8km at its widest point. The island's 55,000 inhabitants are for the most part concentrated around two villages on either side of the island, Muang Khong on the east shore and Muang Saen on the west; an 8km unpaved road links the two.

Most of the surrounding islands – and parts of the mainland – belong to Don Khong district. As his surname suggests, the current president of Laos, Khamtay Siphandone, was born in Si Phan Don – on Don Khong to be exact; there has been talk that the government may carve the district out of Champasak Province to create a separate province called Si Phan Don.

Things to See & Do A tour of the island can be done by bicycle, available through the Auberge Sala Done Khong or possibly other sources. Another possibility is to hire a jumbo for the whole day, though some of

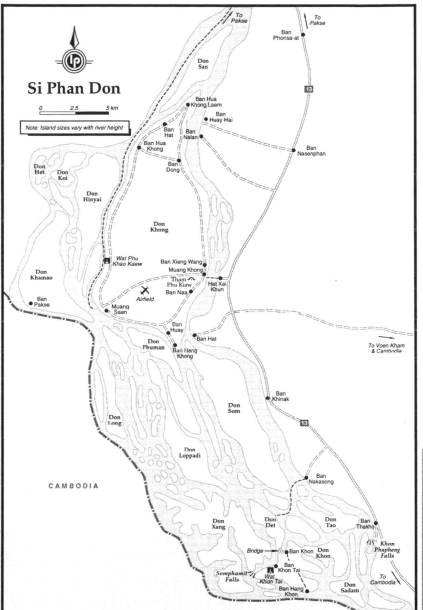

the spots described below aren't accessible by jumbo.

The island is quite scenic; with rice fields and low hills in the centre and vegetable gardens around the perimeter, punctuated by small villages, most of which have their own village wats. Some of the wats are over 100 years old.

Muang Khong is the largest town in the district and features three hotels and guesthouses, a few small cafes, a market and a couple of wats. The busiest time of day is from 4 to 6 am when the small Muang Khong market is in full swing.

Wat Phuang Kaew sits in the centre of Muang Khong and features a towering modern naga Buddha image facing east towards the river. The locals believe the abbot used supernatural powers gained in meditation to defeat government efforts to oust him after the Revolution.

At Ban Xieng Wang, a neighbourhood at the north end of Muang Khong, is **Wat Jawm Thong**, the oldest temple on the island. Dating from the Chao Anou period (1805-28), the main sim features a unique cruciform floor plan in crumbling brick and stucco with a tile roof. Carved wooden window shutters are a highlight. To the left of the uninteresting cement central Buddha image, an old wooden standing Buddha in one-handed *abhaya mudra* (offering protection) leans in a corner. Some local people say a Khmer architect may have designed this sim; similar floor plans in Nan Province in Thailand suggest Thai Lü design, although it would be unusual for the Thai Lü to travel as far south as here. The sandy wat grounds are shaded by coconut and betel palms and mango trees.

A kilometre south-west of Muang Khong, in some hills more or less behind the mayor's office, a trail leads to **Tham Phu Khiaw** (Green Mountain Cave). Sacred for decades, if not centuries, the cave contains a number of old Buddha images and is the object of local pilgrimages during Lao New Year in April. The remainder of the year the trail becomes overgrown, so you should seek out a local guide for the stiff 30 minute

walk up the hill to the cave. East of here near the river, **Wat Ban Naa** is an atmospheric little country temple typical of the style found on the island.

At the north-west end of the island, **Ban Hua Khong** is well known as the 1924 birthplace of Khamtay Siphandone, who rose from being a postman under French rule to the presidency. Khamtay has refurbished **Wat Hua Khong Pha Nyai**, which other than one old wooden monastic building has little to recommend it aesthetically. The wat is named for the large cement seated Buddha image in the main sim. The area between Hua Khong and Ban Dong (to the east) is heavily planted in rice.

Muang Saen, on the opposite side of the island from Muang Khong, can be reached on foot, though this is a hot walk in the middle of the day since both sides of the road have been cleared for rice fields. A jumbo to Muang Saen can be hired in Muang Khong for 2500 kip each way. By bicycle it's about 45 minutes away. It's a bustling little town with a ferry landing for boats from as far north as Pakse. **Wat Phu Khao Kaew**, on a low hill north of Muang Saen (3km or 4km from the junction of the north-south and east-west roads), was built on the site of some Khmer ruins. Look for a stand of plumeria trees on the east side of the hill to locate the path to the temple, or better yet hire a motor-cycle taxi in Muang Saen for 3000 kip round trip. An unusual bronze gong in the shape of a clock hangs here.

Two smaller villages at the southern tip of the island worth visiting for old wats are **Ban Huay** and **Ban Hang Khong**. At the latter village, **Wat Thepsulin Phudin Hang Khong**, more commonly known simply as Wat Hang Khong, features spacious grounds and a small brick and stucco sim with a collection of Buddha images. A pair of slender wooden standing abhaya mudra Buddhas in front of the main image are obviously highly revered locally as they've been dressed in cloth robes. Smaller images made of crystal and wood line the back wall ledge.

Also of interest is the nearby carved and painted wooden *wihāan* (Buddha sanctuary)

Timeworn French architecture in the southern city of Pakse, one of Laos' colonial legacies along with baguettes and coffee.

Southern Laos
Top: Coconut palm fringed Don Det, one of the Mekong River islands in Laos' deep south.
Bottom: The picturesque and isolated Tadlo Resort, near Salavan.

and the sãaláa lóng thám with folk-quality painted tinwork along the eaves. **Wat Silimangkhalaham** in Ban Huay has some similar features on more neglected grounds.

Festival A boat racing festival (Bun Suang Heua) is held on Don Khong in early December around National Day. Four or five days of carnival-like activity culminate in races next to Muang Khong along the east shore of the island. In times past the islanders celebrated this festival one month earlier at the end of the Buddhist rains retreat (Awk Phansaa), but they now combine the boat races with government-mandated National Day celebrations to save money. Activities at previous festivals have included night-time boxing matches in an outdoor ring.

Places to Stay Prices for accommodation on the island are kept artificially high by the presence of package tour groups. Close to the ferry landing and right next door to Muang Khong's largest noodle shop, *Done Khong Guest House* contains three simple but clean three-bed rooms with shared facilities for 10,000 kip per room. The woman owner can speak good French and a little English. An attached restaurant provides simple meals.

Farther north towards Ban Xieng Wang, *Bungalow Souksan (Suksan Guest House)* offers five cottages, each with two small rooms containing fan and private cold bath for 10,000 kip. Seven larger bungalows with air-con (from 6 to 11 pm only) and hot showers go for US$35 to US$40 depending on size. A separate building farther back features dorm-style accommodation – basically just a mattress on the floor – for 4000 kip per bed. The Souksan has a very pleasant restaurant overlooking the river.

The former manager of the Auberge Sala Done Khong has opened his immaculate traditional teak house as *Villa Kang Khong* to visitors. Each of the six clean and tidy guest rooms comes with two beds, fan and attached western toilet for US$15 a night. There is an impressive sitting area at the front with handmade wooden furniture. The

house faces the boat landing, more or less behind the Done Khong Guest House.

About 200m south of the Muang Khong boat landing, the *Auberge Sala Done Khong* (☎/fax 212077) has spacious, nicely decorated rooms in an old teak house for US$20 per night with fan only, US$25 if you use the air-con (available only from 5.30 pm to midnight). All of the rooms have a private toilet and hot showers. These are the walk-in rates; according to SODETOUR these rates are US$35 and US$45 respectively for package tourists or for those booking in advance through SODETOUR in Vientiane or Pakse.

South of the Auberge Sala Done Khong is the more recently built *Muong Khong Villa* (☎ (031) 212503 in Pakse, (031) 213 011 on Don Khong), a cluster of clean if small bungalows with attractive wicker furniture, air-con (evenings only) and western bathrooms with hot showers. Walk-in rates run US$25 per room; but advance bookings or packages (which are available through Lao Travel Service in Pakse) cost more. The owner can speak good French and some English. There is an associated restaurant with good Lao and French food.

Places to Eat Don Khong is nationally famous for its làu-láo liquor, often cited as the smoothest in the country. It's available in the market or at any restaurant.

Near the Muang Khong pier are a couple of adequate *hâan kpn deum* (eat-drink shops). A large *noodle shop* near the ferry landing also serves khào ñãw and, with advance notice, khào jâo.

The *Bungalow Souksan* has a nice little wooden restaurant overhanging the river. The menu includes vegetarian, Chinese, Lao and western dishes, plus a variety of breakfasts. Along the street that leads to the Souksan are several small *cafes* with fõe and Lao snacks. One of these, *Pon's*, is oriented towards foreigners with menus in English and French and various standard Lao dishes. Although the prices aren't outrageous, a bowl of fõe here costs twice what it normally costs elsewhere in the village.

The dining room at the *Auberge Sala Done Khong* is quite good for Lao and French cuisine; non-guests may arrange meals here if they order in advance. The *Muong Khong Villa* offers similar fare.

Getting There & Away Although in the far south of the country, Si Phan Don is reasonably accessible.

Air Lao Aviation no longer flies between Pakse and Don Khong although it may be possible to charter a 15 seat Yun-7 for around US$150.

The airfield – built by the US air force as a landing site on the Phnom Penh-Vientiane route during the Indochina War – lies 4km from either end of the road between Muang Khong and Muang Saen.

Road From Pakse there are usually two passenger trucks per day to Muang Khong via Hat Xai Khun, opposite Muang Khong on the eastern bank of the Mekong. The 120km trip takes at least five or six hours under the current road conditions; when the road is paved it will speed up substantially. The 4000 kip fare includes the short ferry ride across to Muang Khong. From Pakse these trucks depart between 7 and 9 am (whenever they fill up); from Muang Khong they leave around 6.30 and 7.30 am.

If you miss the Khong-bound bus, you can try for trucks going to Ban Khinak (8 am and 1 pm), Ban Nakasong (10.30 am) or Voen Kham (1 pm); all of these trucks stop at Hat Xai Khun along the way and each costs around 3500 kip per person.

On *wán sīn dáp* (days when there's no moon) there may be only one truck a day – even no truck – due to the lack of passengers; the locals believe it is bad luck to travel on these days. On every other day, prepare yourself for possibly the most crowded ride in Laos.

Hat Xai Khun is about 1km west of Route 13. If you're coming under your own power (or have been dropped off in Hat Xai Khun), you can catch the ferry across to Muang Khong for 2000 kip for foreign pedestrians (500 kip for Lao) or 3000 kip per vehicle. Small boats may be chartered across for 2000 kip to the main landing, 2500 kip to the landing below the Auberge Sala Done Khong.

Rumours persist that the vehicle ferry crossing may move south to Ban Nokhok, opposite Ban Naa on Don Khong, to take advantage of a deeper channel and the slightly shorter distance between mainland and island. If this transpires, small boats will continue to operate from Hat Xai Khun.

River Ferries from Pakse head south around 8 am daily – get to the landing early for space. Be sure to inquire thoroughly before boarding (or the day before) to determine the boat's final destination.

Whether or not the boat goes all the way to Don Khong depends upon the river height. During and immediately following the rainy season, boats can make it to the landing at Muang Saen on the west side of Don Khong. This trip takes 10 hours and the fare is 5000 kip. From Muang Saen to Muang Khong by jumbo costs 1000 kip per person shared or 6000 kip if you charter.

During the late dry months large ferry-boats can't make it to Don Khong and it really becomes quite an effort to piece together a river voyage all the way there. We have found smaller boats going all the way from Pakse as late in the year as the middle of February – it depends on the size of the boat and the height of the river.

When the river level descends farther, boats may only go as far as Ban Munla Pamok (1500 kip), roughly 20km north from the northern tip of Don Khong; from here you may be able to charter a small boat the remainder of the way for around 20,000 kip. There is a guesthouse in Ban Munla Pamok.

In the late dry season when the river level is particularly low, boats from Pakse may terminate on Don Sai (1000 kip), a large river island roughly two-thirds of the distance between Pakse and Don Khong. Although it's possible to stay overnight on Don Sai, boat travel onward as far as Don Khong usually isn't available, even by charter.

The travel agencies in Pakse or Muang Khong can arrange boat charters between the two towns for around US$200 each way in boats that hold up to 20 persons. Smaller 10-person boats cost less but aren't as comfortable for such a long journey. You may be able to arrange something less expensive directly from one of the boat landings.

A company called Indocruise (☎/fax (021) 412740, PO Box 4415, Vientiane) operates a four day, three night trip running between Pakse and Don Khong aboard the *Vat Phou*, a steel-hulled barge topped with wooden cabins, each with two beds and private bath. The all-inclusive fare runs around US$400 per person. The trip can be booked through Lane Xang Travel & Tours in Pakse.

To/From Cambodia From Hat Xai Khun, opposite the east shore of Don Khong, it's 35km east to Voen Kham near the Cambodian border. The crossing between Tha Boei (on the Lao side) and Phumi Kampong Sralau (Cambodian side) is open to Lao and Cambodians only at the moment but Champasak Province officials are hoping to make it open to foreigners in the near future. The Cambodian side of the river is a region that is known for occasional Khmer Rouge and bandit activity.

Ferries from Muang Saen on Don Khong go to the Cambodian shore of the Mekong at Phumi Kampong Sralau. There are also passenger trucks to Voen Kham from Pakse and Hat Xai Khun.

Getting Around Bicycles can be rented from the Auberge Sala Done Khong for 4000 kip per day or at the Done Khong Guest House for 3000 kip; this is a convenient way to see the island. A few jumbos are also available in Muang Khong and Muang Saen for around 500 to 800 kip per kilometre.

Auberge Sala Done Khong, Bungalow Souksan and Pon's restaurant hire 10-person boats for 25,000 to 30,000 kip. Sala Done Khong can also arrange larger 20-person boats for 50,000 kip a day. A typical circuit starts with an 8 am cruise to Don Khon, where passengers get off and walk to Taat Somphamit and the old French bridge between Don Khon and Don Det; then the boat continues on to Ban Nakasong where motorbike taxis are hired to Khon Phapheng Falls. The boat returns to Muang Khong by 2 or 3 pm.

Boat travel to Don Det can be arranged at similar rates.

Don Det & Don Khon

These two islands south of Don Khong near the Cambodian border were an important link for supply lines between Saigon and Laos during the French colonial era. In order to bypass the nearby system of rapids and waterfalls in the Mekong River the French even built a 14km narrow-gauge railway across the two islands, linked by bridge and terminating in concrete piers at either end. Boats that had travelled from Vietnam and through Cambodia via the Mekong had their cargoes offloaded at the southern end of Don Khon onto railway cars, which transported the goods by rail to other boats waiting at the northern end of Don Det for the rest of the upriver trip to Pakse, Savannakhet and Vientiane. Sometimes entire boats would be loaded onto flatbed cars and moved by rail, then lowered back into the river. The train stopped running after Japanese attacks in 1945. The impressive bridge and piers are still intact but much of the rail line has been appropriated by the locals for use as footbridges over streams and gullies around the islands.

Don Khon, the larger of the two islands, is famous throughout Laos for the cultivation of coconut, bamboo and kapok. Some households still make their own incense from the aromatic wood of a local tree, to use in offerings at local temples. In the main village, **Ban Khon**, are several old French colonial villas. **Wat Khon Tai**, towards the south-western end of Ban Khon, is a Lao temple built on the former site of a Khmer temple of undetermined age – possibly from the Chenla era. Large laterite bricks used in the construction of the Khmer temple lie scattered about, along with the foundation and a few pediments and columns. Behind

SOUTHERN LAOS

the wooden sim is a 90-year-old Lao jedi sited next to an ancient Khmer lingam on a modern pedestal.

Another 1.5km west beyond the wat, at the western end of Don Khon, is a raging set of rapids called **Taat Somphamit** (also known as Li Phi Falls). The falls can also be viewed from Don Xang, a large island north-west of Don Khon. On the Don Khon side an 800 kip entry fee is collected. If you cross the bridge between Don Khon and Don Det 800 kip is also collected. If you're coming from the Bungalow Souksan on Don Det, it's a 2km walk to the bridge, then another 2km walk to the falls; save your ticket from the bridge crossing and you shouldn't have to pay a second 800 kip.

Railway Hike & Dolphins On Don Khon you can make an interesting 5km trek across the island by following the old railbed. Near the start of the trail at the north end of the island is a rusting locomotive and boiler; take care not to brush your bare skin against the thicket surrounding the locomotive, as its fruit can cause a rash in some people. Farther along the way you will pass bits of primary forest, rice fields, small villages and singing birds. The south end of the railbed terminates at the old French pier – across the river to the right is Cambodia. The footbridges along the way have deteriorated over the last couple of years and the walk can be just challenging enough that if you're not physically fit you shouldn't attempt it.

Irrawaddy dolphins can sometimes be seen off the southern tip of the island in the late afternoon from December until May (during the rainy season the water is too murky and deep). The best dolphin-viewing area is a small sand island a bit farther south of the island. Boats can be chartered from the pier area to the sand island for 7000 kip. Whether you plan to view from Ban Hang Khon or the sand island, the best time of the day to see the dolphins is early morning or late afternoon.

When there is Khmer Rouge activity nearby, the sandbar trips are cancelled, as happened in early 1998 following a Khmer Rouge mutiny at Anlong Veng.

Although you may hear otherwise, according to Lao immigration and the NTAL the entire island of Don Khon, as part of Don Khong district, is open to unrestricted foreign travel. As always in rural Laos, do tread lightly in order to help preserve local traditions.

Places to Stay and Eat About 100m from the boat landing on Don Det is a branch of Don Khong's *Bungalow Souksan (Suksan)* with three bamboo-thatch huts on stilts costing 3000 to 5000 kip per night depending on supply and demand. Toilet and bathing facilities are shared. The owners say they plan to add a dorm-style facility that will cost less. Simple, cheap family-style Lao meals can be arranged. Fresh coconuts are abundant.

A Lao company from Pakse is restoring the remains of a French colonial hospital on Don Khon with the intention of opening the *Auberge Sala Don Khon*, an inn where rooms will cost US$20 to US$35 a night.

Getting There & Away From Ban Nakasong you can charter a boat to Don Det for 8000 kip or share a local ferry with Don Det residents for 500 kip per person. It may also be possible to charter boats from Ban Thakho near Khon Phapheng Falls.

See the Don Khong Getting Around section earlier for information on chartering boats to Don Det and Don Khon from Muang Khong.

Khon Phapheng Falls

South of Don Khong the Mekong River features a 13km stretch of powerful rapids with several sets of cascades. The largest, Khon Phapheng, flows between the eastern shore of the Mekong near Ban Thakho. A wooden pavilion on the Mekong shore affords a good view of the falls. A shaky network of bamboo scaffolds on the rocks next to the falls are used by daring fishermen who are said to have an alliance with the spirits of the cascades. Any ordinary mortal who

Dolphins Endangered

The rare Irrawaddy dolphin (*Orcaella brevirostris*, called *paa khaa* in Laos) reaches around 2.5m in length at maturity and is native to tropical coastal marine ecosystems as well as freshwater rivers and lakes. In existence since the Holocene epoch, these small, bluish grey-to-black cetaceans swim in small pods of two to three individuals; their bulging foreheads give them a resemblance to the much larger beluga whale.

Although the Irrawaddy dolphin can adapt to either fresh or salt water, it is seldom seen in the sea. It has been recorded in the Padma River in Bangladesh, Ayeyarwady River in Myanmar, and the Mekong in Laos and Cambodia.

The dolphin's continued existence is threatened by gill netting and bomb fishing in the lower Mekong River and its tributaries (principally the Se Kong, Se Pian and Se Kaman), where its overall numbers have dwindled to an estimated 100 to 300 individuals. In the Don Khong area there may be only 20 to 50 left.

Among the Lao and Khmer, Irrawaddy dolphins are traditionally considered reincarnated humans and there are many stories of dolphins having saved the lives of fishermen or villagers who have accidentally fallen into the Mekong or who have been attacked by crocodiles. Hence neither the Lao nor the Khmer intentionally capture dolphins for food or sport. While using nylon gill nets to catch other fish, Lao anglers may unwittingly entangle a dolphin and then refrain from cutting the net to release the animal in order to save the cost of the net. Unable to reach the surface, the entangled dolphin then drowns.

The Laos-based Siphandone Wetlands Project, in conjunction with the Department of Forestry & Environment, is making efforts to encourage a return to traditional bamboo fish traps and small hand nets – along with the creation of deep-water conservation zones in waters 10 to 60m deep – through community-based resource management rather than government prohibition. An attempt to compensate Lao fishermen on Don Khon and nearby Don Sadam for any gill nets damaged by cutting free the dolphins has, unfortunately, met with little success.

Another serious threat to the survival of the Mekong dolphin population is the use of explosives for fishing in Cambodia (a practice that is strictly prohibited in Laos), a country where hand grenades and other small ordnance are inexpensive and readily available. In this ghoulish practice an explosive charge is detonated beneath the surface of the river, and fish killed by the shock waves float to the surface and are scooped up by fishermen in boats with hand nets. As many as 20 charges a day are detonated in the Cambodian stretches of the Mekong River above Stung Treng – the lower extension of the dolphins' prime habitat.

In an attempt to crush local beliefs and to extract oil for their war machinery, the Khmer Rouge reportedly shot thousands of the dolphins in Tonle Sap, a large lake in northern Cambodia, during their 1970s reign of terror. The future of the dolphin's Mekong River survival continues to rest in Cambodia much more than in Laos. Although the deep-water conservation zones in Laos have done much to increase the breeding and maturation of other fish, experts say that at current mortality rates the Irrawaddy dolphin has only 10 years left before it is extinct from the Mekong.

For more information on the dolphins' plight, or to make a donation to the Irrawaddy dolphin project, write to Ian Baird, c/o CESVI, PO Box 860, Pakse, Lao PDR. Those concerned about the fate of the Irrawaddy dolphins on the Cambodian side of the lower Mekong can write polite letters to Prime Minister Hun Sen, Government House, Phnom Penh, Cambodia, asking that the use of nylon gill nets and explosives to catch fish be prohibited and that such prohibitions be enforced.

SOUTHERN LAOS

would try getting closer to the falls via these slim bamboo poles would be tempting death.

Refreshments and toilet facilities are available at a couple of vendor stalls near the falls.

A Thai-Lao company signed a contract in the early 1990s to build a huge 300 million baht resort near Khon Phapheng Falls. The international outcries against the project, which would have seriously threatened the local environment since it involved four 18-hole golf courses and a 21 megawatt hydro-electric plant, have apparently pushed the resort aside – at least for the time being.

On the way to Khon Phapheng you might stop in Ban Khinak to visit the largest market in the district (best in the early morning).

Getting There & Away To reach the falls you need to get to Ban Khinak, a riverfront village accessible by boat from Muang Khong on Don Khong island; there are regular ferries between 6 am and noon for 500 kip per person or you can charter a boat for 10,000 kip. From Ban Khinak you can get a passenger truck to Ban Thakho for a few hundred kip or charter a jumbo direct to the falls for 30,000 kip round trip. Day trips to the falls can also be arranged with the Auberge Sala Done Khong and Bungalow Souksan (both branches).

If you're coming on your own from Don Det you should catch a ferry to Ban Naka-song (500 kip shared, up to 8000 kip chartered) and then hire a jumbo to the falls. The latter will cost about the same from Ban Nakasong as from Ban Khinak.

There are also direct passenger trucks between Ban Muang (opposite Champasak) and Ban Khinak.

Sekong Province

Although this province in the south-eastern corner of Laos, like its neighbour Attapeu, is officially open to tourism, the difficulty of transport means that only a few tourists have ventured here.

Laos' least populous province, Sekong numbers only 63,800 people (less than 1% of the nation), with a population density of just 8.3 persons per sq kilometre. It's also a very poor province in which nearly a quarter of all children die before the age of five. The worst poverty and health problems occur between the Se Kong river and the Vietnamese border, an area UN and NGO aid workers call 'The Zone'.

Malaria is rampant in the lowland areas of both provinces, especially towards the Vietnamese border where the deadly *falciparum* is the most common variety. Take the appropriate precautions.

Few Lao Loum – either ethnic Lao or tribal Thais – live in this corner of Laos, which is the traditional home of several Lao Theung or Mon-Khmer tribes, including the Nyaheun, Chieng, Talieng, Ta-oy (Tahoy), Yai Kayon, Laven, Katang, Nge, Suay, Ye, Katu, Lawae, Chatong and Kakang. Many of these tribes migrate between hilly Sekong and the Central Highlands of Vietnam (where they are known as Montagnards).

Of the several Mon-Khmer ethnicities found in Sekong, the most numerous are the Katu and the Talieng. The latter total around 25,000 and are found only in the district of Dak Cheung, east of the capital and 1500m above sea level. Both groups tend towards monogamy but tolerate polygyny (two or more wives); their belief systems mix animism and ancestor worship.

It's difficult to get around the province because of the lack of roads. During the rainy season the road to Dak Cheung, for example, becomes impassable. At other times you can reach the district by truck in four hours.

According to the police in Sekong you're supposed to have permission to travel outside the provincial capital despite the retraction of the permit system. This may simply be a vestige of the old system clung to by local officials or may be because they regard all foreigners as employees of UN and other aid projects, who often have less freedom to travel around the country than the average

continued on page 313

LAO WEAVING

All together Laos is said to have some 16 basic weaving styles divided among four basic regions. Southern weavers, who often use foot looms rather than frame looms, practise Laos' most continuous textile traditions in terms of styles and patterns, some of which haven't changed for a century or more. One-piece phàa nung are more common than those sewn from separate pieces. Southern Laos is known for the best silk weaving and for intricate *mat-míi* (ikat or tie-dye) designs that include Khmer-influenced temple and elephant motifs. Synthetic and natural dyes are commonly used. In Sekong and Attapeu, borders often contain cryptic-looking symbols; the recent introduction of simple helicopter and aeroplane motifs suggests the beginnings of a possible postwar cargo cult among the Lao Theung. In these provinces, beadwork may be added to the embroidery.

In north-eastern Laos (especially Hua Phan's Sam Neua and Xieng Khuang's Muang Phuan) the Thai Neua, Phuan, Thai Lü, Thai Daeng, Thai Dam and Phu Thai mainly produce weft brocade (*yìap kọ*) using raw silk, cotton yarn and natural dyes, sometimes with the addition of mat-míi techniques. Large diamond patterns

The threads of Lao weaving – modern Lao weaving, represented in these three patterned examples, is both a cottage industry and increasingly an export-oriented business (all photographs by Joe Cummings).

are common. In central Laos, typical weavings include indigo-dyed cotton mat-míi and minimal weft brocade *(jók* and *khit)*, along with techniques borrowed from all over the country (brought by migrants to Vientiane – many of whom fled war zones). Gold and silver brocade is typical of traditional Luang Prabang patterns, along with intricate patterns *(lái* and imported Thai Lü designs). Northerners generally use frame looms; the waist, body and *thin sin* (bottom border) of a *phàa nung* or sarong are often sewn together from separately woven pieces.

In addition to the phàa nung or *phàa sìin* ('end cloth' or skirt), other apparel woven in traditional styles include the *phàa bɪang*, a shawl or shoulder sash for women, and the *phàa set*, a shoulder sash for men. These aren't usually worn in everyday life but are important accessories for festival occasions and basi ceremonies. Certain non-clothing textiles are also be crafted for ceremonial use, such as the *thong* – long, narrow, vertical prayer flags made of cloth interwoven with short lengths of bamboo and sometimes weighted with beadwork. These are commonly hung from the ceiling of temple *sim* by the Thai Lü and Thai Yuan. These same ethnic groups sometimes wrap palm-leaf Buddhist manuscripts in bamboo-stiffened textiles.

One of the common myths about Lao weaving is that synthetically dyed fabrics can't be more than 30 years old (or 40 or 50, depending on whom you're talking to). Synthetic dyes were in fact introduced to Lao and Thai weavers by the industrialised western world in the late 19th century; commercial Chinese dyes were known even before that. Today the only natural dye enjoying consistent, widespread use in Laos is indigo.

Along with the rebirth of Lao weaving, however, has come a renewed interest in natural dyes, which typically create softer but richer colours than their commercial counterparts. Natural sources for Lao dyes include ebony (both seeds and wood), tamarind (seeds and wood), red lacquer extracted from the *coccus iacca* (an insect that bores into certain trees), turmeric (from a root) and indigo. Among tribal Thai weavers, indigo recipes are often the most closely guarded dye secrets. To make indigo dye, a weaver soaks the *indigofera tinctoria* plant in water for several days, then adds lime to activate the colour. Once the dye is active, the weaver works it into a thick paste (which can be thinned later for dyeing) along with an idiosyncratic mix of ingredients (such as lime peels, tamarind, salt) to obtain the correct pH balance, texture and hue.

The basic palette of five natural colours – black, orange, red, yellow and blue – can be combined to create an endless variety of new colours. Other unblended but more subtle hues include khaki (from the bark of the Indian trumpet tree), pink (sappan wood) and gold (jackfruit and breadfruit woods). With all these choices available, it's nonsense to say that one hue or another is a 'new' colour that can only be created synthetically. Brighter colours, however, tend to be synthetic in origin.

Although there are many regional differences, Lao weaving is distinctive for its contrasting colours and geometric patterns. In the south, foot looms are generally used, while in the north weavers tend to use frame looms.

ALL PHOTOGRAPHS BY JOE CUMMINGS

BERNARD NAPTHINE

BERNARD NAPTHINE

CARLY HAMMOND

Common flavourings in Lao cuisine include chili, galingale, ginger and lemon grass. These and other ingredients are sold at the many colourful markets in the cities and towns of Laos, or at Laos' fast-food joints – roadside stalls.

continued from page 310
tourist. There is also a danger of UXO in any off-road travel. In reality we found you could travel just about anywhere in the province – the problem being getting there.

SEKONG (MUANG LAMAM)

The main reason people generally come to the capital of Sekong – also called Muang Lamam (population 18,000) – is to use it as a departure point for river trips down to Attapeu. Carved out of the wilderness less than 12 years ago, the spread-out town features a phalanx of government buildings in the centre, surrounded by areas of wood and thatch stilt homes among the cement and wooden ones. Many households grow kapok trees in their yards.

The Se Kong river wraps around the town on the southern and eastern sides, while the Bolaven Plateau rises precipitously to the west. Another reason why local police may be touchy about visitors is the existence of a prison across the river from town. At the town market, border tribes trade cloth for Vietnamese goods. Attapeu residents envy Sekong for having electric power 24 hours.

There isn't a lot to do in Sekong other than shop for tribal handicrafts. About 20 minutes drive south on the road to Attapeu is a scenic 6m-high waterfall with two swimming holes. Next to the falls are a couple of open-air pavilions where you can camp.

Information

Money The Phak Tai Bank, on the highway through town, changes cash Thai baht and US dollars for kip only. It's open from Monday to Friday from 8 to 11 am and from 2 to 4 pm.

Post & Communications The town post office, a block north-west of the Hotel Sekong, now has a public phone where you can make local and international calls. It's open the same hours as the bank.

Places to Stay & Eat

There's still only once place to stay in town, the fairly decent two storey, 16 room *Hotel Sekong*. The ground floor rooms with fan and cold bath cost 18,000 kip, while rooms on the 2nd floor have hot water and better mattresses for 20,000 kip. The manager is trying to learn English. The *Suksamlan Restaurant* on the premises has pretty good food, and the local Katu and Alak fabrics attractively displayed on the walls are available for purchase. Reservations for this hotel can be made in Pakse at the Suksamlan Hotel or at Lane Xang Travel in Vientiane.

Next door to the hotel restaurant is a restaurant called *Nang Malai Thong*, with similar tribal decor. It functions mostly as a nightclub, with food clearly secondary to booze and live music.

The *Fouang Restaurant*, across from the Hotel Sekong, serves decent Vietnamese food but it's best to order well in advance. Several modest restaurants and föe shops can be found near the market.

Things to Buy

Two small handicraft shops – really nothing more than bamboo-thatch cubicles – behind the Hotel Sekong and across from the post office carry a good range of textiles woven by the Alak, Katu, Nge and Talieng tribes, plus a few baskets and other tribal products, including herbs and lào-láo. This is a good place to sort out the different colours and patterns of the various tribes. Katu cloth, for example, typically shows broad bands of red and black with small white beads sewn into the fabric, while Alak designs use a more refined stripe. Rare Alak or Nge loincloths – long, narrow, heavy beaded affairs – are occasionally on sale from US$50 and up.

Around 200m east of the hotel, turn north onto a dirt street and you'll come to a small weaving district of three or four houses where you can observe Nge people using narrow foot looms.

Getting There & Away

Road Passenger trucks from Salavan leave twice daily at around 7 am and 1 pm; in the reverse direction, departures from Sekong are at 7 am and 12.30 pm. The trip takes about 3½ hours and costs 2000 kip. It is

SOUTHERN LAOS

another 3½ hours and 2000 kip to Attapeu from Sekong. The road is fairly good along both legs.

There is also one truck a day running between Pakse and Sekong (en route to and from Attapeu), leaving around 6 am from either end, for 4000 kip; this is a journey of around six hours.

In Sekong trucks arrive at and depart from the morning market.

River Ferry service down the Se Kong to Attapeu is rather irregular. When they are running, passenger ferries charge around 6000 kip per person. You can also charter a pirogue with a motor carrying up to four persons downriver to Attapeu for 65,000 kip or US$27. The scenic trip takes around seven hours either way; the river parallels the eastern escarpment of the Bolaven Plateau most of the way. During the late dry season, you may have to get out and walk along a path next the river while the boatman manoeuvres the craft through shallow rapids.

Getting Around

Sekong has a couple of jumbos which will take you just about anywhere in town for 1000 kip.

Attapeu Province

Rugged, wild, scenic and difficult to get around, the Attapeu/Sekong region harbours many rare animal species. Tigers aren't uncommon, and there's rumoured to be either Javan or Sumatran rhino near the Cambodian border. A recently discovered trout-like fish grows to 10kg in the Se Kong, and the Irrawaddy dolphin makes an occasional appearance in this river and the adjoining Se Kaman. The districts close to the Vietnamese border contain thick jungle teeming with bird life; parrots, parakeets, bee-eaters and other colourful species are often seen. An Australian-financed dam on

the Se Kaman threatens to inundate pristine river valleys but will provide hydroeletric power for developing infrastructure.

Because the Ho Chi Minh Trail wound through the middle of both provinces, Attapeu and Sekong were heavily bombed during the Indochina War and their already sparse populations have declined further. Of the 11 ethnic groups found in Attapeu, Lave, Nge and Talieng predominate, with Lao Loum, Chinese and Vietnamese concentrated in the capital. There are only 14 Buddhist temples in the entire province.

Relations between the Attapeu provincial government and its adjacent Vietnamese counterparts are close. Even on Lao National Day, a Vietnamese flag flies beside the Lao flag at the government guesthouse in the capital.

ATTAPEU (SAMAKHI XAI)

Officially known as Muang Samakhi Xai (population 19,200), the capital of Attapeu Province is set in a large valley surrounded by mountains and rivers, and is famed in southern Laos as the 'garden village' for its shady lanes and lush flora. The town's location at the confluence of the Se Kong and Se Kaman rivers makes it perfect for exploration by boat. The flat-topped line of mountains about 1000m over the valley floor to the north and west marks the edge of the Bolaven Plateau.

The local police have lightened up considerably on tourists, and they don't seem to care whether you check in with them or not upon arrival.

Electricity is available from 6 to 10 pm only.

Information

Tourist Office The Attapeu Office of Tourism (☎ 212039) can be found in the Provincial Hall on the north-western edge of town. As far as we can tell, the main function of this office seems to be to hire the officer on staff out as a guide for tours around the province. If you ask about going anywhere in the province the reply will likely be that it's OK as long as you hire a

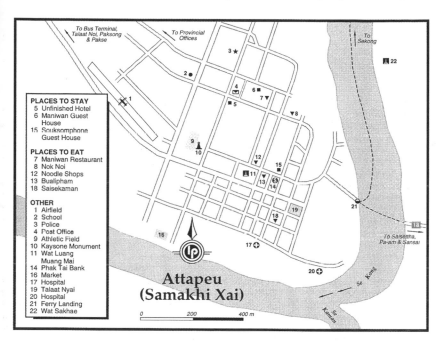

PLACES TO STAY
5 Unfinished Hotel
6 Maniwan Guest
   House
15 Souksomphone
   Guest House

PLACES TO EAT
7 Maniwan Restaurant
8 Nok Noi
12 Noodle Shops
13 Bualipham
18 Saisekaman

OTHER
1 Airfield
2 School
3 Police
4 Post Office
9 Athletic Field
10 Kaysone Monument
11 Wat Luang
   Muang Mai
14 Phak Tai Bank
16 Market
17 Hospital
19 Talaat Nyai
20 Hospital
21 Ferry Landing
22 Wat Sakhae

Attapeu
(Samakhi Xai)

car, driver and guide through the office. In reality there doesn't appear to be any law against going wherever you like, though things will certainly go more smoothly with a guide along.

The problem is that these guide services don't come cheap. We're all for supporting the local tourism industry, it's just a shame the local government tries to monopolise it.

If you need a guide and can't afford the US$50 to US$80 per day fees suggested by the Attapeu Office of Tourism, you might try hiring locally – that is, at the village level – where you can easily find guides for under US$20 a day.

Money The Phak Tai Bank, about 500m south-east of the airstrip, can change cash baht or US dollars to kip in moderate amounts (at rates below even those in Pakse). Despite the fact that other currencies are listed on a board inside the bank,

the staff don't appear willing to change anything but dollars or baht. The overall money supply is very low and depends on weekly deliveries from Pakse.

Post & Communications A post and telephone office stands about 100m west of Maniwan Guest House.

Temples & Shrines
Attapeu is not renowned for its Buddhist temples, but there are a couple of mildly interesting ones around. In the town centre near Phak Tai Bank and the Souksomphone Guest House, **Wat Luang Muang Mai** – more commonly known simply as Wat Luang – was built in 1939 and features some older monastic buildings with original naga bargeboards. The temple boasts around 20 novices and 10 monks, quite a substantial monastic presence for any Lao Buddhist temple these days.

SOUTHERN LAOS

Of similar vintage is **Wat Fang Taeng** on the banks of the Se Kaman river in Ban Fang Taeng, 14km from town on the way to Saisettha. The small but elegant brick and stucco sim dates from 1935-36 and there's a jedi on the grounds that may be older.

Tham Phra is a cave shrine containing Buddhist statuary about 3km north-west of town in the foothills of the Bolaven Plateau.

Places to Stay

The relatively new *Souksomphone Guest House* (no phone yet), right across from the Phak Tai Bank, is a fairly well-maintained two storey building containing eight sizable rooms with fan (which work only when the electricity is turned on in the evening) for 10,000 kip per room. There are three shared bathrooms downstairs. The friendly family who own the guesthouse do laundry and can fix great meals. Reservations can be made at the Suksamlan Hotel in Pakse, the Sekong Hotel in Sekong or Lane Xang Travel in Vientiane.

The once government-owned *Maniwan Guest House* has six rooms in three buildings inside a walled compound. Rooms come with two or three beds with hard mattresses, mosquito nets and shared toilet and bathing facilities; rates are 5000 kip per person or 15,000 kip per room. A desolate restaurant occupies the same compound. The Souksomphone is much friendlier and clearly a better deal.

The government has paid for the construction of a 40 room hotel 'shell' opposite the post office in hope that an investor will come in and finish the project. So far no-one has taken the bait.

Places to Eat

At a small outdoor thatched shelter over tables and chairs next to the *Souksomphone Guest House*, the family who own the guesthouse can do simple noodle dishes as well as baguette-and-eggs breakfasts. More elaborate Lao meals can also be arranged with advance notice, and these can be eaten at tables inside the guesthouse or outdoors. Prices are low.

The *Maniwan Restaurant*, in the Maniwan Guest House compound, offers a good variety of reasonably priced rice and noodle dishes. The manager, Ms Maniwan, speaks some English.

There are several noodle and rice shops between the Souksomphone Guest House and Wat Luang. One of them, *Bualipham*, serves traditional Lao dishes from large pots. Noodle dishes are also available during the morning at *Talaat Nyai*, a day market a couple of blocks south-east of Souksomphone Guest House.

Attapeu's two nightclubs, *Saisekaman* (sign in Lao only) and *Nok Noi*, serve Lao and Chinese meals in the evening.

Things to Buy

Unlike in Sekong there don't seem to be any handicraft shops in town yet. Tribals occasionally wander through the streets carrying stacks of textiles and other crafts, but Attapeu's markets have very little. A small trading house opposite the south-east side of Talaat Nyai has a few tribal artefacts for sale – baskets, fabrics, loincloths, bow and arrow sets, swords and shields.

Getting There & Away

Air Flights from Pakse to Attapeu's airfield – a weedy field scored with two dirt tyre tracks – now appear to be extinct.

Road Attapeu can't be reached by road from the rest of Laos during much of the rainy season. During the dry season the province can be reached by road along three basic routes. The most direct route from Pakse goes across the Bolaven Plateau via Paksong. The road is fairly smooth as far as Paksong (see the earlier Bolaven Plateau Getting There & Away section for details), after which it's rather rough. The scenery east of Paksong – along a new route cut by Korean hydroelectric power developers bypassing Sekong – is spectacular as the road descends along the eastern escarpment of the Bolaven Plateau and follows the Se Kong river. The latter half of this road does not appear on most Lao PDR maps – but it's there! Total driving time is around five to six hours barring any calamities (the last time we did this route it took 12½ hours after two breakdowns and a flat tyre).

In Pakse passenger vehicles leave from the Km 8 southern terminal twice a day, first around 6 am (in a small bus) and again at 9 am (in a large truck); come early for a seat as it gets very crowded. The fare is 5000 kip and the trip takes five hours.

The second way to reach Attapeu by road is from Sekong along a road parallel to the Se Kong. This journey lasts 2½ hours and costs 2500 kip.

The southernmost road – along Route 18 – starts near Champasak on the east side of the Mekong and skirts the bottom of the Bolaven Plateau. Traffic is very sparse along this road but within the next few years the Asian Development Bank is supposed to turn Route 18 into a highway of sorts to Vietnam.

From Attapeu buses and trucks depart from a space next to Talaat Noi at Km 3 north-west of town.

River Attapeu can be reached by boat from Sekong via the Se Kong river. From July to November there are occasional longtail passenger boats for 5000 to 6000 kip per person; during other times of year you can charter a smaller boat for around 65,000 kip or US$27. The seven hour trip goes through stretches of rapids as well as past beautiful mountain scenery.

Getting Around
There are about a dozen jumbos operating in town. Most short trips cost 500 kip per person; to/from the bus terminal costs 1000 kip.

AROUND ATTAPEU
To the east and south-east of the capital are the most heavily bombed districts along the Ho Chi Minh Trail, **Sansai** and **Phu Vong**. Here the trail splits into two, with the Sihanouk Trail heading into Cambodia, the HCM into southern Vietnam. Damaged and destroyed vehicles and equipment can still

be seen lying about in the jungle, along with lots of UXO; don't attempt to explore this area without a local guide (ask at the government guesthouse).

The heavy rainfall, combined with the rugged limestone and basalt terrain of the Bolaven Plateau, means the north-western part of the province harbours several impressive waterfalls; most are inaccessible by road. A waterfall known as **Nam Tok Katamtok**, off the road to Paksong in a cleft in the Bolaven Plateau carved out by the Se Nam Noi river, boasts a spectacular drop of 100m. It's near the split between the Se Nam Noi and Se Katam, between Ban Nong Loi and Ban Kheumkham. **Taat Se Noi**, about 60km north of Attapeu and 25km from Sekong (5km west of the point where the Se Nam Noi feeds into the Se Kong), is known locally as 'waterfall of the heads' owing to a WWII incident in which Japanese soldiers decapitated a number of Lao soldiers and tossed their heads into the falls. Though only a short vertical drop of a few metres, the falls are about 100m wide.

Attapeu Province has one NBCA, **Dong Ampham**, a 1975 sq km area which is wedged between the Se Kaman and the Vietnamese border. Timber poaching, even in protected and managed forests, threatens the pristine environment; a former governor of Attapeu was sentenced to 15 years in prison for smuggling timber. Hydroelectric projects planned for the Se Kaman and Se Su also threaten the integrity of the Dong Amphan NBCA.

The southern mountains of Attapeu may not be safe because of Khmer Rouge or bandit activity; you should make inquiries before venturing in that direction.

Pa-am
At this Alak village in Sansai district, about 30km east of Attapeu via the wide, unpaved Route 18, a Russian surface-to-air (SAM) missile launcher – complete with an unfired missile stencilled in Russian and Vietnamese – has been left intact next to the Ho Chi Minh Trail.

Alak textiles can be bought in the village and you may be able to watch women weaving in their homes – ask first. There are several small cataracts in the Nam Pa river where you can swim in the dry season.

It is another 30km or so farther on to the district capital of Sansai, but the road beyond Pa-am is bad, and requires a 4WD vehicle – or you could walk it in two or three days. It is a beautiful area with many ethnic minorities.

Getting There & Away Passenger trucks to Pa-am leave Attapeu every morning and take only 30 minutes or so to reach the village along the (as yet) unsealed Route 18; you could also hire a jumbo to bring you here.

If you could find someone willing to rent you a bicycle in Attapeu, you could probably pedal to Pa-am without undue strain. To reach Route 18 on the east bank of the Se Kong, you must take a short ferry ride from the main boat landing in Attapeu.

Language

The official language of Laos is Lao as it is spoken and written in Vientiane. As an official language, it has successfully become the lingua franca between all Lao and non-Lao ethnic groups in Laos. Of course, native Lao is spoken with differing tonal accents and with slightly differing vocabularies as you move from one part of the country to the next, especially in a north to south direction. But it is the Vientiane dialect that is most widely understood.

Modern Lao linguists recognise five basic dialects within the country: Vientiane Lao; northern Lao (spoken in Sainyabuli, Bokeo, Udomxai, Phongsali, Luang Nam Tha and Luang Prabang); north-eastern Lao (Xieng Khuang and Hua Phan), central Lao (Khammuan and Bolikhamsai); and finally southern Lao (Champasak, Savannakhet, Salavan, Attapeu and Sekong). Each of these can be further divided into various subdialects; the differences between the Lao spoken in the neighbouring provinces of Xieng Khuang and Hua Phan, for example, is readily apparent to those who know Lao well.

All dialects of Lao are members of the Thai half of the Thai-Kadai family of languages and are closely related to languages spoken in Thailand, northern Myanmar and pockets of China's Yunnan and Guangxi provinces. Standard Lao is indeed close enough to Standard Thai (as spoken in central Thailand) that, for native speakers, the two are mutually intelligible. In fact, virtually all of the speakers of Lao west of the Annamite Chain can easily understand spoken Thai, since the bulk of the television and radio they tune in to is broadcast from Thailand.

Among educated Lao, written Thai is also easily understood, in spite of the fact that the two scripts differ (to about the same degree that the Greek and Roman scripts differ). This is because many of the textbooks used at the college and university level in Laos are actually Thai texts.

Even more similar to Standard Lao are Thailand's northern and north-eastern Thai dialects. North-eastern Thai (also called Isan) is virtually 100% Lao in vocabulary and intonation; in fact there are more Lao speakers living in Thailand than in Laos. Hence if you are travelling to Laos after a spell in Thailand (especially the northeast), you should be able to put whatever you learned in Thailand to good use in Laos. (It doesn't work as well in the opposite direction; native Thais can't always understand Lao since they've had less exposure to it.)

SCRIPT

Prior to the consolidation of the various Lao *meuang* (principalities) in the 14th century, there was little demand for a written language. When a written language was deemed necessary by the Lan Xang monarchy, Lao scholars based their script on an early alphabet devised by the Thais (which in turn had been created by Khmer scholars who used south Indian scripts as models!). The alphabet used in Laos is closer to the original prototype; the original Thai script was later extensively revised (which is why Lao looks 'older' than Thai, even though it is newer as a written language).

Before 1975 at least four spelling systems were in use. Because modern printing never really got established in Laos (most of the advanced textbooks being in Thai, French, or Vietnamese before the Revolution), Lao spelling wasn't standardised until after the Pathet Lao takeover. The current system has been highly simplified by transliterating all foreign loan words according to their sound only, and not their written form.

Lao script can therefore be learned much more quickly than Thai or Khmer, both of which typically attempt to transcribe foreign borrowings letter for letter no matter what the actual pronunciation is.

One peculiarity of the post-1975 system is that it forbade the use of the Lao letter 'r' in words where it was more commonly pronounced as an 'l', reportedly because of the association of the 'r' with classical Thai; although the 'r' was virtually lost in Laos (converting to 'h' in some cases and to 'l' in others), in many parts of Thailand it is still quite strong. Hence the names of former Lao kings Setthathirat and Phothisarat came to be rendered as Setthathilat and Phothisalat in post-1975 Lao script. In the last two or three years the government has loosened its restrictions and although the nasty 'r' is not taught in the school system, it is once again permitted in signage and in historical documents.

Other scripts still in use include *láo thám* (dhamma Lao), used for writing Pali scriptures, and various Thai tribal scripts, the most popular and widespread being that of the Thai Neua (which has become standardised via Xishuangbanna, China).

The Lao script today consists of 30 consonants (formed from 20 basic sounds) and 28 vowels and diphthongs (15 individual symbols used in varying combinations). Complementing the consonant and vowel symbols are four tone marks, only two of which are commonly used in creating the six different tones (in combination with all the other symbols). Written Lao proceeds from left to right, though vowel-signs may appear in a number of positions relative to consonants: before, after, above, below or 'around' (ie before, above *and* below).

Although learning the alphabet isn't difficult, the writing system itself is fairly complex, so unless you are planning to have a lengthy stay in Laos you should perhaps make learning to speak the language your main priority. Lao script for the names of provinces and towns can be found at the end of this chapter so you can at least 'read' the names of destinations in a pinch, or point to them if necessary.

TONES

Basically, Lao is a monosyllabic, tonal language, like the various dialects of Thai and Chinese. Borrowed words from Sanskrit, Pali, French and English often have two or more syllables, however. Many identical phonemes or vowel-consonant combinations are differentiated by their tone only. The word *sao*, for example, can mean 'girl', 'morning', 'pillar' or 'twenty' depending on the tone. For people from non-tonal languages backgrounds, it can be very hard to learn at first. Even when we 'know' the correct tone, our tendency to denote emotion, emphasis and questions through tone modulation often interferes with uttering the correct tone. So the first rule in learning and using the tone system is to avoid overlaying your native intonation patterns onto the Lao language.

Vientiane Lao has six tones (compared with five used in Standard Thai, four in Mandarin and nine in Cantonese). Three of the tones are level (low, mid and high) while three follow pitch inclines (rising, high falling and low falling). All six variations in pitch are relative to the speaker's natural vocal range, so that one person's low tone is not necessarily the same pitch as another person's. Hence, keen pitch recognition is not a prerequisite for learning a tonal language like Lao. A relative distinction between pitch contours within your own voice is all that is necessary. Pitch variation is common to all languages – not tonal languages such as English also use intonation, just in a different way.

On a visual curve the tones might look like this:

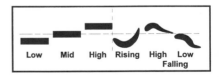

Low   Mid   High   Rising   High   Low
                                        Falling

Low Tone

Produced at the relative bottom of your conversational tonal range – usually flat level, eg *dii*, 'good'. However, not everyone pronounces it flat and level – some Vientiane natives add a slight rising tone to the end.

Mid Tone

Flat like the low tone, but spoken at the relative middle of the speaker's vocal range. No tone mark is used, eg *het*, 'do'.

High Tone

Flat again, this time at the relative top of your vocal range, eg *heúa*, 'boat'.

Rising Tone

Begins a bit below the mid tone and rises to just at or above the high tone, eg *sǎam*, 'three'.

High Falling Tone

Begins at or above the high tone and falls to the mid level, eg *sâo*, 'morning'.

Low Falling Tone

Begins at about the mid level and falls to the level of the low tone, eg *khào*, 'rice'.

TRANSLITERATION

The rendering of Lao words into Roman script is a major problem, since many of the Lao sounds, especially certain vowels, do not occur in English. The problem is compounded by the fact that because of Laos' colonial history, transcribed words most commonly seen in Laos are based on the old colonial French system of transliteration, which bears little relation to the way an English speaker would usually choose to write a Lao word.

A prime example is the capital of Laos, Vientiane. The Lao pronunciation, following a fairly logical English-Roman transliteration, would be Wieng Chan or Vieng Chan (some might hear it more as Wieng Jan). Since the French don't have a written consonant that corresponds to 'w', they chose to use a 'v' to represent all 'w' sounds, even though the 'v' sound in Lao is closer to an English 'w'. The same goes for 'ch' (or 'j'), which for the French was best rendered 'ti-'; hence Wieng Chan (which means Sandalwood City) finishes up as 'Vientiane' in the French transliteration. The 'e' is added so that the final 'n' sound isn't partially lost, as it is in French words

ending with 'n'. This latter phenomenon also happens with words like *lâan* (million) as in Lan Xang, which most French speakers would write as 'Lane', a spelling that leads most English speakers to pronounce this word like the 'lane' in 'Penny Lane' (which is far from accurate).

Many standard place names in Roman script use an 'x' for what in English is 's'. This 'x' stands for a Lao letter that historically was pronounced 'ch' but eventually became 's' in the Lao sound system. There's no difference in the pronunciation of the two; pronounce all instances of 'x' as 's'.

There is no official method of transliterating the Lao language (the government is incredibly inconsistent in this respect, though they tend to follow the old French methods). This book follows the transliteration system which is used in Lonely Planet's *Thailand* guide, since Thai and Lao have virtually identical phonetic systems. The exceptions are where there may be confusion with transliterations that are already in common use (eg *Vientiane* vs *Wieng Chan*, *Luang Prabang* vs *Luang Phabang*).

The public and private sectors in Laos are gradually moving towards a more internationally recognisable system along the lines of the Royal Thai General Transcription (which is fairly readable across a large number of language types). This can also be problematic, however, such as when an 'r' is written where an 'h' or 'l' would be heard, simply because the Lao symbols for these sounds look so much like the Thai 'r' (modern spoken Lao has no 'r' sound).

Recent government maps have finally started using the spelling 'Luang Phabang' rather than 'Luang Prabang'. At the same time the government has begun allowing the use of the once-banned written 'r' for historical Lao names, such as 'Sakkarin' rather than 'Sakkalin', or 'Phothisarat' instead of 'Phothisalat'.

BOOKS FOR LANGUAGE STUDY

Lonely Planet publishes a pocket-sized *Lao phrasebook* which has a complete guide to Lao grammar and pronunciation, along with several chapters designed to make travel in the country easier and more enjoyable, eg 'Around Town', 'Accommodation', 'Food', 'Small Talk' and 'Emergencies'. Lao script and Roman transliteration accompanies all lists of words and phrases. It is available wherever Lonely Planet books are distributed, and it can occasionally be bought in Vientiane at Raintrees and at the Vientiane Department Store.

The *English-Lao, Lao-English Dictionary* by Russell Marcus (Charles Tuttle Co, Suido 1-chome, 1-6 Bunkyo-chu, Tokyo, Japan) is a handy book to have in Laos. Of course you won't be able to read the Lao-English section, but the English-Lao definitions are extensive and the transliteration is more or less consistent. Transliterated Lao words are also accompanied by tone marks (in this case numbers are used for the six tones).

The same company also publishes *Lao for Beginners: An Introduction to the Spoken and Written Language of Laos* by Tatsuo Hoshino and Russell Marcus. This 200 page primer is organised according to situation (eg 'Coming & Going', 'Touring Vientiane', 'Bargaining at the Market'), so the lessons are mostly relevant to everyday needs. The book uses the same transliteration system as the dictionary described above, so the two go together nicely.

A newer and more complete dictionary is the 950-page *Modern English-Lao, Lao-English Dictionary* by Bounmy Soukbandith (contact PO Box 40021, San Diego, CA 92164, USA; or call ☎ (619) 464 3582 for ordering information).

For more serious students, little else is available. Probably the most complete text is the US Foreign Service Institute's *Lao Basic Course, Volumes 1 & 2* (Superintendent of Documents, Washington, DC 20402, USA, 1971). Volume 1 takes students step by step through the rudiments of Lao pronunciation, grammar and writing. Volume 2 is a Lao reader (all in Lao script with no translation) for more advanced students. Both books are oriented towards pre-1975 Laos, with many references to the monarchy and so on.

Most of the books listed above can be purchased in Bangkok at Asia Books, Sukhumvit Rd Soi 15 (and at several other locations).

Not much is available in Laos itself. In Vientiane's Phimphone Market you can find the little blue *English-Lao Dictionary* published by the State Printing Office. This pocket-sized tome contains over 10,000 entries; the Lao entries appear in Lao script only.

A draft copy of the *Lao Language Competencies for Peace Corps Volunteers in the LPDR* by Xamini de Abrew and Thong Khamphasinovanh was distributed in Vientiane in December 1991, just before the short-lived US Peace Corps experiment was shut down before it really got started. Only 30 copies were originally made, but a few photocopies are available here and there. You might also try directing inquiries to the USPC (CHPTO/PACEM, 1990 K St, Washington, DC 20026, USA). This text contains a good selection of structures and vocabulary but some tones are marked incorrectly and there are some minor vocabulary errors.

In Vientiane's government bookshops you can also buy children's first-language primers, which aren't a bad way to start for those who will be staying a long time in Laos and want to attempt to master the written language.

For information on language courses, see the Courses section of the Facts for the Visitor chapter.

If you plan to travel extensively in any Lao Sung areas, Lonely Planet's *Thai Hill Tribes phrasebook* could also be useful.

OTHER LANGUAGES

In the cities and towns of the Mekong river valley, French is intermittently understood. In spite of its colonial history, French remains the official second language of the government and many official documents are written in French as well as Lao. Shop signs sometimes appear in French (alongside Lao, as mandated by law), though signs in English are becoming more common these days. As in Vietnam, the former colonial language is increasingly viewed as irrelevant in a region that has adopted English as the lingua franca of business and trade, and among young Lao students English is now much more popular than French. Lao over the age of 50 may understand a little English, but to a lesser extent than French.

Many Russian-trained Lao can also speak Russian, though the language has drastically fallen from favour. The Russian Cultural Centre now offers more English courses than it does Russian, and the most popular event at the centre is an evening satellite TV program of English-language shows. The occasional Lao who studied abroad in Cuba or Eastern Europe may be able to speak Spanish, German, Czech, Polish or even Bulgarian.

It pays to learn as much Lao as possible during your stay in the country, since speaking and understanding the language not only enhances verbal communication but garners a great deal of respect from the Lao you come into contact with.

PRONUNCIATION
Vowels

Lao vowels can be written before, after, above and below consonants – in the following vowel chart we demonstrate this by using '×' to represents any consonant.

×̂	**i**	as in 'it'
×̂	**ii**	as in 'feet' or 'tea'
ໄ×̌, ໃ×	**ai**	as in 'pipe' or 'I'
×ๅ	**aa**	long 'a' as in 'father'
×̌	**a**	half as long as 'aa' above
ແ×	**ae**	as in 'bat' or 'tab'
ເ×̌, ເ××̌	**e**	as in 'hen'
ເ×	**eh**	like 'a' in 'hate'
ເ×̂, ເ×̂	**oe**	as in 'rut' or 'hut' but more closed
×̂, ×̂	**eu**	as in French 'deux', or the 'i' in 'sir'
×̥	**u**	as in 'flute'
×̥	**uu**	as in 'food'

ເ×̂ົ	**ao**	as in 'now' or 'cow'
×̇	**aw**	as in 'jaw'
ໂ×̌, ××̂	**o**	as in 'phone'
ໂ×	**oh**	as in 'toe'
ເ×ຶອ	**eua**	diphthong of 'eu' and 'a'
×ຽ×, ເ×ຍ	**ie**	'i-a' as in the French *rien*
×ົ×	**ua**	'u-a' as in 'tour'
×ວຍ	**uay**	'u-a-i' (as in 'Dewey')
×ິວ, ×̂ວ	**iu**	'i-u' (as in 'yew')
×ຽວ	**iaw**	a triphthong of 'i-a-w' (as the 'io' in 'Rio')
ແ×ວ	**aew**	'ae-w'
ເ×ວ	**ehw**	'eh-w'
ເ×̌ວ	**ew**	same as 'ehw' above, but shorter (not as in 'yew')
ເ×̂ຍ	**oei**	'oe-i'

Consonants

ກ	**k**	as the 'k' in 'skin'; similar to 'g' in 'good', but unaspirated (no accompanying puff of air) and unvoiced
ຂ, ຄ	**kh**	'k' as in 'kite'
ງ	**ng**	as in 'sing'; used as an initial consonant in Lao. Practise by saying 'sing' without the 'si'.
ຈ	**j**	similar to 'j' in 'join' or more closely, the second 't' in 'stature' or 'literature' (voiceless, unaspirated)
ສ, ຊ	**s/x**	as in 'soap'
ຍ	**ny**	similar to the 'ni' in 'onion'; used as an initial consonant in Lao
ດ	**d**	as in 'dodo' or 'dig'
ຕ	**t**	as the 't' in 'forty' (unaspirated, unvoiced), not as in 'tea'; a bit like 'd'
ຖ, ທ	**th**	't' as in 'tea'
ນ, ໜ	**n**	as in 'nun'
ບ	**b**	as in 'boy'
ປ	**p**	as the 'p' in 'stopper' (unvoiced and unaspirated) not as the 'p' in 'put'

ພ, ຜ	ph	'p' as in 'put' (but never as in 'phone')
ຝ, ຟ	f	same as in 'fan'
ມ, ໝ	m	same as in 'man'
ຢ	y	same as in 'yo-yo'
ລ, ຫລ	l	as in 'lick'
ວ, ຫວ	w	as in 'wing' (often transliterated as 'v')
ຮ, ຫ	h	as in 'home'

Greetings & Civilities

Greetings/Hello.
  sábaai-dii   ສະບາຍດີ
Goodbye.
(general farewell)
  sábaai-dii   ສະບາຍດີ
Goodbye. (person leaving)
  láa kawn (lit: leaving first)   ລາກ່ອນ
  pai kawn (lit: going first)   ໄປກ່ອນ
Goodbye. (person staying)
  sohk dii (lit: good luck)   ໂສກດີ
See you later.
  phop kan mai   ພົບກັນໃໝ່
Thank you.
  khàwp jai   ຂອບໃຈ
Thank you very much.
  khàwp jai lǎi lǎi   ຂອບໃຈຫລາຍໆ
It's nothing. (Never mind/
Don't bother)
  baw pen nyǎng   ບໍ່ເປັນຫຍັງ
Excuse me.
  khǎw thôht   ຂໍໂທດ

Small Talk

How are you?
  sábaai-dii baw?   ສະບາຍດີບໍ?
I'm fine.
  sábaai-dii   ສະບາຍດີ
And you?
  jâo dêh?   ເຈົ້າເດ່
What is your name?
  jâo seu nyang?   ເຈົ້າຊື່ຫຍັງ?

My name is ...
  kháwy seu ...   ຂ້ອຍຊື່ ...
Glad to know you.
  dii-jai thii hûu káp jâo ດີໃຈທີ່ຮູ້ກັບເຈົ້າ
Where are you from?
  jâo máa tae sai?   ເຈົ້າມາແຕ່ໃສ?
I'm from ...
  kháwy máa tae ...   ຂ້ອຍມາແຕ່ ...
Australia
  aw-sáteh-lía   ອອສະເຕເລຍ
Canada
  kaanáadaa   ການາດາ
China
  jiin   ຈີນ
Europe
  yulôhp   ເອີໂລບ
Great Britain
  angkít   ອັງກິດ
India
  india   ອິນເດຍ
Japan
  yii-pun   ຍີ່ປຸ່ນ
Laos
  láo   ລາວ
New Zealand
  níu síiláen   ນິວຊີແລນ
USA
  améhlikaa   ອະເມລິກາ

How old are you?
  jâo aanyuu ják pii?   ເຈົ້າອາຍຸຈັກປີ?
I'm ... years old.
  kháwy aanyuu ... pii   ຂ້ອຍອາຍຸ ... ປີ
How many in your family?
  míi khâwp khúa
  ják khón?   ມີຄອບຄົວຈັກຄົນ?
Are you married (yet)?
  taeng-ngáan lâew
  lěu baw?   ແຕ່ງງານແລ້ວຫລືບໍ່?
Yes, I'm married.
  taeng-ngáan lâew   ແຕ່ງງານແລ້ວ

Not yet.
yáng baw taeng-ngáan ຍັງບໍ່ແຕ່ງງານ
Do you have any children?
míi lûuk lâew baw? ເຈົ້າມີລູກແລ້ວບໍ່?
I have ... child/children.
míi lûuk ... khón lâew ມີລູກ ... ຄົນແລ້ວ

child/children
lûuk ລູກ
daughter
lûuk sāo ລູກສາວ
son
lûuk sáai ລູກຊາຍ
mother
mae ແມ່
father
phaw ພໍ່

Language Difficulties

Can you speak English?
jâo pàak pháasāa
angkít dâi baw?
ເຈົ້າປາກພາສາອັງກິດໄດ້ບໍ່?
A little.
náwy neung ໜ້ອຍນຶ່ງ
I can't speak Lao.
khàwy páak pháasāa
láo baw dâi
ຂ້ອຍປາກພາສາລາວບໍ່ໄດ້
Do you understand?
jâo khào jai baw? ເຈົ້າເຂົ້າໃຈບໍ່?
(I) don't understand.
baw khào jai ບໍ່ເຂົ້າໃຈ
Please speak slowly.
kálunaa wâo sâa-sâa ກະລຸນາເວົ້າຊ້າໆ
Please repeat.
kálunaa wâo mai boeng dụu
ກະລຸນາເວົ້າໃໝ່ເບິ່ງດູ
What do you call this in Lao?
an-nîi pháasāa láo waa nyāng?
ອັນນີ້ພາສາລາວວ່າຫຍັງ?

Getting Around

Where is the ...
... yùu sāi? ... ຢູ່ໃສ?
airport
doen bịn ເດີ່ນບິນ
bus station
sathāanii lot pájam tháang
ສະຖານີລົດປະຈຳທາງ
bus stop
bawn jàwt lot pájam tháang
ບ່ອນຈອດລົດປະຈຳທາງ
departures/flights
thîaw ກຽວ
taxi stand
bawn jàwt lot thaek-sîi
ບ່ອນຈອດລົດແທກຊີ

I want to go to ...
khàwy yàak pại ... ຂ້ອຍຢາກໄປ ...
What time will the ... leave?
... já àwk ják móhng? ...ຈະອອກຈັກໂມງ?
aeroplane
héua bịn ເຮືອບິນ
bus
lot ລົດ
boat
heúa ເຮືອ
minivan
lot tûu ລົດຕູ້

What time (do we,
does it, etc) arrive there?
já maa hâwt yuu
phûn ják móhng? ຈະໄປຮອດພຸ້ນຈັກໂມງ?
Where do we get
on the boat?
lóng heua yuu sāi? ລົງເຮືອຢູ່ໃສ?
I'd like a ticket.
khàwy yàak dâi pîi ຂ້ອຍຢາກໄດ້ປີ້
How much to ...?
pại ... thao dại? ໄປ ... ເທົ່າໃດ?

How much per person?
khón-la thao dại? ຄົນລະເທົ່າໃດ?
May I sit here?
nang bawn nîi dâi baw? ນັ່ງບ່ອນນີ້ໄດ້ບໍ່?
Please tell me when we arrive in ...
wéhláa hâwt ... ເວລາຮອດ ...
bàwk khàwy dae ບອກຂອຍແດ
Stop here.
jàwt yuu nîi ຈອດຢູ່ນີ້
taxi
lot thâek-síi ລົດແທກຊີ
samlor (pedicab)
sãam-lâw ສາມລໍ້
tuk-tuk (jumbo)
túk-túk ຕຸ໊ກ ຕຸ໊ກ

Directions

Which ... is this?
bawn nîi ... nyãng? ບ່ອນນີ້ ... ຫຍັງ?
street/road/avenue
thanõn ຖນົນ
city
méuang ເມືອງ
village
muu bâan ໝູ່ບ້ານ
province
khwãeng ແຂວງ

Turn ...
lîaw ... ລ້ຽວ ...
left
sâai ຊ້າຍ
right
khwãa ຂວາ
Go straight ahead.
pại seu-seu ໄປຊື່
How far?
kại thao dại? ໄກເທົ່າໃດ?
far/not far
kại/baw kại ໄກ ບໍ່ໄກ

north
thit nẽua ທິດເໜືອ
south
thit tâi ທິດໃຕ້
west
thit tạawán tók ທິດຕາເວັນຕົກ
east
thit tạawán àwk ທິດຕາເວັນອອກ

I'd like to rent a ...
khàwy yàak sao ... ຂ້ອຍຢາກເຊົ່າ ...
car
lot (ọh-tọh) ລົດ(ໂອໂຕ)
motorcycle
lot ják ລົດຈັກ
bicycle
lot thìip ລົດຖີບ

Accommodation

Excuse me, is there a hotel nearby?
khãw thọht, mịi hóhng háem yuu kâi nîi baw?
ຂໍໂທດ . ມີໂຮງແຮມຢູ່ໃກ້ນີ້ບໍ່?
hotel
hóhng háem ໂຮງແຮມ
guesthouse
hãw hap kháek ຫໍຮັບແຂກ

Do you have a room?
míi hàwng baw? ມີຫ້ອງບໍ່?
How many persons?
ják khón? ຈັກຄົນ?
one person
neung khón ນຶ່ງຄົນ
(khon diaw) (ຄົນດຽວ)
two persons
sãwng khón ສອງຄົນ

How much ... ?
... thao dại? ... ເທົ່າໃດ?

per night
  khéun-la   ຄືນລະ
per week
  aathit-la   ອາທິດລະ

air-conditioning
  ae yen   ແອເຢັນ
bathroom
  hàwng nâam   ຫ້ອງນ້ຳ
blanket
  phàa hom   ຜ້າຫົ່ມ
double room
  hàwng náwn
  tjang khuu   ຫ້ອງນອນຕຽງຄູ່
fan
  phat lóm   ພັດລົມ
hot water
  nâam hâwn   ນ້ຳຮ້ອນ
key
  kájae   ກະແຈ
room
  hàwng   ຫ້ອງ
sheet
  phàa puu
  bawn náwn   ຜ້າປູບ່ອນນອນ
single room
  hàwng náwn
  tjang diaw   ຫ້ອງນອນຕຽງດຽວ
soap
  sábuu   ສະບູ
toilet
  sùam   ສ້ວມ
towel
  phàa set tọh   ຜ້າເຊັດໂຕ

(I/we) will stay two nights.
  si phak sāwng khéun   ຊິພັກຢູ່ສອງຄືນ
Can (I/we) look at the room?
  khāw boeng hàwng
  dâi baw?   ຂໍເບິ່ງຫ້ອງໄດ້ບໍ?
Do you have other rooms?
  míi hàwng íik baw?   ມີຫ້ອງອີກບໍ?

cheaper
  théuk-kwaa   ຖືກກວ່າ
quieter
  mit-kwaa   ມິດກວ່າ

Around Town
Where is the ...?
  ... yùu sāi   ... ຢູ່ໃສ?
I'm looking for (the) ...
  khàwy sâwk hāa ...   ຂອຍຊອກຫາ ...

bank
  thanáakháan   ທະນາຄານ
barber shop
  hâan tát phōm   ຮ້ານຕັດຜົມ
bookshop
  hàan khāai nāng sēu   ຮ້ານຂາຍໜັງສື
Buddhist temple
  wat   ວັດ
cemetery
  baa sâa   ປ່າຊ້າ
church
  sim khlit   ສິມຄລິດ
hospital
  hóhng māw   ໂຮງໝໍ
museum
  phiphithaphán   ພິພິກະພັນ
park (garden)
  sūan   ສວນ
pharmacy
  hâan khāai yạa   ຮ້ານຂາຍຢາ
post office
  pại-sá-níi   ໄປສະນີ
  (hóhng sāai)   (ໂຮງສາຍ)
stupa
  thâat   ທາດ

I want to change ...
  khàwy yàak pian ...   ຂອຍຢາກປ່ຽນ ...
money
  ngóen   ເງິນ

travellers cheques
sek dôen tháang ແຊັກເດີນທາງ

telephone
thóhlasáp ໂທລະສັບ

international call
thóhlasáp rawaang páthêt
ໂທລະສັບລະຫວ່າງປະເທດ

long distance (domestic)
tháang kại ທາງໄກ

open/closed
pòet/pít ເປີດ/ປິດ

Shopping

I'm looking for ...
khàwy sàwk hāa ... ຂ້ອຍຊອກຫາ ...

baskets
ká-taa ກະຕ່າ

clothing
sèua phàa ເສື້ອ ຜ້າ

embroidery
phàa thák saew ຜ້າກັກແສ່ວ

handicrafts
kheuang fĭi-méu ເຄື່ອງຝີມື

pottery/ceramics
kheuang dìn/ ເຄື່ອງດິນ/
kheuang thùay ເຄື່ອງກ້ວຍ

stationery
keuang khĭan ເຄື່ອງຂຽນ

traditional long
sarong for women
phàa nung ຜ້ານຸ່ງ

cotton
phàa fàai ຜ້າຝ້າຍ

leather
nāng ໜັງ

linen
phàa lĭnin ຜ້າລິນິນ

silk
phàa māi ຜ້າໃໝ

wool
phàa sákálaat ຜ້າສັກກະຫລາດ
(phàa khōn sát) (ຜ້າຂົນສັດ)

How much (for) ...?
... thao dại? ... ເທົ່າໃດ?

this
an-nîi ອັນນີ້

per piece
an-la ອັນລະ

both
thâng sāwng ທັງສອງ

I'd like to see another style.
khāw boeng ìik
bàep neung ຂໍເບິ່ງອີກແບບນຶ່ງ

Do you have
something cheaper?
mĭi thèuk-kwaa
nîi baw? ມີຖືກກວ່ານີ້ບໍ່?

The price is very high.
láakháa pháeng lāai ລາຄາແພງຫລາຍ

(latex) condoms
thăng yạang anáamái ຖົງຢາງອະນະໄມ

sanitary napkins
phàa anáamái ຜ້າອະນາໄມ

soap
sá-buu ສະບູ

toilet paper
jîa hong nâam ເຈ້ຍຫ້ອງນ້ຳ

toothbrush
pạeng thūu khàew ແປງຖູແຂ້ວ

In the Country

forest
paa ປ່າ

jungle
dọng ດົງ

mountain
phúu khāo ພູເຂົາ

rice field (wet)
náa ນາ

river
mae nâam ແມ່ນ້ຳ

sea
thaléh ທະເລ

swamp
beung ບຶງ

trail/footpath
tháang thíaw/ ທາງທຽວ/
tháang nyaang ທາງຍາງ

waterfall
nâam tók tàat ນ້ຳຕົກຕາດ

Health

I'm not well.
khàwy baw sábạai ຂ້ອຍບໍ່ສະບາຍ

I have a fever.
pẹn khài ເປັນໄຂ້

I have diarrhoea.
lóng thâwng ລົງທ້ອງ

It hurts here.
jép yuu nîi ເຈັບຢູ່ນີ້

I've vomited several times.
hàak lāai theụa ຮາກຫລາຍເທື່ອ

I need a/an ...
khàwy tâwng-kạan ... ຂ້ອຍຕ້ອງການ ...

ambulance
lot hóhng māw ລົດໂຮງໝໍ

doctor
māw ໝໍ

dentist
māw pụa khàew ໝໍປົວແຂ້ວ

accident
ú-bát-tí-hèht ອຸບັດຕິເຫດ

allergic (to)
phâe ແພ້

anaemia
lọhk lêuat nâwy ໂລກເລືອດໜ້ອຍ

asthma
lọhk hèut ໂລກຫືດ

diabetes
lọhk bạo wāan ໂລກເບົ່າຫວານ

diarrhoea
lóng thâwng ລົງທ້ອງ

malaria
khài paa ໄຂ້ປ່າ

pregnant
thēu pháa-máan ຖືພ້າມານ
(míi thâwng) (ມີທ້ອງ)

toothache
jép khàew ເຈັບແຂ້ວ

Days

Sunday
wán ạathit ວັນອາທິດ

Monday
wán jạn ວັນຈັນ

Tuesday
wán ạngkháan ວັນຄັງຄານ

Wednesday
wán phut ວັນພຸດ

Thursday
wán phahát ວັນພະຫັດ

Friday
wán súk ວັນສຸກ

Saturday
wán sāo ວັນເສົາ

today
mêu nîi ມື້ນີ້

tonight
khéun nîi ຄືນນີ້

this morning
sâo nîi ເຊົ້ານີ້

this afternoon
baai nîi ບ່າຍນີ້

all day
talàwt mêu ຕລອດມື້

now
diaw nîi/tạwn nîi ດຽວນີ້/ຕອນ ນີ້

sometimes
  baang theua ບາງເທື່ອ
yesterday
  mêu wáan nîi ມື້ວານນີ້
tomorrow
  mêu eun ມື້ອື່ນ

Months

January
  deuan mángkawn ເດືອນມັງກອນ
February
  deuan kumpháa ເດືອນກຸມພາ
March
  deuan mináa ເດືອນມີນາ
April
  deuan méhsāa ເດືອນເມສາ
May
  deuan pheutsápháa ເດືອນພຶດສະພາ
June
  deuan mithúnáa ເດືອນມິຖຸນາ
July
  deuan kawlakót ເດືອນກໍລະກົດ
August
  deuan sīnghāa ເດືອນສິງຫາ
September
  deuan kanyáa ເດືອນກັນຍາ
October
  deuan túláa ເດືອນຕຸລາ
November
  deuan phajík ເດືອນພະຈິກ
December
  deuan thánwáa ເດືອນທັນວາ

Numbers & Amounts

0	*sūun*	ສຸນ	6	*hók*	ຫົກ
1	*neung*	ນຶ່ງ	7	*jét*	ເຈັດ
2	*sāwng*	ສອງ	8	*pàet*	ແປດ
3	*sāam*	ສາມ	9	*kâo*	ເກົ້າ
4	*sii*	ສີ່	10	*síp*	ສິບ
5	*hàa*	ຫາ	11	*síp-ét*	ສິບເອັດ

12	*síp-sāwng*	ສິບສອງ
20	*sáo*	ຊາວ
21	*sáo-ét*	ຊາວເອັດ
22	*sáo-sāwng*	ຊາວສອງ
30	*sāam-síp*	ສາມສິບ
40	*sii-síp*	ສີ່ສິບ
50	*hàa-síp*	ຫາສິບ
60	*hók-síp*	ຫົກສິບ
70	*jét-síp*	ເຈັດສິບ
80	*pàet-síp*	ແປດສິບ
90	*kâo-síp*	ເກົ້າສິບ
100	*hâwy*	ຮອຍ
200	*sāwng hâwy*	ສອງຮອຍ
1000	*phán*	ພັນ
10,000	*meun (síp-phán)*	ໝຶ່ນ(ສິບພັນ)
100,000	*sāen (hâwy phán)*	ແສນ(ຮອຍພັນ)
million	*lâan*	ລ້ານ

first	*thíi neung*	ທີນຶ່ງ
second	*thíi sāwng*	ທີສອງ

Emergencies

Help!
  suay dae ຊ່ວຍແດ່
Fire!
  fái mài ໄຟໄໝ້
It's an emergency!
  súk sōen ສຸກເສີນ
There's been an accident!
  míi úbátíhet ມີອຸບັດຕິເຫດ
Call a doctor!
  suai taam hāa mǎw hài dae
  ຊ່ວຍຕາມຫາໝໍໃຫແດ່
Call an ambulance!
  suay ôen lot hóhng mǎw dae
  ຊ່ວຍເອີ້ນລົດໂຮງໝໍໃຫແດ່
Call the police!
  suay ôen tam-lùat dae
  ຊ່ວຍເອີ້ນຕຳຫລວດແດ່

Could you help me please?
  jao suay khàwy
  dại baw? ເຈົ້າຊ່ວຍຂ້ອຍໄດ້ບໍ?
I've been robbed.
  khàwy thèuk
  khá-móhy ຂ້ອຍຖືກຂະໂມຍ
I've been raped.
  khàwy thèuk
  khòm khēun ຂ້ອຍຖືກຂົ່ມຂືນ
Stop!
  yút ຢຸດ !
Go away!
  pại dôe ໄປເດີ!
Where are the toilets?
  hàwng sùam yuu sāi? ຫ້ອງສ້ວມຢູ່ໃສ?
I'm lost.
  khàwy lōng tháang ຂ້ອຍຫລົງທາງ

Food & Drinks

FOOD
Appetisers (Drinking Food)
Lao have a category of dishes called *káp kâem*, which are meant to be eaten on picnics or while drinking alcohol.

fried peanuts
  thua jẹun ຖົ່ວຈືນ
fried potatoes
  mán falang jẹun ມັນຝະຣັ່ງຈືນ
shrimp chips
  khào kìap kûng ເຂົ້າຂຽບກຸ້ງ
fried spring rolls
  yáw jẹun ຢໍຈືນ
fresh spring rolls
  yáw díp ຢໍດິບ
toasted pork
  pîng mūu ປີ້ງຫມູ
spicy grilled chicken
  pîng kai ປີ້ງໄກ່
spicy green papaya salad
  tạm màak-hung ຕຳຫມາກຮຸ່ງ

Soups
mild soup with
vegetables & pork
  kạeng jèut ແກງຈືດ
mild soup with
vegetables & bean curd
  kạeng jèut tâo-hûu ແກງຈືດເຕົ້າຮູ້
soup with chicken,
galingale root & coconut
  tọm khaa kai ຕົ້ມຂ່າໄກ່
fish & lemongrass soup
with mushrooms
  tọm yám pạa ຕົ້ມຍຳປາ
whole rice soup with ...
  khào pìak ... ເຂົ້າປຽກ ...
fish
  pạa ປາ
chicken
  kai ໄກ່
pork
  mūu ຫມູ

Eggs
hard-boiled egg
  tọm khai ຕົ້ມໄຂ່
fried egg
  khai dạo ໄຂດາວ
fried eggs with a
sliced baguette
  khào jii khai dạo ເຂົ້າຈີ່ໄຂ່ດາວ
plain omelette
  jẹun khai ຈືນໄຂ່
scrambled egg
  khai khùa ໄຂ່ຂົ້ວ

Bread & Pastries
plain bread
(usually French-style)
  khào jii ເຂົ້າຈີ່
baguette sandwich
  khào jii pá-tê ເຂົ້າຈີ່ປັດເຕ໌

croissants
  kwaa-song   ຄົວຊ່ອງ
'Chinese doughnuts'
(Mandarin *youtiao*)
  pá-thawng-ko   ປະກ້ອງໂກະ
  (khàonōmkhuu) (ເຂົ້າໜົມຄູ)
butter
  bǫe   ເບີ
French bread with butter
  khào jii bǫe   ເຂົ້າຈີ່ເບີ

Rice Dishes

fried rice with ...
  khào phát   ເຂົ້າ ຜັດ
  (khào khùa) ... (ເຂົ້າຂົ້ວ) ...
chicken
  kai   ໄກ່
pork
  mǖu   ໝູ
shrimp/prawns
  kûng   ກຸ້ງ
crab
  pǫu   ປູ
steamed white rice
  khào nèung   ເຂົ້າໜຶ້ງ
sticky rice
  khào nīaw   ເຂົ້າໜຽວ
curry over rice
khâo làat kǫeng ເຂົ້າລາດແກງ

Noodles

flat rice-noodle soup with
vegetables & meat
  fõe   ເຝີ
flat rice-noodles with vegetables
& meat, no broth
  fõe hàeng   ເຝີແຫ້ງ
yellow wheat noodles in broth,
with vegetables & meat
  mii nâam   ໝີ່ນ້ຳ

flat rice noodles with gravy
  làat nàa   ລາດໜ້າ
fried rice noodles with meat
& vegetables
  fõe khùa   ເຝີຂົ້ວ
yellow wheat noodles
without broth
  mii hàeng   ໝີ່ແຫ້ງ
fried rice noodles with
soy sauce
  phát sáyûu   ຜັດສະອິ້ວ
white flour noodles served
with sweet-spicy sauce
  khào pûn   ເຂົ້າປຸ້ນ

Fish

crisp-fried fish
  jǫun pǫa   ຈືນປາ
fried prawns
  jǫun kûng   ຈືນກຸ້ງ
grilled prawns
  pîng kûng   ປີ້ງກຸ້ງ
steamed fish
  nèung pǫa   ໜຶ້ງປາ
grilled fish
  pîng pǫa   ປີ້ງປາ
catfish
  pǫa dúk   ປາດຸກ
eel
  ian   ອ່ຽນ
giant Mekong catfish
  pǫa béuk   ປາບິກ
sheatfish
  pǫa sa-ngùa   ປາສະຫງົ້ວ
carp
  pǫa pàak   ປາປາກ
serpent fish
  pǫa khaw   ປາຄໍ
freshwater stingray
  pǫa fǎa lái   ປາຝາໃລ

Sweets

custard
sangkha-nyāa ສັງຂະຫຍາ
egg custard
khào-nōm màw kaeng ເຂົ້າໜົມໝໍ້ແກງ
banana in coconut milk
nâam wāan
màak kûay ນ້ຳຫວານໝາກກ້ວຍ
sticky rice in
coconut cream
khào nīaw daeng ເຂົ້າໜຽວແດງ
sticky rice in coconut
cream & ripe mango
khào nīaw
màak muang ຂ້າໜຽວໝາກມ່ວງ
sticky rice cakes
khào nōm ເຂົ້າໜົມ
sticky rice in coconut
milk cooked in bamboo
khào lāam ເຂົ້າຫລາມ

Fruit

custard-apple (July to October)
màak khìap ໝາກຂຽບ
rose-apple – small, apple-like texture, very
fragrant (April to July)
màak kiang ໝາກກຽງ
banana (year-round)
màak kûay ໝາກກ້ວຍ
durian
thulían ທຸລຽນ
guava (year-round)
màak sīi-daa ໝາກສີດາ
lime or lemon (year-round)
màak náo ໝາກນາວ
longan
màak nyám nyái ໝາກຍ່ຳໃຍ
lychee (July to October)
màak lînjii ໝາກລິ້ນຈີ່
mandarin (year-round)
màak kîang ໝາກກຽງ

mango
màak muang ໝາກມ່ວງ
jackfruit
màak mîi ໝາກມີ້
mangosteen
màak máng-khut ໝາກມັງຄຸດ
pineapple (year-round)
màak nat ໝາກນັດ
papaya (year-round)
màak hung ໝາກຫຸງ
rambutan
màak ŋgaw ໝາກເງາະ
watermelon (year-round)
màak móh ໝາກໂມ

Useful Food Sentences

I eat only vegetables.
khàwy kin tae phák ຂ້ອຍກິນແຕ່ຜັກ
I don't like it hot (spicy).
baw mak phét ບໍ່ມັກເຜັດ
(I) like it hot & spicy.
mak phét ມັກເຜັດ
What do you have
that's special?
mīi nyáng phi sèt? ມີຫຍັງພິເສດ?
Do you have ...?
mīi ... baw? ມີ ... ບໍ?
I didn't order this.
*khàwy baw dâi
sang náew nîi* ຂ້ອຍບໍ່ໄດ້ສັ່ງແນວນີ້

DRINKS

drinking water
nâam deum ນ້ຳດື່ມ
boiled water
nâam tom ນ້ຳຕົ້ມ
cold water
nâam yén ນ້ຳເຢັນ
hot water
nâam hâwn ນ້ຳຮ້ອນ
ice
nâam kâwn ນ້ຳກ້ອນ

weak Chinese tea
  nâam sáa ບ້ຳຊາ
hot Lao tea with sugar
  sáa hâwn ຊາຮ້ອນ
hot Lao tea with milk & sugar
  sáa nóm hâwn ຊານົມຮ້ອນ
iced Lao tea with milk & sugar
  sáa nóm yén ຊານົມເຢັນ
iced Lao tea with sugar only
  sáa wăan yén ຊາຫວານເຢັນ
no sugar (command)
  baw sai nâam-ṭaan ບໍ່ໃສ່ບ້ຳຕານ

hot Lao coffee with milk & sugar
  kaa-féh nóm hâwn ກາເຟນົມຮ້ອນ
hot Lao coffee with sugar, no milk
  kaa-féh ḍam ກາເຟດຳ
iced Lao coffee with milk & sugar
  kaa-féh nóm yén ກາເຟນົມເຢັນ
iced Lao coffee with sugar, no milk
  òh-lîang ໂອລຽງ
hot Nescafe with milk & sugar
  net nóm ເນສນົມ
hot Nescafe with sugar, no milk
  net ḍam ເນສດຳ
Ovaltine
  oh-wantin ໂອວັນຕິນ

plain milk
  nâam nóm ບ້ຳນົມ
yoghurt
  nóm sòm ນົມສົ້ມ

beer
  bịa ເບຍ
orange juice (orange soda)
  nâam m ak kîang ບ້ຳໝາກກຽງ
rice whisky
  lào láo ເຫົ້ລາລາວ
soda water
  nâam sah-ḍaa ບ້ຳໂສດາ

Place Names

Ang Nam Ngum
  ອ່າງບ້ຳງື່ມ
Attapeu
  ອັດຕະປື
Attapeu Province
  ແຂວງອັດຕະປື
Ban Nape
  ບ້ານນາແປ
Ban Phanom & Mouhot's Tomb
  ບ້ານພະນົມ & ສຸສານທມູຫົດ
Ban Phapho & Kiet Nyong
  ບ້ານພາໂພ & ກຽດຍ້ອງ
Ban That Luang
  ບ້ານທາດຫລວງ
Bokeo Province
  ແຂວງບໍ່ແກ້ວ
Bolaven Plateau
  ທົ່ງພຽງບໍລະເວນ
Bolikhamsai & Khammuan Provinces
  ແຂວງບໍລີຄຳໄຊ & ຄຳມວນ
Boten
  ບໍແຕນ
Champasak
  ຈຳປາສັກ
Champasak Historical Heritage Museum
  ຫໍພິພິດທະພັນປະວັດມູນເຊື້ອຈຳປາສັກ
Champasak Province
  ແຂວງຈຳປາສັກ
Don Det & Don Khon
  ດອນເດດ & ດອນຄອນ
Don Khong
  ດອນໂຂງ

Dong Dok University
ມະຫາວິທະຍາລັຍດົງໂດກ

Friendship Bridge
ຂົວມິດຕະພາບ

Hat Sa
ຫາດສາ

Haw Pha Kaew
ຫໍພະແກ້ວ

Heuan Hin
ເຮືອນຫີນ

Hua Phan Province
ແຂວງຫົວພັນ

Huay Xai
ຫ້ວຍຊາຍ

Kasi
ກາສີ

Kaysone Phomvihane Memorial & Museum
ຫໍພິພິດຫະພັນ &
ອະນຸສາວະລີໄກສອນພົມວິຫານ

Khon Phapheng Falls
ນ້ຳຕົກຕາດຄອນພະເພັງ

Kuang Si Falls
ນ້ຳຕົກຕາດກວາງງສີ

Lak Sao
ຫລັກຊາວ

Lao Revolutionary Museum
ຫໍພິພິດຫະພັນການປະຕິວັດລາວ

Luang Nam Tha
ຫລວງນ້ຳທາ

Luang Nam Tha Province
ແຂວງຫລວງນ້ຳທາ

Luang Prabang
ຫລວງພະບາງ

Luang Prabang Province
ແຂວງຫລວງພະບາງ

Muang Khua
ເມືອງຂວາ

Muang Ngoen
ເມືອງເງິນ

Muang Sing
ເມືອງສິງ

Muang Sui
ເມືອງສຸ້ຍ

Muang Xai
ເມືອງໄຊ

Nam Kading
ນ້ຳກະດິງ

Nam Noen
ນ້ຳເນີນ

Nambak & Pak Mong
ນ້ຳບາກ & ປາກມອງ

Namo
ນານໍ

National Circus
ໂຮງສະແດງກາຍຍະສີນແຫ່ງຊາດ

National Ethnic Cultural Park
ສວນວັດທະນະທັມຊົນເຜົ່າແຫ່ງຊາດ

Nong Khiaw (Muang Ngoi)
ຫນອງຂຽວ (ເມືອງງອຍ)

Old Xieng Khuang (Muang Khun)
ຊຽງຂວາງເກົ່າ (ເມືອງຄູນ)

Pa-am
ພະອໍາ

Pak Lai
ປາກລາຍ

Pak Ou Caves
ຖ້ຳປາກອູ

Pakbeng
ປາກແບ່ງ

Paksan
ປາກຊັນ

Pakse
ປາກເຊ

Patuxai
ປະຕູໄຊ

Pha That Luang
ພະທາດຫລວງ

Phongsali
ພົງສາລີ

Phongsali Province
ແຂວງພົງສາລີ

Phonsavan
ໂພນສະຫວັນ

Phu Si
ພູສີ

Plain of Jars
ທົ່ງໄຫຫີນ

Royal Palace Museum (Haw Kham)
ຫໍພິພິດທະພັນພະລາດສະວັງ (ຫໍຄຳ)

Sainyabuli
ໄຊຍະບູລີ

Sainyabuli Province
ແຂວງໄຊຍະບູລີ

Salavan
ສາລະວັນ

Salavan Province
ແຂວງສາລະວັນ

Sam Neua (Xam Neua)
ຊຳເຫນືອ (ຊ່ຳເຫນືອ)

Savannakhet
ສະວັນນະເຂດ

Savannakhet Province
ແຂວງສະວັນນະເຂດ

Sekong (Muang Lamam)
ເຊກອງ (ເມືອງລະມ່າ)

Sekong Province
ແຂວງເຊກອງ

Sepon (Xepon) & the Ho Chi Minh Trail
ເຊໂປນ & ເສັ້ນທາງໂຮຈິມິນ

Si Phan Don
ສີພັນດອນ

Suan Hin
ສວນຫີນ

Taat Sae
ນ້ຳຕົກຕາດແຊ

Talaat Sao
ຕະລາດເຊົ້າ

Tha Khaek
ທ່າແຂກ

Tham Piu
ຖ້ຳພິວ

Thanon Phu Wao
ຖະນົນພູວາວ

Thanon Wisunalat
ຖະນົນວິຊຸນນະລາດ

That Dam
ທາດດຳ

That Ing Hang
ທາດອີງຮັງ

That Phon
ທາດໂພນ

Udomxai Province
ແຂວງອຸດົມໄຊ

Um Muang
ອ່າເມືອງ

Unknown Soldiers Memorial
ອະນຸສາວະລີທະຫານນິລະນາມ

Vang Vieng
ວັງວຽງ

Vieng Xai
ວຽງໄຊ

Vientiane
ວຽງຈັນ

Wat Aham
ວັດອາຮາມ

Wat Chanthabuli
ວັດຈັນທະບຸລີ

Wat Hai Sok
ວັດຫາຍໂສກ

Wat In Paeng
ວັດອິນແປງ

Wat Lattanalangsi
ວັດລັດຕະນະລັງສີ

Wat Mai Suvannaphumaham
ວັດໃໝ່ສຸວັນນະພູມອາຮາມ

Wat Manolom
ວັດມະໂນລົມ

Wat Mixai
ວັດມີໄຊ

Wat Ong Teu Mahawihan
ວັດອົງຕື້ມະຫາວິຫານ

Wat Pha Baat Phonsan
ວັດພະບາດໂພນສັນ

Wat Pha That Si Khotabong
ວັດພະທາດສີໂຄຕະບອງ

Wat Phu Champasak
ວັດພູຈຳປາສັກ

Wat Sainyaphum
ວັດໄຊຍະພູມ

Wat Si Muang
ວັດສີເມືອງ

Wat Si Saket
ວັດສີສະເກດ

Wat Sok Pa Luang
ວັດໂສກປ່າຫລວງ

Wat That Luang
ວັດທາດຫລວງ

Wat Wisunalat
ວັດວິຊຸນນະລາດ

Wat Xieng Thong
ວັດຊຽງທອງ

Xieng Khuang Province
ແຂວງຊຽງຂວາງ

Xieng Khuan
ຊຽງຂວັນ

Xieng Kok
ຊຽງກົກ

Glossary

aang – tank, reservoir
aahãan – food

baht – Thai unit of currency, commonly negotiable in Laos; also a Lao unit of measure equal to 15g
ban – pronounced *bâan*, the general Lao word for house or village
basi – pronounced *bạa-sĩi*, sometimes spelt baci; a ceremony in which the 32 *khwãn* (organ-spirits) are symbolically bound to the participant for health and safety's sake
BCEL – Banque pour le Commerce Extérieur Lao; in English, Lao Foreign Trade Bank
bịa – beer; bịa sót is draught beer
bun – pronounced *bụn*, often spelt boun; festival; also may refer to spiritual 'merit' earned through Buddhist religious practices

chedi – see jedi

dhamma – Pali word referring to Buddhist philosophy in general; dharma in Sanskrit
don – island

falang – from the Lao word *falaang-sèht* or 'French'; a term for a foreigner of European descent
fõe – rice noodles, one of the most common dishes in Laos

hái – jar
hãw tại – monastery building dedicated to the storage of the Tripitaka or Buddhist scriptures
héua – boat
hùay – stream

jâeng khào/jâeng àwk – literally inform enter/inform leave; the compulsory rubber stamps entered on your departure card by provincial customs or police
jataka – Pali-Sanskrit word for mythological life stories of the Buddha; *sàa-tòk* in Lao

jedi – also spelt chedi; another name for a Buddhist stupa
jumbo – a motorised three-wheeled taxi, sometimes called túk-túk

khào jịi – bread
khào – rice
khào nĩaw – sticky rice, the Lao staple food
khào-nõm – pastry or sweet; sometimes shortened to *khanõm*
khwãeng – province
khwãn – see under basi
khúu bạa – Theravada Buddhist monk
kip – Lao unit of currency

làap – a spicy Lao-style salad of minced meat, poultry or fish
lák meuang – city pillar
lam wong – 'circle dance', the traditional folk dance of Laos, as common at discos as at festivals
lào-láo – distilled rice liquor
Lao Loum – 'lowland Lao', ethnic groups belonging to the Lao-Thai diaspora
Lao Sung – 'high Lao', hill tribes who make their residence at higher altitudes, for example, Hmong, Mien
Lao Theung – 'upland Lao', a loose affiliation of mostly Mon-Khmer peoples who live on mid-altitude mountain slopes
lingam – a pillar or phallus symbolic of Shiva, common in Khmer-built temples

mae nâam – river (literally means 'mother water'); with river name, usually shortened to *nâam*, as in Nam Khong (Mekong River)
meuang – pronounced *meúang*, Lao-Thai city state; district; often spelt muang
múan – fun, which the Lao believe should be present in all activities

nâam – water; can also mean 'river', 'juice', 'sauce' and just about anything else of a watery nature

naga – *nâak* in Lao; mythic water serpent common to all Lao-Thai legends and art
NBCA – National Biodiversity Conservation Area, a classification assigned to 17 wildlife areas throughout Laos in 1993
NGO – nongovernment organisation, typically involved in the foreign aid industry
nop/wài – Lao greeting, a prayer-like palms-together gesture
NTAL – National Tourist Authority of Laos
NVA – North Vietnamese Army

pạa – fish
pạa dàek – fermented fish, a common accompaniment to Lao food
Pathet Lao – literally, Lao Land, used as both a general term for the country and a common journalistic reference to the military arm of the early Patriotic Lao Front (a cover for the Lao People's Party); often abbreviated to PL
pha – holy image, usually referring to a Buddha
phàa – cloth
phàa nung – sarong, worn by almost all Lao women
phïi – spirits; worship of these is the other main religion of Laos (and exists alongside Buddhism)
phúu – hill or mountain; also spelt phu

sainyasat – folk magic
sala – pronounced *sãa-láa*; an open-sided shelter
sãaláa lóng thám – a *sala* where monks and lay people listen to Buddhist teachings
samana – 'seminar', a euphemism for the re-education and labour camps established following the 1975 Revolution

samlor – pronounced *sãam-lâaw*; a three-wheeled pedicab
se – also spelt 'xe', this is the term used in southern Laos to mean river; hence Se Don means Don River, and Pakse means *pàak* (mouth) of the river
sii – sacred; also spelt si
sim – chapel or sanctuary in a Lao Buddhist monastery where monks are ordained; so called because of the *sima*, or sacred stone tablets, which mark off the grounds dedicated for this purpose
soi – alley
songthaew – pronounced *sãwng-thâew*, literally two-rows; a passenger truck

tàat – waterfall; also *nâam tók*
talaat – market; *talàat sâo* is the morning market
thâat – Buddhist stupa or reliquary
thaek-sii – literally taxi; either a passenger truck or a three-wheeled motorcycle taxi
tribal Thais – Austro-Thai subgroups closely related to the Lao, who have resisted absorption into mainstream Lao culture
thanõn – street or road; often spelt thanon
túk-túk – see jumbo

Viet Minh – the Vietnamese forces who fought for Indochina's independence from the French

wat – Lao Buddhist monastery; depending on the part of Laos you're in, it may be pronounced *vat*
wihãan – from the Pali-Sanskrit *vihara*; a temple building containing important Buddha images and often used by monks for chants and/or meditation

Index

BOXED TEXT

LONELY PLANET PHRASEBOOKS

Building bridges,
Breaking barriers,
Beyond babble-on

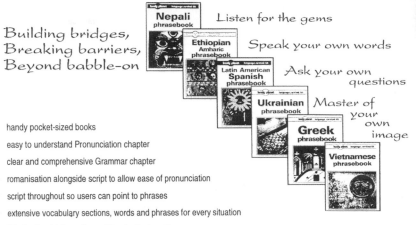

Listen for the gems

Speak your own words

Ask your own
            questions

Master of
         your
          own
           image

- handy pocket-sized books
- easy to understand Pronunciation chapter
- clear and comprehensive Grammar chapter
- romanisation alongside script to allow ease of pronunciation
- script throughout so users can point to phrases
- extensive vocabulary sections, words and phrases for every situation
- full of cultural information and tips for the traveller

'...vital for a real DIY spirit and attitude in language learning' – Backpacker

'the phrasebooks have good cultural backgrounders and offer solid advice for challenging situations in remote locations' – San Francisco Examiner

'...they are unbeatable for their coverage of the world's more obscure languages' – The Geographical Magazine

---

Arabic (Egyptian)
Arabic (Moroccan)
Australia
  Australian English, Aboriginal and
  Torres Strait languages
Baltic States
  Estonian, Latvian, Lithuanian
Bengali
Brazilian
Burmese
Cantonese
Central Asia
Central Europe
  Czech, French, German, Hungarian,
  Italian and Slovak
Eastern Europe
  Bulgarian, Czech, Hungarian, Polish,
  Romanian and Slovak
Ethiopian (Amharic)
Fijian
French
German
Greek

Hindi/Urdu
Indonesian
Italian
Japanese
Korean
Lao
Latin American Spanish
Malay
Mandarin
Mediterranean Europe
  Albanian, Croatian, Greek,
  Italian, Macedonian, Maltese,
  Serbian and Slovene
Mongolian
Nepali
Papua New Guinea
Pilipino (Tagalog)
Quechua
Russian
Scandinavian Europe
  Danish, Finnish, Icelandic, Norwegian
  and Swedish

South-East Asia
  Burmese, Indonesian, Khmer, Lao,
  Malay, Tagalog (Pilipino), Thai and
  Vietnamese
Spanish (Castilian)
  Basque, Catalan and Galician
Sri Lanka
Swahili
Thai
Thai Hill Tribes
Tibetan
Turkish
Ukrainian
USA
  US English, Vernacular,
  Native American languages and
  Hawaiian
Vietnamese
Western Europe
  Basque, Catalan, Dutch, French,
  German, Irish, Italian, Portuguese,
  Scottish Gaelic, Spanish (Castilian)
  and Welsh

LONELY PLANET JOURNEYS

JOURNEYS is a unique collection of travel writing – published by the company that understands travel better than anyone else. It is a series for anyone who has ever experienced – or dreamed of – the magical moment when they encountered a strange culture or saw a place for the first time. They are tales to read while you're planning a trip, while you're on the road or while you're in an armchair, in front of a fire.

JOURNEYS books catch the spirit of a place, illuminate a culture, recount a crazy adventure, or introduce a fascinating way of life. They always entertain, and always enrich the experience of travel.

ISLANDS IN THE CLOUDS
Travels in the Highlands of New Guinea
Isabella Tree

Isabella Tree's remarkable journey takes us to the heart of the remote and beautiful Highlands of Papua New Guinea and Irian Jaya – one of the most extraordinary and dangerous regions on earth. Funny and tragic by turns, *Islands in the Clouds* is her moving story of the Highland people and the changes transforming their world.

Isabella Tree, who lives in England, has worked as a freelance journalist on a variety of newspapers and magazines, including a stint as senior travel correspondent for the *Evening Standard*. A fellow of the Royal Geographical Society, she has also written a biography of the Victorian ornithologist John Gould.

'One of the most accomplished travel writers to appear on the horizon for many years ... the dialogue is brilliant' – Eric Newby

SEAN & DAVID'S LONG DRIVE
Sean Condon

Sean Condon is young, urban and a connoisseur of hair wax. He can't drive, and he doesn't really travel well. So when Sean and his friend David set out to explore Australia in a 1966 Ford Falcon, the result is a decidedly offbeat look at life on the road. Over 14,000 death-defying kilometres, our heroes check out the re-runs on tv, get fabulously drunk, listen to Neil Young cassettes and wonder why they ever left home.

Sean Condon lives in Melbourne. He played drums in several mediocre bands until he found his way into advertising and an above-average band called Boilersuit. *Sean & David's Long Drive* is his first book.

'Funny, pithy, kitsch and surreal . . . This book will do for Australia what Chernobyl did for Kiev, but hey you'll laugh as the stereotypes go boom'
– Time Out

LONELY PLANET TRAVEL ATLASES

Lonely Planet has long been famous for the number and quality of its guidebook maps. Now we've gone one step further and produced a handy companion series: Lonely Planet travel atlases – maps of a country produced in book form.

Unlike other maps, which look good but lead travellers astray, our travel atlases have been researched on the road by Lonely Planet's experienced team of writers. All details are carefully checked to ensure the atlas corresponds with the equivalent Lonely Planet guidebook.

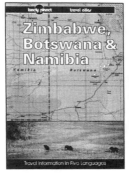

The handy atlas format means no holes, wrinkles, torn sections or constant folding and unfolding. These atlases can survive long periods on the road, unlike cumbersome fold-out maps. The comprehensive index ensures easy reference.

- full-colour throughout
- maps researched and checked by Lonely Planet authors
- place names correspond with Lonely Planet guidebooks
  – no confusing spelling differences
- legend and travelling information in English, French, German, Japanese and Spanish
- size: 230 x 160 mm

Available now:
Chile & Easter Island • Egypt • India & Bangladesh • Israel & the Palestinian Territories •Jordan, Syria & Lebanon • Kenya • Laos • Portugal • South Africa, Lesotho & Swaziland • Thailand • Turkey • Vietnam • Zimbabwe, Botswana & Namibia

---

LONELY PLANET TV SERIES & VIDEOS

Lonely Planet travel guides have been brought to life on television screens around the world. Like our guides, the programmes are based on the joy of independent travel, and look honestly at some of the most exciting, picturesque and frustrating places in the world. Each show is presented by one of three travellers from Australia, England or the USA and combines an innovative mixture of video, Super-8 film, atmospheric soundscapes and original music.

Videos of each episode – containing additional footage not shown on television – are available from good book and video shops, but the availability of individual videos varies with regional screening schedules.

Video destinations include: Alaska • American Rockies • Australia – The South-East • Baja California & the Copper Canyon • Brazil • Central Asia • Chile & Easter Island • Corsica, Sicily & Sardinia – The Mediterranean Islands • East Africa (Tanzania & Zanzibar) • Ecuador & the Galapagos Islands • Greenland & Iceland • Indonesia • Israel & the Sinai Desert • Jamaica • Japan • La Ruta Maya • Morocco • New York • North India • Pacific Islands (Fiji, Solomon Islands & Vanuatu) • South India • South West China • Turkey • Vietnam • West Africa • Zimbabwe, Botswana & Namibia

The Lonely Planet TV series is produced by:
Pilot Productions
The Old Studio
18 Middle Row
London W10 5AT UK

For video availability and ordering information contact your nearest Lonely Planet office.

Music from the TV series is available on CD & cassette.

PLANET TALK

Lonely Planet's FREE quarterly newsletter

We love hearing from you and think you'd like to hear from us.

When...is the right time to see reindeer in Finland?
Where...can you hear the best palm-wine music in Ghana?
How...do you get from Asunción to Areguá by steam train?
What...is the best way to see India?

For the answer to these and many other questions read PLANET TALK.

Every issue is packed with up-to-date travel news and advice including:

*   a letter from Lonely Planet co-founders Tony and Maureen Wheeler
*   go behind the scenes on the road with a Lonely Planet author
*   feature article on an important and topical travel issue
*   a selection of recent letters from travellers
*   details on forthcoming Lonely Planet promotions
*   complete list of Lonely Planet products

To join our mailing list contact any Lonely Planet office.

Also available: Lonely Planet T-shirts. 100% heavyweight cotton.

LONELY PLANET ONLINE

Get the latest travel information before you leave or while you're on the road

Whether you've just begun planning your next trip, or you're chasing down specific info on currency regulations or visa requirements, check out Lonely Planet Online for up-to-the-minute travel information.

As well as travel profiles of your favourite destinations (including maps and photos), you'll find current reports from our researchers and other travellers, updates on health and visas, travel advisories, and discussion of the ecological and political issues you need to be aware of as you travel.

There's also an online travellers' forum where you can share your experience of life on the road, meet travel companions and ask other travellers for their recommendations and advice. We also have plenty of links to other online sites useful to independent travellers.

And of course we have a complete and up-to-date list of all Lonely Planet travel products including guides, phrasebooks, atlases, Journeys and videos and a simple online ordering facility if you can't find the book you want elsewhere.

www.lonelyplanet.com
or
AOL keyword: lp

LONELY PLANET PRODUCTS

Lonely Planet is known worldwide for publishing practical, reliable and no-nonsense travel information in our guides and on our web site. The Lonely Planet list covers just about every accessible part of the world. Currently there are nine series: *travel guides, shoestring guides, walking guides, city guides, phrasebooks, audio packs, travel atlases, Journeys – a unique collection of travel writing and Pisces Books - diving and snorkeling guides.*

EUROPE

Amsterdam • Austria • Baltic States phrasebook • Berlin • Britain • Canary Islands• Central Europe on a shoestring • Central Europe phrasebook • Czech & Slovak Republics • Denmark • Dublin • Eastern Europe on a shoestring • Eastern Europe phrasebook • Estonia, Latvia & Lithuania • Finland • France • French phrasebook • Germany • German phrasebook • Greece • Greek phrasebook • Hungary • Iceland, Greenland & the Faroe Islands • Ireland • Italian phrasebook • Italy • Lisbon • London • Mediterranean Europe on a shoestring • Mediterranean Europe phrasebook • Paris • Poland • Portugal • Portugal travel atlas • Prague • Romania & Moldova • Russia, Ukraine & Belarus • Russian phrasebook • Scandinavian & Baltic Europe on a shoestring • Scandinavian Europe phrasebook • Slovenia • Spain • Spanish phrasebook • St Petersburg • Switzerland •Trekking in Spain • Ukrainian phrasebook • Vienna • Walking in Britain • Walking in Italy • Walking in Switzerland • Western Europe on a shoestring • Western Europe phrasebook

Travel Literature: The Olive Grove: Travels in Greece

NORTH AMERICA

Alaska • Backpacking in Alaska • Baja California • California & Nevada • Canada • Chicago • Deep South• Florida • Hawaii • Honolulu • Los Angeles • Mexico • Mexico City • Miami • New England • New Orleans • New York City • New York, New Jersey & Pennsylvania • Pacific Northwest USA • Rocky Mountain States • San Francisco • Seattle • Southwest USA • USA phrasebook • Washington, DC & the Capital Region

Travel Literature: Drive thru America

CENTRAL AMERICA & THE CARIBBEAN

•Bahamas and Turks & Caicos •Bermuda •Central America on a shoestring • Costa Rica • Cuba •Eastern Caribbean •Guatemala, Belize & Yucatán: La Ruta Maya • Jamaica

Travel Literature Green Dreams: Travels in Central America

SOUTH AMERICA

Argentina, Uruguay & Paraguay • Bolivia • Brazil • Brazilian phrasebook • Buenos Aires • Chile & Easter Island • Chile & Easter Island travel atlas • Colombia Ecuador & the Galápagos Islands • Latin American Spanish phrasebook • Peru • Quechua phrasebook • Rio de Janeiro • South America on a shoestring • Trekking in the Patagonian Andes • Venezuela

Travel Literature: Full Circle: A South American Journey

ISLANDS OF THE INDIAN OCEAN

Madagascar & Comoros • Maldives• Mauritius, Réunion & Seychelles

AFRICA

Africa - the South • Africa on a shoestring • Arabic (Moroccan) phrasebook • Cairo • Cape Town • Central Africa • East Africa • Egypt • Egypt travel atlas• Ethiopian (Amharic) phrasebook • Kenya • Kenya travel atlas • Malawi, Mozambique & Zambia • Morocco • North Africa • South Africa, Lesotho & Swaziland • South Africa, Lesotho & Swaziland travel atlas • Swahili phrasebook • Tunisia • Trekking in East Africa • West Africa • Zimbabwe, Botswana & Namibia • Zimbabwe, Botswana & Namibia travel atlas

Travel Literature: The Rainbird: A Central African Journey • Songs to an African Sunset: A Zimbabwean Story

MAIL ORDER

Lonely Planet products are distributed worldwide.They are also available by mail order from Lonely Planet, so if you have difficulty finding a title please write to us. North American and South American residents should write to 150 Linden St, Oakland CA 94607, USA; European and African residents should write to 10a Spring Place, London NW5 3BH; and residents of other countries to PO Box 617, Hawthorn, Victoria 3122, Australia.

NORTH-EAST ASIA

Beijing • Cantonese phrasebook • China • Hong Kong • Hong Kong, Macau & Guangzhou • Japan • Japanese phrasebook • Japanese audio pack • Korea • Korean phrasebook • Mandarin phrasebook • Mongolia • Mongolian phrasebook • North-East Asia on a shoestring • Seoul • Taiwan • Tibet • Tibet phrasebook • Tokyo
Travel Literature: Lost Japan

MIDDLE EAST & CENTRAL ASIA

Arab Gulf States • Arabic (Egyptian) phrasebook • Central Asia • Central Asia phrasebook • Iran • Israel & the Palestinian Territories • Israel & the Palestinian Territories travel atlas • Istanbul • Jerusalem • Jordan & Syria • Jordan, Syria & Lebanon travel atlas • Lebanon • Middle East • Turkey • Turkish phrasebook • Turkey travel atlas • Yemen

Travel Literature: The Gates of Damascus • Kingdom of the Film Stars: Journey into Jordan

ALSO AVAILABLE:

Brief Encounters • Travel with Children • Traveller's Tales

INDIAN SUBCONTINENT

Bangladesh • Bengali phrasebook • Delhi • Goa • Hindi/Urdu phrasebook • India • India & Bangladesh travel atlas • Indian Himalaya • Karakoram Highway • Nepal • Nepali phrasebook • Pakistan • Rajasthan • Sri Lanka • Sri Lanka phrasebook • Trekking in the Indian Himalaya • Trekking in the Karakoram & Hindukush • Trekking in the Nepal Himalaya

Travel Literature: In Rajasthan • Shopping for Buddhas

SOUTH-EAST ASIA

Bali & Lombok • Bangkok • Burmese phrasebook • Cambodia • Ho Chi Minh City • Indonesia • Indonesian phrasebook • Indonesian audio pack • Indonesia's Eastern Islands• Jakarta • Java • Laos • Lao phrasebook • Laos travel atlas • Malay phrasebook • Malaysia, Singapore & Brunei • Myanmar (Burma) • Philippines • Pilipino phrasebook • Singapore • South-East Asia on a shoestring • South-East Asia phrasebook • Thailand • Thailand's Islands & Beaches • Thailand travel atlas • Thai phrasebook • Thai audio pack • Thai Hill Tribes phrasebook • Vietnam • Vietnamese phrasebook • Vietnam travel atlas

AUSTRALIA & THE PACIFIC

Australia • Australian phrasebook • Bushwalking in Australia • Bushwalking in Papua New Guinea • Fiji • Fijian phrasebook • Islands of Australia's Great Barrier Reef • Melbourne • Micronesia • New Caledonia • New South Wales • New Zealand • Northern Territory • Outback Australia • Papua New Guinea • Papua New Guinea phrasebook • Queensland • Rarotonga & the Cook Islands • Samoa • Solomon Islands • South Australia • Sydney • Tahiti & French Polynesia • Tasmania • Tonga • Tramping in New Zealand • Vanuatu • Victoria • Western Australia
Travel Literature: Islands in the Clouds • Sean & David's Long Drive

ANTARCTICA

Antarctica

THE LONELY PLANET STORY

Lonely Planet published its first book in 1973 in response to the numerous 'How did you do it?' questions Maureen and Tony Wheeler were asked after driving, busing, hitching, sailing and railing their way from England to Australia.

Written at a kitchen table and hand collated, trimmed and stapled, *Across Asia on the Cheap* became an instant local bestseller, inspiring thoughts of another book.

Eighteen months in South-East Asia resulted in their second guide, *South-East Asia on a shoestring*, which they put together in a backstreet Chinese hotel in Singapore in 1975. The 'yellow bible', as it quickly became known to backpackers around the world, soon became *the* guide to the region. It has sold well over half a million copies and is now in its 9th edition, still retaining its familiar yellow cover.

Today there are over 350 titles, including travel guides, walking guides, language kits & phrasebooks, travel atlases and travel literature. The company is the largest independent travel publisher in the world. Although Lonely Planet initially specialised in guides to Asia, today there are few corners of the globe that have not been covered.

The emphasis continues to be on travel for independent travellers. Tony and Maureen still travel for several months of each year and play an active part in the writing, updating and quality control of Lonely Planet's guides.

They have been joined by over 80 authors and 200 staff at our offices in Melbourne (Australia), Oakland (USA), London (UK) and Paris (France). Travellers themselves also make a valuable contribution to the guides through the feedback we receive in thousands of letters each year and on our web site.

The people at Lonely Planet strongly believe that travellers can make a positive contribution to the countries they visit, both through their appreciation of the countries' culture, wildlife and natural features, and through the money they spend. In addition, the company makes a direct contribution to the countries and regions it covers. Since 1986 a percentage of the income from each book has been donated to ventures such as famine relief in Africa; aid projects in India; agricultural projects in Central America; Greenpeace's efforts to halt French nuclear testing in the Pacific; and Amnesty International.

'I hope we send people out with the right attitude about travel. You realise when you travel that there are so many different perspectives about the world, so we hope these books will make people more interested in what they see. Guidebooks can't really guide people. All you can do is point them in the right direction.'

– Tony Wheeler

LONELY PLANET PUBLICATIONS

Australia
PO Box 617, Hawthorn 3122, Victoria
tel: (03) 9819 1877 fax: (03) 9819 6459
e-mail: talk2us@lonelyplanet.com.au

USA
150 Linden St
Oakland, CA 94607
tel: (510) 893 8555 TOLL FREE: 800 275-8555
fax: (510) 893 8572
e-mail: info@lonelyplanet.com

UK
10a Spring Place,
London NW5 3BH
tel: (0171) 428 4800 fax: (0171) 428 4828
e-mail: go@lonelyplanet.co.uk

France:
71 bis rue du Cardinal Lemoine, 75005 Paris
tel: 01 44 32 06 20 fax: 01 46 34 72 55
e-mail: bip@lonelyplanet.fr

World Wide Web: http://www.lonelyplanet.com
or *AOL keyword: lp*